THE
RECOVERY
BOOK

COMPLETELY REVISED AND UPDATED

THE
RECOVERY
BOOK

ANSWERS TO ALL YOUR QUESTIONS ABOUT ADDICTION AND ALCOHOLISM AND FINDING HEALTH AND HAPPINESS IN SOBRIETY

AL J. MOONEY, M.D.
CATHERINE DOLD
HOWARD EISENBERG

WORKMAN PUBLISHING • NEW YORK

Copyright © 1992 by Al J.Mooney, M.D., Arlene Eisenberg, and Howard Eisenberg;
2014 by Al J. Mooney, M.D., Catherine Dold, and Howard Eisenberg

Library of Congress Cataloging-in-Publication Data is available.

ISBN 978-0-7611-7611-4

The Twelve Steps and Twelve Traditions are reprinted and adapted with permission of Alcoholics Anonymous World Services, Inc. Permission to reprint and adapt the Twelve Steps does not mean that AA has reviewed or approved the contents of this publication, nor that AA agrees with the views expressed herein. AA is a program of recovery from alcoholism— use of the Twelve Steps and Twelve Traditions in connection with programs and activities which are patterned after AA, but which address other problems, does not imply otherwise. Neither is approval or endorsement implied.

Design by Sarah Smith

Workman books are available at special discounts when purchased in bulk for premiums and sales promotions as well as for fund-raising or educational use. Special editions or book excerpts also can be created to specification. For details, contact the Special Sales Director at the address below, or send an email to specialmarkets@workman.com.

Workman Publishing Co., Inc.
225 Varick Street
New York, NY 10014-4381
workman.com

WORKMAN is a registered trademark of Workman Publishing Co., Inc.

Printed in the United States of America
First printing October 2014

10 9 8 7 6 5 4 3 2 1

CONTENTS

THE RED ZONE

THE YELLOW ZONE

THE GREEN ZONE

Foreword

As anyone in recovery from alcohol or other drug abuse knows, the recovery community is comprised of a huge group of incredibly diverse people from all walks of life who live in all corners of the world. The only things most of us have in common are our addiction, our recovery, and our desire to keep the latter. This alone makes us, as large and varied as we are, one of the most tight-knit groups of people known to mankind. When we find something good—such as the *Big Book* of Alcoholics Anonymous—something that speaks to us, something we "get," we don't tend to keep it a secret. Step 12 tells us that if we want to keep what we have, we need to give it away. And so we share. We share our best recovery resources with our fellow travelers, with other "friends of Bill," and with anyone who will listen. This leads to the fact that many of us in the recovery community rely on the same trusted resources to pull us out of a recovery rut by inspiring, motivating, educating, illuminating, or doing whatever it takes to keep us on the recovery path. And this, my friend, is how recovery classics—literature no person in recovery would want to be without—are born.

The Recovery Book falls into the "recovery classic" category. First published in 1992, this useful book gradually wound its way through recovery circles, including mine. When I was in early recovery, I bought *The Recovery Book* on a friend's advice. At the time, I read whatever recovery material I could get my hands on. I needed to absorb what people like me—those who had gone before me—went through, what they did to stay in recovery, what they understood recovery to be. I absorbed this information until it became mine—until I could define my unique needs and shape my own recovery. All of this information is based on a universal code, a universal 12-step message that works for each of us individually, despite how different each of us is.

As much as I was reading at the time, *The Recovery Book* stood out. First, it answered most of my questions as a newcomer, but it also showed me there was a way out of addiction, which gave me something even more important than answers to all my questions. It gave me hope.

The second edition of *The Recovery Book* holds all of its original charm and substance with some new and exciting updates. Dr. Al's Recovery Zone System in particular is worth mentioning for how it uses color to categorize three "zones" of recovery. Readers, especially those who are visual learners, will quickly learn an important and often underestimated fact: Recovery is a process. I don't know of anyone who stops drinking or using and finds that life is suddenly a bowl of cherries. It takes work, and we build on our progress until we reach the next "zone," or higher level of being. The Recovery Zone System spells out what needs to happen before we reach the next zone—and makes it crystal clear that we sometimes take two steps back before going forward. Dr. Al doesn't predict our path for us, but, by showing us the process, he takes our hand and guides us through it, giving us an indication of what to expect and, all the while, ensuring us that we are not alone— millions of others have experienced the same ups and downs on the road called recovery.

I have enormous respect for my dear friend Dr. Al Mooney. I first met Dr. Al at a conference, years after I had read his book. We exchanged pleasantries, and I told him what his book had meant to me. Now, Dr. Al and I are good friends, and to this day, I find Dr. Al's book to be an invaluable resource for myself and my patients at the Betty Ford Center in Rancho Mirage, California. Dr. Al's engaging mind and traditional yet creative approach to 12-Step abstinence-based recovery are exemplary. I feel honored to be part of the second edition of this recovery classic, which promises newcomers and old-timers alike a wealth of solid information about recovery, as well as new information based on recent science regarding the disease of addiction and changing technologies.

If you've read this far, *The Recovery Book* is already in your hands. Don't put it aside. Read it. Use it. It can help guide you step by step out of the gloom of addiction hell into the bright light of the world of recovery.

HARRY HAROUTUNIAN, M.D.

Physician Director, Professional and Residential Programs, the Betty Ford Center; Author, *Being Sober: A Step-by-Step Guide to Getting To, Getting Through, and Living in Recovery*

The Mooney Family Story

My name is Al Mooney, and I'm not an alcoholic or addict, but many others in my family are—my parents; my brothers, Jimmy and Bobby; and our sister, Carol Lind. Drinking and using drugs are more than just a challenging medical problem to me. They're personal. Very personal.

When I was growing up in Statesboro, Georgia, alcohol and drugs were in charge of our family. My father, John Mooney, was a wonderful physician—who drank at night and used pills during the day. My mother, Dot Mooney, was doing her best to be a good mom, but she popped codeine for her hangover headaches, tranquilizers for depression, and barbiturates so she could sleep.

One night in our living room, my father went into a convulsion from an overdose. That started him on a series of visits to psychiatric hospitals to "dry out." Each time my mother tried to cover up his absence by telling us kids—and his patients—that he was at a medical conference. Meanwhile, she was doing her best to cover up her own drinking and drug use. She would drive us to Sunday school every week, and then hide in the back of the room so no one could smell the liquor on her breath.

Like so many first-born children of alcoholic/addict parents, I felt I had no choice but to do what I could to keep the family going—getting the kids up for school in the morning, alerting Mom when the car she was driving was drifting off the road, covering up for Dad's absences. At the age of ten, I should have been just a kid playing in the backyard, but that wasn't the way my family worked.

It all finally turned around when my father, who had written himself hundreds of phony prescriptions, was sent to prison for six months. It was a big wake-up call for him, as well as a blessing. With the help of an AA member who visited him there, by the time he was released from prison, he was finally ready for sobriety.

Back home, after a few months of solid sobriety, an interesting thing happened. Dad's friends in recovery started asking him to provide care for their alcoholic friends. It turned out he was pretty good at it. Mom, who by then had also sworn off anything stronger than coffee, helped out. As their reputations grew, people began coming to them for help from all over the Southeast. Several hundred people were treated at our big old house on Lee Street; the dining room was set aside for detox.

Eventually, however, their good works outgrew the house (and the patience of our neighbors). So, Mom and Dad built an addiction treatment hospital in Statesboro. My mother named it Willingway. Today it is a successful, fully accredited, 40-bed treatment facility. My parents worked there for the rest of their lives, helping countless people. Despite our family's difficult early years, I'll always remember them not as hopeless addicts but as wise teachers and wonderful parents.*

As a young adult, I always knew I wanted to be a doctor like my dad, but I wasn't at all sure I wanted to work with addicts and alcoholics. I'd seen far too much of that world already—I was set on being a surgeon. Ironically, it was my surgical rotation in medical school that changed my mind. While stitching up trauma patients, I realized that it didn't matter whether the person on the table was there because of a

stabbing, a car accident, or family violence. In nearly every case, the root cause was alcoholism or addiction. I realized I could do more good helping people to turn their lives around *before* they ended up in surgery. I returned to Statesboro and eventually served as the medical director of Willingway.

Given my family's history, all my life I have done everything I could to avoid alcohol and mood-altering drugs. Addiction is a disease that runs in families, for both genetic and environmental reasons. I kept to the only sure way I knew of to prevent it from taking control of me—total abstinence. You might think that, seeing the mess alcohol and drugs had made of our parents' lives, my siblings would have done the same. No such luck. All of them spent a few years in active addiction. Eventually, however, each one found recovery—and a way to help others find recovery, carrying on the legacy of our parents.

For many years, whenever I discharged patients from Willingway, I longed to send them home with a guide on what to expect while living in recovery. I wanted a book that would help the whole family stay afloat and avoid relapse when our staff was no longer around to hug, love, and counsel them. I wanted a book that would answer all of their questions about practical things that often aren't covered in treatment or fellowship meetings, such as medical crises, going back to work, and fixing relationships. I

---

* If you'd like to read more about my family and the founding of Willingway, read *When Two Loves Collide*, by William G. Borchert.

wanted a book that would also help folks who didn't have the means, or perhaps the need, for inpatient treatment at a place like Willingway. I believe that the first edition of *The Recovery Book*, published in 1992, accomplished those things.

My coauthors and I hope that this second edition will carry on that tradition and help even more people who are struggling with addiction and alcoholism, including the millions who are now misusing prescription painkillers. We've included some entirely new elements, such as the Recovery Zone System, that gives people an easy-to-follow, three-stage blueprint for getting into recovery, preventing relapse, rebuilding their lives, and staying sober for a lifetime. It is a framework that works well with *all* of today's routes to recovery, including mutual support fellowships, medication-assisted treatment, faith-based support, and others. I believe it will help people incorporate whatever route works best for them—at the right time. We've also included exciting new information on neuroplasticity—the brain's ability to change and heal after addiction—and how people can make use of that in their own recoveries.

For decades, ever since my parents got sober and I began treating people with the disease of addiction, I've known that living in recovery can make for a content and purposeful life. I've seen many wonderful people get into recovery and find that life. I hope the new edition of *The Recovery Book* will help many others find that peace.

AL J. MOONEY, M.D.
Director of Addiction Medicine
and Recovery, Willingway

THE
RECOVERY
BOOK

Welcome to Recovery

W e're glad you're here. If you're new to the world of recovery, you might be feeling overwhelmed right now. Maybe you've finally accepted that you have a problem with alcohol or drugs and you need to do something about it. Maybe you're not quite sure you have a problem, but you're worried—or everyone around you is worried. In any event, you're probably confused about where to go from here. We can help.

The Recovery Book is your guide to restoring sanity and living the rest of your life as a sober person. We'll help you explore everything you need to do to immerse yourself in the culture of recovery, turn your life around, and live a long, healthy, and fulfilled existence. We don't promise it will be easy. It takes time, and you will have to do the work. But with our guidance, support from your local recovery community, and perhaps professional treatment, you *can* do it. One day at a time.

In these pages you'll find lots of straight-up information detailing how addiction is a disease of the brain (and how that makes it hard to stay sober at first), your many options for treatment, and how getting involved in a 12-step fellowship or other support group can help.

You'll learn ways to handle cravings and compulsions. You'll find out how you can rebuild your relationships, your career, your very life. You'll also learn about some revolutionary new brain science, and how you can harness the amazing power of your brain to heal yourself and live in sobriety—serenely. Without being a slave to alcohol or drugs.

Sound impossible? It's not. Dr. Al Mooney has been helping alcoholics and addicts get their lives back for more than thirty years. He has helped thousands of people find recovery in his private practice; at his family's treatment center, Willingway; and through the first edition of *The Recovery Book*. (He's actually been living in the world of recovery ever since he was a teenager, when his newly sober parents, Dr. John and Dot Mooney, started treating fellow alcoholics and addicts in the family home.) Over the years, Dr. Al has learned what works, what doesn't, and where the biggest risks of relapse lie. We've packed as much of it into this book as we could.

Turning your life around sounds like a lot of work (especially when you feel rotten and all you can think about is your next drink or fix). We understand. But the good news is *you don't have to do it all at once.* Dr. Al's Recovery Zone System, new to this edition, breaks the recovery process into three distinct zones. We'll give you clear guidance on what you need to do and when—in regard to treatment, joining a fellowship, healing your brain, step work, avoiding relapse, restoring relationships and your health, and much more. First up is the Red Zone, where you focus on saving your life to the exclusion of nearly everything else. Next is the Yellow Zone, where you start to rebuild your life. Last is the Green Zone, where life is really sweet. Follow this system (which works hand-in-hand with the 12-step philosophy) and you can build a strong recovery with minimal risk of relapse.

Right now you might feel like you're the only person in the world with this problem. You're not. Addiction and alcoholism are huge health issues, and far too many people continue to suffer. Fortunately, these diseases *can* be treated and managed. You *can* avoid more years of suffering and the risk of an early death. You *can* join the millions of people who have turned their lives around and found recovery. In fact, you've already started. Just by picking up this book, you've told your brain to start focusing on recovery.

So take a deep breath and keep reading. The first days are the hardest, but we promise it gets better. Much better. There's a beautiful life ahead, just waiting for you.

Who Needs Recovery?

WHAT IS ADDICTION? WHAT IS ALCOHOLISM?

Addiction is a disease of the brain. It is not due to a moral failure or a lack of willpower. It doesn't happen because you are a "bad" person. It is a chronic disease, just like diabetes or high blood pressure.

The first time you took drugs—cocaine, oxycodone, meth, heroin, whatever—it was a choice. Maybe it was just part of an evening with friends. But over time, as you continued to use drugs, your brain changed, affecting your ability to make good choices and control your actions. Eventually you were addicted: You had strong cravings for drugs and you compulsively sought out more, even when you knew that the end result could be devastating—going to jail, losing your family, even dying. Those fun party nights were but a distant memory.

The picture is similar if you have an "alcohol use disorder," which is just another form of addiction. In the early days, alcohol use was optional. But over time, it became more and more important, and you had stronger cravings for a drink. Then you probably couldn't stop drinking once you started, and you might have had withdrawal symptoms when you ran out. You might have also found you needed ever greater amounts of alcohol to get the same buzz. As happens with drugs, alcohol became all-important, pushing aside and doing great harm to other parts of your life, such as relationships, work, school, and health.

ARE YOU AN ALCOHOLIC OR ADDICT?

There is no blood test to diagnose drug addiction or alcoholism. Your doctor won't necessarily pick up on it, though he may notice some telltale signs, like liver damage. Your family and friends might have noticed problems, but you've probably brushed off their concerns (maybe for years).

The only way to be sure you need help is to take an honest look at your life. Read through the questions below. If you answer yes to two or three of them, you might have a problem. If you have even more yes answers, you should seek help now.

- Have you been drunk or high more than four times in the past year?

- Do you ever drink more than you mean to, or for a longer period of time? Do you sometimes stay drunk for days at a time?

- Are you taking any illegal drugs, such as cocaine or heroin?

- Are you taking any prescription drugs that were not prescribed for you, or using them more than was prescribed? Do you use them to change how you feel?

- Have you ever asked more than one doctor to prescribe a drug for you? Are you buying prescription drugs on the street?

- Have you ever gone to work or driven a car after drinking or getting high?

- Do you do things while under the influence that you wouldn't do otherwise? Do you regret them later?

- Do you ever wake up in the morning with no memory of the night before? Are these blackouts happening more often?

- Have you ever felt bad or guilty about your drinking or drug use?

- Have you ever felt you should cut down on your drinking or drug use, or have you ever tried to control it?

- Do you find you need more alcohol or drugs to get the feeling you're looking for?

- Can you handle more than before? More than most people?

Or do you suddenly find you can't handle as much?

- Do you get anxious if you have to go someplace where there won't be any alcohol or drugs? Do you feel uneasy when your supply of pills gets low?

- Do you scrounge for extra drinks at parties because you feel you aren't getting enough? Do you keep going when everyone else has had enough?

- Do you sometimes carry booze or drugs around with you? Do you create situations where you can drink—like arranging a work meeting at a bar?

- Have you ever kept on drinking even though it was making you anxious or depressed, or making another health issue worse?

- Do you tell yourself you can stop drinking or using drugs any time you want to, but find you keep going back to them?

- Have you ever switched from one kind of drink to another, hoping it would keep you from getting drunk? Or from one drug to another to prove you're not addicted?

- When you don't get alcohol or drugs, do you have withdrawal symptoms, such as shakiness, sweating, nausea, a racing heart, or trouble sleeping?

- Do you ever take a morning eye-opener to steady your nerves or get rid of a hangover?

- Do you ever need chemical help to do something (such as start the day, have sex, or socialize) or to change how you feel (sad, scared, anxious, depressed, or angry)? Do you use chemicals to banish shyness or bolster your confidence?

- Do the people you spend most of your time with drink a lot or take drugs? Do you tend to avoid other friends and family when you're drinking?

- Are alcohol or drugs sometimes more important than other things in your life—your family, your job, your school work, your values? For example, is smoking pot every evening more important than taking that last course you need to get a degree?

- Do you find yourself lying to your partner, your kids, your friends, or your boss to cover up your drinking or drug use?

- Has your substance use caused trouble at home or work? Are those around you annoyed by it or concerned about it? Are you annoyed by their concern? Do you get defensive about it?

- Have you had other problems related to your drinking or drug use in the past year (a DUI, missed workdays, failed exams, financial problems, car accidents)?

- Has a doctor found signs of alcohol damage and warned you to stop drinking or cut down?

- Have you ever thought your life might be better if you didn't drink or take drugs?

- Have you ever thought that maybe life just isn't worth living? (If you are having suicidal thoughts, call 800-273-8255 right now.)

ARE YOU AT RISK OF HAVING A PROBLEM?

After reading through the questions above, you might be thinking, "Hey, I'm still working. I'm still going to class. I've never had a blackout." Even so, you might have a problem. Drinking and drug use don't have to be out of control to damage your brain and your body.

Here's a simple question: How many times in the last year have you had four or more drinks in one day (five or more if you are male)?

If your answer is one or higher, you are what we call a "risky drinker."

You might not be an alcoholic now, but you should think about a future plan for dealing with your drinking. Will you go to rehab? Go to Alcoholics Anonymous (AA)? It's best to come up with a plan now, because later on you might well try to deny the problem.

IS DRINKING DAMAGING YOUR BODY ALREADY?

Even if you're not yet addicted to alcohol, you might be inflicting major damage on your body. Alcohol affects every cell in your body, and there is virtually no part of you that won't suffer. In fact, more than 350 illnesses have been linked to alcohol.

Drinking can damage your liver, nervous system, brain, reproductive system, muscles and heart, and impact your blood pressure. Heavy drinking is related to several types of cancers. And the wreckage doesn't stop there. Heavy drinking also puts you at higher risk of depression, stroke, and sleep problems. It can cause you to have trouble managing other chronic conditions, such as diabetes and high blood pressure, adding on all the complications that those conditions can cause.

Bottom line? If you're a man, you risk damaging your health if you have more than two drinks a day. If you're a woman, you can start to damage your body with more than one drink daily.

Alcohol also raises your risk of being killed or injured. It's a factor in far too many tragic events: 60 percent of drownings and fatal burns, 50 percent of severe trauma injuries and sexual assaults, and 40 percent of all fatal car crashes, suicides, and falls. It's also often a factor in homicides. Globally, alcohol causes 3.3 million deaths each year, or about 6 deaths every minute. That's more than the number of deaths due to AIDS, tuberculosis, or violence.

And by the way, you can't fudge on the definition of a drink. It's anything that contains about 0.5 ounce of alcohol. That includes a 5-ounce glass of wine, 12 ounces of beer, or a 1.5-ounce shot of 80-proof spirits (such as vodka or whiskey).

WHY DO SOME PEOPLE BECOME ADDICTS AND NOT OTHERS?

Addiction can happen to just about anyone: you, your spouse, your adored big brother who was the star of the football team, your best friend who planned to go to medical school, your favorite teacher. There is no single factor that can pinpoint who will become addicted to drugs or alcohol. There are, however, some risk factors that can indicate who is more likely to have a problem.

Family genetics. Some genes you inherit from your biological parents can put you at higher risk of alcoholism. But it's not as simple as having "the gene" for alcoholism. More than one gene is involved, and some can actually lower your risk. Furthermore, sometimes these genes are activated, or turned on, and sometimes they're not; they can be influenced by your environment. Scientists say that overall, genes are responsible for about half your total risk for alcoholism and about three-quarters of your risk for addiction to drugs. That means they are pretty strong factors in the overall picture. (If a biological parent is an alcoholic, however, you're about four times more likely than others to have a problem.)

Environment. Many factors relating to where you grew up and the experiences you've had can affect your risk. These include your family life, friends, relationships, socioeconomic status, quality of life, peer pressure, stress, and more.

Trauma. People who have experienced trauma in their lives are at increased risk for addiction. Many events can be traumatic, including sexual, physical, or emotional abuse, domestic violence, seeing combat, being bullied, childhood neglect, the death of a parent, having an incarcerated parent, or living with a parent who is mentally ill or an addict. And those who have experienced more than one type of trauma in childhood are even more likely to develop addiction.

Mental health disorders. If you have a disorder such as depression, anxiety, bipolar disorder, posttraumatic stress disorder (PTSD), or attention deficit hyperactivity disorder (ADHD), you are at greater risk of addiction.

Age. Those who start taking drugs early in life are much more likely to become addicted. In fact, the vast majority of addicts started using before age twenty-one.

Remember, though, none of these risk factors means you or anyone else absolutely *will* become an addict. They do raise your risk, but a person can have every single one of these factors and not become an addict or alcoholic.

Moving into Recovery

WHAT IS RECOVERY?

"Okay," you say. "I admit it. I accept it. I've got a problem. I could be an addict. I might be an alcoholic."

Now the question is, do you have an honest and ongoing desire to be sober? Do you have a true yearning to stop using all mood-altering chemical substances and change your life?

If so, congratulations. You have taken your first step toward a life in recovery.

Getting to that point is not easy, as many people can tell you. A sincere desire to finally get sober often comes only after years of denying that you have a problem and many attempts to get things "under control." You might be afraid of what's coming, of what sobriety might feel like, both physically and emotionally. Getting ready for a major overhaul of your life is a tough place to be in, but it's also the first step toward a better life.

As you'll see in the coming pages, there are many paths you can take to move into a life of sobriety. Some people can quit drinking and using on their own. Many need to detox (get all drugs out of the body) under a doctor's care. Many also need some professional treatment to help them get through those tough first days and weeks. Most people also find that getting support from others in a 12-step fellowship such as Alcoholics Anonymous or Narcotics Anonymous (NA) is crucial.

Getting and staying sober will be your first priority. But what you'll soon learn is that recovery is about so much more. Here are some basic truths about living in recovery.

Recovery is a way of life. Recovery is about building and *enjoying* a better life for yourself in sobriety. It's about finding and developing loving relationships, solid friendships, strong community ties, satisfying work, and invigorating play. It's about spending your life in good health and good spirits. It's about living a good life steeped in the culture of recovery.

Recovery is about healing. Over time you'll notice that your body is healing. Even better, your brain will be healing as well. Addiction hijacked your brain, making it very hard for you to make good choices. As you focus your thoughts and actions on sobriety and recovery, your cravings will disappear and your thoughts will no longer focus solely on getting your next fix. Thinking about recovery, and building your life around it, will be your new normal.

Recovery is a process. It takes time. You can't expect it all to happen overnight. You need to build your new life one day at a time, on top of a rock-solid foundation. That means following the Recovery Zone System, where you focus first on saving your life and then on rebuilding it. Eventually, you'll reach the point where you can celebrate your life and share the gift of recovery with others.

For many people, the process also means sticking with a 12-step support fellowship like AA or NA. In fact, these two pathways—the Recovery Zone System and the 12-step philosophy—work hand in hand.

Recovery is one of the biggest clubs on the planet. And that means that you don't have to do it alone. Millions of once "hopeless" alcoholics and addicts have gone down this road before you. Instead of dying of alcohol poisoning, or a car accident, or a drug overdose, they are now living happy, productive, sober lives. Many of them live in your area and are more than willing to help. They're just waiting to welcome you.

WHAT'S REALLY IN IT FOR ME?

It takes time, patience, and hard work to fully engage in the healing processes of recovery. But you *will* get to live a life that is better than you've ever imagined. You might be skeptical right now, but we have seen it happen again and again.

Here are some of the rewards, partially adapted from *Alcoholics Anonymous*, also called the *Big Book*, pages 83–84, that you can look forward to in sobriety. You will:

- Regain a sense of joy, happiness, and serenity.

- Rediscover peace of mind—or find it for the first time.

- Find a healthy new attitude and view of life.

- Feel a new sense of freedom.

- Regain the freedom to make choices.

- Start caring about others and benefit from a new honesty in your relationships.

- Find pleasure again in friends, family, nature, art, music, work, and hobbies.

- Escape from your fears—of people, experiences, financial turmoil.

- Shed your feelings of uselessness and self-pity.

- Feel comfortable with yourself and with others and feel loving and lovable.

- Lose your need to control people, events, and other things.

- Learn to solve your problems with thoughtful actions instead of covering them up with dishonest behaviors and chemicals.

- Find meaning in what you have experienced so far.

- Understand how your past experiences can help others and learn what you can do to improve the lives of others.

- Break the cycle of addiction.

How Did This Happen to My Brain?

HOW DID YOU GET HERE?

You might be wondering how you got to this place in your life. You surely weren't born an alcoholic or an addict—though, like many people, you might have been born with a genetic tendency to become one. And maybe for a while you didn't have a problem with alcohol or drugs. You honestly believed you could indulge only on weekends or special occasions. Your chemical of choice seemed like a good friend who helped you wind down after a hard day—until you started needing it every day. You trusted that the pain pills your doctor prescribed were only a temporary fix—until you started buying them on the street. So how did you get to the point where those chemicals seem to be running your life? And why is it so hard to change that? It's all about the brain.

In the last few years, scientists have discovered that repeated use of alcohol and drugs can actually *change the structure of your brain and how it works*. Your brain "molded itself" around and adapted itself to your drug or alcohol use—a complex process of change known as neuroplasticity. The end result: Your ability to exert self-control and make good decisions was severely weakened. That means that your addiction is *not* due to a lack of willpower or a moral failing, despite what an angry relative or friend might have told you. Your addiction is a chronic disease of your brain. No wonder it's so hard to stop.

The good news is that many addiction experts now believe that the same process also happens in recovery. Just as your brain molded itself around addiction, it can, with time, be molded around recovery and heal. If you commit to and follow a recovery plan, your brain *will* change. And in time, staying sober will be as normal for you as drinking or using drugs once was.

YOUR BRAIN IN ADDICTION

Your brain is made up of billions of nerve cells, or neurons. Working with nerves throughout your body, these neurons direct everything you do—thinking, breathing, enjoying a bowl of ice cream, everything. Touch a hot stove, and the nerves in your fingers zip a message up to your brain and you think, "Ouch, hot!" Catch a whiff of a burger on the grill and you think, "Time to eat!"

Your brain does all this by passing around messages in the form of electrical impulses. An impulse travels the length of one neuron, leaps across a gap to a nearby neuron, travels the length of that neuron, and so on. Brain chemicals called neurotransmitters help the electrical impulses move across the gaps (which are called synapses). When an impulse arrives at a synapse, the neuron releases a particular neurotransmitter, depending on the type of message. The neurotransmitter flows across the synapse and then, like a key in a lock, docks at a particular type of receptor on the next neuron, delivering the message and activating the impulse anew. This happens billions of times every second.

Now add alcohol or drugs to the system. The first time you indulged in your drug of choice, you probably felt a rush of pleasure, a surge of confidence. That was due to a neurotransmitter known as dopamine, one of the body's "feel-good" chemicals. The drug you took launched a message in your brain. The message then traveled through particular regions of the brain—known as the reward system—with the help of dopamine at each synapse. And the flush of dopamine felt good to you. Your brain said, "Wow! I like that!"

But dopamine isn't there just to make you happy. The reward system's goal is to teach you to do good-for-you, life-sustaining things by rewarding you with those pleasurable feelings. Eat good food, feel a nice dopamine high, and you'll want to do it again; you learn to fuel your body with nutrients. Have a drink, get a nice buzz; you learn to seek out alcohol. With the reward system, your brain is simply telling you, "Yeah! That was good. Do it again. And again." It's a very powerful teaching system.

Here's the problem: In some people, alcohol and drugs hijack the reward system. They overstimulate it in a number of ways, causing the release of very large amounts of dopamine and other chemicals, making you feel *really* good, even euphoric. And so you want another drink, another hit. Right now.

For a while, you were probably a social user: The alcohol- and drug-seeking behavior you learned didn't disrupt your life too much. But repeated social use reinforced what you learned, reinforced the reward. And over time, your brain underwent some complex and profound changes in the reward system and other areas—changes that stuck around long after the high had faded.

For example, depending on the drug you used, your natural neurotransmitter levels were increased or decreased (your brain throttled back its own production of dopamine, for example), and the ability of some neurons to interact with neurotransmitters was damaged. Some neurons were physically altered, neural pathways were strengthened or damaged, and some of the genes that control activity in your brain got more active. Part of this damage, unfortunately, occurred in the frontal lobe area of your brain—the "executive brain" that's responsible for high-level thinking and decision making. At first, these brain changes were reversible, but as your usage continued, some of them became permanent.

As your brain's structure and functioning changed, so did your behavior. The drug-seeking urges got stronger, and soon they started crowding out other things in your life—important things like family, friends, and work. Eventually, the reward, learning, motivation, and self-control systems in your brain were so altered that you found it impossible to resist those urges. It was also impossible to *stop* drinking or using once you started. At that point, seeking out alcohol or drugs was no longer a conscious decision. It had become a compulsion that could not be ignored, as ingrained in your brain as breathing or looking for food when you're hungry. You were powerless over your need to get more—and you did it even though you knew there could be very serious consequences. You had no desire to change your ways, either (in fact, you probably thought everything was just fine). You might have also found that you weren't even getting much of a high anymore—your neurotransmitters were so messed up that you needed drugs to jack them up just so you could feel *normal*.

The end result was that rational thoughts were no longer steering you to make good decisions, and you had lost the "brakes" of impulse control that might have stopped your bad moves. Your brain had molded itself around an intense need for drugs, and you had the disease known as addiction.

Scientists have only recently figured out how addiction happens in the brain, but the early members of AA nailed it decades ago, when they described it as a "physical allergy coupled with a mental obsession."

Unfortunately, many of these changes to your brain are likely to be permanent—they stick around long after you've stopped using alcohol or drugs. Those permanently altered neural pathways, in fact, may account for why some people relapse even after decades of sobriety—one trigger, one cue, can make those long-dormant circuits come roaring back to life.

YOUR BRAIN IN RECOVERY

Alcohol and drugs changed your brain, but you can use these same brain processes to stay sober. As we've noted before, *you can remold your brain around recovery*.

It won't happen overnight. It will take some time and effort. But if you commit to and follow a good recovery plan, your brain *will* change. Your brain *will* heal. Eventually, staying sober will become your routine way of life, and you won't feel like you are constantly fighting off urges to use alcohol or drugs.

How do you do that? You use the power of your brain to focus your thoughts and actions. You focus on the principles and activities of recovery, and on the sweet rewards coming your way, such as the return of your loving family and better health. You do all you can to avoid stress as well as cues and triggers, which can reactivate the drug-seeking pathways.

And you do everything you can to think positive thoughts and banish negative thinking. Over time, you'll develop *new* neural pathways—ones that are not focused on addiction—to guide your life and your decisions and actions. Slowly but surely, rather than thinking about your next drink all the time, your brain will change and you'll more naturally focus on recovery. You will have fewer negative thoughts and more positive ones. Your cravings and anxiety will subside, and sobriety will become your way of life.

Now you're thinking, "That sounds crazy. Just by thinking a certain way I can heal my brain?" Exactly. And there's nothing crazy about it. The scientists who study neuroplasticity point to many instances where people have created new pathways in their brains in this manner. For example, people who have had a stroke, which damages parts of the brain, have developed new pathways that allow them to use an arm, or to speak. The damaged part of the brain was not repaired. Rather, with lots of practice, they formed new routes to send the messages that carry out various tasks. Likewise, psychotherapy—which of course involves a lot of thinking and talking—has been shown to help people develop new pathways in the brain.

Our current understanding of this new brain science, based on scores of recent studies, is that over time, by directing your thoughts, actions, and experiences, challenging your mind, and taking good care of your body, you can:

- Spur the growth of new neurons

- Create new connections between neurons and prune away old connections

- Substitute new areas of neural connections for older or lost areas

- Strengthen or sensitize some neural connections and desensitize others

- Restore normal production of neurotransmitters

- Restore the ability of neurons to work with neurotransmitters

- Restore a strong relationship between the high-level thinking part of your brain (the frontal lobe) and more primitive, emotional part (the limbic brain), restoring your ability to use good judgment, make good decisions, tame your cravings, control impulses, and control your behavior

- Strengthen and expand your emotional capacity, keeping emotions and desires under control

In sum, you can rewire your brain. This ability of the brain to change in response to thoughts and actions may, in fact, help explain why 12-step programs like AA work so well. The founders of AA, Bill W. and Dr. Bob, surely never heard the word *neuroplasticity*, but changing their thoughts and actions is exactly what they did more than seventy-five years ago. They talked about their problems with their peers, they focused their minds on staying sober, and they tried to help others find sobriety. In so doing, they molded their brains around recovery. They healed their brains. They called it the "psychic change."

HEAL YOUR BRAIN WITH TAMERS

If you're stuck in the endless cycles of addiction, you might find it hard to believe that just thinking positive thoughts and focusing on sobriety can help in your recovery. But we promise it can. You just need to stick with it. It's like going to the gym. Keep going, week after week, keep challenging your body, push through some discomfort, and pretty soon your body is in great shape. You can do the same for your brain.

Best of all, you don't need to learn all about brain science to heal your own brain. Just remember TAMERS:

Think about recovery & Talk about recovery

Act on recovery, connect with others

Meditate & Minimize stress

Exercise & Eat well

Relax

Sleep

That's pretty much it. Include TAMERS as part of your complete recovery program, and your brain will heal.

So every single day, think about recovery, talk about recovery, read about recovery. Meditate on recovery. Focus your actions on recovery. For the next several months, make recovery the foundation of everything you do. Follow your treatment plan. Join a mutual-support fellowship and spend lots of time with others in recovery. Also be sure to follow the Recovery Zone System, which is laid out in the next chapter. It will help you see what you need to focus on now to build a strong recovery, and what you can put off until later.

Soon, staying sober will be much easier and will feel completely natural to you. Soon, as the book *Alcoholics Anonymous* promises, you will "know a new freedom and a new happiness."

A DRUG IS A DRUG

It doesn't matter whether your drug of choice is alcohol, cocaine, oxycodone, methamphetamine, or another mood-altering substance. The problems you face in recovery will be the same as those everyone else faces, for the most part. Likewise, most of the solutions raised in this book, even when they refer to a specific drug, are relevant to everyone.

To bring this fact home, we use the terms alcoholism and addiction almost interchangeably. Likewise, when we talk about alcohol, drugs, mood-altering chemicals, or chemical substances, we mean all drugs that exert an effect on the brain, including alcohol. When we mention AA or NA or another group, we mean it to represent all the 12-step fellowships and most non-12-step mutual-support fellowships, unless otherwise noted.

We also discuss many different types of drugs. Most fall into one of a few broad categories, with similar effects: alcohol; other central nervous system depressants; stimulants (such as cocaine, crack, and methamphetamine); opiates/narcotics (morphine, heroin, fentanyl, oxycodone, and other pain relievers); marijuana and other hallucinogens; dissociative drugs (ketamine, PCP); inhalants; and antidepressants and antipsychotic drugs.

CHAPTER

Your Recovery Plan

To build a good recovery you need a plan. This chapter outlines the key elements of what it means to truly embrace recovery, and also explains how you can use the Recovery Zone System to develop your own recovery plan and rebuild your life.

You'll also learn how you can use this system to stay sober for the rest of your life, even when your world gets rocked by major events, such as divorce, the death of a loved one, loss of a job, or surgery.

The Key Elements of Your Recovery Plan

Your life in recovery can be full of serenity, honesty, and peace. It can be a meaningful and happy existence—without alcohol and drugs.

But you can't get to this happy state by waving a magic wand or popping a pill. It will take time. If you're used to immediate payback, the slow process may be hard at first. But you didn't get into trouble with alcohol or drugs overnight, and you can't put your life and your health back together that fast either.

But one step at a time, one day at a time, you can make it happen. Do the work and your brain *will* heal. You *will* move forward in your life, to a more stable, stronger state of recovery.

Many people think there is nothing more to recovery than not drinking and not taking drugs. Sobriety is crucial, of course, but there is so much more to building a strong recovery. The foundation of your journey will be the four key elements of your recovery plan:

- Commit to sobriety.

- Get active in a mutual-support fellowship.

- Be patient and let your body and brain heal.

- Follow the Recovery Zone System, your step-by-step guide to life in recovery.

Embracing these Key Elements will help you build a strong, rock-solid recovery and enjoy a lifetime of health.

Commit to Sobriety

Your first task is to get sober. When you do quit drinking or using, you may go through detoxification, or "detox," and experience withdrawal symptoms. This phase is sometimes best done under a doctor's care.

Along with detox, you may need some professional treatment, such as a stay in a rehab facility or meetings with a therapist. Some people can make the commitment to sobriety without treatment. Many others, however, need some help.

Once you have gotten through detox and initial treatment, you'll need to learn how to *continue* to live sober—how to recognize and avoid the temptations and triggers that could lead you to relapse.

Get Active in a Mutual-Support Fellowship

We are big advocates of the 12-step methods embraced by Alcoholics Anonymous and other fellowships. For most people, taking part in one of these groups is a major factor in how they stay sober.

There are many 12-step groups in addition to AA: Narcotics Anonymous, Cocaine Anonymous, and others. We strongly suggest you find a group near you and start going to meetings and working the steps. Reach out to the people there, find a sponsor, and let people help you.

Millions of alcoholics and addicts around the world can tell you from experience that getting involved in a 12-step fellowship really works. Indeed, these fellowships are known to be the most effective life-long "treatment" available today for people with addiction.

Some people, however, find that groups that don't use the 12-step approach work better for them.

Be Patient and Let Your Body and Brain Heal

You probably won't feel better physically or mentally overnight. Alcohol and drugs may have caused a lot of damage to your body, but fortunately, your body can repair a lot of that damage over time. You also need to give your brain time to rebuild strong neural connections and lay down those new pathways that are focused on recovery.

Remember, even when it feels like you are not moving forward, if you do the work and stay sober, your body and brain *will* be healing.

Follow the Recovery Zone System

Living in recovery can entail a complete overhaul of your life, including many things besides sobriety: relationships, family, friends, career, finances, hobbies, health. Trying to stay sober while dealing with all of these areas at once would be overwhelming. That's where the Recovery Zone System comes in. It is a blueprint for rebuilding your life and living in recovery. It gives you a step-by-step plan for addressing each of these "life domains" at the right time without risking your sobriety.

In this system, your life is divided into three phases: the Red Zone: Stop. Activate Your Recovery; the Yellow Zone: Proceed with Caution. Build Your Life; and the Green Zone: Go. Celebrate Your Life.

You will use the Recovery Zone System to move forward in recovery, moving from Red to Yellow to Green as your sobriety grows more solid. You can also use it throughout your life to take stock of where you are in recovery on any given day—even after years of sobriety—and avoid relapse.

The Recovery Zone System

HOW IT WORKS

Over many years of treating alcoholics and addicts, Dr. Al saw that two issues were jeopardizing recovery for many people.

- People in early sobriety often had no idea how much time and energy they needed to focus on recovery activities. Some tried to do too much—such as beginning a rigorous grad school program after only two weeks of sobriety. Others failed to address crucial areas, such as rebuilding ties with their kids or repairing their health. Far too many people who truly wanted to be sober ended up feeling overwhelmed by it all, or they built a shaky recovery that was full of holes.

- People with many years of recovery sometimes lost their focus on these activities as the years passed. They stopped living in the culture of recovery.

All too often, these situations led people into a downward spiral and put them at high risk of relapse. So Dr. Al developed an easy-to-follow guide for rebuilding your life slowly but surely, while reducing the risk of relapse.

His Recovery Zone System (see chart, page 22) gives you clear guidance on when to address the various areas of your life—treatment, fellowship activities, relationships, socializing, education, career, finances, recreation, and health—now that you are putting your life back together. It helps you to identify how and when you are ready to move forward in each of those areas. And it helps you to see when you might need to move *backward* for a bit, to avoid a relapse. (In this case moving backward is not a negative thing—it could save your life.)

The Recovery Zone System strengthens and simplifies the concept of "living in recovery." Here's how it works.

Your life in recovery is divided into three distinct zones:

THE RED ZONE: Stop. Activate your recovery.

For the first eighteen months or more of recovery, you focus on saving your life. Nothing else is as important. Nothing.

THE YELLOW ZONE: Proceed with caution. Build your life.

Once you have a solid foundation of sobriety, you can move into the Yellow Zone, where you put your energy into building (or rebuilding) the life you want.

THE GREEN ZONE: Go. Celebrate your life.

After you have a few solid years of sobriety behind you and have done most of the work of rebuilding your life, you'll move into the Green Zone. Then it will be time to celebrate. You will focus on what you can do to live a long, fulfilled, and happy life, and also on how you can help others find the gift of recovery.

When you are in early recovery, in the Red Zone, you'll focus almost exclusively on the activities that will save your life: detox, inpatient or outpatient treatment, getting involved in a 12-step fellowship. It is not the time to worry about going back to college or lobbying for a promotion at work. You'll need to do only minimal work on fixing relationships. When you think you are ready to move on from the Red Zone, the Are You Ready questions in chapter 16 will help you assess whether you have truly done the work needed to move forward.

When you do move into the Yellow Zone, you'll focus on building the life you desire, really repairing relationships, and making your existence more fulfilling for yourself, as well as for those close to you. In the Yellow Zone, you can find a new job, start a new relationship, become the expert fly fisherman you always wanted to be, or finally get that degree.

After you've been in the Yellow Zone for a while, and have rebuilt your life, you'll move into the Green Zone (usually after four to six years of sobriety). Again, Are You Ready questions (chapter 21) will help you assess whether you are ready to move on.

By the time you get to the Green Zone, life can be pretty great. That's where you'll find that wonderful life of serenity, honesty, and peace that we promised you.

Chapters 3, 16, and 21 outline what you'll need to do in each of the recovery zones.

RECOVERY ZONE RECHECK

There is no "cure" for addiction. You can live in recovery, but you will be at some risk of relapse for the rest of your life. And relapses can be devastating: You can end up right back in the hole of active addiction and not get out of there for *years*—if ever.

Once you have a few years of sobriety behind you, your risk should be pretty small. But sometimes, out of the blue, you may find yourself in a situation that leaves you at a very high risk of relapse: perhaps a "critical life event," such as having surgery or starting a new job. Or you might find yourself feeling overwhelmed by stress, the blues, or just a really long to-do list.

To grab control of those situations long *before* they can drag you down, take stock of your life regularly with the Recovery Zone ReCheck. To do a ReCheck, at least once a month take a good look at where you are and how your life is going. This will help you to recognize when changes in your life are coming up—in relationships, work, finances, health, and other areas—that could put added stress on you and upset your recovery. These changes can be anything from a simple dental procedure to the death of a spouse. Good events, too, can rock your world, like getting a raise or moving to a new town. Or rather than one big event, it might be just an accumulation of smaller events or emotional upsets that is threatening to upend your progress.

When you see such roadblocks ahead, what do you do? You move *back* a zone or two, and you stay there for a while. You brush up on the guidelines of that earlier zone, recommit to sobriety, and refocus your thoughts and actions on the basics of recovery. You revert to your earlier recovery practices, such as going to meetings daily instead of once a week, or reworking some steps. You wave a flag asking for help and get your sponsor more involved in all your actions and decisions. And you think about what else you can do to avoid a relapse, given the upcoming event or whatever is upsetting you. All this will help you refocus your mind on everything that you know about recovery and how you can avoid a relapse—long before you head to the bar or pop a pill.

Here are the steps to doing a Recovery Zone ReCheck:

1. Take stock of your life regularly by using a personal inventory (see How the Twelve Steps Can Help You, chapter 8), talking with your sponsor, writing in your journal, or using another method that works for you. Choose a regular day to do this every month.

2. Look for current and upcoming events—good and bad—that could upset your stable life and threaten your recovery.

3. When an event arises, ask yourself (and your sponsor) these ReCheck questions:

Potential effects. How might this event affect my sobriety?

Recovery Zone. What Recovery Zone should I go back to in order to avoid a relapse (and for how long)? What recovery activities should I resume or increase in frequency?

Other actions. What else can I do to avoid a relapse?

For example, imagine that after many years of sobriety, you need to have elective surgery. You've been cruising through life and going to fellowship meetings regularly, but you feel your recovery is solid and you don't think about it as much as you once did. You go in for a checkup, expecting everything will be fine. But your doctor says you need surgery to fix something (a knee, a hip, whatever). When you get that news, you might not be focused enough on recovery activities to realize that this could put you at high risk of relapse.

If you are regularly taking stock of your life with Recovery Zone ReChecks and watching out for such events, however, you will quickly recognize that surgery, even something elective, poses a real danger to your sobriety. You'll get in touch with your sponsor or other advisors and talk about the situation.

Here's how you might answer the ReCheck questions:

Potential effects. You've talked with your doctor and know that you are likely to have some pain after the surgery. You know that taking any mood-altering drug for pain control, even under a doctor's supervision, could put you at risk of relapse. Being in an unfamiliar environment, vulnerable, and isolated from your usual recovery resources also poses threats.

Recovery Zone. You decide that a week or more before your surgery, you'll return to the Red Zone to focus more intensely on recovery activities. You plan to go to three meetings a week, meet with your sponsor twice a week, and run all important decisions by him. You plan to renew some step work to recommit to recovery. You plan to keep up this schedule for at least a month after the surgery. You also schedule a few bedside fellowship meetings for the first days after surgery.

Other actions. You realize that you need to investigate options for drugs that won't put you at high risk of relapse. You make plans to talk with the anesthesiologist and your doctor about what drugs you might be given during and after the procedure, and find out if you have any other options. If you must take any risky drugs, you and your doctor will devise a plan to strictly limit your drug usage and have someone else control access to the pills.

Likewise, if you sense that you and your partner are heading for a split, taking stock with a Recovery Zone ReCheck will help you recognize, long before you break up, that stirred-up emotions could trigger an urge to drink, and that you need to start going to more meetings now. Or if you are planning a business trip, you'll recall that being alone in a new city could trigger a sense of vulnerability or anonymity and that you need to move back a zone and also find some meetings to go to as soon as you arrive.

You and your sponsor will need to assess each situation, think about how threatening it might be, and develop a plan. In less risky situations, you might need to only go back to the Yellow Zone.

Some people might resist "going backward" in their recovery. "I've done all this work to get here! I don't want to go backward now," they protest. But it's perfectly fine. The Recovery Zone System is not a one-way street. It's absolutely acceptable to move back and forth among the zones as needed. Most moves to an earlier zone are only temporary, and they are the best thing you can do to protect your long-term recovery. If you are at the point where you are sponsoring other people, you might even ask one of them to do a temporary role reversal—let others get a little practice sponsoring you.

By keeping the Recovery Zone System and Recovery Zone Re-Checks as part of your life forever, you won't be caught unawares by life events. You will be able to *anticipate* times when you'll be at higher risk of relapse and take steps to avoid it.

BEFORE YOU GET STARTED

A word of caution before you jump into the Recovery Zone System: Don't rush. Moving from one zone to another is a big step. Don't move forward until you are really ready. Take plenty of time to work on your program in each zone and think about the issues raised and about your life. Talk about everything with your sponsor and others you trust. Go over the Are You Ready questions at the beginning of each zone section with their help. If you discover at any time that you have unresolved issues, go back and review the related chapters. You can also use the Are You Ready questions at any time to assess your progress in a zone.

If you've been sober for a while and think maybe you should jump straight to the Yellow Zone or Green Zone, go to those section introductions (chapters 16 and 21) and read about what life is like then. Then answer the Are You Ready questions. If you are not ready, go back to an earlier zone guide and start there.

The Recovery Zone System

		RED ZONE
	FOCUS	**Stop. Activate your recovery.** Stop everything you are doing and save your life. Focus entirely on survival and your recovery.
	TIMELINE	First commitment to 1.5–3 years in recovery.
	ARE YOU READY?	• Do you have an honest and ongoing desire to stop drinking or using drugs? • Are you ready to focus exclusively on recovery? • Are you ready to save your life?
RECOVERY ACTIVITIES	**RECOVERY TREATMENT**	Start professional treatment, if needed, with: • Detox • Inpatient or outpatient treatment • Guidance to address issues such as trauma
	MUTUAL-SUPPORT FELLOWSHIP	Start intensive participation in mutual-support activities. Complete steps 1–3 (decision steps) and 4–9 (action steps).
	SPIRITUALITY	Your brain is too foggy for much spiritual growth. Focus on acceptance, preparation.
	LIVING SOBER AND PREVENTING RELAPSE	Learn about cues and triggers that can lead to relapse. Develop a plan to deal with cravings. Your living environment is structured enough to keep your focus on recovery.
LIFE PLAN	**RELATIONSHIPS**	Put relationships on hold and work on yourself. Lay the groundwork for later repairs.
	RECREATION AND SOBER SOCIALIZING	Recreation and socializing are low priorities. Learn how to socialize sober.
	EDUCATION, CAREER, FINANCES	Put education, career, and finances on hold as much as possible. Learn to handle work stress.
HEALTH PLAN	**PHYSICAL HEALTH**	Focus on survival. Take care of immediate needs. Learn about the risks of drugs in health care.
	DIET	Eat to avoid relapse and relieve cravings.
	EXERCISE	Do some exercise, but be sure it is not goal-oriented or isolating.
	MENTAL HEALTH	Symptoms may be due to addiction. Unless they are life-threatening, usually the best approach is to continue your focus on recovery.

YELLOW ZONE	GREEN ZONE
Proceed with caution. Build your life. Maintain your foundation of sobriety and strong recovery. Build your new life.	**Go. Celebrate your life.** Live a long, healthy, sober life. Help others find recovery.
1.5–3 years in recovery to 4–6 years.	4–6 years to the end of your life.
• Do you have a strong and stable recovery? Has the fog lifted? • Have you completed initial treatment? Do you have a relapse prevention plan? • Are you still involved in a recovery fellowship? Have you completed steps 1–9? Are you ready to start steps 10–12? • Have you seen the promises of the *Big Book* come true? • Are you ready to rebuild your life?	• Do you have a strong and stable recovery, and a fulfilled and content life? • Are you still involved in a recovery fellowship? Have you completed steps 1–12? • Have you rebuilt your life (relationships, recreation, education, career, finances)? • Have you restored your health? • Are you ready to help others find recovery?
Professional treatment, if any, should focus on growth in relationships, career, and emotions, and healthy living practices.	Maintain a relationship with a professional for help as needed.
Continue mutual-support activities. If you want to cut back, talk to your sponsor. Welcome leadership and service opportunities. Start steps 10–12 (maintenance).	With your sponsor, find your best level of participation. Continue to practice step 12. Make sponsoring, service, and leadership priorities.
Develop and practice spiritual attitudes and activities.	Be available to guide others.
Continue to be watchful of cues and triggers. Review your plan for cravings often. Do Recovery Zone ReChecks regularly. Your living environment is supportive of your personal goals.	Continue to be watchful of cues and triggers. Review your plan to deal with cravings often. Do Recovery Zone ReChecks regularly. You are strong enough to live wherever you want.
Rebuild or start new relationships with your partner, family, friends, and others.	Relationships should be healed, content, and growing. Address and prevent addiction in your extended family.
Explore recreational and social activities.	Participate regularly in recreational and social activities.
Build or rebuild your education, career, and finances.	Career and finances should be stable.
Stabilize your health. Find a primary care provider and address neglected issues. Avoid all mood-altering medications.	Achieve your best health. Focus on preventive care. Avoid all mood-altering medications.
Learn about nutrition and improve your diet.	Establish good dietary habits.
Find forms of exercise you enjoy.	Set and meet exercise goals.
Focus on quality of life issues.	Focus on quality of life issues.

THE

RED

ZONE

Are You Ready for the Red Zone?

- Do you have an honest and ongoing desire to stop drinking and using drugs?
- Are you willing to focus on your recovery and put other parts of your life on hold?
- Are you ready to save your life?

If you answered yes to all of the above, great! Keep reading.

Please note: If you answered no and you think you aren't quite ready for recovery, don't despair. Keep reading, keep learning, and you might be ready soon. (False starts are not uncommon; read about the stages of motivational readiness in chapter 4.) We'll be here when you are ready.

Stop: Activate Your Recovery

The moment you have an honest and ongoing desire to give up alcohol and other drugs, you have entered the Red Zone of recovery. This is when you *stop what you are doing, activate your recovery, and focus solely on saving your life.*

Right now, your chief concern is surviving. You need to stop your downward spiral and concentrate everything you've got on getting well, to the exclusion of just about everything else. Your family and friends will probably think you are being very self-centered by focusing all your energy on yourself and your recovery. But that's how early recovery has to be.

The Red Zone is a time of learning. It is where you'll learn about options for addiction treatment, perhaps trying more than one until you find something that works for you. You'll also learn about:

- Yourself—who you really are, what you want out of life

- Your addiction—what it's done to you already, what it could do if you don't deal with it now, and how you can manage it long term

- Your brain and how you can help it heal

- Your sobriety—how you can maintain it and live comfortably with it, how to cope with your problems without chemical help, and how to avoid relapse

- Everything else you need to do to live in the culture of recovery

You're likely to experience a wide range of symptoms in the Red

Zone, related to both your addiction and your withdrawal from it. Your body may complain bitterly, with new symptoms related to recovery and with old ones you never noticed when your brain was anesthetized. Your head will probably be shrouded in fog,

Your Recovery Program in the Red Zone

Here's a summary of what you need to do in the Red Zone.

RECOVERY TREATMENT

- Start by reading chapter 4, Committing to Recovery. If you have any lingering doubts about getting into recovery, it will help you resolve those issues.
- Next, explore your options for professional treatment in chapter 5, The Many Roads to a Lifetime of Sobriety. Many people try to get into recovery without professional treatment, but it can be a tough way to go. So do consider all options.
- Once you do quit, you'll have to go through detox, or get rid of all alcohol and drugs in your body. Read about what you can expect in chapter 6, A Closer Look: Detox and Withdrawal.
- If you decide on inpatient treatment to start your recovery, you'll have a lot of questions about what happens there. Read chapter 7, A Closer Look: Inpatient Treatment.

MUTUAL-SUPPORT FELLOWSHIP AND SPIRITUALITY

Most people find that participating in a 12-step fellowship like AA or another group greatly strengthens their recovery. If you choose the 12-step route, start going to meetings and working the steps, preferably with the help of a sponsor. In the Red Zone you'll complete steps 1–3 (the decision steps) and 4–9 (the action steps). Chapters 8 and 9 (A Closer Look: AA and Other 12-Step Fellowships, and A Closer Look: 12-Step Programs and You) give you an in-depth look at 12-step fellowships.

LIVING SOBER AND PREVENTING RELAPSE

Getting sober is just the start. To stay sober, you'll need to learn how to avoid or deal with the triggers and cravings that can trip you up. These issues are covered in chapter 10, First Steps: Living in Sobriety and Preventing Relapse.

Another issue is where you'll live. For now, it should be structured enough that you can keep your focus on recovery. If you check into an inpatient facility, these needs will be taken care of, at least for a while. Another option is a sober living home, which is also covered in chapter 10.

and your emotions will flip-flop often.

For many people, this is the toughest part of recovery. But it's also the time when they see the most dramatic changes.

The Red Zone typically lasts about eighteen months.

RELATIONSHIPS, RECREATION, AND SOBER SOCIALIZING

The Red Zone is not the time to try to repair relationships or make big changes in your life. Still, you can't ignore the people who care about you; you can't hide out at home forever. You might also have to contend with rumors about what you did in blackouts, the effects of sobriety on your sex life, and your new role in your family. Read about all of those issues in chapter 11, First Steps: Relationships, Recreation, and Socializing in the Red Zone.

EDUCATION, CAREER, AND FINANCES

You'll probably have to go back to work once your initial treatment is done. Chapter 12, First Steps: Education, Work, and Finances in the Red Zone, covers how to handle work and financial issues when you're in early recovery.

PHYSICAL HEALTH, DIET, AND EXERCISE

You've put your body and your brain through the wringer. Right now you need to focus first and foremost on survival. Later on, you can worry about getting back into shape or training for a marathon. Medical issues will come up regularly, however. Chapter 13, Your Physical Health in the Red Zone, covers just about everything you'll need to know about your body in early recovery, including avoiding risky medications and dealing with ailments that are common in early recovery.

MENTAL HEALTH

You're likely to feel some pretty strong emotions in the Red Zone—maybe some that you haven't felt in a very long time. Chapter 14, Your Mental Health in the Red Zone, covers some of the issues that might come up and how to deal with them in safe ways.

Note to teenagers and young adults: Most of the information in these Red Zone chapters also applies to you. But at your age you have a whole other bunch of issues to deal with in recovery: fitting in, peer pressure, bullying, going back to school, and more. Chapter 15, For Teens and Young Adults in Recovery, is for you.

Your Brain in the Red Zone

Right now your brain is still pretty foggy. It still sees drugs as a nice reward. Your decisions are not the best, and it's not easy to fight off those cravings. Your thinking and emotions are still all wrapped up in drugs. But with abstinence, you are starting to heal.

As you read in chapter 1, you can use the power of neuroplasticity to heal your brain and make sobriety your new normal state of mind. It's simply a matter of focusing your thoughts and actions on recovery, immersing yourself in the culture of recovery, and practicing TAMERS.

Think about recovery & Talk about recovery

Act on recovery, connect with others

Meditate & Minimize stress

Exercise & Eat well

Relax

Sleep

You will see vast improvements in the Red Zone, but complete healing of your brain may take as long as 5 to 10 years. The frontal lobe, the executive brain, is often the last to return to normal.

Most of your recovery activities will help heal your brain. Below are some more tips for getting the most benefit for your brain.

Recovery Treatment

- Accept in your mind that you have a disease, and formulate your plan for healing.

- If you have professional treatment, give it everything you've got—the behavioral therapies especially will engage your mind in recovery.

- Deal with any emotional trauma from your past. In tough times, the more primitive limbic part of your brain determines your behavior. The animal drive kicks in. In order for your higher-level frontal lobe to jump into the action and start healing, you need to first feel safe and secure. Only then will rational thinking start to guide your life.

Mutual-Support Fellowship and Spirituality

- Get your brain engaged in fellowship activities. Talk about recovery with others; build connections with them. Set up chairs and make the coffee. Share your story. These new "playgrounds and playmates" will help embed recovery practices in your brain.

- Meet with your sponsor or advisor regularly to talk about recovery. His wisdom will serve as a template for your own brain.

- Start working the 12 steps with the guidance of your sponsor. Step 1 is an acknowledgment that you are powerless over your addiction—because of the changes in your brain. Steps 1–3 prepare your brain to move forward with openness. Steps 4–9 include actions that help reestablish healthy thinking and brain function. (Steps 10–12, in the Yellow and Green Zones, will help you maintain your healthy brain.)

- Every day, do a personal inventory and think about where you are in recovery.

- Practice recovery every day, just as if you were an athlete in training. You need to exercise your brain every day for it to heal and stay fit.

Living Sober and Preventing Relapse

- Surround yourself with people, places, and things that support your recovery.

- Form new habits for living. Learn healthy routines by spending time with people who have proven track records of recovery. Let their experiences be embedded into the blank canvas of your brain.

- Learn about the cues and triggers that were wired into your brain in addiction and could fire up those old neural pathways of drug seeking and cravings and trigger a relapse.

- Get rid of all the temptations, cues, and triggers at home that could pull your thoughts back to drugs or alcohol, and arrange your life so you can avoid them outside your home.

- Write up a Relapse Prevention Plan—figure out exactly what you will do to avoid a relapse if you run into any of those temptations, cues, or triggers or have any fleeting thoughts of using.

- Start a recovery journal. Write about what you've been doing for your recovery, what you've learned about yourself and your triggers, what you'd like to accomplish, how you are feeling, and so on. Think about what you are grateful for and write it down. Banish negative thinking. Review your journal regularly to encourage your brain to process events rationally, not purely emotionally.

- Live in a safe, low-stress environment. Your brain needs to be in a safe place in order to change; only then can your "survival brain" take a rest and let your "social brain" take over and rebuild healthy connections.

Relationships, Recreation and Sober Socializing, Education, Career, and Finances

- Think often about the many rewards of life you will soon have: being responsible and honest, finding a sense of

purpose, rebuilding ties with loved ones, having fun sober, making a new start at work, rebuilding your finances. Think about your hopes and dreams for the future.

Physical and Mental Health

- Take care of immediate health needs—a healthy body supports a healthy brain.

- Avoid all mood-altering drugs and supplements; they can reactivate the old neural pathways and prevent the formation of healthy new ones.

- Improve your appearance, so you think of yourself as a person in recovery.

- Protect your brain from trauma; wear a helmet for sports that require it, a seat belt in the car.

- Get plenty of sleep; your brain needs it to function.

- Avoid toxins.

- Eat foods that nourish the brain.

- Keep your blood sugar balanced; low blood sugar is associated with low activity in the frontal lobe of the brain.

- Do some gentle exercise to stimulate the brain.

- Learn and use tools for avoiding or managing anxiety, depression, and stress.

- Learn how to calm your mind; explore mindfulness, meditation, and visualization.

- Replace negative thoughts with positive ones.

Committing to Recovery

You say you have an honest and ongoing desire to get sober and change your life. Great. Now you need to follow through. It's time to face your fears and concerns and make a commitment to getting sober.

Everyone else seems to think it's no big deal to quit drinking and using. "Just stop," they say to you (or scream at you). If only it were that easy. Maybe your spouse is after you to quit drinking. Or your parents asked you to leave, with a warning not to come home again until you got sober. Or your doctor cautioned that if you keep abusing your body, you're headed for an early grave. You know they're right, but still you drink and use drugs. That's because your brain has changed, and making good decisions and carrying them out is not easy at all. It's much easier to find reasons why you should just continue what you are doing.

- It's easier to say that you really don't have a problem—your life is not that bad.

- It's easier to put the blame elsewhere—you wouldn't use drugs if your partner paid more attention to you.

- It's easier to find reasons why you can't take on quitting right *now*—hey, you haven't hit bottom yet, and besides, that big work project is coming up.

- You've already tried quitting, and frankly, it's too hard.

- You don't know what sobriety will be like, and you're scared.

You've got lots of excuses, lots of reasons why you don't really need to change now. To your family, your friends, and your doctor, though, just one thing is clear: Continue to drink and use drugs, and your life will continue on a downward spiral until it's over. But *you* have to believe that. You need to break through those barriers to healing. The choice between life and an early death is yours alone, and you have to want to choose life. So let's look at some of the issues that might be holding you back. See if you recognize yourself in any of the stories that follow.

I Don't Think I Have a Problem

"I may have some problems with booze, but I'm not like those other people. I'll think about quitting drinking, even though I'm sure I'm not an alcoholic."

Most people who have a drinking problem are sure they aren't that terrible "A" word: alcoholic. And most drug users don't think they are addicts, either. They're all sure they're not like "those other people." "Terminal uniqueness" is a major symptom of the disease of addiction. But in reality, it doesn't matter who you are or where you come from. Chemicals don't play favorites; addiction is the great equalizer. The Ph.D. and the dropout, the loving mother and the prostitute, the start-up entrepreneur and the homeless guy—they can all end up dead years ahead of schedule if they don't stop drinking and drugging. It's the similarities you share with these people, not the differences, that are significant—take a close look and you'll find more of those similarities than you would have thought possible. And it's those similarities that you'll have to confront in your recovery. If you're doing a fair amount of drinking, your mind isn't working on all cylinders—though you probably don't see that. It may take months, or even a year or more, for the fog to clear and for you to be able to look back at your behavior and evaluate it objectively. Meanwhile, don't let terminology get in the way of getting help. You don't have to be an alcoholic to quit drinking, or a drug addict to stop using. You only have to *want* to quit.

////////////////////////////

"My wife wants me to go to AA, and I think that's ridiculous. I never drink during the week, and on the weekends I drink nothing but beer—and only after four p.m. Maybe I do get a little drunk, but it's only a couple of nights a week."

Anyone who gets drunk periodically, whether it's once a week or once a month, has an alcohol problem. Most drinkers just don't drink enough to get drunk. That you can go for days, weeks, or even months between occasions of drunkenness doesn't prove a thing. The question is, when you do drink, do you feel like you have to control it? Do you ever lose control of your drinking? If you're getting drunk, then the answer is yes. What you are drinking and the time you start drinking are irrelevant. You can have an alcohol problem drinking hard liquor (scotch, vodka, gin, whiskey), beer, wine, Kahlúa, amaretto, wine coolers, rubbing alcohol, cough medicine, or vanilla extract. And you can start drinking first thing in the morning, never touch a drop until late in the day, or get drunk only on the second Saturday night of every month and still be an alcoholic. If you're drinking enough to become intoxicated, you're drinking enough to damage your health.

////////////////////////////

"I've been wondering if I have a drinking problem. Most of the time I can control it, but every once in a while I go off the deep end. I've talked about it with my wife and my parents, and they all think that I'm exaggerating. Who's crazy?"

When friends and family suggest someone has a drinking problem, they're probably right. When they brush it off, as your family is, they're almost certainly practicing denial (which is almost as common in people around alcoholics as it is in alcoholics themselves). In some cases, the denial is rooted in the family members who also have unacknowledged problems. Your family is probably trying to block out the unpleasant reality that you could have a problem. They might think it would reflect badly on them if you turn out to be an alcoholic, so subconsciously they resist the truth. Luckily, you seem ready to confront that reality.

If you are worried that you're drinking more than you should, don't let yourself be talked out of your concerns. Right now there is no blood test or biopsy that detects early alcoholism. So you will have to assess the situation yourself. Ask yourself the questions in Are You an Alcoholic or Addict, chapter 1, and go to a few AA meetings as an observer.

It may be that you've recognized your disease early. That means you can treat it before the more serious consequences begin to occur, and before everyone knows you have a problem. It also means that you can do something about it before denial of the problem gets so entrenched it's almost impossible to overcome. Don't ignore your own feelings, and don't let anyone talk you out of them.

////////////////////////////

"I take a few oxycodone pills each week. My girlfriend gets them from the pain clinic at the mall and shares them with me. They help with my stress. They're prescription pills, so they must be safe, right? Usually I take them with a glass of wine or two. I think I'm okay."

Oxycodone is a strong prescription pain reliever that should be used only under a doctor's care. Taking it on your own is very dangerous and can lead to addiction. Oxycodone (and other painkillers, drugs known as opioids or narcotics) acts on your brain and nervous system. It can make you feel relaxed and even euphoric. You might think that because it's a prescription drug it's safe, but that's not true. Opioids can cause serious health problems, including depression, low blood pressure, and confusion. They can also cause problems with fertility, as well as immune system issues, diabetes, and osteoporosis. Over time, you'll probably find that you need more of the drug to get the same relief.

Even worse, these narcotics can kill you. They slow down your breathing and your heart rate, and this can cause death—especially when you use them with alcohol, as you are, or snort or inject them.

Prescription drug abuse is far more common than it used to be. In fact, of the two million people who were admitted to rehab programs in a recent year, a third of them were there due to using opioids. A decade earlier, it was just 8 percent.

If you try to stop taking oxycodone yourself, you may have withdrawal symptoms, depending on how dependent on it you are. You might feel restless and have some muscle and bone pain, diarrhea, vomiting, and cold flashes. These drugs are not as harmless as you think.

You might not think you are addicted or out of control, but you do need some help. Read more about treatment in chapter 5, The Many Roads to a Lifetime of Sobriety.

///////////////////////////

"My friends and family think I have an alcohol and drug problem, and they're after me to quit. Sometimes I think they're right. But other times I think, 'Hey, if they're wrong, I'll be giving up the stuff for nothing.'"

Maybe you have a problem, and maybe you don't. If you do, the odds are good that you are not able to see it clearly—self-deception is a frontline symptom of alcoholism and addiction. It helps you escape from an unpleasant reality.

There are some good ways to find out whether or not you have a problem. None of them requires you to go dry until you're ready.

- Answer the questions in chapter 1, Are You An Alcoholic or Addict?

- Get a copy of the book *Alcoholics Anonymous* (also known as the *Big Book*) and read it. Do you see yourself in any of the life histories? Remember, focus on what you have in common with these people, not on what is different.

- Go to a few open AA or NA meetings (see How Do I Find a Meeting, chapter 8). Do you see yourself in any of the speakers?

- Write a mini life history, with some focus on your history of drinking or drug use. Be as honest as you can. Look at how the quality of your life was affected by your use, rather than just listing how much and how often you drank or used. Note opportunities missed, money spent, the impact on your family, job, friendships, and other aspects of your life. Denial often keeps addicts from seeing the problems they are causing, so in order to see yourself as others see you, you should probably talk candidly and patiently to some of those around you.

- Write up a family history of alcoholism or drug use. Have any others in your family had trouble with alcohol or drugs? A predisposition for alcoholism and addiction can be inherited; if you have relatives with this problem, you may have it as well.

And remember, you don't have to be 100 percent convinced you're an alcoholic or addict to quit drinking or using, to go to AA, or to get treatment. If your drinking or drug use is causing problems in your life, or if someone who cares about you believes it is, it could be time to give sobriety a try.

EVERYBODY DRINKS—IT'S GOOD FOR YOU, RIGHT?

"Ever since I was a kid I remember alcohol being a part of our family life. A lot of dishes were cooked with it. It was used when someone in the house was sick and for babies who were teething. Plus, everyone says that drinking is good for your heart. It's hard for me to believe that it can really be harmful."

Believe it. Alcohol is harmful enough to kill more than 100,000 people in this country every year. It kills in two ways: by damaging the body (it's linked to more

than 350 medical problems, from cancer to brain damage) and by causing accidents.

The medicinal benefits of alcohol are essentially nonexistent. Some research has shown that alcohol, particularly red wine, can be good for the heart by increasing the amount of "good" cholesterol and increasing antioxidant activity. But—and this is a big but—the benefits seen in those studies might have been due to other factors, such as being physically active and eating a diet with lots of fruits and vegetables and low in saturated fat. Besides, you can get some of the same benefits from red grape juice—without the risk.

If you want a healthy heart, there are other ways to get it: Control your blood pressure, cholesterol, and weight; eat a healthy diet; and get active. There's really no need to drink for health benefits.

THE DENIAL DILEMMA

Why do some people with certain illnesses—for example, cancer, alcoholism, and addiction—practice denial? It's not because they are bad or stupid or just plain pigheaded. They are genuinely unable to see the truth in their conscious minds, and they deny they are ill to protect themselves from facing a fearsome reality.

The cancer patient doesn't want to know about their illness out of fear of the unpleasant treatments that might be needed, and an even greater fear of the consequences should treatment fail. The alcoholic or addict doesn't want to know because of the stigma attached to the diagnosis, and an even greater fear of having to give up their trusty chemical life supports.

Denial is known in psychiatric jargon as a defense mechanism. It is a primitive mechanism—a self-deception that can be useful for a short time but is destructive over the long term. This self-deception is common in addiction; your psyche is struggling to resolve what it knows is unacceptable behavior with a strong drive to keep using alcohol or drugs.

Learning about addiction and the hope and happiness that treatment provides—by reading this book and other recovery materials and by going to AA meetings—can help overcome denial and open the door to recovery.

It's Not My Fault

MY LIFE IS A MESS

"If only my husband didn't work such long hours; if only he had time for me; if only he would help with the kids . . . If only things were different, I wouldn't have a problem."

Most people with substance abuse problems feel just the way you do. It's a spouse's fault. Or a parent's. Or a boss's. But they're wrong. They (and you) have problems with alcohol or drugs because they are doing the wrong and destructive thing, not because someone else is.

You're the one who drinks the double Bloody Mary or smokes the meth or eats all those oxys long after the pain from surgery is gone. You may be unable to change what a neglectful spouse does. Or a harsh parent. Or an unfair boss. All the wishing (or drinking) in the world won't make them live up to your high hopes and expectations. But you can change what *you* do. And that's what recovery is all about.

Oddly enough, when you change your own behavior in sobriety, your feelings will improve even if your partner doesn't. You will feel better about yourself. And when you do, your partner may change his behavior. Either way, your involvement in a recovery program can help you deal with the relationship in a much more rational way.

///////////////////////////

"We lost our child in an auto accident. That's when I started drinking and taking pills. I don't think I can live without something to keep me from thinking about that horrible moment."

You've got a better excuse for using drugs than most people. But (and this isn't meant to sound cruel) it's still only an excuse. Many people have gone through equally life-shattering, traumatic experiences without drinking or taking drugs to cope. Only someone with this disease called alcoholism/addiction deals with life's problems —big and small—by turning to chemical substances. And in truth, your chemicals are not helping you cope with your issues at all. They are only obscuring them, covering them up. They are not helping you create solutions or find a way to live with what happened.

You now have two problems to deal with. One is your disease, and the other is the devastation you feel about losing your child.

Treating the disease—and quitting those chemicals—has to come first. You need a clear mind so your brain and emotions can process and heal from this trauma. Not until your mind is clear will you be able to work out your feelings, face what happened, and learn to go on. And you will need to process it somehow—unresolved traumas can be a barrier to really healing in recovery.

Grief counseling will probably help, as will taking part in a support group for parents who, like you, have lost a child.

The ache in your heart will probably never completely go away. But it will get duller, especially if, instead of numbing your brain, you give yourself a chance to mourn. You wouldn't want to deaden or lose those memories completely.

Alcoholics/addicts often drink and drug to try to get rid of feelings. But feelings, good and bad alike, are what make us human. They are also the way we learn and grow. One day, you may even find that the pain you feel now will let you help others work through similar tragedies— giving even more purpose to your life in recovery.

"I've tried to get sober before, but every time I do I just want to kill myself. My father did terrible things to me when I lived at home; things I don't want to think about."

Most people can get sober and do just fine without psychotherapy. But some can't stay both sober *and* alive unless they face the deep-seated problems in their lives. So while it's crucial for you to get treated for your addiction, as your clarity of thought returns it will also be necessary for you to deal with the abuse you have gone through. It may be very painful, yes. But if you don't deal with it, it could become a barrier blocking you from recovery.

The ideal treatment for you may be a program designed to help people who have addiction along with other psychological problems. Do seek help immediately. You *can* live sober, but you're unlikely to get there without skilled treatment.

"I started drinking when my husband left me and my whole life went down the tubes. What good will quitting do? My life will still be miserable."

Ask yourself, "Has drinking made my life better? Or has it made things even worse?"

You may not feel the misery as much when you're smashed, but it's there just the same. And it won't go away until you start calling the shots, instead of letting alcohol call them for you. Your misery is likely to fester and grow until you take an honest look at the breakup of your marriage, mourn it, and move past it.

About one in ten people respond to a life crisis (separation, divorce, a major setback at work, a serious illness) by drowning their sorrows in drink or drugs. It's not that their problems are worse than everybody else's. It's just that they turn to chemical substances instead of using the more effective coping mechanisms used by the other nine.

Many people also manage to simply *create* crises in their lives to justify their use of chemicals. Deep down, they don't really want things to be okay, because then they would lose their reason for drinking. When a marriage breaks up, they are more likely to blame the spouse than the drinking. If they move into other relationships and continue drinking, predictably they will fail again—unless, as sometimes happens, they find a drinking-buddy partner. Then they may get along fine all the way to the cemetery.

You may find that once you're in recovery, the pain of your divorce will ease up and you'll feel much better about your life.

I NEED TO FIX OTHER THINGS, NOT MY DRINKING

"Our marriage is a mess. My husband says it's because of my drinking. I think if we get some counseling, everything will be okay. He thinks I've got to stop drinking first."

You might ease some of your marital problems by seeing a counselor, but unless you deal with the underlying alcohol problem, you will still be at risk. Your marriage will be a classic case of curing the symptom while the patient dies of the disease. It doesn't make much sense, after all, to try to solve a communication problem, which is at the core of many troubled marriages, when a mind is so anesthetized that it can't communicate.

That is one of the reasons why we strongly suggest that when someone is in the Red Zone, they need to put aside everything else and focus solely on recovery. Right now, you need to focus solely on your alcoholism.

Once you get sober, you can take some initial steps to at least keep your marriage intact (see chapter 11). But leave the work of really rebuilding your marriage for later on, once you're in the Yellow Zone. At that time, be sure that any professional you see for marriage counseling is also experienced in treating drug and alcohol problems. Those with experience in both areas will know that it sometimes takes years of brain healing before a person can work on relationship skills.

It's Too Hard to Quit

PRESCRIPTION DRUGS

"I'm having a horrible time trying to get off these painkillers. I had no idea they would be so hard to kick! I

thought we were just having fun. My friend at school said it's because they are so pure. Is that true?"

Your friend is right. Prescription drugs like the painkillers Vicodin and OxyContin can be very addictive. In part this is because they are so pure. Whether you get them from a doctor or a street dealer, you are probably getting the real 100 percent deal—pure pharmaceutical-grade drugs. In contrast, "street" drugs like cocaine or heroin are often cut with substances like baking soda, so you sometimes get less of it. In addition to the purity factor, the longer you've been on these drugs, the harder it is to quit.

You might have thought these drugs were safe to use because they were prescription. That's absolutely not true. They can be safe when used as prescribed for a valid medical condition, under a reputable doctor's care, but they are often prescribed in situations where they are not really necessary. And all too often they are used illicitly—not as prescribed. In fact, prescription drug misuse is now a major epidemic in the U.S.; in a recent survey, more than twelve million people age twelve and older reported non-medical use of these drugs. In recent years, in fact, *all* drug-related visits to emergency rooms—and overdose deaths—have increased sharply. It's hard to believe, but more people now die of drug overdoses than die in traffic accidents.

Because these drugs are so strong and so addictive, and you've had such a hard time trying to kick them, you'll need to seek professional help. But you *can* get off them—before it's too late.

A DRUG FOR A DRUG?

"I heard that I can just take another drug to treat my addiction. That sure sounds like an easier way to do it."

It might sound easy, but it's not likely to help you in the long run.

There are some new drugs approved by the FDA to treat addiction, but they are best used only for a short time—to help someone get engaged in a meaningful recovery, maybe to get through detox. They can be abused, and none of them has been proven to be effective long term when compared with 12-step and other abstinence methods. Moreover, trading a drug for a drug is *not* going to help you find a full recovery. It will only get you dependent on another drug.

ALCOHOL VERSUS OTHER DRUGS

They say that alcohol kills by inches, cocaine by yards, crack and meth by miles. The alcoholic may take twenty years to reach the point where his life is a mess and he desperately needs help. The cocaine addict may get there in a few years. The crack and meth addicts will likely get there in just a few months.

They may also have very different experiences in early recovery.

Alcoholics, burned out after the long, gradual downhill slide, are often ready to change their lives. But they may have difficulty because their behavior is so deeply ingrained and the damage to their brains is severe.

Crack and meth addicts have usually plunged from the first high to the bottom in a brief span of time. But because they haven't been using for as long a time, they may not see their situation as serious. They are also often younger and less mature. They may not be ready to change their lives, to open their minds to what they need to do to get well. If they do, however, their chances of success are good.

I'm Not Ready

YOU DON'T HAVE TO HIT BOTTOM

"Okay, I agree that I drink a lot. But I function okay. I take good care of my family. I'm not a falling-down drunk. Don't you have to crash and burn, really hit bottom, before you go on the wagon?"

Each person's "bottom" is different—and it can be wherever *you* decide it is. You don't have to wait until you think you can't go any lower.

Some people realize early on that they are in trouble. It can happen when they don't feel in control of their drinking anymore. When the dinner table becomes a nightly battleground. When they lose a promotion or mess up a deal. When they're booked for a DUI for the first time. Or when their kids start having problems in school because nobody's paying enough attention to them at home.

Others wait until they have nearly run out of options. Their spouse walks out, and they lose their job. They seriously hurt someone while driving under the influence. Their child runs away from home. Or liver disease lands them in the hospital.

Still others stubbornly hold out for an even more extreme bottom: They are given a long jail term, or they end up on the street, penniless, homeless, jobless, friendless.

What you need to ask yourself is, "How far down do I want to go before I make an effort to come back up? How much am I willing to risk the chance that I'll never make it back up?"

WHEN *WILL* YOU BE READY TO CHANGE?

"My friend and I both started using pain pills in high school. At college we both started snorting them, and then tried heroin and even using needles. But he turned his back on it all, got sober at some rehab, and got a great job. He's been sober for three years already. I'm still using. I don't think there's any big problem with it, really. Maybe I can't do this forever, but I don't see any need to quit now."

Different people are ready for and motivated to get help at different times. It sounds like your friend was ready. You are not—yet. That's not to say you won't ever be ready.

There are five stages of motivational readiness:

Precontemplation. There is little, if any, awareness that you have a problem, and pretty much no intention of doing anything about it.

Contemplation. You are somewhat aware there is a problem.

Preparation. You know there is very likely a problem, and you start figuring out what to do about it.

Action. You've made a decision on what you will do to fix this problem, and you do it. (In the case of addiction, this is when you get into treatment and start building a solid recovery.)

Maintenance. You do what you can to stay on track, to stay sober.

It sounds like you are at the contemplation stage. You have an inkling that there is a problem, but you are not ready to do anything about it.

Even if you think you don't need to quit anytime soon, give it some thought. Stay open-minded, consider the possibility that you might need some help. Think about how much better your life might be without drugs. Talk to your friend about his sobriety and how his life has changed. Talk to a counselor or someone else you trust. And go to some Narcotics Anonymous meetings, just to listen.

It's very likely that, as you start to see the advantages of making a change, you'll soon move into the preparation stage. You'll find yourself saying, "Yes, this is a problem. Now what am I going to do about it?"

I CAN'T AFFORD TREATMENT

You're worried about the high cost of treating your alcohol or drug habit? Flip the coin over: Think about how much money you're going to *save* by living sober.

Add up how much you spent on alcohol and drugs each week. Now add in all the *other* related expenses: legal fees, speeding fines, penalties for missed mortgage payments, late charges and interest on credit cards, alimony and child support, the costs of replacing or fixing ruined clothing, cars, furniture, rugs, and so on.

Don't stop there. Be sure to add in the cost of missed shifts, missed promotions, and lost jobs. Any fees for courses you needed to repeat. And the valuables you lost or damaged, such as cameras, phones, and other expensive gadgets. What about health care expenses? How much money have you spent on doctors for problems related to your drinking or drug use? How much higher are your health and auto insurance premiums, given your history?

Did you lose your house to foreclosure due to your drinking? Add in the extra cost you now have to pay to rent a house, compared to your old mortgage payments. Don't forget the equity in the home that you lost—and won't be building in the future.

Total it all up, and you have the financial cost of your drinking or drugging. How much did it cost you (and your family) each year? Each month? Do you really want to *keep* putting out that much cash?

As you can see, even if you opt for a fairly expensive residential treatment, sobriety will reimburse you in a fairly short time. Once you are back on your feet financially and you are paying all your bills on time, open up a special bank account. Each week sock away just half of what you would have spent on alcohol or drugs. Before you know it, you'll be amazed at your balance.

Another way to sock away some savings once you get sober: Every time you have a craving, put a coin in a big jar, or move a few dollars online into your savings account. By the end of the first year of recovery you could be rich. By the second year, you may find your savings doesn't grow for weeks on end. But that's not so bad, either.

I CAN'T MESS UP MY JOB

"I agree that I need to get treated for my drug problem, but I can't spare the time now. I've got a big deal pending."

What about the next big deal? And the next? And the one after that? One of them is going to be your *last* deal if you don't get serious about getting treatment.

If your doctor diagnosed heart disease and said you needed immediate surgery or the disease would kill you, what would you do? Very likely, you would have the surgery. Doesn't it make sense to give the same kind of attention to your addiction, which is just as dangerous to your health?

Be honest. Can the deal wait? Can someone else handle it? If so, drop it for now, or hand it over to a coworker. Then get some help for yourself immediately. Your productivity at work may suffer for now, but in the long run it can only benefit from your sobriety.

If not completing this big deal really will sink your business, leave your family destitute, or otherwise wreak havoc in your life, then by all means take care of it—assuming you're sober enough to see it through safely. (You may think you are, but even small amounts of drugs and alcohol can have a detrimental effect on your thought processes, and thus on your business dealings.)

At the same time, set a definite date for getting sober, put down a deposit for treatment, and start going to fellowship meetings now. You will be welcome at NA, AA, and other mutual-support meetings even if you haven't stopped using yet.

Be wary, however, if every time you consider sobriety you find there's another big deal or crisis to hold you back. You are either creating these diversions to avoid facing your problems or you've got too much cooking on your stove. Either way, you need to put everything else on the back burner and turn up the flame under your recovery.

"The doctor says my liver is acting up and I've got to give up drinking. There is no way I can do that in my business. Drinking is part of courting the clients."

If you worked on a loading dock and had a heart attack and the doctor said you had to give up heavy lifting, would you say, "No way"? Your condition is every bit as life-threatening as a bad heart.

Fortunately for you and others, these days there is little or no stigma to saying you don't drink. Many people in our society don't drink at all, and many others drink only every now and then. It is entirely acceptable to order sparkling water, iced tea, or other non-alcoholic beverages, even at high-powered business dinners. You might not have noticed this change; maybe you were too busy drinking.

Your situation isn't unusual. All kinds of people connect drinking or drugs with their work: rock musicians who are convinced (wrongly) they can play only when high ("It makes me creative"); assembly-line workers sure they'll be bored stiff if they have to work without having a drink first ("I wouldn't be able to stand doing this stuff anymore"); salesmen who fear they won't make any deals if they're sober ("I need a shot to make a good sales pitch").

Such fears are understandable. If you've been doing something for a long while with what you see as the friendly support of chemical substances, of course you're going to worry about functioning without them.

The fact is, there are many fine musicians who don't do drugs, factory workers who are teetotalers, salesmen who can sell snowballs in Siberia on nothing stronger than decaf coffee.

You can do your job sober, too— probably a lot better than you're doing it now.

///////////////////////////

"I've promised my family and my employer that I will check into an alcohol and drug treatment center next week. They want me to get sober now in preparation. I say, 'No way.'"

You are right. It usually isn't a good idea for someone to try to get sober before going into treatment, for a couple of reasons.

One is that once sober you may think, "Hey, I don't need treatment. I've quit on my own." And then celebrate your self-control by getting high as a kite, further delaying treatment.

Another is that, cold sober, you may not have the courage to turn up for treatment. Few patients arrive at a treatment facility with a completely clear head. Many are draining the last dregs from a bottle as they come through the front door.

Perhaps most important, some people develop serious complications from abrupt detox and withdrawal. In some cases, these can be life threatening. When a person is addicted to more than one drug, the process can be complex to deal with, even for trained medical professionals. You're doing well if you agree to treatment; don't push your luck by playing doctor (even if you are one).

I'M PREGNANT

"I just agreed to go for treatment for drug dependency. Then I found out I was pregnant. I don't know what to do."

The first thing you should do is commit yourself to getting treatment. No matter what decision you make about your pregnancy, getting sober has to be your number one priority.

As far as your pregnancy, there are several things to think about.

- How far along are you? If it's been less than six weeks since you conceived, and any serious damage was done to the embryo, you are likely to have a miscarriage. If you don't miscarry, and get sober and stay that way, chances are good the baby will be okay. If it's two or three months since you conceived and you used or drank heavily during that time, your baby could still be born okay if you get sober now. Every day of sobriety you have raises the odds of having a healthy baby. Every day you continue to drink or use drugs lowers them.

- How likely are you to have a healthy baby if you quit now? That depends on the types of drugs you've been using, and

how long and how heavily you've used them. Prenatal tests may be able to provide some information. If it's not clear what the chances of a healthy baby are, or you're not sure how to evaluate information you've been given, ask for a consultation with a doctor, preferably one certified by the American Society of Addiction Medicine, or with a genetic counselor familiar with pregnancy and addiction. They can help you understand what is going on. (See page 88 on how to find medical professionals with experience in addiction.)

- What are your feelings about having a baby now? Do you have a good place to live, a safe place to raise a baby? Do you have a way to support yourself and a child? Is the baby's father able to contribute emotionally and financially?

- How will your having a child now affect others? The father? Your parents? Any other children?

- Does the treatment program you are considering accept pregnant women? Most do not. If you intend to continue your pregnancy, you'll need to find a treatment program that will accept you. (Read more about finding treatment in chapter 5.)

- If you think the risk of birth defects is too high, what are your thoughts on terminating the pregnancy?

If your medical advisors say you are likely to have a healthy baby, and you think you can care for it and give it a good home, then you might want to continue the pregnancy. You should also be sure you'll have enough support to be able to handle both a new baby and a new recovery. They can both be very time-consuming.

Often the answers aren't clear-cut. If the baby has a fifty-fifty chance of being damaged, if you are unclear about your feelings on terminating a pregnancy, if having a baby would be overwhelming financially—talk it all over with a counselor before making a decision.

Once you make your decision, no matter what it is, accept it and learn to live with it. You did the best you could under the circumstances.

There's No One There Like Me

I DON'T THINK I'LL FEEL COMFORTABLE

"I'm Asian American and ready to go for treatment. But I've talked with some people at the inpatient rehab my company's insurance plan wants to send me to, and there are no Asian counselors there. It seems to serve a community different from the one I relate to well. Should I go there?"

Many people worry about feeling uncomfortable with the other patients and counselors when they go to treatment. Some of this may just be due to nervousness about jumping into a new environment, a new experience. Some, certainly, may be due to concerns about being with people who are somehow "different" from you. This issue can come up for people from *any* community—blue-collar, indigent, rich, African American, Caucasian, Middle Eastern, Native American, gay, straight, bisexual, women, men, transgender, gender variant, intersex, married, single, monogamous, monogamish, polyamorous, Christian, Jewish, Muslim, Buddhist, atheist, agnostic, parents, non-parents, adopted, biological, young, older, liberal, conservative—well, you get the picture.

In truth, however, most alcoholics and addicts, whatever their backgrounds, have much more in common with each other than they have differences. They all have the problem of addiction, and that is what you need to address when you go to treatment. So if you go to that program your company recommends, try to push aside any concerns you have about cultural differences. Focus instead on what you all are looking for—a good life in recovery—and give it everything you've got. You may be surprised at how well you can relate to everyone else there after all.

You can ask your company's benefits manager about other treatment options. You can also look at other programs you might pay for yourself, if you have the means. But you might not find one that feels perfect for you. Most people don't. And that's okay. This is a time to make changes and shake things up. Being uncomfortable at first is not necessarily a bad thing right now. (Of course, you should never tolerate any discrimination against you or others in a treatment program.)

This is not to say that we are all alike in every way. Many people have issues related to the way they were brought up, how they live now, the experiences they've had, and other factors of their lives. And many will need to address those issues in recovery. Some options for doing that:

- When you look into a treatment program, see if they have any regular meetings or classes for people of various communities.

- Look for a treatment program that *does* focus on your community.

- When you return home from treatment, find some AA or NA meetings that focus on your personal issues. There are certainly more specialized meetings than there are treatment centers. Read more about getting involved in these fellowships in chapters 8 and 9.

"I live on an Indian reservation. I recently got married and think I may be pregnant. But I can't seem to stop drinking. Where can I get help before I hurt my baby?"

Contact the alcohol and substance abuse coordinator at the Indian Health Service office nearest your home (see chapter 13). This professional should be able to give you information on Native American alcoholism and addiction counselors, on AA groups run by Native Americans, and on culturally sensitive in- or outpatient treatment, if you need it. Also contact the maternal/child service department or a local obstetrician. You can also do some research on your own into programs that accept pregnant women. But move quickly. Your baby's future depends on your becoming sober as soon as possible.

If you're like many Native American women, especially those from matriarchal tribes, you may feel more comfortable seeking help from a woman with a background like your own.

"I know I drink too much. I think it's because I've known since I was young that I'm gay, but my parents just don't understand or accept that. My father says if I started dating girls at my school, I'd get my sexual orientation straightened out, and I could stop getting drunk."

Many LGBT people start drinking or using drugs in their teen years. They use chemicals to mask the loneliness and isolation they may feel in being different from some of their peers. They often think that only drugs or drink can keep them from falling apart completely. And if they are hiding their orientation, that stress often contributes to the problem.

But the idea that you can change your sexual orientation and that will get rid of your need to drink is a delusion. Your father is wrong. Your sexual orientation is something you're born with; it's not a problem and it's nothing to be ashamed of.

Your drinking, on the other hand, is becoming a problem. And you can do something about it. If you work at sobriety, not only will you not fall apart but you might feel whole for the first time in your life. If you also need to work at accepting who you are, get some counseling from a therapist who understands both alcoholism and gender issues.

//////////////////////////

"I've got a long-term problem with alcohol and prescription pills, but I'm so embarrassed about this kind of thing at my age—I'm past sixty. I can't even talk to my doctor about it. I want to stop on my own, but I can't seem to."

No professional is going to blink an eye at seeing an older person with an addiction problem. There are literally hundreds of thousands of you. In fact, by some estimates, about 17 percent of people over sixty-five have an alcohol problem.

If you shrink at the idea of bringing your problem to your own doctor, you can find an addiction specialist. (See Find a Health Care Professional, page 88, for how to find help.) Discuss your problem with a doctor or another professional and work out a plan for treating your illness.

If you go to an inpatient treatment program, try to find one that specializes in older patients, or at least treats many older people and has programming, staff, and facilities suited to their needs. In some cases, a program that treats older people with a variety of problems (including addictions) may work better than a drug rehab program for people of all ages. In others, getting help in a mixed-age program may work better, as long as your living space gives you enough privacy to meet any special needs you may have.

When you look for a 12-step support group, you will also want one that includes some other seniors. Instead of spending your time alone drinking and looking forward to nothing but empty days and nights, you can find new hope and purpose in your life in recovery.

VETERANS AND SUBSTANCE USE

"I recently came back from Afghanistan, and I'm worried I might have a problem. After I was discharged I started drinking a lot more than I ever did before, and I'm taking extras of the pain pills the doctor gave me to help with my injuries. Okay, a lot extra. I'm holding it together, but I'm worried. My dad's uncle was in Vietnam, and he came back with all kinds of problems. He ended up homeless and a heroin addict. I don't want to end up like that. I'm only

twenty-three. But it seems like a sign of weakness to ask for help."

You are smart to be concerned. Substance misuse among veterans is very common, especially with younger people. In your age group, the eighteen- to twenty-five-year-olds, one-quarter of all vets have a substance problem, ranging from abuse to addiction. Vietnam veterans like your great-uncle certainly had many problems with substance abuse. But it's even more common among those who served in Iraq and Afghanistan. There are several reasons for this: Soldiers are serving longer and more numerous tours in tough situations; they're spending more time away from their loved ones; and rates of post-traumatic stress disorder (PTSD) and traumatic brain injury (TBI) are higher than in earlier wars. Those who suffer from PTSD or TBI are at particularly high risk of addiction. Even just being exposed to combat increases the risk of addiction.

The drugs of choice are different, too. Your great-uncle, like many of his time, used heroin. In today's young vets, we're seeing lots of alcohol and prescription drug use (mostly painkillers), as well as meth and cocaine. Some get hooked on the stimulants they used to stay alert in combat.

Veterans and active duty staff face a lot of issues that can make an escape into drugs and alcohol look awfully tempting. Even before leaving the U.S., many had to contend with the fear of being deployed. Seeing conflict and witnessing the death of friends can be very traumatic. And because phones and laptops have made it much easier to stay in touch with home, many soldiers today also deal with the day-to-day issues of keeping a marriage together and being a parent. It's nice to stay in touch, of course, but for many that only adds to the stress level. Female soldiers also have reported high rates of sexual abuse and rape while being deployed; that can be traumatic, and puts them at higher risk of substance abuse.

When you came home, you probably had even more pressures: finding a job, reconnecting and fitting in with your family and friends after a long absence, losing the camaraderie of being with the people in your unit, maybe a shaky marriage and shaky finances, and problems sleeping, not to mention recovering from physical injuries.

For too many soldiers, the situation gets out of control and results in depression, anxiety, and nightmares. Many fall into the trap of using drugs and alcohol to try to escape their memories and problems. Suicide has become far too common among veterans and active duty military—and in many of those situations, drugs or alcohol were involved.

You need to address this now, before it gets any worse. We understand that asking for help can feel like a sign of weakness, but remember that addiction is a disease, not a personal failure. And the long-term health effects of this disease can be severe: liver disease, high blood pressure, stroke. Asking for help is a sign of how *strong* you are, and how concerned you are about your health.

The Department of Veterans Affairs can help. They now have many programs for dealing with addiction—partially because of the issues the Vietnam vets had. You can find out more at va.gov or by calling 800-827-1000. Or you might want to contact a VA Vet Center. These community-based centers focus on helping returning vets and their families. You can find out more at vetcenter.va.gov or by calling 877-WAR-VETS (927-8387).

In particular, make sure you are assessed for PTSD. If you have it, getting treated for it at the same time greatly increases your odds of successful addiction treatment.

If you're in crisis now, call the confidential Veterans Crisis Line at 800-273-TALK (8255). They're open 24/7. You can also chat online with someone at veteranscrisisline.net.

Many people, we know, are reluctant to seek help through military channels. They worry about the stigma of being labeled an addict by other soldiers or their superiors. Some worry about confidentiality issues, or being kicked out of the service if they are still on active duty. (Many also don't want their families to know they are having problems.) You do have other options. Check out local AA and NA meetings and county mental health services. Ask your family doctor for a referral. And if you get involved in AA or another mutual-support fellowship, try to find a sponsor (or co-sponsor) who also has military experience. It can be a big help to talk with someone who knows where you are coming from and who understands military jargon and culture right off the bat. You can also look for someone with that background if you work with a private health care provider, but it's not always easy to find. Another option is to try to find a provider who has had special training in working with military. (See chapter 5 for more ways to find help.)

A strong soldier takes this on. Get some help.

WOMEN AND SUBSTANCE USE

Women *are* different from men. Health care professionals once thought women were simply "small men" in terms of their medical needs, but most understand now that women are different both physically and mentally. They experience life very differently, as well, and as a result, many experts now agree that gender-based treatments can offer distinct advantages.

That is certainly true in the case of treatment for addiction. A woman's experience with drugs and alcohol is often very different from that of a man, from the reasons she starts using to the effects on her body, and even the issues she considers when thinking about treatment. Many treatment programs now take these factors into account.

So how are men's and women's addiction experiences different?

- Women are more likely than men to progress to being a substance abuser after their first taste of alcohol or drugs.

- They progress to injecting drugs faster than men do.

- Their bodies process alcohol differently, so they get drunk on smaller amounts.

- They develop related health problems earlier and at lower consumption levels, including liver and kidney diseases, high blood pressure, heart problems, and some forms of cancer.

- They are more vulnerable to contracting sexually transmitted diseases.

- Women alcoholics and addicts are more likely than men to also have some "process addictions," such as eating disorders.

- And, of course, women still carry the babies. If you are pregnant and using drugs or alcohol, you are putting your baby at risk for many complications, including prematurity, low birth weight, drug addiction, and fetal alcohol syndrome.

The reasons *why* women get caught up in using chemicals differ, too. Some trace their drinking habit back to being given alcohol to treat menstrual cramps. Many suffered a traumatic event, such as childhood sexual abuse or domestic violence, which raises the risk of addiction. In fact, as many as 70 percent of chemically dependent women have experienced some form of sexual abuse. That often leads to having a first drink at a young age, as well as low self-esteem and depression.

As a woman, your intimate relationships are also likely to have a big impact on your drug and alcohol use. If you live with someone who is a heavy drinker or drug user, you are likely to do the same. If you inject drugs, you were probably introduced to it by a sexual partner. Chances are you feel a sense of emotional intimacy when you share needles and drugs.

Other relationships influence you, too. Women are more likely to misuse substances if they are single, separated or divorced, unemployed, have no children, or have children who are grown.

If you're in the business world, you might feel like you need to prove you can keep up with the guys—all the way to the bar. In fact, women who work in male-dominated professions are more likely to drink.

What's more, compared to men, women who abuse substances are much more stigmatized by society. They tend to have significant feelings of shame and guilt, as well as low self-esteem.

Such feelings, along with little support from family, can make it very hard to seek help. How can you go to treatment if there is no one to care for your kids or your aging mom? Will your ex-husband reopen the custody battle if you seek help? Men don't worry about these issues nearly as much.

For women to succeed in recovery, these issues have to be addressed. Today, many treatment programs are taking into account the entire context of your life: your social and economic world, your health issues and trauma history, your role as a caregiver, your support systems, your relationships.

When women's needs are taken into account from the start, treatment simply works better. So finding a treatment facility where gender-specific methods are understood and practiced may help speed your recovery.

If you're a woman with a substance abuse problem, today you have a better chance than ever before of getting help and controlling your disease.

Okay, I'll Go—But What Do I Tell Everyone?

TELLING YOUR FAMILY

"They gave me a choice at work: either go into a residential treatment program or get fired. I'm going to get treatment, but I don't know how to tell my wife and kids about it."

Chances are, no one will be happier than your family to know that you're finally going to do something about your problem.

Tell your wife first. She probably won't be surprised by the news. Unless she's your drinking buddy, she knows you need help. She may be upset that you'll have to be away from home or that you will be devoting so much time to recovery, but she'll be happy you're trying to get well.

What else should you talk about with her? Tell her how important her support is going to be. Tell her that you realize now that alcoholism/addiction is a disease that affects the whole family, and that though recovery is something you've got to do yourself, you're going to need a lot of family support. Have her read chapter 26, For Family and Friends, and urge her to start going to Al-Anon or Nar-Anon meetings while you're away. She will probably be invited to attend individual and family sessions toward the end of your inpatient stay. (She will also be welcome in AA or NA if she drinks or uses drugs and wants to stop.)

Your wife needs to know that moving into sobriety will not be easy for you or for the rest of the family. But if you all try to understand the disease and the recovery process, you will have a better chance of making recovery work.

Tell your children as soon as you can. They will sense something is going on—especially if you go away for treatment, but even if you only go as an outpatient or go to AA meetings every night. Telling them the truth will be less shattering than what they might imagine is going on. Children sheltered from the truth often blame themselves for the bickering and other family problems they see or sense. This, in turn, sets them up for another generation of family dysfunction. (For ways to help your kids stay sober, see chapter 23.)

The best way to tell the kids is at a family conference. If you're not used to holding such meetings, now is a good time to start. They're a great way to foster communication, which is going to be very important in your lives from now on. Explain that you are sick, that it is the drugs or alcohol that have made you sick, and that you are going to a hospital that teaches people how to live without them.

Make it clear to your kids that they are not the cause of your problem (and never have been). Let them know that you will need their help to get better. Ask them if they will consider going to Alateen (the 12-step programs for teenaged children of alcoholics) or another group that helps children of alcholics or addicts, which will help all of you.

Finally, tell them that if you all work hard at recovery, it will soon be easier for everyone to talk to one another, to understand one another, and to show love to one another. It may be tough for a while, but the result—a happier family— will be worth waiting for.

TELLING FRIENDS

"I've been drinking after work with the guys for fifteen years. How can I tell them I can't drink anymore? They're going be wondering what kind of man can't hold his liquor."

A man with the disease known as alcoholism. That means all kinds of men: weight lifters and computer geeks, shortstops and longshoremen, farmers and scientists.

All kinds of men have problems with alcohol, but many find it hard to admit. This is often due to cultural expectations: Men are supposed to be tough, never cry, refuse to be defeated, and always be in control.

It's sometimes easier to tell the guys you can't drink anymore if you have a better-understood condition, like heart disease. But even then, some men won't admit they have to give up the booze and instead continue to drink themselves to death.

You have that option. Or you can be a real man and acknowledge that you're an alcoholic. It takes strength to stand up and be counted, and even more strength to do what it takes to beat alcoholism. And besides, a whole lot of guys today are proud to say they are in recovery. (Don't be surprised when some of your friends ask how you did it, and if you'd give them a hand.)

TELLING YOUR EMPLOYER

"I've got a good job and I'm afraid I'll blow it if I go into treatment and the boss finds out. He's sure to fire me."

If your boss doesn't already know something's up, he's sleeping on the job. In any case, he'll know about it before long. Addiction is a progressive disease. If you don't get better, you will get worse. At some point there will be no way in the world you'll be able to cover it up.

Still, you're wise to be wary about telling your boss outright that you're going in for treatment. Many people still don't accept those with addiction. Not every employer is understanding; some still think it's a moral issue, not a disease. Others have their thinking tainted by their personal alcohol or drug problems or those of family members. Some may tolerate an employee who drinks a lot or is using addictive prescription drugs, but not one who openly admits to being an alcoholic or addict.

If you work for a large company, you may be able to find the official policy on addiction and treatment resources posted online.

Another way to find out how the company might respond: have your doctor, lawyer, a friend, or counselor call human resources, the employee assistance program counselor, or whoever is in charge of employee policy and ask some questions anonymously. This person can say, "I have a patient [or client, or friend] who works for you. He's interested in getting help, but is unsure how you will look at this. What's your company policy on alcoholism/addiction? [Most companies have one.] Do you have an employee assistance program? Will you pay for treatment? Does the

employee have to pay a portion out of pocket? Will your knowledge of this person's disease prevent future advancement? Could this knowledge mean immediate firing?" Then the caller can ask for a written or electronic copy of the company policy on the subject.

Most of the time, the response will be, "We like to keep our employees on and will do anything we can to help." Smart companies know that it costs more time, money, and effort to fire and replace someone than to it does to rehabilitate an alcoholic/addict. This is especially true when employees have special skills. Employees who are unskilled or recently hired are less likely to get support.

If you work in a field that involves public health or safety (pilots, bus drivers, doctors, and so on), you may have to agree to more conditions. For example, you might have to agree to regular drug testing, mandatory treatment, or immediate dismissal if drugs are found. Fortunately (for you and for the public), many leaders in these safety-sensitive professions have learned that punishing people for the disease of addiction only serves to hide the problem, and that only undermines the security and safety they are entrusted to protect—with potentially tragic results. Good managers have learned that treatment is a much better option.

If you work for a small company, you may be able to rally support from your boss or coworkers just by acknowledging your problem and seeking help. If you can, share your situation with one or two trusted coworkers, so they'll feel like partners in your decision and can help others understand it. But if that's not an option, don't let concern about how others will respond stand in the way of getting help. Get it and then worry about the consequences. In the long run, recovery is *always* the better option for you.

Working for someone who doesn't understand—and doesn't want to understand—the disease you're battling won't help you over the long haul. You'd probably be better off finding a new job after treatment.

Be sure, however, that in your anxiety you don't misinterpret the reaction you get at work. When your boss says, "It's okay—take all the time you need," he's not saying, "Don't bother coming back—we don't want you anymore."

CONFIDENTIALITY CONCERNS

"I need help. But everyone will know I have a problem if I go for treatment."

You're probably kidding yourself if you think your coworkers, boss, family, and friends don't already know you have a problem. Even the most discreet of heavy drinkers or users sends out a steady stream of signs of addiction.

Still, if you want to keep your recovery private, you have that right. Federal laws protect the confidentiality of any professional treatment you get. And for some people, keeping the first phase of their recovery under wraps—for either professional or personal reasons—makes sense.

If you're planning on inpatient treatment, you might want to go to a program in another state or another part of the country. Tell everyone you are taking "a long-overdue vacation." That way you can immerse yourself in recovery without embarrassment or the fear of being discovered. If you fear being recognized, you may want to try using an assumed name when registering. If you have outpatient treatment at home, you can see an addiction professional, who is bound by law to respect your privacy.

AA (Alcoholics *Anonymous*) was the pioneer in making anonymity possible for its members. It does this from the beginning by using only first names at meetings ("Hello, I'm Jan, and I'm an alcoholic"). And AA tradition insists that who is seen and what is heard at meetings never goes beyond the meeting-hall doors. Other 12-step programs are equally anonymous. If you're still worried you might bump into an acquaintance, try some meetings in nearby towns or neighborhoods. Remember, if you do bump into anyone you know at a meeting, he will be just as eager as you are to keep the encounter quiet.

Wanting to protect your privacy while building up a good sobriety track record is understandable. But it's not a good idea to keep your recovery a secret forever. We have long known that people with good recoveries share, rather than hide, their problem. An important part of staying well is helping others who are ill—by talking about your own experiences.

This is also true for people with many other serious health problems. Talking about experiences builds a bridge of empathy and empowerment, and that helps everyone deal with issues more successfully.

I'm Still Wary About Living Sober

"I know that drinking and using have messed up my life. I know it's time to get some help. But the thought of life without my 'best friends' scares me. It's been years."

You've leaned on your chemical friends for a long time now, not just to enjoy life but to help you cope with it. You've used your chemicals to "solve" your problems, endure your job, cheer you up, calm you down, alter your thinking, help you forget what a mess your life has become. In short, to survive. As you read in chapter 1, using your chemicals has become just as routine as eating or breathing.

Not surprisingly, you're afraid that living without those friends could be very painful.

Furthermore, you don't know what to expect in sobriety. How will you talk to your spouse if you don't have your favorite substance to prop you up? Cope with your boss's demands? Survive an all-day conference? Or even have fun?

Life with alcohol and drugs may be hell right now, but it's a familiar hell. The unknown, the darkness out there, is a lot scarier. But what will help is flooding that darkness with light, and that's what you'll find in this book. You'll learn all about what you can expect when you get sober and get into recovery. You may have some difficult months ahead, but knowing what is coming will make it easier to take those first tentative steps.

The months ahead will also be less scary if you work with a qualified counselor in an inpatient or outpatient treatment setting, or with others in a mutual-support group like AA who've been there before you. It won't be enough for you to simply stop drinking and drugging. You will need to develop skills for dealing with your partner, your family, your job, your social life—without chemical assistance. A structured program based on the successful experiences of others can help you do this best.

In the end, you will be surprised to see how, as the darkness dissipates, the world out there becomes brighter than it *ever* was when you were "looking for God in a bottle."

CHAPTER

The Many Roads to a Lifetime of Sobriety

What do you *do* when you finally make that commitment to stop drinking or using? Do you wake up one day and tell yourself, "Okay, this is it—I'm sober from now on"? Do you go to an AA or NA meeting and announce, "Hi, I'm Sue, and I'm an addict"? Do you check into a treatment facility?

This chapter describes the many routes you can take to get sober and start building your life in recovery. It covers the potential costs of each and who is most likely to benefit, and includes guidance on how to find a good program or provider. It will help you decide which recovery option is most likely to get you started on your new life.

You Have Many Options

Your options range from going it alone to intensive treatment from a doctor or therapist:

- Quitting on your own

- AA or another 12-step fellowship (with or without additional treatment)

- Other mutual-support fellowships (that don't use the 12-step method)

- Outpatient treatment in a comprehensive program

- Outpatient treatment by a physician or other addiction specialist

- Outpatient treatment by an addiction counselor, psychologist, or other therapist

- Outpatient treatment by a psychiatrist

- A sober companion

- Inpatient treatment

- A therapeutic community

- A recovery residence

- A combination of two or more of these approaches

The route you choose depends on many things, such as your needs, your drug of choice, your history, finances, and insurance coverage, and your current living and family situation. You can decide on a route yourself, but if your mind is still fuzzy it's a good idea to ask others to help you explore options.

We suggest you start by reading more about all of the options and then finding out who in your circle of friends or your community might have some experience with these issues or might be able to refer you to a professional for more help. Ask your neighbor, your family doctor, your spiritual advisor, your friends, your coworkers, and the human resources person at work, if they know anything about addiction or know someone who does. Call a treatment center and ask to talk with someone there (they can often do a brief assessment of your situation over the phone). Call a local mental health agency and make an appointment with a counselor. Figure out who in your extended circle of friends and relatives is an old-timer in AA or NA (there are bound to be some). Go to a fellowship meeting on your own and ask the people there for recommendations.

Here's a quick rundown of the variety of health care and other services you might come across as you explore your options:

- Assessment of your addiction: current use, past use, past treatment, and attempts to quit

- Assessment of your current physical and mental health and your HIV and hepatitis C status

- Assessment of your physical and mental health history, any trauma in your past, and your behavioral history (including sexual history)

- Assessment of your current living situation, as well as legal and financial problems, cultural issues, child care needs, relationships, employment history, vocational training, educational level, and referrals to related services

- Stabilization of your condition: stopping the use of alcohol or drugs; supervised detox; ongoing substance use monitoring

- Management of your disease with psychosocial therapy

- Involvement in a mutual-support fellowship such as AA

- Management of your disease with pharmaceutical therapy

- A continuing care program

- Management of other physical conditions, with referrals to specialists

THE RED ZONE

- Advice regarding healthy habits, such as diet, exercise, and smoking cessation

If you search online for treatment options, you are likely to come across people who will promise the moon and the stars, who will swear they can cure your addiction with little effort. Be skeptical; be wary. Treatment for addiction takes time, and in our view, long-term abstinence from *all* mood-enhancing drugs is usually the best route. Before you make any decisions on treatment (certainly before you hand over any money) be sure to read our criteria for choosing an inpatient treatment program (page 75). They can be used to assess any treatment program.

Once you do choose an option, give it 100 percent of your effort. Most people need at least three months of treatment. If you give it a halfhearted try and fail, you'll never know whether it might have worked. But if your first choice doesn't work, don't give up. It doesn't mean you're a hopeless case. It probably just means you need a more intensive or different pathway. So try something else. (It could also mean that you are not quite ready to embrace recovery. Sometimes it takes a few tries. Read more about the stages of readiness in chapter 4.) And many times, you need more than one approach, or a treatment plan that changes over time—just as you might for any other disease.

If you're already sober, but periodically feel the ground tremble beneath your feet, a refresher course of treatment might help.

It All Starts with Detox

Your first step toward a life of sobriety is detox—you stop taking drugs or drinking alcohol and you wait until all the "leftovers" leave your body. This process can cause a variety of physical and emotional withdrawal symptoms; you might have only mild discomfort or you might feel really miserable symptoms. It all depends on the drugs you've been using, how long you've been using them, your age and health, and other factors.

In some cases, it's best to detox under a doctor's care. Others might be able to do it at home, with the assistance of a friend or a detox helper.

Read more about detox and withdrawal in chapter 6.

Quitting on Your Own

Trying to do it all on your own—detox, early sobriety, living in recovery—is the rockiest road. Once in a while someone can "just say no" and have it work, but that's not very common.

It's hard to do it on your own because there is so much more to recovery than simply abstaining from chemicals. You may need help to detox from your drug of choice. Then, if you've been drinking or using for years, you'll need to learn new ways to cope with life. Depending on your current lifestyle, that can be nearly impossible. If you live in an environment that encourages addiction (high-flying coworkers who snort coke before every sales meeting, meth dealers on every corner), trying to get sober at home will be really tough. If your social life revolves around drinking or drugging, you're likely to find working on sobriety on your own a lonesome business. In either case, you will have a much better chance of succeeding at recovery if you do it with other people who are also working on living sober.

Plus, many of those people who do manage to get sober on their own later find that their recovery is pretty shaky, and that being dry is not enough. The wise ones sign up for some inpatient or outpatient treatment, or they head over to Alcoholics Anonymous (or another peer-empowered program) for support. Most people find that mutual-support fellowships like AA offer a social ingredient that is essential to healing—even though the addict within them originally voted for the isolated approach.

Going it alone *does* work for some people. But it's mostly those newcomers who were using drugs because of peer pressure or shortsighted medical advice, rather than an entrenched addiction.

Even if you want to try to quit on your own, we urge you to still read about the other options mapped out in this chapter. They may come in handy later on.

Alcoholics Anonymous and Other 12-Step Fellowships

For most people, getting involved in Alcoholics Anonymous or a similar 12-step program is a key part of successfully living in recovery. In fact, it is widely understood that *not* including such a program in an overall treatment plan can put a recovering addict on the road to relapse. And for some folks, taking part in a mutual-help group is all they need to get sober and stay that way.

Alcoholics Anonymous (aa.org), the granddaddy of the mutual-help movement, is a nonsectarian, nondenominational, nonpolitical, loosely organized fellowship. AA sees alcoholism/addiction as a disease, a physical allergy coupled with a mental obsession. It is a disease that can be treated into remission, but never cured. Once an alcoholic or addict, says AA, always an alcoholic or addict.

The heart of AA's program is lifetime abstinence from alcohol and other drugs, one day at a time, sharing "experience, strength, and hope" at meetings, and working the Twelve Steps for recovery. Millions of people can attest that it works, and the program's basic tenets have held up under scientific scrutiny. AA has earned the backing of innumerable doctors and therapists—many of whom have worked with alcoholics and addicts for decades. Another great thing about AA is that it offers an entire program of recovery in a very simple package: show up at meetings and work the steps. And it's free.

AA has spawned many similar groups: Narcotics Anonymous, Cocaine Anonymous, Crystal Meth Anonymous, Overeaters Anonymous, Gamblers Anonymous, and more. These groups operate on the same principles and use the 12 steps, but deal with other addictions. Altogether, about five million people in the U.S. are involved in AA or one of these programs.

The dropout rate is high, but many return to try again. Those who stick with the program have a good chance of getting sober and staying sober: More than a third of the current two million members of AA have more than ten years of sobriety. Moreover, those who get involved in a group like AA or NA after their initial treatment for addiction are more likely to stay sober than those who don't join a mutual-support group.

The only requirement for membership in AA is a *desire* to stop drinking. The basic therapy is "sharing." Members share their past experiences with alcohol and drugs, their present fears, and their hopes for the future.

The concept began in 1935 when two alcoholics, Bill W. and Dr. Bob, began meeting to share their stories and feelings with each other. They were soon amazed to find that through this sharing, from helping each other, they experienced relief from their once insatiable compulsions to drink, which had nearly destroyed their lives. They went on to share their experience with others, and developed a suggested program of recovery—the Twelve Steps. AA members—who also work through the steps—have been making the same discovery ever since. As members often say at the close of AA meetings: "Keep coming back! It works if you work it."

One commonly misunderstood aspect of AA is its spirituality. AA is *not* a religious organization. You do *not* have to believe in any god to join it or benefit from it.

For more details on AA and other groups, see chapters 8 and 9.

WHO CAN BENEFIT FROM AA OR NA ALONE?

Some alcoholics and addicts can move into a life in recovery with no treatment other than regular attendance at Alcoholics Anonymous or another 12-step program. This may be all you need if:

- You don't need medical supervision of your detox (see chapter 6).

- You are a social being, used to spending a lot of time with your drinking or drug-using buddies. You'll find the same friendly folks at AA. The only difference is that now they socialize without chemical help.

- You are ready to change your relationship with alcohol and drugs.

- You are disciplined and motivated (you'll have to talk yourself out of your excuses and into attending meetings every day for at least three months to start).

- You have a good support system at home—especially family members who are active in Al-Anon or who have been in AA for a long time.

For some people, AA is their only option. They might not have insurance or access to effective low-cost treatment, and they can't afford to pay for a residential or outpatient program. Even if you don't meet the above criteria, AA is worth a try. And it's certainly better than doing nothing.

WHAT DOES IT COST?

With no dues or membership fees, AA (and other fellowships) is far and away the least expensive treatment option. At most meetings the hat is passed for donations to cover rent, coffee, cookies, and other expenses.

CHOOSING THE RIGHT FELLOWSHIP HOME GROUP

Each AA group has its own personality, a composite of the attributes, attitudes, and histories of its members. You may want to visit a few groups to see where you feel most comfortable.

Most people like to find a home group, a meeting they go to regularly with the same bunch of people. The home group becomes their anchor; it offers a sanctuary of familiarity and support. It's where they take on service roles, such as making coffee and greeting newcomers, as well as leadership duties.

To find a home group that works for you, you'll have to do some in-person research on the local meetings. Which groups are mostly male or female? Which are made up mostly of professionals, or blue-collar workers, or pilots, or stay-at-home moms? Which ones are small (where you can get to know people and confide in them), and which are large (where you can absorb the wisdom of the "old-timers")? Which welcome babies or young kids? Which ones work with your daily schedule? Which tend to be more religious or more agnostic? Check out several meetings and get to know the people there to find one you like. (For more about finding a group, see chapter 8.)

Your home group meetings won't be the only ones you attend. Most groups don't meet often enough to fulfill the needs of those in early recovery: ninety meetings in ninety days. You may want to go to lunch-time meetings on Tuesday and Thursday near your shop or office, your home group on Monday, Wednesday, and Friday evenings, and yet a third group on weekends.

CONCERNS ABOUT FELLOWSHIPS

Many people who could benefit from AA or NA don't try it, because they have a skewed idea of what these meetings are like. Are you wary of going to an AA or NA meeting because you fear it will resemble the drunk tank at a county jail (it's as civilized as a PTA meeting), or you're afraid you'll be pushed to talk about yourself (you won't be), or you fear it's too religious (it's not a religious organization), or for any other reason? If so, read chapters 8 and 9 to find out what AA is really like. You can also learn more about it by reading *Alcoholics Anonymous* (also known as the *Big Book*) and other publications from AA and watching some videos that help acquaint newcomers with the program.

12-step system. Some focus on a less spiritual path, some on a more religious approach. For others, the concept of staying sober one day at a time is rejected in favor of a decision to never drink or use again, period. Some encourage people to attend meetings regularly, while others don't hold any meetings.

These groups have not been around as long as AA, nor do they have nearly as many members. But they do work for many people, and some also find that getting involved in one of these groups is a way to ease into recovery. So if you are inclined, give them a try.

- Celebrate Recovery: celebraterecovery.com

- LifeRing: lifering.org

- Rational Recovery: rational.org

- Secular Organizations for Sobriety: centerforinquiry.net/sos

- Smart Recovery: smartrecovery.org

- Women for Sobriety: womenforsobriety.org

Other Mutual-Support Groups

AA, NA, and other organizations that use the 12-step approach are the most popular mutual-help recovery organizations today. But there are other recovery groups that don't use the

Outpatient Treatment

Outpatient programs vary widely, but in general they are less intensive than inpatient programs. Because patients don't stay overnight, they are also less expensive.

Ideally, outpatient treatment starts after you have gotten sober—your mind can't absorb much while it is still clouded by drugs. So you may need to first go through a supervised detox, on an inpatient or outpatient basis. (Read more about detox in chapter 6.)

Outpatient programs include the following:

- An evaluation and assessment interview, including family history

- A physical exam (including a urine drug screen, tests for liver disease, and other blood tests)

- Regular visits with a doctor, and possibly pharmaceutical therapy

- Individual, group, and family therapy

- Ongoing drug-use monitoring (urine screens; family and work reports)

- Outside confirmation that you have attended mutual-support meetings, counseling, or other services

- Referrals to social support services, such as legal, employment, and housing help

- Videos, books, and other materials on recovery

- An introduction to AA, including guided study of the *Big Book* and the Twelve Steps, an explanation of the ninety-meetings-in-ninety-days program, and how to work with a sponsor

- Special individual or group sessions, as well as Al-Anon meetings for your family.

Programs can range from three hours a week to several hours a day, or even full-time. But compared to an intensive inpatient program, you'll have fewer hours of daily programming each week, so you might attend an outpatient program for months or even a year or more, with follow-up care. In contrast, inpatient programs usually last four to six weeks.

An outpatient program can be risky for people who are close to relapse. Dredging up deep feelings could lead to dropping into a bar afterward, or to dropping out of the program entirely. (It's not so easy to walk out of an *in*patient program, and participants have time to work through traumatic feelings before being sent back out into the real world.) Some people also find it hard to concentrate on recovery issues while work, family, and other outside factors continue to tug at their emotional strings.

Some professionals think that learning to stay sober in the real world, rather than in a sheltered facility, is an added bonus of an outpatient program. But some studies have found that a secure and low-stress inpatient facility, where you are free of day-to-day distractions, is a better place to embark on recovery.

In the end, the quality of a program and whether or not it fits your needs is more important than whether it is inpatient or out. If you are very motivated, a good, lower-cost outpatient program may be better for you than a high-cost inpatient program. It will surely be better than a poorly run inpatient program.

Of course, you might have to experiment to see what works for you. You can choose outpatient, find it isn't enough to keep you sober, and so try an inpatient facility. Whatever you learned as an outpatient will help you get even more out of an inpatient experience. Or you could complete an inpatient program, find you still need help when you leave, and enroll in outpatient treatment back home. Again, the one-two punch may be better than either alone.

WHO CAN BENEFIT?

You are a good candidate for outpatient treatment if:

- You've been having problems with alcohol or drugs for only a short time and have decided to take action before your life is a total mess.

- You are already sober, or your doctor says you are not at risk of serious problems with detox, or you plan to go through detox as an inpatient and then move to an outpatient program.

- You have done an inpatient program but feel your recovery is not strong enough yet to move into a less intensive continuing care (aftercare) program.

- You are not seriously depressed, manic, or psychotic, and haven't been thinking about suicide.

- It would be extremely difficult for you to leave your job or family.

- You *don't* work in a safety-sensitive job (such as piloting an airplane) where you can endanger others.

- You have a stable and supportive home environment and are sure family and friends won't sabotage your treatment. Your family is open to going to Al-Anon and open AA meetings.

- You don't feel you need residential treatment, but you want a program that is more structured than AA alone.

- You are motivated. You are ready to give up some control and accept direction from others. You admit to your addiction and you are determined to do something about it.

- You are open to intensive involvement in AA or another mutual-support fellowship.

- You tend to put more effort into something you (or your employer) pay for. For you, a free peer-run group might not work.

WHAT DOES IT COST?

Outpatient programs cost about half as much as inpatient treatment. They range from about $6,000 to $20,000, depending on the part of the country, how much treatment is needed, and the length and type of program.

CHOOSING THE RIGHT OUTPATIENT PROGRAM

Outpatient programs are offered in many settings: community mental health clinics, local health agencies, counselors' offices, hospitals, inpatient facilities, and elsewhere.

There are good and bad programs, and a higher cost doesn't necessarily mean a better program. Most of the same features that make for a good inpatient program (see Inpatient Treatment, page 71) also make for a good outpatient one. Try to meet the staff before you sign up. Do you feel you can trust them? Will you listen to them? You don't have to feel comfortable about *everything* they are going to ask you to do, though. A little discomfort is often the route to a comfortable recovery.

There are still many areas that have no good outpatient programs, or any at all. If you live in such a town, you may need to work out your own program with a doctor, counselor, or therapist—one that includes group and individual counseling plus daily AA or NA meetings. (See more about working with an individual advisor below.)

Outpatient Treatment by a Physician or Addiction Specialist

Seeing a doctor or addiction specialist on your own is essentially going the outpatient route, with the doctor as the counselor or as part of your treatment team. Your care might include assessment of your condition, stabilizing your condition and supervised detox, management with or referral to psychosocial therapy (see What About Therapy?, page 84), management with pharmaceutical therapy (see Drugs for Addiction, page 87), treatment for other physical conditions and referrals to specialists as needed, and advice and management regarding health habits.

As with any outpatient program, patients are also usually urged to go to Alcoholics Anonymous or a similar support resource.

If the thought of going to AA makes you break out in a rash, your doctor may ask you to build your own recovery plan with some similar healing elements: counseling, group meetings, personal inventories, meditation, reflection, and changing your ways. There are so many approaches to treatment these days that it's possible to develop a successful personalized plan for everyone.

Whatever you do, don't go to a doctor who wants to treat you *solely* by writing a prescription. Some medications can be very useful to help a person get through detox and early sobriety, but you need much more than that to move into a solid life of recovery. Simply trading one drug for another is not the solution.

Also avoid a physician (or any other professional) who assures you with a parting slap on the back that you can eventually return to drinking or using. There is absolutely no good evidence that alcoholics or drug addicts can do this.

WHO CAN BENEFIT?

The same people who are good candidates for other kinds of outpatient treatment may also benefit from treatment by their own skilled, well-qualified doctor.

WHAT DOES IT COST?

Costs will vary depending upon the physician's fees, the number of visits, and how long treatment lasts. In most cases, it will cost less than residential treatment, and maybe less than a more complex outpatient program.

CHOOSING THE RIGHT SPECIALIST

Many doctors today have little knowledge of or experience with addiction, but thankfully, the medical profession is changing. More people are recognizing the significance of addiction issues, prompting more doctors to get training in this field. Some do fellowship programs like the one at Willingway; some take courses from the American Society of Addiction Medicine (ASAM), the American Academy of Addiction Psychiatry (AAAP), or other medical societies.

A doctor who is trained or certified by one of these organizations should be able to work with you on your alcohol or drug problem, or help you look at other options. Another good prospect is a doctor—even without certification—who is recommended by old-timers in AA. Those who have been around a while often know where to find the local experts. Finding a doctor who is in recovery himself can be a good bet, too.

Outpatient Counseling by an Addiction Counselor, Psychologist, or Other Therapist

Many counselors and therapists with a variety of professional training now treat people with addiction. Their approach usually includes individual and group therapy as well as referral to AA.

The effectiveness of the treatment will vary, depending on the training, skill, and orientation of the counselor. One advantage to working with a professional who does not have the ability to prescribe drugs is that they are more likely to focus on emotional healing through *non*chemical means.

WHAT DOES IT COST?

Like other outpatient treatment, this is less expensive than an inpatient program. Non-M.D. therapists are usually less expensive than M.D.s. Total cost also depends on how long your therapy runs.

CHOOSING THE RIGHT COUNSELOR OR THERAPIST

An unqualified person can do more harm than good, especially if he fails to focus on the alcoholism/addiction issue from the start.

Counselors who are in recovery themselves often have a good grasp of the issues and can identify with their clients. To be sure that your therapist is qualified and will tackle addiction issues first, it's best to find one who is a certified or licensed addiction or alcoholism counselor.

See more in How to Find Treatment, page 88.

Outpatient Treatment by a Psychiatrist

If you want to go this route, be sure to ask how much experience the doctor has in addiction, and whether he will focus on abstinence. Once you find a psychiatrist who will focus on abstinence, your treatment will be similar to that given by other savvy doctors.

You'll likely be asked to get involved in AA and to follow the AA guidelines to get sober. Once you are solidly sober, the psychiatrist will look at personality traits that need fine-tuning and help you build self-worth. He will also work with you on feelings that may be keeping you from being fully engaged on your new path, such as rage, shame, aggression, or anxiety. You might also talk about self-care issues.

If you have any psychiatric problems—such as deep depression—that are interfering with your addiction treatment or are putting you or others at risk, you'll be treated for those right away.

For many people, addiction comes hand in hand with traumatic experiences. Those events can create lifelong scars—and make numbing your feelings with drugs seem like a good idea. A good therapist will frame those events as incentives for change.

If you do choose psychiatric treatment, don't con yourself into thinking that once your psychiatric problems are "solved" you will be able to safely drink or use drugs again.

WHO CAN BENEFIT?

If you have a serious mental illness or unresolved trauma along with your addiction, you should certainly consider treatment from a psychiatrist.

This is especially true when:

- You might be a danger to yourself or to others.

- You can't benefit from treatment for addiction because your mind is so muddled by the disorganization of schizophrenia or mania, or so numbed by depression, that concentration is impossible.

- You are still troubled by the effects of sexual or other abuse or serious trauma or loss in your life.

If you are functioning well enough to get sober first, it's often a good idea to get in three to six months of sobriety and then see if your psychiatric symptoms are still there.

Once you're sober and working a good recovery program, however, if you are still suffering from deep depression, big mood swings, serious mania, or schizophrenic symptoms, do see a psychiatrist.

WHAT DOES IT COST?

The cost depends on the therapist's hourly fee (usually from $100 to $250) and on the number of sessions you have. Of course, if you need treatment for a mental illness as well, the cost could be much higher. This additional cost, however, may be covered by insurance. And sometimes treatment for addiction will be covered if a psychiatrist bills for a dual diagnosis on insurance claims (specifying that mental illness coexists with the addiction).

If you get psychiatric treatment in an inpatient facility, the cost will be similar to that of any hospital admission.

CHOOSING THE RIGHT PSYCHIATRIST

Many older psychiatrists in the U.S. were never trained to identify or treat drug and alcohol problems.

Those trained more recently know more about these issues, but unfortunately, many have not been well trained in nondrug treatments for addiction, and instead default to treating it with yet more drugs. You may have to look around to find one who will work with you on a program based on abstinence, but in the long run you are likely to have more success going that route.

A psychiatrist who is familiar with good treatment of alcoholism/addiction also knows that it often masquerades as mental illness. He can help you sort out what is really going on and see if you honestly do need treatment for anything beyond addiction (often the answer is no—you can do just fine without those antianxiety drugs and antidepressants). A psychiatrist with this background also will not routinely use mood-altering drugs to treat addicted people once they are sober, unless there is a life-threatening psychiatric problem; he knows that those drugs can raise the risk of relapse. And he will be strongly supportive of the AA principles of recovery.

Like physicians, psychiatrists who are addiction experts may be accredited by the American Society of

Addiction Medicine or the American Academy of Addiction Psychiatry. The one you trust your life to should have plenty of hands-on experience in treating chemical dependency. Try to get a recommendation from someone in AA who has a strong recovery, or from a physician or counselor with experience in addiction.

Help from a Sober Companion

As we've said, recovery is best done with the help of all kinds of support: medical professionals, a mutual-support group, a sponsor, family, friends.

A relatively new piece of this mosaic is the sober companion. Variously called sober coaches, peer support specialists, or recovery coaches, these folks can provide hands-on help to the person in recovery: guidance, fellowship, discipline, support, education, accountability, safe travel, and more.

Most sober companions, however, are *not* treatment professionals. They should be seen as an adjunct to treatment. Read more about sober companions in chapter 10.

Inpatient Treatment

Inpatient treatment is the most intensive, most structured, and most immediately time-consuming approach to getting well. But for many people, inpatient treatment, combined with good follow-up care, is the best way to get sober and stay that way.

In these programs, alcoholics and addicts live together in a therapeutic environment and are totally immersed in learning about their disease and developing coping skills for living sober after they return home. Programs typically last four to five weeks for alcoholics and six weeks or longer for those who are on other drugs or are cross-addicted.

In quiet, comfortable, and supportive surroundings, patients can take part in both individual and group therapy. They are encouraged to examine their lives in a safe place where they can open up and be vulnerable. They are able to focus entirely on getting help and getting well: learning how to break free of old patterns, how to deal with family and psychological problems, how to avoid relapse, and how to develop new skills for living. With few distractions and plenty of time for introspection and interaction, patients often end up with answers to questions they didn't even know to ask. The counselors and other staff also can sometimes help patients sort out other practical issues, such as parenting or housing.

Many programs combine an initial inpatient stay with an outpatient program of several weeks in a dedicated residence or halfway house.

Before patients come in for treatment, they typically have no choice but to continue their self-destructive tailspins. The goal of treatment is to give them back the choice to live sober, by creating an environment where it is sure to happen—at least for the few weeks they are in treatment. It's a choice they will then have to make for themselves every day for the rest of their lives.

Some inpatient treatment programs have their own detox facilities. Others will have you detox elsewhere before admitting you.

WHO CAN BENEFIT?

Not everyone needs inpatient treatment. Consider it if:

- You've had severe withdrawal symptoms when going without your drug of choice before, or fear you may have a hard time detoxing (see chapter 6).

- You've relapsed after failing to stick to a less-intense plan.

- You have rejected AA or NA or it hasn't worked for you, and outpatient treatment is not an option.

- You've failed to stay sober after previous treatment.

- You have medical problems (such as liver disease, lung disease, AIDS, or heart disease) that could complicate recovery.

- You have medical problems that could make a relapse life-threatening.

- You have psychological, behavioral, or emotional problems (such as major depression, bipolar disorder, or schizophrenia) that could possibly complicate recovery, or you are at risk of suicide.

- You work in a safety-sensitive or highly responsible field (such as airline, railroad, or trucking employee, doctor or nurse, power plant worker, or police officer), so the fallout from a relapse could be critical to the public and coworkers as well as to yourself.

- You have a very stressful or drug-oriented environment at home.

- You are addicted to both alcohol and other drugs, or to more than one drug.

- You are still in denial about your disease and can't look at yourself honestly (you may not be able to decide this for yourself).

- You are still in your teens and need to work through some behavioral and accountability issues before you take on the job of recovery on your own.

- You feel total immersion in a controlled environment would give you the best start on the road to recovery.

- You want to really understand the nature of your disease.

- You want to start your recovery in a place that minimizes risk and maximizes good outcomes.

- You're just plain scared that if you don't do something drastic soon, you're a dead duck.

WHAT DOES IT COST?

Inpatient treatment can cost anywhere from $9,000 to $50,000 or more for a four-week stay.

You won't necessarily get a better program by paying more. Some of the best programs have endowments that help keep costs down. Others keep costs down by not providing medical services and sending patients with medical problems or detox needs elsewhere.

Some very expensive programs provide resort-like accommodations. Such an approach may cater to a person's self-centeredness and ego, but it's not going to ensure a better treatment outcome (and in fact can distract you from treatment).

Some states fund their own inpatient programs for those who are unable to pay for private treatment. The cost of those programs may vary depending upon patients' ability to pay.

When you compare programs, be sure that *all* fees are included in the price quote: detox, lab tests, psychologist, doctor, other professional fees, medical evaluation, X-rays, participation of family members, and continuing care. Don't forget to factor in the cost of round-trip transportation for yourself, as well as for anyone who plans to visit you.

When looking at programs, you'll need to find out if they qualify for reimbursement under your health insurance policy or your company's Employee Assistance Program. Insurance policies often say that treatment is covered, but what kind of treatment and to what extent can vary widely from one policy to another.

What often happens, too, is a patient is denied treatment during the preadmission certification, even though the policy does cover addiction and medically necessary care. Patients then have to appeal that decision.

Get advice from your treatment center as well as your employer's benefits counselor before you apply for insurance benefits.

CHOOSING A TREATMENT CENTER

Addiction treatment centers—inpatient and outpatient—can be quite varied. Some specialize in alcohol rehab, others focus on drugs. Some are just for women, others are just for men, and some are for teens only. Some focus on the LGBT community, particular ethnic groups, chronic pain patients, or those with a dual diagnosis.

When you start looking for a treatment center, consider several basic criteria:

Location. Can the patient as well as others in the family travel to a treatment center that is across the country, or is a center close to home preferred?

Treatment. What types of treatment are offered and what is the philosophy of treatment?

Certification. Are the counselors certified? Are there doctors on staff?

Expense. How much does it cost? Do they accept insurance? Do they have a payment plan?

Aftercare or continuing care. Is an extension program available near your home?

Success rate. What does the program claim?

Reputation and reviews. What do others say about the program?

Using the resources listed in How to Find Treatment (page 88), find some programs that meet the basic criteria of most concern to you, perhaps location and costs. Then take a closer look at those programs and see which ones measure up, using the APGAR score as well as the more detailed treatment criteria listed below. Read their online materials. Call them up and talk to the admissions counselors (many have people on staff who are waiting for your call). If you can, talk to former patients and visit the facility in person. Ask local AA members or a counselor who works with recovering people what they recommend. As you learn more about each program and what you want, toss out some of your options; you should end up with a good list of finalists.

This may seem like a lot of work, but it is important to find a quality program. Such a facility will increase your chances of successfully getting sober—and a poor one may sour you on treatment forever.

TREATMENT PROGRAM APGAR

When a baby is born, doctors do a quick assessment of its condition using what is known as an APGAR score. You can do a quick screening of treatment programs using *this* APGAR system, which rates a treatment program on a scale of 0 to 10 on the basis of whether or not the most critical components are present. Any program that gets a score of 7 or above is probably good. You should be able to get the answers from websites or program materials, and also by asking a program director, counselor, or admissions person the following questions. Award one point for each positive response. Unknown, ambivalent, and negative responses all score zero.

Alcoholism as a primary disease:

> Does written program material state that the staff believe that addictive illness is a primary disease?

> During the program is a patient required to complete a written life history?

Professional qualifications:

> Are at least half the doctors on the attending medical staff certified by the American Society of Addiction Medicine?

› Are at least half the counselors in the program certified or licensed as addiction counselors?

Groups specially designed for addiction treatment:

› Does the program have group meetings to discuss the 12 steps of AA and NA?

› Does the program have group meetings for families and to meet other special needs of patients?

Abstinence orientation:

› Are more than 90 percent of patients discharged abstinent from all mood-altering drugs and medications?

› Is there a hospital policy that clinical staff remain abstinent from alcohol and other mood-altering drugs?

Recovery priority of the program:

› Are more than one third of the clinical staff recovering from alcohol or drug problems themselves?

› Are patients given the opportunity to attend and join AA or NA during treatment?

TREATMENT CENTER CRITERIA

There are no industry-wide quality standards for addiction treatment programs, and no two programs are exactly alike. In general, however, the best programs have the following qualities.

A philosophy that puts patients and their sobriety first. Patient needs come before staff convenience or financial issues. You can probably find this out only from someone who has already been through the program. Ask around at AA meetings and check with your counselor or Employee Assistance Program staff person at work about any program you are considering. You might also read some online reviews, but they can be written anonymously by anyone, so take them with a grain of salt.

A medical approach to alcoholism/ addiction. Alcoholism/addiction is seen as a disease. Alcoholics/addicts are treated as sick people who come to get well, not crazy people who need to get sane, bad people who need to reform, or undermedicated people who just need more drugs.

A detox facility, if you need one. It makes sense to go through detox and treatment in the same facility—not only because you could get derailed between detox and treatment at the first bar you pass, but because it will mean better care. There won't be any conflicting philosophies to confuse you. If you have any prolonged medical effects of detox they will be dealt with more easily. Plus, those who are treating you will be more familiar with your case from the start, and will be able to ease your transition from detox to the other areas of the program.

An opportunity to learn about 12-step methods. The staff introduces patients to what these fellowships are, what they do, and how patients can work with them. It's best if patients can leave the treatment center once in a while to go to real community AA meetings with counselors and others in their program. That way, they will be less hesitant to attend them when they get back home. Next best is having AA meetings at the facility, inviting people from the local area.

Enough treatment time. A minimum stay of four weeks for alcoholics and six weeks or longer for those addicted to other drugs or who are poly-addicted has been traditional for many years. More recently, however, there has been a trend toward shorter inpatient programs coupled with intensive outpatient continuing care. This is largely due to everyone trying to rein in costs. But research clearly shows that longer treatment means better results. If you can swing the longer stay, go for it. Many people also benefit from spending time at a halfway house or long-term residential facility after their inpatient treatment. Ask if the facility you are looking at has any such programs.

A professional environment. While a relaxed, homelike atmosphere is good, a setting that is too informal or too posh can undermine treatment. It could divert you from the work you need to do for recovery. You should feel like a patient at a medical facility, not a guest at a resort. Features such as TVs, cell phones, tennis, golf, computers, and shopping outings may sound appealing, but they are distracting and can sabotage therapy.

An educational program. The better you understand this disease, the more ammunition you will have to fight it. You should learn about topics such as:

- The disease concept of addiction
- History and statistics on the drug epidemic
- How it's possible to break through the self-deception or denial of addiction
- Information on tolerance, dependence, and withdrawal symptoms
- The actions and effects of drugs and cross-addiction
- The possible medical consequences of alcohol and drugs and how they can affect recovery
- How alcoholic/addict families function and what kinds of family complications can be expected in recovery
- How to prevent relapse
- How to move forward in your life as a sober person (and work on all of the life issues listed in the Recovery Zone System)

- How to protect your children from addiction

These subjects are best taught through a combination of lectures, group interactions, and recordings and videos. Recordings, books, and online resources should all be available for patients to use during their leisure time to reinforce what they have learned. (It is reasonable to restrict Internet activity during treatment; in that case, the staff should supply materials from online resources as needed.)

Quality staff. A mix of trained professionals and recovering alcoholics/addicts is best. Be wary of any program run entirely by recovering people without any support from professionally trained staff. Also be wary of one that has few recovering people on staff. Counselors should have national or state certification or licensing in the addiction field. Staff physicians should be certified by ASAM or AAAP. Such specialists can handle most medical and behavioral complications of addiction. (See also How to Find Treatment, page 88, for more on credentials.)

A big-name hospital with lots of specialists may seem appealing, but often there are too many chiefs and not enough communication among the staff. Then patients—and sometimes their families—are able to manipulate the staff, play one against the other, and tell one story to person A and another to person B. They can split the staff and derail their own treatment.

Enough staff. A good ratio is one counselor for every seven patients or so. The best programs have counselors with added expertise in areas such as marital and family problems, women and addiction, pregnancy and child issues, ethnic issues, LGBT, HIV/AIDS, hepatitis C, and the issues unique to teens.

Full-time staff. Even the best of staffs can't do the best of jobs if they are around only from nine to five. There should be qualified people for patients to talk to whenever the need arises, day or night, weekdays and weekends. Visit or call a facility you are considering after hours or on the weekend and ask to speak to a counselor. If you are put off until the next morning, reconsider. At the very least, counselors should be available until 11 p.m. or midnight seven days a week, with other support staff on hand around the clock.

A sound policy on the use of medication. The use of medication to ease the symptoms of withdrawal is proper procedure, and can even be lifesaving. But continuing to use drugs long into your recovery, except in rare cases, places time bombs on the road to recovery. Ask how many patients get mood-altering drugs after detox. Any program that medicates more than 5 to 10 percent of patients long-term is probably not the best place for first-time treatment, except for those with severe mental illness. (The rate of medicating will probably be higher at psychiatric facilities, which usually treat individuals with coexisting psychiatric problems. Those patients may indeed need to be treated with medication if their mental issues are more life-threatening than the addiction.)

A self-discovery approach. Patients should have the chance to really look at themselves, preferably by writing a life history and confiding as much as they wish of it to a counselor. You should not be required to show this life history to anyone, and it should be routine policy that it is burned or otherwise destroyed after you've talked about it with your counselor. Steer clear of programs that fail to offer a structured opportunity for this kind of valuable and honest introspection. Also avoid those that require you to read your life history to a group or insist you save it to be read in the months or years ahead.

Plenty of group sessions. There should be at least three daily patient group meetings, led by a professional. There should be more group meetings if there is not a lot of one-on-one work being done. Some meetings should be educational (nutrition, health, pharmacology), others therapeutic (talking about feelings and experiences). Group sizes should range from six to twelve for counseling sessions and twenty-five to fifty for larger educational lectures and AA-type meetings. Group meetings that run from sunup to bedtime are a red flag. They may leave no time for intro-

spection or informal "sharing" with other patients.

Programs for diverse communities. Many treatment centers have group sessions that focus on the issues of women, men, families, teens, older people, LGBT, repeaters, and other communities. And as we've said, some centers focus solely on those communities. Before you decide on such a program, ask questions to see how committed the facility really is to a community. For example, an online directory listing that says a facility has programs for LGBT clients may not tell the whole story. How *often* do the specialized groups meet? If it's just once a month, the center probably is not really taking those needs into consideration. On the other hand, if a large facility has daily meetings for the LGBT clients, that's a better sign. Have all of the staff been trained in diversity issues? How often do they get such training? What percentage of their patients are typically from this community? Are there any people on staff from this community? If a center says it focuses on Native Americans, are there any Native Americans on staff? How many? How would the staff deal with someone who made derogatory racial or ethnic remarks toward others? Do they have policies in place for such situations?

One-on-one therapy. Patients should have scheduled time with a counselor at least twice a week. These counseling sessions are critical in motivating a patient to put in some hard work, even if the work becomes painful. Counselors should be skilled enough to use this time to identify and remove any blocks to successful treatment.

A comfortable schedule. The daily routine needs to be designed for the benefit of patients, not staff. The philosophy of some programs is to stick to a very rigid schedule: patients are roused at an early hour, then herded from one activity to another throughout the day. Others practice a looser schedule, placing more responsibility on patients to get out of bed, get to meals, and get to meetings. This allows counselors to identify (and give extra help to) those who have trouble structuring their own time, while not penalizing those who can handle these small responsibilities, and it more closely simulates the real world of recovery back home, where you will have to get up on your own, get to meetings, and so on. Looser scheduling also allows more time for patients to talk about and process what went on in meetings, to learn to engage each other in casual conversation, to do some self-evaluation and study in their rooms, and to seek help when and how they need it.

Treatment centers usually have a set bedtime so that patients get into a normal day/night pattern. Some, however, allow patients who can't sleep to talk with a staff member after lights out.

A mix of patient and staff ages. Sharing with others in different age groups can improve communication skills and open up solutions to emotional problems. It can also foster empathy for others and initiate resolution of family problems. Older patients and staff bring their experience and wisdom to the treatment environment and young people bring vitality and optimism. Together they create a surrogate family atmosphere.

Family involvement. A good program will involve your family in the recovery process. It will urge your loved ones to go to Al-Anon meetings during the treatment period and afterward. It will also invite them to participate in the treatment program itself, usually toward the end of your stay. The family program may include individual, couples, and family counseling. This helps the worried folks at home to better understand the process of recovery and gives them a chance to ask their own questions (they're bound to have a lot of them). The best programs will arrange even more support by putting you in touch with patients and families in your own town who are doing well in recovery.

Recreational therapy. It's not enough for a treatment center to tell patients not to use drugs. It also needs to teach them the importance of learning new things to do with their time (other than go to AA meetings). Recreation preparation can include art, music, exercise, indoor or outdoor games, arts and crafts, or hobbies. The activities

THE RED ZONE

should not be too focused on competition. They should encourage positive interaction and communication with others, rather than isolation. A good recreational therapist helps patients see that—surprise!—*they can have fun sober*, and begins teaching them how.

Most patients in early recovery are not ready for a strenuous exercise program, such as running or other high-stress aerobic activities. They may not have been very active lately, and could have damage to their muscles, nerves, and bones. Walking, swimming, light use of exercise equipment, and water aerobics are okay for most at this point.

Question the validity of a program that puts too much focus on exercise or other recreational activities that can distract from treatment. You should also question any program that sends people—usually kids—out into the wilderness for "treatment."

Confidentiality assurance. The center should not give out any information—including the fact that you are a patient there—to anyone except people on your "approved" list. (See more on this in Treatment Confidentiality, page 92.)

Patients should also be cautioned not to pry into each other's full names or backgrounds (though they are free to divulge their own names if they wish). They should also be advised not to take photographs of or share identifying information about other patients when talking with family or friends.

A passing grade on the Kleenex test. Boxes of tissues placed throughout counseling areas, group rooms, and in sleeping rooms tell you that patients don't need to hide their emotions, and that having a good cry is just fine. It's an important and positive part of emotional recovery for some.

Snack stations. Recovering alcoholics and addicts are subject to snack attacks. Snack stations with healthy foods such as fruit, nuts, and pretzels, as well as noncaffeinated drinks, are another sign of a place that cares. The focus should be on healthy snacks, but sometimes a sugary snack can satisfy a craving for drugs. Having a candy bar or two is certainly better than leaving treatment to get drugs.

Healthy foods. Good nutrition is a must in recovery. Many programs now provide healthy meals developed by a nutritionist. They also provide nutritional advice and sometimes recipes to take home. The daily diet should focus on whole grains and plenty of fresh fruits and vegetables, while downplaying bad fats, salt, refined foods, and sugar.

A good referral network. A good program will be able to give you the names of satisfied graduates as well as professionals in your home area who can vouch for its work.

Beware of programs that advertise heavily. That can jack up the cost of treatment. It could also be a sign that the program is having trouble filling beds through professional referral channels, because ineffective or it's overpriced. Ads can also give you unrealistic expectations of the center, leading you to think you're going to a resort, for example. They can lead you to choose a cushy, but ineffective, program.

A continuing care (or aftercare) program. Treatment is not just the end of a life of alcohol and drugs. It is the beginning of a new drug-free life. To continue the process begun in treatment, you will need to follow through with an ongoing program of support, meetings, and maybe counseling or outpatient treatment when you go home. The treatment center should be ready to set up a continuing care program for you.

A convenient location. The quality of a program is more important than its location, but location is a factor to consider. Sometimes being far from home can be a real advantage. It might even improve your chances of successful treatment. Out of your neighborhood, away from your usual sources of drugs and alcohol, it will be easier to focus on changing your life. You'll have fewer distractions and temptations. On the other hand, you may be uncomfortable in a place that feels foreign to your usual way of life. Plus, you might not have the funds to allow family members to travel there. You will have to decide what is best for you.

A quality facility. There is no sole national accreditation required for inpatient treatment facilities. To further complicate things, facilities offer different levels of care, so different licensing requirements may apply. Some are licensed or accredited by a state health or mental health agency, but those requirements vary from state to state.

Voluntary accreditation is offered by some organizations, such as the Commission on Accreditation of Rehabilitation Facilities (CARF), The Joint Commission, and the Council on Accreditation (COA). If you want to check this out, just ask, "What accreditations do you have?" A facility should be happy to fill you in on its background.

THE RIGHT TREATMENT PROGRAM FOR YOU

You are going to experience some discomfort during your drug or alcohol treatment. If you don't, then you aren't exploring your innermost feelings, and you probably aren't being honest with yourself or anyone else. You are unlikely to make much progress.

But discomfort when you feel you are among people very different from yourself can hinder progress. So when you choose an in- or outpatient program, be sure there are other people you can relate to, not only among those in treatment, but among the counselors.

If you come from a rural area or a sophisticated suburban one, an inner-city program may not work for you. If you come from a strong African American tradition, a program where the patients and staff are all Caucasian or Asian might feel awkward. If you are a female, a program filled with men might not work.

On the other hand, a program where everyone is just like you may not be the best choice. You may end up focusing on issues common to your particular community, rather than your recovery needs. In most cases, a program that serves a variety of people but is also attentive to the particular issues of various groups is ideal.

Socioeconomic level. Are most of the patients poor, working-class, middle-class, wealthy? What are the counselors' backgrounds? Will you feel comfortable with the mix?

Male-female ratio. Are there enough patients and counselors who are the same sex as you? Do you prefer a female-only or male-only program, or a mix?

Age. Are there several other patients in your age bracket? Are counselors experienced in dealing with your age group?

Language. If you aren't fluent in English, is there someone on the staff who speaks your language? Are there other patients who do?

Social, cultural, and ethnic backgrounds. Are there others on the staff and in the patient population whose backgrounds are similar to yours?

Community background. Are people from similar areas (city, inner city, suburban, rural) or with similar lifestyles involved in the program? If any of your specific issues are not addressed in the program, will you have access to visitors, talks, videos, or other resources to help you address those needs?

Cultural competence. Do you get the feeling from talking to program representatives that people from diverse backgrounds are respected? Do you get any hint that you might be treated as a second-class patient because you are poor, African American, Hispanic, Jewish, Muslim, Christian, Native American, LGBT, old, young, female, or just from a different part of the country?

Special needs. If you are disabled, multi-addicted, or have any other special requirements, will those needs be met? If you have any dietary restrictions, can those be met? Does it seem that counselors are willing and able to deal compassionately with issues such as trauma, a history of sexual or physical abuse, self-hate, low self-worth, and bias toward your group?

A Therapeutic Community

Therapeutic communities (TCs) are a unique type of treatment center. They provide a drug-free residential setting that focuses on increasing levels of responsibility while peer guidance and other group processes help residents develop good social skills.

Many residents of TCs come from very unconventional lives. They may need "habilitation" (learning how to live) rather than rehabilitation (relearning how to live). The goal is to change the negative patterns of behavior, thinking, and feeling that predispose a person to drug use, and to replace them with the values (honesty, responsibility, accountability, social concern, community involvement) that make up a responsible drug-free lifestyle.

Detox is not usually part of the TC program. Most residents are detoxed before admission or are admitted and then sent to a medical detox facility.

When TCs were first developed, the programs were generally run by recovering people. This is still true, but most TCs also have a staff of professionals (who may or may not be recovering).

The primary "therapist" is the community itself, including both staff and other residents. Therapy is based on peer pressure and finding one's own strength in the group, along with counseling and 12-step work. In order to help residents understand that behaviors have consequences, they may be expected to live up to a contract, with infractions resulting in extra chores, fewer privileges, or recovery-oriented exercises.

The therapeutic community offers a supportive but demanding surrogate family in a tightly structured environment. Sometimes the residential part of the program is located in a rural area, with outpatient and continuing care programs back in the neighborhoods from which clients came. But many TCs have thrived in urban locations, where peer empowerment and a strong commitment to recovery help residents face up to the active drug culture around them and push for a healthier new culture.

To prepare residents to return to society, most TCs provide job training and help finding work. Those programs geared to teens and young adults also have ongoing education during treatment, and some are especially geared to adolescents who are also having behavior problems. Many provide for extensive family involvement.

Traditionally, TCs required a commitment of fifteen to twenty-four months or longer. Today, most offer several options, including long- or short-term treatment and outpatient or day treatment. Length of stay seems to be the single best predictor of successful recovery in a TC; a longer stay means a more stable recovery. (This is true, of course, for all forms of treatment.) Random drug testing is used by most TCs to be sure residents are living up to their commitments.

WHO CAN BENEFIT?

Many see TCs as an alternative to the criminal justice system.

They are a way for those otherwise doomed to revolving-door jail terms to learn discipline, gain self-respect, develop a notion of right and wrong, and build productive lives. Originally designed to help the most alienated members of society addicted to hard drugs, TCs are now more diverse and are attracting more "mainstream" alcoholics and addicts, as well as homeless people. They can be especially useful for young people who are out of control and are not being helped elsewhere.

WHAT DOES IT COST?

TC treatment can be very cost-effective. It averages from $13,000 to $20,000 a year, less than the cost of a four-week stay at most inpatient programs. A few cost as little as $9,000 a year. Fees are often based on a sliding scale; in some cases insurance covers all or part of the tab. Since many people served by TCs are indigent and already rely on public support, programs such as welfare, food stamps, and Medicaid can also help subsidize the treatment.

CHOOSING THE RIGHT THERAPEUTIC COMMUNITY

Look for recommendations from alumni of a TC or from a professional who has worked with graduates. No reputable TC allows drinking or the use of marijuana or condones physical or other brutal punishment. Avoid any program that does. Also look for at least some medical personnel and other professionals on the staff; they can be recovering addicts, but they should also have the necessary credentials (see Find a Health Care Professional, page 88). A good TC will also be ready to refer clients to outside resources when situations arise that are too complex or difficult to be dealt with via peer interventions. A day-long visit is one way to get a good sense of the atmosphere and the people at a TC.

Recovery Residences

Recovery residences are not the same as treatment facilities. They are more of a safe transition zone for people in early recovery—a temporary home from which you can practice the recovery tools you have learned in treatment, and also be surrounded by and supported by others in recovery.

There are many different types of recovery homes, with varying levels of oversight. Read more about them in chapter 10.

What About Therapy?

You may encounter several types of therapy once you are in treatment. Some will help you manage the physical and emotional symptoms so common in recovery, while others will improve your skills for dealing with relationships, families, communication issues, and temptations to use.

Beware of relying on any single panacea to turn your life around. One technique or another might help you avoid drinking or using drugs at first, but unless you follow a complete recovery program, it won't keep you sober.

BEHAVIORAL THERAPY OPTIONS

Behavior modification techniques look at a person's current behavior patterns and try to change them for the better. In a sense, the 12-step approach to alcoholism/addiction is a form of behavior modification. Its goal is to change the way you've been doing things, the way you've been living.

Supportive psychotherapy. Not psychoanalysis (which delves into the subconscious), but counseling or psychotherapy (solo or group) aimed at changing behavior.

Contingency management. With this method, a system of rewards for good behavior and consequences for unwanted behavior gives patients a reason to change for the better. For example, if you stay abstinent and go to meetings, you may be rewarded with money, vouchers, or more freedom and responsibility. If you take a drink, you will lose privileges such as Internet access or talking with friends. This tool works well with teens, who may not see that abstinence is its own reward.

Skills development. This involves learning cognitive and social skills, such as decision making, assertiveness, relaxation tools, and stress management. Many people never developed these skills growing up, so they never found appropriate ways to handle emotional and other issues in their lives. Consequently, they turned to alcohol and drugs to try to cope.

Peer support self-help groups. These groups help change behavior through various peer-oriented means, such as sharing, support, and example. They have gotten more popular in recent years, and several training and certification programs are now available for those peers who want to do more to help others.

Cognitive Behavioral Therapy (CBT). This arose as a form of behavior modification. In this technique, the therapist helps the patient become aware of maladaptive behaviors and find ways to replace them with less destructive and even positive behaviors. Once these "better" thoughts and behaviors are developed, the therapist helps the patient to reinforce them so they become natural. These new behaviors can augment the attitudes and skills instilled by other treatments and 12-step work.

Dialectic Behavioral Therapy (DBT). This helps you improve control of your emotions. In this approach, the therapist combines standard CBT techniques with other methods, such as distress tolerance, acceptance, and mindful awareness. This helps a person make better decisions in handling their life circumstances.

DBT is based on Buddhist meditative practices. It works well with 12-step philosophies that also focus on meditation, and can be used with people who need professional help working on the 12 steps (especially steps 3 and 11).

Motivational Interviewing and Motivational Enhancement Therapy. The biggest barrier to recovery is often a person's inability to see his own destructive path—a self-deception commonly known as denial. Motivational interviewing (MI) and motivational enhancement therapy (MET) techniques can help reduce this denial in a supportive, nonconfrontational manner, and increase a person's level of motivation and commitment to get and accept help.

In MI and MET, the therapist builds an atmosphere where self-confrontation can take place. To start, when the patient has little or no motivation to change, the therapist encourages some gentle self-evaluation. He asks questions about how the person would like to live their life ("What do you want life to bring you?" "Does your using help you get there?"), while the patient typically tries to justify their behavior. These questions help expose the conflict created by addictive behaviors. The therapist then raises opportunities for the patient to see a need for behavioral changes, which can be found in treatment and recovery. The patient drops his defensiveness, and moves toward what he now sees as important. He can now be more easily guided to constructive solutions.

This "therapeutic alliance" between counselor and the patient can then be paired with other, more direct, treatment plans. This can result in greater success than more aggressive approaches.

Therapeutic communities were among the first to use aggressive confrontation strategies. These broke through a patient's denial, but often at a high cost. Anger and depression were common results. MET is a better way to reduce denial.

12-Step Facilitation Therapy. This helps patients get actively involved in a 12-step fellowship.

Family Behavior Therapy (FBT). This is a combination of behavioral modification and contingency management. It focuses on the substance use disorder as well as other issues in the family, such as conflict and child abuse. It typically includes other family members along with the patient.

THERAPY FOR TEENAGERS

Some of the psychosocial therapies discussed above, such as cognitive behavioral therapy and family behavioral therapy, are also effective in treating teenagers with addiction. Treatments that include a strong family component work very well for them.

You may want to look for a therapist who is trained in family therapy techniques, such as the following:

Multidimensional Family Therapy (MDFT). An outpatient family-based program.

Functional Family Therapy (FFT). A three-month program that focuses on the many factors known to influence teenage behavior, including the family.

Multi-Systemic Therapy (MST). A family-based program that addresses risk factors associated with anti-social behavior in young people who misuse substances.

Some Others. Brief Strategic Family Therapy (BSFT), Adolescent Community Reinforcement Approach (A-CRA), Assertive Continuing Care (ACC).

What About Pharmaceutical Therapy?

DRUGS FOR ADDICTION

A few prescription medications are now approved by the U.S. Food and Drug Administration for treating addiction. Most act on brain receptors and other pathways to produce various results,

including reducing craving, ing withdrawal symptoms, ing the physical "reward" fr addictive substance. One, ...um-ram, blocks the breakdown of alcohol, resulting in headache, sweating, chest pain, and other very unpleasant symptoms if one drinks.

Currently approved drugs include:

- acamprosate (Campral): for alcohol
- disulfiram (Antabuse): for alcohol
- buprenorphine/Naloxone (Subutex, Suboxone, Zubsolv): for opioid addiction
- methadone: for opioid addiction
- naltrexone (ReVia, Trexan, Vivitrol): for alcohol and opioid addiction

These drugs can be helpful early on, when someone is in the Red Zone and needs help getting engaged in recovery. They can help a person taper off narcotics legally, detox, and then be ready to move to a residential treatment program. But they can be misused, and they can cause side effects. And so far none has shown long-term effectiveness in promoting recovery.

More important, for most people, treating drug addiction with another drug is not a good long-term solution. A maintenance plan that relies on one of these drugs can lock you into physical dependence for years while postponing the start of a recovery that is based on abstinence. Plus, these drugs can be very expensive. If you are ever told by a doctor that you will absolutely need medication forever to treat your addiction, get a second opinion.

Some doctors think that these drugs can be used for life—but experience shows that abstinence from all mood-altering chemicals is still the best foundation for successful treatment and life in recovery.

DRUGS FOR OTHER MENTAL HEALTH CONDITIONS

Some people with addiction also have other mental health conditions, such as depression, anxiety, or schizophrenia. Psychoactive drugs such as antidepressants, anti-anxiety drugs, and mood stabilizers can be very helpful for some people. But their use should be limited to those who have a *severe* mental illness unrelated to their addiction.

Very often, the symptoms that look like one of these conditions are nothing more than symptoms of addiction. When the addiction is treated, the other conditions "magically" go away. So if your doctor agrees, try to wait until you have several months of abstinence before starting any of those medications. A new assessment might find that your other condition is no longer an issue.

Keep in mind, too, that research has now shown that in many people, antidepressants work through the placebo effect. If you and your doctor

strongly believe you will get better with those drugs, you will. A better option is to put your strong belief in a cure into your recovery work.

How to Find Treatment

FIND A HEALTH CARE PROFESSIONAL

Although your first instinct might be to ask your family doctor for help or a referral to a treatment center, you might find out that he has little or no knowledge of the issue. Most health care professionals are not adequately trained to diagnose and treat addiction, and there are no national standards for certifying or regulating treatment providers or facilities. There *are* many very good addiction physicians, therapists, and counselors—but you might have to do some digging around to find one.

The guidelines and resources below can help you find professionals and look at their qualifications. We've also included some of the training and certification options you can look for. Of course, specialized training in addiction is a plus, but it doesn't guarantee quality care. And some of the best experts may not have had special training, but have many years of experience.

Physicians. Medical doctors need a state license to practice medicine. Most, however, had little training in addiction in medical school. With additional training, they can be certified in addiction medicine by the American Board of Addiction Medicine (ABAM).

- Find doctors certified by ABAM: abam.net/find-a-doctor

- Find members of the American Society of Addiction Medicine, a professional organization: community.asam.org/search

Mental health counselors/therapists. Most of these professionals are licensed by states and must have a master's degree in counseling or a related field. With additional training, they can be certified as master addiction counselors by the National Board for Certified Counselors (NBCC).

- Find a counselor certified by NBCC: nbcc.org/CounselorFind

Addiction counselors. Addiction counselors are also called substance abuse counselors, credentialed alcoholism and substance abuse counselors, and alcohol and drug counselors. These professionals may be licensed or certified by states; the requirements vary widely from one state to the next. Some states require a master's degree, while others require only a high school diploma. In some states, certification is voluntary. Some states use the certification processes of professional organizations, such as the International Certification and Reciprocity Consortium

(IC&RC) or the National Certification Commission for Addiction Professionals (NCCAP), which is affiliated with NAADAC, the Association for Addiction Professionals. There are several levels of certification.

- Find a substance abuse professional: naadac.org/sap-directory

To find out what agency or group licenses addiction counselors in your state, go to the Addiction Technology Transfer Center Network's Certification Information directory at attcnetwork.org. You can also find U.S. and international credentialing agencies at the IC&RC site: internationalcredentialing.org.

Buprenorphine prescribers. Not many doctors are certified to prescribe buprenorphine, so it can be hard to find one near you. Your first stop should be the Buprenorphine Physician & Treatment Program Locator (from SAMHSA, the federal Substance Abuse & Mental Health Services Administration): buprenorphine.samhsa.gov.

Before you explore this option, be sure to read our cautions about using yet more drugs to treat addiction (see Drugs for Addiction, page 87). It can help people get engaged in recovery, but it's usually not a good idea for long-term recovery. Also, the Drug Enforcement Administration requires doctors who prescribe this drug to have a few hours of additional education on it, but many of those doctors know little

THE RED ZONE

about treating addiction. If you use this drug, you should also work with an addiction professional.

Psychologists. Also regulated by national boards, psychologists must have a doctorate: a Ph.D or Psy.D. The licensing board, the American Psychological Association, used to offer a Certificate of Proficiency in the Treatment of Alcohol and Other Psychoactive Substance Use Disorders, but that program was discontinued. Psychologists are not allowed to prescribe drugs (in the case of treating addiction, this is a good thing).

- Find a psychologist: locator.apa.org

Psychiatrists. Psychiatrists are specialized medical doctors, also subject to state licensing. With additional training, they can be certified in addiction psychiatry by the American Board of Psychiatry and Neurology (ABPN) (abpn.com).

- Find members of the American Academy of Addiction Psychiatry, a professional organization, at the AAAP Patient Referral Program: aaap.org.

FIND A TREATMENT PROGRAM

The Substance Abuse & Mental Health Services Administration (SAMHSA), a federal agency, maintains the Behavioral Health Treatment Services Locator, which lists more than 11,000 alcohol and drug abuse treatment facilities and programs in the U.S., as well as more than 8,000 mental health facilities and programs. Many of these are local agencies that provide free or low-cost treatment.

- Search this directory for local resources: findtreatment.samhsa.gov.

- You can also call the SAMHSA Treatment Referral Helpline: 800-662-HELP (4357) or 800-487-4889 (TDD). The helpline is available twenty-four hours a day in both English and Spanish.

Another option is to contact your state substance abuse agency, which you can find at findtreatment.samhsa.gov/locator/stateagencies.

About.com has a state-by-state list of Alcohol and Drug Treatment and Rehab Centers: alcoholism.about.com/od/pro.

FIND A MUTUAL-SUPPORT FELLOWSHIP

Descriptions and directories of many mutual-support fellowships can be found in chapters 8 and 9.

Who Will Mind the Kids?

"God knows I need treatment. Alcohol has totally ruined my life. But I have two kids and nobody to take care of them."

For single parents, what happens to your kids when you go to treatment can be a major concern. The kids have usually suffered a lot already, and you don't want to expose them to more trauma. Still, a less-than-perfect care situation for the short term may mean less trauma and upset in the long run than continuing to live with a parent who is actively drinking or using—or losing an only parent to the disease. Sometimes you need to make compromises if you want your family to become whole again.

There are several options to be explored.

The other parent. Sometimes a parent who has left the home because of his spouse's drinking is willing to return—at least temporarily—to care for the children while the other parent undergoes treatment. Or the children can be moved for the time being to the nonaddicted parent's home. Of course, this isn't an option when the absent parent is also addicted or is abusive, irresponsible, or untrustworthy.

The grandparents. In many families, loving grandparents are the best choice for temporary caretakers. Though some older people can't handle kids on a permanent basis, most can do the job well for the short haul. One way to ease the burden is to have another relative or friend come in regularly to help out.

Other relatives or close friends. Other relatives or friends who know the children may also be an option. Of course, you have to feel confident that anyone you ask to help is not a substance abuser and that they will provide a safe environment for your kids. Someone from your religious community, if you belong to one, is often a good choice.

A combination solution. If you have several kids and none of the above options will work for them all, think about combining two or more plans. For example, the grandparents and other relatives or friends might alternate child care. Or an older child could stay with grandparents while a younger one lives with friends who have kids the same age. Or maybe you can find day care for the kids, with family members taking over after work. With a little creative thinking, you should be able to find a solution.

A residential treatment program with child care. A few treatment programs do provide child care for patients. In some cases, federal subsidies are provided to help keep families together when a parent needs treatment. Ask the counselor or physician who is advising you about this option. You can also call your state's substance abuse agency or the SAMHSA Treatment Referral Helpline and ask if there are any nearby programs that help with child care.

Outpatient treatment. If there is a good outpatient treatment program nearby, you might be able to spend your day in treatment and be home each night. If your children aren't yet in school or day care and the program doesn't provide child care, ask your counselor to help you find a temporary daytime place for them. But before you select this option, keep in mind that outpatient treatment probably won't work if you have already tried to get sober several times and failed, or if your problem is overwhelming.

Foster care. Sometimes you have no option but to allow the state or county to take custody of your child until you are well. Try to find out more about the child protective services available in your state so you'll know how you can safeguard your children as well as your rights as a parent. You can find links to all state agencies, as well as many private organizations, at childwelfare .gov. In many cases, you can call your local agency and get at least an overview of the services and benefits that might be available. If you think you'll need to place your children in foster care while you are in treatment, be sure to talk to a legal aid lawyer or case manager so you understand what you are doing.

In almost all cases, child protection staff prefer to return children to their homes and to improve family functioning rather than break up a family. So they will likely do whatever they can to help you get good treatment and child care. Though foster care isn't ideal, if you take your treatment seriously it won't be forever.

After you finish treatment, be sure to arrange for supervision by a counselor or doctor and agree to a structured aftercare program; that may help you get your children back sooner. Or you might be able to get into an extended-treatment facility or halfway house with facilities for children.

In the end, you and your children will probably realize that getting treatment was the best thing for all of you, and that it helped you be the best parent you can be.

Treatment Confidentiality

In the U.S., your private health information with regard to substance abuse treatment is protected by two federal laws, the Confidentiality Law (42 CFR-PART 2-Confidentiality of Alcohol and Drug Abuse Patient Records) and the Health Information Portability and Accountability Act of 1996 (HIPAA).

The first law applies specifically to people who are being treated for substance abuse. It was enacted in the 1970s when Congress recognized that people considering treatment for substance abuse worried about the stigma of being labeled as a drug user. The second law, HIPAA, applies to all people who are getting any kind of medical treatment. Your privacy is also protected by state laws.

In general, these laws mean that people and organizations who provide you with substance use disorder treatment cannot release any information about you without your permission. This includes doctors, nurses, pharmacists, hospitals, clinics, and others.

So if your nosy mother-in-law, your boss, or anyone else calls your doctor or a clinic and asks if you are being treated there, the facility will *not* be allowed to tell them unless you agree to disclose it. In some circumstances these rules are waived, such as if you need emergency treatment or you commit a crime at the treatment facility.

The HIPAA law also gives you the right to see your medical records and the right to specify how you want to be contacted by a health care provider (which phone number you would like them to use and whether they can leave a message, for example).

When you first see a new provider or check into a facility, you will probably be asked to sign some papers regarding your privacy rights and who you want to have access to your information. If you are not sure what you agreed to in the past, ask your health care provider.

Willingway's privacy guidelines are a good example of how a treatment facility will protect you. Read about them at willingway.com/privacy.

For more on your health information privacy rights (including several video presentations) or to file a complaint, see the Health and Human Services website at hhs.gov.

Paying for Treatment

Addiction treatment can be expensive, depending on what kind of care you get. AA and other 12-step programs, of course, are free. Inpatient treatment tends to be the most expensive option.

USE YOUR BENEFITS

Some options to consider:

Health insurance. If you have health insurance, you may have extensive benefits. Most insurance plans are now required to include some mental health care as well as treatment for drug addiction and alcoholism, under the Patient Protection and Affordable Care Act of 2010. If you are enrolled in college, you may be paying for an insurance plan or may have access to health care professionals at an on-campus health center.

Employee Assistance Programs. Some companies offer health-related benefits beyond insurance, including alcoholism or addiction treatment.

The Family and Medical Leave Act. This law entitles many employees to take up to twelve weeks per year of unpaid time off from their jobs to deal with a medical issue (their own or that of a family member). During that time, your job is protected and your health insurance stays intact. You do *not* have to tell your employer the nature of the illness; all you need is a letter from a doctor (this letter can be from your family doctor, which is not as revealing as a letter from a treatment center). Those with family members in the military may qualify for additional time.

Heath savings account (HSA) or flexible spending account (FSA). These accounts generally allow you to save money for certain expenses, primarily medical and dental expenses. The money you put aside is usually tax-deferred, so using these funds can save you money on out-of-pocket costs, including transportation to a facility.

Veteran benefits. If you are a veteran, you and your family may be entitled to benefits from the Department of Veterans Affairs. See va.gov/healthbenefits or call 877-222-VETS (8387).

If you are not sure what your plan provides, ask. Ask the human resources staff where you work for an explanation of what is covered. Call your insurer directly and ask for a written list of what is covered. Ask to talk with a case manager at your insurance company; they often have extensive knowledge of resources, and can help you get the most out of your benefits. Look online to see if your employer or your insurer has posted a list of benefits. Even if you are sure you were not covered for addiction or mental health treatment in the past, check again. Your coverage may well have

changed due to the 2010 Affordable Care Act.

One note of caution: You may be tempted to try to get the "best deal" by using your insurance or letting your company pay for treatment. However, treatment for addiction and alcoholism can still carry a social stigma and can lead to discrimination. Your diagnosis and treatment are *supposed* to be private, but there are no guarantees in life. Private information, including medical records, is sometimes disclosed or lost or stolen, so your insurance records may not be as private as you think. In addition, an agency called the Medical Information Bureau tracks your medical history, akin to how credit agencies track your credit history. If you are worried about anyone learning of your issues, you might want to think about paying for treatment out of pocket.

"My husband and other family members have persuaded me to get help for my drinking. But I'm not sure whether I should just quietly sign up for treatment somewhere or admit to the people in our Employee Assistance Program that I've got a problem."

The recovering alcoholic (or addict) needs all the help she can get. Employee Assistance Programs (EAPs), available at larger companies, can help employees deal with substance use disorders as well as issues like child care, elder care, parenting, and financial problems. If your company has a good EAP, they may be able to arrange for treatment at a program they know has a good success record and then help you devise a quality continuing care program.

They can also help after treatment. Once you have been treated, your alcoholism is considered a disability under the Americans with Disabilities Act. So when you are back on the job, the EAP should be able to help you arrange your work schedule to accommodate your disability. They may also help you find other support services that will help in recovery, such as couples counseling or treatment for the physical effects of substance abuse. They may even help other family members deal with their own substance problems.

EAPs act as advocates for the employees, even though they are paid for by the employer. The company doesn't pay for this out of the goodness of its stockholders' hearts, but rather with the goal of increasing productivity.

It's smart to think about whether you really want to go through an EAP, however. It's probably a good idea to look into the confidentiality protections first. If you do talk to an EAP staff member about a problem—any problem—what you discuss should remain confidential. Effective EAPs are not arms of the personnel or security departments (at least, the vast majority are not) and do not hire and fire. Ask what the confidentiality policy is *before* you divulge any personal information (or see if you can find

a written policy on the company website). Talk with others at your company who have turned to the EAP for help. Were they satisfied with the treatment they got? Was their privacy respected? Another option is to check credentials— most EAP staff are certified, either as Certified Employee Assistance Professionals (CEAPs) or addiction counselors (see Find a Health Care Professional, page 88).

If you want to get information before making any admissions, try the old "I've got a friend who . . ." routine. This generally works, and most EAPs will respect your privacy and not pry further. Or call from a pay phone (if you can find one) and ask your questions: How do I know I have a problem? What can I do about it? How can the EAP help me? Once you've established rapport, you can make an appointment to see the EAP counselor. (You can also try blocking your number from Caller ID by dialing *67 first.)

While you can usually feel free to contact an EAP, going to the human resources department about a drug or alcohol problem may not be a good idea. Some are still uneducated about addiction and have been known to be less than humane. Unless you are sure your best interests will be protected, you're probably better off going elsewhere for help and not divulging your problem until you're sober. Once you are sober, it is illegal—again thanks to the Americans with Disabilities Act—for you to be fired on the basis of your alcoholism or drug addiction. Should you relapse, however, that protection is gone.

MEDICAID

If you are on Medicaid, the health coverage program for low-income people, you might be able to get addiction treatment as a benefit. It depends on your state's plan. If you are looking for treatment for your child, ask about the Children's Health Insurance Program (CHIP) at the local Medicaid office. It might be an option, even if your family is not eligible for Medicaid.

MEDICARE

Medicare, the program that provides health coverage for older people and some people with disabilities, does cover some services when "medically necessary," including detox, inpatient rehabilitation, clinic-based treatment, and more.

IF YOU HAVE NO INSURANCE OR MONEY

If you don't have health insurance or the means to pay for a program yourself, look through the treatment directories for programs that are run by your state, county, or a nonprofit agency. Many of these are free or very low-cost. Some admit people on a sliding scale—you pay according to what you can afford. And don't forget about AA, NA, and other fellowships—they are always free.

Another option is to explore taking part in a clinical trial, where the cost of treatment might be covered for you. Go to clinicaltrials.gov and search for "addiction" and other related terms.

If you have no money, just try to figure out a way to get into a good program, and worry about how you will pay for it afterward. We are talking about saving your life here. When you are sober and back on your feet, your earning potential is likely to be *much* better, so you will be able to find a way to pay for the treatment then.

TALK TO A TAX PROFESSIONAL

Some treatment costs might be tax deductible as medical expenses. This might even include some things you hadn't considered, such as the cost of travel to treatment for both the patient and family members.

CHAPTER

A Closer Look: Detox and Withdrawal

Deciding to get sober was your first major decision on the road to recovery. Getting the chemicals you've been using out of your body—detox—will be your first major hurdle. Knowing what's ahead won't make the experience any easier, but it can make it safer and more comfortable.

Before You Get Started

As dangerous as it is to start taking drugs without medical supervision, it can be even more dangerous to stop them abruptly on your own. So please be sure to read this chapter and follow its recommendations—including the need for medical advice—before going through detox and withdrawal.

Before you get started, you (and anyone who has signed up to help you through the rough spots) need to think about:

- The kind of help you might need—how your detox goes will depend on what drugs (including alcohol) you were using as well as your personal history

- When it's best to detox in a hospital or other medical facility

- Why you'll need a 24/7 attendant if you choose to detox at home and how this person can help you

- The kinds of withdrawal symptoms you can expect and how long they might last

- What can be done to make detox less of an ordeal

It's important to realize up front that detox is *not* the same thing as treatment. It's just the first step in moving into recovery. To stay off drugs and alcohol, you will need to follow up with one or more types of treatment and involvement in a mutual-support fellowship.

If you've already gone through detox, you may find that this chapter will heighten your understanding of the experience and help you to see that what you went through was normal and expected.

A Guide to Detox and Withdrawal

Detox, or detoxification, is the process of getting rid of the alcohol and drugs in your body. Withdrawal refers to the physical and mental symptoms you experience as a result of stopping the use of alcohol or drugs.

At least in part, the symptoms you may have during withdrawal are a result of your body's attempts to get back to normal—to compensate for the chemical ups and downs caused by the use of alcohol and mood-altering drugs.

When you first took a drug that numbed or slowed down your body

and mind (such as alcohol or sedatives), your body tried to resist the change you imposed on it by speeding up. If you took a drug that sped up your body (such as cocaine), your body tried to slam on the brakes and slow down.

In each case, as the effects of the drug wore off, your body continued to overcompensate—by sprinting or foot-dragging—as it struggled to return to its normal baseline functioning. That made you edgy and uncomfortable, so you responded by taking more of the drug. You felt a temporary rush of relief, but then the new dose forced your body to struggle even harder to return to normal.

As this tug-of-war continued, you found you needed even larger doses of the drug to overcome your body's stubborn resistance. You had developed a drug "tolerance." Ironically, the chemical substance that caused your internal warfare was the only thing that could establish a shaky truce. So soon your body craved it and needed it continuously, and you felt compelled to use the drug—even when you knew there could be harmful consequences.

Enter detox and withdrawal. When your supply of chemicals is cut off completely, your body gets even further off balance. It continues its overcompensation in the expectation that the usual dosage of drugs will soon arrive. This can produce a variety of unpleasant effects: withdrawal symptoms such as shaking, sweating, mood swings, hallucinations, and many others.

The goal of detox is to eliminate the drugs from your system and let your body and brain start to heal. You may feel downright miserable for a while, but remember, it is temporary. The process may take anywhere from several days to a week or more to complete.

After you go through withdrawal you are probably going to feel like there is a void in your life, a hole that needs filling. Don't worry. We will help you to fill it with something much better—the joys of recovery and living a drug- and alcohol-free life.

WHAT DETOX AND WITHDRAWAL ARE LIKE

You'll feel worse before you feel better. But you *will* feel better eventually. The symptoms you have will depend on the drug or drugs you've been taking, how long you've been taking it, and your own body's response. So while a large number of common withdrawal symptoms may be listed below for the drug you've been using, you may have only one or two of them. Or you may have some of the less common symptoms. It's impossible to predict exactly what will happen for each person. We do know that almost everyone will have mood swings and sleep problems, both of which can continue for months.

In some cases, it may feel like a roller-coaster ride as you soar from the low of withdrawal up to a giddy high and plunge down again, even though you haven't been anywhere

near your chemical of choice. That high isn't a hallucination. It's a true intoxication that occurs when the drug you've been using is released from storage in your fat cells during withdrawal (this often happens in marijuana withdrawal). With luck, it will be your last chemically induced high. Others may have withdrawal symptoms continue for months or even years after they start detox. This delayed discomfort is known as post-acute withdrawal syndrome (PAWS).

Medical approaches to managing detox differ from one person to the next. Some people are given drugs or nutritional supplements to prevent the most serious symptoms of withdrawal and to ease the psychological pain. If you are going to detox in a facility, before you check in ask if any such options will be available to help you get through it. Keep in mind, though, that these treatments are used primarily for detox and withdrawal—they are not a substitute for treating your addiction. That process comes *after* detox.

The person overseeing your detox may ask if you've had suicidal thoughts, which are very common in alcoholics and drug addicts. If you have, don't be afraid to talk about them. It's understandable that you don't like yourself or the way your life has been going. You may feel desperate to change it at all costs—even by taking your own life. But if you stick with your treatment plan, you'll find there's a much better way to change.

THE RED ZONE

Are You Detoxing for Two?

If there is any chance that you are pregnant, do a home pregnancy test before you go through detox and withdrawal. Some of the drugs used to help people with withdrawal symptoms can harm a fetus. If you are pregnant, talk with a doctor about your detox.

SHOULD YOU DETOX IN A FACILITY OR AT HOME?

Detoxing and withdrawing from alcohol or other drugs is a stressful experience. It can also be dangerous. That's why for most people it's best to go through detox and withdrawal in a hospital or treatment center with a detox unit. A well-run unit will not only make the whole process safer, it can make you more comfortable.

Consider detoxing in a medical facility if:

- You have already had withdrawal symptoms when you needed a drink or a fix, such as extreme nervousness, tremors, or hallucinations (hearing voices or seeing things). This is a sign that you are physically addicted. (If you are only psychologically dependent on the drug, you may be upset but you won't have physical symptoms.)

- You're middle-aged or older and have been drinking heavily for many years.

- You have severe or chronic health problems other than addiction, such as heart disease, liver disease, chronic lung problems, diabetes, or hepatitis C.

- You are severely depressed.

- You feel life is not worth living, have tried suicide in the past, or have been having self-destructive thoughts.

- You've had episodes of violent behavior while intoxicated or during withdrawal.

- You've had seizures or convulsions in the past.

- You recently had a head injury or you were hurt in an accident and have injuries that have not been evaluated.

- You're afraid of doing it alone or have been unsuccessful at previous do-it-alone attempts.

- You are taking any type of opiate drugs.

- You have been regularly taking barbiturate or benzodiazepine sedatives.

Of course, some alcoholics and addicts who fit one or more of the above categories have gone through detox and withdrawal on their own, without medical oversight. This has worked best for those who were not yet physically dependent on their drug, and thus did not have serious side effects when it was withdrawn. But it's risky to try—and *should not be tried at all* if you've had severe withdrawal symptoms when you've needed a drink or a fix. It's also unwise if you've been using alcohol, benzodiazepines, narcotics, or stimulants (cocaine, etc.) daily.

Another option is a "social detox," which might be thought of as a step down from a medical facility. Here you might get professional supervision of your detox, plus a comfortable room, meals, and plenty of TLC. Some of these facilities have a staff person who can prescribe and dispense medications, some don't. You'll also get plenty of help deciding on your next steps for treatment.

Sometimes a home detox can work—if you can set up a very supportive home environment, complete with frequent visits with a doctor, carefully allotted medication, and round-the-clock attendants. If you opt for a home detox, you have to be very careful to see your doctor as scheduled and take medication *only* as directed. This is best done with the help of someone you can trust to hold your medications and dole them out on schedule. Be ready to switch to inpatient detox if your withdrawal symptoms get really bad or you feel overwhelmed by cravings. If you have any of the symptoms in When to Call for Emergency Help, page 106, get medical help right away.

If You Detox at Home

YOU'LL NEED A HELPER

Though you may be able to safely detox at home, you should *never* try to do it alone. You need to have someone with you around the clock until all symptoms of withdrawal have passed. This attendant or helper could be an AA or Al-Anon member (those doing step-12 work are often happy to help), a sober coach or companion, or a friend or relative who is not a drinking or drugging buddy. The helper should read the information below before withdrawal begins.

INFORMATION FOR THE HELPER

Sitting with an alcoholic or addict in detox is a major responsibility and a difficult task. These tips will help you see someone safely to the other side of addiction.

Prepare for Detox

- Read this chapter so you will know what to expect and what you will need to do.

- The patient should be examined by and supervised by a doctor or nurse familiar with addiction and withdrawal. The provider should be willing to make home visits, if necessary. In some areas, an experienced visiting nurse may be available; ask the doctor for a referral to a service, search online for "visiting nurses," or look in the phone book.

- Find others to share the watch duties. A detox can last several days, so line up a team of people who can help out at various times. Shifts can be twelve hours long, eight hours long, or even shorter if there are several people helping. Schedule the helpers on a paper calendar or set up a shared online "care calendar" that allows people to sign themselves up to cover shifts, bring meals, or handle other tasks. Include the helpers' phone numbers, so if someone is late for their shift, they can be called.

- Prepare a list of emergency contacts, including numbers for the police (in most areas, it's best to call 911 if you have an emergency), a nearby hospital emergency room or urgent care center, and the doctor handling the case. If possible, also include one or more strong neighbors who have agreed to help if your charge gets violent. Send the list to everyone on the detox team. Make sure they all add them to their own phones.

- Prepare a list of all other medical issues the patient has: allergies, any medications or supplements they take, and any chronic conditions they have, such as high blood pressure or diabetes. If there is an emergency, the first responders will need this information. Share the list with the other helpers.

- Print out a few days of hourly calendars and use them to track symptoms, eating, sleeping, emotions, and any significant events.

- Print out copies of all your lists and put them in a file folder that will be left with the patient. Leave it near the house phone or on the kitchen table so everyone can find it. Include a map to the nearest emergency room as well. You might also post copies on the refrigerator door or other prominent places that are easy for first responders to find.

- Make sure the environment where the detox will take place is "clean." Search it thoroughly for hidden drugs and alcohol. Clear out the medicine cabinet and the bar. Also check everywhere else in the house: kitchen and bathroom cabinets (for vanilla extract, other high-alcohol flavorings, and gel hand sanitizer), the first-aid kit (for rubbing alcohol—alcoholics will drink it when desperate), under beds, inside drawers, deep in laundry hampers, behind books, under computer towers, taped underneath keyboards, under sofa cushions, in toilet tanks, handbags, luggage, makeup cases, backpacks, coat pockets, and so on. Be suspicious of everything. Overlook nothing. You should also remove any weapons.

During the Detox

- Be sure your charge is never left alone until all severe withdrawal symptoms are gone.

- Set up a calm atmosphere. Lights should be on, but not too bright. Soft music and conversation are okay; loud noises are not. There should be a comfortable chair for the patient, as well as a low bed for resting and sleeping (a restless sleeper could fall from a high bed and be hurt).

- Give the patient unconditional love and care. Forget about lectures and sermons. It's important that he feels worthy of your efforts and attention. Just be there for him. Follow his lead. If he wants to be quiet and listen to music, or nap, let him. If he wants to eat, that's fine. If he wants to watch movies, okay. Let him occupy his time doing whatever activities (within reason) help him get through the days and nights.

- When he seems up to it, you can encourage your charge to talk about his feelings. Be a good listener, and don't try to give a lot of advice. It's best to communicate with open-ended questions and discussion (see Have Helpful Conversations, page 105, on how to motivate someone with friendly conversation). Do give direct accurate answers to the best of your ability, and don't be evasive.

Be careful not to act as though you don't believe or trust your patient.

- Don't allow any unsupervised phone or computer use, to prevent your patient from contacting his dealer or friends who are still using. Do not allow visits from anyone who is not connected to and supportive of the recovery plan. One well-meaning but ill-advised visitor at a critical point could take your charge from "almost there" to back out on the streets.

- Do not give him any mood-altering drugs or medication without an order from the doctor.

- Take any talk of suicide seriously and get professional advice for dealing with it (see When to Call for Emergency Help, page 106). Please note also that if your charge begins to cheer up after talking about suicide, this is *not* always a good sign. More people commit suicide when they're emerging from depression than when they are in the middle of it. Fortunately, as the fog of withdrawal lifts, a person's brain function improves, inhibiting such ideas, and suicide becomes less likely.

- Remember the therapeutic value of touch. Handle your charge gently, and "lay on hands" (pat shoulders or arms, hold hands) to calm anxiety and reassure the patient that he or she is not alone. Much of our communication comes from body language. Keep your posture open and welcoming, lean toward the person who is detoxing, and make lots of eye contact. Such gestures can stimulate brain chemicals that help with withdrawal.

- Remember that any anger or hostility aimed your way is not meant personally. It's just part of the process. But if violence seems about to erupt, get help immediately. Often a strong neighbor or friend or two can help to restrain the violence (by holding the patient's arms and legs), but if this doesn't work, be ready to call the police to protect everyone's safety.

- If your charge seems to be afraid of you, try to be reassuring. Use a soothing tone of voice and calming words. Again, this is nothing personal; it's just another reaction to the withdrawal of drugs. If you're afraid, try not to project your fear, because people in withdrawal tend to pick up the feelings of those around them. Ideally, act as you would like your charge to: calm, relaxed, positive, optimistic.

- Shower him with positive affirmations—remind him that you know he has the personal qualities to make it through this, and he can surely stick to the recovery path he is now on.

- Hallucinations (seeing or hearing things that aren't there) are common. The patient may not tell you about the hallucinations in so many words; you may have to deduce their existence from your own observations. The most common tip-offs are glancing looks or other inappropriate eye movements (seemingly aimed at nothing), incongruous actions or words (directed at empty space), and picking at the skin (as if to remove insects).

- Hallucinations are very real to the person experiencing them and often very frightening. Try to play along. You don't have to lie and say you see something that is not there, but it's okay to respect what is reality for your charge and not argue about it. If you laugh at them or deny they exist, that could be interpreted as a lack of support or concern. Challenging the patient in the hope that the visions will go away may only make things worse. Instead, acknowledge that they exist in your charge's mind and try to calm him with reassurances that they can't do any harm and will soon go away.

- Although hallucinations are not harmful in themselves, you should report them to the doctor supervising the detox. Note them on the daily calendar as well. Later on, it's important to be sure that the patient understands that the hallucinations were not real (see Detox: Alcohol, page 106).

- Let your charge drink all the fluids he desires. Provide high-carbohydrate (fruit, pretzels, muffins, crackers) and high-protein (nuts, cheese and crackers, yogurt, peanut butter sandwiches) snacks. These can help relieve the compulsion to use alcohol or drugs and also reduce the risk of dangerously low blood sugar. If sleep is a problem, try warm milk. Honey mixed with lemon juice and warm water may soothe a cough (see also Colds and Flu, on page 500). A heating pad will make physical aches and pains more tolerable.

- You might suggest the patient try some alternative methods to ease the jitters and anxiety of withdrawal symptoms, such as visualization or meditation recordings, yoga, and light exercise (see chapter 14).

HAVE HELPFUL CONVERSATIONS

If you are trying to help a friend get through detox (or trying to help them decide to get some help), it's best to engage in nonthreatening, open-ended conversations. Focus on building and strengthening a relationship. Don't focus on how "wrong" they are about what they are feeling, what they are experiencing. Making changes to a situation will come easier if it is layered on top of a bond of friendship.

Some tips:

- Show empathy and respect.

- Avoid arguments, but point out discrepancies between their current behavior and desired behavior.

- Discuss options, rather than dictating what you want.

- Ask open-ended questions, such as "How would you like to handle that?" and "What do you want to do now?" and "How can I help?"

- Listen without interrupting or judging.

- Compliment and reward good actions and decisions.

- Don't try to make them feel guilty or shameful, don't make any threats, and do not preach to them or judge them.

- Connect with love and compassion.

- Express hope for good outcomes.

- Try to make decisions together.

Detox and Withdrawal Scenarios

Below are descriptions of what is possible when detoxing from these classes of drugs:

- Alcohol and other central nervous system depressants

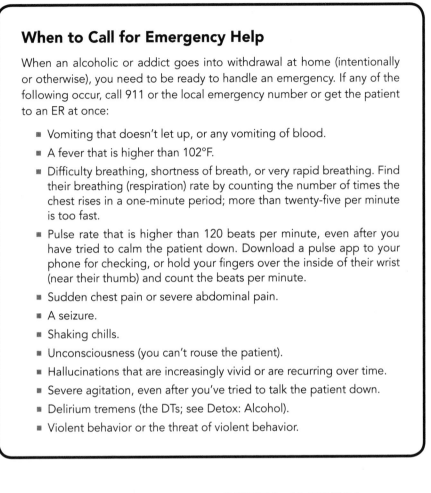

When to Call for Emergency Help

When an alcoholic or addict goes into withdrawal at home (intentionally or otherwise), you need to be ready to handle an emergency. If any of the following occur, call 911 or the local emergency number or get the patient to an ER at once:

- Vomiting that doesn't let up, or any vomiting of blood.
- A fever that is higher than 102°F.
- Difficulty breathing, shortness of breath, or very rapid breathing. Find their breathing (respiration) rate by counting the number of times the chest rises in a one-minute period; more than twenty-five per minute is too fast.
- Pulse rate that is higher than 120 beats per minute, even after you have tried to calm the patient down. Download a pulse app to your phone for checking, or hold your fingers over the inside of their wrist (near their thumb) and count the beats per minute.
- Sudden chest pain or severe abdominal pain.
- A seizure.
- Shaking chills.
- Unconsciousness (you can't rouse the patient).
- Hallucinations that are increasingly vivid or are recurring over time.
- Severe agitation, even after you've tried to talk the patient down.
- Delirium tremens (the DTs; see Detox: Alcohol).
- Violent behavior or the threat of violent behavior.

- Stimulants, such as cocaine, crack, and methamphetamine
- Opiates and other narcotics
- Marijuana and other hallucinogens
- Antidepressants and antipsychotics

Remember, detox scenarios differ from one person to the next, and you will not necessarily have all of the symptoms listed.

DETOX: ALCOHOL

Alcohol is a central nervous system depressant. Because it affects virtually every cell in the body, withdrawal can be very complicated.

What Is It Like?

Alcohol withdrawal symptoms usually begin six to twelve hours after the last drink; they can start even while you still have significant amounts of alcohol in your blood. Symptoms are classified as minor (tremors, restlessness, sweats, insomnia, mood swings, anxiety) or major (seizures and delirium tremens, or DTs). The goal of treatment during detox is to prevent progression to the major symptoms.

First, the minor symptoms. In the first stages of withdrawal, your mind and body will race in response to the withdrawal of the alcohol, a depressant. An early sign of this hyperactivity will be tremors, commonly known as the shakes or jitters. They may be so bad you can't function, or no more than a faint fluttering inside. Loss of appetite, nausea, and vomiting are common. You may have had these symptoms before when you urgently needed a drink, particularly first thing in the morning. Though you may feel unusually alert, you may also be irritable, a bit disoriented, and easily startled. You may be agitated, restless, and unable to sleep, while at the same time, oddly enough, desperately craving rest and sleep. Your face may be flushed, your body sweaty, your pulse racing, your blood pressure high, and your manners not at their best. Other possible minor symptoms include diarrhea, anxiety, mood swings, fear, loss of memory, and depression.

Most of these symptoms—the shakes and loss of appetite, for example—will ease up within a few days. (Before you decided to get some real help, you might have already learned that a sip or two of alcohol made these pains go away.

But in the long run, of course, that only serves to dig the hole deeper.) Other symptoms, such as sleeplessness, may take weeks to improve.

About 25 percent of people in alcohol detox have hallucinations. These usually occur twenty-four to forty-eight hours after the last drink. The first sign of hallucinations may be fleeting shadows. The person may progress to seeing or hearing (or sometimes smelling or feeling) things that aren't there, or he may complain of bad dreams or nightmarish episodes. These hallucinations, which are usually more vivid and intense at night, are most often of people, animals, or insects—frequently enlarged, shrunken, or gruesomely distorted. Snakes, roaches, and rats may swarm in the windows. The air may be filled with disembodied voices, haunting music, or blood-curdling screams and sounds.

Though often terrifying both to the person experiencing them and to bystanders, shakes and hallucinations are not serious in themselves. But if they occur, report them to the doctor overseeing the home detox or to the attendant at the hospital detox unit.

Next up, the major symptoms: seizures and DTs. Seizures or convulsions (also called "rum fits") may happen on the second day, but can occur anytime from six to seventy-two hours after the last drink. These don't usually recur and are rarely life-threatening. They can almost always be prevented in a good medically monitored withdrawal program.

The DTs are a complex of sudden and severe mental and nervous system changes, also described as delirium. (They are more elegantly referred to in Latin as *delirium tremens*, or "shaking frenzy.") The DTs usually occur two to three days after the last drink, but can show up as late as the second week, especially when there is cross-addiction to other drugs (which can delay their onset). The minor symptoms discussed above become more severe and hallucinations more graphically intense. There is usually severe shaking, sweating, paranoid delusions ("Everyone's trying to get me!"), inability to sleep, irritability, and increased blood pressure, pulse, and temperature.

The patient may lose touch with reality, see helpers as enemies, fight to escape caretakers, or even get violent. When severe, the DTs can be fatal. It's suspected that the dehydration, shock, and heart irregularities induced by an extra-heavy adrenaline flow and the super stimulation of the nervous system in withdrawal are responsible.

The DTs are a medical emergency that requires hospitalization. They can usually be prevented, however, by early and intensive medical treatment.

Overall, the symptoms of alcohol withdrawal can last for several days or weeks. The shakes are usually at their uncomfortable worst on the third or fourth day, but they can continue for a few weeks. The risk of seizures is much lower after four days. The DTs, in a heavy-duty alcoholic, can continue for two weeks and (rarely) even longer.

Often the hallucinations experienced in a severe withdrawal are later remembered as vividly as if they were real. It's possible to really believe that the doctor, nurse, or other person who was with you at the time was trying to kill or hurt you. If you have such hallucinations, you may have to be "debriefed" later, to challenge your distorted memories and replace them with reality. Otherwise, you may go through life believing your delusions were real. If you are in any way confused or worried about what happened during withdrawal hallucinations or the DTs, talk about your feelings with the professional caring for you.

If you have really severe withdrawal symptoms, your doctor should check to be sure there are no other underlying causes, such as an undiagnosed illness or injury.

Detox and Withdrawal Treatment Options

The lurid movie scenes of alcoholics shaking violently through the DTs, strapped to their beds to keep them from harming themselves or others, is *not* how drying out has to be. Carefully supervised medical withdrawal can head off the worst symptoms, making you more comfortable and putting you at virtually no risk.

It's likely that you'll be given medication—often phenobarbital, lorazepam (Ativan), or another sedative replacement drug in decreasing doses for five or six days, to ease the symptoms. You may be given magnesium sulfate, thiamine (100 mg), folate (1 mg), and perhaps a multivitamin, which also reduce the risks of seizures and the DTs. You may also be given a variety of other medications to relieve specific complaints, such as pain or sleeplessness. In some cases, particularly during an outpatient detox, the doctor may prescribe naltrexone, acamprosate, or disulfiram, all of which are approved by the FDA for treatment of alcoholism.

These medications may be helpful in early treatment, when the goal is to engage the patient in recovery. In the long term, however, none of them has been shown to work as well as 12-step methods and abstinence.

After Detox

The alcohol you've flooded your system with for years has overpowered your body's metabolism, but with detox there will be a rebound. In the early weeks of sobriety, your long-abused body works hard to fix the damage. Your liver swelling will go down, your muscle tissue will come back, and your bone marrow will improve its performance in your immune system. Your kidneys will release excess fluids (increasing your visits to the john). Most of this repair work is done by the end of four weeks, but some damage may be permanent. While you were drinking, brain cells may have died, your liver may have become scarred (cirrhosis), and your heart muscle may have been damaged. Now only long-term abstinence can supply the resources to compensate for such changes.

Mood swings, often with severe depression, might continue for months, or sometimes as long as two years. Many addicted people are *mis*diagnosed with depression or bipolar disorder because of these addiction and withdrawal symptoms. It is rarely necessary to treat these symptoms with medication. Such treatment can reactivate the entire addictive process and put you back at square one.

DETOX: OTHER CENTRAL NERVOUS SYSTEM DEPRESSANTS

Central nervous system (CNS) depressants include barbiturates, benzodiazepines, sleep medications, and several other tranquilizers, sedatives, and hypnotics that are less commonly used. Many of these drugs are cross-reactive with each other and with alcohol. That is, the withdrawal symptoms of one of these drugs can be eased by any other one. As a result, many addicts routinely use them interchangeably to ward off withdrawal and often mistakenly believe they're not addicted to any of them.

What Is It Like?

Every act of courage has its price, and flushing your last vial of sedatives down the toilet is no exception.

Withdrawal from these drugs is similar to what alcoholics go through, but the time scale can vary. Symptoms may start anywhere from twelve to twenty-four hours after the last drug dose, or even several days later. The onset depends on the amount of the drug used and how long it remains in the body. (How long any drug stays in the body depends on its half-life, a standard measure of the time needed for half of it to leave the body. A drug's half-life is often used as a gauge of when withdrawal might start and how long symptoms might last.)

Because these drugs are less acutely intoxicating than alcohol, their withdrawal symptoms tend to be less severe (at least to observers). But because their effects are longer-lasting, the symptoms can continue for a much longer time, making you miserable for weeks.

In the case of barbiturates, withdrawal can lead to very serious medical complications and is *not* for do-it-yourselfers. Without medical supervision, it can be fatal. Starting eight to twelve hours after the last dose, patients can expect nervousness, tremors, and general hyperactivity. They may also have fever; nausea and vomiting, loss of appetite, and stomach cramps; sweating; and generalized aches, pains, and muscle cramps. A few days later, seizures, often with a loss of consciousness, may occur. Sometimes the seizures are localized, affecting only one part of the body. These seizures may recur periodically for months. Delusions and hallucinations, or even full-blown psychotic delirium akin to the DTs, sometimes occur. Fortunately, we don't see people abusing barbiturates as often as we did in the past.

With benzodiazepines, the pattern is somewhat different. Since many of them have a long half-life and linger in the body, it's not necessary to use them daily to produce physical dependence and withdrawal symptoms. So even casual users—including those who've used the drugs for as little as two or three weeks—can have withdrawal symptoms. These can include anxiety, panic attacks, depression, and distorted senses. In the past, such symptoms were often mistaken for a new or reemerging emotional problem, but they are now known to be a normal outcome of detox and withdrawal. As detox progresses, patients often have alternating good and bad days, with the good days eventually outnumbering the bad ones.

Because these central nervous system depressants have such a long half-life, withdrawal symptoms also last longer than they do with most other drugs. With benzodiazepines, symptoms peak in three or four weeks but can last to some degree for months. Effects may still be noticed more than a year after drug use is stopped. But the severity does lessen with time, and in almost all cases, all symptoms disappear eventually.

Detox and Withdrawal Treatment Options

Generally, another drug in the same class is given in decreasing doses to minimize the effects of withdrawal. For sedatives, barbiturates or benzodiazepines are usually used. With benzodiazepines, medication may be needed for weeks or months.

In inpatient detox, the sedatives used for withdrawal are gradually tapered off over a period of two weeks and then stopped. In outpatient management, the usual procedure is to use the sedatives on alternate days, then twice a week, then weekly. It sometimes takes as long as three months to complete the process. When the process is completed, the drug can be stopped with minimal side effects.

DETOX: COCAINE, CRACK, METHAMPHETAMINE, AND OTHER STIMULANTS

Many cocaine users also use alcohol, sedative drugs or narcotics to take the edge off the agitation or jitteriness they can get from cocaine. This sets the stage for severe or fatal overdose and withdrawal complications if the detox plan doesn't strictly ban the use of those drugs as well as cocaine.

Besides cocaine, there are many other stimulants abused by addicts. Methamphetamine (aka ice, crank, crystal meth) is one of the most commonly used. Prescription stimulants include amphetamine and methylphenidate (Ritalin). Ecstasy, sometimes called a "club drug," is also a stimulant, as are the newest kinds of drugs, bath salts.

Cocaine: What Is It Like?

Symptoms of cocaine withdrawal—often called the post-cocaine crash—begin about nine hours after the drug is last taken.

Abstinence causes deep depression and unhappiness—the cocaine blues (what doctors call dysphoria). The earliest symptoms are agitation, depression, loss of appetite, and strong craving for another hit. In the next couple of days, depression continues and fatigue replaces agitation. Insomnia becomes a problem even though there is great sleepiness. After three or four days, the patient is exhausted, drowsy, sleeps a lot, and notices no craving.

By the end of the first week, sleep patterns are more normal, mood levels off, and anxiety is reduced. Unfortunately, at this point there is typically a gradual return of cravings, which after several weeks become very strong. This often leads to a return to the drug, followed by a repeating cycle of drug use followed by a crash. If this cycle is interrupted, however (by a lack of money or supply, incarceration, or treatment), there is a period of several weeks during which the ordinary pleasures of life (food, sex, friends) don't seem very pleasant, when doing anything at all seems difficult to impossible, and when anxiety begins to build. Suspiciousness, even actual paranoia, can persist for weeks.

By the end of ten weeks, most people start to enjoy life again and have more energy. But periodic cravings—sometimes out of the blue and sometimes triggered by specific cues—are still a problem. Because memories of the adverse effects of cocaine use often dim with time, cravings can provoke a relapse.

Cocaine: Detox and Withdrawal Treatment Options

Most important is round-the-clock support, preferably from people in long-term recovery. Symptoms can also be eased by keeping the patient comfortable during the first few days, and providing individual and group therapy as soon as the patient is able to benefit. Medications may be used to relieve specific symptoms, but there are no medications that have proven to ease the detox itself.

Methamphetamine and Other Stimulants: What Is It Like?

Withdrawal symptoms usually start twenty-four to thirty-six hours after the drug was last taken. You may feel depressed, anxious, moody, fatigued, physically and mentally slow, and very sleepy. At a time when you need the support of others the most, you may feel suspicious of everyone, even paranoid or suicidal. Your appetite, impeded by the drug, bounces back. But because the gastrointestinal tract has also slowed down, you are likely to have indigestion and bloating as you resume normal eating.

These stimulants deplete the natural supplies of norepinephrine (a chemical necessary for normal brain function) in the brain. Deprived of home-grown norepinephrine, you may have strong, periodic compulsions to take more of the drug, which acts as a replacement for these chemicals.

Withdrawal from stimulants is not often life-threatening in itself, but trying to detox without medical help isn't wise. Without close supervision, a strong craving could lead to violent or reckless behavior. And that could threaten not just the patient's life but the lives of others as well.

It often seems that patients recover very quickly from withdrawal. After a few days, appetite, sleep patterns, and sex drive all return to normal, producing a false sense of security. But this can be deceptive. The most dangerous withdrawal symptoms—a nagging craving for more of the drug and impaired judgment—continues for many months during the post-acute withdrawal period. The danger is that the recovering addict feels so good, he begins to wonder, "Why not give in to that craving?" See chapter 10 for how to deal with temptations.

Methamphetamine and Other Stimulants: Detox and Withdrawal Treatment Options

In most cases, supportive treatment and efforts to deal with the underlying addiction are all that are needed to help the patient through detox.

If a person is also addicted to alcohol or mixed drugs (many who use uppers use depressants to bring themselves down), many addiction specialists will add a sedative drug to the stimulant detox regimen.

DETOX: OPIATES/ NARCOTICS

Prescription drugs in this category include meperidine, methadone, fentanyl, tramadol, hydrocodone, and others. One of the most commonly abused drugs today is oxycodone (OxyContin). Many of these drugs were created for the legitimate pursuit of pain control.

Heroin is an illegal (nonprescription) opiate/narcotic.

What Is It Like?

Narcotics disrupt the way the frontal lobe of the brain works, greatly impairing functions such as logic and reasoning. The mind becomes incapable of making decisions, even those that help ensure the addict's own survival.

When detox starts, this "insanity" becomes even more extreme. Patients are likely to manipulate, wheedle, demand, and plead for more of the drug. They may pretend to have symptoms or greatly exaggerate them.

Symptoms of withdrawal from all of these drugs are similar, characterized by the disruption of the autonomic nervous system (the one that carries on the day-to-day functions of life that we don't consciously think about, like breathing).

These symptoms are often classified by severity, from 0 to 3, with 3 the most severe. Grade 0 symptoms usually start eight to sixteen hours after the last dose. Grade 3 symptoms start about thirty-six hours into withdrawal. Symptoms start earlier when the drug being withdrawn is a short-acting one (like fentanyl), which leaves the body in a hurry. And they may be delayed in the case of long-acting narcotics (such as methadone, Subutex, or Suboxone).

- Grade 0: Symptoms start with anxiety; drug craving; drug-seeking behavior.

- Grade 1: Symptoms worsen and progress to yawning; sweating; tearing of the eyes; runny nose; restless, broken sleep.

- Grade 2: Withdrawal progresses to dilation of pupils; goose flesh; muscle twitches; leg cramps; loss of appetite; irritability.

- Grade 3: At their worst, symptoms can include weakness; insomnia; low-grade fever (under 100°F); increased respiratory rate; increased blood pressure; restlessness; abdominal cramps, nausea, vomiting, diarrhea; weight loss.

Symptoms usually become more pronounced over time, peaking at about forty-eight to seventy-two hours after the last drug dose, and then gradually begin to decline. Most symptoms are gone in seven to ten days, but sleeplessness, anxiety, weakness, and muscle aches can persist for a few weeks. Periods of craving may continue for months.

Detox and Withdrawal Treatment Options

In the past, slowly tapered doses of the addictive drug methadone were used to wean addicts off their opiate/narcotic of choice. A newer drug, buprenorphine (Suboxone, Subutex), is now used more often. It is an addictive drug that can be substituted for the narcotics the addict was taking. It acts on the same receptors in the brain as opiate drugs, so it suppresses withdrawal symptoms and relieves cravings for the drug. When used along with other methods to help a person engage in recovery, it can be helpful in making the transition to healing.

Clonidine (Catapres), which blocks many of the withdrawal symptoms, is a very effective alternative withdrawal medication. It is usually given (via a skin patch or orally) for four to six days—often longer for patients who have used longer-acting narcotics. It can cause blood pressure to drop below normal, so that needs to be carefully monitored. Lowering the dose or having the patient lie down flat can help.

DETOX: MARIJUANA AND OTHER HALLUCINOGENS

These distorters of reality include marijuana, K2, Spice, PCP, LSD, mescaline, and psilocybin.

What Is It Like?

The onset of withdrawal symptoms varies, depending on how quickly the drug in question acts in the body and how quickly it leaves.

Marijuana has a long half-life. It is stored in fat tissues and leaves your system slowly, so users tend to be fairly lethargic and unmotivated in the early days of withdrawal. They may even be too apathetic to crave more of the drug. Anxiety, confusion, depression, and irrational behavior are common. Sometimes the only personality changes obvious to others in the first two weeks are self-centeredness and slowed thinking. Energy doesn't begin to replace apathy until the end of the first two or three weeks of abstinence. Then high energy levels return and the patient becomes more active and attentive. He may become restless and start acting out, and may begin to crave the drug once more.

There are no life-threatening side effects from withdrawal of LSD, but flashbacks (hallucinations that appear out of the blue when the drug has not been taken) can occur. With PCP there can be very dramatic effects from intoxication, but the withdrawal symptoms—depression, craving, and confusion—are mild compared to drugs in other categories. The panic, anxiety, violence, and behavior changes (some permanent) sometimes seen in withdrawal are actually a continuation of the effects of the drug as it wears off.

For reasons that are not fully understood, the effects of K2, Spice, LSD, and PCP can persist long after these drugs have left the body—for months, or even for a year or more. Some personality changes may be permanent.

Detox and Withdrawal Treatment Options

Rest, emotional support, good nutrition, and adequate fluid intake are all basic to the treatment of marijuana withdrawal. The process is not life-threatening, so medication isn't required. But in some cases a sedative schedule like that used in alcohol withdrawal will ease symptoms.

Withdrawal from LSD, K2, Spice, or PCP doesn't usually require medication, but the lingering symptoms of intoxication may require medical care in a very supportive environment. The hallucinations associated with these drugs can be disorienting and anxiety-provoking. The medical staff often has to use visual and auditory cues to help the patient remember who he is, where he is, and why he's there. Focusing on these interactions helps to dampen the overwhelming hallucinogenic effect. Without this kind of support, patients might believe that they really can fly, a belief that could have serious consequences.

DETOX: ANTIDEPRESSANTS AND ANTIPSYCHOTICS

Both antidepressant and antipsychotic drugs play important roles in the treatment of some forms of depression and other mental health issues.

Narcotics Detox and Withdrawal for Two

Expectant mothers tend to be very motivated to change, and addiction treatment can be very effective at this time. The best option for pregnant women addicted to narcotics is a mid-trimester detox, followed by a drug-free delivery.

Some doctors think methadone or buprenorphine (Suboxone) maintenance is the best way to detox pregnant women from narcotics. But while mothers treated this way do have healthier babies than addicted mothers, the babies still have many serious problems, including addiction to the maintenance drugs.

A better option is a slow and closely supervised detox from all narcotics, giving the mother ever smaller doses of methadone, buprenorphine, or clonidine. Such treatment is best done in an inpatient medical facility or extended-care residence. The staff must be able to provide good prenatal care as well as intensive addiction treatment to ensure the mother does not relapse during pregnancy.

For the good of both mother and baby, a structured continuing care program (see page 133) is essential.

However, these drugs are often prescribed to alcoholics and addicts even though there is little evidence they will help—symptoms in these people are often a result of substance use, not an underlying mental condition. If that's the case, withdrawing the drugs can enhance the recovery process. If you are on such medications and are being treated for addiction (to alcohol or other drugs), then it is likely that these drugs, too, should be withdrawn—*but only under close medical supervision.*

What Is It Like?

Contrary to popular belief, these drugs, especially antidepressants, do lead to physical dependence and withdrawal symptoms. The onset of symptoms varies, but they generally start two days to a week after stopping the drug.

Antidepressant withdrawal symptoms are similar to those of benzodiazepine withdrawal (but not including seizures). Possible symptoms include confusion, depression, anxiety, agitation, mood swings, fatigue, insomnia, muscle aches and spasms, nightmares, psychosis, vertigo, loss of coordination, tremors, nausea and vomiting, headache, unjustified fears, and a sensation that feels like an electrical shock.

Although these symptoms can be uncomfortable and disabling, they are not life-threatening. How long they last depends on the drug, its half-life, the usual daily dose, and other factors. But in general, most symptoms are gone in a matter of weeks. It may take six to eight months for your brain to heal, and your emotions to get back to normal.

Detox and Withdrawal Treatment Options

Tapering off these drugs over two to three weeks can make coming off them easier. Apart from that, emotional support, rest, good nutrition, and adequate fluid intake are often all that is needed during the initial withdrawal period. Sometimes sedatives are used to reduce symptoms. This is particularly useful if other drugs have been taken by the patient, whether or not they admit being addicted to them.

You Can Make It Through Detox

STAY WITH IT

During withdrawal, you may feel a very strong desire to leave treatment, use more drugs, or escape the therapeutic process. These feelings are normal. Painful and difficult as it may seem at the moment, try to hang in there—things will get better a minute, an hour, a day at a time. Meanwhile, there are things you can do to make it easier.

Be sure you are not alone. At a medical or social detox facility, a supportive, caring staff is crucial. If you are at home or elsewhere, have an experienced attendant with you.

Talk with others who are further along in the process than you are, or who have gone through it before. You can probably find someone to talk with you at an AA or NA meeting, if you are feeling up to it, or you can read about the experiences others have had in an online forum (see What About Online and Phone Meetings?, page 161). It can help to know you're not the only one who has ever felt so awful and out of control, and that others survived the ordeal (and, in fact, now feel better than ever).

Stop resisting and relax. Try to give up your need to control things, so you can ultimately be a better manager of your life. It may not make sense to you now, but millions of alcoholics and addicts have found that letting go, surrendering, relinquishing control, is helpful during this extremely difficult period.

Make sure that you are in a calm and comfortable environment. Activity, noise, and people who upset you will all make withdrawal more difficult. Don't tempt yourself or risk setting off triggers by looking through old party photos online or texting with your old drinking and using buddies. Keep looking forward, not backward. Focus on your new life.

Try some alternative therapies to help you relax: yoga, meditation or guided visualization, acupuncture, hypnosis (see chapter 14).

Write about how you are feeling. Start a private journal or share your feelings online in a recovery forum or blog (you may want to do it anonymously).

Try some light exercise with a friend: a walk around the neighborhood, a stroll in the woods. Appreciate what is around you, now that you are sober.

Start counting your days sober. Mark them on a calendar, use an app, or just check off the days in a notebook.

WATCH OUT FOR THOSE FEELINGS OF POWER AND SUCCESS . . .

At some point in detox, you may start to feel *really* good. This can be dangerous if you then conclude, "Great, I'm done with my addiction. I'm back in control. It's back to business as usual." However, now that you're detoxed, you're just *starting* to deal with your problem. For at least the next year, while you're in the Red Zone, the business of recovery will have to be the focus of your existence. And you'll need all the help you can get.

. . . AND THE SELF-DESTRUCTIVE FEELINGS

There are two self-destructive mind-sets that can make withdrawal an especially high-risk period for the alcoholic/addict.

One is "I'm scared that I'm slowly killing myself with chemicals, but it all seems hopeless. I might as well just die now instead of piece by piece." The other is "I'm afraid of life without drugs. I'd rather be dead than sober." Both of these are conscious feelings, brought about by the hopelessness and despair that are common to this illness. Such thoughts often seem to drown out your will to live.

If you find that such self-destructive ideas are dominating your thoughts, even briefly, talk about them. Talk to a doctor, nurse, or attendant if you are at a medical detox facility, or to a friend or relative who is helping you through withdrawal. Don't let shame or guilt about these feelings (neither of which is warranted) stand in the way of unburdening yourself.

There is perhaps even a positive side to such self-destructive thoughts. We know that change is so hard for the addict. If you are now willing to consider a self-destructive plan, it shows that *you have finally surrendered to the need to change.* Of course, hurting yourself is not the kind of change you need; your treatment team will show you that there are much better options. But nevertheless, this tiny glimmer of willingness to change can lead to a healing outcome.

Fortunately, self-destructive feelings usually begin to lessen as the initial withdrawal period ends. You will start to get glimpses of the light at the end of the tunnel. When you notice that you've felt better for a few days in a row, you've probably passed the period of greatest danger. Depression and despondency may crop up every once in a while, but the down periods should become fewer and farther apart as the months roll by.

If the self-destructive feelings come back, talk about it right away with your sponsor, counselor, or doctor. Or call the National Suicide Prevention Lifeline at 800-273-8255 (see Suicide Prevention and Crisis Intervention Lifelines, facing page).

WHAT ABOUT RESTRAINTS?

Rarely, patients become agitated enough during a severe detox to need physical restraints. They sound medieval, but as long as restraints are used in a loving and supportive way, they can provide a welcome sense of security to patients who feel out of control. And they can protect violent or self-destructive patients from harming themselves (perhaps permanently) or others. Restraints should never be used as a substitute for attention from the staff, and there must be strict accountability to ensure they are used in the most therapeutic and humane way possible. (They should be used *only* in a medical facility—never at home.)

If at any time during your detox you feel you are about to lose control, tell an attendant. Restraints might make you feel safer. And if you do feel violent, don't be afraid that this is "the real you" emerging. Such Mr. Hyde feelings are simply an aspect of withdrawal. They will pass.

Suicide Prevention and Crisis Intervention Lifelines

If you are having thoughts of suicide or are having an emotional crisis, help is available around the clock. The services listed below are for people who are in crisis as well as those who are worried about them and want to help.

- If you or someone else is in immediate crisis, call 911.

- Call the National Suicide Prevention Lifeline number at 800-273-TALK (8255). Spanish speakers, press 2 after dialing, or call 888-628-9454. The Lifeline also has interpreters for other languages (TTY: 800-799-4889). In a time of crisis, at any time of the day or night, whether there is talk of suicide or not, they will connect you with a counselor in your area. suicidepreventionlifeline.org.

- Chat online at suicidepreventionlifeline.org/ GetHelp/LifelineChat.aspx.

- Veterans may also contact the Veterans Crisis Line (veteranscrisisline.net). Call 800-273-TALK (8255) and press 1 (TTY: 800-799-4889). Text a message to 838255.

Chat online: veteranscrisisline .net.

- LGBT youth may also contact the Trevor Lifeline: 866-4-U-TREVOR (866-488-7386). Chat at Trevor Chat thetrevorproject.org/chat.

- Chat online at crisischat.org/chat.

- Chat online at imalive.org.

- Find other online crisis services (including a few local organizations that will text with you) at Online Suicide Help Wiki (unsuicide.wikispaces.com/ Online+Suicide+Help+Wiki).

- Teens, text "listen" to 741-741 (crisistextline.com). If you need a safe place to stay, text "safe" and your location to 69866.

Some local help services also provide support via texting. To find a local service, search online for "suicide hotline" or "mental health" plus your town or state.

If someone you know is posting on a social media site about being in crisis:

- If you know where the person is, call the police or 911.

- Call one of the numbers above for guidance on how to help your friend.

- Post a message to your friend, urging them to call one of the numbers above.

- Report your concern to someone at the social media

site. Responses vary, but most will send the user an email with the National Suicide Prevention Lifeline number. Some will connect the person with a crisis worker.

- Facebook: facebook.com/help/contact/305410456169423

- Twitter: support.twitter.com/forms/general

- Tumblr: Go to tumblr.com/help and let them know that someone is in crisis, including the URL of the person's Tumblr blog.

If you are not in the U.S.:

- Find a crisis center near you at websites of the International Association of Suicide Prevention (iasp.info/resources/Crisis_Centres) or Befrienders Worldwide (befrienders.org).

Mental Health First Aid USA (mentalhealthfirstaid.org/cs) is a certification course that helps people learn how to recognize and respond to a person who is having a mental health crisis. They learn a five-step action plan that allows them to help the person in crisis with appropriate questions and resources.

A Closer Look: Inpatient Treatment

I f you've never been in an inpatient program, you probably have no idea what to expect. This chapter describes what happens in an effective inpatient program, and helps you determine if one would be right for you.

Should I Consider Inpatient Treatment?

F or many people, a course of inpatient treament is the best way to get started on a lifetime in recovery. If you have tried to stop drinking or using on your own and it hasn't worked, checking into a facility might help you make the leap into sobriety. Think of it as a safe harbor. Often, we're able to make big changes in our lives only when we (and our brains) feel safe—safe enough to challenge ourselves with something new. A structured, focused day-to-day program might give you that safety, making it easier to get started on your Red Zone recovery work. Having constant access to recovery professionals—all of whom are there to help you get well—will also help you get started on those big life changes.

Inpatient treatment is not only for those who are still trying to get sober. It can also help strengthen the recovery of those who have been sober for some time. Have you been sober for a while, but don't seem to be feeling better, or don't feel like you are moving beyond the Red Zone? Is your recovery a little shaky? A short stint at a good treatment facility may be just the booster shot you need.

Keep in mind that inpatient treatment is just one step on the road to recovery. Some people come out ready to resume their daily lives, ready for a life in recovery bolstered by fellowship meetings and the tools they learned in treatment. For most people, however, a course of inpatient treatment is not enough time for thinking to become completely clear, for new ways of living to become truly second nature. That often doesn't happen until well into the Yellow Zone. If that's the case for you, you might find that a stay in an extended-care program or sober-living situation will solidify your recovery before you return home.

Regardless of which route you choose, you will also need a continuing care plan to guide you when you are back on your own.

What Happens in Inpatient Treatment?

WHAT IS TREATMENT LIKE?

"I know that I can get treatment at a very good rehab hospital. But I feel like I'm headed into the unknown. It's very scary."

Feeling scared is normal. Ease your anxiety by learning as much as you can about the rehab program you're going to. Check out their website, see what kind of programs they offer, see what the rooms and grounds are like. Chances are it's a comfortable, safe environment, a place where you will feel secure. If the facility has a Facebook page or other site where people can leave comments, see what others have said about it. See if you can tell what kind of experiences they had there, and how happy they (or family members) were with their care. You might also even be able to chat online with staff to explore recovery strategies. You can also call the facility and ask to speak with an admissions counselor or other staff person. They can often ease your fears by giving you a detailed description of what your daily life will be like. They might also refer you to some patients who have already been through treatment there and are willing to share their experiences.

The following outline, based on a typical stay at Willingway Hospital, may also help. Though treatment is a little different in each rehab center, the basic pattern is often the same. And remember, everyone is there to support *you* in your quest to get help.

First Days

A friendly hello. A staff member will greet you. An on-the-spot evaluation will see if you need emergency treatment for withdrawal or overdose. If that is the case, most other intake procedures will be put aside until later. Likewise, if you have to go through nonemergency detox first, you won't be fully integrated into the program until you've done that.

Getting to know you. Once you're feeling comfortable, and assuming you're not heavily intoxicated or in the middle of withdrawal, a staff member will go through an extensive admissions interview with you and (with your permission) any family members or friends who came with you to treatment.

The interview will include questions about your alcohol and drug use. Pride, embarrassment, and memory lapses often keep patients from being totally open, but be as truthful as you can. Dishonest answers will only make your treatment more complicated, and longer. If you'd rather that those who came with you not hear all the gory details, you can speak privately. And if you are not ready to talk about everything in your past yet, just say, "I'm not ready to go there yet." (There will be time later—once you have a little more trust in the process.) Some of this data-gathering can also be done by phone or email before you arrive.

Family orientation. Your friends and family will get a tour of the facility; they need to be satisfied that you're in good hands.

Tech check. Good inpatient programs are designed to help you focus like a laser beam on recovery. This means distractions—anything that is not directly supportive of this very early stage of recovery—are strongly discouraged. You may be asked to leave at home your laptop, phone, tablet, and video games (think of it as a "digital detox"), as well as musical instruments, and even books that are not related to recovery. In addition to freeing up your ability to focus, there are other reasons for banning these toys. Some people whose self-worth is at its lowest due to addiction try to fill the gaps in their lives with things and toys; giving them up for a while can help them explore those issues. Also, some facilities limit possessions to prevent a patient-environment split between the "haves" and "have-nots."

A luggage search. Does that sound like the staff doesn't trust you? Well, do you trust yourself right now? The search is done for your protection and to preserve a drug- and alcohol-free environment for everyone—the only environment that's safe for you and your fellow patients right now. It will be thorough. Staff members have seen it all—cocaine in baby powder containers, pills buried deep in toothpaste tubes, alcohol in makeup containers. It isn't likely that you'll get anything past them.

Settling in. A staff member will take you to your room and give you time to settle in. You may have a private room or a share, depending on the facility and your arrangement.

Assessment. The staff will assess your physical and mental health. You'll have a physical exam, as well as lab tests and interviews. The staff will look at your condition from all angles:

- **Medical.** Is there a physical issue or disability that could interfere with treatment, or an illness that needs treatment?

- **Psychiatric.** Are there feelings of depression, anger, grief, or trauma that need attention so they are not barriers to healing?

- **Social.** Are you concerned about your relationships with your kids, parents, spouse, partner, or others, or perhaps unhappy about a lack of close relationships in your life?

- **Recreational.** Is most of your leisure time spent focused on alcohol and drugs?

- **Spiritual.** Are you moving away from or feeling alienated by your religious background, or maybe searching for a new spiritual home? Are you looking for some spiritual help for your addiction?

- **Intellectual.** Do you understand that addiction is a disease?

This initial assessment will be discussed and evaluated by the staff. They will then work with you to develop a treatment plan that best fits your needs.

Medication. For some people, medication or particular nutrients can help ease withdrawal or ongoing cravings.

Orientation. In most cases, you'll get an orientation to the facility within the first twenty-four hours. If you arrived in a blackout and wake up to find yourself in a treatment facility, don't be afraid to ask questions about where you are and what is happening. Even if you don't ask, you can expect to get a lot of information from the nurses, counselors, and others.

One caution: Be careful about getting too much information from other patients right now. Identifying with their pain and desperation can be a powerful motivator to make changes in your life. But those patients are probably also in the Red Zone. Like you, they are finding their way and aren't likely to have all the answers you need.

Day-to-Day Life

Schedules and rules. Every facility has schedules and rules. At some, you will have virtually no free time. At others, patients who seem able to use their time constructively are allowed more freedom. There may or may not be a set wake-up hour; there almost certainly will be a lights-out time.

Your daily routine will include meals, group meetings, individual counseling sessions, and probably some time to familiarize yourself with recovery—through classes, reading, videos, recordings. There may also be time for exercise and other opportunities to unwind.

Rules vary. Phone calls, visitors, outside work, Internet access, email, TV, and trips off the grounds (except group trips to AA meetings) may be limited or banned entirely. Whatever the rules, they will apply to everyone—the movie star, the truck driver, the dot-com entrepreneur, the dad on welfare. Leveling the playing field tends to reawaken a sense of humility. You might find living like this annoying if you've been shoring up your emotional or spiritual life with material things, along with power and control. But you will find it to be healing as well.

Meetings, lectures, and counseling sessions. These will be the heart of your treatment.

- You will hear talks on many topics, including the disease of alcoholism/addiction, the tools you can use to stay sober and avoid relapse, the living skills that can help you have a happy and productive life, and the risks of using *any* mood-altering substances in recovery.

- You will have one-on-one sessions with a counselor, where you can explore issues.

- You will also go to group meetings and counseling sessions, where patients will share with each other their thoughts, feelings, and experiences, past and present.

Though the idea of speaking at a group meeting may be unnerving at first, you'll have plenty of time to get used to it. You'll start by talking about yourself with your counselor. Then you will share with a small group, and finally in larger groups.

Most people are comfortable with "sharing" by the time they leave treatment.

You will learn a lot at these sessions, but keep in mind that knowledge doesn't equal true healing or recovery. You will be building skills, learning the tools that will allow you to live a life without the need for alcohol or drugs. Your counselors will show you what you need to do. But just as if you were an athlete training for a race, it's only with practice, practice, and more practice that you'll really get good at it, heal your brain, and succeed at what you need to do. (Be sure to review your brain TAMERS, page 30, and keep up those practices.)

Introduction to 12-step fellowships. You will have a chance to learn about Alcoholics Anonymous, Narcotics Anonymous, and other 12-step fellowships. You'll get familiar with their meeting formats and how you can start working the steps. You will probably go to AA meetings in the facility, and maybe out in the community as well.

A life history. At some point, you may be asked to write a life history. You will have to dig deeply and honestly into your past. You may be asked to share some parts of your history at a meeting. And finally, you may ceremoniously burn your life history—and leave that part of your life behind.

The family visit. Since alcoholism/addiction is a family disease, your treatment should include some of the important people in your life: spouse, partner, children, parents, siblings, close friends. Your visitors will have a chance to learn about the disease of addiction and how Al-Anon might help them.

Getting Ready to Leave

Continuing care conference. At this session, which may stretch over a few days, you and your counselor will plan how you'll continue your recovery after you return home. You will write it up as a Continuing Care Plan (sometimes called an aftercare plan). This is a critical part of your treatment. As you know by now, inpatient treatment is just the first step in a lifetime of recovery.

Final meetings with staff. Your counselors and doctor will share with you their assessment of your progress to date, along with any concerns they have. This is also the time for you to bring up any unanswered questions and to raise any concerns.

Going home. You will likely return to your home after treatment. But most facilities will urge you to stay in touch. This might include going to homecoming weekends, getting together with other graduates in regional meetings, or following the facility through newsletters or online venues. Later on, once you are a recovery veteran in the Yellow or Green Zone, you will also be able to say thank you to those who helped you during treatment by sharing your experiences with newcomers.

Although you may feel wary or scared when you arrive at treatment, you may find yourself even more worried about leaving. It likely turned out to be a warm and loving environment, and you may fear leaving this security. Be sure you share these concerns with your counselor and deal with them in your continuing care plan. Being scared of leaving is perfectly normal; in fact, your counselor would probably be concerned if you *weren't* a little apprehensive about leaving.

I'M AFRAID OF REHAB

"I've agreed to go to an alcohol treatment center, but the whole idea is driving me to drink even more. Being away from my family, away from work, spending all my savings, and worst of all, being locked up like a criminal—I can't deal with it."

If you'd had a stroke and had to go to a rehab hospital, the conditions would be pretty much the same. You'd have the same worries—about leaving your family, not working, spending your savings, being in an institution. But you'd go because your only other option might be death.

Your situation right now is just as serious as any medical crisis. In fact, it *is* a medical crisis. But fortunately, good treatment exists and it works, and there's a lot of evidence that says you really don't have a choice at this point. If you keep drinking you will become a hostage to alcohol and maybe to drugs, if you aren't already.

What's the worst that can happen if you go to treatment? You'll feel lonely? You'll fall behind on your work? You'll end up broke? Everyone will know you're an alcoholic? You'll end up sober and ready to live a much more fulfilling life in recovery?

On the other hand, what's the worst that could happen if you *don't* go? You could be permanently lonely, losing your family for good. You could do much worse than fall behind on your work—you could be out of a job. You could lose more than your savings—you could lose your home, your car, everything. And not only will friends know you're an alcoholic, they'll know you are an alcoholic who hasn't done anything to help himself. Finally, instead of sober, you could very well end up dead.

Going off to treatment may be easier if you prepare for it beforehand, assuming you're in a condition to do so. Here are some ideas:

Accept your fears as normal. Everyone has some fears when going into a hospital—for any reason. That's compounded right now by many other fears you might have: fear of detox and withdrawal; fear of being with all those alcoholics and addicts; fear of getting sober, of losing your escape valve, of being cut off from your source; fear of losing your friends and your lifestyle; fear that you'll never again have any fun; fear of learning about yourself, and having that self exposed to others; fear of finding out that

you have brain or liver damage, or other addiction-based health problems; fear of embarrassment once the word is out. And vague nonspecific fear—a common symptom of addiction. You may even have a fear of getting well and being expected to do better in life; many people do.

Though these fears are understandable, they are based on your unrealistic view of your life and your situation. Most of them will fade away as treatment progresses, your brain heals, and you learn more about yourself, your disease, and the real world that you've been avoiding.

Express your fears. Of dying. Of getting sober. Of being with strangers. Of leaving home. A counselor at the treatment center should be available to talk with you before you take the plunge.

Get a preview. Get some information about the program you're entering. Go to their website, watch their videos, read their brochures. Talk with others who have been there. What's a typical day like? What will be expected of you? You may find it's a lot more appealing than you think. Some people look back upon their stay in rehab as a peak life experience.

Keep the home fires glowing. You'll feel better checking into a facility if you know that your loved ones are supporting you and getting help themselves. So urge them to go to Al-Anon, Nar-anon, or Alateen (see chapter 26).

HOW LONG DOES IT TAKE?

"I've been in this treatment center for nearly a week. I feel great. I'm cured. Why can't I leave now?"

Because the euphoria you are feeling won't last. Anyone who wants to cut treatment short takes a big risk—those who leave early usually relapse.

You're no more cured than the strep throat patient who feels better after taking an antibiotic for two days. If he stops the drugs the moment the pain goes away, instead of completing the full ten-day course, he is almost sure to find that he's much sicker a few days later.

Moods in recovery can be fickle and fleeting—you may feel deliriously happy today and miserable tomorrow. You also might be a poor judge of just what "feeling great" is. After all, it's been a long time since you got there without the help of chemicals. You could be mistaking "not feeling miserable" for being as good as it gets. Alcoholics/addicts often fall short of their own goals early in life and compensate by lowering their standards. But your life can get a *whole* lot better.

In the past, you might also have fallen into the habit of not completing jobs that you started. Now is the time to start reversing that trend by doing the one thing that can change your life—sticking with treatment. For some people, a few weeks of inpatient treatment will be enough to kick-start their recovery; others will need a longer course. Wanting to leave treatment early is often just an urge to drink or use in disguise. So follow the guidance of the people treating you. They've been down this road before. They know where the potholes are and they know how to help you steer around them.

I'M NOT COMFORTABLE WITH THE COUNSELORS

"I had the bad luck of being assigned to a counselor who seemed pretty prejudiced against LGBT people. As part of my treatment I wrote up my history—marriage to a woman, divorce, then marriage to a man, and a split from him. When my counselor read it, he asked, 'Well, do you think your wife would take you back?' Like now that I am sober I should be able to go straight."

Unfortunately, there are still some people—including counselors—who hang on to their prejudices. But don't let one person's ignorance deter you from *your* goal: recovery.

Relay the conversation to the people who run the facility and ask if you can work with a different counselor. Tell them you prefer someone who is experienced in working with the LGBT community, or at least is not stuck in biased, old ways of thinking. (There are many counselors today who specialize in working with the LGBT community.) If there is no one else, try to make the best of an awkward situation. Explain to the counselor that "going straight" is not an option (think of this chat as an educational opportunity, not a confrontation). Try to take in whatever good advice he has about recovery. After all, most of what is important about recovery is true for everyone, straight or LGBT. Later on, you might want to seek out some LGBT-focused AA groups.

////////////////////////////

"The counselor I've been assigned to is so different from everyone I know. I'm not sure we can really connect. I don't feel comfortable talking with him."

We have heard from a number of patients who at first were uncomfortable with their counselors. Often it was because the patients had no experience talking with people from other races or cultures. Other times it was due to their own addiction-related resentments or closed-mindedness.

If your counselor is just different from the people you normally run into in your life, try to give the relationship a chance. Take the time to get to know him; you may find that you have far more in common than you think and that you can learn a lot from this person. (It's also a good exercise in learning how to be a little more open-minded yourself.)

However, if you think your counselor is clearly racist or sexist or in some other way bigoted, by all means, talk to the people who run the facility. No one has to put up with that.

I CAN'T GIVE UP CONTROL OF MY LIFE!

"I know I need treatment, but just thinking about having someone else control every aspect of my life is driving me crazy."

Many people going to treatment feel just the way you do. What they forget is that they've been controlled for years by alcohol or drugs. As they struggled to take that control back, to limit their use of alcohol and drugs, their need to control things bubbled over into every other part of their lives.

For now, try to relax, and recognize that sometimes you have to let someone else do the driving. That's not a sign of weakness. A willingness to be guided by others and accept help may, in fact, be the surest sign of inner strength. Admitting that you are not in total control of your life now will, in the end, put you back in the driver's seat.

Get All You Can from Treatment

HOW TO SUCCEED AT TREATMENT

Treatment for alcoholism/addiction is not something someone does to you. It's something you do for yourself. Even the best program can't help you if you are not motivated, ready to make a change, and ready to live up to your responsibilities.

Here are some ideas on how you can have a better chance at success:

Be ready to practice HOW. Try to approach every part of your treatment and recovery with HOW: honesty, openness, willingness.

Do some soul-searching. If you want to come out of treatment successfully sober, try facing your past instead of going into the usual I-don't-want-to-talk-about-it denial dance. That means taking a hard look at your life up to now. When your counselor gives you the go-ahead, sit down in a quiet corner and write a life history, starting with "I was born . . ." No one else has to see that history unless you choose to share it.

If you're totally honest, this look at your past will probably be filled with surprises. It should help you discover where you got lost along the way and how you can find your way back. See page 154 for more on writing your history.

Listen and observe. Let it all soak in. Even when people are talking about something that doesn't seem relevant to your life (say, you're a high-powered drinker from a big city and the topic is meth in small towns), listen and learn. You never know where you will find nuggets of wisdom that can turn your life around. And try to remember that it is more therapeutic to identify than to compare. Focus on the things that you share with others, such as common emotions, fears, and experiences, rather than comparing yourself to them.

Share your thoughts, feelings, and experiences. Though some people are eager for the strong sense of relief they get from opening up to others, others are reluctant and uncomfortable sharers. But everyone benefits from the exercise, even if you have an audience of just one. There's been ample evidence since Bill W. and Dr. Bob had their first meeting of what later became AA that, in some miraculous way, sharing the experience helps heal your brain and relieve the compulsion to drink or use drugs.

Be honest. Honesty is the foundation of every good recovery. If you share only half-truths or untruths, you will subconsciously start to believe those tall tales. That will only sabotage your recovery efforts.

As you move toward the Yellow and Green Zones, you will draw comfort and strength from the fact that you are no longer burdened by secrets. They will no longer hold back your healing. Can you imagine having nothing in your thoughts or life that has not been shared with at least one other person, having nothing left to hide? Can you imagine living your life every day without having to deal with the lies you needed to tell to keep up your addiction? How freeing would that be?

Commit to a mutual-help program. No matter where you start your recovery, plan to continue it by taking part in AA, NA, or another mutual-help fellowship. Commit to your fellowship for the long haul.

Be patient. You didn't become an alcoholic or addict yesterday, and you won't feel wonderful the day after tomorrow. It will take time and effort before your brain heals and you feel like a new man or woman. Judge your progress one day at a time. If you feel better today than yesterday, or last week, or last month, then you are headed in the right direction. But never forget that nobody—addict or not—feels great all the time.

HOW TO FAIL AT TREATMENT

Just as there are some basic steps you can take to improve your chances of a successful recovery, there are some you can take to ensure you'll fail and return to a life of drugs and drinking:

- Spend all of your time playing video games, watching TV, texting with friends, or building your biceps, rather than learning about recovery.

- Insist you have to answer dozens of emails every day or your company will go belly-up.

- Repeatedly threaten to jump ship, then leave before your course of treatment is done.

- Go through the motions to appease your counselor. Pretend you're feeling better and paying attention when you're really not.

- Stubbornly resent the fact that "they" have taken away your freedom. Ignore the fact that this feeling of bondage is actually due to your untreated addiction. Dwell on your feeling that you're cut off from the love of your life or your buddies. Show that resentment by fighting treatment every step of the way.

- Wallow in self-pity. Tell yourself: "Poor me; nothing ever goes right for me. So treatment won't work either. I only drink (or use drugs) because of all my problems, and my problems won't go away." While you're at it, ignore what is really going on: You drink or take drugs because you have a disease called addiction. Everybody has problems, some a lot worse than yours, and not everybody turns to chemicals to deal with them.

- Be a know-it-all. "What do counselors know anyway? They're just addicts, too. Besides, I'm smarter than all those other people. I don't need a string of clichés or bumper sticker sayings to live my life by, or a sponsor to tell me what to do. I can take care of myself."

- Romanticize the drink or the drug. Spend as much time as you can looking through old party photos on Facebook, reliving those "good old days." Talk about all the fun stuff that happened when you were using. (And, of course, conveniently forget about the awful consequences.) Daydream a lot about drug paraphernalia.

- Try to start up a romance with someone at the treatment center, so you are both sure to lose your focus on recovery.

Leaving Treatment

YOU NEED A PLAN

"I'm finishing up my residential treatment in a week. I know I have to go to AA or another fellowship when I graduate. Anything else?"

Plenty. You've got a great start on things, but recovery is not a process that gets completed in four or six weeks at a treatment program. It is something you'll need to live with and attend to for the rest of your life. What you do during the first year after your initial treatment—especially in the early months—can make the difference between staying sober forever and relapsing into an ever-downward spiral of active alcoholism/addiction.

Your treatment program should set you up with a clear plan for your next steps—a continuing care or aftercare plan. You and your counselor should work out all the details before you leave. Your plan should outline all the things you need to do (and not do) in order to stay sober—touching on every part of your life, including meeting with a temporary AA sponsor as soon as you get home. It should also include a relapse prevention component—clear guidelines on what you will do to avoid a relapse in various situations.

Some of the continuing care services you'll use may be included in your treatment tuition. Or you might need to pay fees to a continuing care or outpatient program back home.

As you think about what to include, be sure to review the Recovery Zone System (chapter 2), as well as the three zone introductions (chapters 3, 16, and 21). The Recovery Zone System covers your recovery treatment as well as all the big life issues (school, relationships, work, and more), and gives you guidance on when to tackle each one without risking your recovery. It can help you formulate a good continuing care plan.

While you talk through each topic with your counselor, sketch out on paper how you will address it. Try to pinpoint what makes you nervous. For example, you may be thinking, "I'm scared to death that when Saturday night rolls around, my friends will be calling me to party and I'll want to go." Your counselor will have some solutions for you, based on things you've learned in treatment and what he knows about your home situation. You can then work out practical responses together, rehearsing until you've got your lines down pat.

A major goal of your plan is to build your own supportive social structure wherever you will be living, rather than allowing your former destructive network to reel you back in. You might not have all the answers right now for dealing with every aspect of your life in recovery.

That's okay. You're just getting started. For now, just get a basic plan in place so you can continue your recovery activities and avoid relapse once you leave treatment.

Just know that people who stick with a well-defined plan—and follow the Recovery Zone System and don't let their focus on recovery wander—are more likely to succeed.

The Recovery Zone System Continuing Care Plan

The continuing care plan topics below are grouped according to the Recovery Zone System. You can use this continuing care plan not just for the initial weeks after treatment, but throughout your life, updating it as you move from one Recovery Zone to the next and take on new challenges.

RECOVERY ACTIVITIES

Recovery Treatment

Professional treatment. You may need to continue with professional care. These solo and/or group sessions usually deal with the transition back to planet Earth and with issues you'll face in early sobriety: how to find a good AA home group, how to cope with your job and your family, and so on. Your continuing care therapy may be provided by a doctor, counselor, or therapist trained in addiction, or by the continuing care arm of a local treatment program.

Crisis resources. What will you do if you have a crisis in the middle of the night? Who will you contact? Even if you don't continue with intensive professional care, get a referral to an addiction professional so you have somewhere to turn in an emergency. You should also be able to contact the counselor you were closest to and others at your treatment program if you have questions or concerns over the next year or two.

Additional counseling. If you need marital counseling, therapy to deal with sexual or other abuse in childhood, or another type of therapy in addition to addiction treatment, it should be set up before you leave.

Mutual-Support Fellowship

A temporary AA sponsor. Your plan should list someone back home who will be your temporary AA sponsor (until you have time to find someone who agrees to be your permanent sponsor).

This should be someone your counselor knows and respects—maybe a past patient with many years sober.

Mutual-support fellowships at home: when, where, and how often. Your plan should include details on AA or NA groups in your hometown and how many meetings you and your counselor decide you will go to. If there are absolutely no meetings nearby, you may want to delay going home and instead move into a sober-living home. Another option is online meetings, though nothing really compares to the fellowship of an in-person meeting.

Living Sober and Relapse Prevention

Relapse prevention. What do you need to do to avoid a relapse? What people, places, activities, and emotions do you need to avoid? What will you do instead? What skills have you developed for avoiding triggers and not giving in to cravings? How will you handle holidays and special occasions?

Emotional care. How will you manage stressful situations, disappointments, negative thinking, conflicts with others, boredom, loneliness, anxiety, sadness, guilt, rejection, and other emotions?

Retreat plan. You'll need a carefully mapped retreat path—one that will take you back to some kind of safe harbor or treatment without much effort on your part in case your recovery falters. With such a plan, you'll know what to do right away if things get dicey.

Recovery Zone ReCheck. What system will you use to take a daily inventory of where you are in life and your recovery, in order to anticipate events that could trip you up? Writing in a journal? Meetings with your sponsor? (See Recovery Zone ReCheck, page 18.)

Housing and Related Issues

Living situation. Where will you live when you leave inpatient treatment? Can you return to your home? Should you consider a sober-living house or a campus recovery home?

Transportation. How will you get yourself to appointments and meetings?

Social services. Do you need some help through welfare, food stamps, child custody issues, housing, or other social services?

LIFE PLAN

Relationships

Family issues. Do you need to mend relationships with your spouse or family members? Who can you turn to for support, and who should you avoid for now? Is anyone else in your family doing drugs or drinking heavily?

Recreation and Sober Socializing

Free time. How will you now fill the time that you used to spend drinking or drugging? What hobbies, sports, or other positive activities will you engage in? What will you do to avoid old drinking buddies? How will you build a network of sober friends?

Education, Career, and Finances

Work issues. Are you ready to return to work? Do you have a job waiting? Do you need to find a new job? Do you need to line up child care?

Legal issues. Do you have any legal issues pending, such as a DUI, divorce, or custody hearing? What is your plan for dealing with them?

HEALTH PLAN

Primary health care. Your counselor should make sure you have a doctor or other primary care provider to see at home, and may even make an appointment for you before you leave. If you don't have a doctor, the counselor will probably recommend one with addiction experience.

Treatment medication. If you will be taking medication after you leave the facility, you or your counselor will need to get in touch with a doctor back home who can prescribe it, as well as review your ongoing need for it.

Medication avoidance plan. You may also be given a list of medications that could cause problems for you in recovery and should be avoided (including some over-the-counter drugs that you might have thought were safe).

FEAR OF RETURNING TO THE "REAL WORLD"

"I really didn't want to go to treatment—my husband pushed me into it. But it turned out to be great. Now I'm worried about going home."

A little fear at this stage is a good thing. It probably means you've learned quite a bit about addiction.

It's very much to your advantage to leave your treatment program with a healthy respect for the powerful disease of addiction and concern about what's to come in the crucial next phase of your life.

It's overconfidence that's dangerous. The person who feels sure of herself on discharge is often the one who refuses to live what she learned in treatment, skips recovery meetings, brushes off advice from sponsors, and is most likely to fall off the wagon.

But you don't have to panic. Take a good look at yourself and you'll see that you aren't the same person you were when you entered treatment.

- First of all, you've been sober for several weeks now. Your brain is early in the process of healing and being rewired, but the "psychic change" that people in recovery talk about has already started.

- Second, you've gained some valuable new skills that will help you to not only stay away from alcohol and drugs, but to cope with the everyday problems of life. You just need to keep practicing those skills and internalizing them.

- Third, you're probably leaving with a very detailed continuing care plan that will help you through the rough days.

- Finally, you are going to take life just one day at a time. And one day (or one minute or even one second), no matter how difficult, is rarely more than you can handle—especially if you follow the Recovery Zone System. It lets you know what you need to work on in these early months—and what you can put aside to deal with later. You don't have to take on *everything* at once.

You should figure on being in the Red Zone for at least a year after you leave your initial treatment. This might all seem rather daunting right now, but if you keep working at your recovery and follow your plan, you *will* be able to move out of this shaky early stage and into the Yellow Zone, where you will feel more stable and you can start rebuilding your life.

////////////////////////////

"I am about to get out of treatment for the second time. I'm worried about what's going to happen when I get back to my neighborhood, where it's all too easy to buy meth."

Neighborhoods where drug dealers are a standard part of the scene are not good places to live while you are trying to stay sober— at least not until you have at least several months of solid sobriety.

Many who return to drug-drenched areas after treatment find that dealers are waiting for them with open arms—and open hands. "Here, try this stuff. You never had anything like it. It's on me." Friends who still use are often enlisted to lure former drug customers back ("Just this once won't hurt!"). If your former dealers still have your contact information, you may find them texting you day and night with offers of freebies. Even with your good intentions, these could be just the cues that trigger a relapse.

If you can, go to a sober-living home or enroll in an extended-care program away from your old neighborhood. You need a safe environment where you can spend several months working on your sobriety.

When you do go back to your hometown, be sure to have several NA, church, or other sober contacts to build your new life around.

Staying sober won't be easy, but if you want it badly enough and you do the work, you can be a success. Make it clear to all through your actions that staying sober is now the most important thing in your life. Forget that even for a moment, or let others forget it, and your recovery is in big trouble.

You can prepare yourself for that return by thinking ahead and planning every aspect of your life. Where are the 12-step meetings in your area and how will you get to them? Who will you turn to when you're upset, lonely, tempted? Try to imagine every possible scenario: running into your former dealer; being offered a hit; seeing pictures on Facebook of your former friends partying and having fun; getting a text from a friend who is still using. Rehearse what you will do and say in these situations with a counselor, an AA sponsor, or a friend. That way you'll know what to do when your moment of truth comes along.

Do what you can to *prevent* tempting situations from happening before you go home. Change your phone number. Make sure you have the numbers of your new recovery contacts in your phone for quick calling or texting when you need some support. Unfriend those former friends who are still using, delete their numbers, and block them from texting, emailing, or calling you. If they do call, just don't answer. Remove as much online evidence of your former drug life as you can. If you don't want to unfriend everyone right now, at least limit your time on social media, or temporarily hide their profiles. Make a plan for handling your money, too, so you aren't tempted to buy alcohol or drugs (see page 216).

THE RED ZONE

A Closer Look: AA and Other 12-Step Fellowships

Joining a fellowship that focuses on the 12-step philosophy is a top priority for most people seeking long-term sobriety. Participating in such a group doesn't guarantee a successful recovery, but it sure does improve your odds. And it's free.

This chapter will introduce you to Alcoholics Anonymous and other fellowships, how they function, the 12 steps, how to find a meeting, sponsors, your Higher Power—which you can interpret however you want—and more.

The Serenity Prayer

Grant me the serenity
To accept the things I cannot
*   change;*
Courage to change the
*   things I can;*
And wisdom to know the
*   difference.*

A Beginner's Guide to AA and Other Fellowships

Bill W. and Dr. Bob, the New York stockbroker and Ohio surgeon who founded AA back in the 1930s, started something amazing—a not-for-profit fellowship that gives a lot, asks for little in return, and whose only membership requirement is a desire to stop drinking.

AA works on the principle that members stay sober by sharing their experiences at group meetings and by working the 12 steps (though these are "suggested," not required).

Indeed, AA defines itself quite simply: *Alcoholics Anonymous is a fellowship of men and women who share their experience, strength, and hope with each other that they may solve their common problem and help others to recover from alcoholism.*

In the years since AA was born, it has helped millions of people around the world get sober and live a life in recovery. Many other fellowship groups patterned after AA have since emerged, including Narcotics Anonymous, Crystal Meth Anonymous, Marijuana Anonymous, and others. Most of these groups follow the same general format as AA, both in their structure and in a focus on the 12-step method. The AA approach has proven so successful that today you can find 12-step fellowships to deal with just about any type of addiction.

People who've never been to a fellowship meeting tend to have a distorted view of them. They may picture a room of drunks in tattered clothes sitting around, sipping black coffee, and sharing horror stories. They may imagine people who have no control over anything in their lives, who have decided to give themselves over to some kind of religious cult. Nothing could be further from the truth.

In reality, members of AA and other fellowships come from every walk of life. Executives, musicians, athletes, teenage dropouts, retired grandpas, out-of-work blue-collar workers, professors—all can be found in AA meetings. Members come from every religion, race, culture, and sexual orientation. Possibly in no other setting are differences erased as completely as they are at an AA meeting. Everyone is welcome. All are equals. Most of them are there because they *want* to be there. And contrary to what some think, AA and most other fellowships are *not* based on religion.

Here's what a mutual-support fellowship really is:

- A place where people meet to share their problems and help each other, where they form no-strings friendships in a compassionate, nonjudgmental atmosphere. You will find all kinds of people there. Many have backgrounds like yours, others have very different backgrounds, but they all suffer from the same disease. For many people, it's a second family; for others it's the only real family, or at least the only supportive family, they've ever known.

- A place where you can try again (and again and again) in your quest for recovery, without fear of rejection or recrimination if at first you don't succeed.

- A place where you can start to be honest with yourself and with others in an atmosphere of trust.

- A place where you can learn from other people's mistakes, and others can learn from yours. It's a mirror in which you can see yourself by looking at others—and find out you're not so bad after all.

- A place where you can learn about living in recovery and make contacts for help and support on your own. Your fellowship community can be your base camp, where you'll find coffee, advice, and hope available almost around the clock. It can be your security blanket, filled with people you know you can always turn to for help and support. Many members feel more secure just knowing that their group is there for them.

- A place where, ultimately, sobriety is contagious, just as drinking is contagious at a bar or a party.

- A place where you can socialize and interact with others without the crutch of chemicals.

- A place where you can develop and practice basic living skills—the kind of skills that some alcoholics/addicts may never have learned, such as responsibility, accountability, communication, empathy, and assertiveness.

- A place where you can explore your spiritual side, reflecting on concepts that are foreign to those who only live materially.

- A place where you can be as anonymous as you wish. There is no registration required, no form to fill out, no dues to pay.

Wherever there are people, there are people addicted to alcohol and other drugs. And where there are alcoholics, there is AA. Currently, AA (aa.org) is the fellowship of choice for more than two million alcoholics in the U.S. and more than 170 other countries around the world. As an AA member, you will find support wherever you go.

WHY SHOULD I JOIN A FELLOWSHIP?

Does an alcoholic/addict really need a mutual-support fellowship to make a good recovery? The answer is almost always yes, for many reasons.

One, it works. Millions of people have turned their lives around with the help of AA and other fellowships. You *can* try to do it on your own, but it doesn't usually work. AA and the 12 steps work. All you have to do is follow the recipe and do what others have done, with the guidance of your sponsor.

Two, you will know you're not alone. When you join a mutual-support fellowship, you can talk with others in the same situation; you can learn from those who have been through what you've been through. It's partly genetic: We are tribal beings. We are prewired to be connected to one another for safety, security, and mutual support. Cancer patients, people with diabetes, and abused spouses all do better when they participate in support activities with others in the same boat. So do alcoholics and addicts.

Three, a support group replaces the drinking or drugging social group you once bonded with. It acts as a positive substitute for some of the dependency needs your old group filled. People in recovery share a bomb-shelter camaraderie: Alone you die, united you live. And the early, fixed structure of 12-step programs, followed by their later open-endedness, allow for maximum personal growth. Stick with the program and you can have a life better than you ever dreamed of.

Four, sharing your story helps others and it helps you. Forging connections with a community of other people in recovery is a key part of healing your brain.

If you've had in- or outpatient treatment, or have been seeing a doctor or therapist about your addiction, it's likely you have been urged to join a mutual-support fellowship. In fact, studies have shown that even the best treatment is likely to unravel if it's not followed up by taking part in such a group. So at least give it a try.

AA FOR BEGINNERS

If you are in early recovery, maybe still dealing with the brain fog of addiction, you might find it hard to grasp what is going on at an AA meeting. To help you get your bearings, here's a quick rundown of the basic AA principles:

- You admit you're in trouble and can't get out of it on your own.

- You recognize there's some Higher Power—God, your AA

group, whatever (it doesn't matter what, as long as it's not you or your chemicals)—and you turn to that Higher Power for solutions.

- You start telling yourself the truth, to your fullest capacity.

- You talk about your problem with others who've gone through it before you.

- Later on, you think about those you've harmed and try to make up for the damage.

- Once you are well on the road to getting better, you start helping others as you've been helped—both for your sake and for theirs.

THE TWELVE STEPS

The Twelve Steps, based on the experiences of the earliest AA members, are your guide to recovery. When you first go to an AA meeting you will hear about the steps; see literature on them; possibly see them posted on a wall. Your sponsor will guide you through them, if you choose. But nobody will push them on you. You can start working your way through the steps when you are ready, and others will be there to help you.

The first three AA steps are often called the "decision steps." They are sometimes paraphrased as "I can't. He can. Let Him." Steps four through nine are the "action steps," where you are doing the hard work of recovery, including personal inventories and making amends.

Steps ten through twelve are the "maintenance steps," where you are doing what you need to do to *stay* in recovery and also help others. Most other fellowships use the same steps, or something very close. Following are the 12 AA steps, reprinted here with the permission of Alcoholics Anonymous World Services, Inc.

Step 1: *We admitted we were powerless over alcohol—that our lives had become unmanageable.*

Step 2: *Came to believe that a Power greater than ourselves could restore us to sanity.*

Step 3: *Made a decision to turn our will and lives over to the care of God as we understood Him.*

Step 4: *Made a searching and fearless moral inventory of ourselves.*

Step 5: *Admitted to God, to ourselves, and to another human being the exact nature of our wrongs.*

Step 6: *Were entirely ready to have God remove all these defects of character.*

Step 7: *Humbly asked Him to remove our shortcomings.*

Step 8: *Made a list of all persons we had harmed, and became willing to make amends to them all.*

Step 9: *Made direct amends to such people wherever possible, except when to do so would injure them or others.*

Step 10: *Continued to take personal inventory and when we were wrong promptly admitted it.*

Step 11: *Sought through prayer and meditation to improve our conscious contact with God as we understood Him, praying only for knowledge of His will for us and the power to carry that out.*

Step 12: *Having had a spiritual awakening as the result of these steps, we tried to carry this message to alcoholics, and to practice these principles in all our affairs.*

WHAT ARE MEETINGS LIKE?

If you've never been to an AA meeting before, you probably have no idea what to expect. At the very least, we guarantee you won't be bored.

The atmosphere is that of an informal social group, though less raucous (nothing stronger than coffee is served) and more interesting. Real people tell real stories; stories very much like your own, stories probably more emotionally gripping and sometimes funnier (fun poked at the speakers by themselves) than anything you've ever seen on TV or in the movies. Since people are not judged by what they say, most feel free to speak up—under the cloak of anonymity if they wish. Others prefer to remain silent, at least at first. No one participates at any meeting except voluntarily. Nor is anyone pressured to admit to a drinking or drug problem.

Meetings start on time, so people often arrive early to chat with friends. Meetings usually open with one or more readings (the Twelve

Steps, the Twelve Traditions, the Serenity Prayer, or other AA material). Then there may be one or more scheduled speakers, then an open discussion, or "sharing," on a topic.

An *open meeting* welcomes guests who are not alcoholics, as well as those who are not sure if they are. Going to one of these is a good non-threatening way to see what AA is like. People who are having trouble with alcohol, but who consider themselves "smarter than those alcoholics," often find this a good way to ease into getting help.

Closed meetings are more intense gatherings of people with one common bond—they have all decided they want to stop drinking and stay sober. These meetings are not open to outsiders.

Meetings last about an hour—sixty minutes crowded with emotional recollections of personal struggles, revealing insights, practical suggestions, and a lot of tears and laughter. Surprised flashes of "Well, at least I'm not the only one!" are common as listeners identify with speakers they recognize as co-tenants of what they'd thought was their own private hell. Many close with a recitation, such as the Serenity Prayer or a silent meditation, followed by coffee, tea, and conversation. Sometimes refreshments are served.

Group size varies from a handful to a hundred or more (with occasional regional meetings attended by thousands). Meeting formats are scheduled well in advance, usually by some form of group leadership, so people can plan ahead to attend meetings specific to their current needs and interests. Meetings may focus on one group, such as beginners, women, gay men, teenagers, or Spanish-speakers. Some focus on specific topics, such as *Big Book* study or working on a particular step. Local meeting schedules (which are often posted online) will indicate which type of meeting is planned. Each type of meeting serves a different purpose. All can be helpful.

YOUR FIRST MEETING

If the thought of going to your first AA or NA meeting makes you sweat as much as a letter from the IRS, find someone to go with you. Ask an AA member you know, your partner, a parent, a friend. (If the person is not an alcoholic/addict, be sure to choose an open meeting.) Or call the local Alcoholics Anonymous phone number (if there is one) and ask if they can put you in touch with an AA veteran who will go to a meeting with you.

At the meeting you don't have to do anything but listen. No one will pressure you to get more involved than you want. If you're asked to identify yourself, you can give your first name and simply say "I pass"; if even that makes you uncomfortable, make up a name. If you're embarrassed to tell anyone about your drinking or drug problem, use that old standby: "I'm here for a friend." If you really don't want to talk to anyone, arrive five minutes after the meeting starts and sit in the back. If you feel ready to start meeting people, come fifteen minutes early or plan to stay for coffee afterward. You will likely find others who are happy to talk with you and get you started with the group.

Keep in mind as you look around the meeting that you're surrounded by people very much like yourself. They too were deep into drinking or using drugs, before it wrecked (or almost wrecked) their lives. Now they'll cheerfully assure you (if their recovery is well along its way) that they have even more fun sober.

You'll have many choices for your first meeting if you live in a large city, fewer if you live in a small town. Beginners Meetings are geared toward newcomers and could be especially helpful. But if there is no Beginners Meeting, go to an Open Speaker, Open Discussion, or any other meeting you can find. Just go.

Be sure to pick up some of the reading materials on display, including a list of local meetings. You can also find a lot of these materials online.

If you don't have one, get a copy of the *Big Book* (formally titled *Alcoholics Anonymous*) at the meeting or elsewhere. In paperback, the current (fourth) edition sells for under $12 and used copies for as little as 99 cents. Ebook versions are available at online bookstores. You can also read it online for free at the

AA site: aa.org/bbonline or aa.org/bigbookonline. An audiobook version is available at audible.com and other websites.

YOUR HIGHER POWER

"I'm not a religious person. What's the deal with turning everything over to a Higher Power?"

It's a common misunderstanding that AA is based on religion. It's not. You do not have to believe in any particular religion or religious concepts to benefit from AA, and you can be sure there are many AA members who feel just as you do.

The concept of a Higher Power is anchored in the idea that a person needs to gather strength from something outside himself in order to heal. Think of it as whatever "force" is helping you change your destructive behavior. Many people do consider God (however they define it) to be their Higher Power. Some came into AA with that belief; some came to believe it as they struggled with recovery.

Others believe there is simply a power out there, stronger than they are, that can help them with their alcoholism/addiction. Your Higher Power could be the unknown force that created the universe. It can be your love for your family, your ancestors, or your beloved dog. Maybe it's the beauty and wonder you see in nature, or the power of your AA group's love and acceptance. It can simply be something that is unknown, but has the opposite energy of what threw your life off track in the first place.

Whatever form it takes, believing that this power can help them change has proven to be important to the recovery of millions of people with drug and alcohol problems.

Think about it this way. You've already seen how powerful it was turning your life over to a different Higher Power—the negative power of alcohol or drugs, which took you where you never planned to go. From there it's no great leap to accepting that there must be a positive equivalent: a power that can help you find a way to overcome addiction. Now you just need to find that good source of power.

In the earliest days of AA, Higher Power was intended as a reference to God. But as the membership grew, it soon became clear that people who had no religious affiliation whatsoever also got sober by working the steps, as did those who subscribed to a wide variety of religions and beliefs. The founders of AA wanted them all to feel welcome: Even in the early texts of AA, they were careful to refer to the Higher Power with the qualifier "as we understood Him." In fact, they were so concerned that nonbelievers not feel excluded that they devoted an entire chapter of the *Big Book* to talking about the approximately 50 percent of the original group that felt as you do. Read that chapter ("We Agnostics") and see if it offers some help.

So don't let yourself be put off of AA because of the concept of a Higher Power. Bottom line, your Higher Power can be whatever it is that works for you, whatever interpretation you want.

///////////////////////////////

"When I was young, my parents taught me that 'God helps those who help themselves.' That's why I have trouble with the idea of surrendering and turning it all over to God."

Your parents were right. God (however you choose to define it) can't do it alone. You can't expect your Higher Power to take over and change your life while you sit back and relax. You've got to do your part: go to meetings, talk to your sponsor, work the steps, look at your behavior, do what you can to help your brain heal. Only then can you ask your partner in recovery— your Higher Power—to remove your defects, keep you sober, and make you a better person. You and your Higher Power need to be *cocreators* in reshaping your life.

ABOUT POWERLESSNESS AND CONTROL

"How can admitting I'm powerless and turning control of my life over to a Higher Power help me control my drinking?"

When life spirals out of control, our usual instinct is to try to exert more control. That can work for some people, but it's different for those with the disease of addiction. The more control you try to exert, the greater the compulsion to drink or use. With more use, more bad things happen, which leads to more attempts at control, and the cycle continues.

The need to control often spills over into other aspects of life—family, work, recreation—and this can foster a false sense of also controlling one's drinking or drug use. But no matter how much control is exerted, the compulsion to use doesn't go away. In fact, with each renewed effort at control, it grows and again overwhelms.

Instead of trying to seize more control, alcoholics need to stop trying to dominate the compulsion. With no tug-of-war, the compulsion diminishes. As they say in AA, "The surrender stops the battle."

Surrendering control of your life, of those around you, of your drinking and drug use, isn't easy for the alcoholic/addict. For most, running the show (usually into the ground) has become a way of life. But in the end, "turning it over" *will* make your life more manageable.

HOW CAN I GET INVOLVED?

It's easy to get involved with AA and other fellowships. All you have to do is show up.

You'll find AA meetings in union halls, schools, hospitals, community centers, homes, churches, synagogues, other houses of worship, and online—virtually anywhere some inexpensive meeting space or an Internet connection can be found.

You don't have to pay any dues to belong to AA. The hat is passed at each meeting, and contributions are welcome but never mandatory. Most people drop in a dollar or two (not bad for a little therapy and a spiritual boost). In fact, one of AA's few policies is that no one may contribute an amount so large that it might give him influence over group policy. The funds are used for rent, coffee, literature, and support of the central office.

Each AA group is autonomous and is organized in its own way, guided by the Twelve Traditions. Leadership roles rotate. In most groups there is a chairperson, a secretary, and a treasurer, as well as a general service representative (GSR) who may represent the group at larger assemblies of AA groups. There may also be a steering committee or other group that helps guide the group; it is usually made up of people with long-standing sobriety.

AA FOUNDATION STONES

AA is guided by several basic elements, which we call the Foundation Stones. Most other fellowships have similar guidelines.

The Twelve Steps. These form the basis of recovery in AA, each step taking members a little further along in the struggle to turn their lives around.

The *Big Book*. Officially titled *Alcoholics Anonymous*, the *Big Book* is the basic text for AA. The life histories chronicled in its pages show how alcoholics from all walks of life, from the time of the founding of AA, have benefited from the program. First published in 1939, it was last updated in 2002.

The Serenity Prayer. This nondenominational affirmation, while not an official AA element, has helped millions in AA and other fellowships cope with their problems.

The Twelve Traditions. The traditions cover group organization, function, funding, anonymity, and relationships within and outside the group.

Starting Your Fellowship-Based Recovery Program

WHAT IT MEANS TO "WORK YOUR PROGRAM"

Many people new to this type of healing wonder what it means when people talk about "working your program." For each person it may mean something different, but overall, working your program is your way to a successful recovery. It means including all of the following in your life:

- Working the 12 steps

- Having frequent and regular contact with your sponsor

- Meditating or praying daily

- Going to fellowship meetings

- Reading or listening to fellowship materials

THE TWELVE STEPS AND THE RECOVERY ZONE SYSTEM

In chapter 2, Your Recovery Plan, we described the Recovery Zone System, which coordinates nicely with the Twelve Steps:

- In the Red Zone, you focus on steps 1, 2, and 3, the decision steps, which provide a foundation for the better life you are seeking, as well as steps 4 through 9, the action steps, which produce the results.

- Once you move into the Yellow Zone, you will build on that foundation with steps 10, 11, and 12, the maintenance steps.

- In the Green Zone, you will continue to practice all the steps, revisiting them as needed.

We introduce all of the 12 steps in this section, even though you won't be focusing on the last three until you have moved past the Red Zone.

HOW THE TWELVE STEPS CAN HELP YOU

Newcomers often observe that AA members seem to put the Twelve Steps right up there with the Ten Commandments. What gives the steps the power they seem to have? The answer is simple: *They work.* That's the best recommendation any set of guidelines can have.

The Twelve Steps date back to the early days of what later became known as Alcoholics Anonymous. In searching for ways to deal with their compulsion to drink, the founding members realized that telling other alcoholics about their weakness for alcohol—and its negative effects on their lives—actually helped relieve them of their obsession with drink.

Sharing their stories, they found, was truly "the fuel of sobriety." The stresses of day-to-day living depleted this fuel rapidly, however, and the AA members quickly learned that an *ongoing* sharing of experience, strength, and hope was needed to ward off the need to drink.

The AA founders knew that what they were doing was working. But how could they pass it on? They dissected the process of their recovery and codified it into 12 steps. At first some thought they ought to impose these steps as "commandments" for AA newcomers to follow. But wiser heads prevailed, and instead of being a list of "thou shalts," the Twelve Steps were written down as a simple history of how these recovery pioneers succeeded at staying sober: "*We* admitted *we* were powerless over alcohol . . ." and so on. The steps became a "suggested" part of the recovery program for each arrival into the fellowship.

The following explanations of the Twelve Steps are a blend of some common views of these valuable recovery tools. But they aren't the only way to view them. Each individual interprets and uses the Twelve Steps in the way that is most helpful to them personally.

How exactly do you "work" the steps? Read them. Study them. Think about them. Make them your own. Talk about them with your sponsor, your counselor, your therapist, and others. Write about them in a journal or online forum. Read them and work through them with the help of a study group. But most important of all, follow them. They have worked for millions of others. They can work for you.

Step 1: *We admitted we were powerless over alcohol—that our lives had become unmanageable.*

It's no fun to admit to being powerless. The more you see your world unraveling around you, and the more unmanageable your life becomes, the more frightening is the prospect of giving up what little control you have left.

But, as those early AA members learned, the urge to control is just another obsession, and this loudly proclaimed dominance over drinking behavior ("Hey, I can handle it!") inevitably gives way to the drive to drink.

They found that admitting they couldn't control their drinking allowed them to go on to address the problem in a way they couldn't when they were still wrestling for control. And, as a dividend, it enabled them to develop humility—which not only aided the recovery process, but made them better human beings.

Grasp this step and you grasp the problem.

Step 2: *Came to believe that a Power greater than ourselves could restore us to sanity.*

If you take the first step and accept that you have a problem, what's next? You can either give up entirely, or you can make the leap of faith that says there is hope, that you don't have to continue living with the insanity of alcoholism or addiction.

In step 2, you recognize that *there is a solution.* You also acknowledge that you yourself are not the solution (otherwise you wouldn't need to agree to step 1).

Step 2 verifies what you've been hoping for, praying for, or just plain betting on: There is some positive power—it may be God, your AA group, a counselor or sponsor, or just some unnamed entity—that can help restore you to sanity.

Step 3: *Made a decision to turn our will and lives over to the care of God as we understood Him.*

After thoroughly working through step 1 and step 2, you clearly see that there is a problem and that there is a solution outside of yourself. Now it's time to put those two assets together and begin the work of healing.

In step 3, we make a decision to take action, to actually hand over control to that Higher Power. Again, this is not necessarily a religious Higher Power; read more on how others view this concept in chapter 9.

Turning the reins over won't be easy. You'll find yourself chafing at the bit every time you want to take one road and your Higher Power directs you down another. Learn to relax and let things happen. You'll find you'll get to where you really want to go in the end.

Step 4: *Made a searching and fearless moral inventory of ourselves.*

Now the action begins. Everything up to now was kind of a head game—admitting, believing, deciding. Now, in step 4, it's time for an honest and thorough appraisal of your life.

The ability to be truly honest at this point is a major distinction between those who successfully live in recovery and those who don't. Most alcoholics and addicts have long been living lives of dishonesty. Making this step toward honesty can be painful, but to avoid it is like sweeping garbage under the rug. It's going to come out eventually.

This step involves not just thinking, but producing a chronicle of your life, a document that measures your life as it now exists. There are many ways you can complete this step, including following a study guide, receiving coaching from your sponsor, reading fellowship materials, and using other ideas you may get from your 12-step network. If you choose to work this step by writing a life history, take a look at page 154 (Writing Your Life History), for some ideas on how to do that.

However you proceed, if you're as searching as you are fearless, you will be rewarded with knowledge of the good things you have done as well as the bad. You will find your character strengths as well as your defects. Many behavior patterns, both healthy and destructive, will become clear. Outside influences that you hadn't noticed earlier will also become apparent.

Step 4 is one that many people return to over and over again—as their lives change, they heal and gain more understanding, or they find themselves in new difficulties. You can do the step with a focus on a special area of your life, such as your relationship with a partner or your work history. A fresh self-examination at times of crisis can be a guide to the best ways to maximize your talents and minimize your weaknesses.

Step 5: *Admitted to God, to ourselves, and to another human being the exact nature of our wrongs.*

Early AA groups learned (and therapists now know) that talking about our problems gives us insight into our lives and problems and makes us feel better. Talking the crippling past "off our chests" gets us out of its control and helps us move into the future with a clear mind and a clean slate. So share your story with your Higher Power and an objective person, such as your sponsor, counselor, or spiritual advisor. Get it all out there. In the end, if there is anything you hold back, anything you have not shared with someone else, you will be inviting trouble. You will be more likely to relapse.

Step 6: *Were entirely ready to have God remove all these defects of character.*

You've seen your flaws and faults. Now, in order to heal, you have to be willing to relinquish them.

For the nonalcoholic, this may seem obvious and simple. For the alcoholic, it can be very difficult to do—your emotions, personality traits, preferences, and values have evolved over a lifetime (or even generations) to justify the urge to drink. Without all that pain, without those defects and flaws, how will you justify a need to drink or use drugs? But you must be willing to have them removed, if you're going to be ready for the next step, and for a life that isn't ruled by alcohol or drugs.

Step 7: *Humbly asked Him to remove our shortcomings.*

Now that you're willing to leave behind those defects of character, you can make it happen. How? You just ask. You ask through prayer, meditation, shouting into a canyon or from the top of a building, while walking in the city or hiking in the woods, or however you best relate to that force greater than yourself. You humbly ask to be rid of those flaws that you dug up and examined in the last three steps.

You probably won't see major changes right away. But you *will* be changing. Eventually, you will start to get some feedback assuring you that those negative traits are in fact loosening their hold and you are coming closer to being the person you want to be. You'll get feedback through your experiences with others (at home, work, and meetings; in casual interactions and in counseling). You'll get it through identifying with life histories and other examples in AA literature, and through keeping your personal inventory and regularly evaluating it. Try to be encouraged by small, steady improvements over time.

You might even see some of your defects change into assets you didn't know you had. Remember that selfishness that kept you scrambling for drugs every day? It could very well turn into a selfishness that serves as a strong focus on recovery—and keeps you sober.

While you're thinking about getting rid of your faults and flaws, you should also be developing positive traits. Start with some small positive changes that are easy to do. Smile at the clerk at the supermarket, say good morning to the bus driver. After a while, with such practice, it will be easier to stay positive at more challenging times. You'll be able to avoid exploding when your kid drags mud in on the new carpet; you'll greet your late-arriving spouse with a joke rather than a nasty remark.

The more you try to be pleasant, the more you think positively rather than negatively, the more you turn to humor instead of anger, the more natural such behavior will become. If you continue to act like a really nice person, before you know it you'll be one.

As you work through step 7, try not to set up a timetable for change in your mind. It's up to your Higher Power.

Step 8: *Made a list of all persons we had harmed, and became willing to make amends to them all.*

If step 4, your searching and fearless moral inventory, is fresh in your mind, it will be easy to draw up a list of the people you have harmed. If not, it may be time to do another review of your life.

When making your amends list, be thorough. Try not to let any name slip by. Resist the temptation to justify your conduct, and don't worry now about *how* you will make amends. Just get every name down, and be *willing* to make up for your past actions.

This is another step you may return to again and again. As your self-centeredness diminishes and your perspective broadens, new names that you had forgotten will pop up.

Step 9: *Made direct amends to such people wherever possible, except when to do so would injure them or others.*

Now comes the task of making those amends, correcting the wreckage of the past without regard for what it does to you.

There are probably as many ways of going about this as there are people you've hurt. And it can seem overwhelming and impossible at the beginning. Some people find it helps to assign those they've hurt to one of three categories:

1. I can make amends with that person *now*.

2. I can probably approach that person *later*.

3. I'll *never* make amends with that person.

With your new list in hand, start approaching the people in category 1. (For some ideas on how you can make amends, see page 157.)

After a while, take a look at the people in category 2 and see if you can move any of them into category 1 and start making amends with them. Don't approach this as a simple to-do list, with people to be checked off as if you were buying items on a grocery list. Rather, look at it with a spiritual perspective. Search for your Higher Power's timing to complete making amends with those people. When there is no one left in category 1 or 2, it's time to look at your "never" list; you might find now that you can approach those people after all.

You will find that guidance from other AA members and your sponsor will be essential in this step. You will also find, long term, that working through this step molds the alcoholic/addict into a tool for good, just as addiction molded him or her into a tool for destruction.

Completing the work of step 9 is a milestone in your recovery. At this point, you have changed your life and arrived at a meaningful, serene existence. Your bondage to alcohol and drugs has been removed, and the joy and rewards of recovery have arrived. The promises of the *Big Book* have come into your life:

We are going to know a new freedom and a new happiness. We will not regret the past nor wish to shut the door on it. We will comprehend the word serenity and we will know peace. No matter how far down the scale we have gone, we will see how our experience can benefit others. That feeling of uselessness and self-pity will disappear. We will lose interest in selfish things and gain interest in our fellows. Self-seeking will slip away. Our whole attitude and outlook upon life will change. Fear of people and of economic insecurity will leave us. We will intuitively know how to handle situations which used to baffle us. We will suddenly realize that God is doing for us what we could not do for ourselves.

With the completion of step 9, you are likely ready to move into the Yellow Zone. Life is good.

Step 10: *Continued to take personal inventory and when we were wrong promptly admitted it.*

With step 10 you begin the work of maintenance, to ensure that your life continues in this direction. Set up a regular schedule of honest review. You might do this through daily review and meditation, via talks with a sponsor or counselor, or by keeping a journal. This kind of a routine maintains accountability, and helps keep character flaws from sneaking back into your thoughts and behavior. Keeping a journal will also help you see how much progress you've made, week to week, month to month, year to year.

We will all make mistakes, and negative traits will always exist, but if you follow step 10 faithfully, these traits are less likely to sneak up on you. You will know about and be able to deal with them.

You'll find ideas for doing personal inventories in chapter 17.

Step 11: *Sought through prayer and meditation to improve our conscious contact with God* as we understood Him, *praying only for knowledge of His will for us and the power to carry that out.*

In step 3 you turned your life over to your Higher Power. You might think that now you can just take back the reins and head off on your own. But the alcoholic or addict is always within you, waiting patiently to reactivate those neural pathways focused on addiction and take over your life again. The honesty, insight, and selflessness of your recovery have starved the addiction, built new pathways, healed your brain, and nourished and brought out the real you. But the illness is part of you and will always be there.

Remember, though, that addiction's destructive power can work *only* if you allow it to have control over your life, *only* if you allow it to influence your thinking and behavior. Delegating your life direction to a Higher Power of your choosing—outside of your own brain—holds the addictive forces at bay.

Step 12: *Having had a spiritual awakening as the result of these steps, we tried to carry this message to alcoholics, and to practice these principles in all our affairs.*

This step takes you full circle, consolidating the work of the previous steps. Here you "carry the message" of recovery to others. Step 12 is a Yellow Zone *and* a Green Zone activity; you will start this work of helping others in the Yellow Zone and continue it for life in the Green Zone.

Just how you'll do that depends on your own strengths and inclinations (for some ideas, see chapter 22). You may want to work directly with other alcoholics or addicts, become more active in the AA fellowship, or volunteer to speak at schools. The longer you are in recovery, the more ways you'll find to help others. Spreading the word may help others deal with their addictions; it will *definitely* help you keep your recovery strong. Performing 12-step service work has proven to be one of the factors associated with long-term, quality recovery.

Summary. If a year or two down the road you feel that you have worked hard on these steps, yet find you still don't have a fulfilling life, it may be because you left out some important element. To avoid this, be sure not to allow your denial to trick you into skipping one or more steps or attending to them halfheartedly. Don't allow shame or guilt to freeze your feelings and make you unable to look at yourself as the steps require. And be sure you don't try so desperately to overcompensate for past wrongs (you now want to be the best employee, best spouse, best parent, best child in the world) that you leave yourself no time to work on your recovery.

More Ideas for Working Your Program

WRITING YOUR LIFE HISTORY (STEP 4)

As we've discussed, the fourth step in AA entails making a searching and fearless moral inventory of yourself. It's even better to go further and do a complete-as-you-can-make-it life history.

You probably haven't written a life history since you were in third grade and drew pictures of your parents, your siblings, and yourself on colored paper. When you did it then it was an important learning experience. Doing it now, at the beginning of your recovery, is an even more important learning experience.

Start with the day you were born and go from there. Don't worry about what you don't remember, but include everything you can recall. The day you first talked back to your mom, when you got your first dog, the first time you saw anyone drink alcohol, the first time you took a drink or a drug. Try to dredge up things you haven't thought about for years. Take your time writing, and describe your feelings. Include everything you've done that relates to your drinking or drug use—speeding fines, fights with your spouse, auto accidents, child abuse, embarrassing moments, jobs lost, and so on—as well as how much money you spent on your chemical highs.

As you work on your life history, answer these questions, always being sure to describe your feelings as well as the facts:

- When and where were you born?

- Who are your parents? Where are they from and what do they do for a living? What are they like as people? How did they influence your life?

- Do you have any siblings? What did you think of them as kids? As adults?

- What was it like growing up? Do you remember your childhood as happy or unhappy? Why? Describe some of the experiences you remember. Were they good or bad? Give specific recollections about how you felt you were treated by others, how family members communicated with one another, about family relationships, and about friends and others in your life.

- What losses have you experienced? Have you lived through the death of a parent or other family member, a close friend, or a pet? What about events where you felt abandoned? Any big disappointments in your life?

- How did you feel about school? Were there any teachers who had a big influence on you? Were you bullied? Were you a bully?

- Did you have any pets? If so, what part did they play in your life? How did you and others in the family treat them?

- Were you ever abused or traumatized as a child— emotionally, physically, sexually?

- How many years of school did you complete? Did you go as far as you would have liked? Did you get out of it all you wanted?

- What do you remember about the first time you noticed alcohol or drugs being used in your home? Outside of it? Were the drugs legal or illegal? How did you feel about this?

- What can you recall about your parents' drinking habits or their use of drugs? Did any siblings use drugs?

- How did alcohol or drugs affect your life when you were growing up? Do those experiences have an influence on your thoughts and attitudes now?

- What did you think the first time you saw someone drunk?

- How and when did you have your first drink? Use your first illicit drug? How did you feel about these experiences?

- When did your drinking or drug use first get you in trouble?

- What other problems were caused by your substance abuse? DUIs? Fights? Problems at school or work? Missed appointments or classes? Accidents? Getting fired from a job? Spouse or child abuse? Parental abuse? Stealing? Lying? Financial turmoil?

- Did your drinking or drug use ever hurt others?

- Have you ever done something you were ashamed of while under the influence?

- How did your drinking or drug use affect your relationships: your love life, marriage, family, friends, neighbors, community, coworkers?

- What about your social life? With whom did you usually spend your time? Where did you spend most of your time? Who was the most constructive influence in your life? The most destructive?

- What kind of work do you do? Do you enjoy it? How has it been affected by your substance use?

- Have you ever gotten sober before, but then relapsed? Describe the experience and what you think triggered the relapse. Describe your previous treatment experiences, if any.

You can't finish the story of your life in one sitting. Give yourself plenty of time—at least a week. Your history should fill at least ten pages, but ideally should be much longer.

Be so candid that you wouldn't want anyone else to see your recollections. To be sure no one else does see it, keep it in a safe place (maybe carry it with you always). If you type it on a shared computer or on a note-taking app on your phone, protect it with a password. If you don't carry a hard copy of your history around with you, do carry a small notebook (or a note-taking or recording app) so you can capture thoughts as they occur.

If you hit a roadblock and come up with some events or thoughts you don't want to record, those are probably just the things you need to write about. Seek out a sounding board. Try talking with your sponsor or spiritual advisor about the issues that are holding you back. Disclosing something—in any way you can find to do it—can make it easier to process the information and move on.

Don't freeze up because you're afraid you won't do a professional job. Style, penmanship, spelling, grammar, and neatness don't count. You don't even have to use complete sentences. Use symbols or shorthand if you like—anything that you can decipher.

If writing doesn't come easily to you, there are some other options. Speak into a recorder, or look for a recording app for your phone. (Because recording your history is not as effective as actually seeing your life in print, you might later transcribe your words.) Tell your story in words or pictures on your computer or online with a free Pinterest, Wordpress, or Tumblr account (you can make it private or anonymous). Download a recovery app to your phone that includes a life history component. All of these methods allow you to work on your story over time, returning to it when you have new thoughts.

Review and Share Your History

Go over what you've written and look for holes. Be sure you haven't left out any major events or periods of time. Also be sure you've described your feelings in each case. If there are any glaring gaps, this could indicate a problem area that was pushed into the background and needs a closer look.

When you finish, try to analyze your story as you would someone else's. Look for insights into what brought you to where you are today. Think about how your experiences might have influenced your current life, your beliefs, and your behavior. Try to track the development of your disease from your first exposure.

It's also a good idea to share your history with somebody—your sponsor; a minister, priest, or rabbi; the physician or therapist who has been treating you; or some other person who can view it objectively. *Don't* show it to your parents, your spouse, your partner, your children, or anyone else who is emotionally involved in your illness. You can be sure that your sponsor and any professional you are working with will not be surprised by or judgmental about anything you've written. They've seen it all—and worse—before.

After reviewing your life history, go through the ritual of getting rid of it—burn a paper copy, delete your digital copy, file it away in a folder you won't see every day, or move it to a flash drive and stash it away in a drawer or a safe. Think of this step as symbolically incinerating the garbage of your past life.

If you can't seem to write your life history at all, it may be a sign that your recovery is in trouble and you need professional help. If there are any particular events in your life that you haven't been able to put on paper, this could also indicate a need for help. But that's okay. Some things (like incest, abuse, or violence) are just too difficult and dangerous to deal with without professional support.

MAKING AMENDS (STEP 9)

"I hurt so many people when I was taking drugs—I don't even know where to start to make amends."

You can start by going through your "fearless moral inventory," which you did in the fourth step, and then making a list of those you have harmed (the eighth step). Divide those people into three groups, as described.

Once your list is complete you'll have to decide how you are going to make up for the pain you caused each person on it. In most cases, saying you're sorry—in person, in a letter or email, over the phone—will be relatively easy. Convincing them you mean it may be tougher.

For example, you can go to your parents, partner, siblings, and others and apologize for all the misery you've brought them. The fact that you have now been sober for a while will help show them you're sincere (something they desperately want to believe) and on the right track. But you'll also have to help convince them by making changes in your behavior—doing things like holding down a job, keeping regular hours, and spending time with them.

In many cases, making amends is best done by taking direct action to remedy the wrong. If you've hurt someone financially, for example—such as by taking money from the cash register at work or from your dad's wallet—try to make amends by paying them back. Steady payments of even a few dollars a week, until you can afford more, prove that you mean what you say.

If you've been lying to your spouse (or parents or friends or boss) for years, apologizing will be a lot less effective than being scrupulously honest from now on. If you regret and owe amends to your children for the years when you missed parent-teacher nights, didn't show up for soccer games, or were too high to help with homework, by all means tell them you're sorry you failed them. (You can take the first steps on serious family work like this now, but be sure you don't let it get in the way of your Red Zone personal recovery work. You will have more time in the Yellow Zone to work on restoring important relationships.)

If you disappointed a teacher by dropping out of school, let her know when you earn your degree. If you told lies about friends that hurt their reputations, make public acknowledgment among your mutual friends that you were wrong. If you ruined a neighbor's garden when you were driving high, offer to replant it or help with the weeding.

If you are not sure how you can best make amends to someone, ask them. They are likely to have some ideas—things you might never have thought of.

Some people put off making amends because of embarrassment. Although some might think that's a poor excuse for inaction, feelings are real no matter what others think. But even if you are embarrassed, you still need to make amends.

There are ways you can ease your discomfort. Try writing out your apology with no fixed plan for what will happen when it's done.

If writing it turns out to be not so hard after all, you may end up sending it by email or letter. Once you've seen it in black-and-white, you may even feel that you can deliver the message in person. Or you may find you are still uncomfortable, in which case you should talk about it with your sponsor. Eventually, you will have to make those amends in order to have a successful recovery.

If apologizing directly would embarrass or hurt the other person or reopen old wounds, you're still not off the hook. You still need to make amends, but you can do it anonymously. Send flowers or a gift, or make a donation in the person's name to a cause he supports. If some of the people you want to make amends to are no longer alive or reachable, then do a kindness for someone connected to each of them, directly or indirectly. Help out a surviving relative or volunteer your time to help an organization that was important to them.

What if you never learned the names of the people you hurt? Can you still make amends? Maybe not directly, but if you're creative, you can come up with something that seems appropriate. You can make "indirect amends." Maybe you stole some gloves and scarves from a street peddler who's long since moved on. Find another peddler and buy some gloves and scarves.

If you can't come up with any amends that fit the crime, do some volunteer work or make a charitable donation, which at least *you* know is meant to make up for a specific act.

Some people also work on making "living amends"—they strive to live their lives differently from here on out, as amends for their past. Indeed, helping others find sobriety is a wonderful way to make amends when you can't make things right with someone personally, for whatever reason.

Sometimes an apology isn't accepted graciously. It might even be rejected outright. That's okay. Though you may feel better after making amends, that's only part of the purpose. The idea is also to make up for the harm you've done to others. If they are not willing to forgive and forget, you will just have to live with that. You tried. Now what you have to do is try to live your life so you never inflict wounds like that again.

One final thought—don't rush to make all of your amends. Rather than trying to race through your list, wait for the right time. By that we mean let God, as you understand Him, determine your schedule. You will be able to recognize when your path in recovery crosses an opportunity for amends—and *that* will be the right time to do it. Be patient; it generally happens in a way that has deep emotional impact.

GIVING A TALK AT AA

"I've been asked to give a talk at our NA group next month. I've gotten used to sharing parts of my story with others, but getting up in front of the whole meeting scares me to death. What if I blank out up there?

Anyway, my life story is boring compared to most of those I've heard."

The huge majority of people have a pounding heart before they speak in front of others. Believe it or not, those relaxed and eloquent speakers at your meeting who now command your rapt attention once felt just the way you do. But when they dove in, they found the water was fine. To their surprise and profound relief, they realized they had a lot more to say than they'd imagined. Things they'd been unable to put into words for years just came pouring out, and in their fellowship's safe and accepting environment, everything was easier to say than they'd thought possible. They felt great accepting hugs and congratulations afterward. You will get there, too.

Think about it. Your topic is one on which you are the world's greatest authority: your life. All you have to do is tell it as you lived it.

The purpose of your talk is to help yourself. So be totally honest. There's no need to make a story "better" with a lot of half-true embellishments and exaggerations. If you're alive and sober, your true story will be strong enough. Focus on what you've done, not on what others have done to you. Your talk shouldn't be a "poor me" story. Nor, if a good recovery is your goal, should it be a just-for-laughs comedy routine.

When you sit down to plan your first talk, answer these questions:

- What was your life like before sobriety?
- What happened to open your mind to recovery?
- What is life like now?

Try to weave into your talk how recovery fellowship principles (the 12 steps, for example) tie in to your life then and now. ("In those days, the more I tried to control my life, the more I used drugs. Now, the more completely I turn my life over to my Higher Power, the easier it is to stay sober.") Look for the themes, the big lessons, the miracles, the meaning you have found in your new life. It will all make your talk more valuable to listeners and to you.

As you move along in your recovery, you'll find the focus of your talks changing from "what was then" to "what is now." You might also be surprised to find that some aspects of your recovery now have a much deeper meaning for you. For example, maybe the pain you had from liver damage was something that prompted you to try sobriety. Now you see it as a gift that allowed you to connect with the new guy who got messed up by taking narcotics for his pain. Or maybe you were originally grateful that you ended up in jail and were forced to check out AA. Now you take meetings into jails, and helping the people there has strengthened your own program in ways you never predicted.

Before you give your first talk, get some practice speaking about feelings and experiences. Speak up in discussion meetings. Start some informal conversations with other fellowship members or your sponsor. Then move on to an audience of two to four people. Continue increasing the group size until you are comfortable stepping up to the podium anywhere.

Ease pre-talk jitters with careful preparation. Write up a few memory-jogging key phrases to speak from, or even write out your story in advance.

Some people find that once they've done this prep work, they can speak—whether in a chair or on their feet—without notes. Others feel more comfortable with a backup in hand—an outline, or notes on paper. Still others prefer to read their story word for word. You might also rehearse your talk a time or two in front of a mirror, a friend, or a family member. Do whatever sends those butterflies in your stomach off to a happy landing.

More About Those Meetings

HOW DO I FIND A MEETING?

Your counselor, doctor, or treatment center may refer you to a specific AA contact. If not, there are several ways to find a meeting.

- Search online for Alcoholics Anonymous (or Narcotics Anonymous, etc.) plus your town. Many local groups list meetings online. If you don't have a computer at home, try a library. Most have computers you can use for free.

- If you don't find local lists of meetings, start at the "find a meeting" sites below and drill down to find resources near you. Some list meetings around the world, and others have links to local listings; some also have phone lines dedicated to meeting information. Some of these sites are also available in Spanish, French, and other languages.

AA: aa.org/pages/en_US/ find-aa-resources

AA outside the U.S.: aa.org/ pages/en_US/find-aa -resources/world/1

Al-Anon: al-anon.alateen.org/ meetings/meeting.html

Cocaine Anonymous: ca.org/ phones.html

Crystal Meth Anonymous: crystalmeth.org/cma-meeting- directory.html

Marijuana Anonymous: marijuana-anonymous.org/ meetings/in-person

Narcotics Anonymous: portaltools.na.org/portaltools/ meetingloc

- Chances are you know someone who is in AA or Al-Anon. If not, someone in your circle of friends probably does. Due to the anonymous nature of the fellowship, your friend can ask for information on your behalf, or pass your phone number on to someone who is a member.

- Check a print phone directory for a local Alcoholics Anonymous number or other fellowships. If you don't find a number for a local fellowship, look for "addiction services," "mental health resources," or a city or county health agency. The people there can refer you.

- Call a local treatment center.

- Ask a librarian. They will almost certainly be able to help you find a meeting.

Many of the online listings above carry extensive lists of meetings. They typically specify the locations and times, as well as whether meetings are open or closed, discussion or speaker, and any special topics on the agenda.

WHAT ABOUT ONLINE AND PHONE MEETINGS?

If you can get to in-person meetings, they are usually your best option. There is no substitute for sharing in person with others, talking one on one with other alcoholics. There's nothing like having a cup of coffee after the meeting with someone who will listen and give you guidance, or sharing a laugh and a hug with a new friend who truly understands where you've been. Of course, an in-person meeting is not always convenient or available just when you need it. When that's the case, a phone or online meeting or discussion forum might help. They can also be a lifesaver on those nights when you wake up at 3 a.m. with a craving and no one to talk to. And if you are still not sure that AA is for you, online meetings are a great way to test the waters.

- Online AA meetings and other discussions are now common in many formats, including email, texting, online chat, audio, phone, and video chat (including ones for users of American Sign Language). Many are listed at aa-intergroup .org. That site also lists meetings in several languages, as well as some for women only, men only, LGBT folks, and other communities.

- Narcotics Anonymous online and phone meetings: portaltools .na.org/portaltools/meetingloc/ index.cfm (enter "web" or "phone" in the Country field).

- Cocaine Anonymous online meetings: ca-online.org/ca_ meetings_online.

- Marijuana Anonymous online meetings: ma-online.org; phone meetings: marijuana-anonymous .org/meetings/phone-meetings.

There are also many online discussion forums for alcoholics, addicts, and their loved ones that are not affiliated with the above groups. Most are not run in meeting format, but they are places where you can share your story and connect with others. Some also have recordings of meetings and other resources. Several are listed in Resources.

YOUR HOME GROUP

Once you decide you want to be part of AA or another fellowship (and that's all you need to do to become a member; there are no official sign-up lists), you will be warmly welcomed at meetings anywhere in the world. But unless you live in a one-meeting town, you will still want to shop for a group you can call home.

The first group you visit may not be a perfect fit—or even the second or third. That's okay. Groups have different kinds of members—some mostly young, others older; some middle class, others working class; some more religious, some agnostic. Some are composed mostly of doctors or lawyers, businesspeople or government scientists, students or people in the entertainment world. There are men's and women's groups, LGBT groups, groups for young mothers, and many others. Just keep trying different meetings and you'll find a home group.

The home group you choose will also depend on your drug or drugs of choice. If you're an alcoholic, the choice is pretty clear: Alcoholics Anonymous. AA may also be the choice if you've abused alcohol as well as other drugs. But although some AA groups do allow talking about drugs other than alcohol, others are less receptive. These days, the thing to keep in mind is that you need to have a desire to stop drinking alcohol to be a member of AA—but that could refer even to those two or three beers that you fear will trigger a desire for drugs. In any event, Open Meetings are open to everyone.

Heroin and pain pill addicts often do well at Narcotics Anonymous meetings. (NA, in fact, welcomes those who are addicted to any drug, including alcohol.) Those addicted to marijuana may be more comfortable at Marijuana Anonymous. Cocaine Anonymous may seem the natural choice for cocaine addicts, but this isn't always the case. Sometimes they find their craving is set off by hearing others at CA meetings romancing the drug. These individuals often do better at AA, especially since they need to avoid alcohol (a gateway drug for them) as assiduously as cocaine. For some alcoholics/addicts, Overeaters Anonymous (OA) or Smokers Anonymous is more congenial and works even better than alcohol- or drug-directed programs.

You'll need to make some choices about which groups you find comfortable. But keep in mind that it's not a good idea to feel too comfortable. Comfort in your old life came from drugs, alcohol, and the life that went along with them. It's best if you are perhaps a bit uncomfortable—and striving to be more like those in the group whom you admire.

Some factors to think about when searching for a home group:

The type of 12-step program. Will AA, NA, CA, CMA, Marijuana Anonymous, or some other group most enhance your recovery?

Location. If the meetings are too far from where you live, you may not go when you need it most—when you're feeling tired, lazy, resentful, self-pitying, depressed.

Meeting times. If they don't work with your schedule, you'll miss meetings.

Compatibility. If you're a young, single, nonsmoking male, you may feel out of place in a group made up mostly of middle-aged women who chain-smoke.

Comfort level. Do you feel at home with the people, the meeting formats, the programs?

Though you'll be most closely associated with your home group, you should still continue to go to other meetings, especially if your home group doesn't meet daily and you need a meeting every day. Going to a variety of meetings will broaden your perspective on recovery and help you grow.

HOW MUCH IS ENOUGH?

The idea of "ninety meetings in ninety days" works for many people in early recovery. A meeting every day for three months makes sobriety a habit and provides momentum. It helps keep newcomers on track, reminding them of the universality of their problem and of the things they need to focus on. It's like a daily booster shot of support.

For some people, a meeting a day is too few—they may go to one before work, brown-bag a second at lunch, and do a third in the evening. Think of your meetings as a person with diabetes thinks about insulin: if the dose is not enough to keep you stable, increase it.

Less important than the number of meetings you go to is your attitude when there, your level of participation, and how seriously you follow the prescription for recovery suggested by your counselor, doctor, or AA sponsor between meetings. You can go to two or three meetings a day and still get drunk. You can go to two or three a week and stay sober. But long-term research has shown that people who incorporate recovery practices and attitudes into their daily lives, and who help others find recovery, have the best life and long-term sobriety.

Ideally, go to as many meetings as you can on a regular schedule. It's not a good idea to adjust the frequency of meetings to the way you feel. The time you *don't* feel like going to a meeting is probably the time you need one *most*. And the feeling that you're getting *too much* AA is sometimes a sign that you're not getting enough. (Be sure to read about doing Recovery Zone ReChecks, which will help you figure out when you might need to increase your meeting attendance. See chapter 2.)

FITTING IN UNDER THE RECOVERY UMBRELLA

As anyone who has ever been to an AA meeting knows, individual differences fade next to the power of the one common tie: the disease of alcoholism/addiction. A blue-collar guy talks about his work issues, and a Ph.D. scientist responds warmly, "I really identify with what you said." Alcoholics and addicts—no matter what their background—have much in common. They share a disease, have similar symptoms, and need the same basic treatment.

Still, if you identify strongly with a certain community (Latino, Asian, or African American, for instance), you may want to also go to some meetings that focus on that community. They might help you explore your questions about your background, about who you are or where you are from, or experiences or relationships common to your community.

But you should also go to meetings that are not limited to your community. You will learn a lot from people at both types of meetings.

Your goal is to overcome your addiction without losing what is precious to your culture or identity. You also need to avoid using those issues as an excuse for not getting treatment.

(Read more about diverse perspectives in chapter 9.)

DRESSING FOR RECOVERY SUCCESS

"A recovery dress code? Seriously? What difference does it make what I wear to a meeting?"

A reasonable question. But think about it. The way you dress is part of your lifestyle. If you want to change your lifestyle—which you clearly do—it makes sense to change your wardrobe accordingly. Say you're a student wearing jeans and T-shirts every day. When you get a job in a law firm, you start wearing suits. If you hang out at nightclubs a lot, you dress differently than if you spend your free time camping or on a golf course.

Even in rags, you'll be accepted at an AA meeting. It's what's inside that counts. But you will probably make better progress if you dress for recovery success. Dressing appropriately shows a basic ability to interact meaningfully with any environment or situation; being able to handle such interactions is something addicts will need to prove to themselves in recovery. It will signal to yourself and to others that you're serious about getting well. Being *unwilling* to see what your attire says about you can limit your success; the look you acquired during your downward spiral into addiction might only attract those who are not as motivated for recovery as you are.

How should you dress for recovery success? Cleanliness is a good start: nails clean, hair groomed,

clothing fresh. Next, think about the style of clothes you usually wear. Does it reflect your drinking and drugging past? If it does, time to make a change. For a new style, take a look at your new sober friends, or your favorite people in your home group. How do they dress? You don't have to give up your own personal style, but perhaps you need to be a little neater, a little less out-there.

In addition, certain items can act as dangerous reminders of your drinking or drugging life: the boots that were part of your favorite club outfit, the T-shirts with logos for beer or party events, the long-sleeved shirts that hid the tracks on your arms. Don't let those items trigger an urge to drink or use; toss them out as relics of your past.

It isn't practical, of course, to buy a whole new wardrobe. So sift through what you have for clothes that can fit your new sober lifestyle and check out some thrift stores for a few items to get you started.

All About Sponsors

For the shaky newcomer to AA or NA, a sponsor is a reassuring lifeline to sobriety. For those who have gone through treatment, a sponsor is an introduction to a mutual-support fellowship and a mirror in which to try out their new reflection in the real world.

And for those with many years of sobriety, a sponsor is a friend who knows them better than anyone else in the world, who is both a sounding board and a security blanket, in good times and bad.

The idea that you, a mature person, need to lean on a stranger might make you uncomfortable. But for the alcoholic and addict, leaning on a sponsor has proven to be a strength. The alcoholic/addict has been likened to two personalities wrestling for control within one body. In early recovery, there's a struggle to keep your addicted half from subduing your still-fragile better half and regaining the upper hand. When you hand over major decisions to someone else—someone with only your well-being and recovery in mind, who knows you and your disease well—you strip the power from the addict inside you. Starved for control, the addict struggles at first, then hibernates, waiting for the next opportunity to stage a coup.

Millions before you have found that leaning on a wise sponsor can help overcome this self-destructive aspect of the disease. Deferring to a sponsor's sober wisdom can be your key to a successful recovery.

FINDING THE RIGHT SPONSOR FOR YOU

Choosing a sponsor is a big decision. It's your sponsor you will turn to when a crisis—big or small—arises. He will get to know your situation, but unlike your family, won't be emotionally involved in your life.

And he will be experienced with sobriety, so the opinions and advice he will offer you are likely to be more valuable than what your own not-yet-reliable emotions will tell you.

Choosing a sponsor is a very personal decision. The sponsor who is right for you might be all wrong for someone else. Still, good sponsors have certain qualities in common:

Long sobriety. If you choose someone who is not much further along in sobriety than you, the relationship could be a disaster for you both. It's best if a sponsor has at least three or four years of sobriety, but some people turn out to be good at the job after just two years.

Quality sobriety. You can judge this from talking to and listening to prospective sponsors at meetings. Look for someone who seems happy with sobriety and life in general and who is respected by the group. While a good personality is a plus, more important is solid sobriety and a strong foundation in your recovery fellowship program.

Broad interests in the recovery community. A sponsor who is active in recovery outside your home group—locally or nationally—can introduce you to a broader fellowship program, such as interesting meetings at other groups.

A record of success. Generally, you want someone who has already had success in helping other sponsees. But of course, there's a first time for every sponsor.

Congeniality. A sponsor should be easy to talk to and listen to—someone you feel comfortable with and have confidence in.

Trustworthiness. You should have complete trust in this person, to the point that you can share your deepest and most intimate feelings and problems.

Objectivity. Your sponsor should be someone who is not emotionally involved in your life, except as it relates to your recovery. A spouse, a live-in partner, or a close friend might seem appealing but would in no way be an appropriate sponsor.

Availability. Your sponsor should live near you so one-on-one meetings are easy to arrange. But you can also choose a distant supplementary sponsor—one who can serve as support in areas where your local sponsor lacks the necessary background or expertise.

And more availability. Think about how you will interact with your sponsor. Face-to-face meetings are often best, but there may be times when you need to text your sponsor for a quick boost or consult. Imagine that you travel frequently, and you sometimes need some help avoiding the airport bar. Would your potential sponsor be available for a quick texting interaction, or is he someone who insists on phone or face-to-face contact?

Toughness. You don't want a sponsor who is a yes-man or yes-woman, but rather one who tells it like it is, even if (or especially if) you don't want to hear it. Look for a person who you think will be willing to confront you if you are headed for another fix or a drink—someone who won't wait until it happens, who will be sure to call you on your BS.

Compassion. While it's important to have a tough sponsor who can point out mistakes and weaknesses, it is also important, especially if your sense of self is poor, to have one who will point out your good points and help you build up your feelings of self-worth.

Compatible lifestyle. Some people find that sponsors who share a similar lifestyle or ethnic and religious background, or who are in the same field of work or come from the same part of the country, are the most compatible since they might immediately understand specific problems. For others, someone with an entirely different background works better, since they can single-mindedly focus on the only thing they have in common: their addiction. They can also avoid the intellectual jousting or competitiveness that can come with sharing other interests.

In some cases, you won't have to go looking for a sponsor. Some home groups assign sponsors to new members.

If you are heterosexual, it's usually best to choose a sponsor of the same gender, so you won't run into any issues with flirting or feeling attracted to them. See page 168 for some thoughts on choosing a

THE RED ZONE

sponsor if you are gay or lesbian.

If you just don't find anyone who really hits home as your preferred sponsor, rather than doing without, choose someone to be your "temporary sponsor." This is an acceptable alternative, and no one will feel insulted.

CAN I HAVE MORE THAN ONE SPONSOR?

Consider multiple sponsors if:

- You have several problems— more problems than one sponsor can handle. For example, you've used both drugs and alcohol and recently returned from military service in the Middle East. You might not find a sponsor who is comfortable dealing with all of these issues.

- You have specific needs that require expertise. For example, you're a recovering doctor, pilot, or other professional, and you need a role model who can guide you on how to get your suspended professional credentials back.

- You are a young LGBT person who would like to have a sponsor close to your own age who is also in the LGBT community, but you would also benefit from an older, more experienced advisor.

- You are very focused on your spiritual growth (or want to be), and would like to have a spiritual advisor who can guide you in that area.

- Your main sponsor travels a lot or has a demanding schedule that limits his availability. In this case, you might want someone who is around all the time and can provide extra help when you need it.

- Someone you admire is too busy to take you on, but is willing to be on call once in a while when you need extra help or guidance. This person can serve as a second sponsor as needed.

Even if one sponsor is enough, you should build strong friendships with others in your fellowship. Call them occasionally. Share a meal. Go to a meeting together. That way, if your sponsor is ill, out of town, or otherwise unable to help, you have somewhere to turn. You should, in fact, have a dozen or so phone numbers of friends in recovery with you at all times, just in case you urgently need to talk to someone but hit a wall of voice mails.

WHAT ABOUT SPONSORS FOR LGBT MEMBERS?

If you're lesbian, gay, bisexual, transgender, or questioning (still exploring and figuring it all out), should your sponsor be the same sex as you or the opposite; homosexual, heterosexual, or bisexual? There are different points of view on this and all have validity. Some options:

- A non-LGBT person of either gender to whom you feel no physical attraction. Such a sponsor would have the advantage of keeping your priorities where they belong: on your recovery, rather than on relationships. It is important that the person you choose be someone who accepts your sexual orientation and is not uncomfortable with it. Of course, neither of you may be aware of any deep-seated prejudices at first. If they do surface, you should resolve them or switch. Just don't use prejudices—yours or anyone else's—as an excuse to squirm out of your recovery responsibilities.

- An LGBT person of either gender to whom you feel no physical attraction (and vice versa). Such a sponsor may be most able to understand your feelings and your needs, and could offer empathy on issues that arise from being part of that community. This could work well as long as the focus of early recovery remains where it should be: on getting better.

- A sponsor team made up of a non-LGBT person to deal with recovery issues and an LGBT person to deal with issues related to your sexual orientation.

The main issue is to avoid someone who you might find yourself attracted to in a sexual way, regardless of their gender or orientation. That could open a Pandora's box of sexual game playing and manipulation, which could hamper the growth of an honest relationship. Be alert to such things. If they

occur and neither of you seem to be able to prevent them (through honest discussion and hard work), you should switch sponsors.

In the end, your sponsor's sexual orientation is far less important than whether the two of you have a true sponsor-sponsee relationship. You will have to be honest with yourself about this one.

REJECTED BY A SPONSOR!

Sometimes a newcomer asks a respected and admired fellowship member to serve as her sponsor, but is turned down. If that happens to you, don't take it personally. The potential sponsor may be so well thought of that he already has as many sponsees as he can handle. Or maybe he has decided, probably wisely, that you two are not a good match. In either case, the rejection is really for the best. Look elsewhere for your sponsor. And don't forget that you can call on many people in the group for advice and encouragement—including this unavailable first choice. Of course, if the response you get feels like a brusque or uninterested rejection, consider yourself lucky. You don't want a sponsor who makes you feel ill at ease. In most cases, the person who turns you down will suggest a couple of other potential sponsors.

One caution: Sometimes newcomers are so afraid of rejection that they hesitate to approach anyone. Fear not. Being a sponsor, as part of working step 12, is a piece of everyone's recovery. You'll be helping your sponsor while your sponsor helps you.

WORKING WITH YOUR SPONSOR

Choosing a sponsor is important. How you use this person in your recovery will be even more important.

Don't just leave contact to chance. In addition to seeing each other at meetings, have a regular time to speak to your sponsor daily—at least until you've been sober for four months. Confer wherever and whenever it's most convenient—at a coffee shop breakfast, in the car on the way to a meeting, on the phone at the end of the day. Personal face-to-face contact is probably best, especially in early recovery, but email, texting, and video chats are all acceptable ways to stay in close regular contact.

Reach out to your sponsor whenever you have a problem or a decision to make, or you need help with a step. Make sure all of his numbers are in your phone, so you can make quick contact when you need it.

You can talk to your sponsor as you talk to no one else, because his only interest in your life is your sobriety. For example, you may have trouble telling your partner, who's worried about money and has a stake in what you do, that you're afraid to ask for a raise. You fear she will tell you to "stand up for yourself for once." A sponsor, on the other hand, will probably respond sympathetically ("I've felt the same way. It's normal.") and offer some constructive advice about how to boost your courage without turning to the bottle. (Later, your spouse or partner may become your confidante. But early in recovery, when so much dirty water has already flowed under the bridge, confiding in a spouse may be difficult.) Or you may find yourself attracted to another person, and you know you can't discuss these feelings with your partner. Your sponsor will hear you out without judging you, and will suggest safe ways of dealing with the issue.

Your sponsor may occasionally make a suggestion that you don't think makes sense. You needn't just swallow it blindly. Be honest, and raise your questions or objections. Your sponsor will then be able to explain the reason for the suggestion, giving you further information on which to base a final decision. Sometimes it will help to talk to a cosponsor or other fellowship friends to get more input. Before you resolve the issue, however, consider that your judgment may be flawed. Your sponsor, with a clearer mind and more experience in sobriety, is more likely to be right than you are. But remember, too, that nobody's perfect. Not even a sponsor.

Some other ideas for working with your sponsor:

- Be honest about your triggers. It's critical for your sponsor to be able to recognize behavior that can lead you to a relapse. So tell him what situations have been triggers for you in the past, such as going out of town, feeling depressed, or seeing old friends.

- When you do your moral inventory or your life history in step 4 (if you haven't already done it in treatment) and are ready to share it, show it to your sponsor and discuss it with him.

- Keep your sponsor posted on what's going on in your life, including troubling physical symptoms; new relationships; job concerns; problems with your partner, children, parents, or friends; and whatever else is on your mind. There's no need to wait until something becomes a crisis.

- Don't make any decisions that could affect your recovery (from taking cold medicine to changing your job) without consulting your sponsor.

- If you're having cravings, aren't working your program, or sense that you are headed for a slip, call your sponsor immediately.

- If you are scheduled to undergo a dental or medical procedure requiring medication or sedation, ask your sponsor to go with you.

- Once you are out of the Red Zone, do regular Recovery Zone ReChecks with your sponsor to anticipate events that could lead to a relapse.

This constant process of keeping your sponsor in the loop on everything in your life might seem like overkill at first, but it is the best way to keep addiction from moving in and taking control of your life once again.

In the end, your sponsor will be only as good as your willingness to take full advantage of the relationship.

AREN'T I IMPOSING ON MY SPONSOR?

Your sponsor is there to help you. Take advantage of this gift, this incredible resource.

If you smoke pot at 2 a.m. because you were too embarrassed to call your sponsor in the middle of the night to deal with a "puny problem"—a compulsion to use—you might think you are acting with both humility and consideration. Actually, you are being arrogant and thoughtless. Arrogant to assume you can handle the problem on your own. And thoughtless to assume your sponsor values his sleep more than your recovery.

Your sponsor has been through it all, has probably woken up *his* sponsor many a night himself. He wants you to call when you're in need—remember, helping you helps him (see chapter 1 on the brain in recovery). So don't hesitate to contact your sponsor if you need to talk, particularly if you have a compulsion to drink or use. If your sponsor doesn't seem to appreciate such calls, then switch sponsors. And when your turn comes to play sponsor, be sure to keep your phone by the bed.

A Closer Look: 12-Step Programs and You

Many people suffer from AA-phobia, dreading the idea of joining Alcoholics Anonymous or any other mutual-support fellowship. They have all kinds of reasons. Going to a meeting admits something they've been denying for years. They fear the stigma of being labeled an alcoholic. They are put off by AA's intimacy, spirituality, and sharing, and by what they see as a kind of public confession. They may worry, too, about bumping into someone they know at a meeting. Or maybe they just don't have the energy to get out of the house.

Well, not going to AA—for whatever reason you might cook up—is about as sensible as a person with pneumonia refusing to go to the doctor for a penicillin shot because he's afraid of the needle. You need AA the way a sick person needs an antibiotic. You've got to at least give it a good try.

Knowing what AA is like before you go should help ease your worries.

Common Issues of AA Beginners

SENSORY OVERLOAD

"I went to my first AA meeting and I was overwhelmed. All that talk about steps and traditions and sponsors and stuff. My head is still spinning."

It is a lot to take in all at once, but as your brain heals, the spinning will stop. In the meantime, don't let the fact that you can't seem to think straight and have a lot to learn about AA keep you from going to meetings.

Don't worry if it all seems to elude you for a while. Right now, there are just two things that you have to focus on:

- One: staying sober, one day at a time

- Two: going to a meeting every day

That's all. The rest will come with time.

NO MEETING NEARBY

"I stopped drinking two weeks ago. I'm climbing the walls. My brother says I need to go to AA every day for ninety days. But I'm a rancher and there isn't a town—much less a meeting—in easy driving distance."

Your brother is right about your needing AA, but it's obviously not very practical for you to spend the next ninety days in your car. Still, you do need help. And you can get it if you're creative. Below are a number of options. Figure out what will work best for you—then go for it.

- Get a course of residential treatment. At a good rehab program or recovery home you'll learn the tools necessary for rebuilding your life sober. You will also find people— professionals and peers—who can help you when the going gets tough.

- Take some time off—two or three months if possible—and get a sublet in the city. Get in at least one meeting a day during that time. Find a temporary sponsor and utilize him to the fullest. Getting some outpatient counseling during this time may also help.

- Work out a way to get to an AA meeting at least once a week— even if it means a couple of hours' driving each way. Many AA veterans had to drive for hours to make regular meetings, especially years ago when there were not as many meetings available. Listening to AA recordings going and coming, or making the trip with another local person in recovery, will make the time go faster. It will also get you in the mood for the meeting en route and help you think about what you heard as you drive home.

- In addition to at least one AA meeting a week, try to find some other mutual support meetings you can attend more often (see How Do I Find a Meeting? on page 160). Even if you were solely a drinker, if there are Narcotics Anonymous meetings near you, give them a try.

- Find a sponsor and have daily contact with him. If you can find one who lives fairly close to you, great—you can have face-to-face meetings. If not, stay in touch with him by phone, email, video chat, or text.

- Try to find some other folks in your area who are in recovery and see if you can set up your own local AA group. All it takes is two interested people and a coffeepot. You could then go to your new local meeting as well as long-distance ones.

- Try out some online meeting and discussions—there are many regular online meetings these days. You can also meet with other people in recovery by way of email, phone, and video chats.

- On days when you can't get to a meeting, devote at least an hour to written and recorded recovery material. Read the *Big Book*. Download some AA speaker meeting recordings and listen to them. Maybe one of the locals in the AA group in the nearest town could take a laptop or tablet to the meeting and include you by way of video chat, or ask the group if they could record an occasional meeting for you. When you do make it to a meeting, bring along your own recorder and capture the meeting to listen to later. (On these last two options, you will need to first make sure that everyone there is okay with recording the meeting.)

///////////////////////////

"The town I live in doesn't have any public transportation. I don't know how I'm going to get to my Crystal Meth Anonymous meetings without a car."

Did you manage to get to places to buy drugs before you got sober? If so, you can also find a way to get to CMA meetings. People who are serious about staying sober figure it out somehow. Carpool with other fellowship members, get a bike, or consider walking. Raise your hand at a meeting and let other members know about your transportation problem. And plan ahead. Always know how you are getting to each meeting beforehand. Like a lot of other things in your new life, getting to meetings is now your responsibility.

FEELING UNCOMFORTABLE

"I've gone to a couple of AA meetings and felt very uncomfortable. I really don't think it's the place for me."

There are a number of possible reasons why you think that way. First of all, it's a new situation. Most people feel awkward when starting a new job or beginning a new relationship. It takes time and willingness to try to begin feeling at ease. And a couple of meetings isn't enough time. Go to them daily for a month before passing judgment.

Second, as an alcoholic/addict, going to an AA meeting doesn't seem natural to you. AA is the antithesis of what has been the center of your life for a long time: drinking or using drugs. Its very success may threaten the emotional bonds that tie you to your chemical crutch. Again, time and learning about your disease will shift your center—if you let them.

Third, maybe the meeting you picked was not the right one for you. Look for other meetings where you'll feel more comfortable. But don't wander indefinitely, looking for the perfect meeting. AA is a support fellowship—you get out of it what you put in.

Fourth, AA, with its Twelve Steps, Twelve Traditions, and the Serenity Prayer, may seem a little simplistic to you. It *is* simple, but those who have lived with it—including professors, scientists, doctors, lawyers, and a lot of other very smart people—know it's not simplistic. And, above all, they know it works.

Finally, your feelings may have nothing to do with AA and everything to do with your own attitude. Your rejection of AA may be part of your disease—just another form of denial.

Whatever your reasons, the fact is that those who participate in AA or another program that uses the 12-step method adjust to sobriety more easily and completely than those who don't. And they are more likely to *stay* sober.

At this point, you have a few options:

- Continue to go to AA even if you are uncomfortable. Treatment for any disease is not always pleasant, but you could die without it. With time, your comfort level is sure to rise.

- Attend another AA group that seems more your style. Ask people at various meetings for recommendations of other good meetings, and check out a few options.

- If a different AA group doesn't work, try other recovery fellowships, such as Celebrate Recovery or Smart Recovery (see chapter 5).

- Seek treatment as an outpatient or inpatient, with a qualified doctor or counselor. (Eventually, most will urge you to join AA or at least follow its principles. But by then you may find that the meetings no longer seem so foreign.)

- Try to stay sober on your own. This is the most difficult and least promising path to take, and not one we recommend. Recovery is not just about abstaining from your chemical of choice. It's about rebuilding your life and healing your brain in such a way that the chemicals you once thought you couldn't live without become unnecessary. This is tough to do without others who've gone before to show you the way. Still, if this is your choice, it will work best if you borrow the successful AA principles for the underpinnings of your recovery (the 12 steps, daily discipline, use of a sponsor), as embodied in the *Big Book* and other AA literature, even if you don't go to meetings.

But you should always be ready, if you begin to falter, to turn to more traditional paths for help.

////////////////////////////

"I have been going to recovery meetings that don't use the 12 steps. I find them more helpful than AA. Your book seems to be built around AA, so I'm not sure it can be useful to me."

Yes, it's true that this book focuses heavily on AA's 12-step philosophy and methods. The AA methods are the most widely available and they have been tested by millions of now-sober people over several decades; in fact, studies have shown that many of the principles and practices of 12-step recovery are effective.

But you may find other fellowships that use similar techniques work better for you. Whatever the source, if it strengthens your recovery and helps you stay sober, great! Apply it in your new life. But don't ignore solid advice from other sources. Most of the advice in this book—particularly the Recovery Zone System, the Zone ReChecks, TAMERS for your brain, and the material on detox and withdrawal, physical and mental health, relationships, work, and helping others—is valid for everyone in recovery, whether they go to AA, go to another group, or go it alone.

I'M NOT INTO SHARING

"I'm not into touchy-feely, woo-woo, new age stuff. Words like 'sharing'

irritate me. That's why the idea of getting involved in AA turns me off."

You're not the only one. Many people feel they are too sophisticated, too shy, too smart, too whatever to get involved in something so touchy-feely. They don't like the idea of sitting around with a bunch of strangers and sharing (yes, it's a tired word, but nobody's come up with a better one) their most private thoughts. Still, most of them eventually come to terms with the need to talk the past out of their systems, especially when they realize there's no obligation to share all of the intimate details with everyone.

Try to open yourself up—just a bit. Start by going to a few open meetings. Sit in the back and take it all in. Once you hear the stories of others and find that most of these people are very much like you, you may find it easier to tell your own. You may even feel a strong urge to share your story. Many people find that this story-swapping helps reduce their "nobody hurts like I hurt" self-centeredness. And when you feel there's no way out of the blackness of your tunnel, it can really help to meet people who've already seen the light at the end of theirs—even if all you do for now is just listen.

If the desire or ability to be more vocal and unload some of the burden you've carried so long doesn't come right away, don't worry about it. A nod of your head, a smile, or a laugh at a meeting are all fine, too. Those are basic ways to show your feelings. Think baby steps. Once you've tried that, verbal interaction is just another step away. One-on-one conversations, particularly with the person you choose for a sponsor, will also help you get used to sharing with others. And suddenly one fine day you'll hear yourself speaking at a meeting, even if it's just to say, "I'm really glad to be here." Of course, if you're still not convinced you have a problem, you could just say, "I don't think I'm an alcoholic. I am a little worried that I may be on the way to becoming one." Remember, the only requirement for membership in AA is the *desire* to stop drinking. You can start there.

When you do share something, you can be sure no one will judge or condemn you (cross talk is strongly discouraged). And no matter what you say, no one will be surprised or shocked. You'll be accepted as you are—fears, doubts, warts, and all. There aren't many other places where that's true.

It's important to keep in mind that the sharing that goes on at AA meetings isn't exhibitionism. It's a necessary part of the recovery process—and, like other forms of group therapy, it works. Research suggests it actually triggers mood-lifting brain chemicals. People who talk about their experiences with alcohol and drugs, and who describe the ravages and wreckage these substances caused in their lives, find relief from the wounds of pain, guilt, and anger, and the beginning of freedom from the need for mood-altering chemicals.

There is no obligation to "spill your guts" or share the most personal details of your life. But many in the recovery community also know that secrets are the fuel of addiction. Secrets give addiction power over our lives. Honesty, and sharing those secrets, drains addiction's fuel tank to empty. So give some serious thought to talking about it all. It doesn't have to be in front of a meeting. Many people choose to share their most intimate life details only with their sponsor. You can, too.

If you really find it impossible to open up at AA meetings, or even to go to them, you might look into professional help from a doctor, psychiatrist, or counselor with experience in treating addiction (see chapter 5). Many alcoholics and addicts have had traumatic experiences that impede their ability to share and process life events. For some, professional help is needed to break through those barriers, and only then will they find a mutual-support group helpful.

MUST I BE HONEST?

"I don't understand how anyone can get up in front of a group like AA and bare their souls. Does it really help?"

Yes, it does. Decades of experience have shown that those who honestly disclose their personal stories in a general way to others greatly improve their chances of long-term sobriety. Self-deception is dishonesty at its most foolish and dangerous. It breeds attitudes that lead inevitably to relapse.

As is the case in many spiritual movements, self-examination followed by confession to others nurtures healthy emotional growth. This cleansing process is particularly essential in recovery. Since what's said at meetings is held in strictest confidence, participants can share without fear of having their stories leave the meeting room. After all, *everyone* there has a stake in maintaining privacy.

Alcoholics and addicts have more trouble being honest about their feelings than most people. They're used to smothering feelings with chemicals and have turned self-deception into an art form. But part of recovery is learning to recognize and express feelings, even negative ones. Everybody has them. It's only actions that can be right or wrong. And when you are sober, acting on a feeling is optional—and under your control.

At first you may not even realize that the feelings are there. They've been frozen for so long they'll take a while to thaw. Once they do, try to learn to accept them—and then to share them.

The goal of sharing feelings is not simply to confess and unburden yourself. That is a big step, but the next step is bigger: going on to change your behavior.

////////////////////////

"The things I did while I was using drugs were so awful. Do I have to tell everyone at my fellowship meeting?"

Absolutely not. First, you'll want to omit the name of anyone who might be damaged in any way by your account, as well as events that could identify and put others in harm's way. Second, it's fine to talk about your history generally ("I still can't believe the things I did when I was living on the streets") rather than giving details ("I sold my body for drugs; I slept with anyone who would help me get a fix"). Many speakers do get into specifics, but how much you open up will depend on your own feelings, how it might affect others, and on your fellowship group. Talk about it with your sponsor before you plan a talk.

If there are feelings or experiences you need to talk about with someone but don't want to discuss publicly, talk about them with your sponsor, therapist, or counselor. They can serve as discreet, understanding, and nonjudgmental sounding boards.

I DON'T HAVE THE TIME

"I've been sober for three months now. From what I've been hearing, I've got to devote my life to NA in order to keep my recovery going. How can I do that when I have a family to support and a busy social life? Can't I cut back on meetings now?"

That's an interesting question; one that is raised by many newly sober people. But let's answer it with another question. How much time did you devote to using drugs? Probably a lot—maybe almost all your time. All you're being asked to do is to put part of the time and energy you put into getting high (or thinking about it) into getting well.

Basically, you have two choices: devoting a lot of time to NA in order to get well, or skimping on NA time, relapsing, and not being able to take care of yourself, your family and job, or any of those other responsibilities you need to attend to in order to feel good about yourself. Common sense strongly recommends the first choice.

For some practical guidance, take another look at the Recovery Zone System in chapter 2. It will help you prioritize your activities as you move into a solid recovery. When you're in the Red Zone, as you are now, you need to focus primarily on your recovery. When you're ready to move into the Yellow Zone, you can focus more on rebuilding those other parts of your life, including relationships, career, education, and more.

This doesn't mean letting *everything* else in your life go by the wayside. Just strip your life down to the essentials, the way you would if you were recuperating from a heart attack. Go to work, of course, but don't work longer hours than are absolutely necessary. Spend time with your family or close friends. But drop other activities—hobbies, volunteer work at your church or synagogue, community work, heavy socializing, home improvement projects, sports—until your recovery is on solid ground, probably after the first year or so. Three months sober is great, but it's way too early for you to take your focus off your recovery.

If you try to do everything now, ignoring the need for a solid foundation for recovery, your new world will eventually collapse like a house of cards. Take the time to do it right.

////////////////////

"When can I stop going to AA?"

You can stop tomorrow. But as long as it's today, you need to go. That's AA's one-day-at-a-time philosophy, which urges people to focus on the present. Stay sober today. Go to a meeting today. Tomorrow will take care of itself. Of course, for some of us that's a difficult philosophy. We've been trained to worry about tomorrow.

It's clear that many people gradually reduce the number of meetings they attend over the years. Many go to meetings for the rest of their lives. Some eventually stop, but their recoveries almost always suffer if they don't continue to live the AA principles—meditating, personal inventories, listening to recordings, reading AA literature, talking to and socializing with AA friends, persuading other alcoholics or addicts to get help. Once AA thinking and behavior become ingrained (and wired into your healing brain), the structure of regular meetings may not be required. Still, there's solid evidence that people who stop going to meetings and stop helping others are at higher risk of relapse than those who continue.

More About Spirituality and Religion

WHAT IS SPIRITUALITY?

"A lot of people at AA and NA talk about spirituality. But some of them haven't seen the inside of a church in forty years. What do they know about spirituality?"

Spirituality isn't found only in a church. It isn't necessarily related to religion. And it doesn't mean the same thing to everybody. Dr. John Mooney used to say that we had three types of existence: the body, the mind, and the soul. The body is pretty easy to understand. The mind is becoming more so. The soul is the toughest part to fathom.

In a practical sense, spirituality can be said to embrace the sweet mysteries of life, those things that are outside the realm of science and intellect: faith, trust, love, truth, compassion. Focusing on our spirituality in recovery and working to strengthen it in ourselves can help carry the benefits of traditional medical care beyond its physical limits.

Achieving real spirituality takes a long time for most people. That's probably why the notion of a spiritual awakening isn't mentioned until the last of the 12 steps. For many people, a *rude* awakening comes long before a *spiritual* one.

HAVING A SPIRITUAL EXPERIENCE

"It may sound unbelievable, but I felt more spiritual when I was high—having to do with the effects of the drug, but still pretty great. Since getting sober, I haven't had any spiritual experiences."

Recovery is not one long spiritual experience. None of us is a saint, and those spiritual moments happen only rarely for most people. But when they do, we know it.

The spiritual experience that helps recovery—the *Big Book* calls it a "spiritual awakening"—doesn't come with a flash of lightning, a thunderclap, and a vision of a white-bearded holy man on top of a mountain. It's something that happens deep inside. It's the moment when you finally realize you are willing to surrender, to stop fighting, to turn yourself over to that Higher Power. It's the moment when you realize that this Higher Power is going to do for you what you couldn't do for yourself.

For some people, meditation and prayer can lead them to a spiritual experience. For others it comes through peace and serenity, and a faith that everything is going to be okay. Through putting hopelessness, guilt, and self-pity behind you. Or through accepting life as it is, knowing it's not always going to be the way you want it to be.

It might come in doing something for someone else and putting aside selfish wishes. In seeing the beauty in a walk in the woods or a baby's smile, things you couldn't process and probably never even noticed when you were high. Maybe it comes in feeling good—naturally—almost for the first time you can remember. Or when you have the option to choose between doing something right and doing something wrong, and you choose doing right. Now, that's a powerful spiritual experience.

Some people, particularly those with a strong commitment to intellectualism, have trouble with the concept of spirituality. They're likely to refuse to recognize a spiritual experience even when it comes complete with thunderclaps. That's unfortunate, because people in recovery who expand their spirituality seem to do better than those who don't.

Everyone Is Welcome at 12-Step Fellowships

ADDICTION IS AN EQUAL OPPORTUNITY DISEASE

As you have probably figured out by now, alcoholism and addiction are equal opportunity tyrants. They are found in every community—every profession, race, culture, orientation, and faith. No group is immune. Even more importantly, AA and other recovery fellowships welcome people from every walk of life, every community. So no matter what your own background is, know that you will be welcomed at a recovery meeting.

This is not to say our diverse backgrounds don't matter. For most of us, our family interactions, personal histories, relationships, and communities have all played a role in how we got to where we are now. They can also play a role in the issues we may need to address in order to heal.

So while you will be welcome at any AA meeting, we do understand that you might feel uncomfortable if everyone seems different from you. If you have experienced discrimination, harassment, or even violence because of who you are, you may prefer to talk about those issues with others who have had similar experiences. Let us offer a couple of thoughts.

One, addicts and alcoholics have a lot more in common with each other than they have differences. We urge you to go to meetings with a diverse crowd, with people you might not meet in your everyday life. You may be surprised at how well you can relate to them, and how much you can learn from them. At those meetings, try to focus on your commonalities, not your differences. Spend some time learning about the culture of recovery, and how you can get involved in *that* community.

Two, try to also find opportunities to share with people from your own community, if you want. You might benefit from going to meetings that focus on health care professionals, Native Americans, women, men, Asians, Latinos, and so on. The people at those meetings may have an understanding of particular issues that would be hard to find elsewhere, and you may also find a cosponsor who can help you with specific issues. If you can't find a meeting locally, look for one online.

So, we urge you to go to both kinds of meetings. The most important thing is to find what works for you, what helps you to get and stay sober.

RACIAL DIVERSITY

"I'm a newly sober African American and the local AA group is all white. I've gone a couple of times and felt totally out of place."

Most people, no matter what their background, feel out of place at their first couple of meetings. But don't automatically assume that the color of your skin matters to anyone else. Although it's certainly possible to find bigots at AA, to most AA members, a drunk is a drunk, whether he is black or white. Still, your discomfort is real and not uncommon, so try to find a group with people from a variety of backgrounds, or an all-black group, to go to at first, even if that means extra travel and effort. Attending such a group will allow you to get used to participating at AA meetings in an atmosphere that might feel more comfortable to you.

Once you feel at home with recovering African American alcoholics, you will likely find you feel more comfortable at other meetings.

Different meetings have different personalities, so you might also try out some other groups nearby, even if they are predominantly white. If you ask a friend or two to go with you, you might feel less intimidated and able to participate more freely.

It might also be that your discomfort stems from a cultural difference, not a racial one. If AA meetings don't seem to fit you, you might want to try NA, CA, or MA meetings, or another 12-step fellowship.

Whatever you do, don't use the fact that the only AA group available to you is predominantly white as an excuse not to go. The fact is that AA people, no matter what their skin color, may understand you better than anyone else.

///////////////////////////

"I grew up on a reservation where a lot of people were heavy drinkers. A lot of them did drugs, too. I moved to the city, but I still drink a lot. A friend said I should try AA, but the only AA meeting I ever went to was very foreign and uncomfortable."

Your reaction isn't unusual. Many Native Americans have the same issue with their first AA encounter. The trick is to shop around for the right meeting. In areas with a large Native population, there are usually one or more AA groups that are run by and for Native Americans, and are tied closely to that heritage. As at other AA meetings, spirituality is an important element, but at these groups, Great Spirit and God may be used synonymously with Higher Power. The focus is on recovery at several levels, beginning with the inner self, moving on to the family, then the ancestors, and finally Holy Beings.

With several hundred American Indian and Native Alaskan tribes, each with its own language and customs, it's not surprising that a wide variety of traditions have grown up at AA meetings in different parts of the country. As at other AA meetings, there is no judging, and no feedback other than support.

Keep looking for a fellowship that is focused on Native Americans. You can also check with the Indian Health Service or another program in your area for information. If there is no Native American–oriented AA group near you, there are some steps you can take to make yourself more comfortable at another group:

- Look for a group that does not play up Christian thinking, if that makes you uncomfortable.

- If you're the lone Native American showing up at an AA meeting, you may feel more comfortable going to an open meeting and taking a friend along.

- If you can't find the perfect AA group, settle for what you can get. If there's a lot of talk about God and Christianity, then try substituting the "Creator" or the "Great Spirit" in your mind. You, like everyone else at the meeting, are free to interpret the words however you choose.

- Get additional preparation for recovery. A good way to do this is by getting inpatient or outpatient treatment, which will help you feel more at ease in AA groups. Of course, the ideal program will be one that focuses on American Indians or Native Alaskans, or at least has some counselors from those communities, but such programs are not found everywhere.

Many Native Americans are discovering that AA and its spirituality, far from being foreign, can become very comfortable—especially when intertwined with old traditions.

///////////////////////////

"I'm black and I've been going to an almost all-white NA group. It's been okay. The people are nice and I'm pretty comfortable. But it's the social stuff that I seem to get left out of—like when everybody goes out for coffee after meetings."

That is a major problem for a lot of people who attend groups where they feel like outsiders. And though it may seem like it's okay just to go to meetings and go back home alone, you really do miss out on an important factor—the camaraderie of fellowship groups. Part of a good recovery is building social relationships with others in recovery. So this isn't just a social issue; it's also a recovery issue.

To remedy the situation, there are several things you can try:

- Become more active in the group. Arrive early and help set up chairs. Offer to make coffee, greet newcomers, pick up cookies, or take care of other jobs.

- Take the initiative. Invite a couple of people you're friendly with at meetings out to coffee after a meeting. If they accept, you will have broken the ice; maybe next time they will ask you along. If they don't accept, ask some other people.

- If you have friends in other NA groups, ask them to come to yours or start attending theirs—at least some of the time. That will give you some ready-made friendships. Or spend time socially with them at times when you don't have meetings.

- Find some friends—of any race—who you think could benefit from NA and invite them to your group.

- Try some other NA groups. Each one has its own personality. You may find one that's more friendly.

- Volunteer to do service work with some of the more experienced members of the group. You might join them for some step-12 work, such as taking meetings into institutions, or go with them to a regional meeting.

- If all else fails, try starting your own group with a few friends.

CULTURAL AND COMMUNITY DIVERSITY

"I'm supposed to go to an NA meeting every night. But my home group— the one in my neighborhood—meets only three times a week. The only other meetings I can get to are in a neighborhood with people much better off than me. They all live in their own homes, and I lost my house to foreclosure after I went to jail. I'm just getting back on my feet. I'm going to feel like I don't belong."

If you qualify for NA (or AA or CMA or another support fellowship), you belong, no matter what kind of people are in the group. Of course, telling you that may not change the way you feel or make you more comfortable when you first go to that meeting. Still, there's no escaping the fact that you need those daily meetings. So what can you do?

First, double-check to see if there are any other options. Maybe there's another group near where you work that meets before or after work, or at lunchtime. Or maybe you can get together with a few members of your home group every day for a while. If not, you're going to have to give in and try the meetings in the other neighborhood.

If that's the case, it's okay to slowly ease your way in to the other group (while still meeting your daily obligations). For now, plan to do most of your participating in your home group. At the new one, just show up and listen for a while. As you get more comfortable in your own group and start to feel like an NA old-timer, you'll find yourself more at ease in the other group. Faces will become familiar, and so will stories. You'll find you have comments to make and things to add from your own experience— which, because your background is different, will be of special interest to the others. You'll find, too, that although these people seem to have more money than you, their problems with drugs are very much the same. (And honestly, they may not be any better off financially than you; appearances can be deceiving. That guy who drives up in the nice car? He might be borrowing it from his sister, who was kind enough to let him live in her spare room after he got out of treatment.)

Don't dread these meetings. See them as an opportunity, a way of getting to know people from other backgrounds in a comfortable situation where, for all the differences, you do have a lot in common. It all adds to your recovery experience. If you can learn to be at ease with people outside your personal orbit, doors may start to open—not just to NA meetings, but to jobs and other opportunities as well.

////////////////////////////

"My doctor recently told me to stop drinking because of my health and suggested I start going to AA meetings. He also said I should stop smoking pot. I'm not sure about going to meetings—I just turned sixty-four and I have a feeling I'm going to be the only baby boomer there."

We promise that you won't be the only baby boomer at AA. Far from it. You'll find many boomers and seniors in there—in fact, more than 20 percent of all members are over sixty.

Most of those folks have long years of sobriety behind them. But many got into recovery only recently. Some became problem drinkers late in life, or were among the lucky few to have survived years of alcohol misuse. Others were lifelong moderate drinkers who suddenly found they had a problem with alcohol—not because they were drinking more, but because they were using prescribed or over-the-counter drugs, such as pain pills. And some found their aging bodies could no longer handle alcohol as well as before. (Because it takes older people longer to eliminate drugs from their bodies, withdrawal is usually prolonged. This should be taken into account during detox.)

Those who start problem drinking later in life may have previously been light drinkers or occasional bingers or even abstainers. Later in life they turned to alcohol for a variety of reasons: increased isolation and loneliness; loss of spouse, job, friends, family; reduced status, self-esteem, and sense of usefulness; declining financial resources; too much leisure time and boredom; poor health, physical disabilities, and pain; sleep problems; thoughts about mortality; depression and suicidal feelings. Some have even gotten in trouble with alcohol for the first time because they gave in to peer pressure to drink in their retirement communities.

You probably won't be the only person there who is trying to kick marijuana, either. Illicit drug use is also common among older adults, and the numbers have increased sharply in recent years. Much of this is due to the boomers getting older; they have always had high rates of illicit drug use.

The good news is that more of them are also looking for help, like you. In fact, many of the people you'll meet at meetings are just like you—they started smoking pot in the sixties, and they never stopped.

At most meetings you will find a good mix of folks, with members in every age group, from teens to seventies and eighties, and they'll have a lot of wisdom to share.

////////////////////////////

"I went through detox in a jail cell. They told me I can go on probation if I start going to a 12-step program, but I can't walk in there and face all those people. I've been living on the street, selling my body for meth. I'm so ashamed."

You have a disease; a disease that makes people do things they may later feel terrible about. But so do all the other people at Alcoholics Anonymous, Narcotics Anonymous, Cocaine Anonymous, Crystal Meth Anonymous, and other fellowships. Most of these people also felt ashamed about their past behavior once they got sober.

If you walk into a meeting and look around, you might think, "Hey, these people look pretty good. They couldn't have done the terrible things I've done." But that isn't true. They only look good because they've been in recovery for a while. If you had known them while they were using, you probably wouldn't recognize them now. Listen to their stories, and you'll hear many that sound a lot like your own.

If it makes you feel more comfortable, try to find a friend who is sober (or would like to get that way) to go with you to your first few meetings. And when you've been around a bit yourself and you want to speak, remember that you don't have to go into any gory details that make you uncomfortable.

Keep going to those meetings, and one of these days you will be one of those sober people that newcomers think "look pretty good."

LANGUAGE ISSUES

Since Alcoholics Anonymous is an international fellowship, many AA publications are available in a number of languages, including Afrikaans, Arabic, Chinese, Dutch, Finnish, Flemish, French, German, Icelandic, Italian, Japanese, Korean, Norwegian, Portuguese, Spanish, Russian, and Vietnamese, among others. Some Al-Anon materials,

THE RED ZONE

too, are available in numerous languages. You can order those materials at aa.org.

Another option is to use a service such as Google Translate. At translate.google.com you can cut and paste text into a box and have it translated instantly into one of dozens of languages. You can also type in a website address there and have the site's content translated. Google Translate also has an app you can use on your mobile device. Of course, these tools are not perfect yet, but they can help.

If you are looking for health information in languages other than English, MedlinePlus (nlm .nih.gov/medlineplus/healthtopics .html) is a great option. Run by the National Institutes of Health, it reviews and links to expert health information from many sites, and offers much of that information in many languages.

///////////////////////////

"My first language is Spanish and I feel very uncomfortable at an English-speaking AA meeting. I haven't been able to find any Spanish-speaking meetings near me."

Most people who learned a language other than English as a child—even those who speak English well now—feel uneasy when they are at an AA meeting or a counseling session where English is spoken.

Speaking from the heart about fears, problems, or experiences may be easiest in your native language.

You might also find the experience easier when at least some of those you are sharing your thoughts with come from a similar culture. They may better understand what your family life is like, what things are important to you, and what kinds of problems you have in trying to deal with those outside your community.

But communication is much more than words. Many of those who go to meetings held in an unfamiliar language absorb far more than they ever expected to. Feelings, fears, and emotional support can supersede words when we are honestly seeking help. You might want to try a few different groups and see where you get the most benefit.

FOR WOMEN ONLY

Some women find that women-only fellowship groups best meet their needs, and there are many women-only groups in AA, NA, and other fellowships. There is also a group called Women for Sobriety (WFS). Based on thirteen positive-thinking statements, the program emphasizes that women are capable, competent, confident, caring, and compassionate. Instead of focusing on past miseries, discussion centers on present concerns and questions as well as successes. The emphasis is on building self-esteem. Many of the women in WFS are also AA members. For information see womenforsobriety.org. (For more on women and addiction, see page 51.)

RELIGIOUS DIVERSITY

"I've been through a treatment program for alcohol and drug addiction and I've been told I have to attend Alcoholics Anonymous meetings as part of my continuing care program. This worries me since I'm Muslim and AA is a Christian-oriented organization."

This is a common misconception, but AA is not a Christian organization. It isn't even a religious organization. It's a fellowship of men and women of all faiths and of no particular faith who have joined together with a common goal: sobriety. In fact, the most rapidly growing region of 12-step recovery fellowships is in the Middle East, which is primarily Muslim. Muslims often resonate quite well with the principles of AA: They have a strong religious tenet of surrender, as well as a strong conviction to "do God's will," two concepts that work very well with the 12-step philosophy.

If you want to get sober, whatever your beliefs and background, then AA (and NA) is the place for you. You may be able to find some AA or NA groups that are primarily Muslim, too. See chapter 8 on how to find an AA group.

////////////////////////

"I'm a Jewish alcoholic. I went to my first AA meeting, and I was really uncomfortable. The way they talked about spirituality somehow seemed un-Jewish to me. Then they read the 12 steps, which are so Christian, and ended with the Lord's Prayer. I'm not sure I should go back."

Many Jews (as well as atheists and other non-Christians) have felt uncomfortable with AA because prayers are recited at some meetings or because they sense there is a Christian theme behind the 12 steps. However, many Jewish experts have clarified the words and thought behind the 12 steps and see no cause for religious concern among Jewish recoverees. The 12 steps, for example, do not run counter to Jewish thinking at all. There are parallels for each of them in rabbinic Judaism. The twenty steps in Rabbeinu Yonah of Gerona's *The Gates of Repentance*, for example, are full of similar ideas. So is the service for the Day of Atonement, with its vocal public confession. In fact, the more familiar Jews become with the 12 steps, the more they recognize the echoes of Jewish thinking in them.

The Lord's Prayer, sometimes recited at the close of AA meetings, appeared in the New Testament and has over years of use taken on a Christian image. But its foundations are thoroughly Jewish, with almost every phrase finding a direct parallel in the Kaddish, the Eighteen Benedictions, or in one or another of the rabbinic writings.

If the prayer nevertheless is one you do not want to say, look for a group in your area that uses the Serenity Prayer instead or is willing to substitute the Twenty-Third Psalm, or another verse from the Book of Psalms. Some groups close with the "I am responsible" statement, rather than a prayer. You can also simply remain silent, or say any prayer you feel is appropriate. You are not required to participate in the recitation. The Lord's Prayer is not an official prayer of AA; even Bill W. couldn't recall how the custom of reciting it started.

The Serenity Prayer, frequently recited or quoted at AA meetings and in AA literature, was written by a Christian clergyman, but it is by no means exclusively Christian. Its theme is universal.

However, many rabbis have pointed out that even if one chose to recite the Lord's Prayer at an AA meeting in order to participate in the program, it would be within Jewish law to do so. It is simply a matter of "saving a life," which outweighs all other laws.

You may want to find an AA group that is primarily Jewish, or look into some Jewish organizations for support in addition to AA. The JACS program at the Jewish Board of Family and Children's Services supports existing 12-step programs (such as AA and NA), but is not a substitute for them. It helps addicted Jews and their families integrate Jewish traditions and heritage into their recovery programs. It also serves as a resource center for information and education.

SEXUAL ORIENTATION DIVERSITY

"I haven't shared the fact that I'm transgender with anyone but my girlfriend and a few others. I don't think I'm ready to talk about my personal life publicly at an NA meeting."

Telling others about your transition is a personal decision, and how and when it happens are up to you. Members are encouraged to talk about their lives in a general way at NA; they do not have to share every detail. Only you can decide how open you want to be with your group.

It may help to test your comfort level by first sharing this part of your life with someone you trust— your sponsor, for example, or a close friend from your home group. You can also ask other LGBT NA members what their experience has been and if there are some meetings they prefer. If you don't know of anyone at your local meetings, you will surely find helpful people at online meetings and forums.

Hopefully you will find a group with which you can be completely honest and open, or at least as open as you want to be. When (and if) you feel the time is right, you might choose to tell others about your transition in an LGBT-focused NA group, of which there are many.

///////////////////////////

"I'm gay and completely open about it with people. But the first NA meeting I went to, I was totally turned off. One woman was talking about a boyfriend who abused her. A guy was complaining about his wife not understanding him. It was so hetero, there was no way I could talk about

the problems I'm having communicating with my husband."

There are two issues here. One, did you go to the meeting in the right frame of mind? And two, was this the right meeting for you?

As to the first, it may be that you were so focused on what made these folks different from you (their sexual orientation) that you were ignoring what you all have in common: chemical dependency. The truth is that there may have been little difference between the roots of their problems and your own. Try to listen with an open mind. You will gain more healing from identifying with others than from comparing yourself to them. Focus on your common ground.

As to the second issue, maybe you would feel more comfortable—at least early in your recovery—sharing at a meeting that is primarily gay men. Or going to an LGBT meeting once a week. Do what makes you feel most comfortable and able to embrace recovery.

Most gay and lesbian alcoholics and addicts find that once they become comfortable at LGBT-focused meetings, they are able to attend and benefit from other meetings.

Whatever you do, just keep going to meetings.

FOR PEOPLE WITH DISABILITIES

"Because I've got cerebral palsy, I'm pretty much a loner. That's probably why I developed a drinking problem. I think I can stop drinking on my own, but my doctor says I really should go to some kind of mutual-support meeting. I dread it."

Just like everyone else, people with physical disabilities are susceptible to alcoholism/addiction. In fact, many people with disabilities became handicapped through their use of alcohol or drugs—usually through accidents, but sometimes through the toxic effect of their chemicals of choice.

For many people with disabilities, AA is a haven where they can meet friends and talk about their fears and concerns. As we've said before, it's a place where its best to focus on what you have in common with the others there, not what makes you different.

Of course, if you've been a loner most of your life, no one should presume to tell you it will be easy to face strangers. Still, if you have to meet new people, you won't find many who are more open to meeting new friends than the folks at an AA meeting. We urge you to at least give it a try.

Check in advance to be sure that there is handicapped access to any meeting you are planning to attend, if you need it (meeting schedules often include this information). If you can't find a meeting with easy access, ask one of the leaders of a nearby group if they can work with you to make it easier to attend meetings.

First Steps: Living in Sobriety and Preventing Relapse

Staying sober, especially in the first weeks and months, is going to be tough at times. You are going to face temptations. But if you set yourself up to live immersed in the culture of recovery, and you know what kinds of problems to expect and how you can deal with them, you *can* remain chemical-free. You *can* heal your brain and live your life sober.

Here are a few key things to keep in mind as you begin your new life:

- While you're not responsible for your disease, you are responsible for your recovery. Once you recognize that you are an alcoholic or addict, it is your responsibility to get sober and stay that way.

- Changing your "playmates, playgrounds, and playthings" is an absolute must if you are to avoid chemical seduction in the future.

- Fear, anxiety, insecurity, uncertainty, and confusion are just some of the feelings you can expect to have in recovery. Through a good recovery program, you can learn to deal with them sober.

- It takes constant vigilance to neutralize the cues (things you see, hear, smell, taste, and feel) that can trigger cravings and compulsions. Those cues were wired into your brain while you were in active addiction; now you need to be careful to avoid them, while also rewiring your brain to focus on new things.

- What you have to do to make a successful recovery from any disease is not always fun, but it is often necessary for survival. Just as if you had diabetes or high blood pressure, lifestyle changes will be a crucial part of your efforts to stay healthy.

- Don't just go through the motions at meetings and other recovery activities. Really listen to what is being said. Talk with other people. Put away your phone, unplug, and immerse yourself in the culture of recovery.

- Working your program—including practicing TAMERS (see chapters 1 and 3)—will help your brain heal, making it easier and easier over time to stay sober.

Moving into Your Lifetime of Sobriety

CAN I DO IT?

"I just got home from four weeks of inpatient treatment. But I'm nervous. I've tried to quit drinking before and never succeeded. I don't know if I can this time, either."

At your next AA meeting, look around you. How many people are there? Twenty, thirty? Most of them have succeeded at staying sober, right? Now multiply that by the more than one hundred thousand AA groups around the world. You don't have to be a mathematician to realize that literally millions of people have managed to stay sober through AA. The trick is to use the tools you were given in treatment. Neglect them, and you will almost certainly fail.

To improve your chances of making it, follow the guidelines laid out in your continuing care plan. Here's a short version of what you need to do now:

- Immerse yourself in AA, NA, or another 12-step or mutual-support fellowship.

Take It One Day at a Time

You'll hear a lot of "one-day-at-a-time" talk among recovering alcoholics and addicts. That's because it works. You might even notice that it seems oddly similar to your old drinking and drugging lifestyle.

One day at a time is how you lived day after miserable day: "I'll drink today and quit tomorrow." "Just a few more pills today, then never again." Now all you have to do is worry about getting through one more day *without* drugs or alcohol. So for now, just worry about today. Tomorrow will take care of itself. You'll take care of it when it becomes today. One day at a time.

- Attend meetings more than once a week, and participate in the group.

- Work the 12 steps.

- Find a sponsor.

- Later, sponsor others.

This may seem like a tall order, but it works. Moreover, if you don't follow the recommendations given to you during treatment or at AA, then your odds of long-term survival are about as poor as those of the person with diabetes who refuses to take insulin. Those odds, as you know, aren't very good.

In bed tonight, just before you fall asleep (the hardest time for most of us to lie to ourselves), ask yourself, "How much do I really want to stay sober?" If you tell yourself, "More than anything in the world. I'll do anything to get myself straight!" you've got a good chance of making it. If you hesitate, if you're not ready to make a total commitment to the effort, you are on shaky ground. But there is still hope if you do the work.

Remember that when you wanted booze or drugs, you did whatever you had to do to get it. You let nothing stand in your way. Transfer that same determination and creativity to your recovery, and you'll be stacking up more sober anniversary chips before you know it. And remember, too, your brain is changing and healing. Take a little faith in that.

SET YOUR PRIORITIES

"I've been sober for six weeks and I feel as though I'm being pulled in four directions at once—family, work, church, AA. I don't know what to do first."

Getting well is what you need to do first. You are still in the fragile early stages of recovery— the Red Zone—and you need to focus on your recovery as much as you can. Right now, saving your life from addiction has to come before your job, your family, your hobbies, or anything else. You can work on all of those other parts of your life when you get to the Yellow Zone. As a matter of fact, if you put anything before recovery, you will probably lose it anyway, as you'll be more likely to relapse.

If you were recovering from a heart attack, this intense focus on your health would be pretty obvious to you and those around you. It is less obvious to everyone when someone is recovering from alcohol or drug addiction. But what your family needs more than anything else is for you to be sober. For good.

For now, your top priorities need to be your fellowship meetings, aftercare meetings, meditation periods, and counseling sessions. Take another look at the Recovery Zone System in chapter 2 for more guidance on just what we want you to put off until later, and what you need to focus on now.

THE RED ZONE

LEARN TO PLAN AHEAD

"I was on my way out the door to an NA meeting when I knocked over a pot of coffee. Coffee, grounds, and glass splinters were all over the kitchen floor. I didn't know whether to just walk out and go to my meeting or clean up the mess. Instead of deciding, I just sat down and cried."

That was a lot better than reaching for a pill or a drink, but it wasn't the best response. If you're going to make recovery your number one priority, you have to keep it at the top of your list all the time. A better way to deal with a messy situation like this would have been to block the entrance to the kitchen door so no kids or pets could walk in and get hurt, and explain to your spouse or babysitter that you have to get to your meeting and will clean up the mess when you return. Or you could have done a quick cleanup and gotten to your meeting a little late. Bottom line, don't let a little mishap like this turn into an excuse for missing a meeting.

One way to avoid this kind of problem—and avoid the cliff-hanging you've probably specialized in for years—is to cultivate the art of thinking ahead. Plan on leaving for your NA meetings twenty minutes early. Then, if a snag pops up that could delay you, you can deal with it without worrying about being late. If there's no snag, no sweat. You'll get to the meeting early.

KEEP A JOURNAL

If you haven't already started keeping a journal, now would be a good time. It doesn't have to be fancy—you can get your thoughts down in a spiral notebook; email memos to yourself; use a recovery app; or just start a computer file. You can write about whatever you want—no one has to ever see a word of it—so be honest. Some ideas:

- Your emotions today
- Feelings about being in recovery
- Your overall recovery plan
- Your feelings after a meeting or therapy session
- Triggers you have identified
- Your plans for avoiding triggers and dealing with cravings
- Things you are grateful for
- Thoughts on seeing old friends
- Thoughts on making amends
- Thoughts on patching things up in relationships
- Your current priorities
- Your motivations to stay sober
- Your current strengths and weaknesses
- Thoughts about finances and work issues
- Your victories and progress in recovery
- Your new view of yourself

- An exercise log and new activities you want to try

- Meditation and relaxation practices you'd like to try

- Thoughts on diet

- Short- and long-term goals

- Reflections on your progress

- Your hopes and dreams for the future

Writing things down can be a very powerful way to process your feelings and get them "out of your head." Often, problems don't seem quite so big or so awful once you've worked through them on paper. A journal is also a great way to keep an eye on your progress over time. A year or two from now, you might look back on what you wrote and be astonished at what you have accomplished.

FIND YOUR VALUES

Values are the moral and ethical framework by which we live. When we are unsure which road to take, our values act as a guide for our actions and attitudes. They help us see which way we should turn and what is the right thing to do.

An important part of learning who you are in recovery is finding out what your values are. They are in there somewhere, buried deep in your mind. The odds are pretty good that you gave little thought to your values while you were under the influence.

So now is the time to unearth your values—and start living them.

The sad truth is that people who don't live up to their value systems in recovery usually don't stay sober. (As we've said before, lies and secrets are the fuels of addiction.)

How do you dig up and identify your values—and live by them?

Prioritize the positive. Make a list of the important things in your life: family, religion, work, school, play, friends, pets, hobbies, music, art, nature, sports—whatever matters to you. Then arrange them in order of importance.

Evaluate. If you started drinking or using drugs at an early age, you may not have had the opportunity to form a sound value system. If you started later and used for a long time, the values you did have may have become distorted. So see how your list of priorities stacks up against those of people you respect. Compare what you think is important to what is important to your spouse, parents, children, minister, sponsor, and others you trust. Now go back over your own list and refine it with newly gained insights.

Identify what you could lose. Take a look at what you could lose if you return to drugs and alcohol. You say your family is your top priority. Are they likely to stick around through a relapse?

Nullify the negative. Make a list of the things that you'd like to banish from your life for good. This will probably include alcohol and drugs. It may also include promiscuous sex and extramarital affairs; lying, cheating, and other forms of dishonesty; laziness and procrastination; unkindness; wallowing in guilt or self-pity; and pessimism.

Draw boundaries. Once you know what aspects of your life you want to banish, draw some clear boundaries to keep those things out of your life. If you find yourself crossing the line to even dabble in any of those activities, take it as a red flag, an alert that you need to get back on track, pronto.

Plan ahead. Think about the ways you can build and enrich those parts of your life that are most important to you. Think about ways to rid your life of more of the negatives.

Keep looking in the mirror. Do a regular personal inventory (technically, this is part of step 10, but you can jump ahead and read about it now in chapter 17). When you look back at your actions, notice whether you behaved in ways that reflect the things you value most. If family is important, did you remember to call your partner when you realized you'd be late for dinner? Did you make a special effort to go to your child's school play? Likewise, did you avoid those negatives you are trying to eliminate? Did you lose a promotion by watching football instead of working on a proposal for a new client?

If you keep asking yourself questions like these, and answering them honestly, you'll not only find your values; you'll begin to live them. In the process, you'll come to love and respect yourself a lot more.

Sober-Living Homes and Sober Helpers

"One of the women in treatment with me said she is going to move into a sober-living home. What is that? Is it something I should consider?"

Many people feel nervous about leaving the highly supportive and structured environment of inpatient treatment. Although they no longer need the intensive (and expensive) treatment environment, they are not yet ready to go home. Maybe they don't have supportive surroundings to go home to, or they need to do more work on building recovery skills. Or maybe they simply worry that without the day-in-and-day-out, intense focus on recovery, they will falter.

These people need something in between—a recovery residence. These are community-based residences, ranging from small private homes to larger facilities, where people in recovery live together and work on staying in recovery. They have been around for quite some time, and are now more popular than ever. According to the National Association of Recovery Residences (NARR), thousands of such residences now exist in the U.S.

A recovery residence might be just what you need when you leave treatment. Think about it this way: Your initial treatment gave you the tools for sober living; living in a recovery home will let you practice using those tools in a secure and supportive setting.

These residences go by many different names, including sober living houses, halfway houses, sober living environments, transitional living, recovery homes, and extended-care programs. The services provided at each vary greatly as well. Some are mostly run by the residents, with minimal oversight, while others are run by professionals and feature extensive in-house services.

Recovery residences usually are homelike environments. If a resident slips and gives in to the urge to drink or use drugs again, people he trusts are right there to help him get back on his feet. Residents often have access to counseling and to a house manager who is an empathetic person in recovery, an addiction professional, or both. Residents also have one another around the clock—for support; group meetings; trading hopes, fears, and feelings; and working out problems.

Residents share the household chores, go to meetings, and, when ready, work in the community—usually at a low-pressure or volunteer job. They learn how to live in and maintain a household and how to socialize without chemical support. (A modest goal, but no small thing for an addict.)

The families of those in a good extended-care program are not forgotten. They receive encouragement and support to build their own recovery programs. Once the patient and the family are well on their own roads to solid recovery, they can start working on rebuilding their ties to one another. Family visits with the patient—along with joint counseling, workshops, and other activities—begin the healing process and improve the odds of rebuilding a healthy family.

Dating and forming new intimate relationships are usually forbidden during extended care, at least for the first year.

Stays at some recovery homes may be covered by insurance. At others, residents pay fees or rent. Costs range from a few hundred to thousands per month. You may have some control over your own finances, but you probably will not be allowed to have credit cards, take out a bank loan, or otherwise add to your stress by accumulating debt. If you are working, a portion of your wages may be set aside by the home for you to use later on.

If living in a recovery residence isn't an option for you, you can find extra support by taking part in a strong continuing care or outpatient program near your home.

DO YOU NEED A SOBER HIGH SCHOOL OR COLLEGE?

"I've spent several months getting my life back on track. First rehab, and then a sober-living house. I'm

ready to go back to college, but I'm wary about being there. It's a total party environment. Almost everyone is into heavy drinking and smoking weed—not to mention all the so-called study drugs they live on at finals. That's what helped me get into trouble in the first place."

You are smart to be thinking ahead. Even with several months of sobriety, it can be hard to stick to your recovery plan.

You have a few options. First, can you take classes at a college near where you live now? Avoiding a big change in your environment might help you stay on track with your program. Another option is to move to a school that has a Recovery Campus (sometimes called a Collegiate Recovery Community, or CRC). These programs allow people to go to school while living in an environment that supports recovery as well as academic and social success. Programs vary. Some schools have housing floors or entire dorms for those in recovery; some will find you a roommate who is also in recovery. Some have classes on how to prevent relapse and other recovery-related topics. Georgia Southern University, for example, has an extensive recovery program that was set up in cooperation with Willingway. You can read more about it at jphcoph.georgiasouthern.edu/centers/addiction/welcome.

You can find a list of recovery high schools and colleges at the Association of Recovery Schools (recoveryschools.org) and the Association of Recovery in Higher Education (collegiaterecovery.org). Most of these schools and programs do not provide treatment for addiction; rather, they offer an educational setting that has extra services and support for students who are in recovery. It's always best to get your treatment *first*, and then, only after you have a solid recovery under way, go back to school in a supportive environment.

If you decide to return to your original school, make sure you'll be able to build your own network for abstinence and support. Where is the local AA or NA community? Are there meetings close to campus, or even on campus? What will you do to find some new friends who are either sober themselves or supportive of your sobriety (fellowship meetings are a great place to start)? Also give a lot of thought to the triggers you might encounter in that setting; recognizing them now will help you avoid them later. You can even write up a Recovery Zone System Continuing Care Plan that focuses solely on returning to school—it can help you anticipate all kinds of problems and solutions (see page 133).

Be careful, though. If you can't find or build a supportive recovery network at your school, you are probably better off staying away from the lure of campus life for the first two years of your sobriety.

SOBER COMPANIONS AND PEER SUPPORT SPECIALISTS

Sober companions and peer support specialists are a fairly new part of the world of recovery—they try to enhance your sobriety by keeping an eye on you and helping you navigate through various situations.

These folks—professionals and volunteers alike—are not a substitute for going to treatment, getting involved in a fellowship, working the steps, working with a sponsor, or meeting with a therapist or addiction counselor. But for some people, they can be a big help in avoiding relapse and getting settled into comfortably living in sobriety.

The services they offer vary widely (as do their titles: you may hear of sober coaches, companions, and escorts; recovery coaches; peer support specialists; and others). Some will move into your home and keep watch over you round the clock, while others offer shorter-term services such as regular in-person meetings or phone support. Some focus on helping families navigate the world of recovery, including running an intervention and getting their loved ones into treatment. Some of the common services:

- Remind you to go to meetings

- Escort you when you travel to treatment or back home, or make any other transition where you might face temptations to drink

- Go with you to work, while shopping, on business trips, and on vacations

- Ensure that your environment remains free of alcohol and drugs

- Manage and hold on to your money, phone, and email and social media accounts so you are not tempted to buy alcohol or drugs or contact friends who are still using

- Talk with you about your life and help you make good choices throughout your day and as you transition back to daily life

There are no national standards defining who can be a sober coach or companion, so just about anyone can call themselves one. Most are not trained therapists or doctors and are not qualified to provide you with any sort of treatment. They tend to focus more on practical issues, rather than therapy. Nor are they "sponsors for hire." They will not necessarily help you work the 12 steps. They should be viewed more as companions and peers, people who will try to steer you in the right direction.

How do you find a good sober coach or peer support specialist? It's best to start with referrals: ask your doctor, therapist, addiction counselor, treatment center staff, fellowship members, and others you trust in the world of recovery if they can recommend someone. You might also find some on staff at an agency or facility (which will have already vetted their abilities). If you

THE RED ZONE

find some candidates, interview them, ask about their approach and services, and ask for references. Have someone else who has your best interests at heart also interview them. You might also ask your doctor or therapist to meet with them and try to assess their professional abilities.

Avoid a Relapse— Resist Temptations

WHAT IS RELAPSE?

In the medical world, a relapse means that signs and symptoms of a disease have returned after an apparent recovery. You can have a relapse with the flu—and you can have one with the disease of alcoholism/addiction. In neither case does your prognosis have to be grave. It's likely you will recover from both, but while the flu will probably go away on its own, you'll have to take very positive steps to recover from relapse into alcoholism/addiction.

Many think a relapse starts when someone starts drinking or using drugs again. But in fact, the "relapse train" starts moving much earlier— when a person starts *thinking* that it might be okay to drink or use again, even though he is well aware that to do so could destroy everything. His subsequent behavior might quickly spiral out of control, or he may try to control it for a time. A slip, as we use the term here, implies a brief return to drinking or using—and getting help before going further.

Of those who relapse after a solid foundation in treatment, most will eventually have a successful recovery. These people come to understand relapse not as a failure, but as a lesson in how not to succeed.

YOUR RELAPSE PREVENTION PLAN

As you read through this chapter, think about what factors might lead you to a relapse and write up your own plan for dealing with each one.

MYTHS ABOUT RELAPSE

Because relapse is shrouded in shame and embarrassment, many myths have grown up around it—myths that can endanger recovery if they aren't recognized as such.

"Relapse is inevitable." Sometimes people hear so much about relapse that they think it's part of getting better. "I might as well have my slip now and get it over with" is often heard. But in fact, many sober people have never relapsed. In the long run, your chances of staying sober are better if you don't relapse and don't even consider it an option.

"Relapse means failure." For some people, relapse *is* an important part of recovery. They aren't truly committed to sobriety the first time around; they haven't experienced enough discomfort to persuade them that they can't safely drink or use drugs. But they learn something each go-round, they get more motivated to stay sober permanently, and eventually they have the tools they need to get the job done.

"Relapse can't be prevented." The truth is that relapse is optional. Avoiding it is much less a matter of willpower than of knowing what causes a relapse, how to minimize the risk, what the signs of impending relapse are, and what to do if a slip is about to occur.

"Relapse after a period of sobriety, and it will take months or years to hit bottom again." Alcoholism/addiction is a progressive disease. It continues to get worse in a kind of shadow progression during recovery. Those who relapse usually find that when they wake up "the morning after," they are in worse trouble than when they first swore off. In fact, it generally takes only a few hours to a few days to reach bottom in a relapse.

"Using a different drug doesn't count as a relapse." Some treatment professionals have started using the world "lapse" for situations where a person has started using a new drug. But returning to *any* drugs or alcohol is a relapse. The drug of choice is almost beside the point; a relapse is a return to ideas and behaviors of addiction. Lapse equals relapse.

IDENTIFY YOUR PERSONAL TEMPTATIONS

A major part of avoiding relapse and staying sober is just avoiding temptation.

Some temptations are quite obvious: A friend invites you for a beer after work. Your mom leaves the painkillers from her surgery out in plain sight.

Others are not so obvious. Many times your resolve will be tested by subtle cues, signals to your brain that seem to pop up out of nowhere. You see some powdered sugar spilled on a glass table and it looks just like a line of coke; you hear a song that was a favorite during your drug years; you happen to drive by your once-favorite bar.

You may also experience a variety of situations and emotions that can leave you open and vulnerable to temptation: You feel hurt and abandoned by a partner who suddenly decides to leave you; a parent dies before you ever had a chance to make amends; your friends at work are not so friendly anymore.

To avoid falling victim to all of these siren calls to "come on back," you need to be able to anticipate them, recognize them (even when they are not obvious), avoid them when possible, know how to outmaneuver them, and know how to confront their seductive come-ons. You also need to take steps to relapse-proof your home and your life, so those situations don't even have a chance to come into your world.

RECOGNIZE AND CHANGE YOUR CUES

In recovery you need to change or avoid the old negative cues. AA refers to them as the playgrounds,

THE RED ZONE

playmates, and playthings you associate with drinking or using.

Playgrounds

Most of our daily routines are linked to specific places. You don't whip out your toothbrush in the car, but when you walk into the bathroom at night, you reach for it without thinking. Likewise, you have no trouble putting alcohol out of your mind all morning in the office, but as soon as you step out to lunch and pass your favorite bar, you want a drink.

Familiar places can dredge up old feelings, emotional memories that trigger cravings. Those feelings can run the gamut from troubled (tension, anxiety, and what seem to be withdrawal symptoms) to titillating (pleasant expectancy, with salivation, giddiness, and an imagined inner warmth).

That's why recovering alcoholics and addicts are urged to avoid the places where they did their drinking or drugging, especially in early recovery. It's vital that you stay away from the bars, clubs, dances, parties, rock concerts, and liquor stores where you're known by your first name. Steer clear of the restaurants, sports events, and memorable street corners where you once drank or used drugs. Drive or walk a few blocks out of your way to avoid them. Also try to avoid any place you might associate with drinking or using drugs, even if you've never been there before. If you are looking for a new restaurant to try, choose one with no liquor license,

or at least no bar area. If you go to a sporting event, get seats in the no-alcohol area. If you're not clear where your quicksand lies, do a special personal inventory (step 4) to remind yourself.

If you drank or used in places you can't avoid—at home, at work—use some of that old addict ingenuity to erase the danger signs. Get rid of the table you prepared your cocaine on, as well as the paraphernalia. Dump your pills down the toilet. If you always popped pills in the bathroom, get rid of the familiar bathroom water glass. If you need to take prescribed medication, do it in a different room. If you always drank beer when you watched football on the living room TV, watch the game in the bedroom. If prescription meds were part of your addiction, avoid doctor's offices, urgent care centers, and emergency rooms unless it's absolutely necessary—and then bring someone with you.

Spend more time in places where it's impossible, or at least not easy, to drink or use drugs: museums, stores, the gym or health club, AA meetings, your workplace, churches and synagogues.

If you spend any time in places where drinking or drug use is an option, plan ahead to avoid peer pressure to drink or use. At the theater or a concert, for example, bring your own soft drink for intermission, so you won't have any reason to go anywhere near the bar. Even if you think you can safely buy a nonalcoholic drink, don't risk it—have someone else do it.

When you plan your day or your week, think about where you are going and who you will be with. Always be sure you are not setting yourself up for failure.

Playmates

Just as places can turn on your cravings, so can a specific cast of characters: the people you always drank or used with. Stop seeing them for now. And remove any reminders of them that could pop up on your online social networks. Delete photos on Facebook and other social networks, and unfriend people. If you don't want to banish some people entirely, add them to custom lists of people, and look at only your lists of "safe people" for now. Consider deleting your social networking accounts entirely and starting fresh with just the people who you know support your recovery. Looking at the old photos can just stir up FOMO (fear of missing out), and the feeling that everyone else is having lots more fun than you are (it's not necessarily true). It's best if you do this clean sweep with your counselor or sponsor by your side, because it might trigger emotions or cravings that need to be dealt with. (See more ideas in Clean Up Your Online Life, page 233.)

If you really want to connect with people online, check out some of the new sober social networking sites, such as IntheRooms.com. Those online networks and friends can come in handy in the middle of the night, too, when you suddenly feel like you want a drink.

If there is an old friend you really want to see, arrange to meet in a coffee shop or at your home, and bring along your sponsor or another friend in recovery. A true friend will be happy to see you getting better and won't object to your bringing a chaperone.

Renew friendships with people who don't drink or use, the ones you stopped seeing when you started getting heavily into your addiction. You may find there are more of them than you thought, and that you really enjoy their company. And make new friends. You'll find a host of great candidates at fellowship meetings—people like you, no matter what you're like. Outgoing people who've learned how to have fun without chemicals. Calm, serene people who are comfortable with themselves and with others now that they are sober.

Playthings

It won't be enough to change the scenery and the cast of characters. You'll also have to be wary of the props that surround you as well. In our society, we are constantly bombarded by images of alcohol and drugs. Any of these stimuli—visual, psychological, even random smells—can bring on the signs of physical craving, with sweaty palms, a fast pulse, and agitation.

You'll have to be constantly on the alert for such cues. If they trigger fear rather than craving the first few times you come across them, don't be tricked into believing you're forever safe. The fear reaction is common in early recovery, but repeated exposure to the same cue can dilute and finally wash away the fear. So learn to recognize these cues and avoid them.

TV ads for beer or wine. Leave the room or change the channel immediately when they come on. Even better, record the shows you want to watch so you can zip right through the ads. These commercials are most dangerous when they show drinking scenes that dredge up pleasant memories: romantic dinners with wine; exhilarating moments sailing on a sunlit bay with glasses raised; exciting moments celebrating the home team with a frosty beer. (Of course, the ads never show the drinkers weaving drunkenly home, being pulled over for DUI, puking on the carpet, or waking up with a pounding head and foul breath the next day.)

TV ads for prescription drugs that promise to help with your emotions. As with most ads, these commercials promise more than they can deliver. Listen closely to the "fine print" at the end; the appeal of these drugs should fade when you hear the warnings about side effects, sickness, and potential death.

Liquor ads—everywhere. You may find your cravings triggered by posters in subways and buses, by roadside billboards, or by print ads.

They all show gloriously happy people building enduring friendships, improving their already enviable sex lives, and generally having a wonderful time thanks to booze. So change your seat, avert your eyes, or turn the page in a hurry.

Online ads for liquor or anything that could remind you of your drinking and drugging days. If you are a golfer, and you always drank with the guys at the "19th hole," chances are your computer browser knows you like golf. It may try to "help" you by serving up ads for things you might enjoy. But seeing images of golf clubs in ads, or happy people on a new course—even if they don't include liquor—could be a trigger for you. Install an ad-blocking extension such as Adblock (adblockplus.org) on your browser. It can block all ads on social networking sites, news sites, and other online venues.

TV shows and movies in which the drink's the thing. As much as you can, skip the movies and shows that feature casual drug use and drinking.

Books about drinking and using. Addiction memoirs are popular. While they might hold some good lessons, those that replay scenes of drinking and drugging days could dredge up cues for you. You are likely to hear lots of these stories at meetings as well, but that's a safer place to hear them. Also avoid novels in which drinking or drug use is part of the story.

Loose sugar, baking soda, cornstarch. All of these, when spread on a table or dish, are uncomfortably reminiscent of cocaine. Avoid leaving any of these items lying around. Buy sweeteners in packets, rather than loose. Don't dump any of these substances on the table and play at cutting them, even just for "fun." If you use them for cooking, they should go directly from the container into the food you're preparing. In recovery, you can never be too careful.

Windex and similar glass-cleaning preparations. These have an odor strikingly similar to cocaine. Let your windows and mirrors stay a little dirty for now, or use a cleaner with a citrus odor or other scent.

Vinegar. Some say it smells a lot like heroin. Don't bring it into the house.

Drug paraphernalia. The very sight of it can trigger an irresistible drug craving, and a relapse. Dump all of yours and maintain a safe distance from anyone else's. You might not consider a mirror to be drug paraphernalia, but if you prepped your coke on one, that's what it was. Banish mirrored trays and other horizontal mirrored surfaces from your home. (Plus, even the possession of paraphernalia is a crime in some places. You don't want to get stopped for a missing taillight and find yourself going to jail for having an old crack pipe in your glove box.)

Your favorite liquor store or bar. Try to avoid passing it, even if it means going far out of your way. If beer, wine, or liquor is sold in your supermarket, make a wide detour around that part of the store when you shop.

Your old drug dealer. If you have to pay an old debt, ask a friend to do it for you. More than one recovering addict has been rehooked in the process of paying up—especially when the dealer, eager to win back a lost client, made an offer he couldn't refuse: "Hey, this stuff is on me. For a friend."

Hot-weather activities. Fishing, boating, hanging out at the beach or boardwalk, barbecues, even mowing the lawn can summon up drinking memories for some people. Avoid them if this is true for you, or engage in them only in a controlled situation where booze is out of the question—such as with another AA member.

Cold-weather activities. Some people associate snowstorms with hunkering down in a cozy cabin and drinking the night away. You can't control the weather, but you can close the blinds or go to a meeting when the flakes start falling.

The end of your workday. If this was when your drinking day began, change your routine. Maybe go straight to a meeting after work, go out for a run as soon as you get home, or go to the gym to work up a sweat instead of a thirst.

The corner where you used to buy drugs. Even driving *close* to that part of town could be a trigger, so avoid it. If there's no way to get around it, sail through under escort with an NA buddy.

Nostalgic music. Hearing rock music, club music, or a song or band you associate with drugs or alcohol could send you right back to drinking and drugging. Even marching band music might do it if you always drank at college football games. If that's the case, steer clear of such music entirely until your sobriety is solid, and even then, do your listening in safe surroundings. For now, get those tunes off your phone or music player. Download some AA recordings or music from an entirely new-to-you genre.

Romantic dinners. If a dinner without wine seems as unromantic as a traffic jam, try substituting candlelight, soft music, and flowers. When dining out, look for restaurants that don't have a bar. If you find yourself in a restaurant that serves alcohol, decline the wine or beer list, and ask the waiter to remove any wineglasses from the table. If there's a bar, ask to be seated far, far away from it.

Sporting events and concerts. Many arenas offer alcohol-free seating sections now. Request them when you buy tickets.

Stimulating situations. Situations as diverse as skydiving, playing poker, and trying to con someone can all trigger a rush of adrenaline, which can in turn trigger a craving for cocaine or other drugs. For now, focus on moderation in your activities, and move away from thrill-seeking to limit that response.

Pharmacological perils. If cough medicines or other over-the-counter items were among your drugs of last resort (or you used them to cook up other drugs), stay away from those aisles at the store. If a bottle of vanilla extract turns you on, steer clear of the spice section. Find this difficult? Shop with a buddy, or place your order online and have your groceries delivered.

Pain and other medical ills. A backache, a splitting headache, or a runny nose can send you to the pharmacist for what seems like a good reason. But before you know it, you don't even remember why you're reaching for the medicine. Instead, learn how to prevent your most common ailments, and how to treat them without drugs when prevention fails (see chapters 13 and 24 for lots of ideas).

Hospitals, emergency rooms, and medical clinics. Now that addiction to prescription drugs has become a huge problem, the health care environment is an especially risky place for addicts and alcoholics. If you go in for medical care, you may find people offering you addictive or mood-altering drugs—a very likely trigger. It can be especially hard to resist these offers because they come from someone in a position of trust; someone who is supposed to be helping you. If you need medical

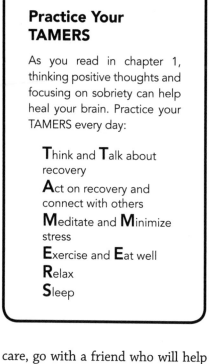

Practice Your TAMERS

As you read in chapter 1, thinking positive thoughts and focusing on sobriety can help heal your brain. Practice your TAMERS every day:

Think and **T**alk about recovery

Act on recovery and connect with others

Meditate and **M**inimize stress

Exercise and **E**at well

Relax

Sleep

as powerful as the old negative cues that led you to drink and use.

Some ideas for your good cues:

- Seeing your sponsor and other AA friends
- Meditation and prayer
- Seeing your loved ones
- Your sober image in the mirror
- Listening to recovery recordings
- Reading recovery books and watching videos
- A good job review, a good grade on an exam, or a word of praise from a boss or teacher
- Things you've obtained since sobriety (a car, a new TV)
- Finishing dinner—associate it with going to a meeting, rather than with drinking

Use technology to reinforce these messages. Set up your computer screen saver to flash an inspirational message or photos of your sponsor or your happy new life. Download some apps that will ping you with positive messages during the day. Ask a friend or your sponsor to check in with some recovery-related text messages a couple of times a day, or when you know you will be most vulnerable. For example, if you know that on your bus ride home from work you have to pass your old dealer's neighborhood, arrange to text with a supportive friend at that time, or schedule some of your own email

care, go with a friend who will help you say no, and tell the staff that the use of *any* mood-altering medication puts you at risk of a relapse that could lead to death. And remember, you don't *have* to take whatever they suggest. Ask if there are other options. This is a very risky situation; read more on page 290.

ADD SOME GOOD CUES

While doing your best to avoid those dangerous old cues, look for some new cues and rituals for recovery. Write up a list of them—and every time you see or hear one, take it as a reminder to remain sober. Get this wired into your healing brain by consciously thinking about these cues when you encounter them. These can be just or text reminders to be delivered at those times. A timely email with a photo of your daughter might be just the thing to help you avoid hopping off the bus.

WATCH OUT FOR EMOTIONAL CUES

Certain feelings—known as "emotional memories"—can be as hazardous to recovery as bumping into your drug dealer. Identifying these feelings and learning how to handle them can keep them from triggering cravings.

Good Feelings

In early recovery, it might seem like you will never again have any fun. But eventually, a pleasant experience will make you feel wonderful and give you an emotional high. It might be the first time in many years you've felt that way without the use of chemicals. Great! Enjoy it. Revel in it. But be wary. When that good feeling *wanes*, your still-healing brain may confuse that with coming down from a drug-induced high. You could start craving the drug as the cycle of addiction tries to rekindle itself.

It's all related to how drugs affect your brain. When you engage in an activity that leads to an emotional high, your brain's reward system is activated. You get a rush, a feeling of pleasure. This reward is our survival mechanism. Something feels good (love, sex, eating), so we repeat it. We learn to do what helps us survive. Drugs also activate the reward centers of the brain, producing a similar rush and feelings of pleasure. But

they confound the system: You get the reward without engaging in an activity related to survival, or in fact any activity at all (except taking the drug). Instant gratification, instant reward. Drugs, in essence, hijack the reward system of your brain. You are then driven by cravings, not by intellect or thinking. (Read more on this in chapter 1.)

So right now, your brain is still used to associating those good feelings, whatever their source, with the drugs you used to take. Like any other cue, this can trigger a craving.

That doesn't mean you have to go through the rest of your life wearing a frown. Just be aware that right now, your body may interpret feeling good as a drug high, so don't let it fool you.

Bad Feelings

Rage and resentment, feelings that come from a part of the brain that is more primitive and powerful than the higher-level "thinking" region, can sometimes cause a rush that feels like a cocaine or other drug rush and can trigger a strong craving. Try to avoid such feelings. If you have them, learn how you can get rid of them as quickly as possible. (See page 329 for tips on handling anger and resentment.)

Other feelings—such as distress, depression, shakiness, apprehension, jumpiness, a knot in the stomach, fear of dying, or a feeling of sickness or of being out of control—are also associated with strong cravings. Tension, unease, irritability, restlessness, insecurity, self-disgust, vague guilt, and annoyance are associated with mild cravings—which may be only steps away from strong cravings.

That's why pure white-knuckle abstention is rarely enough to maintain sobriety—you are not going to stay sober if you are constantly stressed and having these kinds of feelings. Your recovery program needs to help you learn how to feel good about yourself and how to deal with emotions like these quickly and effectively.

In an odd way, all of these emotions that we would normally try to avoid are actually helpful. They become fodder for good discussions at meetings and talks with your sponsor. Sharing the pain and struggles of these issues strengthens the healing bonds of fellowship.

Defense-Lowering Feelings

In addition to triggering cravings, feelings can lower our defenses against the other "Oh hell, why not?" cues that assault us daily. We are most susceptible to temptation when we are *hungry*, *angry*, *lonely*, or *tired* (just remember HALT), or bored, sad, worried, nervous, or depressed. This is particularly true in recovery. Try to avoid those mental states as much as you can.

Keep busy, but not so busy you're always exhausted. Get enough rest and relaxation. Eat regularly and wisely. Learn to deal with resentments and anxieties, possibly using stress-reduction techniques. And do things that make you smile a lot.

BE WARY OF FLEETING THOUGHTS

A fleeting thought about "the good times" may seem innocent, but it's not. Here's what can happen. The thought leads to fantasizing (a more organized, scripted mental picture of a longed-for event). The fantasy becomes a preoccupation (a focused pattern of thought about the event). The preoccupation becomes an obsession (the thought develops a self-fulfilling control over the person). Now that not-so-innocent, not-so-fleeting thought is in charge. The obsession turns into a compulsion and the need to take action. It's not far from there to the nearest bar.

So, the moment it surfaces, banish that fleeting thought. Redirect your thinking. Say some affirmations; meditate; listen to recovery recordings. (See chapter 14 for more.)

ROMANCING THE DRINK OR THE DRUG

Recovering surgery patients like to talk about their operations. Recovering alcoholics/addicts often like to talk about their drinking and drugging days. But while reminiscing is harmless for bypass patients, it can be fatal for people in recovery. They tend to remember the good stuff, rather than the hangover, the dent in the car, and the sudden fear on waking—"Did I hurt anyone when I blacked out?"

Fantasizing about the good times of drinking and drugging,

sometimes called "romancing the drug (or the drink)," is dangerous because it can change your focus. Rather than concentrating on your sobriety and building your knowledge and skills of recovery, you could start to think only about missing drugs and how you long to use them again. The romantic pull of prescription drugs can be especially subtle. Romancing, like other visual and psychological temptations, can easily lead to preoccupation and obsession, and then to cravings. And it's a short distance from the craving to the bar, your dealer, or a doctor with a prescription pad.

If you hear such conversations starting, leave in a hurry. Don't worry about being rude. Worry about staying alive. Conversations should focus on living, not drinking; on answers, not problems.

GET RID OF TEMPTATIONS AT HOME

The Liquor Cabinet
Should you ban all alcohol from your home? There's no simple answer to that question. But in most cases there are sound reasons for keeping the temptations far away.

You don't want to have something around that can trigger cravings all day, every day. It's like stashing a box of doughnuts in the fridge when you're trying to diet. Every time you open the door to get some baby carrots, temptation winks.

You also don't want to make it easy to fulfill any cravings—especially those that pop up seemingly out of nowhere. If you are suddenly assaulted by the "I've gotta have a drink" blues, but you have to get in the car and drive somewhere to fulfill the craving, time and distance are on your side. Having to take action may well disrupt the craving, and the desire may pass before you've buckled your seat belt and headed down the street. If, on the other hand, the object of your affection is in the next room, your romance with alcohol could be back on in a half-dozen steps.

If you're willing, and especially if you're eager, to keep alcohol in your home, you're not as free of your compulsion as you'd like to think. You're trying to keep an escape hatch open—just in case.

The Medicine Cabinet
It's also a good idea to not keep any mood-altering drugs (such as tranquilizers, painkillers, antidepressants, and stimulants) in the house. You've spoken to your doctor about your prescriptions by now, so get rid of any leftover medications lying around. This is especially important in regard to narcotic pain relievers, which now cause more overdose deaths than all illegal drugs. If a condition comes back and those kinds of drugs are absolutely necessary, you can see the doctor again and get a new prescription.

If a family member needs to take any mood-altering prescription drugs, see if they can be stored elsewhere (such as at the office). That will keep the home supply small enough that if any pills go missing it can be easily detected.

Making mood-altering drugs less accessible can be good for the whole family. It provides extra incentive for everyone to develop a lifestyle that doesn't rely on drugs. This approach will also unify and focus the family's attention on its primary problem. A casual approach toward drugs could, on the other hand, undermine your newfound recovery.

In addition, many young people today are starting down their own path to addiction not by buying drugs on the street, but by swiping them from medicine cabinets at home—and from the homes of friends. So it's a good precaution to *always* dispose of or lock up any drugs in your house. Even if your drug of choice was alcohol, and you never had any problems with pills, those painkillers left over from your knee surgery could be what starts your daughter's best friend on the road to heroin addiction.

Secure your current medications.

If you do have any medications in your home, take steps to make them less accessible to others. Keep them all in a single location that is off-limits to your kids and visitors, perhaps in a locked box or small case in your bedroom closet or personal bathroom. Another option is to install a locking medicine case inside your bathroom cabinet.

Get rid of unneeded medications.

Why leave them sitting around your home? It's like leaving a loaded gun unsecured. Flushing drugs down the toilet is not always the best option, because they can get into the environment. Three options for disposal:

- Find a safe place to dispose of them. The U.S. Drug Enforcement Administration sponsors National Prescription Drug Take-Back Day events across the country, in cooperation with pharmacies, law enforcement agencies, and other local sites. Ask your pharmacist or police department about upcoming events or ongoing disposal sites. Or check with the DEA (dea.gov, 800-882-9539).

- Throw them out in the trash. Take pills out of the bottle and mix them up with some used kitty litter or coffee grounds so they will be less appealing. Put it all in a plastic bag so the pills aren't easily spotted and won't get spread around, then throw it in the trash. Before you throw out the pill bottles remove your personal information.

- Flush them down the toilet. The FDA says some drugs, if they can't be disposed of at a take-back program, should be flushed down the toilet. That will prevent people in recovery, as well as children and pets, from getting access to them. In general, this is recommended for some very strong drugs that could be fatal, such as Fentanyl patches and lozenges, as well as OxyContin and morphine. Used patches should also be flushed, as they can still contain some medication.

You can find disposal instructions for some medications on the DailyMed site (dailymed.nlm.nih.gov/dailymed/about.cfm) from the National Library of Medicine. It contains package inserts for most drugs, as well as other facts. (It is also handy for identifying unlabeled medications.)

AVOID HIDDEN TEMPTATIONS: IN FOOD AND ELSEWHERE

Alcohol doesn't come only in a glass or a bottle. It can come in bowls and plates, too. And what you don't know *can* hurt you. One reason, of course, is that even a small amount of alcohol can trigger a relapse. How much does it take? A tiny drop? A small glass? There is no definitive answer, so it's best to avoid all alcohol and keep your risk as low as possible. Another reason is the psychological risk: the taste plus the "thrill" of knowing that you're consuming alcohol could turn on a compulsion to drink. Remember, the addiction is in the person, not the substance; it's critical to stay away from that slippery slope of guessing what might be risky for you.

So to be sober rather than sorry, always be sure your food has been prepared completely without wine or spirits.

At home, that should be easy. In other people's homes or in restaurants, it doesn't have to be much harder. You don't have to offer long explanations—just say that you are not allowed to have anything with alcohol in it. To be sure your hostess or waiter takes you seriously, you can add, "My doctor's given me strict orders." And because we now know that addiction has a genetic basis in some people, you can honestly say, "I'm allergic to alcohol and can't have it in any form." Raising legitimate medical issues usually helps to dissuade those people who (for some reason) feel a need to push something on you.

Be very careful of the following:

Foods cooked in wine or other spirits. The old wisdom—that if wine or liquor is simmered for five minutes or more, the alcohol cooks out—is wrong. Even an hour or more of cooking will not eliminate all the booze. (In addition, if you try to push this boundary you could easily cross into that area where cues threaten to wake up that sleeping giant you're trying to put to rest.) So avoid any dish that includes alcohol, even minute amounts, as an ingredient. And don't use it when you're doing the cooking, for yourself or when hosting company. With a chef's hat on your head and a bottle in your hand, that old one-for-me-one-for-the-pot feeling could easily come back.

Some dishes announce their alcohol content loud and clear: beef bourguignon, coq au vin, fettuccine with vodka cream sauce, and rum pecan pie. Others are standard recipes that you can be pretty sure are made with alcohol: cumberland sauce, sole véronique, cheese fondue, Welsh rarebit. And of course, Irish coffee and all the other drinks that are full of alcohol.

Many other dishes are not so obviously made with spirits. Often only the cook knows for sure. If this is a possibility, ask your waiter to have the chef make you something strictly without alcohol. There are so many people in recovery these days that no one should balk at your request. And a good chef is likely to accept the challenge.

To play it safe, always ask whether soups, sauces, marinades, or salad dressings are made with any alcohol-based beverages.

Uncooked foods flavored with alcohol. Of course, alcohol can be hiding in a great many dishes where it hasn't been cooked at all, and is as powerful as it was in the bottle. Dips can be spiked with brandy or other spirits. So can desserts such as holiday fruitcake, hard sauce, zabaglione, baba au rhum, or berries romanoff.

Flaming dishes. Main courses and desserts that are served flaming (flambé) use alcohol to fuel their flames. Avoid them.

Extracts and flavorings. When cooking at home, use vanilla and other extracts that are made without alcohol (at 40 percent alcohol, it's like holding a hand grenade without the pin). Don't worry about eating commercial ice creams or baked goods flavored with vanilla, almond, or other nonalcoholic flavorings, or such items made by friends. The amount of alcohol in a single serving will be negligible and the taste will not be apparent at all. But avoid such foods with rum or other spirit flavors, whether or not they actually contain alcohol (many fancy cakes and gourmet ice creams do). The flavor alone can trigger a craving.

Wine vinegars. There is no alcohol in commercial vinegars—so don't worry about salad dressings in restaurants or in other people's homes, unless the vinegar is homemade. Don't keep wine vinegar at home, however. Just the look and smell of it could conjure up old feelings and lead to a craving.

Sugar-free sweeteners. The liquid extract versions of some sweeteners (such as stevia) contain alcohol. The solid versions are fine.

Nonalcoholic beverages. When counterfeit wines and beers came on the market, it seemed to be a boon to the recovery community. But they are less boon than booby trap. "Nonalcoholic" does not mean 0 percent alcohol, but rather no more than 0.5 percent. That doesn't sound like much, but it may be enough to trigger a craving.

Other products say they "contain no alcohol," and should be 100 percent alcohol-free, but they can still be a problem. Here it's the psychological feeling of drinking, of participating in a drinking lifestyle, that could put your recovery at risk. So school yourself in the recovery culture and avoid them, particularly early in your sobriety.

Likewise, avoid those fancy non-alcoholic drinks that look like margaritas or other party drinks. They, too, can trigger cravings.

Energy drinks and shots. These products contain a lot of caffeine and can give you a buzz. Avoid them.

Foods you link to drinking. If you always drank beer with your pizza, bypass the pizzeria for a while. Do the same with other foods you always had with a drink. They are as likely to trigger a craving as a sip of alcohol.

Nonstick vegetable sprays. Some of these use alcohol as a propellant, but the chemical evaporates as soon as it hits the air. Still, if just knowing there's alcohol in the can makes you edgy, look for an alcohol-free brand. There's another reason to avoid vegetable sprays—some people use aerosol sprays to get high. They inhale the fumes in a variety of ways; this is sometimes called "huffing." Use a nonspray alternative.

Mystery foods. If you are not sure what is in a packaged food or a restaurant item, do a little sleuthing. Most ingredient lists are posted online.

AVOID TEMPTATIONS AWAY FROM HOME

On the Road

Some people are at high risk of slip-ups in old familiar places, but others are more likely to be tempted when they're on the road.

On a business trip or vacation, with your support and accountability systems left behind, you can be anonymous. "No one knows me. No one will know if I have one little drink or do a few lines." Far from home and your normal routine, your safety net can fall away all too easily. Don't let this natural tendency for a bit of self-deception turn your trip into a disaster. Plan ahead.

At this early point in your recovery, when you are in the Red Zone, vacations shouldn't be a top priority. If you do take one, though, the safest options are AA group weekends or retreats. Check out the listings at the AA Grapevine magazine (aagrapevine.org/calendar) and at Sober Travelers (sobertravelers .org). Many tour companies also now offer sober tours, from cruises to camping trips. A great benefit of going to these retreats is you'll meet people in recovery from all over the country. On later travels, you'll have sober friends to look up in many places.

For people in later recovery, there are also "recovery tourism" opportunities, which combine travel and recovery service work. Some of the schools with recovery programs have study abroad programs that focus on helping alcoholics and addicts start recovery programs in other parts of the world.

Another option when you travel is to find a local group that is hosting related sober events. This can be a safer way to go to a big event like a music festival, an alumni weekend, or a business conference. For example, Queer and Sober, a group in New York City, sponsors a "3-day sober pride experience" for those coming to the city for Gay Pride weekend. At the South by Southwest Conferences and Festivals held in Austin, Texas, each year, a Safe Harbor Room is set aside every day so those in recovery can meet informally.

If you are going on a trip that is not sober-focused, travel with a recovery buddy or a friend or family member who doesn't drink or do drugs, if possible. If you have the funds, you can even hire a sober companion to go with you.

Whenever you travel, be sure to line up some meetings at your destination. You'll find a warm welcome and support at local AA and NA groups around the world. You'll even be welcomed at meetings held in languages you don't speak.

- Do you have any recovery friends in the town you're headed to? Get in touch with them before you leave, and plan to go to some meetings together.

- If you don't know anyone there, do some research beforehand. Search online for your destination plus AA, NA, Cocaine

Anonymous, or another group. Line up meetings and contacts at your destination. (See How Do I Find a Meeting?, page 160.)

- If you can't line up meetings in advance, check the phone book for Alcoholics Anonymous the moment you arrive. Waste no time; go to a meeting your first evening.

If you're going to a professional conference out of town, the organizers may have added recovery meetings to the schedule. Check the website. If no meeting has been arranged, try to set one up. Post it on the meeting site, or ask the sponsors to announce it. Post it on Twitter using the conference hashtag. All you have to say is "Any friends of Bill W. here?" or "Open 12-step meeting at . . ." You'll be amazed at the turnout.

When planning any trip, before you go make sure the activities won't revolve around drinking, and that you'll have access to alcohol-free beverages. If travel is *really* risky for you—if you have a history of impulse drinking—get a prescription for a few days of Antabuse from your doctor. It can give you an extra layer of protection.

When you've moved into the Yellow and Green Zones, later on in your recovery, you can expand your travels—go abroad, go to "civilian" resorts. But even then, be sure to line up some recovery activities at your destination *before* you get there, just to be safe.

In the Air

Flying can be really hard for some people in recovery, especially those who used to overcome their fear of flying by drinking. Planes don't have "no alcohol" sections, so it's possible that the person sitting in the very next seat will order something alcoholic. What do you do?

Ideally, fly with someone you know—someone who knows you are in recovery and will avoid drinking during the trip.

If you're flying alone and feeling vulnerable, explain your situation to the flight attendant. Ask if he can help you change your seat if anyone seated next to you orders anything stronger than tomato juice. Even on a crowded plane, where there is goodwill there is a way; swapping seats is almost always possible. If you do get stuck next to a drinker, close your eyes and meditate. Put your headphones on and zone out to music, or watch the movie. If you have Wi-Fi on the plane, email or text your sponsor or a friend for support.

If you can, carry on some soda or coffee so you have something to sip even before the beverage service starts. If you can't manage that, ask for water or coffee as early in the flight as possible. Also bring along some AA literature to read, or listen to recovery talks. A long flight is a perfect time to catch up on material.

If you worry you'll be tempted to stop at a bar on the way to the airport or inside the terminal, have a friend or your sponsor drop you off at the airport and then stay in touch with you via phone, text, or video chat until you get on your plane and the cabin door is shut.

MONEY MATTERS

Carrying a lot of cash or an ATM or debit card can be a trigger to use again. You'll need to develop a plan for managing your money. If you are in residential treatment, try to do this before you go home. Some ideas:

- Have your employer deposit your paychecks directly into your account. Don't put yourself in a position of carrying a lot of cash or a check you can quickly turn into cash.

- Make it hard to get cash. Use a bank that doesn't have many local branches and doesn't have ATMs on every corner. Make a trip across town to draw out money only as you need it.

- Even better, tell your bank you *don't* want an ATM or debit card linked to your account. If you do have a card, see if you can set a very small daily withdrawal or transaction limit. Don't carry it with you every day. Lock it away so you have to make an extra effort to get to cash, or ask someone you trust to hold on to it for you. Having a little more time to think about your actions may help you avoid making a bad decision.

- Use online bill pay to pay your bills, so you rarely have cash or checks in hand.

- Don't carry credit cards with you, either. With the advent of credit card readers that plug into phones, it's all too easy to use a card for illicit purchases, including drugs from your friendly neighborhood dealer. Also ask your credit card company to remove the cash advance option from your cards.

- You might also consider a restricted credit card. One prepaid credit card (nextstepcard .com) is designed for people in recovery. It does not allow transactions at liquor stores, bars, ATMs, and other sites. The person in charge of the card, such as a family member, can put a limited amount of funds on the card, limit the number and amount of transactions, and get text alerts when transactions occur. The card has a monthly fee, however.

- You can also set up many types of accounts to send email or text alerts whenever certain transactions are made, such as an ATM withdrawal of a certain amount, a transaction over a certain amount, or an online transaction. You can set these up so someone else is keeping an eye on your transactions, which might help you avoid temptation.

If you feel shaky about taking any financial responsibility right now, ask a trusted friend or family member to handle your funds for you, paying your bills and doling out only what you need. Your sponsor, or a banker or financial advisor in recovery, will probably be glad to help, too. Or give one of those people access to your online accounts, so they can monitor what you are spending. Of course, these approaches aren't long-term solutions, but they can help when you're in the Red Zone. Later on, you can take back control of your funds, when you are more stable. Right now, you can't afford to let down your guard. If you do, you could very quickly end up right back in the throes of addiction.

Avoid a Relapse— Deal with Cravings and Compulsions

You might do everything you can to avoid the cues and temptations to drink or use drugs, and *still* have cravings or strong compulsions.

HOW LONG DO CRAVINGS LAST?

"I haven't had a drink in two months. But not a day goes by that I don't think, 'God, I want a drink.' When will the cravings go away?"

Hard to say. It's different for each person in recovery. Some claim their cravings went away the moment they quit—almost miraculously. But for most people, the compulsion to drink or use drugs only gradually loosens its grip over the first year or so. It happens day by day. In the beginning, there may be a constant gnawing. Then cravings pop up only several times a day. Suddenly you realize you haven't had a craving in a week, or a month. Nobody continues to crave chemicals forever (though the addiction is always there).

If your cravings continue after a year of sobriety, it's time to get extra help from a counselor or doctor with addiction accreditation. You may even need to consider in- or outpatient treatment if you've never had any, or a brief booster visit if you have.

Continued cravings could also be due to concerns about whether recovery can work for you, or conflicts of a spiritual nature. You might benefit from talking with a spiritual advisor.

Living with frequent or constant cravings over a long period of time can be pretty miserable and could hinder your recovery. Worse, it could cause you to stumble down the rocky road to relapse. Read on for some tips on what to do when a craving strikes.

HOW TO KEEP CRAVINGS AND COMPULSIONS UNDER CONTROL

Cravings come from a deep, animal-like part of our brains. Unless you deal with them quickly, they can feel so strong that they overcome your memory of the wreckage that drugs or alcohol caused in your life.

As your brain heals, your cravings *will* come less often and feel less intense. For most people, they eventually go away entirely. But especially in early recovery, you may not be able to completely wipe out the last vestige of desire for your drug of choice. Over time, people in successful recovery develop their own strategies for dealing with these feelings. We've listed many of them below. The moment you feel—even fleetingly—that you want to drink or use, put one of these options to work.

- Call or text your sponsor, your counselor, your doctor, or your treatment center, and save the numbers of ten or twelve other people from your fellowship in your phone for just such an emergency. Even if you don't reach anyone, by the time you've run through your list of people the craving is likely to have eased up or gone away. If you do reach someone, share how you feel if you can, but if you can't, just talk about anything at all. Ask them not to leave you alone.

- Find a fellowship meeting and go to it. Right now. If it's the middle of the night or you can't leave the house, find an online meeting.

- Figure out what might be triggering your craving, then remove yourself from it. Do a quick inventory. Are you with friends who set off the urge? Did you drive past a favorite bar from your past, hear a song, or have another experience that launched this craving?

- Distract yourself at home. Play a video game, wash the dog, take a shower. Or leave the house and go someplace where drugs and booze are not available—a hike in the country, a movie. By the time you head home, the craving should have passed.

- Remind yourself that you are helpless against drugs (step 1). That once you start, you can't stop, and you'll be right back in that downward spiral. Reinforcing your commitment to surrender could scare off your craving. Say it out loud. Then say it again.

- Try to stay sober for just one minute. Then two minutes. Then start doing something (wash the dishes, read the newspaper), and set your alarm for five minutes. When you've managed to get through the first five minutes, try for ten. Keep increasing the time. Tell yourself you only need to focus on not drinking this minute, this hour, this day.

- Get in a quick workout. Do some push-ups or run up and down the stairs. Head to the gym or go for a run or a brisk walk.

- Pray. Ask your Higher Power to remove your craving. Recite the Serenity Prayer or another comforting prayer. Read it out loud, or stare at it. Focus on each word, one at a time.

Many successful people in recovery start their mornings by askingtheir Higher Power to relieve them of the compulsion to use and end their nights saying a thank-you for having gotten through the day without drinking or using.

- Practice visualization with the help of a recording. Promise yourself that you will not give in to your craving at least until the recording ends. If the craving is still there at the end, listen to it again.

- Meditate.

- Read the *Big Book* or other AA materials. Read the Bible, the Koran, or other religious literature, if that helps you. Watch your favorite recovery video or listen to a recorded meeting or another AA recording.

- Remind yourself that, for you, using alcohol or drugs is just not an option. Your disease has gotten to the point where a drink or a drug means instant pain and illness. Remind yourself that this disease is a fatal one. If you do slip, you could wind up dead.

- Remember the bad old days. Pull out the letter, video, or photo collection in which you described them. Look it over again. Or simply think about those days—the DUIs, the DTs, the degradation, the horror of waking up and wondering if you've hurt anyone, the hangovers, the black abyss. Just one drink or drug and you'll be headed right down that road again—only further. The pain and the consequences of drinking or drugging are worse than anything you can be feeling now.

- Remind yourself of the good things in your life. Look at a picture of someone you love. Think about your job, your family, your home, your friends. Think about how far you've come in your recovery, about how much better your body and your brain are feeling. Think about the fact that your brain is healing, even if it doesn't feel that way quite yet. Do you really want to throw it all away?

- Think about the number of days you have sober. Feel that AA attendance chip or NA key ring in your pocket. Look at your calendar of days sober. Do you really want to start all over?

- Have a snack. Have a low-calorie drink, such as juice, soda, water, milk, or decaffeinated coffee. If that doesn't work, forget the calories—better to blow your diet than your sobriety. Eat anything that satisfies you.

- Take the money you are thinking of spending on drugs and spend it on a treat for yourself, or put it in a piggy bank for a future treat. Use an online calculator or spreadsheet to remind yourself how much money you blew on alcohol or drugs in the past, or how much you stand to lose in the near future if you give in to this craving.

- Instead of thinking about drinking or drugging, think about *not* drinking or drugging. Think about all the things you can do with your life now that you are sober. Think about all the dreams you are now free to pursue.

- If you really can't stop thinking about drinking or using, think the scenario through to its likely end point. Another DUI to deal with? A couple of years in prison if you violate your parole? Think about all the dreams you now have for your life that you'll lose if you give in.

- If you want to drink or use because you're depressed or anxious, see chapter 14 for tips on dealing with these emotions. If your compulsion was triggered by a problem in your life, try to deal with it honestly instead of shoveling pills or powder onto it.

- If you're out of town when a compulsion strikes, find a meeting immediately and talk to the folks there.

- Remember, cravings and compulsions will pass. If you can hang on, they *will* go away.

HOW TO KEEP THOSE ODD COMPULSIONS UNDER CONTROL

Wanting a drink or a drug may not be the only compulsion you have in recovery. You might come up with a whole range of substitute compulsions. If you're prepared, you have a better chance of handling them.

The random compulsion. You wake up one fine Monday morning and feel a sudden burst of inspiration. You know exactly what you need to make your life complete: a motorcycle. Red. A Harley-Davidson. By the time the sleep is out of your eyes, you're on the computer, comparing prices at dealerships. If you're not careful, you could own one before noon. Instead, give your compulsion some time. Wait until Thursday and see if the need is still pressing. (It's not likely to be.) If it is, then start comparing deals. But be sure to find out not only what it will cost, what the insurance would run you, where you would keep it, how you would learn to drive it, what the risks are, and so on. Don't take any final action for at least two weeks. By then, if the urge to buy was indeed fueled by the addictive you, you'll probably have lost interest. If it's a small thing you think you must have, simply postpone the gratification for a few hours.

The repeated compulsion. You're getting addicted to food or work or video games or sex or Snickers bars,

just like you were once hooked on drugs or alcohol. It's all you think about, and it's getting in the way of having a normal life. Deal with this compulsion the same way as your chemical addiction. Recognize that you have no control or power over these habits. Seek help to deal with them—from your Higher Power, your sponsor, your counselor. Try meditation, apply the first three steps to your problem, or recite the Serenity Prayer. Find and join a 12-step program geared to this emerging new addiction. But also know what your behavior may be telling you—that you have not yet applied yourself completely and earnestly to recovery.

The dangerous compulsion. If your compulsion is hurting you or someone else (such as food binges or purging, sexual acting out, violent behavior, or gambling), get professional help right away.

////////////////////////////

"I haven't smoked meth in two months. I'm not really missing it, but I seem to be going for food with the same urgency."

Addicts and alcoholics are compulsive. Their addictions are obsessive attempts to help them get rid of bad feelings, to help them feel good inside by changing the world around them. Where other people can deal with occasional bad feelings (sorrow, anger, pain), addicts/alcoholics try to bury them with chemicals. When that escape is gone, they may turn to other "highs" to fill the hole: eating an entire pizza, nonstop shopping, video games, cleaning a house that's already spotless. The problem is that the good feeling gained this way quickly fades. Then they need to compulsively repeat their actions again. And again.

These substitute compulsions often lead right back to the original one: drinking or drugging. Or they become self-destructive themselves. Some compulsions that can turn hazardous are overeating, smoking, gambling, excessive spending, promiscuous or inappropriate sex, and overworking.

It would be nice to get rid of all destructive obsessions. It would be nice to change the addict's pattern of thinking, to help them acknowledge and accept bad feelings as normal. But this can be tough and it takes time. And, once treatment is over and outside controls relax, people in recovery often fall back into their old obsessive ways.

Finding a positive compulsion to replace the destructive one is often better for your recovery than trying to uproot all compulsive behavior down to the last twitch. Going to AA or NA meetings and working your program is one such positive compulsion. (Even if it becomes an addiction, at least it will save your life rather than take it.) Exercise is another. But don't let running, swimming, or biking grow into such an obsession that it takes over your life and distracts you from the more vital work of recovery. Like so many situations in sobriety, this is a time when you need to learn balance.

If you find yourself hobbling along on the crutch of a substitute compulsion in early recovery, ask yourself if, in the long run, you wouldn't be better off learning to deal with your feelings rather than covering them up. Get some help from your sponsor in deciding which behaviors can stay and which must go. You might also consider a higher level of care, such as seeing a counselor, increasing the number of visits with a counselor you already see, returning to inpatient treatment, or moving into a recovery residence where you'll have more support and structure.

SEXUAL COMPULSIONS

"While I was using drugs, sex was no big deal. It was a way to get drugs. Now suddenly I want to go to bed with every guy I meet."

You've probably substituted one compulsion (sex) for another (drugs). Both of them tickle that "feel-good" part of your brain. This isn't a healthy switch, though, especially with HIV, hepatitis C, and other sexually transmitted diseases still running rampant. But it is a very common one.

People who have the disease of addiction often have a hard time with relationships. They seem unable to achieve true intimacy, to communicate with loved ones much beyond a superficial level. Drugs or alcohol can camouflage these issues.

When your chemical cover-ups were removed, your need for intimacy came bounding back. Confusing *intimacy* with *intimate acts*, you are trying to satisfy your hunger for love and intimacy through sex—with different partners, over and over again. But it's not fulfilling because those hookups never give you the rewards of a genuinely loving relationship.

The compulsion may extend further, to reckless sex or even criminal forms of sex. That person wants to believe that the pleasures of sexual conquest will conquer his inner turmoil, just like those lines of coke once did. But shortly after orgasm, the feelings of worthlessness, regret, and shame are likely to return. In the end, the bad feelings are even worse.

When recovery is well under way, these compulsions tend to fade—especially when relations with one's own partner improve or when an enduring new relationship develops. If they don't, a 12-step program may help. In extreme cases, especially if your behavior could be risky, you should look into professional help.

Acting on your sexual compulsions could derail your recovery. Talk to your counselor or sponsor about this. You may feel embarrassed or awkward talking about something so personal. But an inability to open up about real feelings is a major part of why you have this problem in the first place. Talking about it may help

unblock the channels of communication and lead to your being able to enjoy what you really crave: a truly loving relationship.

I Thought I Would Be Happy by Now

WHY AM I STILL SO MISERABLE?

"I've been off oxys for two months. This time around, I feel like I finally kicked that habit, after years of being addicted. Everything should be great. So why do I feel so miserable?"

Most addicts expect their upside-down world to immediately turn right side up, but if you've been abusing oxys (or other drugs) for a while, your brain will need months or even years to set itself right. Coming to grips with the idea that sobriety is not instant heaven is an important step in recovery.

It's not surprising that you are feeling miserable. You are now suddenly out in the world without your favorite tool for coping with life, and in some ways you are at square one: no easy fix in a pill, no drug-using pals, no drug parties, no ego, no self, no nothing. You probably feel a bit like a black hole.

Now you have to find new ways of coping, and at the same time you have to start mopping up the mess you made of your life. Taking a close look at your emotions and your life as an addict won't all be fun and

The Superhuman Multitasker

You've seen him. You may even *be* him. He gets up before dawn. Before he's even out of bed, he's scanning emails and texts on his phone, sending responses to colleagues around the world. He's plowing through the news and Twitter, looking for overnight developments that could affect his company. After an early-morning workout at the gym, it's back home to get ready for work, gulping down coffee while watching the news and reading more emails. Then he's dropping the kids off at school, late again, and rushing to work, all the while checking his phone at every red light.

At work, he's a nonstop workaholic, trying to prove to everyone he's no longer an alcoholic. Every other week he flies cross-country to meet with employees, squeezing in as many meetings as possible, plus a run every morning that he's on the road. He volunteers to take on new, highly visible projects at work. Even on vacation, he can barely tear himself away from the laptop and phone. He pushes on, trying to do it all, trying to show everyone that everything is "just fine now."

But in fact, he's putting his health and his recovery at risk. Believe us when we say, "You can't do it all." Especially when you're in the Red Zone. You can't do it all without paying a high price. Exhaustion is a major risk factor for relapse. It interferes with good judgment and rational behavior. And while you might think you are just working really hard, and the boss will be impressed, you are probably exhausted.

To avoid falling into this trap, set your priorities and limit your commitments. Use shortcuts when you can: cut back on your workouts, ask your partner to take the kids to school, cut back on the business trips and make do for a while with conference calls or video meetings. Review the priorities you promised to focus on while you are in the Red Zone. Above all, keep your recovery job number one.

---

games. But if you continue to work your program and follow our suggestions, life will get better. Take it slow. Think progress, not perfection.

For the time being, don't worry about the future—how you will get through the next year, month, or week. If you can make it through until it's time to go to bed tonight, that's all you need. Just get better one day at a time.

Remember, you are still in the Red Zone, where you need to focus on saving your life. Use the tools available to you: a 12-step program; the continuing care plan you developed at treatment or on your own; an outpatient program; your sponsor, counselor, physician, or psychiatrist; others further along in recovery than you.

You might have forgotten during your years of addiction that nobody is always happy. Life is full of highs and lows, which you are just beginning to feel again. For a while during recovery they are going to be exaggerated—you'll feel *very* up or *very* down. But that will change. As you learn to cope with ordinary feelings and everyday problems, your moods will settle down.

You may also find that part of your discontent is linked to the work of recovery. You might not find it fun to go to seemingly infinite numbers of aftercare and NA meetings, or to study your recovery resources, or to meditate. You may find working your steps the hardest work you've ever done. But the person with diabetes doesn't think it's fun to inject insulin every day. Nor does the average kidney patient look forward to his regular dialysis appointment. They accept these uncomfortable treatments in order to save their lives. And that's exactly why you should faithfully follow your recovery program.

If nothing seems to help and you aren't finding any good days among the bad, get professional help.

I'M FEELING REALLY GREAT!

"Since I got out of treatment, I feel like I could kiss the world. I can't believe how good I feel."

You'd be smart not to believe it, because it's unlikely to last. You may be on top of the world today and in the pits tomorrow. Some recovering people enjoy more good days than bad, some more bad than good, but virtually all have their ups and downs.

It's not uncommon for people in recovery to feel reborn and omnipotent after a week or ten days of sobriety. If they're in treatment, they decide it's time to go home. If they've been going to AA or NA, they're ready to taper off. If they're in outpatient treatment, they start missing appointments.

Some manage to stay sober while the good feelings last. Then the moment a dark mood engulfs them, they fall off the wagon. Others, lulled by feelings of euphoria, conclude there's been some mistake and they were never addicted at all. They return to their old ways and right back into the downward spiral of their lives. Still others manage to stay sober for a while, but then they dive back into their overcommitted lives, neglect their recoveries, and end up back in trouble.

It's okay to appreciate feeling good. But it's a bad idea to read too much into it or to expect it to last forever. You need to faithfully and patiently follow your program, keep a lid on your activities and emotions, and give yourself time to heal.

WHEN THE EUPHORIA WANES

"I felt so good for the first month, so proud of myself for not doing any drugs. Now suddenly the thrill is gone. I'm so depressed."

You're right on schedule. If you kept feeling great, that would probably interfere with your recovery and keep you from looking at yourself and working your program as seriously as you need to now.

A real recovery goes beyond the first pink clouds and the novelty of being sober. Reality has its ups and downs, and as you get well it's normal to feel its variations. We all do.

You may also be reacting to being off antidepressants or other mood-altering drugs, if you stopped taking them while in treatment. That can cause anxiety, irritability, and other side effects, as well as a return of depression symptoms. Another possibility is what some call the "post-acute withdrawal syndrome," or PAWS. Some people go through a kind of mini-withdrawal about a year or more after their initial detox—complete with mood swings, emotional upheavals, insomnia, depression, cravings, and other symptoms. Doctors don't know exactly why this happens, but it's not uncommon. It's probably all part of the brain working its way back toward normal functioning.

For most people, being depressed, anxious, or confused at this stage simply serves as a reminder that you still have a way to go in recovery. Such feelings should help to point you toward further growth in sobriety—toward, for example, a couple of extra fellowship meetings. The "down" of depression is really where the no pain, no gain part of your recovery begins. Now it's time for the hard work.

If your emotions become disabling, however, or really impede you from being able to engage in your recovery program, talk to a doctor about it immediately.

UH-OH—MORE EMOTIONS CREEPING IN

Be on the lookout for any of the following feelings and attitudes. They can sometimes be as harmful to your sobriety as alcohol or drugs. If you notice one or more of them creeping into your recovery, do something about it right away. You can find out more about dealing with these issues in chapter 14.

Fear. A little fear is not only normal but healthy. Too much fear can be debilitating.

Guilt. While guilt that leads you to make amends is useful, guilt that hampers you from getting better is not.

Unrealistic expectations. Dreams and hopes are what keep us going. But expecting the impossible can leave us chronically dissatisfied.

Resentments. Clinging to anger against others for past or recent hurts doesn't harm them, but it can hurt you and your recovery. You have to learn to forgive and forget.

Low self-esteem or self-worth. If you don't feel good about yourself, if you don't feel you deserve the joy of recovery, or that you carry value into your new life, you are sure to "punish" yourself and slip back into alcoholism/addiction.

Procrastination. If you don't deal with problems promptly, they'll grow such hard shells that you may decide you need alcohol or drugs to dissolve them.

Dishonesty. Lying to yourself and to others usually becomes an entrenched trait in addiction. You lie about your drinking or drug use; about where you've been and with whom; about why you haven't met responsibilities; about your feelings and values. Dishonesty may be protective in active addiction, but it's downright harmful in recovery.

HOW CAN I EVER FORGIVE MYSELF?

"Ever since I started drinking, my father's been telling me I am bad. Now that I'm sober, I know he was right. How could I have ever done the things that I did?"

Your father was wrong. The fact that you did some bad things— maybe even a lot of them—while you were drinking doesn't mean *you* are bad. The idea that drinkers or addicts are bad people just isn't true. Yet many in recovery drown themselves in guilt.

In truth, the alcoholic/addict is no more evil than the person who has allergies and coughs during a quiet church service. They both have a disease. To understand why alcoholics do things when they are high that they would never do sober, you (and your father) have to understand the way alcohol affects the brain. Alcohol is an anesthetic to the central nervous system, which includes the brain. Even small amounts of alcohol can

impair activity in the cerebral cortex (the most sophisticated part of our brain). It can distort the workings of the part of the brain that gives us thoughts and behaviors different from those of other animals. Long before alcohol causes us to stagger or slur our speech, it has numbed the part of the brain that we use for judgment and that controls our value system, our memory, and some of our feelings and emotions. Some drugs, such as those that depress the central nervous system (sedatives, for example) work in a similar way; others somewhat differently. But all affect the brain and, thus, our behavior.

With even just a little alcohol or a single dose of a drug, we are ready to flout the law and ignore what's right and wrong. We are ready to behave in ways totally unlike our sober concepts of good and evil. What tends to come out are more primitive emotions, the kinds associated with survival, such as aggression, inappropriate sexual urges, and the fight or flight response to a perceived threat. In fact, studies show that most crime in this country, particularly violent crime, happens when people are under the influence of alcohol and other drugs—not because everyone who drinks or uses drugs is bad, but because their controls, moral and otherwise, were turned off.

As one friend said, "I didn't get into trouble every time I got high, but every time I got into trouble I had used or was drunk. Now that

I'm in recovery, I realize I might be a better person than what my behavior back then showed."

So respectfully reject your father's idea that you are inherently evil. You aren't. Do examine your life for the things you've done that you aren't proud of, that have caused others pain. As you move forward along the steps in recovery, do what you can to make amends. To be sure that you avoid causing pain in the future, never again take that first drink or drug. That's the one that will open the door to all the others and get you into trouble. Remember, one drink is too many. A thousand is not enough.

THE SIX-MONTH SNARE

"I picked up my six-month chip last night and I feel like a million bucks!"

Picking up that six-month chip is a significant "I did it!" point. It *is* an important achievement—something to be rightfully proud of. But it's no time for overconfidence.

There is strong evidence that you need to work just as hard over the next six months to solidify your recovery and take it to the next level. Those who relapse before they pick up their one-year chips usually are the ones who get complacent: they attend fewer meetings, stop working the steps, or kiss their sponsors good-bye.

You've come this far. Don't fall into the trap now of telling your Higher Power, "See you later! I've got it under control now." If you continue to work hard at your recovery during the second six months, you greatly improve your chances of long-term sobriety.

LEST YOU FORGET: REMEMBERING THE BAD OLD DAYS

We humans have a wonderful ability to block out bad memories. That ability allows a mom who has endured hours of labor to return to the delivery room two years later, ready to do it again. It allows a person who had an awful first marriage to try again with a new partner. And, unfortunately, it allows alcoholics and addicts to forget how awful things were—for themselves and everyone else—when they were drinking or using. It allows them to think, "I can control it this time."

You won't be able to control it, though. You know that now. But you might have to remind yourself of that fact once your bad memories have faded. As many in AA advise newcomers, "Remember your last time." Let your bad memories be an incentive to stay sober.

How? Capture them in words or pictures. While the images are still vivid in your mind, write yourself a letter describing the misery of your life before you became sober. Be honest, and don't spare any details.

If you have any photographs to document your words, gather them up as well. Did anyone take a photo of you passed out on the kitchen floor? Maybe they thought it was a fun party photo, perfect for Facebook. But you probably remember how awful you felt the next day when you were so hungover, not to mention how embarrassed you were that the whole world saw you like that. How about a shot of the car you totaled? Or the wife or child you screamed at? If you have a video camera or video app on your phone, record yourself telling your story. While you're talking, hold your photos up to the camera, or zoom in on them on your computer screen, and describe them. Talk about how you felt in each of those shots, and afterward. Talk about what you had to deal with after each incident (and what you might still be dealing with today, such as legal issues or a divorce or the sky-high insurance payments you now have to cover).

Now, what to do with your story? Some people like to have the "evidence" right in front of them at all times. Others prefer to tuck it away, knowing it is there if they need it. The choice is yours. Think about what would work for you, what will help you stay sober.

You might want to stick a few photos up on the fridge or inside your locker at work as ongoing reminders. Or you might tuck one in your wallet for a more discreet but handy reminder. You can file it all away in a "memories" folder on your computer or on a closet shelf. One person we know put everything on a small flash drive that he carries in his pocket. Every time he pulls out some change, the flash drive shows up in the palm of his hand. Nobody but him knows what is on it, but it

does the trick. You can also hand over your file to a trusted friend or your sponsor and ask them to show it to you if you ever seem on the brink of using again.

As some say, "If you ever forget your last drunk, you probably haven't had it."

Keep Your Life on Track

DO I HAVE TO TELL EVERYONE I'M IN RECOVERY?

"I've been on the wagon for six weeks, faithfully going to AA. But I haven't told any of my friends about this—it's very embarrassing."

Many people are embarrassed to talk about some life events—having depression, getting a divorce, losing a job. It's natural. But as millions of people have learned in all kinds of support groups, talking about our problems rather than burying them really helps.

The word "anonymous" is used so often—Alcoholics *Anonymous* and similar groups are, after all, the center of the world for most recovering people—that those in recovery sometimes take this to mean that they should keep it all a deep dark secret. That's not true.

Anonymity has long been a tradition at 12-step meetings. This is due to a couple of factors. Those who wrote the *Big Book* were all volunteers, and they were concerned they would not be able to handle the many requests for help once it was published. Later on, the request for anonymity was directed at the media—full names were not to be divulged in the press, radio, TV, or online. And, of course, AA wants newcomers to be able to come to meetings without fearing that their names will be disclosed to people outside the fellowship.

However, this does *not* mean you need to keep your recovery a secret.

First of all, there is much less stigma to being identified as an alcoholic or addict these days. Nearly everyone knows someone who is in recovery and is very open about it. Many people in recovery willingly share this information with others at some point. Even during meetings, while members use only first names to introduce themselves ("I'm Leslie, and I'm an alcoholic"), most share their identities, as well as their problems, fully and openly with other members. It's your choice. You may feel reluctant to tell people about your recovery now, but later on you may feel comfortable opening up about it.

Second, it's important to your recovery for others outside of AA to know about it. If, for example, your drinking buddies don't know you've given up alcohol, they may lead you into temptation without intending to. Telling them "I don't drink anymore" will give them a choice: They can either support your efforts or bow out of your life.

Third, being open about recovery is significant not just for you. When you let it be known at a party that you don't drink, or you talk openly about going to NA meetings, you offer support and encouragement to others who are thinking about sobriety but are afraid of taking the leap. You just might be the catalyst that gets someone else started on recovery.

CAN'T I HAVE JUST ONE?

"My husband says that he's heard that instead of abstaining completely, it's possible for an alcoholic to return to controlled drinking."

Sorry, but no. File this one under "impossible dreams."

Some drinkers are able to control their consumption for a while. They take just one drink a day for a few weeks and persuade themselves they don't have a drinking problem. Then they say, "Okay, I've proved I'm not an alcoholic. I can control my drinking if I want to. I just don't happen to want to right now." Pretty soon they are right back where they started.

Bottom line, there is no doubt that those with alcohol and drug problems who continue to drink or use will die much sooner than those who don't.

MY PROBLEM WAS PILLS, NOT ALCOHOL

"I drank for years and never had a problem with alcohol. But after I had back surgery, my doctor prescribed pain pills and I got really screwed up

with them. I've finally gotten that under control. So I should be able to drink again, right?"

No—even though every recovering addict who asks this question hopes the answer will be yes.

Many people have tested that theory before you, usually with painful results. Before they knew it, they found themselves back on their drugs, worse off than when they quit. Or they suddenly had a new problem: alcohol. Some can manage controlled drinking for a while, but usually not for long.

Those addicts can all tell you from personal experience what they learned the hard way: Switching poisons can be lethal for addicted people.

It's no better for the alcoholic who pops a few pills. Many people in AA have mistakenly believed that alcoholics can safely take mood-altering prescription drugs. And AA doesn't specifically address drugs other than alcohol. But even seemingly innocent drugs (over-the-counter cold pills, for example) can trigger relapse.

Fortunately, many people now realize that addiction is addiction is addiction—they need to be just as vigilant about drugs as they are about alcohol, and vice versa.

If you're addicted to alcohol or other drugs and value your sobriety, you need to stay away from *all* mood-altering substances, except in life-and-death situations. (Read more about this on page 290.)

LIVING IN THE REAL WORLD

"My husband always said I was irresponsible when I was drinking. I really didn't think I was that bad—I had a full-time job and was a pretty good wife and mom. But now I see a lot of responsibilities I wasn't aware of before."

Reality dawns. When an alcoholic/addict's life isn't in a shambles, sometimes it's because she managed through superhuman effort to stay responsible. But more often it's because the things she neglected were handled by someone else: a secretary who came up with excuses for missed meetings, a nurse who lied to patients about "emergencies" when the doctor didn't show up for work, a partner who took over all the child care duties.

Now that you're well, it's likely that many of those people have stopped filling in for you. Suddenly your list of tasks looms large; maybe too large for someone in early recovery. This is not the time for you to try to run the whole show. A reduced schedule at work and at home is a good idea while you get back on your feet. It also means learning to say no to other obligations that can be put off for now. Otherwise, you and your recovery could be at risk.

Gradually, as your recovery becomes more secure, you can take on all of those things again—and build the life you want.

THE RED ZONE

HANDLING PROBLEMS

"Every time I mention to my sponsor that I have a problem at home or at work, she tells me to go to an NA meeting. That seems like a crazy way to handle a problem."

Was doing drugs a saner way to handle problems? That was almost certainly your old method of handling disappointments, frustration, or anger, and almost anything would be better than that. But though more than a few NA members at first thought that going to a meeting was "a crazy way to handle a problem," most of them have found that, through some mysterious mood-changing alchemy, it works.

What else can you do to work through your problems?

- Figure out what is troubling you. Be honest. Whether it's back taxes, a court date, or a relative you're not speaking to, don't ignore it—define it. Putting it down in writing may help. When you look at it in black-and-white, it may not seem as bad as when it was swirling around inside your head.

- Talk about it. Problems we keep to ourselves seem to get bigger and more out of our control, and often eventually cause an explosion. Those that we talk about get smaller and easier to get a handle on and conquer. Talking about them safely relieves the pressure that's building up inside. You're also likely to get some new ideas, sound advice, and a new perspective on what works and what doesn't from others who have been there before you and really do know how you feel.

- Decide how you want to deal with the problem. Take a step-by-step approach. First, collect all the information you can on the subject. Next, sort out the information and write out your options, listing the risks and benefits of each, and how they will affect you and others. Then talk about your options with your sponsor and other trusted advisors. Finally, pick an option to follow, based on the information you've collected as well as on your values and goals. Carry out your decision and take responsibility for it. At this point you might be surprised—moving forward with assertive action often solves a problem more easily than you expected. And at the very least, once you've addressed an issue, it doesn't get to live rent-free in your head anymore.

- Don't put things off. Deal with problems as they come up instead of keeping them on the back burner until they boil over. This doesn't mean handling them on impulse—that's as bad as procrastinating. As has long been the case, "Think before you act" is a good motto to live by.

- Use some stress-reduction techniques to help you function more effectively (see chapter 14).

CLEAN UP YOUR ONLINE LIFE

If you're like many people, you live a good portion of your life online. You've been sharing bits of yourself on Facebook, Twitter, MySpace, Flickr, message boards, and other online venues for years. If you've been drinking and doing drugs pretty hard, some of what you and others have shared about you may be less than flattering. Now that you are entering into your life in recovery, you might want to get rid of some of that evidence of your past behavior. You also need to get rid of any photos or comments (or online friends) that could act as a trigger.

Do this cleanup for yourself so you can avoid running into reminders of your past life and can concentrate on where you are going now. Do it also so you can project a better image for future employers and others. (You might want to do some of this mop-up with your counselor or sponsor by your side; it could trigger cravings or strong emotions.)

You also might want to simply limit the time you spend on social media right now. A digital detox for a few weeks or months might help you focus better on recovery as well as make solid real-life connections with others in the recovery community (which is crucial to brain healing).

See what's out there. Do a search on your name in Google, Bing, Yahoo!, and other search engines. Put your name in quotation marks to limit results to exact matches, and try a few variations of your name. Also do a Google Image search and a Google Blog search on your name.

Check all the sites where you have a profile and where others might have posted about you, such as Facebook, Twitter, Flickr, MySpace, YouTube, Google Plus, Instagram, Tumblr, and Yahoo!. Search within those sites, and also do a Google search of them. To do a Google search of Facebook posts, for example, type "'your name' site: Facebook.com" in the search box.

Delete and clean up what you can. On your own social networking pages you can delete your own posts, photos, and videos. It might be harder to get rid of other stuff.

- Ask people who have posted about you on their pages to remove their comments and photos. If they won't delete a photo, you can usually "untag" yourself, so at least the photo won't show up in a search.

- If there are news articles, blog posts, or other mentions about your less-than-stellar history, you can politely ask for them to be removed. Not everyone will cooperate, but it's worth a try. In the long run, it's best to push them down in search results with good stuff (page 234).

- Quietly unfriend the people in your life who might post unflattering things about you, as

THE RED ZONE

well as those who have their own tainted reputations to deal with. You don't want to show up as linked to them.

Lock down your pages. You can't remove everything. But you can lock down some content.

- Change your privacy settings on sites so only select friends are allowed to see what you post.

- Limit what others can post about you. For example, in Facebook's privacy settings you can prohibit other people from tagging you in photos without your permission.

Drown out the bad old stuff with good new content. Search engines love new content, so eventually newer items about you will rise in search engine results and show up on the first pages when someone searches for you. Make sure that everything you post from now on, anywhere, reflects your new life— post only positive comments and pictures. Post enough of it, and you can drown out the old bad stuff. It will still be there, but further down in the results. (It's important, however, that you don't think of this as "rewriting the past." You can't eliminate the consequences of your past actions. This is simply focused on presenting a true picture of your life as it is now.) Some ideas:

- Delete old accounts and set up squeaky clean new profiles on Facebook, Google Plus, LinkedIn, Tumblr, Instagram, and others.

- If you used a nickname in the past and all of your online profiles use that name, delete them and start over with your full proper name, or vice versa. Go to namechk.com to see where a new username is available.

- Start a new Flickr or Google Plus photo-sharing account and add your name to all the photos you post, even those that are not photos of you. Post a picture of your dog? Add your name to it. A picture of your garden? Add your name to it.

- When you get involved in healthy activities, allow others to tag you in photos and list your name. Tag yourself in photos that others post of you. Let the good news shine through. A photo of you playing softball in a community game, helping at a church fundraiser, or volunteering at a shelter will speak volumes about your new life.

- Send news to your alumni newsletter, write a thoughtful letter to the editor about a local issue, and allow organizations to list your name online when you volunteer. All those mentions will eventually show up online.

- If you want to post comments on an online forum that you would rather others didn't see, such as a recovery discussion site, don't use your real name.

- Set up a website or blog of your own. It doesn't have to be fancy.

You can post just a few pictures and a few words about yourself. When you find other positive mentions of you, link to them from your blog. You can get a free blog at wordpress.com or blogger.com.

- Set up an account on Google and fill out your Google Plus profile. Google usually puts these on the first page of search results. Do the same with a LinkedIn account.

- Monitor your online reputation. Set up a Google Alert (google .com/alert) for your name (and all variations), and you'll be notified of any new mentions.

- Keep in mind, as you do this cleanup, that you are simply trying to present to the world an accurate picture of what you are like now—as a sober person in recovery. You should *not* be doing this as an attempt to wash away and forget all the negative consequences of your life before recovery, or to feed your ego.

An unfortunate new trend is online sites that post mug shots. They can show up even when someone has not been convicted of anything. Some of these sites say they will take them down on request, but others ask for payment. A better option is to bury your old mug shot in good content.

Bottom line, treat anything you might post online like a tattoo. Will you like it five years from now?

THIS SOBRIETY STUFF WAS NOT MY IDEA

"I was pushed into treatment and now I'm going to AA—all against my will."

You're not alone. A lot of people come into treatment with footprints on their backsides and a drink in their hands. It may be the footprint of their boss, of a family member who gave them an ultimatum, of the judge presiding over drug court, or of some life crisis.

Many of these people aren't as honest about their feelings as you are. They don't own up to the fact that it's against their will, that they don't really want to change their way of living, that they bitterly resent being forced to end their drinking days. They just go through the motions, pretending to want sobriety.

But that doesn't doom them—or you—to failure. It's said that "if you bring the body, the mind will follow." All that's necessary is to be open to change. The odds are that down deep somewhere that's what you want, or you wouldn't have gotten involved in recovery no matter what pressure you were under.

You've come this far. Give sobriety a chance. Give your brain a chance to heal. Life down the road could turn out to be a lot more enjoyable sober than you expect. Give it your best shot by learning the options available to you and working your program faithfully. And give it some time. Enough time so you're over

THE RED ZONE

the first discomforts of withdrawal and abstinence and your head has cleared. Usually this takes about a year—though it may seem like ten.

Then evaluate the situation, using your own judgment and the impressions of those around you. Is life more satisfying? Are you feeling better? Have your relationships improved? Are you doing your job better? One thing is sure: Your health will be better. And we'll bet that at some point you will be quite accepting of your sobriety, even though it began under duress.

THE DRY DRUNK

"I heard a couple of people talking about a guy being in a dry drunk. What did they mean?"

Now that you're in recovery, you'll hear the term "dry drunk" fairly often. Just what it means depends on who is using it, but there are at least two interpretations.

One is fairly obvious: the person who acts intoxicated—giggly, hysterical, uncontrollable—though he has not had a drink or used any drugs. The second type is the person who acts like an active addict—resentful, inconsiderate, not going to meetings, denying his addiction, ignoring his family—while staying sober. (You may hear the phrase "white-knuckle sobriety" to describe similar behavior.)

The dry (but unhealed) alcoholic or addict creates a need for alcohol or drugs to make his life complete, and if his attitude doesn't improve,

they'll be back in his life very soon.

If you ever find yourself in a dry drunk, immediately take steps to rev up your recovery. Double up on meetings, share your feelings, talk to your sponsor about doing more step work, and pray for relief.

If you have frequent emotional dry benders, take a good look at your recovery program. Are you doing all the things suggested for the Red Zone? Are you going to meetings, working the 12 steps, talking with your sponsor regularly? The odds are you are slipping up somewhere, and that's the reason for your behavior. Another possibility: Something is going on at home or at work that is souring your mood. If so, you may need family or other counseling in addition to your recovery work.

What If I Slip?

"I really want to stay sober, but I keep worrying that I'm going to slip and blow it."

If you're worried, you're in good shape. It's the folks who *don't* worry who are more likely to relapse.

You are still in the Red Zone. Even if you have a few months in and you're feeling pretty good, you still need to think of yourself as being in the very first stage of sobriety. You need to keep a constant vigil on your recovery. Worrying about it is okay.

To make sure you stay on your feet, work your program religiously. Heed the suggestions of your counselors, sponsor, and other advisors, and follow the recommendations in this book.

Still, you never know when a trigger will jump into your path. Have a fight with your spouse, lose a promotion at work, and suddenly you're feeling very tempted to pick up a drink.

If at any point you feel shaky and fear a slip is near, see the tips for forestalling relapse earlier in this chapter. If, in spite of all your efforts, you do relapse, don't feel it's the end of your world. Like most negative experiences in life, a relapse can have a positive side if you take the time to look for it. Examine your stumble and what led up to it with your team, and turn it into a "therapeutic slip." Learn from it, then move on in a positive manner, knowing that "I don't have to prove that again." You have the power to take what looks like failure and transform it into success: a more solid recovery next time.

///////////////////////////////

"I went to my cousin's birthday party and though I tried hard to stay away from the bar, I finally told myself I could have just one drink. Of course, I didn't have just one. I got drunk. I'm so ashamed."

Some recovering alcoholics/addicts stop drinking or using, period. They never have another drink or use another drug. But many have at least one slip. What often happens is that "sobriety lost its priority." Or SLIP. Either you stopped giving enough attention to your recovery, or you were never serious about quitting in the first place.

Though anyone can slip anytime (even with decades of sobriety), slips seem to be most common in the early months of recovery. Eventually, as the months roll by and your brain heals, your cravings will be fewer and your interest in the "old scene" will lessen.

The good news is a slip doesn't necessarily doom you to a swift downhill slide back to your pre-recovery life. In the one-day-at-a-time philosophy, slipping today doesn't automatically mean forfeiting tomorrow. Most people are resilient enough to climb back on the wagon. You probably need to adjust your program—maybe go to more meetings, meet with your sponsor more often, or go for a course of outpatient or inpatient treatment. Be sure to also read the tips on sober socializing in chapter 11—before you head to another event.

MANUFACTURING RESERVATIONS

"A speaker at last night's meeting referred to 'reservations.' What did she mean?"

A pilot likes to be sure he can safely eject if his engine conks out. A shopper buying shoes online likes to know she can return them

THE RED ZONE

if they are too tight when she tries them on. And the alcoholic/addict likes to know there's a way out if sobriety proves too tough. That's why many create "reservations" that will allow them to return to their chemicals "just in case." Some call them "escape hatches."

The kinds of reservations that signal trouble ahead include:

- Keeping a secret stash of money or a credit card—just in case you decide you need to use again.

- Failing to firmly notify your dealer that you are absolutely not interested in more drugs. Saying "Well, not right now" is a way of leaving the door ajar.

- Refusing to let anyone remove liquor, drugs, or pills from your house while you're in treatment.

- Allowing liquor to remain in your home because your spouse or someone else drinks. Ask yourself: "Am I worried about *their* not being able to take a drink—or *my* being unable to have one?" This kind of behavior shows a preoccupation with alcohol; if we don't need it, why keep the risk around? No one obsesses over whether to keep an old film camera or other obsolete tech toys around. When we are healthy we easily move on in life.

- Accepting gifts of liquor.

- Not telling the family doctor, who prescribed the pills you got addicted to, about being in recovery—just in case you need to go back to the well again.

- Planning an out-of-town trip alone or with coworkers who don't know you're in recovery and failing to line up an AA contact at your destination.

- Insisting on going to a party, wedding, or other event where you know there will be drinking—though you barely know the people involved.

- Keeping, or discreetly acquiring, a hideaway that people who are aware you're in recovery don't know about.

- Not cutting off an extramarital affair or a special friendship in which drinking or drug use played a major role.

This kind of "reservation" thinking indicates a pretty flabby commitment. You should see it as a red flag warning you how fragile your desire to stay sober really is.

If you find yourself leaving open escape routes back to your past, consciously or subconsciously, reevaluate your recovery and talk to your sponsor about what you can do to strengthen it.

First Steps: Relationships, Recreation, and Socializing in the Red Zone

///

I f you're like most alcoholics and addicts, you've left a long trail of wounded relationships behind you. Family members, friends, spouses, girlfriends, boyfriends, coworkers, neighbors—it's likely that many of them long ago reached the end of their patience and bowed out of your life, sometimes with a whole lot of sparks flying.

///

Early recovery might seem like the ideal time to pick up the pieces. It's not. The Red Zone is the time to concentrate on your recovery and nothing else. Repairing and renewing those fractured relationships (and starting new ones) is best built on a solid personal recovery; it needs to wait until you're in the Yellow Zone.

Still, you can hardly live in this world without relating to others. You can't exactly ignore everyone around you. So how do you keep old relationships from souring even further and avoid starting distracting new ones? How do you persuade others you're serious this time? How do you deal with rumors of your past behavior? How should you start relating to your partner, kids, friends, and others now that you're sober?

This chapter will help you navigate relationships in the Red Zone.

As you do, there's one crucial point to remember: You can't change other people—you can only change yourself.

Rebuilding Relationships

CONVINCING OTHERS YOU'RE SERIOUS

"I've gone to several AA meetings and haven't had a drink in three weeks. My wife says I'll soon be back at the bars, just like every other time I quit. How can I persuade her that this time I really mean it?"

You can't do it with words. Only with actions. You've lost her trust and you're not going to regain it with a kiss and a promise. You'll have to earn it.

Start by telling her you finally realize what alcohol has done to you, to her, and to the family, and that you're trying to do something to end the devastation. Ask her to judge you one day at a time. Invite her to come to an open AA meeting with you. Urge her to go to Al-Anon and to read materials for friends and family, both in the *Big Book* and in chapter 26 in this book. She needs as much support as you do right now, because she's been through so much, heard so many promises, and had her hopes shattered so many times. She may have been so thoroughly betrayed and confused by your self-serving addictive logic

and behavior that she thinks *she's* the one who's crazy.

An important lesson of recovery is to understand that you can't change how others think. You can only change yourself, and you have a wonderful opportunity now to do that. So work on changing your own attitudes. Try not to be controlling or overbearing, hostile or aggressive; don't push. Give your spouse time, distance, and space. Let her decide for herself whether this time really is different.

Whether it will be different depends on you. The AA program comes with unconditional love, but no unconditional guarantees. If you're honest, open-minded, and willing to do whatever is necessary to get well, you can greatly improve your odds of success.

///////////////////////

"How can I let my friends know that this time I'm sober for good? I know they're sick and tired of hearing me say I'm going on the wagon."

And probably even more tired of seeing you fall off. This time, don't bother to announce your intentions. Just change your behavior and take full advantage of the culture of recovery that will help make you better. Immerse yourself in your new life.

Pretty soon, your friends will notice that staying sober is as much a way of life for you as staying drunk was. But trust isn't built in a day, so although they're rooting for you, it may take a while for them to believe you're serious.

If they ask you what's happening, tell them that you're sober today, and that you're determined to stay that way for the rest of today. Be honest—that's part of your recovery—but don't preach or promise the world. Use a little humor to ease the tension; you're the one who has to set the tone for your relationships.

Some friends will ask a lot of questions and want to know all about your alcoholism. Be candid with them. Invite them to go with you to an open meeting to see for themselves. It might do them some good, too, either personally or in dealing with a family member.

For those who have little interest in the details, tell them only as much as they want to hear. In most cases, it's enough to say that you've turned over a new leaf, and you're going to do your best to stay on this new path.

You may also feel bad about the way you treated your friends in the past. But that past behavior is history now—and this is not the time to try to fix it or change it. In fact, trying to rewrite history while you're in the Red Zone could detract from what you need to do to live well in the here and now. If you are in a 12-step program, you may have noticed that the steps are in a specific order. Steps 1–7 focus on *you* (in fact, they take advantage of your self-centeredness, a trait most addicts have perfected). Further down the road, in steps 8 and 9, the focus shifts to making amends and fixing what you can of what you've done to those around you. You will have plenty of time to do this later. In the meantime, good friends will forgive you; with others, it will take time to regain their trust.

I WANT TO FIX THINGS, NOW

"I hurt so many people—my husband, my parents, my friends, my boss—when I was using meth. All I cared about was myself. I don't know how I can ever make it up to them."

First things first. Right now, your recovery comes first. This may seem selfish and self-centered, both to you and to those around you. But for now, it's the way things have to be. In the long run, self-centeredness in *getting your recovery right* will benefit not just you but everyone you know.

Ask those people to be patient a little longer. You will have plenty of time later to make amends. Right now, the best thing you can do is focus on and strengthen your recovery. It's like triage in a hospital emergency room: If the patient bleeds to death, it won't matter how well the broken leg is set, so they stop the bleeding first. In your case, stem your addiction now; deal with the other damage later.

In the meantime, watch out that your guilt over past behavior doesn't wreck your recovery by making you feel unworthy of a new and better life. Everyone who works at recovery is worthy of a good life. Including you.

///////////////////////////

"Some of the things I did when I was using drugs will haunt me all my life. The worst was when this little kid was killed. My friend was driving, but we were both high. He was arrested, but I wasn't. Still, I feel guilty."

Nothing you can do will bring that child back. Nothing you can say is likely to make his parents feel any better. The important thing now is that you concentrate on your recovery. That way you can ensure that, at the very least, you will never again be involved in such a tragedy. You can't change the past, but you can let your memory of this horrible incident help you keep your focus on recovery.

When your recovery is more solid and you are ready to make amends, you can take steps to help prevent others from making similar mistakes. Probably the best way is by telling your story, completely and honestly. You can tell it to schoolchildren, AA groups, NA groups, driver's ed classes, DUI classes, drug courts, and programs sponsored by MADD (Mothers Against Drunk Driving; madd .org) or SADD (Students Against Destructive Decisions; sadd.org). You can also share your experience in online forums. When people hear what it feels like to have a part in erasing another person's life, how

it feels to live with it for the rest of your life, they may look for help for their own addictions.

SHOULD I TELL ALL?

"While I was drinking and using I did some things that were so bad I don't even want to think about them. But now I'm trying to be honest with my mom. Should I tell her everything?"

Do you think she really wants to know everything? If it hurts you to think about some events, just imagine how she would feel hearing about it. For your mom's peace of mind as well as your own, focus on your current positive life, not the negative events of your past.

When the subject comes up, however, don't minimize or ignore past behavior. While your mom's feelings might be a reason to avoid confessing all, your own embarrassment or shame is not. Relapse feeds on secrets. It's best if you have none. You don't have to confess to your mom, but some other person should know about all of those past events (what you can remember, anyway). Your sponsor and AA or NA group can help you get it off your chest. They've all been there. (This is likely to be an ongoing process—as your brain heals, new memories will emerge.)

If your mom finds out things you'd rather she didn't, or if she finds evidence of your past on Facebook or elsewhere, consider it to be for the best. But it will be easier for her to deal with the details if she gets active in Al-Anon.

////////////////////////////

"I'm so ashamed of what I did when I was drinking. I would proposition perfect strangers at parties. I had a crush on my boss. And that's just what I remember—God knows what I did during blackouts. I keep wondering if I should tell my husband about all this now."

Honesty is important in any relationship—as long as it doesn't hurt someone. Telling your husband everything could very well hurt him, and it won't help your marriage. Odds are he has suspicions, but doesn't really want to know any more. So bury the messy debris of your past life; burn it all with your life history; and as best you can, clean up any physical or online evidence he might stumble across in the future. Instead, focus on your newfound recovery and tell your husband how he can help you through it.

Not talking about past mistakes doesn't mean you don't have to take responsibility for them, however. As you move on in recovery it will be important to work the ninth step and make amends. If you had sex with someone other than your husband while you were drinking, you might have picked up a sexually transmitted disease. See a doctor about getting tested (see chapter 13). If you get a clean bill of health, then you can forget about telling your spouse. If, on the other hand, you do have an STD, you will need to be treated and your spouse will need to be tested.

SURVIVING THE RUMOR MILL

"Hardly a day goes by that one friend or another doesn't tell me some wild story he heard about me. How can I shut down the rumor mill?"

You can't. If some of the stories are true, you can't change the facts. If some aren't true, they aren't worth your attention.

What you *can* do is act in a way that shuts down the rumor mill of the future. If you're sober and going to meetings and acting responsibly, what can they say about you?

If rumors continue to pop up, you can ask friends to help set the record straight. Have them calmly and politely tell the storyteller that you were a mess for a long time and you know it, but now you'd be grateful if they would give you a second chance.

There may be some people who insist on passing the stories around. They may be the ones who are still drinking or using drugs and don't want to see you go straight. Ignore them. Try to understand that for them, your new direction in life may feel like a threat to their continued use of alcohol or drugs. Someday they may come to you for help.

Another thing you can do to put some of those old stories to rest is to clean up your online persona. See how to do this on page 233.

FEELING ANGER TOWARD OTHERS

"I know you're supposed to get rid of your anger in recovery. But after what my parents put me through—the physical and emotional abuse from the earliest time I can remember—I don't know if I ever can."

Letting anger continue to simmer can sabotage your recovery. It can prevent your growth, boil over into a relapse, and hurt you even more.

That doesn't mean your anger isn't justified. Anyone who has been mistreated has reason to feel angry. But you can get past it. You might not be able to forgive and forget, but you can accept what happened and move on.

- Express your anger. Talk about your hurt. You might not be ready to talk to your parents about it just yet, but you can discuss it with your counselor or sponsor. It might help, too, to write a letter to your mother and father explaining your feelings. You don't have to send it; just getting it down on paper can be therapeutic.

- Examine your anger. Are you angry at your parents? Or are you angry at yourself because you think you somehow triggered their mistreatment? Many abused children feel they deserve what they get. If you do blame yourself, you need to recognize that no child ever deserves to be abused, including you. You also need to build your own sense of self-worth.

- Try meditating as a way to banish your anger, or ask your Higher Power to release you from it. Remember, as long as you retain the anger, your parents' abuse is still hurting you.

- Try to understand their behavior. Was there so much hate and anger between them that there was no room in the house for love? Could the abuse you felt have been a side effect of their own wretched relationship? When spouses constantly pick at one another, the kids are often the ones who feel the hostility and hatred. Knowing the reason doesn't make the abuse okay, but it should help you understand you were not responsible for it.

Once your recovery is more solid, you'll need to reevaluate your relationship with your parents. After what they did, you may never be able to love them with real enthusiasm again. But you may feel better if you can manage to forge some kind of peace with them.

TRYING TO BE HONEST

"Everybody at NA keeps talking about the importance of honesty in relationships. Boy, I don't know where to begin. It's been so long since I told the truth."

Dishonesty becomes a way of life for most addicts and alcoholics. They lie to themselves and they lie to others. They lie about feelings. About substance use. About money.

About where they've been and what they've been doing.

In part, lying is a way of protecting their drinking or drug use. In part it's because their minds are so messed up and their emotions so muddled, they can't even tell the difference between their lies and the truth.

Quite often, lying becomes ingrained as a coping skill that helps the addict survive. (Imagine what your dealer would have done if you honestly told him you'd smoked up all the drugs you were supposed to sell.) In fact, dishonesty can become so second nature to the addict that he will lie even when the truth would have served him better.

As you've found, the tendency to lie doesn't magically go away when you swear off drugs. It has to be unlearned. And that can be hard. You developed an innate trust in this pathological trait after it served you well in the past, and you need to move beyond that. You also need to overcome your fear that telling the truth (to a boss, a spouse, or your friends) could be disastrous. Neither of these challenges is easily met. But you can't have a good recovery otherwise.

- Start with yourself. The first person you have to start telling the truth to is you. If you don't level with yourself, you can't level with anyone else. You already took the first steps in that direction when you admitted you had a chemical dependency problem and wrote a life history or made a searching personal inventory. Keep going. It might not be easy. You may be so used to beating up on yourself that you've come to believe you have no good traits. But being honest with yourself means acknowledging your good qualities as well as the not-so-good ones.

- Tell the truth to others, even when your first instinct is to lie. It may seem hard at first, especially when you aren't used to it. But in the long run, with practice, it does get easier. And it's a relief: You don't have to keep tabs on what story you told to whom. You don't have to worry about getting caught in a lie, and you don't have to feel the guilt of deceiving someone.

- At first, others may not be ready to accept your word as gospel. Your dishonesty is something they have long known to expect. You will have to practice honesty in your relationships for a long time before others will accept it as the norm.

- The fear of telling the truth about yourself is almost always unfounded. Most people will appreciate hearing the truth. The few who do not probably have problems of their own that they aren't facing. You may be uncomfortable with a negative reaction to the truth, but that's better than not knowing how the other person feels.

- Honesty to the point of hurting others is as wrong as direct lying. "Brutal honesty" is more brutal than honest, and the motivation is often to hurt.

- No one can be perfectly honest all the time. Sometimes we really don't mean to lie to people. We unintentionally mislead them (or ourselves) about our feelings or intentions because we are really trying to please them. We can forgive ourselves for that. But we can also learn to be smarter about evaluating ourselves and others so we can avoid these situations in the future.

If you try to take these ideas to heart, but still find it very hard to stay honest, you may want to take another look at your behavior. Take a focused honesty inventory by talking with your sponsor or someone else you trust. Are you continuing to lie in early recovery? When you lie to others, you lose their trust, and you also lose their help. And without the trust and help of others, the world is a very lonely place.

Repairing the Family

REASSIGNING RESPONSIBILITIES

"I understand why my husband took over running our family—handling the finances, organizing the kids'

lives—while I was out of it and taking pills. But I'm sober now. Why can't I take those jobs back?"

That may sound reasonable to you. But it isn't. Not yet.

First of all, you need to concentrate on recovery, not on trying to juggle a lot of other stressful responsibilities. For now, consider yourself lucky that your spouse has taken over most family responsibilities; that will help secure your recovery.

Second, before you regain the right to help run the family, you have to regain trust. Every day you need to prove in little ways that you are ready for more responsibility. You can do that by staying sober, working on your recovery, and fulfilling whatever tasks you still have, even if it's just getting to work and then home on time. Many people in early recovery find that's about all they can handle anyway.

Finally, early recovery is delicate, and some people do have slips. If you had one after taking back these responsibilities, you could seriously damage the family's finances, mess up the kids' lives, take the family in the wrong direction.

So don't struggle to regain any major responsibilities until you are further along—preferably in the Yellow Zone. Then you and your spouse can start to look at your family as a joint responsibility and renegotiate the division of labor. At that point, he'll no longer feel the need to handle everything to keep the family from falling apart, and may be only too happy to have you as an equal partner again.

"I'm seventeen, and I've been sober for nearly two months. Now my parents are dumping all kinds of family jobs on me. Drive my brother here. Take my sister there. Babysit both of them. I feel so overloaded I want to scream—or worse."

You haven't had a drink or a drug in two months. You're acting pretty much like a normal person. Why shouldn't you start participating in family life like a normal person? That's how your parents see it, as do many others who live with people in recovery.

What they clearly *don't* see is that for you this is a period of recuperation. Like recovery from the flu or any other illness, getting back into full activity too soon often leads to relapse. The less stress in your life in the months ahead, the better your chances of staying engaged in a successful recovery and getting to the Yellow and Green Zones, where life is more normal. Explain that to your parents, and ask them to read chapter 26. Also have your counselor or sponsor talk with them. That should help them understand where you are now and take some of the pressure off you.

That doesn't mean you don't have to help out at home. In fact, taking on a few chores is a good idea. It will give you a sense of accomplishment, which is good for your recovery. So wash your own clothes, keep your room neat, and don't add to the clutter around the house. Offer to clean the kitchen each night after you return from your meeting. Taking on these jobs will also help ease family tension by showing others that you are indeed healing.

FEELING READY TO TAKE CONTROL AGAIN

"I'm sober now. Why can't my family just accept that and let me take back my job as head of the family? My parents moved in to help care for my kids. I'm grateful for their help, but I'm ready to be back in charge."

For years your family has been tiptoeing around you. Now you're the one who has to tread lightly. That's probably not an easy change for you to make.

People in active addiction often want to control things. They try to control their use of chemical substances, but find that hard, so they try to control everything else in their lives—including their families.

In sobriety, that urge to control often remains strong. But it's unrealistic. You can't just walk in and announce to your family that from now on you're in charge. Over time, they adjusted to getting along without you, and they will resist your interference—sometimes fiercely. Your parents, like many family members, made major changes in their own lives to keep your family together. Understandably, they may be too angry and resentful to welcome you back as dictator.

If you want to be head of the household again, you're going to have to earn it—with a long period of sobriety, and by slowly regaining everyone's trust and respect. That means that you can't tell your spouse how to spend the money or organize the house. You can't tell your mom how to handle getting the kids to school and soccer games. Nor can you dictate to your children what your relationship with them will be, who they can hang around with, or how much time they should spend at home or with you.

The alienation that came about because of your drinking or drug use isn't going to go away just because you're sober. Things will get better, but it won't be as easy as walking into a room and switching on the lights. It will be more like waiting patiently for the sun to rise in the hours before dawn. In fact, much as you'd like to rush it, the major part of rebuilding your relationships shouldn't come until later in recovery, in the Yellow and Green Zones.

In the meantime, you can take some steps to win back your family. Staying sober and in recovery is the most important by far. You also need to take small steps—every day—to nourish these relationships. You can do that by treating your loved ones with honesty, respect, consideration, and love.

Ask your spouse to watch a movie with you, or your mom if she'd like to go somewhere special for lunch. Invite your kids to go for a bike ride, or ask *them* what they'd like to do

with you. But don't be resentful if they turn you down. Just give them more time, then try again.

BUILDING BRIDGES WITH YOUR KIDS

"I've been going to AA and haven't had a drink in six weeks. My kids should be glad, but they still treat me like an ax murderer. At the same time, they keep complaining I never have time for them."

Some of the anger and confusion your children are expressing is probably related to your inattention now, since you are so focused on your recovery. A lot of it is also held over from when you were drinking.

Kids generally don't let you in on all they're really thinking. This is especially true in alcoholic/addict families. Your children developed many of their personality traits by adapting to and imitating yours. Dishonesty and deceit are things they've both experienced and been forced to practice. But stuffing or disguising all those feelings takes its toll, and the result in many children is anger, either expressed or thinly concealed.

As with everyone else in your life, earning back the respect of your kids is going to take time and plenty of good, constructive behavior. In the meantime, you should give your children, even very young ones, some explanation of what is happening.

Exactly what you say depends on their ages. A very young child needs only a brief explanation. A teenager can probably read this entire book, or at least chapter 26, which is for family members.

Above all, be honest. You can't make promises (you made and broke too many of those while you were drinking), and you can't make demands (you haven't earned that right). Below are some issues you can try to convey to them.

- Your drinking wasn't their fault. When something is wrong in a family, children tend to blame themselves. Make it clear to your children that nothing they did caused either your alcoholism or the things you did because of it.

- Alcoholism/addiction in a family member is nothing to be embarrassed by or ashamed of. It's an illness, like any other illness. People who have this illness try to make themselves feel happy by drinking liquor or taking drugs. These chemicals mix up their thinking, making them do things like fight with others, forget promises, and say mean and hurtful things. The only way they can get better is by not drinking alcohol or taking drugs. If someone they know has a chronic condition that needs ongoing care, such as diabetes, point to it as a way of explaining your own.

- It's normal to feel scared, confused, embarrassed, ashamed, angry, or guilty when a parent has this disease. The anger and disappointment they feel about you (because of broken promises, abuse, or whatever else you did) are absolutely justified.

- They are not "bad" because they are angry at (or even feel they hate) a parent who has treated them poorly. Tell them it's okay to have those feelings, and it's important to get them out in the open. Encourage them to talk about them with you, in an Alateen meeting, or with a counselor. To find an Alateen meeting, see How Do I Find a Meeting? on page 160.

- You want them to tell you how they feel—even if they feel angry. You'll do your best not to lose your temper, to give them support, and to stop and think before you react.

- For a while, recovery has to be the number one priority for your family. You are sick and you have to do a lot of things to get well, like going to AA. Ask them to understand. Tell them you hate to miss doing things with the family, like going to their basketball games or school plays. When they see you going to AA meetings instead of doing something with them, they need to remember it's just like going to the doctor's office. And it won't be forever—once your sobriety is solid you can spend more time with them. In the meantime, you promise you'll try hard to be easier to live with than you used to be.

- You want them to continue asking you to do things with them, and you will try hard to spend time with them.

- If you start drinking or using drugs again it won't be their fault—no matter what you might say under the influence. If you do start again (and you hope you never will), they shouldn't feel as though they have to lie or cover up for you to keep you out of trouble.

- If everyone tries very hard, you can all get to understand and know each other better than ever before, and the love you have can become stronger and stronger. Things won't get better overnight, but they will get better.

You do need to focus on your recovery, but make an effort to do a few special things with your kids. Come back from your AA meeting with a quart of ice cream, or play a video game together. Arrange a time every week to do something with the family. These little things can mean a lot and will help to reestablish the idea that they can count on you.

As you get more involved in your children's lives, try to make them a part of your new life, too. Invite them to open AA meetings and other recovery activities, especially those for families. Introduce them to the new people in your life and their children. Plan outings with these other people, and invite them to your home. This will help your children feel more comfortable about your rushing off to meetings every evening. Instead of feeling threatened by all this activity, they'll feel part of it. Just as important, they'll start to understand that there are many other families who have gone through the same thing, that you really do have a disease, and that drinking was not something you did to punish them. It will make it easier for them to separate you from your disease and start to believe you can get better.

A couple more things to keep in mind:

- Avoid making promises like "I know a lot of people who got better and can now do more things with their kids. Pretty soon we can do that, too." This might seem like a good approach, but it likely sounds to them like a drinking promise, the kind you've made but never kept.

- Don't fall into the trap of trying to buy forgiveness and acceptance. Plying your kids with gifts may ease your guilt, but it only trivializes the real issues that need to be addressed.

Gradually, your kids will see that your priorities have changed. If you're consistent in your behavior and love, and you stay sober, they'll likely come around eventually. Children learn to trust again more quickly than adults; they are also more forgiving. And they want to be able to love you.

MY PARENTS DON'T UNDERSTAND

"My parents are still reeling. In one week they found out that I was a drug addict, an alcoholic, and gay. Thank God, they haven't rejected me, but I don't think they've stopped crying since they heard the news."

Your parents, like the parents of any person in recovery, need to understand what is going on in your life and how they can and can't help you. The first thing they should do is go to Al-Anon meetings. That will help them understand the disease of alcoholism/addiction.

You might also suggest they get in touch with a local chapter of PFLAG—Parents, Families and Friends of Lesbians and Gays (pflag .org). This organization helps parents and others understand and accept their gay and lesbian loved ones. If they are not interested in a group like that, suggest private counseling. The counselor should be qualified in alcoholism/addiction and should also understand the LGBT community.

But more than that will be needed. You, too, will have to try to improve communications and build trust. This will be hard and may take time (even years), since trust has not been a part of your relationship for a long time. And communication has probably been almost totally disrupted—or at least reached a level so superficial as to be meaningless. Be patient with your family, if you can. They will be dealing with many of the issues that you are struggling with or have already put behind you.

Some parents are troubled by alcoholism/addiction and homosexuality on religious grounds. Whether or not they can get help from their present spiritual advisors depends on their affiliation and the individual clergyperson. In general, those who are involved in the More Light Presbyterian organization (mlp.org) or Dignity USA, a Catholic organization (dignityusa.org), as well as Reformed and Reconstructionist rabbis and organizations, can offer the most support.

Remember that your family does not have to accept your sexual orientation for you to stay sober or be happy—though it would be nice if they did. AA and NA will provide you with the support, the steps, and the tools to be okay no matter what your family does.

You will need to make amends for the *effects* of your alcoholism/addiction and the hurt that resulted. But you do not have to apologize for the illness itself. You didn't cause it. As for your sexual orientation, you have nothing to apologize for.

Issues with Your Partner

THE STRAIN OF SOBRIETY

"If I had known what a strain sobriety would be on my relationship,

I'm not sure I'd have quit drinking. My partner and I have been fighting more than ever."

Your partner, like many people, might have thought that all the alcoholic or drug user needs to do is quit drinking or using and the couple will live happily ever after. Just about every family dealing with addiction hopes this is true. You know now that it's not.

Back in your drinking days, whether you seemed to be getting along well or your relationship was clearly in trouble, there certainly were deep-seated problems. Those can't be cured just by erasing whiskey and pill bottles from the family portrait. And now, added to those old problems is a new one: men and women become different people when chemical dependency drops out of their lives.

That's why, for almost all relationships, the first year of sobriety can be painful. For some, it can mean the end of the relationship. In most cases, the best medicine is AA or another fellowship for the newly sober partner and Al-Anon for the codependents. If the problems are severe, your family might also need therapy with an addiction counselor or other qualified person.

Remember, your goal is to get closer, to share with each other. It isn't to prove who's right and who's wrong. Don't keep rehashing old or new problems. Instead, discuss an issue once—twice, at most—and then move on. Secrets, too, are a block to understanding. When you start telling each other the truth (though not truths that hurt your partner), a light goes on. Trust and new hope naturally follow.

Even if the relationship seems to be in terrible trouble during early recovery (and it often does), it's a bad idea for either partner to rush off to see a divorce lawyer unless abuse, active addiction, or other serious problems exist. As with other areas of your life, it's best to put big decisions on hold while you are in the Red Zone. Don't make any decisions about breaking up a relationship until sobriety is well established—usually by the end of the first year. If marital stress is interfering with recovery, you might try a friendly temporary separation.

With some effort, you may be able to rebuild your relationship. Most of that work, however, will have to wait until you are in the Yellow Zone. Then, working on relationships can be a safe and fruitful part of your recovery.

A SPOUSE WHO IS ALSO NEWLY SOBER

"My wife and I both recently got sober through AA. It sort of puts us in a funny spot. Do we each play both roles—recovering alcoholic and recovering spouse?"

In a sense, yes. You should both continue your AA work—most of the time going to different meetings, if you can, and once in a while going together for a more social time. When both of your recoveries are fairly stable, you can also go to some Al-Anon meetings, separately, to better understand the partner's role in addiction.

Being in recovery together is an advantage; you know what the other has been through. But there is also a disadvantage. If one of you slips, the other one might fall as well. Or if you're dealing with major money issues or other problems and you both begin to think about the "good old days," you could fall victim to romancing the drink.

So be careful to remember that the good old days really were pretty bad, most likely awful.

A SPOUSE WHO IS STILL USING

"I've been sober for three months. I thought my husband was, too. I got a real shock this morning when I borrowed his car—I found some meth in the glove box. If I hadn't had the presence of mind to flush it down the toilet, I don't know what would have happened. But what do I do now?"

You get help. Now. Call someone you trust and tell them what happened. You need to stay somewhere else as long as your husband is there. What you found could sorely test your sobriety, obviously. It could also have legal consequences that you really don't want to add to your plate. If you can, go stay with family or friends until the issue of your husband's drug use is resolved.

Once you're in safe living quarters, talk with a professional about doing an intervention with your husband. This could be someone who has been treating you or someone recommended by your sponsor or doctor. Your first goal will be to get your husband into treatment for his drug problem. If that doesn't work, you'll need to let him know you can't live with him under the circumstances.

If you value your recovery, don't agree to meet with your husband alone or to move back in with him under any circumstances. If you love him, set a good example and continue to urge him to get some help. But remember, you can't do it for him. And don't feel guilty if he doesn't. That kind of guilt can wreck your own recovery.

Be sure to read chapter 26 for more information about all of these issues.

HOME DRUG TESTING

If you are a partner in recovery and you come home late from work, you can expect doubt, dirty looks, and nasty comments. Better than inviting a suspicious mate to smell your breath ("Sure, you've switched to vodka!") or check your car for drugs is to do a quick home test for drugs and alcohol.

Over-the-counter drug tests can detect marijuana, cocaine, opioids, amphetamine, methamphetamine, Ecstasy, PCP, barbiturates, benzodiazepines, methadone, and oxycodone. Most test the urine, but some use a hair sample. Most give the results immediately—you don't need to send a sample to a lab.

Several over-the-counter alcohol testers detect alcohol on the breath. There are also some that test the saliva, such as the AlcoScreen (available at chematics.com; 800-348-5174).

You may resent having to prove you're sober, but you have to remember how many times you've angered and disappointed your spouse in the past. Until doubt moves out and trust moves back in, home drug tests can be a good ally.

BREAKING UP

"I've been in a relationship for the last few years. But now that I've been sober a few months, this guy doesn't seem right for me. He's never been violent before, but I'm a little scared about how he might react if I leave him. Should I stay put?"

No. If you are really sure the relationship has gone sour, you don't have to hang in there. Get out, and fast. Otherwise, you may find that the tension of living in a bad situation could be a risk to your recovery.

If you don't live together, breaking up will be somewhat easy. If you can simply explain to him that it's over and that is that, do so. If he doesn't agree and keeps trying to win you back, stand your ground. Write a clear, firm letter or email. Ignore phone calls, unfriend him on Facebook (and change your relationship status), and block his texts. Turn down invites to see him. Refuse to be civil. That may seem cruel, but it will probably end things faster.

If you live with him, cutting the cord may be tougher. If it's your house, tell him that he needs to move by a certain date (giving him some time to find a new place). If it's his place or you share it, you'll have to pick up and leave. If he does react badly, you may be best off just leaving as soon as you can, avoiding any altercations. If he continues to bother you, you may have to get a court order to force him to stay away. If he threatens you in any way, or is stalking you, call the police.

DOMESTIC AND DATING VIOLENCE

He swears at you. He threatens to kill your cat if you ever leave. He picks you up at work every night and never lets you go out with friends, or even talk to them on the phone. It's been so long since you've seen them, they've given up on you. Your sister begs you to leave him. "Oh, but he's never hit me," you say. "He's not that bad."

Yes, he is. Domestic violence is not just physical abuse. It also includes things like verbal abuse, keeping you from going to work or school or seeing family or friends, threats of violence, destroying your property, forcing you to have sex, threatening to expose your sexual orientation if it is not public, harming or threatening to harm your pets, and many other scenarios. (And it tends to run in families, so you might well have seen similar behavior in his relatives.) Domestic violence is *never* okay.

If you are in a relationship that includes any kind of domestic violence, you need to get some help. If it is an emergency, call 911. For help with safety planning, information, and referrals to local resources, such as shelters, that can help you get out of your situation, contact the National Domestic Violence Hotline at 800-799-SAFE (7233); TTY: 800-787-3224); email contact@thehotline.org; or visit facebook.com/NationalDomestic ViolenceHotline. The Hotline can also help people who are concerned about someone else's safety. Services are available in English and Spanish, and they have access to interpreters of more than 170 other languages. Their website also has more information, including a list of many state organizations (thehotline.org/help/resources). The Hotline's sister organization, loveisrespect.org, focuses on abuse in dating relationships. They offer help through peer advocates at 866-331-9474 (TTY: 866-331-8453), as well as live online chats (loveis respect.org/get-help/contact-us/ chat-with-us) and texting (text "loveis" to 22522).

You can also ask for help from your doctor, a local women's center, a mental health center, or the courts. If he never leaves you alone, make an appointment with your doctor and ask for help in the privacy of the exam room. Or borrow someone else's phone when you're in the ladies' room at a restaurant. Or slip a note to a friend when you are all out to dinner or at an event.

Be aware that it is very easy for someone else to monitor your computer and phone use. You may want to use a different phone or computer if you reach out for help (try a friend's phone, a computer at the library, or a phone at work or in your doctor's office). Also check your car for GPS devices; they can be used to track your whereabouts.

Sexual Intimacy

You may have heard your sex life is likely to be a mess in early recovery. Sorry to say, it's true. This section will help you and your partner understand why it seems like you're failing Sex 101, and what you can do about it.

An AA joke tells of a wife explaining why she's still a virgin after ten years of marriage to an alcoholic: "All he ever did was sit on the bed and tell me how good it was going to be." But the problems people in recovery—both men and women—have with sex are no joke. Though many think getting sober will remove all the barriers to a great sex life, they quickly find that is just wishful thinking. Just about every sexual problem—erectile dysfunction (ED), premature ejaculation, painful intercourse, lack of interest or response—is common (though not universal) in the early days.

There are many reasons why lovemaking is almost always not so great in early recovery. Some are related to the person in recovery, some to his or her partner. Read through the issues below; they can help you figure out what's going on in your bedroom—or give you an opening topic so you can discuss things with your partner, your therapist, or your doctor.

YOUR ISSUES

Many factors contribute to making men and women in early recovery less than ideal partners:

Hormone havoc. In male alcoholics, alcohol lowers levels of testosterone. At the same time, liver damage raises levels of estrogen (the feminizing hormone). As a result, men who drink heavily lose interest in sex. It's also why they sometimes develop female traits, such as breast enlargement and loss of body hair. Marijuana, because it is similar to estrogen, can also wreak havoc and cause feminization in men.

In early recovery, these symptoms can persist because the reproductive hormones have not yet returned to normal. But as hormone levels start to come back into balance (which can take a few weeks to several months), these changes taper off and sexual desire returns.

Women don't escape unscathed. As their testosterone levels slide, so does their interest in sex.

For both men and women, what starts out as a short-term physical problem can end up as a long-term psychological one, if you start to fear there is something permanently wrong with your sexuality. Patience is the best cure; your body will heal itself over time.

A battered nervous system. Alcohol damages the nervous system, including the nerves leading to and from the penis and the clitoris. With such damage (often compounded by blood flow or vascular issues), men can have trouble getting or holding an erection and women can have a hard time with orgasm. In most people, the nerve endings and blood vessels return to normal in the first six months to a year of sobriety, and erection and orgasm again are possible.

Medication. Certain drugs, such as some that treat high blood pressure and most that treat psychiatric illnesses, can interfere with sexual performance. Some can also compound the bad effects of addictive substances.

Low self-esteem. People in recovery often lack confidence and feel insecure and less in control of their lives, all of which can add to the problems of ED, lack of desire, and not-so-great sex.

Lack of practice. Many alcoholics/addicts had no sexual activity for a long time before they got sober. Many alcoholics simply couldn't perform, or their partners found them repugnant and refused them.

Losing the chemical security blanket. During active addiction, many people get used to having sex in a chemically induced haze, sometimes with anonymous partners. Some have never had sex any other way. Now they have to learn, or relearn, how to make love sober.

Bad memories. Sex under the influence was often unsatisfactory, unsavory, abusive, dull, or even disastrous. It can take a while for the act of lovemaking to be rehabilitated in your mind.

Fear of failure. If you had trouble with sex for years, you may fear the problems will continue when you are sober. This can become a self-fulfilling prophecy.

Guilt. Remorse over how you treated your partner before you got sober, or about infidelities, can make it hard to perform sexually. A poor performance then doubles the guilt, further worsening performance.

Sex-drug associations. For some people, sex is entangled with the use of cocaine or meth. They used cocaine or meth to get sex, and sex to get the drugs. Or doing drugs together was a core part of the intimate relationship. Once in recovery, just thinking about sex fires up fantasies in their minds. Since they are trying to avoid drugs, they also try to avoid sex, often subconsciously.

Self-centeredness. Some people in recovery are not ready for the unselfish giving that is needed for real sexual intimacy. In early recovery, it's often tough for them to recognize, understand, and be sympathetic to the feelings and needs of partners.

Stunted sexual development. People who started using or drinking in their teens may find that their sexual development (like other parts of their personality) got stuck in childhood or adolescent immaturity. They will have to put some effort into growing up before they'll have good sexual relationships.

A Madonna complex. A man may view his long-suffering wife as saintly—unapproachable, at least by someone as "unworthy" as he. Unable to satisfy sexual desires with his spouse, he may look for fulfillment elsewhere.

Menstrual irregularities. In early recovery, irregular periods can complicate efforts to avoid pregnancy, causing anxiety.

Painful activity. A woman who had pain during sexual activity (because of dryness or endometriosis, for example) but numbed it with alcohol or drugs may suddenly become painfully aware of the problem when she gets sober.

Menopausal changes. In older women, there may be hormonal and physical issues that arose but were masked by substance use.

Age-related changes. If both members of a couple are older and have been together and addicted for many years, they may not have had any good sex in a very long time. If they are in their forties or fifties now, sex will not be the same, even when it's good. It almost certainly will be less frequent (it takes men longer to recover between ejaculations), a man's erection may be softer (but it may last longer), and a woman's vagina, if she is postmenopausal, may be dry (lubrication will help).

Fear of passing on an STD. Many people worry they might have contracted a sexually transmitted disease during under-the-influence sex, and they worry about passing it on. Most of these infections can be easily detected and treated. With new treatments, even HIV infection has become a disease requiring ongoing care, rather than being the death sentence it once was. So it makes sense to seek medical attention quickly, rather than let the fear of a perhaps nonexistent disease ruin your pleasure.

Sexual inhibitions. Many people don't know they can talk about sex if it's a problem. Others don't want to admit failure between the sheets, or they don't know who they can talk to about it. Doctors and counselors may be uneasy about it themselves and never give patients an opening. And because these issues often are not suitable for a mixed group, no one brings them up at fellowship meetings. The result: Many suffer in silence.

YOUR PARTNER'S ISSUES

The nonaddicted partner may not be eager to jump back into a sexual relationship with the newly sober person for many reasons.

Bad memories. Making love with someone who reeks of alcohol, is high on drugs, is sloppy, or is abusive rarely leaves happy memories.

Resentment. When the alcoholic was out of it, the partner suffered, fully aware, through everything. Resentment about that can be a huge obstacle.

Lack of trust. Sex without trust is not a truly satisfying experience, and many people are not yet ready to trust their newly sober partners.

Lack of forgiveness. There may be bitterness over past affairs. Even if the partner has consciously forgiven, the body, led by the subconscious, may still register anger.

Fear of inadequacy. Many partners of those who had affairs fear they won't measure up to that sexy other woman or other man.

Misunderstanding and confusion. Lack of sex drive and interest on the part of a newly sober partner often is seen as a sign of rejection, rather than as part of the normal pattern of recovery.

IMPROVING LOVEMAKING IN RECOVERY

You could just ignore any sexual problems you're having in recovery and hope that they go away. But taking this tack could increase anxiety, damage an otherwise good relationship, or send you right back to drinking or drugging. If you don't want that to happen, take some steps to improve your sex life.

A sexual relationship is the culmination of an intimate relationship. As the personal relationship wilted during your active addiction, so did its sexual component. Depending on the problems you've had, you may find some of the following tips helpful in coaxing your relationship back into full flower. But remember, as with other parts of your life, you can't expect it all to be normal until at least the end of the first year.

Lower your sights for now. Don't expect great, or even good, sex right away. Although it's possible, the odds are against it. There is even a good chance there will be no sex at all until your recovery progresses and your relationship has time to heal. Most people are unsuccessful weeks into recovery. For many, the issues last even longer. With so many other things on your mind and so many challenges to meet in your early months of recovery, set your sights low. Don't feel you have to make love or meet any performance standards. And don't judge the rest of your relationship by the quality or quantity of your sexual encounters.

Set your sights realistically for the long run. The average couple has average sex. A few couples have fantastic sex. Some find they have little interest in sex. All these variations are normal and none prevents a couple from having a loving relationship. What's right for you is what you are comfortable with and not disappointed by.

Focus on communicating. The non-threatening kind of communication, where each partner has the freedom to express feelings without fear of being attacked. Share your feelings about lovemaking—when, where, how, and how often—openly and honestly. Talk about pain, fears, what feels good and what doesn't. Try to avoid sparring over who's right and who's wrong.

Do a little self-examination. Are you really interested in your partner's sexual pleasure, or only in your own? Sex is a way of sharing with the one you love, so share the pleasure. Self-centered sex is not only likely to be unsuccessful; it could be a warning that you aren't working hard enough at your recovery.

Get romantic. Focus on the nonsexual part of your relationship. Work on rebuilding trust and showing you care through deeds, not words. Put your focus on love, intimacy, and romance rather than physical sex acts. Renew your courtship—get to know each other again. After all, you are not the same two people you were during active addiction. Hold hands, touch, kiss, hug, cuddle, enjoy massages, pleasure each other. The rest can follow when the time is right.

Understand your partner. He or she may need as much help as you do now. While you may have had in- or outpatient therapy and have attended many AA meetings, your partner may not have had any support or professional treatment. They may still be confused about what is going on. They may feel and act as though you're still an active addict and be torn between wanting to go and wanting to stay. Al-Anon and counseling can help.

Help your partner. When people are not interested in sex, it's often because the demands of everyday life have sapped their energy: work, kids, dealing with too many emails and texts, running a house, caring for parents and pets, community work, and so on. Make sure you are holding up your end of the partnership. If you do that, you may find your partner has more energy when bedtime rolls around.

Evaluate failure. If a lovemaking jaunt goes awry, try to figure out what went wrong. Discuss the problem openly and honestly; that's often half the journey to a solution. Try to identify the problem and fix it before the next try. If the problem is that one or both of you developed poor lovemaking habits during active addiction, try to slow down and improve your technique. Read some books on sex and try some new things. Of course, in many cases the problem may be deepseated: a hurt that will simply take a long time to heal.

Accept abstinence. If neither of you feels like making love for weeks or even months, but your relationship is still getting better, don't worry about it. That's normal for some couples, especially in the Red Zone. And contrary to rumors, there are no ill effects—physical or emotional—due to sexual abstinence.

Get ready, get set. When you do feel ready to make love, set the scene with care. Be sure you are both relaxed (try relaxation exercises or meditation if it helps; see chapter 14). Get rid of distractions. Turn off the TV and the phone. If your bedroom is a warehouse for so many bad memories that either of you feels inhibited there, try another part of the house, a vacationing friend's apartment, or a night at a hotel. Put on some romantic music. If a certain type of clothing—or no clothing at all—helps, go for it. Indulge in fantasy, use some sensuous lubricants or oils, try out some new sex toys, watch a video, or read an erotic book together if it helps arouse your libido.

Have fun. Don't forget the foreplay. Kissing, caressing, and touching each other's erogenous zones will help both of you become physically and emotionally ready for more sexual activity. Sometimes foreplay alone is enough to send you to sleep with a smile on your lips. The other good stuff can come later.

Concentrate on giving. The odds of successful sex increase when each partner focuses on giving pleasure, rather than just on receiving it.

Take care of yourself. Work on your recovery. A good recovery will raise your feelings of confidence and security, which in turn will improve your prospects for good sex. Take care of your health, too. Do what you can to stick to a good diet, get plenty of exercise, set aside time to relax and meditate, and give up smoking. These can all boost energy levels and so improve sexual performance. (You will also have plenty of time later to really focus on these lifestyle changes, once you are in the Yellow and Green Zones.)

If all else fails. Sometimes couples need outside help to achieve a satisfying sexual relationship or to reconcile differences in what they want. Consider a therapist if sexual dysfunction threatens the relationship.

Look to the future. Remember that with time—and given patience, love, and care—sex often becomes more satisfying with sobriety than it ever was before.

What About a New Relationship?

"I feel like I'm starting a new life now that I'm sober. I want to find someone nice to share it with, to support me in my sobriety. Should I start looking around?"

That wouldn't be quite as risky as looking around for your old drug dealer, but it's still a bad idea. Most recovery experts suggest you don't start any new romantic relationships in the first year. A new relationship takes time and energy, both of which you need to devote to staying sober. So resist early emotional entanglements as you would an alluring hotel bar. And keep the following in mind:

- People who are in the Red Zone of recovery are often so needy they're likely to feel that *anyone* who smiles at them is Ms. or Mr. Right. Your judgment right now is not stable enough to make important decisions.

- Sobriety is very fragile in the first year. Most people are better off without the stress, disappointments, and upsets that can go along with a new relationship. Focus on your recovery now and do the work that will help you move into later zones of recovery; you will be rewarded with a life you never thought possible, possibly including a fabulous new partner.

- You'll be a poor partner in any relationship until you have value yourself. Addiction freezes personality development. If you started drinking or using in your teens, you may be socially and emotionally still a teenager, no matter what age you are now. Spend the first year of recovery maturing and building your interpersonal skills.

- There is a tendency in any relationship to lean on the other person. This can give you a false sense of strength, which at this early stage could be a fatal weakness. The minute alcoholics/addicts feel powerful, they figure alcohol and drugs can't get them into trouble. And *poof!* The genie of denial pops out of the bottle and takes charge. Again.

- Though we don't often notice it at the time, many relationships in early recovery are largely selfish. Deprived of our chemicals, we are looking for other ways to feel good or worthy, and the applause of an old friend provides that. But as with drugs, this kind of dependent relationship can backfire. It says to you: "You are incompetent; you can't feel good or worthy on your own. Someone else must run your life for you." It's just trading one kind of bondage for another.

- Any heavy relationship in early recovery—even a nonsexual one—in which you let your security get caught up with another person can put your recovery at risk. Should the other person flounder or fail in some way, you may, too.

All this doesn't mean you're doomed to a year or more of monkish solitude. There's a relationship continuum that starts with shy glances and ends in commitment. Until your recovery is more solid, you've got to stop somewhere in the middle. Start getting to know new people. Talking with others at meetings or over coffee is okay. Going out in groups is, too. It's good

to build a network of people who nourish your recovery. But there's an invisible line (which you can usually sense) past which a relationship turns more intimate and more dependent, and that's where it can ultimately become destructive. For now, keep your focus on friendships that have no potential for intimacy.

There are some red flags that should tell you to hit the brakes on a budding relationship:

- You're spending more time with this person than with anyone else.

- You begin to have sexual fantasies about him or her.

- You place this person on an emotional pedestal.

- You exchange gifts or favors, or intimate texts or emails.

- The relationship lures you away from recovery activities.

- The relationship becomes a substitute compulsion.

Many people assume that although other liaisons are taboo, a relationship with someone in your support network is a good bet. Sorry, but no. You are still likely to focus your energies and attention on the object of your affection rather than on your recovery.

Of course, you might meet someone and, without trying, believe you've fallen in love. You can't change the way you feel. But you don't have to *act* on those feelings. Don't trade short-term good feelings for long-term serenity and happiness, as you have in the past. If this is the real thing, it will still be real after you've moved into the Yellow Zone.

Sober Socializing

YOU WILL HAVE FUN AGAIN

"I'm twenty-two and fresh out of treatment after eight years of drinking and drugs. I'm glad I'm sober, but I'm pretty depressed, too, when I think that there's going to be no more fun—no more parties in my life."

What will really be missing from your life is the DUIs, trips to seedy neighborhoods, hangovers, cold sweats, and blackouts.

You *will* have plenty of opportunities for fun down the road, with friends who truly care about you. It may not seem that way at first, as you struggle with staying sober. But it will happen. Many people, in fact, report that their social lives really didn't take off *until* they got sober. Most people in this world do not misuse alcohol or take drugs. And sober, nonusing people have plenty of fun.

You've probably already noticed at AA, NA, or other recovery meetings that the folks solidly into recovery seem to be having a great time. If you think about it, it may strike you that they aren't so different from your old drugging and drinking pals. And you'd be right. They

are the same kinds of people—gone sober. At the beginning of their recovery, they spent most of the time they used to spend drinking and drugging at meetings instead. But they soon added other activities. In time, you'll do the same.

The fact is, there are many more fun things you can do when you're sober, compared to when you're not. Most people who drink and take drugs spend all their time feeding their habits, with little time for anything else. True, you remember the good times rolling at parties and bars (though you may have blocked out what really happened). But do you remember doing anything *else* in your life that was fun?

You can still go to parties. But now you'll choose parties with no alcohol or drugs. You'll enjoy activities you never had the patience for before, like movies or plays. As your recovery gets stronger, you'll have fun doing things you didn't have the stamina or coordination for, like swimming, running, playing basketball, or hiking. And you'll be able to do things you couldn't sit still for, like reading, video games, crossword puzzles, painting, photography, or playing an instrument. In fact, you will probably find lots of people in recovery fellowships getting together to do many of these activities.

Once you are in the Yellow Zone, with your sobriety well under way, you can expand your recreational outings even more. You'll be free to do things that would have been downright dangerous when you

THE RED ZONE

weren't sober—skiing, playing ice hockey, horseback riding, mountain biking, whitewater rafting. (It's not a good idea to try these high-exhilaration activities early in recovery, since they can cause an adrenaline rush that could lead to a compulsion to drink or use.) And later you'll be fit to confront the ultimate danger: going to parties and places where alcohol is served.

Vacations can still be fun as well. While it's best to wait until the Yellow Zone before heading off on a trip, there are many options for sober travel. At first, you can arrange yours around AA-focused retreats, and you'll find compatible people and plenty of fun in safe surroundings.

Soon you'll find enjoyment in the most mundane activities—taking a course, talking with a friend, spending time with your family, watching newcomers to AA turn the corner, earning your first-year chip. Even watching the flowers grow in spring and the leaves change color in the fall—things that passed you by when you were drinking or using—will give you a high.

"Since getting sober, my social life has ceased to exist. In our town, all the gay socializing is in bars."

This can be an issue in some small towns, and one that isn't easily solved.

Going to a bar is obviously too dangerous for you now; you could be tempted to drink as soon as you walked in the door. Even if you resisted drinking for a while, the people you meet at a bar are probably going to be drinkers, and starting friendships with them could lead you back to drinking eventually.

Of course, going to a bar can also lead to more than drinking—it can lead to emotional relationships and sex. Your first year or two of recovery is not a time for new emotional relationships. At a time when your life is in shambles, you may be tempted to use the sexual element of a relationship to control others and to escape from your own feelings. That isn't healthy. It can interfere with your recovery and also be damaging to partners.

If you belong to an LGBT-focused recovery group, or a group with several LGBT members, ask how they handle this issue.

One solution could be to establish a social group with friends from AA—in a restaurant or club room somewhere. You can have music, dancing, everything a bar usually has, minus the booze. You might also organize some non-bar-focused activities with others you meet in recovery—LGBT or straight. Start a restaurant club, go skiing, or try some of the other activities listed above. Check out some local Meetup groups (meetup.com) that focus on an activity you enjoy; you may find some new friends that way. (Remember, your goal for now is to build relationships that are not based on sexual attraction.)

GET READY FOR SOBER SOCIALIZING

How do you handle parties, business dinners, and other occasions where you previously drank, and where just about everyone else still does? Ideally, just avoid them early in your recovery. Sometimes, of course, that's impossible. You may have no choice but to attend your brother's wedding or your boss's party. If that's the case, these tips will help you get home sober:

Evaluate your motivation. Why do you want to go? The experienced alcoholic usually has a credible motive or two up his or her sleeve: "I love to dance." Or "People will be insulted if I don't show up." Or "It's important for business." Evaluate those reasons. Are they honest? Or deep down do you still fantasize about the good old lifestyle, still long for the good old drinking and drugging days?

Alcoholics often insist the only reason they go to clubs is because they love to dance. But once there, they do very little dancing and a whole lot of sitting at the bar. So forget the rationalizations, and avoid wet events unless you have strong reasons that have nothing to do with drinking.

Evaluate your feelings. Do you feel nervous when alcohol in any form is around? That's an okay feeling, and maybe for the time being you should beg off all wet parties. But be even more wary if you feel the bravado of the alcoholic. "Hey, I can handle it!" are some famous last words in the recovery world. You're safest not accepting an invitation if you still feel just a bit hesitant.

Forewarn your hosts. If they're not already aware, let them know in advance that you don't drink alcohol. That way you can be pretty sure there will be some risk-free alternatives. It's not a good idea to attend any event at which there are no options other than alcohol or water.

Forearm yourself. Decide in advance that there's no way in the world that you will drink or use drugs at the event. Ask for help from your Higher Power, because you may need it. Go to a few extra meetings in the days before the event. Know and rehearse exactly what you will say if someone asks "Would you like a drink?" or "Want to do a line in the bathroom?"

Don't go it alone. Think of yourself as swimming in deep swift waters, and take an AA buddy or a hired sober companion. If that's not an option, take someone at the party into your confidence (the host, a good friend, or even a waiter), keeping in mind that candor will serve you better than pride, embarrassment, or guilt. Tell them that you can't drink, and enlist them as bodyguard. It will make the event easier for you and could keep you from winding up in a relapse.

Don't go late. You're safest arriving early, before everyone is cheerfully high or roaring drunk and you're sucked into the maelstrom.

Serve yourself. If you can, bring your own water bottle or glass full of soda, so you don't even have to go near the bar. If you don't bring your own, head straight to the liquid refreshments when you arrive and help yourself to a safe option, such as sparkling water. (If you choose a Virgin Mary or rumless piña colada, examine your motives. Is this your choice because it's alcohol-free or because it's the closest thing to a familiar friend? It's safer to switch to something without even a faint resemblance to your old "usual"). Keep a beverage in your hand for the rest of your time at the party, and refill it as needed. That way you won't have to keep turning down offers of something more to drink.

But if you set your drink down while you're dancing or when you step into the bathroom, get a new one when you return. Don't take a chance on anyone having accidentally switched drinks or good-naturedly topped yours off, or even worse, slipped a drug such as Rohypnol (the "rape drug") into it.

If you can't serve yourself, just make it clear that you prefer your alcohol-free option. Nine out of ten people will serve you without blinking. The tenth person, of course, will be one with a problem of his or her own. Move on with a "No, thank you" when you hear "Oh, come on. Just one. To drink to the . . ." If you do drink a toast, you can drink it every bit as sincerely with your soda.

Don't be a barfly. Once you have your beverage, put plenty of space between yourself and the bar. Dance, circulate, or sit and chat. Keep a safe distance from the source, and give your sobriety some elbow room.

Curb resentment. You're almost sure to run into someone who'll say with a smile, "Do you mind if *I* have a drink?" Your automatic answer will most likely be "Oh, no, I don't mind." The truth is you probably do resent it. You're as good as the other guy. If he can drink, why can't you? (Maybe he's got genes that allow him to drink and you don't—a small point it would be rash to ignore.) If you feel resentment building, make your excuses and find your sober buddy, slip out to a meeting, or head to the hallway and call or text your sponsor. Whip out your phone or tablet for a quick check-in with a recovery app or a mobile meeting. Or head home and go to an online meeting (they can be lifesavers in the middle of the night).

Be ready to leave. Keep your car keys or taxi fare in your pocket. Should drugs appear, or should you suddenly feel overwhelmed by temptation, leave immediately. Do not try to test yourself. It's too soon. In the Red Zone, you are not ready to test your willpower.

Beware of hidden trouble. If food is served, be sure it won't sabotage your recovery with hidden alcoholic ingredients (see page 212).

Don't linger. Let the host know you won't be able to stay longer than a half hour or so. The more tired you are, the more vulnerable you become. (Once you're more secure in your sobriety, you won't have to check out that soon.)

Take inventory the next day. When you're in the Red Zone, the day after you go to an event with alcohol you may well fall into self-pity mode. "Why can't I have fun like those other people?" Don't let those feelings and ideas simmer. If they do, they can push you right over the edge into a relapse. Immediately after you go to one of these "must-attend" events, plug into your recovery program. Call or text your sponsor, double up on meetings, and read your literature. Be honest about any feelings that arose from being around the drinking/using scene.

TAKE A BUDDY ALONG

Just as you shouldn't swim in deep water without a buddy, as an addict in early recovery you should not wander alone. Whether it's an NA meeting, a wedding, your mom's birthday party, or just a walk past your old happy hunting grounds (bar, liquor store, drug corner), don't do it solo. Go with a buddy.

Your buddy can be a spouse or partner. It can be your sponsor or someone from your sober-living house. Look for people in your fellowship who have similar interests and whose social networks fit with yours, so you can do things together.

Spending time with others in recovery also means less time to wander off on dangerous tangents by yourself. It also gives you the chance to build some strong friendships.

BEING ALONE AND NOT LONELY

"I'm fine when I'm at a meeting or having coffee with friends. I'm even okay at work. It's just when I go home and have to be with myself that I feel like I want to climb the walls—or get high. I can't even go online for a little chat with others. All of my 'friends' were users, so I had to delete my accounts."

Many people never learn to enjoy their own company. From the time they're babies, someone's been there to entertain them. When they find themselves alone as adults, they are jumpy and anxious—especially if they haven't learned to like themselves. Alcoholics/addicts use chemicals to try to transform themselves into better company. Once the chemicals are gone, they're back to feeling lonesome.

But why feel lonely? You can be good company for yourself.

Get loose. Learn relaxation techniques, such as the ones in chapter 14, to make it easier to enjoy your solitude. Prayer and meditation have a similar effect, and they help you get in touch with yourself, which is necessary if you are to become a good companion.

Get busy. Take up a serenely solo hobby, such as reading, knitting, or woodworking—anything that will occupy you when you are alone (but nothing that will keep you from doing recovery work). The time you spend alone will pass more quickly and pleasantly, and mastering a hobby can give you a nice sense of achievement.

Get physical. Set up an exercise program at home or at the gym, or start running in the park. Sign up for a yoga class. The activity will keep you happily busy and will also pump endorphins through your brain and lift your mood.

Get educated. Increase your self-awareness by reading the *Big Book* and other recovery materials, and by listening to or watching recordings on recovery. At first this may make you a little less comfortable with yourself, but in the long run, as you realize how much you've got going for you, it will become a recovery plus.

Get serious. Take an inventory or work on your journal; this is solitary but important work.

Get out. Limit your time alone to a minimum until you are further along in recovery. Plan more activities with others from your group or groups. Sign up for some activities (like ski trips, hikes, or movie nights) with a local recovery-oriented program.

Get connected. Before the loneliness gets to be too much, phone or text your sponsor or another AA friend. Connect with others in recovery in online groups (see page 161). Start a new Facebook account, and connect with others in recovery.

THE HOLIDAY BLUES

For recovering people (and millions of others), holidays can be times of tension, sadness, and depression. They are also a time when temptations to jump off the wagon seem to multiply. The following tips can help you beat back the blues:

- Keep your expectations realistic, so you don't set yourself up for an emotional letdown. Being sober doesn't mean your life will suddenly be a piece of cake. Other people in your life probably haven't changed, and many of the conflicts that cropped up at family reunions will doubtless crop up again. Accept it, roll with the punches (and away from the rum punch), and rein in the urge to control everything. It will be enough to just take care of yourself.

- Limit the amount of time you spend with relatives who make you crazy. If the clan is gathering for a holiday, including your brother who drinks like a fish, plan on an overlap of just a day or two while he's there. (If he's arriving on Christmas Day and staying the week, you can arrive a couple of days before Christmas, help your parents prepare, enjoy a quiet Christmas Eve, and leave the next day.)

- If the holidays mean being away from your home group, plan to attend meetings wherever you are. Find a meeting before you get there. This will give you a nice booster shot of support. You'll have a chance to say, "Sure, I love my family, but sometimes they drive me up the wall" or talk about whatever it is that almost drives you to drink.

- Plan activities that will make for pleasant memories. Try to avoid just sitting around and gabbing—which in many families means sitting around and drinking. Movies, museums, holiday concerts, skating, skiing, long walks, sledding with the kids, snowball fights, a workout at the gym, sports, and religious services can all help fill the time with fun and limit stress. If the weather keeps you inside and you want to keep the conversation from getting out of hand, try some activities that will keep everyone busy, such as baking and decorating cookies, playing board games or video games, having a dance contest with the kids, or watching old movies.

- If the holidays mean visiting your old hometown, take time to see old friends whose company you enjoy. Avoid those you used to drink or get high with.

- Get plenty of rest, watch what you eat, and get your usual exercise. Take time for meditation. Find a little slice of solitude where you can, as a haven for self-care—even if you have to go sit in the car for a half hour with your mittens on. Keep up your recovery routine as much as you can.

- If the celebration includes alcohol (such as wine at Passover), make sure in advance that substitutes are available.

- If you aren't going home for the holidays, plan to celebrate with AA or NA friends. If you haven't been invited anywhere, do the inviting yourself. Follow your old family traditions or start some of your own.

- During winter holidays, make sure there is plenty of light in your life. Keep the lights bright at home, try to get outside when the sun is shining, or light a cheery fire in the fireplace. Winter solstice darkness and drabness can be psychologically (and physiologically) depressing.

CHAPTER

First Steps: Education, Work, and Finances in the Red Zone

W hen you get sober, you'll look at your life through different eyes. You might regret having dropped out of school before getting your degree. You might find you like your job better than you thought you did—or a lot less. Maybe you'll figure it's time for a change of career.

You might also realize that you didn't cover up your "problem" nearly as well as you thought. Maybe your employer doesn't want you to come back to work, or you now see that a boss who pushed you to get treatment really was a good guy after all.

As we've said before, while you're in the Red Zone, try to put off making any big moves in your work or school life; wait until you're in the Yellow Zone to take on those areas.

You need to build a solid recovery first.

Of course, most of us can't afford to avoid those issues forever. And for many people, work also provides important structure and support. This chapter will help you learn how to juggle work and recovery in the Red Zone without dropping either ball. It will also help you to start getting your financial house in order. As always, honesty will be your most important tool.

Your Professional Life

SHOULD I GO BACK TO SCHOOL NOW?

"I just got out of treatment and they say I'm ready to go back to work. I never really liked my job, though. It seems to me it's time for a change. I think I'll go back to college instead."

Making significant changes of any kind in the Red Zone—a career change, a relationship change, a location change—can put your recovery at risk. So while your ambition is laudable, now is *not* the time to go back to college.

Near the end of your first year of sobriety, when your recovery is more solid, you can think about a change. Then you can start to explore going back to school, applying for education loans, maybe moving to a campus. Be sure to read in chapter 10 about recovery campuses.

If your employer welcomes you back to your old job, consider yourself lucky. Plant yourself there for the next year or so while you focus on recovery. Even if you don't like it, stick it out. Looking for a new job now would mean a lot of stress and anxiety, which could make it hard to stay sober. And learning the ropes at a new job would almost surely turn your energy and focus away from recovery, where it needs to be.

You might decide later on that you don't want to make a change after all. Feelings you remember now as job dissatisfaction may really have been job scapegoating. Think about it: You didn't want to be there—you wanted to be out drinking or drugging. It's likely some of your coworkers didn't want you there either, because of frictions due to your addiction. But you're a very different person now. You may find the job is different, too. Or you might find that you'd like to hang on to that job and take classes in the evenings.

Of course, if you return to the job and find you're still unhappy with it, and your discomfort is strong enough that it could put your recovery at risk, then you might have to look for a new job. Talk about it with your counselor or sponsor.

A NON-PRESSURED JOB MIGHT BE BEST

"I started drinking in college and barely managed to graduate. I've been sober for almost a year, and I'm working as a dishwasher. This makes my parents crazy. But for the moment, I'm happy with this low-pressure work."

Mom and Dad don't always know best. In this case, you're absolutely right to stick for a while to a job where the demands on you are minimal. This allows you to put your focus where it belongs: on recovery. When your recovery is more stable, you can start thinking about moving on. At that time, with a clearer head, you're likely to have some good ideas about careers you might want to explore. If your folks have trouble understanding this, ask them to read chapter 26.

MAKING A FRESH START

"I've been through treatment, and now I'm ready to go back to work. Things were very sticky before I left. My boss said it was treatment . . . or else. If I mess up now, I'm history."

You're lucky to have a boss who cared enough about you, as a person and as an employee, to push you into treatment—and, on top of that, to welcome you back.

Now it's your turn to show those you work for (and with) that they're lucky to have someone as reliable and productive as you on the payroll. A lot will depend on keeping your priorities straight and on avoiding possible pitfalls.

- Prove you're serious about sobriety by staying sober.

- Be sensitive to your coworkers. Steamrolling in and trying to make up for all those lost days is admirable—but not if you step on a lot of people's toes in the process. Think how *you* would like a returning coworker in recovery to act. Then, do likewise.

- If any of your colleagues were covering for you while you were addicted, they may now be a little put out to find that this part of their job has been wiped out. Be sensitive to their situation.

- Don't try to run the show. Most alcoholics/addicts in the Red Zone still feel a need to control things. In most cases, your coworkers won't be any more willing to put you in charge now than your family is.

- Toe the line. Chances are your work history includes frequent absences, missed deadlines, and forgotten meetings. Most of us can get away with dropping the ball once in a while, but you don't have that luxury. If you oversleep and come in late just once, everyone will assume you were out on a binge. Don't stress over it. Maybe everybody *is* watching you, but they have reason to distrust you. Now quietly go and earn their trust.

- Think about setting up a continuing care work plan with your employer (see page 277). If your company has an Employee Assistance Program, ask the staff there for advice on making the transition back to work.

- Honesty in all things is very important, and that also applies to your workplace. If you do your job well and stay sober, you shouldn't have any reason to lie on the job. But if, say, you find you won't be able to complete a task on schedule, you need to tell the truth. Lying to anyone, even to keep a job, could jeopardize your long-term recovery.

- One side effect of your treatment you might not have expected:

The skills and strengths you are developing in recovery will also help you at work. You will know more about how to interact well with coworkers. You will be better able to focus, set priorities, and complete projects.

WHAT DO I TELL MY COWORKERS?

"I've been away from my office for six months, going through treatment and then a stint at a sober-living house. I'm very nervous about going back, mostly because I haven't been in touch with any of the people I work with. I don't know what they know about my absence, or at this point how much I should tell them."

Ideally, it's best to take one or two respected coworkers into your confidence before you leave for residential treatment. With them you can discuss how and when others at work will be told what is going on in your life. They will feel like partners in your decision, and can support you while you're away by squashing wild rumors before they start to fly.

If that didn't happen, the first thing you need to do now is set the record straight. It's likely that rumors flew while you were gone, and also that some coworkers were talking about your situation because they truly care about your well-being. If your company has an Employee Assistance Program, ask a counselor what might be your best way to approach your coworkers. If there is no such program, arrange to have lunch with a coworker whom you like and whom others respect. Here are some ideas for what to say:

- Explain exactly what has been going on—treatment, sober living, and so on—and how long you've been sober.

- Make it clear that you'll be staying sober from now on, one day at a time.

- Point out that you'll work hard to prove you're serious about sobriety this time.

- Also point out that, just as if you were recovering from a heart attack, you still need time to recover from your illness. For now, you won't be able to put in lots of extra hours on the job. You won't fall down on the job, but for now your most important job is solidifying your recovery.

- Admit honestly that you know you've let them down in the past, if this is the case.

- Explain that their support and patience now will be a big help to you.

Ask this friend to get the word around to others at the office so that you won't have to explain one on one to everyone. Of course, if someone asks, feel free to talk about your recovery. You'll find that those who ask the most questions often have drinking or drug problems of their own or in their families. Your success could guide them to the help they need. And that will feel pretty good.

"I've heard conflicting advice on whether or not to tell the folks you work with that you've been out because of an addiction problem."

As with so many issues, there is more than one point of view. Some counselors say keep your business to yourself. Keeping quiet may work for some people, but there are several problems with this approach.

- Avoiding the truth gives you an out, a way to sneak back to using. "If no one knows I've been to treatment, they won't notice if I have a drink."

- Avoiding the truth leaves you much more exposed to temptation. If your coworkers aren't aware of your problem, they won't know it could be harmful to urge you to join them at the local pub after work.

- Lying has a way of catching up with people. This is a time for you to rebuild trust. What if you say you were out with some vague complaint, and later the truth comes out? How will you look to others then? This doesn't mean you have to announce your condition with a company-wide email, or that you need to "confess" to every client. But should people ask where you have been, an honest answer is best.

Since you are probably going back to a workplace where you were often drunk or high and operating at less than your best, think ahead of time about how you'll respond to people there. You might be embarrassed to face them. You might all be uncomfortable. One approach that can help is to acknowledge the issue, defuse any anger, and give them some "ownership." Try responding to pointed comments with something like: "Yeah, I can't believe I did that either. Can you help me to not dig an even deeper hole for myself now?" They may very well respond with kindness and concern.

WORRIED ABOUT OVERDOING IT

"I've been back at work for three months. I've been working night and day to prove that I'm not the drunk that I used to be, that I can do as good a job as anyone. But my sponsor says I'm doing too much, and I should slow down. I don't see why."

If you weren't so busy at work, you'd quickly see the wisdom of what your sponsor is saying. You would have time to look at your life and realize that spending so much of your day buried in your job is taking time away from your recovery work. It is also—as you transform yourself from alcoholic to workaholic—building up more stress than you may be able to handle.

So let a more experienced person guide you. Listen to your sponsor and slow down for a while. Get through the Red Zone of recovery before picking up the pace at work.

CAN I WORK WITHOUT CHEMICAL HELP?

"I always needed something to get me to work in the morning, then something more at noon to get me through the rest of the day. I'm about to go back to work, and I don't know how I'll get through the day."

Now that you are in recovery, you are better able to handle the tensions and stress of your job, compared to when you jump-started your motor with chemicals. That doesn't mean that it will be easy.

These tips may help:

- Don't try to be a superhero. Remember your new mantra: "Nobody's perfect—not even me." Don't try to make up for lost years in a day or a week. And don't take on more than is practical while you're in early recovery. Setting your expectations (and everybody else's) too high will make it impossible for you to live up to them.

- Base your approach to work, as well as to everything else, on moderation. Rebuild your work life slowly, one day at a time. Tackle a single task, complete it, then move on. Do it again. That will send an important message to your coworkers: You can be relied on.

- When you start to feel tense or uneasy at work, take a few moments to meditate (see

chapter 14). If that isn't enough, call or text your sponsor or another AA friend. Or stop in to see the Employee Assistance Program person. Find a fellowship meeting to go to at lunch or after work.

- If you're in a highly skilled profession, find out if there is a local AA or NA group made up of your peers— doctors, lawyers, pilots, engineers, or nurses, for example. Taking part in such a group can offer support not just for recovery, but for revamping your work life as well. It will give you a chance to discuss issues related to your job (such as dispensing drugs if you're a nurse). If you work for a large company, seek out others with similar jobs who are also recovering. Some large companies and government agencies are supportive enough to have on-site meetings.

FEELING RAILROADED

"A friend of mine went into treatment about when I did. He did it voluntarily, and it seems nobody at work bothers him. My boss reported me to the company EAP and I was railroaded into treatment. Now they never take their eyes off me."

It might not seem fair, but this is actually a good thing for you. In reality, the guy who did it on his own may be more likely to relapse than you are, because his recovery program is not getting the scrutiny yours is. If someone had taken more notice of his substance abuse (and his slipping job performance) and reported it, he would have had closer monitoring—and a better chance of a successful recovery. That's what you are getting, even if it doesn't feel so great right now.

In general, alcoholics and addicts whose jobs are on the line if they fail to stay sober have a much better rate of recovery. That's because they're painfully aware of what they will lose if they fail, and also because they are more closely supervised by the EAP. So getting help in the workplace means added incentives to work hard for recovery, as well as more accountability. The guy who sends himself to treatment may dictate his own treatment terms, fail to follow recommendations, and end up relapsing.

It's possible, of course, that your friend will make it, mostly because it sounds like he has a positive attitude about getting involved in recovery. It's also possible, because of your negative attitude, that you won't make it. That won't be because of unequal treatment at work, but because of how each of you responds to your recovery responsibilities.

That's *not* to say alcoholics and addicts should wait until someone else forces them to get sober. But those who initiate action on their own often need to keep firing up their own motivation to stay on track.

I'M AFRAID OF BEING FIRED

"I've been out on sick leave, getting treatment for my alcoholism. But I didn't tell my boss. It's a high-pressure business, and I'm afraid if I tell him I'll get canned. Can't I just keep the whole thing a secret?"

Dishonesty is the fuel that powers active addiction. A good recovery is based on honesty, so don't start your efforts to rebuild your life with a lie. It's more important to save your life than to save your job. Besides, you aren't likely to get away with it.

Your bosses probably know you had some kind of substance problem. So call, email, or talk in person and explain what's going on. If your employer wants to know more about your treatment, you can put him in touch with your counselor, doctor, or therapist. They can help your employer understand why you are now likely to be a better worker than ever before.

If you're a good worker, a wary employer may be swayed into keeping you on with a strict continuing care work plan. In such a plan, a professional monitors your recovery and sends periodic "fitness for duty" statements to your employer, showing them that you are toeing the line.

And, in fact, if you are in recovery and stay sober, you can't be fired for alcoholism or addiction. You are protected under the Americans with Disabilities Act. You are not protected when you are using, or if you relapse, but once sober, you are. Also, your medical information is private under federal law. Your boss cannot get access to your medical records, or talk to your doctor, without your permission.

If you are fired—even in a tough job market—try to see it as something good. You don't want to work someplace where there is no support for people in recovery. If you follow your recovery program faithfully, not only will you be able to find a new job but you'll be a better employee than you ever were before.

A CONTINUING CARE WORK PLAN

Your employers might respect your talents and your past contributions to the business. But they might still be wary of keeping you on, given your history.

To protect them and yourself, suggest a tough, no-loophole work agreement for the next year or two. This continuing care work plan should require:

- Your full participation in a fellowship such as AA or NA.

- Random drug screens on request from your employer or a medical monitor.

- Quarterly reports from your doctor or counselor verifying your sobriety. This could include a "fitness for duty" letter, which ensures recovery accountability

for safety-sensitive jobs, such as bus driver or pilot. Make sure the report or letter has an expiration date and clearly requires periodic renewals so it doesn't imply permanent clearance.

- Immediate loss of your job if you fail to uphold your end of the plan.

Getting Back into a Work Routine

I THOUGHT I KNEW THIS JOB SO WELL

"I've been back at work for a week, and I can't seem to focus at all. Today I tried to use a computer program I should know well, and my mind went blank. I'm afraid I've had some kind of permanent brain damage."

Alcohol and other drugs do damage the brain, but in most cases the brain eventually recovers. It's likely yours will, too. Still, the fogginess and lack of concentration can be scary if you don't realize they are normal at this stage. Many people report they can't concentrate well enough to read anything longer than a text message. But the fog gradually clears, and the ability to sit still and apply yourself to a task gradually returns.

Not remembering how to run a computer program, however, may be related to what is known as "state-dependent learning." If you learned to do something (run a machine, work a program, do a dance step) while you were in a particular state (such as high on a drug), you may have to learn it all over again once you get sober. This problem is most common with people who used alcohol and benzodiazepines, but it can happen to those who used other drugs, too. Fortunately, the second time around, since the motor memory is there somewhere, it won't take you as long to learn what you seem to have forgotten.

SHOULD YOU GO BACK TO HIGH-RISK WORK?

"I was a floor nurse in a big hospital before my treatment for drug addiction. My supervisor is hesitant to take me back. And to tell you the truth, I'm a little nervous myself about being face-to-face with the drug closet with a key in my pocket."

You are both wise to be wary of a day-in-and-day-out proximity to drugs. It can be just too much temptation.

Recovering doctors, nurses, pharmacists, and others who may handle scheduled drugs should change positions for a while, at least for the first year. If that's not possible, then very close supervision of that part of the job is needed—with someone else holding the key to the drug closet. An employment contract might also be useful.

You may also be required to participate in a professional monitoring and assistance program run by a state agency or licensing board or by your employer. These programs, and their requirements, vary from state to state. You might have to agree to continued counseling, random drug tests, and other requirements. These programs improve your chances of recovery; they also protect the public from injury.

WORKPLACE DRUG TESTING

Many companies do drug tests on current employees as well as those applying for jobs. This is now routine in many industries and mandatory in some safety-sensitive jobs, such as pilot, ship captain, and rail operator. Some high schools and colleges also now randomly test students for drugs.

The most common type of testing is pre-employment, which is meant to weed out drug users from job applicants. But the purpose of testing among current employees, drug experts believe, should not be to get people fired, but to get them into treatment (unless, of course, their drinking or drug use leads to some kind of catastrophe—a train crash, a fire, an explosion—in which case they may be fired on the spot).

In some companies, employees are screened across the board, usually randomly. In others, testing is "for cause"—it is limited to those whose behavior at work (absenteeism, accidents, possession of drug paraphernalia) makes their supervisor suspect current drug or alcohol abuse. It may take place for those in recovery, who may have agreed to frequent testing, and for those who have recently had an accident on the job. These tests can show if a person has used drugs in recent days, but they cannot detect if someone is a chronic user or addict.

WHAT SHOULD I SAY WHEN LOOKING FOR A NEW JOB?

"My boss fired me. I don't blame him. But now that I've gone through treatment I need to find a new job. Do I have to tell a prospective employer about my past?"

Yes. Honesty—with yourself and others—is such a key element in recovery that you really have no choice but to tell all. Most people will be impressed with your frankness. In addition, many employers are wise enough to know that those who have gone through the rigors of treatment often are better candidates for a job. Many have honed their coping skills, are more honest and responsible, and relate better to others. Of course, that doesn't mean every employer will be happy to hear that the six-month gap in your résumé is due to alcohol or drug usage or treatment. But anyone who turns you down on that alone, after your honest attempts to turn your life around, is probably not the right employer for you anyway.

Not leveling with an employer can not only put your recovery in jeopardy, it can put your job on the line. If the employer finds out about your history from someone else, they will wonder about your integrity. There could be legal implications if you lie on an application. On every level, honesty is the best policy.

Being honest, however, doesn't mean you can't use a win-win strategy (good for you, good for the employer) while job hunting. One way to do this is to withhold your alcohol/drug history from your original application and résumé. Addictive illness is a protected disability, as well as private medical information, so employers should not be asking about diagnosis or treatment for drug or alcohol problems on applications anyway. Then, when you are called in for an interview, put your best foot forward, make a great impression, and get the job offer. Finally, before you accept the job, explain your history. Don't make too big a deal of it. The more emphasis you put on your problem, the larger it will loom in the eyes of others.

If it seems appropriate or necessary, suggest writing up an employment contract similar to the continuing care work plan described above, in which you agree to certain conditions. You might also write an undated letter to your employer saying that you have not met your recovery responsibilities and so are probably back on drugs or alcohol. The letter is held by your counselor, doctor, or sponsor, and is sent in the moment you miss an appointment without good cause, stop going to meetings, or fail to meet other recovery tasks. This option puts the onus on you to stick to your recovery.

Legal and Financial Troubles

I DON'T WANT TO GO TO JAIL!

"I've got a jail sentence hanging over my head—I stole some stuff so I could sell it and get drugs. Now that I'm sober, is there any way to get out of serving the time?"

Possibly. Some judges will not bend and will want you to serve the time, but others may give you a suspended sentence *if* it's clear you're serious about recovery. You may have to agree to being supervised by a doctor, counselor, or outpatient program, as well as a probation officer.

Another option is to have your case heard in a drug court. These specialized courts can offer the option of treatment instead of jail time—they aim to break the cycle of repeated incarceration, which is all too common for people with addiction. They are often limited to nonviolent offenders. You would be closely supervised throughout your addiction treatment and subject to random drug testing. You would also meet regularly with a judge or other court officials so they could monitor your progress. You'd be legally responsible for completing treatment; if you

didn't make it through, you could be sent to jail.

There are also several other specialized courts that can help people with drug problems avoid jail: juvenile drug courts, where treatments and sanctions are tailored for younger people; mental health courts, which help people with mental health issues; Tribal Healing to Wellness Courts, which work with the Native American community; and Campus Drug Courts, which work with college students.

Ask whoever is treating you if they know someone who can help. Most people in the recovery field have been down this road before and can direct you to a lawyer who will know how to handle your case. If he can persuade the judge that you're a new person and there's no reason to put the old you behind bars, you might be able to get off with just probation.

If you don't have the money to hire your own lawyer, you may be assigned a public defender. You can also try to find some low-cost or free legal services and information from various nonprofit organizations. To find a service near you, do a search at LawHelp.org. Many of these services can also help with issues such as bankruptcy, divorce, and other noncriminal matters.

I'VE MADE A MESS OF MY FINANCES

"I came out of treatment owing money everywhere. My credit cards are maxed out, and I'm behind on

my mortgage and my car payments. I don't have two cents in the bank. How can our family survive?"

Most people find that the walls start tumbling down around them about three months into recovery, when creditors start turning accounts over to collection agencies. So your situation, though dire, is not unique.

One option is to get help from a nonprofit debt counseling service, which can help you develop a debt management plan, counsel you about bankruptcy and housing issues, and also provide other services. Be wary, however—there are some less-than-reputable debt management companies out there. Your best option is to look for one that is a member of the National Foundation for Credit Counseling (nfcc.org). You can also ask around for leads at fellowship meetings; you might be able to find a financial professional, such as a banker or an accountant, who is in recovery and is willing to help you get your finances in order.

You can also write up your own financial recovery plan. Some ideas:

Call your creditors to let them know what's happening. Calmly explain that you've been through a long illness and you're now on the road to recovery, but you need some time to regroup. If they will work out an extension, you'll repay them—slowly, but surely. Mention that if they're not willing to work with you, you'll be forced to declare bankruptcy and they'll get little or nothing. Assure them that in the meantime you won't take on any more debt.

Avoid using credit cards. Instead use cash or a debit card with a daily withdrawal limit. Either way, watch what you spend very carefully. But it's not always a good idea to simply close your credit accounts; that can hurt your credit score. You might ask a trusted friend to hold on to your cards for a while so you won't be tempted to use them. Or you can just cut them up so they're not handy. (See page 216 for more tips on avoiding temptation by controlling your money.)

Cut back on expenses. You know where your spending may be excessive, and where you can best cut it. If you're not sure, keep a diary for a month, writing down where you spend every penny.

Keep to a budget. Decide in advance where every incoming dollar will go, and then stick to your budget. Use a free online expense tracking service like mint.com or a software program like Quicken to track your income and expenses. Keep a calendar of when bills are due, and check it often to make sure you are on time. Better yet, pay your bills online, and schedule them all at the start of each month.

Start a savings account. This may seem impossible with all the creditors at your door, but plan to pay yourself before you pay them, even if it's just $5 a week.

Accept help—with a caveat. Do you have family or close friends willing to lend you cash or cosign a note to pay off some of your creditors? Swallow your pride and accept their help, but make an ironclad plan to pay it back. Write up a letter or contract that spells out all the details. It's important for your recovery that ultimately, *you* accept responsibility for your life. That means *you* pay the bills *you* owe.

Learn more about finances and how to live on less. There are several good (free!) blogs where you can learn more about taking financial responsibility, frugal living, and saving. Check out *Get Rich Slowly* (getrichslowly.org/blog), *WiseBread* (wisebread.com), and *MintLife* (mint.com/blog) for starters.

Declaring bankruptcy might look like an easy out. Some lawyers will tell you it's a simple way to get rid of old debts. But that should be your last resort. You risk losing your home, car, and everything else if you go that route. Plus, you need to take responsibility for your past actions as much as you can.

///////////////////////////

"I was sober for sixty days and feeling pretty good—until I got this nasty note from the IRS. With all the debts I'm behind on, there's no way I can pay what I owe."

Get a letter from your counselor, therapist, physician, or treatment center explaining that you're in early recovery and it will be a while before you are on your feet financially. Contact the IRS (meet with someone in person if possible), show them the letter, and explain that you do want to pay, but it will be a while before you can. You may be able to work out a payment plan. Or they may work out a loan for you with your credit union or bank so you can pay off your debt that way. If you run into resistance, ask to speak to a supervisor.

If that doesn't work, or if you owe several thousand dollars or more, you will need professional help to cut a deal with the IRS. Consult a tax lawyer or a tax-savvy certified public accountant (CPA), preferably one who used to work for the IRS or who appears in tax court often. Recovery publications often run ads for such professionals, some of whom are recovering themselves. But discuss their fees up front to be sure they're not going to sink you even deeper into your hole.

Another option is to ask around at your AA group for a good CPA. You're not the first person in recovery to find himself in debt to the IRS. Someone's sure to know of an expert who can help. (Don't forget that medical expenses—including some related to addiction treatment—are tax deductible.)

Your Physical Health in the Red Zone

You might be tempted to jump into a rigorous health and fitness plan so you can get into tip-top shape now that you are sober. But that's not a good idea. Right now you need to focus most of your time and effort on staying sober and working your recovery program.

So forget about trying to do an instant turnaround. Forget about training for next month's marathon. That's the old you, the addict, talking. The new you is going to go slowly, to solidify your recovery foundation first. For now, you just need to stabilize your health and ease your way into a healthier lifestyle. Your priorities now:

- Take care of any pressing medical and dental needs.

- Give your body time to recover. You may have lingering symptoms for a few months or longer, but many things will resolve on their own with time.

- Learn about the risks of medication and safe ways to treat illness. Taking mood-altering medications can put you at a huge risk for relapse, so you'll need to learn about other ways to deal with illnesses. In fact, you'll need to be very wary about taking *any* drugs—prescription or over the counter.

- Start taking better care of yourself. Learn about the initial steps you can take toward a healthy lifestyle with better eating, hygiene, and exercise.

Start with these small, easy steps now, and your body will start to heal. Pretty soon, you'll start feeling much better. When you move into the Yellow and Green Zones, you can think about overhauling your diet, ramping up your exercise routine, and losing those nagging extra pounds. *Then* you can start training for a marathon.

But honestly, for the time being, if it comes down to possibly relapsing versus eating half a pizza or a pint of double-fudge ice cream, go for the food.

Your Health Priorities Now

TAKE CARE OF PRESSING HEALTH NEEDS

Your body may have been subjected to a lot of abuse while you were drinking or using drugs. Now that you are sober, you'll have to clean up the damage. While you're in the Red Zone, it's best to address only the most severe or immediate health needs—those that could turn into life-threatening issues.

- If you were an IV drug user or you had unprotected sex, get tested for hepatitis C, HIV, and other diseases that can be transmitted through needles or sexual contact.

- If you were a heavy drinker, have a doctor assess your liver.

- Consider having screening exams for high blood pressure, diabetes, high cholesterol, and other common conditions.

If you were treated at an inpatient program, you might have already addressed these issues. If not, and if you don't already have a family doctor, you have a few options for getting low-cost care. Look around for county health agencies, Planned Parenthood offices, health fairs, low-cost immunizations and flu shots at grocery stores and pharmacies, and free screening days at local hospitals. Pharmacists are always happy to give free advice about prescriptions. Also check the many directories listed in Calling Dr. Google: How to Find Good Health Information (page 286).

Once you move into the Yellow Zone and have more time and energy to devote to your health, you can look around for some health care providers you'd like to work with long-term. You'll be able to take the time then to find someone who knows how to work with patients in recovery, will work with you on fixing all those smaller gripes, and will also guide you on what you can do to ensure a lifetime of good health. And by the way—if you plan to use an Internet search engine to figure out what is ailing you (as most of us do these days), read our tips for healthy health searching starting on page 286.

GIVE YOUR BODY TIME TO RECOVER

Most people are amazed at how much their health improves in early recovery, simply by removing the poisons they were consuming. But many also notice a host of new physical symptoms and ailments at that time. Some even wonder if maybe they were healthier when they were drinking and drugging.

No way.

What's happening is simple: You're just much more aware of what your body is saying now. Twitches, aches, and odd sensations went unnoticed before. Or if you did notice them, you just treated them with more alcohol or drugs. Now that you're sober, they are amplified. This is also partly because your body's own natural pain-easing chemicals are not yet back in full production.

Some of these symptoms are normal aches and pains, some are a result of the damage alcohol and drugs did to your body, and others are related your body's efforts to rebound from chemical abuse. Still other symptoms may be rooted in emotional distress. You may also still be having some withdrawal symptoms.

The best approach is to be patient and give your body time to recover. Many of your aches and pains will go away on their own, some within hours of your last drink or fix. Others may take months or even a year or more to fade away. Of course, you may need medical attention for some situations; talk with a doctor about anything that doesn't seem to be at least easing up. Symptoms of depression and anxiety are also common, even normal, in early recovery. You can read more about those and other mental health issues in chapter 14.

THE GOOD NEWS: CONDITIONS THAT TEND TO IMPROVE IN RECOVERY

The health news in the Red Zone isn't all depressing. The good news is that some conditions clear up or improve rather quickly once you stop using drugs and alcohol.

Diabetes. Alcohol damage to the pancreas and liver tends to worsen diabetes; alcohol also adds excess calories to the diet. When they quit drinking, many people who started taking oral medication for diabetes find they no longer need it. Even some insulin-dependent diabetics improve enough to be able to give up their insulin shots. If you have diabetes, watch your blood sugar levels closely and have your doctor reassess your disease very early in recovery so your treatment can be altered if necessary.

Hypertension. Heavy alcohol consumption can raise your blood pressure. With abstention, blood pressure often returns to normal. Many people who were on medication suddenly find they can do without it when they quit drinking. You can check your blood pressure for free at many drugstores, or you can buy an inexpensive device to check it at home. Don't stop taking medication without checking with your doctor, of course, but do have your hypertension evaluated once you are in recovery. You may be pleasantly surprised. As a precaution, check your blood pressure often during recovery to be sure it doesn't sneak up again. To help keep it down, don't smoke, eat a diet low in sodium, watch your weight, and get regular exercise.

Calling Dr. Google: How to Find Good Health Information

Most of us turn to one of the big search engines such as Google or Yahoo! to start an online search for health information. But while your search results may contain some very helpful medical news from a prestigious medical association, the very next link could be some sketchy guy who promises to cure your addiction or whatever ails you just as soon as you send him some money. And he doesn't always *look* sketchy.

The good news is there are many sites that do offer quality, accurate information that is reviewed by medical professionals. Stick to the sites listed below and in the Resources section and you should find only good, solid information.

Start at MedlinePlus

MedlinePlus (medlineplus.gov), a site from the U.S. National Institutes of Health, is hands down *the* best place to start looking for health information and news. In the Health Topics area you can look up conditions by body system (heart, bones, etc.), types of disorders, age group, gender, and more. Once you find a topic of interest, you'll see some basic descriptions, along with an entire page of well-organized links to more information—overviews, news, diagnosis, treatment, videos and graphics, anatomy, support organizations, current clinical trials, related issues, and more. These links all go to reliable, high-quality sources of information, such as other government agencies, medical societies, medical journals, and hospitals. All of the information is vetted by the MedlinePlus staff according to their quality guidelines. In essence, MedlinePlus does your information search for you. (Just be sure you don't wander far. Once you click through from MedlinePlus to another site, you might come across questionable ads or links to other sites that are not of such high quality. It's best to go to a link, then head back to the MedlinePlus page to do some more exploring.)

MedlinePlus also has information on prescription and over-the-counter drugs and on herbs and supplements; a medical dictionary and encyclopedia; easy-to-read materials; and videos, for people who prefer that medium. For many conditions, it also has materials in several languages, such as Spanish, Arabic, Khmer, Russian, Tagalog, and others.

The MedlinePlus Directories (nlm .nih.gov/medlineplus/directories .html) is an extensive list of helpful medical directories that were produced by other organizations. These directories can help you find doctors, surgeons, physical therapists, dietitians, medical centers, free clinics, Indian Health Service facilities, and more. (These have not all been vetted, however.)

How to Assess Websites

When looking at other websites, how do you know if they are any good or not? Here are some things to look for:

- Who sponsors the site? Is there a major institution behind it, such as a university, a hospital, or a government agency? They usually have accurate information. Look for sites that end in .edu (educational), .gov (government), or .org (usually a nonprofit organization). Read the About Us section on the site.

- Does the site have professional medical reviewers or editors? Read what you can about how the site's information is written and reviewed. Check out their editorial or review policies.

- How often is the information updated? Do the articles have dates on them?

- Be skeptical. Does the site promise a "miracle cure"? Does it claim that "the government doesn't want you to know" about this cure? If so, it's likely a waste of time and money.

Protect Yourself

Online communities (forums, chat rooms, mailing lists, blogs, and so on) where people with a common condition or situation provide support for each other can be very helpful. But tread cautiously. Use them for moral support; a shoulder to lean on; someone to listen to you. Be very wary of following anyone's advice too closely, however, and do *not* rely on people there for medical advice. Learn what you can from good medical sites and always consult with your doctor.

Never use your real name in any of these communities. People always seem very nice, but there are some who just troll the forums looking for people they can take advantage of. Never disclose any personal information, such as your address, social security number, age, birthday, mother's maiden name, and so on.

OTHER GOOD HEALTH INFORMATION SITES AND PHYSICIAN/CLINIC DIRECTORIES

Below are several high-quality health sites, as well as some directories of low-cost and free health care and assistance. Some of these sites also have apps or mobile versions. (Be sure to also see the sites focused on finding addiction treatment in chapter 5.)

General Health Information

FAMILY DOCTOR (American Academy of Family Physicians)

- familydoctor.org

HEALTHFINDER.GOV
(U.S. Department of Health
and Human Services)

- healthfinder.gov

MAYOCLINIC.COM

- mayoclinic.com/health
  -information

MEDLINEPLUS (U.S. National
Institutes of Health)

- medlineplus.gov

NEMOURS FOUNDATION/
KIDSHEALTH

TeensHealth

- teenshealth.org/teen

KidsHealth

- kidshealth.org/kid

KidsHealth for Parents

- kidshealth.org/parent

WEBMD.COM

- webmd.com

WOMENSHEALTH.GOV (U.S.
Department of Health and
Human Services)

- womenshealth.gov

Condition-Specific Health Information

ACADEMY OF NUTRITION AND
DIETETICS

- eatright.org/Default.aspx

HEPATITIS FOUNDATION
INTERNATIONAL

- hepfi.org/index.html

HIV INSITE (University of California,
San Francisco)

- hivinsite.ucsf.edu/InSite

HIV AND STD TESTING RESOURCES

- hivtest.cdc.gov/Default.aspx

NATIONAL CANCER INSTITUTE

- cancer.gov

NUTRITION FACTS LABEL: HOW TO
UNDERSTAND AND USE IT (U.S. Food
and Drug Administration)

- fda.gov/Food/Ingredients
  PackagingLabeling/Labeling
  Nutrition/ucm274593.htm

U.S. FOOD AND DRUG
ADMINISTRATION: FOR CONSUMERS

- fda.gov/ForConsumers/
  ConsumerUpdates/default.htm

WOMENSHEALTH.GOV: STATE
RESOURCES REGARDING VIOLENCE
AGAINST WOMEN

- womenshealth.gov/violence
  -against-women/get-help-for
  -violence/resources-by-state
  -violence-against-women.cfm

Health Care—Directories of Providers and Resources, Including Some Free or Low-Cost Services

BENEFITSCHECKUP (from the National
Council on Aging, directories of help
for medication, health care, food, legal
help, transportation, housing)

- ssl4.benefitscheckup.org

CHILDREN'S HEALTH INSURANCE
PROGRAM (CHIP)

- insurekidsnow.gov/chip/index
  .html

DISABLED AMERICAN VETERANS (help
applying for benefits, filing claims,
transportation, etc.)

- dav.org

FEDERALLY QUALIFIED HEALTH CENTERS

- hrsa.gov/healthit/toolbox/ RuralHealthITtoolbox/ Introduction/qualified.html

FINANCIAL HELP FOR DIABETES CARE (National Diabetes Information Clearinghouse; NIH)

- diabetes.niddk.nih.gov/dm/pubs/ financialhelp

FIND A HEALTH CENTER (Health Resources and Services Administration; U.S. Department of Health and Human Services): Directory of Free and Low-Cost Services

- findahealthcenter.hrsa.gov/ Search_HCC.aspx

FIND RYAN WHITE HIV/AIDS MEDICAL CARE PROVIDERS (Health Resources and Services Administration; U.S. Department of Health and Human Services): Directory of Free and Low-Cost Services

- findhivcare.hrsa.gov/Search_HAB. aspx

HOMELESSNESS RESOURCE CENTER (Substance Abuse and Mental Health Services Administration)

- homeless.samhsa.gov/Resource/ LocalResources.aspx

INDIAN HEALTH SERVICE: FIND HEALTH CARE

- ihs.gov/forpatients/ findhealthcare

MEN'S HEALTH MONTH DIRECTORY OF FREE AND LOW-COST HEALTH CARE (not only for men)

- menshealthmonth.org/ freehealthcare/index.html

MEDICARE RIGHTS CENTER

- medicarerights.org

MENTAL HEALTH TREATMENT FACILITY LOCATOR

- findtreatment.samhsa.gov/ MHTreatmentLocator/faces/ quickSearch.jspx

NATIONAL ASSOCIATION OF FREE & CHARITABLE CLINICS

- nafcclinics.org/clinics/search

NATIONAL CANCER INSTITUTE: ORGANIZATIONS THAT PROVIDE SUPPORT SERVICES

- supportorgs.cancer.gov/home .aspx?js=1

NEEDYMEDS (many programs that help with medication costs, copays, health insurance, free screenings, transportation, prescription discount cards, and more)

- needymeds.org

PATIENT ADVOCATE FOUNDATION (insurance appeals information and help)

- patientadvocate.org

SUBSTANCE ABUSE TREATMENT FACILITY LOCATOR (including state agencies)

- findtreatment.samhsa.gov
- 800-662-HELP (4357)

Dental and Vision Care—Directories of Providers and Resources, Including Some Free or Low-Cost Services

DENTAL LIFELINE NETWORK (donated dental services)

- dentallifeline.org

EYECARE AMERICA (from the Foundation of the American Academy of Ophthalmology; free eye exams through a volunteer network)

- eyecareamerica.org

NEW EYES FOR THE NEEDY (glasses for those in need)

- new-eyes.org

VISION USA (free eye exams; American Optometric Association Foundation)

- optometryscharity.org/vision-usa

Medication Concerns

BE *VERY* WARY ABOUT MEDICATION

As an alcoholic or addict in recovery, you need to be very careful about *any* medication you take—for the rest of your life. Slip with even a seemingly innocent cold pill, and you could be setting yourself up for a relapse. Yes, it's that risky.

There are two kinds of medications: mood-altering and non-mood-altering.

It's the mood-altering drugs that present the greatest risk to you—and it's not just those strong painkillers or tranquilizers. Even antihistamines can trigger a relapse, even though they are not *all* addictive. They are risky because they can impair your ability to think clearly enough to recognize potential triggers and avoid relapse. The very first dose, like flipping a switch, can transform your positive attitude into a negative one, as it does a number on your brain's frontal lobe. It can also lower your brain's ability to resist mood swings and those fleeting compulsions to drink or use drugs. End result: relapse.

The non-mood-altering drugs are also risky. Alcoholics and addicts can get hooked on an empty capsule if they're convinced it will make them feel better (remember, the addiction is in the person, not the pill). It's not just their vivid imaginations; their expectations trigger disturbed thinking and can even create a drug high.

So, since *any* medication, no matter how innocent, can feed addictive tendencies, consider anything and everything you might swallow, inhale, absorb, or inject to be potentially hazardous to your sobriety. This might sound a bit extreme, but experience shows it really is that important. (In fact, any time you really do need to take a medication, be sure to see if it is available in a form that is *not* similar to your former drugs of choice. For example, if you took pills, see if a patch is available. If you snorted drugs, stay away from saline nasal sprays, no matter how innocent they may be. Toradol, a very effective non-narcotic pain reliever that is often a good choice for people in recovery, is available as an injection, a nasal spray, and a pill.)

Your doctor may think there's no need to make a big deal out of taking an aspirin, but your sobriety will be strengthened by knowing that taking *any* medication is risky. If you follow these precautions, avoiding any and all drugs as much as you possibly can, you'll be less likely to innocently open the door to a relapse. If you do decide to take any optional medication, you should consider it a slip. Be completely accountable and report it to those involved in your recovery: your sponsor, counselor, and doctor.

You will probably need medication less often as you progress in recovery. The reason is chemical: ordinarily, the brain provides its own chemicals (such as endorphins, enkephalins, dopamine, serotonin, and glutamate) to combat pain, depression, and anxiety, as needed. Alcohol and drugs impair these natural defenses by telling the brain to stop making its internal painkillers, because the body is now getting them from an external source. When you sober up, it will take at least a couple of weeks for your still-fuzzy brain to kick in with painkiller production again. But once it does, you will find that a single ibuprofen relieves pain even better than a strong painkiller used to do.

Of course, some medications may be necessary to keep you alive: diabetes medications, cholesterol-lowering drugs, antihistamines to halt a deadly allergic reaction, and so on. See also Medication Exceptions (page 292).

THE MOST MENACING MEDICATIONS

Some of these gateway drugs are not in themselves hazardous. But for people in recovery they can open the door back to addiction even faster than those fairly innocent over-the-counter drugs you are now wisely avoiding. Except for life-and-death situations, do your absolute best to avoid:

- All sedatives (sleeping pills), including all benzodiazepines, barbiturates, and all synthetics

- All narcotics (painkillers), including opioids and synthetics

- All tranquilizers (anti-anxiety agents), including benzodiazepines

- All stimulants, including amphetamines and antidepressants

- All antihistamines (except Claritin and Allegra)

- All combination medications, prescription or over-the-counter, containing narcotics (usually codeine), stimulants (including caffeine), alcohol, or antihistamines

If you are unsure about a particular medication, ask "What would a pilot do?" The Federal Aviation Administration issues guidance on which drugs are okay to take while piloting a plane and which are absolutely not okay. They disapprove of not only drugs that can cause

THE RED ZONE

drowsiness, but also those that can affect memory, judgment, and handling multiple tasks at once. The FAA does not publish this list, but a private organization, Pilot Medical Solutions, posts updated information online; see leftseat.com/medcat1.htm.

See chapter 24 for many alternative remedies that do not rely on drugs (as well as some guidance on when a last-resort situation does call for medication).

THE WILLINGWAY DRUG RULE

"There are two types of drugs: old drugs and new drugs. The old drugs are addictive. The new drugs are nonaddictive. When the new drugs become old drugs, they become addictive and are replaced by new nonaddictive drugs."

What does this mean? Virtually every time a new drug comes out, it is hailed as "nonaddictive." Once it's been around for a while it becomes clear that it is indeed addictive, little comfort for those who have already inadvertently become hooked. So take any claims about a new drug being safe for people in recovery with a grain of salt.

MEDICATION EXCEPTIONS

Mood-altering drugs can be dangerous for anyone in recovery. However, there are some people who really can't move into recovery until they are lifted out of a deep, paralyzing depression, can turn off the voices plaguing them, or can organize their thoughts well enough to use the tools of recovery. Such life-threatening situations demand drastic action, which may mean the use of psychotropic drugs, such as antidepressants, antipsychotics, or lithium. Sedative hypnotics or benzodiazepines are also sometimes used, but because they can trigger a relapse, if possible they should be used only in detox or very early recovery.

If such drugs are deemed absolutely necessary, they are best given during inpatient treatment or doled out in a doctor's office or by a reliable third party. Once brain function is normalized, the patient can, in consultation with a medical doctor, be slowly weaned off the medication—on a trial basis. If he continues to function well, the medication can often be discontinued permanently. If not, it can be continued for a while longer, with another attempt at weaning later. (However, people who have a diagnosed chronic mental illness such as bipolar disorder or schizophrenia may need to take medication for a lifetime.)

One risk of prescribing some of these medications is that once a person escapes from depression, he may assume his addiction is a thing of the past: "Why go to AA? I only drank because I was depressed." To guard against this, many doctors adopt a "no meetings, no meds" policy: If the patient does not faithfully follow an agreed-upon recovery program, the medication plan may be reassessed.

At times during your recovery, you may also have a true need for pain control medication, such as when you have surgery, dental work, or a medical emergency. See chapter 24 for guidelines on safe medical and dental care and pain control.

Your Primary Health Issues Now

HEPATITIS C

About 3.2 million people in the U.S. are known to be infected with the hepatitis C virus, and they are all at risk for serious liver problems in the future.

Anyone who has used intravenous drugs (even rarely) is at risk for hepatitis C. Other risk factors include having unprotected sex, getting body piercings or tattoos under unsanitary conditions, and having had a blood transfusion or an organ transplant before 1992. Many people who have the virus have few or no symptoms, even for decades. If you have any risk factors, get tested.

If you do have the virus, talk with your doctor about treatment. Finding out you are infected can be scary, but keep in mind you might not have to start treatment immediately. Plus, some hepatitis C treatments can have significant side effects and they are not 100 percent effective, so you may want to put it off until you are out of the

Red Zone. See more on hepatitis C and other liver conditions in chapter 20.

HIV/AIDS

"I was an IV drug user and I'm terrified that I am HIV positive—so terrified that I don't want to know."

You're not alone. Many people feel the same way. But there's good news. These days, the future for most people who have HIV (human immunodeficiency virus) is much brighter. Treatment with antiretroviral drugs is now very effective, and many people with HIV now live long and healthy lives and never develop AIDS (acquired immune deficiency syndrome). So there are good reasons for you (and everyone in recovery) to find out if you have the virus. The earlier it is discovered, the earlier you can start treatment. And that's good for your long-term health.

As you probably know, intravenous (IV) drug users are at high risk of contracting HIV, mostly because they often share contaminated needles. Their sexual partners (male or female) are also at risk. But they aren't the only ones at risk. *All* drug and alcohol users are, because they may have weakened immune systems and may have had risky sexual contact with a number of partners (heterosexual or homosexual).

So even if you restricted all your use to clean needles and have absolutely no symptoms of AIDS, it's a good idea to get tested.

If you are HIV positive, you should be scrupulous about not engaging in activities through which you can pass the virus to others. You should also notify anyone you shared drugs with or had sex with so they can get tested. In most states there are programs to help with contact notification.

Remember, testing positive for HIV does not mean you have AIDS or that you will develop it in the near future—just that you have the virus. With today's treatments, you might *never* develop AIDS. But while a positive HIV test is no longer a death sentence, it is a warning: to get the best possible treatment, take the best possible care of yourself, and be alert for symptoms.

Of course, you'll also need to pay close attention to your recovery program, for a variety of reasons:

- Without sobriety, treatment is sure to be compromised. People who are drunk or high often forget to take their medication or keep doctor's appointments, and in general fail to take good care of themselves.

- Alcohol suppresses the immune system and can lower the body's resistance to fighting off the virus.

- Sobriety will reduce the likelihood of behaviors that could pass the virus to others.

- Abstention can slow the progression of the disease.

You will also need emotional and social support, good nutrition (which helps strengthen the immune system), and a positive attitude, which might include using relaxation techniques such as meditation and prayer.

If you don't have the virus and you later relapse and return to using IV drugs, talk to your doctor about starting antiretroviral treatment as a preventive measure. Studies have found that among IV drug users, those who had such treatment were half as likely as others to become infected with HIV.

For more information, call the national HIV/AIDS hotline at the Centers for Disease Control, 800-CDC-INFO (232-4636), or your state or local health department.

OTHER SEXUALLY TRANSMITTED DISEASES

"I've gotten a clean bill of health where AIDS is concerned. Are there any other diseases I could have caught while having sex?"

Today, all sexually transmitted diseases (STDs) are on the rise. Even syphilis, once believed to be almost wiped out, is showing up more often. What this probably means is that people are not taking precautions against STDs.

These diseases are passed along through sexual intercourse or other sexual contact (such as oral sex) that allows the germs or viruses from the infected person to pass to his partner through a body opening or torn mucous membrane lining. The most common transfer areas are the mouth, the vagina, the penis, and the anus.

The leading villains are gonorrhea, herpes, venereal warts (caused by the human papilloma virus, or HPV), chlamydia, trichomoniasis, and syphilis. If you think you might have picked up something while under the influence, then you would be wise to get tested for all the possibilities. Many infections are asymptomatic, so you can't rely on symptoms giving you a warning.

If you are infected, you should be treated immediately. Any sexual partners should also be informed and treated as necessary. Until the infection clears, avoid intercourse, or use condoms to block transmission of germs.

Of course, if you notice any symptoms of an STD, see a doctor right away. If you have not yet received the HPV vaccine, ask your doctor about it. We strongly suggest it for women and men under the age of twenty-seven.

URGENT DENTAL ISSUES

People who have used meth often have some pretty severe dental problems (sometimes called meth mouth). Those who used other drugs also may have a lot of dental issues, due to years of neglect. Dental work is expensive and time-consuming, and it can be tempting to just put it off. But if you ignore any urgent issues now, they are only likely to get worse, and you may lose teeth.

So see a dentist fairly early in recovery. At the very least you can get a good cleaning and identify any work that needs to be done. If you need something for pain relief before you get to the dentist, try nonsteroidal anti-inflammatory (NSAID) pain relievers. If you have severe pain, Toradol, a non-narcotic but very effective pain reliever, is an option. Toothaches are almost always due to infection or abscess and should respond to the antibiotic amoxicillin.

If you can't afford dental treatment at this time, there are still some options: getting care at a dental school, looking for a low-cost clinic (see Health Care—Directories of Providers and Resources, Including Some Free or Low-Cost Services, page 288), and working out a low-interest payment plan with your dentist. Be candid with your dentist about what you can afford, and work out a plan to address your most urgent needs first.

BASIC HYGIENE

Many alcoholics and addicts don't take very good care of their personal hygiene when they are in active addiction. If that was the case for you, it's time to start fresh with good personal habits.

This means bathing and washing your hair regularly (daily, for most); using deodorant daily; brushing your teeth twice a day, plus flossing; trimming your fingernails and toenails; keeping your hair (including any facial hair) trimmed and clean; shaving as needed; washing your hands after using the bathroom; using makeup appropriately; and covering your mouth when you cough or sneeze.

A Healthy Lifestyle in the Red Zone

Your lifestyle and your health are inextricably intertwined. What you eat, drink, and smoke (or *don't* smoke), how you spend your free time, how you conduct your love life—all affect your health and longevity. Eventually, you may want to overhaul your lifestyle and set some major goals for yourself so you can be healthier and live longer (and maybe run that marathon). Right now, however, you need to concentrate on recovery to the exclusion of pretty much everything else. So don't worry about setting any major lifestyle goals right now (other than staying sober). Limit your changes to some small moves that will point you in the right direction.

EATING WELL IN RECOVERY

"I've never eaten very well. Should I worry about my diet during recovery?"

For now, worry only about the dietary changes that will help you to stay sober. The Clean and Sober Diet for the Red Zone will do just that. It includes six simple recommendations, all of which can enhance sobriety.

Five of these recommendations are very easy to do, yet they can have a big payoff: Good nutrition results in fewer episodes of low blood sugar (which can be mistaken for a craving), less alcohol craving, and a better chance of staying sober.

The sixth recommendation, dropping sugar from your diet, is tougher for some people. You can skip it for now if you want (it's always better to eat a chocolate bar than to relapse!).

Once you get into the Yellow and Green Zones you can put more energy into improving your diet, with additional Clean and Sober Diet guidelines.

THE CLEAN AND SOBER DIET FOR THE RED ZONE

Plan for a "safe relapse." From time to time in the Red Zone, your cravings for alcohol or drugs may be really tough to ignore. You might try all the methods in chapter 10 for dealing with them and find that nothing works. You're still crawling up a wall. What will often work then is giving in to a "safe relapse"—feasting on a milk shake or a large pizza with all the toppings. Be prepared for those major cravings by having some alternative treat in mind. Yes, this could be called "stuffing your face," but if it saves you from a relapse and another trip to detox, it's a win. (As your recovery gets stronger, these crises should occur less often.)

Eat three squares a day—plus. It may not be easy to get into the habit of eating three meals a day if you've been living on junk food, eating at odd times, and getting most of your calories from alcohol. But it's a habit worth cultivating. It's particularly important in recovery because skipping meals or eating junk food can lead to episodes of low blood sugar, and that can make you jittery, depressed, confused, or anxious—all of which are feelings that can bring on a compulsion to drink or use.

To get into a regular eating program, start with breakfast. If you have little time in the morning, fill your bowl with dry cereal (whole grain is best) and fruit the night before; in the morning just add milk and eat. If you're a coffee drinker, prepare the ingredients (preferably decaf) at night, too.

If your work schedule is so busy you can't find time for lunch, you're working too hard. Make time for lunch.

Most people manage to have a meal in the evening, so you shouldn't have too much difficulty with that one. If you've already had two solid meals, you'll find less need to eat a lot in the evening.

Many people can't get from meal to meal without a drop in blood sugar. To avoid that (and the risky consequences), have light between-meal snacks—fruit, raw vegetables, string cheese, whole grain crackers, a spoonful of peanut butter.

Get your fill of fluids. Alcoholics, though they drink constantly, can suffer from dehydration. Now it's important to keep your body hydrated. Bring a water bottle to work and sip throughout the day. An easy way to see if you are getting enough fluids: watch the color of your urine. If it's dark, drink more water.

Focus on B vitamins. They are vital for the repair of the nervous system, so try to increase your intake. That means more whole grain cereals and breads as well as some meat or dairy products daily.

Catch up on calcium. Alcohol depletes the body of calcium, robbing the bones of this vital mineral and often weakening them. The resulting conditions, osteopenia and osteoporosis, can occur in males as well as females. The sooner you start replacing the calcium you've lost, the better. Try to drink at least three glasses of milk daily, or eat the equivalent in other foods.

Shun sugar. For some, eliminating sugar is akin to trying to kick one more addiction. So use your judgment. If you aren't suffering from cravings or annoying mood swings, and attacks of low blood sugar don't seem to be a problem, you can wait a while before moving on to this step. On the other hand, if you are often shaky, irritable, depressed, or tired, or have trouble concentrating a few

THE RED ZONE

hours after having a sugar-loaded snack, it makes sense to adopt this Clean and Sober Diet guideline early.

But remember—if a quick sugar fix is going to help you avoid a relapse, by all means, go for it.

SHOULD I EXERCISE NOW?

"I'm really eager to get into a good exercise routine. Is there anything special I should know because I'm in the Red Zone?"

Yes—take it very, very slowly. While every sedentary person who gets into an exercise program should start slowly—starting out with just a few minutes a day—this is even more important for those in recovery. Your muscles, joints, and reflexes, and maybe even your bones, are probably far from normal. Depending on how long you were drinking or using, your muscles may be weak or shrunken from disuse and chemical damage. Your joints may be inflamed because of mistreatment or gout. Your reflexes are probably slow because the connections between muscles and brain are all off-kilter. And your bones may be brittle because of alcohol-related calcium loss. Plus, your heart is likely not ready to be challenged just yet.

If you push yourself too hard and too far, it can also result in injury, disrupted sex hormones (throwing the menstrual cycle out of whack in women and lowering sperm count and sex drive in males), an impaired immune system, and even an increased risk of osteoporosis.

For now, some mild exercise such as brisk walking or swimming is plenty. Try to work it into your day in a way that helps you build connections. For example, you might plan to meet others from your home group and walk to a meeting together a couple of evenings each week. Try to avoid isolating exercises. If you want to swim, join a swim club rather than doing laps by yourself. And don't do anything more strenuous until your doctor says you are ready. That will happen in the Yellow or Green Zone.

THE RISKS OF EXERCISE

For newly sober alcoholics and addicts, exercise poses another risk: You can get addicted to it, possibly risking your sobriety.

Exercise stimulates the feel-good chemicals in your brain, just like drugs and alcohol do. We all know people who get that "runner's high" with intense exercise. The problem is that some people who chase that feeling neglect family, work, and other healthy activities. If you have to work out rather than go to meetings or finish a paper for school, or if you go out running in spite of foul weather or serious injury, exercise is a problem, not a solution.

Even if your exercise routine doesn't become your new addiction, spending too much time on it could keep you from working on recovery or relearning interpersonal skills. Getting involved in daring or thrill-seeking activities, such as skydiving, can also be very risky now, as they can reactivate those brain pathways that focused on living on the edge. Your goals have to be focused on recovery, not on running more miles each week, ramping up your weights routine, or seeing how fast you can ski.

The greatest danger, ironically, is that exercise can make you feel *too* good. So good that you think, "Hey, I'm healthy again, I don't have to work my program. Now that I'm healthy, I can control my life. Maybe I can even drink again."

Of course, you can't. The fact that you can control your life enough to exercise doesn't mean you can be a "controlled drinker." Do not allow this central fact to slip your mind: Alcoholism/addiction is a disease, and diseases can't be controlled through willpower.

Like everything else in your life now, moderation in exercise should be the goal. And just to be on the safe side, ask your sponsor, counselor, or addiction specialist to monitor your exercise program.

DO I HAVE TO QUIT SMOKING NOW?

While fewer people smoke these days, it's still very common among alcoholics and addicts. If you didn't quit while you were in treatment, you need to decide whether to stop now or to wait until your recovery is more solid.

There is one good reason to wait: Quitting later can act like a booster shot for your recovery. Many people get a little complacent about recovery once they have a year to a year and a half behind them. Taking on quitting smoking at that time can rekindle your recovery skills, further solidifying your sobriety.

Whenever you are ready to toss away your last pack, read chapter 25.

I'M WORRIED ABOUT MY FERTILITY

"I've got a very spotty past where drugs and alcohol are concerned. How is this going to affect my getting pregnant and having healthy babies in the future?"

Once the drugs and alcohol are out of your system, you're well into a solid recovery, and your physical condition passes muster with the doctor, you should be able to conceive and carry a healthy baby.

But here is a big *but*: That is assuming you stay sober. If you have any doubts about being able to do that, *do not try to conceive now*. The risk of devastating effects of alcohol and other drugs on a fetus is too great. Plus, it can be a distraction from the work of recovery. Even if you managed to stay sober during a pregnancy in the Red Zone, you could easily relapse under the stress of parenting.

Ideally, put off getting pregnant until you've done a lot of recovery work and are in the Green Zone. By then you should be emotionally ready to have a baby, and all the effects of the chemicals you have been using should be gone from your body.

Your fertility is likely to improve rapidly as recovery progresses, so be sure to get some form of birth control and use it faithfully. In fact, if you assumed you were infertile because you never got pregnant while you were using, you may be in for a surprise. So use birth control even if you don't think you need it.

If you do get pregnant now, and want to carry the baby, that's certainly not an impossible task. But you will have to work very hard at your program, because you have only nine months to establish a really solid foundation that will give your child the gift of a sober mother. See chapter 24 for more on having a safe pregnancy and a healthy baby.

Common Health Issues in Early Recovery

As you'll see below, there are many puzzling, unexpected, and disquieting physical symptoms that a person in early recovery might experience. Most are recovery-related and resolve themselves given time.

But some of these conditions, such as sleep problems, gastric discomfort, and pain, may be due to diseases unrelated to addiction. So

if you experience any of them, be sure to see your doctor—especially if they continue or get worse after your first weeks or months in recovery. That's true, too, of any other unusual symptoms you may have that are not listed here.

If your doctor doesn't find any unrelated medical problem, it's very possible your symptoms are just slower to disappear than most. It is also possible, however, that unresolved symptoms are alarm bells warning that your recovery is shakier than you think.

For some people, unexplained physical ills (aches and pains, minor infections) or emotional symptoms (mood swings, depression) are a substitute for a compulsion to use; they can be a sign of impending relapse. So talk to your sponsor, counselor, or doctor about your concerns, and together decide what you can do about it. Going to more fellowship meetings may help. Another preemptive strike: Get some outpatient treatment, or even a short relapse-prevention inpatient treatment booster.

Now that you've stopped abusing it, your body is on speaking terms with you again; it will tell you when there is a problem. Sometimes quite loudly.

Described below are many of the common health issues that tend to come up in early recovery, from abdominal pain to wheezing.

Abdominal pain. There are many reasons why your stomach might hurt. The stomach lining usually protects the muscular wall of the stomach from acidic digestive juices. But alcohol can damage the lining, leaving the stomach open to a number of problems, including bleeding.

Abdominal pain may be due to gastritis (stomach inflammation), a consequence of your favorite rotgut "rotting" the stomach lining. Or it may be caused by other stomach problems. Mild pain that is clearly related to the use of alcohol or other drugs will probably go away on its own, sometimes within a few days of initial sobriety. Antacids and a light or liquid diet may help rest the stomach until it is healed. Over-the-counter medications such as Pepcid, Zantac, and Prilosec can help with minor stomach problems and are safe to use for a short time in recovery.

More severe pain or soreness, especially if there is any sign of internal bleeding (such as bloody or black, tarry stools), requires a careful medical workup to be sure there is no serious or life-threatening condition.

Cocaine addicts sometimes have abdominal discomfort in the form of bloating, cramping, and gas. This usually lasts only a few days after their last fix. Recovering narcotics addicts can expect cramping and gas to last a bit longer, but these symptoms usually clear up in the first few weeks.

Abdominal soreness. Soreness or tenderness below the right rib cage, often with a feeling of deep pressure, usually is related to liver damage or pancreatitis. In most cases, abstinence reverses the condition over time.

Aches and pains. The theory that alcohol numbs pain is true but deceptive. It's like a shopping spree on your credit card—sooner or later, you have to pay it back with interest. That's because alcohol interferes with the body's own ability to handle pain; when the alcohol wears off—as it does in sobriety— your body isn't ready to deal with it. Consequently, for a while you'll be noticing aches and pains more than ever before. But as your body gets back to normal, so will your reaction to pain. In most cases this will take two or three months, but if you used the slower-acting sedative drugs, antianxiety drugs, or narcotics, the discomfort will be slower in fading away.

You may find that the addict in you, now sidelined by your decision to put your life back in order, sees any kind of discomfort as an excuse to start using drugs of any kind. But don't let those minor annoyances point you down the road toward relapse! See Pain in chapter 24 for ways to deal with pain without falling back into the pain-drug-pain-drug cycle. Also see *Nerve pain; Muscle pain.*

Acne. Though dermatologists don't recognize a link between alcohol and acne, some alcoholics, particularly young ones, report outbreaks.

This may stem in part from poor personal hygiene in active addiction, which sometimes continues into early recovery. There are also immune system and hormonal changes that can contribute. Often the problem seems worse than it is to the young person in recovery whose self-image is already in tatters—so talking about it with a doctor, your sponsor, or someone else you trust may help put it in perspective. It's rarely a lifetime sentence, since the culprit hormones level off after the teen years. See Skin Problems in chapter 24 for ways to deal with acne safely.

Anemia. Alcoholics often suffer from anemia, a shortage of the red blood cells that carry oxygen. There are several reasons. For one, alcohol damages the bone marrow, which produces red blood cells. For another, there may be internal bleeding due to alcohol's interference with clotting, stomach and intestinal inflammation, or hemorrhoids. Bleeding can also result from being injured in a fight or a fall during a drinking or drug binge. Since normal blood clotting depends on healthy liver function, damage to the liver by alcohol makes it even tougher for the body to plug the leak, making the bleeding more severe and anemia more likely. Dietary factors also play a role in anemia (most alcoholics eat poorly), and to compound the problem, alcohol depletes the body of important nutrients or interferes with their absorption. Iron, vitamin

D, and the B vitamins, particularly B6, B12, and folic acid, are the most affected by alcohol, and inadequate stores of any of these can contribute to anemia. Many drug users also suffer from anemia—usually because of poor diet or the secondary use of alcohol.

There may be no symptoms with mild anemia, but extreme fatigue, weakness, palpitations, breathlessness, and even fainting are possible in more severe cases. Check with your doctor if you have such symptoms. A simple blood test can confirm or rule out anemia. The doctor should also make certain that the anemia is the result of past alcohol use and not a symptom of a serious but unrelated disease. Since a red blood cell's life expectancy is about 120 days, it may take several months of sobriety for the cells you now have to be replaced and for alcohol-related anemia to be corrected.

Anxiety attacks. These are extremely common in recovery, and there is much you can do about them. See chapter 14, as well as Anxiety in chapter 24.

Bowel problems. See *Constipation*; *Diarrhea*. These may alternate in recovery, which can sometimes be confusing to both the doctor and the patient. In some instances, the cause of this seesaw bowel activity is psychological; it's also a common problem in children who grew up in families with alcoholism/addiction. It usually doesn't require any treatment other than more fiber in the diet and a good recovery.

Narcotics users often have small, frequent bowel movements for one to three weeks in early recovery. This may be a sign of withdrawal for those who suffered from constipation during active addiction, and it will pass.

Breathlessness or shortness of breath. This is common in those who smoked cocaine or marijuana, and it can hang on for as long as a year. Sometimes it is severe enough to seem like an asthma attack. Until this symptom abates, limit any activity (such as strenuous exercise) that brings it on. It will most often ease up with a better overall physical condition later in recovery.

Shortness of breath may also be a problem for alcoholics who have done damage to their hearts, as well as for former narcotics users. This is a symptom that requires medical evaluation, especially if it gets much worse with exercise or when you lie flat.

Bronchitis. Bronchitis is an inflammation of the bronchial tubes (air passages leading to the lungs) that triggers coughing. It can be acute (lasting a short period of time, usually no more than a few weeks) or chronic (lasting more than a few weeks). It may be associated with smoking tobacco or other drugs, or it can be caused by a virus or bacteria. When there is a bacterial infection, coughing generally produces phlegm (often thick,

yellow or greenish, and possibly foul-smelling). If it doesn't resolve in a few days on its own, an asthma inhaler or antibiotic treatment may help. Those with chronic bronchitis from smoking are more susceptible to acute infections of the bronchial tree. See also *Cough.*

Chest pain. The stress on the heart caused by cocaine use can trigger chest pain and heart attack. The pain usually clears up once drug use stops. If it doesn't, major heart damage may have occurred and you should get to a hospital immediately. (Do the same with any acute chest pain that lasts for more than twenty minutes and radiates to other body parts—the arm or jaw, for example. You could be having a heart attack, and fast medical attention can reverse or at least minimize heart muscle damage.)

Constipation. Constipation (infrequent and difficult-to-pass bowel movements with hard stools) is not unusual in early recovery. In fact, it is a universal side effect of using opiates. It may alternate exasperatingly with diarrhea (a combination of symptoms often referred to as irritable bowel syndrome, or IBS). Constipation is not only uncomfortable in itself, it can also bring on hemorrhoids, so it's not wise to ignore it. Once you are in recovery, it may take a few weeks for bowel activity to return to normal. For ways to prevent and treat the condition, see chapter 24.

Coordination problems. The nerve connections between your muscles and your brain may not be working at their best in early recovery, so the muscles may not always do what the brain commands. Give your body time to heal. In most cases it will do so within six months. However, some neuromuscular conditions caused by alcohol and drug use are permanent.

Cough. People who use marijuana, crack cocaine, and other inhaled drugs (including tobacco) often develop a chronic cough, due to irritation of the respiratory tract. When the drugs are stopped, the cough may get worse instead of better, and dark gray mucus may be coughed up. That's probably because the cilia, the tiny hairs that sweep the respiratory tract clean, were until recently paralyzed by the drugs, and suddenly got back to work. Now they are triggering coughing to expel the junk that was built up during drug use. For ways to treat a cough, see chapter 24.

If you have a cough along with a fever over 101 degrees (even if you've had a smoker's cough for as long as you can remember), or you cough up any blood or have chest pain, see your doctor. Also call the doctor if you have a cough that lasts more than a few weeks into recovery; some dangerous strains of tuberculosis are on the rise.

Coughing is, of course, a perpetual problem for smokers. In recovery, they often find they are coughing more and are more sensitive to cigarette smoke. (See chapter 25 if you are ready to quit smoking.)

Diarrhea. Alcohol, which burns like the devil's pitchfork when poured on an open wound, irritates the delicate lining of the digestive tract and often causes diarrhea, nausea, and vomiting. These symptoms may continue for a couple of weeks after withdrawal, but should disappear then. If they don't, or if you see blood in your stool (it may look red, black, or tarry) or in your vomit, check with the doctor. There could be internal bleeding.

Narcotics users may experience diarrhea, or diarrhea alternating with constipation, in recovery. See chapter 24 for treatment tips.

Ear symptoms. Ringing, buzzing, and roaring in the ears are most common among benzodiazepine users in recovery. There may also be a heightened awareness of sound in general, or a reduced ability to hear and discriminate sounds. Most of these symptoms start to diminish in the early months of recovery.

Changes in immune system function, chemical irritation, and poor hygiene can all contribute to itching or pain in the ear canal or outer ear due to inflammation. Try to avoid cleaning out your ears with swabs, and let them heal. If the symptoms don't clear up after three weeks of sobriety, check with your doctor. If fever, redness, or other signs of infection occur, however, call your doctor immediately.

Erectile dysfunction (ED, or impotence). This condition is very common in early recovery. Distressing, yes, but take heart. It's not likely to last and there is treatment available (even though your sponsor might call it a blessing in disguise).

Eye symptoms. Dry eyes can be a problem for alcoholics. As alcohol is excreted from the body in tears and other body fluids, it can cause dehydration of tissues as well as chronic irritation. This in turn decreases the ability of the eyes to self-lubricate, leaving them dry and itchy. Time will remedy this. In the meantime, soothing and lubricating eye drops may help. See also *Visual disturbances*.

Fatigue. Some of the "I'm tired all the time" feeling experienced in recovery is the result of your body working overtime to get back to normal. It may also be the result of vitamin deficiency (particularly folic acid), which could be causing anemia. So be sure to eat nutritious food, and ask your doctor about taking a vitamin supplement.

Some of your extreme tiredness, however, could be caused by your doing too much too soon—in your eagerness to make up for lost time, you may be setting a pace that is unrealistic for anyone, especially someone recovering from a severe health problem. This is not the time to play Superman or Superwoman. Do only what is necessary for your recovery at this point; be sure to

review the Recovery Zone System chart in chapter 2 and the Zone outlines (chapters 3, 16, and 21) to make sure you are not taking on too much. You not only do not have to do everything at once—you *can't* do it all and survive. Be sure to include relaxation and stress reduction, exercise, adequate sleep, and good nutrition in your daily schedule. They will all help reduce fatigue.

To wake yourself up when you're feeling zonked, get up and walk around (outside, if you can), do some stretching exercises, take a few deep breaths, drink a glass of ice-cold water, or talk to someone. Make sure the room you're in is well-ventilated.

If over time you don't see any lessening of your fatigue, talk with your doctor. He may want to check for anemia, a thyroid condition, diabetes, a blood pressure problem, or other issues; all can lead to fatigue.

Flaking of the face or peeling skin. During the first week of recovery some people, particularly African Americans, have what looks like and itches like dandruff of the face. The reason is unclear, but it may be related to the fact that alcohol leaches oils and proteins out of the skin, leaving it dry. The condition may have existed during alcohol use, unnoticed by the sedated drinker. Other skin conditions, such as rosacea, are also common in addiction and early recovery.

Flashbacks. Flashbacks—the sensation of having used a drug when you haven't—can occur during abstinence with many different kinds of drugs, including alcohol. You may seem to relive a past using experience, complete with visions, feelings, and even physical symptoms. Some former cocaine users experience a cocaine taste in the back of the mouth, often with a numbing feeling, even late in recovery. This appears to be a conditioned response of some kind, often to some stimulus in their environment (a dish of powdered sugar, perhaps). Narcotics users may be suddenly overcome with nausea, as though they have just shot up with heroin. And former users of hallucinogens (such as PCP, LSD, or marijuana) may suddenly feel high, though they haven't been near the drug in weeks or months. Flashbacks are also common after the use of the synthetic marijuana drugs K2 and Spice. Fortunately, flashbacks are usually short-lived and tend to go away over time.

It's not always clear whether a particular episode is a flashback or not. But it really doesn't matter what you call it as long as you realize it isn't harmful (unless it leads to a craving). When a flashback strikes, take it as a reminder that you're still vulnerable.

Fungal infections. Male alcoholics are very susceptible to jock itch and athlete's foot. But again, they might not be particularly bothered by either one until they get sober. Then suddenly the itching and discomfort become unbearable.

Over-the-counter medications such as Tinactin (tolnaftate), Lotrimin (clotrimazole), or Lamisil (terbinafine) usually can quickly eliminate the fungus and its discomforts. (Be wary of any oral—taken by mouth—medications for fungal infection, as they can affect the liver.) If the problem persists, see your doctor. Female alcoholics are also susceptible to fungal infection; see *Vaginal infections*.

Gastritis (or inflamed stomach). Early in their drinking careers, alcoholics often conclude that drinking actually makes their heartburn quiet down. But that wishful thinking doesn't last long, and soon the discomfort is worse than ever. They may have a burning or queasy feeling in the area of the stomach (just above the waistline), or a sour taste in the mouth; they may even vomit. These symptoms are caused by the irritation of the inside of the stomach by alcohol and may be mistaken for an ulcer, especially if a doctor isn't aware of your drinking history. This gastritis may become chronic, which is why so many alcoholics also pop antacids or over-the-counter pain relievers (many of which only produce more stomach irritation). In some people, it is suspected that a tolerance to alcohol develops and gastritis becomes less of a problem as the alcoholism progresses.

Fortunately, with sobriety, the stomach lining heals quickly and within days of the last drink there is usually relief from the symptoms. Of course, if they persist or if there is bleeding or black stools, check with the doctor. An upper gastrointestinal (GI) tract examination with an instrument (a gastroscope) may be necessary. If a gastroscopy is required, be sure to follow the medication guidelines in chapter 24.

Gout. Alcohol's metabolic damage inhibits the breakdown of uric acid. As levels of this substance build up in the body fluid, it sometimes crystallizes in joint cavities, causing the inflammation and exquisite pain of gout. The joint most often affected is in the big toe, but gout can also affect knees, hands, the spine, feet, elbows (joints and long bones), and hips. Symptoms may worsen during withdrawal, but then usually begin to improve. With abstinence, the number of gout attacks diminishes, often even if there were other causes of the condition. If alcohol was the prime cause, attacks usually stop entirely within a year, sometimes almost miraculously. If possible, avoid treating symptoms with muscle relaxants and narcotics, since they can lead to a relapse. The pain of gout can be treated with cholchicine or nonsteroidal anti-inflammatory drugs like ibuprofen, rather than with mood-altering drugs. If you have more than a couple of attacks, see your doctor; gout is very responsive to preventive treatment. You may need medication to keep uric acid levels low.

Gums bleeding. Cocaine damages mucous membranes, not only of the nose but of the mouth as well. Bleeding and soreness may continue briefly after cocaine use ceases, but should clear up soon. Alcoholics, too, may suffer from bleeding gums. Damage to the gums and mouth can also be caused by poor nutrition, frequent vomiting of the acidic contents of the stomach, the effects of inhaled drugs (particularly crystal meth), and neglect of dental hygiene. Again, this should clear up with abstinence and better hygiene, along with proper dental care. See chapter 24 for tips on keeping your teeth and gums healthy.

Headache. When the hangovers end, the headaches of early recovery sometimes begin. Some, called "tension headaches," are usually centered in the forehead or the back of the head. They are often said to feel like a constricting band around the head. Others are probably vascular-type headaches that resemble migraines, with pounding and often pain only on one side. In alcoholics, headaches can continue for a month or more after the last drink. In cocaine users, they may continue on and off for months. Some people who never experienced (or at least never noticed) headaches while drinking or using are bothered by them in recovery for the first time.

If you suffer from persistent headaches that are accompanied by nausea or vomiting, disturbed vision (double vision, for example), localized weakness on any part of your body, or poor coordination, see your doctor immediately. For tips on treating headaches, see chapter 24.

THE RED ZONE

Heart palpitations. A rapid or irregular heartbeat may occur during detox—or at any time—because of the use of caffeine, tobacco, or other stimulants (including energy drinks, which can have dangerously high levels of stimulants). Sometimes they occur for no apparent reason. If such symptoms don't speedily resolve themselves after detox, and if cutting back on or giving up caffeine doesn't help, it's time to check with your doctor. An EKG (electrocardiogram) to evaluate heart function, a blood-pressure reading, and other tests may be in order. Heartbeat irregularities (particularly what feels like a skipped beat) are fairly common, and though sometimes disconcerting, they are usually harmless. Don't worry about them, but do mention them to your doctor. If a heartbeat problem occurs along with chest pain or a loss of consciousness, or is set off by exercise, have your doctor check it out immediately.

Heartburn. The alcoholic who lives on beer and antacids, or on scotch with an aspirin chaser, often suffers constant heartburn. If this pain or burning sensation in the center of the chest doesn't disappear after several days of sobriety, try using the over-the-counter remedies that are listed in chapter 24. If that doesn't help, check with your doctor. You may be suffering from gastritis (see above) or stomach ulcers. It could also be related to reflux of stomach acid into the chest or a hiatal hernia.

Indigestion, gas, and heartburn are all common in recovery, no matter what your drug of choice was. This may be because of the accumulation of drug effects on the GI tract, or it could be due to a rebound effect. For example, cocaine stimulates the GI tract; with withdrawal, the system becomes sluggish and starts closing down.

Hemorrhoids. Many people in early recovery suffer from hemorrhoids (piles)—varicose veins of the rectum that can bleed, itch, burn, or ache. It isn't clear why these swollen veins, which resemble a bunch of small grapes, suddenly become a problem at this point. They might result from constipation or diarrhea associated with withdrawal. Or they could be related to liver disease. Or they may have been there all along, a result of poor eating habits, low-fiber nutrition, and straining during bowel movements; they just weren't noticed or were disregarded. Whatever the cause, they can usually be prevented or alleviated (see chapter 24).

Hormonal issues and feminization. Many men would never start using if their dealers had to put a warning on the drugs they peddle: "Use of this drug is hazardous to your masculinity." But, indeed, some drugs are, notably alcohol and marijuana. Alcohol decreases levels of the male hormone testosterone, and (by way of liver damage) increases levels of the female hormone estrogen. As a result, men who drink or use heavily tend to develop feminine character-istics. Their breasts enlarge, they have less body and facial hair, and their fat takes on a more female pat-tern (heavier around the hips). In most cases, hormone levels return to normal in four to six months, but in some men the process is slower. In a small percentage of men—usu-ally those who have been drinking heavily for many years—there is enough damage to the liver and the testes to permanently derail normal hormone levels. If you are diag-nosed with low testosterone in early recovery, your best course of action is to hold off on treatment. Wait until you have a few more months of sobriety and then get retested. Chances are your hormones will have rebounded by then. If not, ask your doctor about treatment.

Infection. Alcohol is no friend of the white blood cells we need in order to fight invading microorganisms. By reducing their numbers and effec-tiveness, it makes drinkers more susceptible to everything from boils, athlete's foot, and the common cold to bronchitis and pneumonia. With sobriety, the white count goes back up and susceptibility back down, though how quickly varies from person to person. To help improve your resistance, get started with the Clean and Sober Diet, exercise, work your program, and deal with tension and anxiety promptly.

Infertility. Alcohol and marijuana, by killing sperm cells in the male, inter-fering with ovulation in the female,

and decreasing sex drive in both, can impede fertility. It will gradu-ally return over the early months of recovery. Just when isn't sure, so don't forget to use birth control.

Intellectual problems. Fogginess, short attention span, and other thinking problems are routine in early recovery. They almost always clear up with good recovery. See chapter 14.

Itching. Because signals can get muddled by your damaged nervous system, you may experience some odd symptoms, such as itching, twitching, and unusual skin sensa-tions. You can try anti-itch oint-ments and colloidal oatmeal baths, but they aren't likely to help much because the problem most likely isn't your skin, but your nervous system. Meditation may help more than calamine lotion. With time, your damaged nerve endings will heal and itching will ease.

Joint pain. Like every other part of your body, your joints are affected by drug use. And like other aches and pains, joint discomfort should ease up in the first few months of recovery. If it doesn't, you may have arthritis; with sobriety, it might improve but it's unlikely to go away completely. See your doctor for diagnosis and treatment (especially if the pain makes you start thinking about taking strong medication). A heating pad is a good first step to remedy the pain. See Arthritis, chapter 24, for more treatment tips.

Leg cramps. Leg cramps due to flabby, out-of-shape muscles are not uncommon. Be sure you're getting enough calcium (through dairy products or supplements) and potassium (try bananas or orange juice). Stretching and moderate exercise may also help.

Memory problems. A variety of these commonly occur; they are almost always temporary. See chapter 14.

Menstrual irregularities. The menstrual irregularities that occur with heavy drinking or drug abuse do not suddenly vanish with sobriety. In recovery, a woman's menstrual periods can be longer or shorter than normal, more frequent or less, heavier or lighter. Or they may be totally absent. This doesn't mean you can't get pregnant—which presents a problem, since an unplanned pregnancy in early recovery is the last thing most women need to cope with. To be safe, rather than surprised, use birth control.

Menstrual regularity usually returns after several months of sobriety, though emotional or physical stress can throw it temporarily out of kilter at any time. If menstrual abnormalities continue beyond the first six months of recovery, talk about it with your physician. (Also see *Premenstrual symptoms or syndrome.*)

If you are in midlife, menstrual irregularities or changes could be due to menopause or perimenopause.

Minor annoyances. Throughout the day, we all experience sensations that we have learned to disregard—a twitch here, a flutter there, an itch, an ache, a pain. But alcoholics and addicts don't learn to disregard these minor annoyances; instead they blot them out with chemicals. Now that your romance with chemicals is over, you have probably become newly and unduly sensitive to these normal body sensations. You may find them annoying, even worrisome, at first.

Some may have an obvious cause (your feet hurt because your new shoes are too tight), and eliminating the cause will usually eliminate the discomfort. Others (accelerated heartbeat during exercise or in stressful situations) may just be normal signs of a busy body at work and can't be eliminated. They can, however, be ignored, which you will gradually come to do. Still others (frequent unexplained headaches or ringing in the ears, for example) are signs that something may be wrong. You will need to learn to listen to and evaluate what your body is trying to say, to sort out the friendly everyday messages from the dire warnings. In general, you should be feeling better as you get further into recovery. If anything gets worse with time, talk to your doctor.

Mood swings. Almost no one escapes these in early recovery. See chapter 14.

Mouth dryness. Dry mucous membranes are common during the first few days of recovery. As traces of alcohol exit the body through the mouth, the evaporation promotes a drying effect. When all of the alcohol has been eliminated, the dryness generally disappears as well. Drinking plenty of water may help keep the membranes moist and you more comfortable. Your salivary glands, which stopped working properly due to alcohol (and sometimes drugs), should get back to normal soon as well.

Mouth irritation and sores. Poor nutrition and dental hygiene, frequent vomiting, and chemical use during active addiction all contribute to making the mouth an uncomfortable place in early recovery. Bleeding gums, canker sores, fever blisters, and infections are all common, but they should clear up with abstinence. Cold sores on the facial skin near the mouth are usually due to the herpes simplex virus. They can often be prevented by using sunscreen on your face and lips, and can be treated with Zovirax or another antiviral medication. Cold sores do tend to recur, so seeing a doctor about them may save you a lot of misery down the road.

Muscle pain (myalgia) and weakness. Muscle tissue rarely escapes the ravages of substance use. It may be destroyed directly by the chemical used or indirectly by a diminished blood supply resulting from infection, scarring, and a narrowing of blood vessels caused by the use of needles. This muscle damage is known as "myopathy." There may be both pain and weakness, particularly in the arms and legs, sometimes accompanied by trembling and twitching. Due to the weakness, even the slightest exertion (walking up stairs, lifting a suitcase) can cause extreme fatigue and pain. A common symptom is not being able to rise from a seated position without bracing your hands on your knees. In alcoholics, myopathy most often weakens the muscles around the shoulders and hips. In recovery, your muscles will begin to regenerate and the symptoms will ease. If the damage is severe, physical therapy may help; ask your doctor.

Sometimes, muscular weakness, pain, and flabbiness are due to plain old lack of use. Many alcoholics and addicts get little exercise; when muscles don't get used, they can weaken and atrophy. Gradually and very gently ease into an exercise program. That will give your muscle tissue some time to rebuild without being subjected to overextension, and will help you avoid injury to joints and ligaments.

A disease called fibromyalgia can cause symptoms similar to the muscle problems associated with substance use and withdrawal, but the conditions should not be confused. Fibromyalgia is a complex condition that can cause pain in several places in the body. It is generally more persistent than other muscle aches after someone gets into recovery. Fibromyalgia is not well understood, but its origins may be similar to some of the brain changes that occur in addiction. This might be good news: The attitudes, activities, and methods used to overcome addiction may also help in relieving the discomfort of fibromyalgia. If you think you need medical help for this condition, start with physical and verbal therapies, rather than drugs.

Muscle spasms or twitches. Your arm suddenly swings out. Your foot jerks back. Your body seems to be operating independently, out of your control. These random movements are the result of damage to the communications system between brain and muscles, and are usually most troublesome at night when you are sleeping or trying to fall asleep. They will eventually improve, but some muscle jerks are normal in the early stages of sleep and may continue. In the meantime, relaxation exercises or meditation (chapter 14) may minimize the problem and help you get some shut-eye. (Severe and extreme uncontrolled movement of your legs, especially at night, could be due to restless leg syndrome.)

Nerve pain (neuralgia). Like muscle tissue, nerve tissue can be damaged by alcohol and drugs, particularly benzodiazepines. A low level of damage can cause pain along the course of one or more nerves. Although the pain usually lessens with time, it can take weeks or even years for it to cease entirely. Though such pain is probably related to substance use, report it to your doctor so other causes can be ruled out.

Night sweats. These are most common during the early months of sobriety, with the first few days being the most uncomfortable. Anxiety may be partially responsible, but the major cause is probably physical withdrawal itself. When the sweats occur, change to fresh clothes to keep yourself comfortable, use a fan or air-conditioner to cool off, and try meditation or relaxation techniques. If sweating suddenly begins later in recovery, it could be due to an infection; take your temperature to see. If you are a woman in midlife, it could be the hot flashes of menopause. If sweating continues for more than two or three weeks, gets worse instead of better, is associated with pain, coughing, stomachaches, back pain, or diarrhea, or is so heavy you have to get up and change your damp sheets in the middle of the night, check with your doctor.

At other times, sweating is normal: during exercise, in hot weather, or when you're under stress, for example. It's the body's way of turning down its thermostat (just as shivering turns it up).

Nightmares. Dreams about drinking and using are common, particularly early in recovery. They can be alarming, but don't worry about them. It's actually *good* if you wake up in a sweat believing you've just blown your sobriety. It means you value your recovery. Start to worry if you find such dreams enjoyable. Many people in recovery also have dreams that are difficult to distinguish from hallucinations; this is particularly true of those who have used hallucinogens and antidepressants. The sudden explosion of vivid, disturbing dreams in recovery is partly psychological, the result of anxiety about recovery plus fear of insomnia (you know you can't take anything to help you sleep). But it's partly physiological, too. While on alcohol or other drugs, you got very little REM sleep—the sleep during which dreams occur. In recovery there is a rebound, as though the mind is trying to catch up with all that missed dreaming. Even fairly harmless dreams may be unsettling when you have gone so long with almost no dreaming at all. This unwelcome overstock of nightly dreams can last a year or two, but dreaming will eventually revert to normal levels. In the meantime, try meditation to help calm you after a particularly disturbing episode.

Nosebleeds and nasal damage. Snorting cocaine can inflame and seriously damage the tissues of the nose, eventually causing a break through the wall between the nostrils. The body responds to the damage by creating extra blood vessels that are larger, more superficial, and less protected from bleeding than ordinary vessels. Breathing (especially dry air) can then irritate them and cause nosebleeds. Sometimes the nose seems to bleed almost constantly. In recovery, the nosebleeds will eventually ease up and stop. Many recovering cocaine addicts also experience uncomfortable crusting and annoying whistling sounds.

The nasal tissues can be surgically repaired, but it's best to wait until you have a year or more of recovery. Early on, even the unperforated nasal tissues are likely to be in such poor condition that the necessary graft may not take. In the meantime, it may help to use a saline nasal spray (Simply Saline, Ayr, Ocean), coat the inside of the nose with Vaseline, or moisturize the air in your home. You can also make your own salt solution by dissolving ¼ teaspoon of salt in 1 cup of warm water. Use a clean atomizer or dropper to administer the liquid with your head tilted back. (For some people, a nasal spray can trigger cravings; if that is likely, try the other options first.)

For small perforations, surgery usually gives a good result. But if the loss of cartilage is more extensive, the nose can collapse, requiring major reconstructive surgery. Most surgeons won't do this challenging and difficult procedure until you have at least a year of recovery, to allow the damaged tissues to recover and your overall health to improve.

Numbness and tingling. Numbness, tingling, and tenderness, with or without pain, are common in alcoholics and some drug users. In alcoholics, the cause is usually peripheral neuropathy, a condition in which nerve cells, particularly in the extremities, are damaged. It seems to be the result of the toxic effect of alcohol on the peripheral nervous system. It usually begins in active alcoholics as a tingling, numbness, and tenderness in the feet, which then creeps up the legs and may later progress to fingers, hands, and arms. Weakness and difficulty balancing can make walking awkward and painful, and even impossible in advanced stages. It can also cause impotence and incontinence.

Abstention from alcohol doesn't bring miraculous relief from peripheral neuropathy. The damage usually persists into recovery. It generally takes months, sometimes years, of sobriety, along with a good diet, plenty of foods rich in the B vitamins, and sometimes medication to eliminate these symptoms. A burning sensation in the feet is a good sign—it means the nerves are slowly coming back to life. If these problems persist, a medical workup is needed to be sure there is no underlying disease.

Some people have found that the B vitamins, particularly B6, B12, and niacin, help reduce the symptoms of neuropathy. But they can be dangerous in high doses, so take them only under medical supervision.

Benzodiazepine users also might experience distorted sensation for many months. But because these drugs don't discriminate as much among body parts, the sensations are just as likely to affect the trunk as the extremities.

Osteoporosis. Alcohol robs the bones of calcium, making men and women who drink heavily (even those who are not alcoholics) more susceptible to fractures because of brittle bones, sometimes at a relatively early age. Ask your doctor if you should have a bone density screening exam.

During recovery, a diet rich in calcium and low in caffeine, combined with weight-bearing exercise, such as walking, bicycling, or running, may help improve bone density. Bisphosphonate drugs such as Fosamax, Boniva, and Recast may slow down or stop the bone loss. Hormone replacement therapy may also help some older women.

Vitamin D is also critical for healthy bones—it helps your body metabolize calcium. But since we need adequate sun exposure to produce vitamin D, many people in temperate climates have lower levels of it in winter—and consequently more bone loss. For both men and women in recovery, taking vitamin D supplements (but no more than the recommended daily allowance) is probably a good idea during the short, dark days of winter. (Also consider it if you are indoors most of the time and don't drink vitamin D–fortified milk.)

Pain. Aches and pains you never noticed before—or that you routinely covered up with drugs—may surface in recovery. Now you need to deal with them in nondrug ways (see chapter 24).

Pancreatitis. Inflammation of the pancreas occurs in many heavy drinkers. Though it happens most often to those who have been drinking for ten or fifteen years, the really serious drinker can do a number on the pancreas in just a couple of years.

The pancreas supplies the digestive juices that dissolve the food we eat; when these juices can't get to the intestines to do their job, they start to digest the pancreas itself. The end result: pain and digestive problems. The pain, usually in the mid-abdomen, is severe and stubbornly steady and may radiate to the back between the shoulder blades. The patient generally feels very sick and is anxious, restless, and distressed, and usually has nausea and vomiting. He may also have mottled skin, cold and sweaty hands and feet, rapid heartbeat, constipation, and fever. Sometimes there are black-and-blue (or blue-green) marks on the flanks or around the navel, indicating internal bleeding. Most people begin to feel better after a week of sobriety, but complications can extend the disease.

Treatment may include suctioning of the GI tract through a tube in the nose, antibiotics, and IV fluids for a few days, followed by a liquid diet and then a gradual return to a regular diet after the intestine has rested. It may also include pancreatic enzymes and vitamins to reverse malnutrition, and drugs (and sometimes insulin) to lower blood sugar levels. You may get some relief from the pain by sitting with your knees drawn up, forearms folded across your abdomen. If the pain is very severe, narcotics may be the only option for relief—taken under carefully controlled conditions, of course (see Pain, chapter 24). A single alcohol binge can bring a rapid return of pancreatitis.

Pancreatitis sometimes becomes intermittent or chronic, particularly in people with an abnormal pancreas. Symptoms include recurrent episodes of abdominal pain of varying intensity; occasional jaundice; and fatty stools that are difficult to flush. The patient often looks thin and malnourished and appears older than he is. The condition can be fatal. Unfortunately, abstinence does not always prevent recurrence in the last stages of the disease.

Pneumonia. A cough associated with shortness of breath, rapid breathing, or chest pain is usually a sign of an infection of the lungs, or pneumonia. The invading organisms may be bacteria, viruses, or other microorganisms. This is more serious than bronchitis because it threatens the ability of the lungs to get oxygen into the body. Active alcoholics and addicts are particularly susceptible to pneumonia. The risk is much lower once you are in recovery, but do report any symptoms to your doctor right away.

Testing for pneumonia includes X-ray, white blood count, and sputum examination. Mild cases can be treated with antibiotics. But if breathing becomes difficult, treatment in the hospital with IV antibiotics and oxygen may be needed. If an abscess of the lung develops (a fairly rare event), it may need to be surgically drained.

Premenstrual symptoms or syndrome. Most women who begin having PMS as teens learn to deal with the discomforts—more or less. The woman who uses alcohol or other drugs deals with them, too, by blocking them out with chemicals. Often PMS becomes a nonissue in active addiction because menstruation ceases entirely, or the symptoms overlap with those of drug withdrawal. When menstruation resumes in recovery, the accompanying backache, cramps, headache, tension, irritability, and depression may come as a shock. Since alcohol is a major contributor to PMS, the symptoms are often at their worst in early recovery, before the body gets back into the business of manufacturing its own painkiller hormones and chemicals again. See chapter 24 for tips on making the best of PMS.

Psychosomatic ills. Symptoms of illness in humans can be caused in a variety of ways: by germs, by the reaction of the body's immune system to foreign invaders, by injury, by genetic mistake, by failure of some body system, or by the mind and the emotions. The illnesses triggered by the last two are as real as the others and are called "psychosomatic,"

meaning that physical symptoms are caused by emotional distress. In fact, we now know that physiologic processes closely link physical and mental well-being.

Psychosomatic ills are common in alcoholics/addicts, who have not been champs at knowing, and clearly and honestly communicating, their feelings. In those who are newly sober, they can represent a conscious or subconscious plan to get back to drug use.

This emotional distress may be expressed in a variety of ways. When things begin to "hurt" emotionally, you may get a headache or a skin rash. Try to interpret the way your body speaks to you when you're not treating it right. If you're honest with yourself, you'll be better than your doctor at figuring out its language.

Of course, neither you nor your doctor should automatically dismiss symptoms because they seem to be psychosomatic. "Psychosomatic" illness often results in real physical damage, so it should always be treated as real.

Restless leg syndrome. These annoying nighttime movements of the arms and legs are common in active addiction and early recovery. The drug treatments for this condition, however, are not very effective long term, and they can trigger an addiction relapse; this is a situation where the treatment is more dangerous than the disease. In severe cases, look into having a workup in a sleep lab and consider the possibility of treatment with non-mood-altering drugs, such as vitamins or minerals.

Runny nose. Sniffling and a runny nose can result from the use and withdrawal of many drugs, particularly opiates. When drugs are taken nasally, membranes in the nose get irritated; they can also be irritated by cigarette and marijuana smoke and the cooking of drugs. The body fights back with its inflammatory response, increasing secretions. These symptoms usually disappear as the irritation clears up, but some drugs (especially cocaine) can cause permanent damage to nasal passages. In the meantime, treat the condition as you would an allergy (see Allergy, chapter 24).

Shakiness. Long after detox and withdrawal are done, some people find they are occasionally shaky and lightheaded, particularly around the time of day they usually drank or took drugs. It feels much like an attack of hypoglycemia (low blood sugar). Liver damage, weakened muscles, and nervous system impairment may all be contributors.

There is also a harmless condition called "benign essential tremor" that results in the shakes. Some alcoholics treat this shakiness with alcohol (clearly not the ideal prescription for you). A high-protein snack may help, but it is probably something you'll just have to learn to live with.

Skin rashes. Some people have recurring skin rashes or boils for months or even a year or more into recovery. This may be due to lowered resistance to infection, as well as a weakening of the skin's protective qualities because of alcohol use. For tips on skin care, see chapter 24.

Sleep problems. Whether you are sleepy or sleepless following detox (and for how long) will depend on the drugs you used and your personal sleep needs and patterns. Humans need widely differing amounts of sleep; most adults can readily describe their normal sleep patterns. But in alcoholics and addicts, the sleep pattern has been chemically disrupted for so long that they usually have no idea what is normal for them.

In early recovery, they aren't likely to find out. Their bodies are still rebounding wildly from the effects of their drugs of choice. Those who had been using alcohol or other depressants usually find it difficult to fall asleep, and staying asleep is just as hard. Those withdrawing from benzodiazepines often can't sleep at all. Those who had been using stimulants, on the other hand, may feel like sleeping around the clock in early recovery, and later have trouble settling into a comfortable sleep pattern. In a sense they're catching up, and even ten hours a night can seem like a mere catnap.

The brain needs time to rehabilitate itself after years of chemical use. Disordered sleep patterns may clear up in as little as five or six days, or it may take a year or more. In the meantime, you'll lose less sleep worrying about your sleep problems if you keep three points in mind:

- There is no such thing as a normal sleep pattern. Don't obsess, complain, or even think about being unable to sleep (or sleeping too much). Even among people who've never misused alcohol or other drugs, that legendary eight hours of sleep is a myth. Sleep patterns vary from person to person, and in the same person at different ages. Some people get along fine on five hours of sleep a night; for others ten is not enough.

- The sleeping pattern you settle into in the months ahead may be entirely different from the one you had before you began drinking or using. You've been sedated or high for so long that your internal body clock may have been thrown out of balance. If you started to use in your teens, you never had a chance to establish an adult sleeping pattern.

- Drugs of any kind are never a good long-term treatment for sleeping problems. If you're not sleeping, or are sleeping too much, see chapter 24 for tips on sleep hygiene and nondrug ways of dealing with these problems.

Slowed reflexes and judgment. Most drinkers assume that once they're on the wagon, their reflexes will quickly return to normal. Not so. You'll probably discover that not only are your reflexes still slower than normal but your overall motor performance isn't up to par either. That means you have to be particularly cautious when driving or operating machinery and, at least for a while, should lower your expectations when participating in sports or activities like video games, which depend on rapid responses. Over the next few months, your coordination will gradually improve.

Most of your impaired thinking will improve in the first several months of recovery. After a year or two, you should be close to 100 percent recovered. However, the critical brain activity that gives us good judgment and decision-making skills can take much longer to get back up to speed. The full return of this "executive-level" functioning can take seven years or more of sobriety.

In the meantime, go slow, especially where risk to yourself or others is involved.

Sore throat. Many alcoholics find their throats are red and raw in early recovery. If not caused by a respiratory virus, this may be due to long-term irritation from downing alcohol and bringing it back up, smoking, and a weakened immune system. Staying away from both alcohol and tobacco will allow the throat to heal in time. For dealing with the discomfort, see chapter 24.

Vaginal bleeding. Some women have excessive vaginal bleeding (not necessarily menstrual blood) during alcohol detox. This is probably related to hormonal changes accompanying the withdrawal of the drug, but it's best to check with your doctor, especially if you are postmenopausal.

Vaginal infections. In the early months of recovery, many women notice symptoms of vaginal infections. If it's a yeast infection, there will be itching and irritation, and possibly redness and swelling of the vulva (the inner folds of the area around the vagina), along with a thick cheesy discharge. With other types of infection there may be a greenish-yellow, foul-smelling discharge. These infections need proper diagnosis and treatment, so call your doctor. Over-the-counter treatments can be used for a yeast infection. If you have a discharge along with severe lower abdominal pain, call your doctor immediately or go to the emergency room—you may have a pelvic infection, which could put your fertility at risk. See chapter 24 for information about prevention and treatment of vaginal infections.

Visual disturbances. Just when your mind begins to see the world more clearly, your vision may become alarmingly blurred. You may also have problems focusing and find it hard to concentrate on reading. Don't run to get new prescription glasses. Alcohol and other drugs apparently alter the sensitive metabolic balance needed for visual sharpness and acuity. If these symptoms are not extremely disabling or inconvenient, wait three

or four months for them to resolve, and then get your eyes checked. Obviously, if your safety or someone else's depends on your visual acuity, you may need to get a transitional prescription immediately and later get another prescription as your eyes stabilize.

Some of the changes you experience may also be related to normal aging of the eyeballs. In the mid-forties almost everyone develops a condition called presbyopia, which makes reading (and other close-up tasks) more difficult. It can often be resolved with an inexpensive pair of reading glasses.

Night blindness from alcohol use may also persist into recovery. This is apparently the result of an ailing liver's inability to metabolize vitamin A, the vitamin that helps your night vision. Until your doctor says your liver is back to normal, you won't be able to take any vitamin A supplements, but in the meantime you should be able to safely eat plenty of carrots, sweet potatoes, and green leafy vegetables rich in beta-carotene. See also *Eye symptoms*.

Wheezing. Addicts can, of course, have asthma apart from their drug use. But some also develop wheezing (noisy, difficult breathing, especially on breathing out) and other symptoms of asthma because of an allergic reaction to inhaled or intravenous drugs, or because of damage done to the respiratory tract by drug use.

Your Mental Health in the Red Zone

Although you'll certainly be hearing from your body while you're in the Red Zone, it might feel like your brain is not saying much at all—or at least not anything clear. A good description of most people at this stage is "jittery or befogged," as they say in the *Big Book*.

The emotional and intellectual symptoms you have will depend on the drugs you used, how long and how heavily you used them, and your brain's reaction to their withdrawal. Overall, though, your mind is likely to be pretty numb and out of focus—so much so that you won't even realize how bad your mental state is until you've passed through it. At times you may *think* your mind has cleared—until the following week when you realize that things are so much clearer than before. Your emotions, too, may seem frozen at first. Then suddenly the cold haze of winter will lift, your emotions will thaw, and feelings you didn't know you had will burst forth and demand a hearing.

Try to be patient. Your mind will improve over time. Most people find that the frontal lobe, the part of the brain that gives us wisdom and judgment, is the last part to revive. A rule of thumb: one month of fogginess for every year of drinking or drug use.

Common Lingering Symptoms

EMOTIONAL AND INTELLECTUAL SYMPTOMS

"I've been sober for nearly two months and I still can't think straight. Can't concentrate. Can't

get anything done. I thought sobriety was supposed to clear my head."

It will—eventually. But the haze won't vanish overnight. The brain is one of the slowest parts of the body to recover from the ravages of substance misuse. Many brain cells are destroyed or damaged during active addiction, and it takes time to grow new ones and "tune up" those that are left. Studies show that the biggest increase in brain function occurs in the first six months of recovery, but gradual improvements in emotional and intellectual function can go on for ten years or more. So it could be a while before your brain feels fully recovered.

A wide range of emotional and intellectual symptoms are likely to trouble you in the first year or two of recovery. Some will go away quickly, some will last longer. Some common symptoms:

- You have fuzzy thinking, problems with judgment, mood swings, or an overall feeling of numbness.

- You feel oddly disconnected from your surroundings, like an outsider looking in.

- Your short-term memory doesn't work well—you're walking down the hall and suddenly can't recall where you're going or why.

- You find it hard to concentrate— you find yourself reading the same sentence over and over.

- You find it hard to solve problems—the problems you routinely solve, such as getting

the kids to school on time, get solved. But taking on a new one, like learning a new computer operating system, is too hard.

- You have problems with spatial relations—you download a map to a new AA meeting and can't make heads or tails of it.

- You forgot skills you learned while under the influence—a condition called "state-dependent learning."

These symptoms can be scary. But they are all very common, and they will all gradually go away. Many people report that the fog starts to lift after three months; others say six months. A few say it took a year. Good short-term memory sometimes does not return until the end of the second year. This process may be particularly slow for people who used certain prescription drugs, but almost everyone can look back at last week, last month, or last year and say, "Hey, I'm doing better!"

SUPERSENSORY PERCEPTION

"Though my brain seems numb, my senses seem extra sharp—as in too sharp. Every sound, every light, seems a thousand times more intense."

Very perceptive of you to notice. Many people in early recovery share this augmented sensory perception. A group of kids walking by sounds like a thundering herd of elephants. The light you usually read by is way too bright. Even your sense of touch may be altered—a wool sweater that never bothered you before now feels so itchy you can't bear it. It's all thanks to the snarled communications system in the brain.

These symptoms will gradually go away over the next few months. But until they do you may feel like screaming, just like a baby who has had too much sensory stimulation.

Instead of screaming, take some time to meditate or do relaxation exercises. You could also try earplugs, a white noise app, or a fan to block the excess noise, and sunglasses to dim the bright light.

PARANOIA

"On my last cocaine binge, I thought everyone was out to get me, including my parents. Most of those feelings are gone now, but after six weeks of sobriety, I still feel a little uneasy, a little threatened."

That's the cocaine talking. Like all stimulant drugs, it alters the chemical communications between brain cells. Many cocaine users have psychotic behavior, including paranoid delusions—the "you're all out to get me" syndrome. Things start to improve when you stop using the drug, but it will take a while before your messed-up neurotransmitter system and brain connections get back to normal. That's why many cocaine users in the Red Zone still feel a bit paranoid. If you're still feeling paranoid, try to relax.

Things will get better. Some guided visualizations or meditation may help you calm down.

In the meantime, you may want to stay in a safe place for a few weeks—a treatment center, a sober-living house, or the home of someone you trust and who is familiar with the needs of recovery. When you are in a place that feels safe and secure, your "survival brain" can rest and let the "social brain" take over and rebuild those healthy connections. If the feelings of paranoia threaten to get out of hand—if you think you are losing touch with reality, or feel you need to *act* on your fears—get some help immediately from an addiction professional.

Mental Health and Emotional Issues

SELF-ESTEEM ISSUES

"I'm sober, but when I look around at other people I realize I just can't measure up. I'm not real smart, and I don't have a lot of talent."

It's the nature of the alcoholic/addict to feel inadequate. Not because they are truly inferior (look at how many beautiful and talented actors become addicts) but because they hold themselves to unrealistically high expectations. And they think others expect that of them as well.

And while they underestimate themselves, they overestimate others. They think everyone else is happier, better-looking, smarter, richer, more talented. Your recovery work will help you rebuild your sense of self-worth. You will learn to accept yourself as you are, to know that what you are is good, and to appreciate your contributions to society.

The following tips can help:

- Stay sober. Get involved in a 12-step fellowship; they are great ways to build self-respect. Work the steps. When you are ready—in the Yellow Zone at the earliest—sponsor newcomers and help others get onto the path that helped you so much.

- Understand—with your heart as well as your mind—that alcoholism/addiction is a disease. People who use or drink destructively have an illness. They are not bad people. That includes you.

- Recognize that there's good in every person. Look for it in others, and in yourself, too. When you do a life history or inventory or write in your journal, be sure to list your positives, your strengths, as well as your weaknesses. You may have fewer negatives than you thought. Those things that were well intentioned but turned out badly, those mistakes you've tried to correct, are not negatives. If there are shortcomings you can change, try to do so, with the help of your Higher Power. If there are some you can't change, accept that.

- Avoid trying to bolster your self-esteem by feeding your ego. The woman who dresses seductively in an attempt to attract men is doing that. So is the man who bullies women. Though both may briefly feel good about themselves, the real emptiness inside is not filled.

- Keep your word—to yourself as well as others. If you can't trust and respect yourself, how can you expect others to do so?

- Learn the difference between self-respect and selfish self-centeredness. Find a few people you really trust, and ask them to let you know when things you do for your "self" are dishonest or at the expense of others.

- Figure out what your values are (see page 195) and take a close look at them to see if they are healthy. If they aren't, now is the time to rebuild them. If they are healthy, live by them.

- Surround yourself with people you respect, people you can learn from, who care about you and accept you for who and what you are. Those are the people who won't be fooled by (or even interested in) the false you.

- Make amends to those you have harmed (step 9). This will help you get rid of unnecessary guilt, which can demolish your self-esteem.

- Keep your goals realistic—which in early recovery means very modest—and work hard to meet them. This is not the time to take risks. Getting your entire life back on track in ninety days is not realistic. Staying sober one day at a time and going to ninety meetings in ninety days are challenging but realistic goals. Getting solidly entrenched in a path that will save your life is realistic.

- Like yourself. You deserve it, especially now. Show your gratitude by how you care for yourself—how you eat, exercise, dress, and treat yourself. Don't do this because you want to look good to others; do it for yourself. The more you act as though you like yourself, the more you will. As they say, "Bring the body, and the mind will follow."

- Think before you act. Ask yourself, "What will I think of myself if I do this? Will I respect myself more? Or less?"

- Stop comparing yourself to others. Everybody's different. And we all have the potential to be wonderful in our own way— you included. We just have to find what that way is. You'll get more out of relationships if you try to identify with others, rather than comparing yourself to them.

///////////////////////////

"My whole life is a disaster. I can't help thinking my alcohol problem is a punishment for being gay and for my dad leaving us. I couldn't stop him. I feel like a total failure."

Your life is messed up because of alcohol, period. It's not because of your sexual orientation or anything you did or didn't do. It's common for alcoholics to think they are being punished for something they have done. They have the idea that things happened to them because they were bad people—that such things don't happen to good people.

First of all, there is nothing wrong with being gay. You might live in a town where it's still not widely accepted, but in many other places, it's completely accepted. To many people, being gay or straight is just not an issue. And that attitude is becoming much more common.

Second, bad things do happen to good people all the time—whether they are gay or straight. No one is immune from bad events. Even those people who look like they've got it made often have bad stuff going on; they just hide it well.

The sense of worthlessness you're feeling is a common symptom of alcoholism. It's also an important contributory factor to alcoholism/ addiction. The feeling may be directly related to any number of causes (lack of support and encouragement while growing up, child abuse, learning disabilities, and so on).

Additional factors can also damage the self-esteem of LGBT kids over the years:

- Hearing from all sides—your family, church, friends, school—

that being gay is somehow "bad." (Again, it's not, and don't let anyone tell you otherwise. If they have a problem with it, it's *their* problem, not yours.)

- Hiding your sexual orientation—and maybe chiming in when others made fun of gays, feeding your guilt.

- Living in fear—fear of your sexual orientation being found out, fear of being rejected or hurt (even physically) if you tell others.

In recovery, your job will be not only to give up drinking but also to build a life that *you* see as having real worth. You may be able to do this just by going to AA or another fellowship and working with a sponsor. Or you may also need counseling with a therapist.

It would be good if you can talk with someone about your sexual orientation and how it has affected your life. If you can't find a welcoming AA group or a local therapist, try some online options. You will surely find support from many other young gay people in recovery who are working through the same issues. You'll also get support from older, and straight, people in recovery who accept LGBT people for who they are.

PANIC ATTACKS

"There have been a couple of times when I was in an uncomfortable situation and my heart began to race and I got all sweaty and had trouble breathing."

You were probably having an anxiety or panic attack. The symptoms usually include strong feelings of fear, worry, and tension. These can be disabling, as your mind runs wild with thoughts of what is happening or what might happen. The mental discomfort can also set off a flood of physical symptoms. Your body launches a defensive response, an adrenaline surge that leads to a rapid, sometimes irregular heartbeat, along with sweating, increased blood pressure, and problems catching your breath. Some people have hot flashes or chills, dizziness, shaking or trembling, choking, nausea or stomach pain, numbness or tingling, and altered senses of sight, sound, and time. If you have rapid breathing, you might also feel faint and have tingling lips and fingers. Many people feel oddly detached from their environment; they feel a sense of impending doom or feel like they are dying or going crazy. A person having a panic attack can be so scared it's hard for others to calm him.

These attacks are common in early recovery. At that time, the brain chemistry is still disturbed and an event can trigger an abnormal survival response. Your brain is no longer being soothed by your chemicals of choice, but neither is it making its own natural tranquilizers yet. So when your anxiety is triggered, there's nothing to calm it down. Panic attacks can also feed off themselves, so even the fear of having an attack can trigger one.

To head off panic attacks:

- First, avoid caffeine. Also avoid its cousin, theobromine, in chocolate and cocoa. Decaffeinated or caffeine-free drinks are okay, and carob is a good chocolate substitute.

- Second, make a serious effort to learn meditation, deep breathing exercises, and other relaxation techniques, which can help break the cycle. They can head off an impending panic attack as well as curb one that's begun. These are excellent tools that have many other uses in recovery, such as dealing with stress, warding off compulsions, and more.

- Third, try to identify your triggers—such as certain people, events, places, chemicals (such as caffeine)—and try to avoid or defuse them. If every time you see your father-in-law there's a blowup, avoid him for now. Then gradually try to work out your issues before resuming contact.

If you have panic attacks very often (four times a week or more), or if they start to interfere with your life, you should seek help. Cognitive behavioral therapy (CBT) and desensitization treatment are two effective treatments that are safe for those in recovery. Both are drug-free and focus on changing thinking and behavior to reduce your sensitivity to stimuli. Another effective approach is EMDR, or eye movement desensitization and reprocessing. It's another good alternative to treatment with drugs, especially for people with a history of trauma.

FEAR OF FAILURE

"I've been in recovery for three months, but I still seem to be living in fear—fear that I'll lose my job or my wife and kids or that I'll have a slip."

For most people in active addiction, fear becomes a way of life; it's a required element of survival. When they get sober, the fear is still there. That's not surprising. The ability to look to the future with self-confidence can be built only on a track record of successes. But this early in recovery, about all you have to look back on is a long, sad history of failures. As you pile up small victories—sober anniversary tokens among them—you'll start to lose your fears and feel more confident that things are going to work out after all.

So do your personal best on the job. Show your wife and children that you care. Be a good friend to others. And follow your recovery program faithfully. Right now, your fear serves a useful purpose, reminding you day after day how important it is to do what's necessary to stay sober. Self-confidence too early would likely sabotage that effort. If at any time your fear becomes disabling—you are unable to go to work, can't relate to your family, or can't get to meetings—get professional (drug-free) help from a physician, counselor, or therapist immediately.

AM I GOING CRAZY?

"Lately, I've been feeling like I'm going crazy."

If you're together enough to think you may be going crazy, you probably aren't.

This feeling is common in early recovery. It's partly because of the lingering effects of the chemicals you used, and partly because of the stress of adjusting to a new life that feels overwhelming. Usually, this feeling rears its head only occasionally and soon passes. Sometimes, however, the feeling pervades your life. That can signal more serious problems beneath the surface. Take a look at yourself. Are you taking any prescription drugs that may be clouding your thinking? Have you gotten away from your recovery program—missing meetings, neglecting to talk with your sponsor, avoiding 12-step work? Or are you abandoning other practices that anchor your recovery success? Getting back to your program can help you feel better. Are you doing too much, too soon? Keeping up a hectic pace can drive anyone to the edge.

If you can't pinpoint a problem that is causing your unhappy state of mind, or if you are having hallucinations or violent thoughts, get professional help right away. See a therapist who works with addiction.

If you are having suicidal thoughts, call 911 or the National Suicide Prevention Lifeline immediately, 800-273-TALK (8255).

GREAT EXPECTATIONS

"So I'm sober. Still, nothing works out the way I hope. What's the use?"

Many addicts and alcoholics expect their lives to be magically transformed and all of their fantasies to come true the moment they get sober. Their families will welcome them back with open arms; they'll land their dream job; life will be wonderful.

Unfortunately, when we have these great expectations, we set ourselves up for a Grand Canyon–size fall. Sure, those fantasies might happen, but they're the exception, not the rule. And they aren't likely to happen on day two of your sobriety, or even day sixty-two.

That doesn't mean you should throw all your dreams, hopes, and aspirations out the window—they're what keep all of us moving forward. So keep working for your long-term goals and dreams (in accordance with the Recovery Zone System timeline). But maybe scale them back a bit. Focus on a smaller goal for now, like getting *any* job, rather than the dream job. And don't expect that things will magically fall into your lap. It all takes time and work.

THE RED ZONE

MOOD SWINGS

"One day I feel great, the next just awful. There doesn't seem to be any rhyme or reason for my mood swings—they just come over me."

Many people in early recovery feel like a punch-drunk boxer in the ring: he's up, he's down, he's up, he's down. These mood swings, as long as they are not drastically altering your day-to-day life, are a normal part of recovery. (However, if you are so up that you go buy a new car you don't need with money you don't have, or so down you can't get yourself out of bed, you should see a doctor.) Why these mood swings happen is not entirely clear, but they may be due to both physiological and psychological factors.

Physiologically, alcohol and drugs can disrupt emotional stability and sabotage the brain's ability to keep our moods in balance. It's as though the brain says, "Hey, with all that Xanax coming in, you clearly don't need my help with your emotions." It stops producing the natural brain chemicals that help regulate moods. But when you stop popping the Xanax (or whatever drug you're using), the brain doesn't pick right up and start producing those chemicals again. It takes a while—sometimes quite a while—for the brain to realize that the external supply has been cut off. Meanwhile, brain function tends to be less organized and predictable than is normal. The result is both emotional instability (which leads to mood swings) and sensory instability (which can lead to itching, ringing in the ears, and other sensory oddities). Hormone changes may also flip-flop your moods.

Psychological reasons, too, add to roller-coaster moods. Emotional maturation stops when you start drinking or using drugs. Now that you are sober, you're trying to zip through missed developmental stages in a very short period of time, with all the up-and-down emotions of a teen. In addition, like anyone coping with a recently diagnosed illness, in early recovery you're going through a great deal of stress. Sometimes you feel good because things are going well; sometimes you feel bad because they're not, or because you're afraid the good days can't last.

The solution is to keep working your recovery program, including practicing all components of TAMERS (see chapters 1 and 3). If you do this faithfully, your brain will heal, and eventually the mood swings will subside.

EXTREME REACTIONS

"I feel like such a fool. I seem to over-react to everything and everyone. I cry when my boss tells me to redo a project, get angry when my husband asks if I picked up dinner on the way home from work, and am ecstatic when I hear from an old friend."

In case you don't recognize them, those are emotions you're feeling. Everybody feels them—everybody, that is, except active alcoholics and addicts. They take the edge off their emotions with chemicals. Their intention may be to get rid of the bad feelings, but of course the good ones get smothered, too.

Emotions don't usually resurface in early recovery. For the first months, and sometimes longer, you are likely to feel pretty numb. But once those emotions come back, they spill out all over, like a flood. And dealing with them is difficult because they've been dammed up for so long that they're strangers.

So what can you do? Recognize that overreacting is normal, and that it won't last forever. Usually by the end of the first year of recovery, the extremes begin to pull back; eventually they will disappear almost entirely. In the meantime, talk to others who've been through this. This is no time for stiff-upper-lip toughness. Sharing will be more important now than at any other point in your recovery. Trust your comrades in recovery with those thoughts, fears, and feelings that you've been keeping a secret (sometimes even from yourself). Do that and you will get to a degree of recovery stability that would not have been possible if you had toughed it out alone.

FEELINGS OF ANGER

"I find myself angry a lot of the time. I know that's not good, but I don't know what to do with my feelings."

Everyone feels angry sometimes, and anger can be a catalyst for good. Anger about a child being killed by a drunk driver can lead to tough legislation. Anger about what alcoholism/addiction is doing can help you save your life and your family.

But anger can also be unleashed in unhealthy ways. A parent angry at a crying baby can lash out and harm it. Anger can also blind us to possibilities, to truths, to our own shortcomings. And of course, a person in recovery can use his anger as an excuse for a relapse.

Acting on your angry impulses can be risky to your recovery, even if you don't relapse. It can serve to further cement those unhealthy behaviors into your emotional memory. Then anger becomes an unconscious tool you use more as a reflex than as a rational and desirable reaction.

Deflecting anger—turning it toward someone completely unrelated to the situation—can also be bad for everyone. Your boss chews you out at work; you snap at your partner when you get home. Your mom mistakenly throws out some of your important papers; you start screaming at your kids. This kind of anger solves nothing and only spreads the misery. Also futile is anger that is a result of exhaustion, lack of sleep, poor planning, guilt, and other feelings that have nothing to do with the final trigger.

Letting your anger simmer or covering it up isn't the answer. Anger has been linked to health issues such as high blood pressure, heart disease, headaches, skin disorders, and gastrointestinal problems. And pent-up anger, like uncontrolled anger, can lead to relapse.

Still, many people are afraid to express anger, afraid that they will antagonize others. This is especially true of those who grew up in families ruled by alcohol or drugs. Expressing anger when they were young meant being humiliated, being physically abused, or having love withdrawn. Expressing it now is still scary.

So what can you do with your anger? Recognize that it exists. Accept it. Realize that it's okay to be angry. It's what you do with it that really counts.

Keep track of the situations that tend to infuriate you, with either a notebook or an anger management app. Then try to figure out why these situations set you off and what you can do about them.

- Sometimes we are angriest with others when there is a grain of truth in what they are saying. When that's the case, don't shoot the messenger. Figure out what you can do to fix yourself.

- Sometimes anger is justified—as when someone has treated you poorly, or has been dishonest, cruel, or unkind. But even justified anger can be dangerous to your recovery at this point. The emotional energy you spend in expressing it is much better spent on recovery work. When possible, wait until later in

your recovery to start venting righteous indignation.

- Often there is no good reason for your anger. You could resent your boss for not giving you a promotion, or your family for not appreciating the miracle of your hard work and discipline in recovery, or the judge for not throwing your DUI case out of court. Try to be more realistic in viewing these events. You could say, "Okay, I was drunk for twelve years. What can I expect from people in six months?" When you put yourself in other people's shoes, you may find that they had no choice and you would feel the same way. Or that they had problems of their own that led them to hurt you, and they deserve empathy rather than anger. It's a matter of being a pessimist or an optimist. The optimists of this world always do better handling affronts. If you just can't find a positive spin to the situation, reserve judgment for now.

Also try some new ways to manage and express your anger.

- Try to settle down before you express your feelings. If the old "count to ten" doesn't work, count to one hundred—or wait an hour, or twenty-four. Then be calm and assertive rather than angry. Anger just leads to more anger, and it's nearly impossible to get your point across clearly when your mood's black and you're seeing red.

- When you can't get rid of anger directly, do it indirectly. Tell someone else how you feel, someone you trust and who isn't emotionally involved. Or tell yourself; write down your feelings in your journal. Or talk it out with yourself, recording it on your phone. Be careful about capturing your anger in digital forms such as email. Angry emails and online rants have a way of reaching the people who weren't supposed to see them.

- One of the best ways to get rid of your anger is to unburden yourself at a fellowship meeting. Or try using prayer and meditation to ask your Higher Power to free you from your anger. Some people use a "God Box" or "Higher Power Box" to deal with feelings: When they have a problem, they write it out on a piece of paper and put it in the box for handling.

- If your anger is directed at a situation, do something positive to eliminate it. If you're angry about your car breaking down every day, get it fixed, switch to mass transit, or carpool.

- Sometimes, the best way to get rid of anger is to turn your mind to something else—watch a movie, head for the gym, or listen to your favorite music.

- Look for the humor in the situation.

- Try stress reduction techniques (see Getting Healthy, page 333).

However you deal with your anger, your goal is to get rid of it, not to fuel it and keep it simmering. Once you've talked about it or done something about it, it's time to forget it and move on.

If you can't seem to deal with your anger at all—if you can't express it, or you're afraid that if you do you'll hurt someone or be hurt yourself—you need to share this feeling with others. Talk to your sponsor first. If you continue to fume, if your fuse is too short and explosions come too often, it could be a warning sign that your recovery is in trouble. Find an anger management class or get professional help.

Finally, turn your anger into a positive force in your life. Use your anger at the misery in your past as a motivation to work hard at your recovery. As you move along in recovery and get into the Yellow and Green Zones, you should be feeling anger less often and be able to handle it better.

If anger is directed at you, responding to it with anger serves no constructive purpose and can elevate the problem, causing damage you never intended. Instead, try to deal calmly with the issues. If you do start burning, use the above suggestions to cool off.

Listening attentively to someone else's angry tirade can also be a way to make amends for the things *you* did in anger during your active addiction.

DEPRESSION

"My boyfriend and I both got sober at the same time. Six months later I still seem to be depressed a lot, but he hardly ever is. Why is that?"

How depressed you are in recovery can depend on a lot of factors. One is the drugs you used. Those who used cocaine or amphetamines are more likely to be severely depressed than those who used alcohol or other drugs. Another is your gender. In general, more women than men get depression.

Another factor is the expectations you have for yourself. Some people who get depressed have high expectations for themselves, but not much confidence in their ability to reach those goals. Others are perfectionists, expecting everything to be perfect. When it's not, they're depressed. In addition, some people find it hard to go to others for help. With no outlet for their emotions, they turn the heat inward, setting the stage for depression.

A major reason for depression in recovery is biochemical. All emotions have a healthy purpose; depression is no exception. When your body is fighting illness, proteins produced by the brain can make you depressed. That's nature's way of telling you to slow down, go to bed, and give yourself time to heal. Plus, some of the symptoms that look like signs of depression (such as sleep problems and difficulty thinking clearly) are actually a normal part of early recovery. They will pass.

There are times, however, when professional help is needed. If you have an ongoing lack of pleasure in the things you used to like to do (at home, at work, or at play), if you feel somehow that you don't deserve to be happy, if your low mood keeps you from functioning at all, seek help from your doctor, therapist, or counselor. But be absolutely sure the person you see understands the problems that can arise from using medication in recovery. You don't want to risk falling back into active addiction. If you're having self-destructive thoughts, call 911 or the National Suicide Prevention Lifeline right away (800-273-8255).

WHEN FEELING SAD IS NORMAL

A death in the family, a divorce, the loss of a job—all such events can evoke sadness and depression. These feelings are normal and part of the necessary grieving process. How long they last and how deep they are depends on the kind of loss and our own reaction to it. If we don't allow ourselves to express these feelings soon after the event, the bottled-up emotions will eventually spill out in some less appropriate way.

So allow yourself to grieve when something bad happens. Then, when the pain begins to dull, gradually use the antidepression ideas later in this chapter to help you start feeling even better.

FEELING LONELY

"Sometimes I feel totally alone in the world, more cut off from my family and my friends than when I was using drugs. I don't understand why."

Alcohol and drugs anesthetize the brain, the organ that allows us to live at peace with others. Many active alcoholics/addicts think they are relating well to others, but this is rarely the case. At best, they make superficial connections.

Theoretically, because sobriety reverses the anesthesia, the wall of isolation should come tumbling down in recovery. But there are a couple of reasons why this doesn't always happen. One, some people in recovery claim that "being a loner is the way I am." In truth, this is because they're afraid people won't like them. Since they fear rejection, or they don't have the social skills to interact with others they way they think they should, they pretend (even to themselves) that they prefer to be alone. Two, many people failed to develop crucial social skills before they started using drugs, especially if they started in their teens. Many in active addiction use chemicals as a way to make friends instead, so they feel lost when they get sober.

The solution is to build your confidence and to work on skills such as listening, sharing, caring, and helping. The best place to do that is in the secure and welcoming environment of AA or another mutual-support fellowship. In addition to going to meetings, join some sober activity groups. Hanging out with others in a casual atmosphere will give you the chance to make friends and learn more about how to relate to people.

It's very important you address this feeling of isolation. It's a one-way street to relapse if you don't. Fortunately, if there is any truism in successful recovery, it is that you don't have to be alone anymore.

Getting Healthy

YOUR OPTIONS FOR MENTAL HEALTH CARE

As you see, there are many common mental health issues that can come up in recovery. Most often they will resolve on their own as your brain heals and your recovery gets stronger.

- Prevention is always the best option. Learn how you can prevent depression, anxiety, and other conditions from ever getting hold of you. Sometimes it's as simple as making sure you go to fellowship meetings.

- Drug-free self-care methods, such as meditation, yoga, and visualization, can work very well to tend to or prevent mental health woes. They may sound kind of New Agey, and they do take more effort than taking a pill—but they work. So give them a try.

- Also helpful: getting more involved in a community, getting some exercise, volunteering, and making other small changes in your life. You might be surprised at the immense benefit some simple habits can bring about.

- Seek help from a professional if your symptoms hang around for a long time or interfere with your daily life. Start with the people who are treating you for addiction. If you're not working with someone now, read about the types of health care professionals who work in mental health in chapter 5. If you do see a new health care provider, be sure to tell him you are in recovery, and *you very much prefer not to use any mood-altering drugs of any kind.* That includes antidepressants, antianxiety drugs, and others that can alter moods. If he suggests drugs anyway, insist that you try other options first. Don't be pushed into taking drugs; this is *your choice.* Then work with him to do everything you can to address your issues with nondrug means. Mood-altering drugs are usually unnecessary, and they *will* raise your risk of relapse. You haven't

come this far only to get turned around by a well-meaning health professional. Those drugs, ideally, should be used only in a life-and-death situation. (Read more on page 290.)

If you don't have health insurance, or money to pay for mental health care out of pocket, you still have options. Many counties and states offer free and very low-cost mental health care. See chapter 5 for some tips on finding local treatment programs. You might also find local programs in the phone book.

If you are having thoughts of suicide or of harming yourself, please call for help *right now.* Call 911 or the National Suicide Prevention Lifeline, 800-273-TALK (8255).

PREVENTING DEPRESSION, ANXIETY, AND OTHER MENTAL HEALTH ISSUES

You *can* lower your chances of developing depression and anxiety. Here's how:

- Work hard at your recovery program. But don't try to do everything at once; follow the Recovery Zone System to take on rebuilding the parts of your life at the right time.

- Try to anticipate events that could upset your smooth recovery. Do regular Recovery Zone ReChecks to keep an eye on upcoming events and know when you should increase your recovery activities to avoid a relapse.

- Practice TAMERS so your brain heals and becomes as healthy as it can be.

- Learn coping, decision-making, and communication skills.

- Learn to express your feelings and share worries.

- Avoid procrastination. A long to-do list can be depressing and anxiety-provoking.

- Keep busy with positive, healthy activities, but not so busy that you are exhausted or have no time for recovery work.

- Organize your time to reduce stress; keep track of your schedule on a calendar so you have an overview of everything that's going on. Be sure to reserve time for exercise, meditation, and relaxation.

- Keep your expectations realistic; don't expect perfection.

- Stay honest. Getting caught in a lie—or fearing you'll be caught— is a major cause of anxiety.

- Keep an eye out for medications that might contribute to the blues. Some that you might not suspect, such as blood pressure medications, can depress your mood.

- Explore the blues-prevention tips below and incorporate what works for you into daily life.

NONDRUG WAYS TO DUMP (OR PREVENT) DEPRESSION, ANXIETY, STRESS, AND THE BLUES

We have seen every one of these tips work for someone. With a little trial and error, you'll figure out what works for you. And don't wait for the blues to hit before you start experimenting—find some things that work for you and make them a regular part of your life.

Get out. You've heard it before. Now hear it again: Go to a meeting. *Especially if you don't feel like going.* You become what you do. It's an act of faith (and brain health), and it works.

Get your feelings out. Call your sponsor, a fellowship friend, your partner, your best friend, or someone else you trust. Talk with them about your feelings or your problems, specifically and honestly. Sharing the load makes it lighter. Can't reach anyone? Find an online meeting or pour your heart out in an online forum. Write in your journal or your blog. Take your dog for a walk and have a chat with him.

Get up and do something. Depression can be paralyzing; some days you just want to crawl into bed and hibernate. Don't give in to it. Do something—anything—even if it's just a walk around the block, preferably with someone you like.

Check out (temporarily). If the news stresses you out, take a time-out. Avoid the TV and news sites for a while. If ambient noise bugs you, make a practice of listening to music or white noise on the bus, on the plane—wherever you can't control your surroundings. Get a massage. Watch some funny movies, or animal or baby videos.

Learn from others. Read recovery materials. Browse through your daily meditation resource to find topics that apply to your current situation. Read the Bible or another inspirational book. Listen to some reassuring AA talks and recorded meetings and get a lift from other people's experiences. (See chapter 8.)

Be with others. When you feel down, avoid being alone. If you need to stay close to home for illness, ask some AA or NA friends to come over for a bedside meeting, or go to an online or phone meeting.

Do for others. The selfish component of depressed feelings can make things worse. You can reverse this if you stop thinking about yourself and do something for someone else. Send your mom some flowers; write a poem for your sister's birthday; take over a household job your roommate usually handles. Spend a night helping out at a homeless shelter; cheer up an elderly relative with a visit; plan a movie night with the kids. Sign up as a volunteer dog-walker or kitty-cuddler at an animal shelter. If you're far enough along in recovery (usually the Yellow or Green Zone), and your sponsor approves, do some step-12 work

helping another alcoholic or addict who is worse off than you. Studies show that volunteering makes people feel better physically and mentally, lowers their stress, and fosters a deeper sense of belonging to a community.

Make a recovery program checklist. Are you going to meetings, talking with your sponsor, doing personal inventories, and helping (not controlling) others? Go to a few extra meetings. Many people find they need more meetings when they're going through rough times—just like the person with diabetes who needs more insulin when they eat more carbs. Read earlier chapters of this book and review the Recovery Zone System guidelines in chapter 2 to make sure you are not skipping anything or taking on too much at once. Are you worried about an upcoming event or situation that you fear might tempt you to relapse? Prepare for it by doing a Recovery Zone ReCheck. Read over the many ways you can help your brain heal in chapter 3 and try some new options.

Make a gratitude list. Be thankful for what you have. Make a list of people who like you, who love you. Count the miracles that have happened to you, including sobriety. Draw up a balance sheet comparing what you are now to what you were when you first got sober. Your progress will probably surprise you.

Make a top ten list. What are the top ten best parts of your day? Best people in your life? Most fun activities? Future vacation spots?

Make a worry list. List all the things that are bothering you, then cross off all those you don't have to take care of today. You can worry about them tomorrow. Next to the remaining worries, write down what steps you can take to deal with them. Then start dealing. Avoid catastrophizing—don't turn a problem into something bigger than it really is.

Look to the future. Think about where you expect to be in a year— another year sober: maybe back in school or back at work, with a few dollars in the bank.

Take care of yourself. A healthy body supports a healthy mind. Be sure to eat well, get regular exercise, and get a good night's sleep.

Get outside—regularly. Many people have little or no connection with nature, but a regular dose of nature can do wonders for mental health. So make a regular habit of walking in the woods, having lunch by a lake, watching birds, smelling the pine trees. You don't have to climb a mountain every day; if you live in a city, even spending time in a small park watching the squirrels can help.

Try distraction. Divert yourself with something you enjoy—a crossword or jigsaw puzzle, a movie, organizing your photos, knitting, needlepoint, a good book, a bike ride, a hike with a friend, or another hobby (if you don't have one, start

looking). Call your favorite aunt. Or tackle something that needs doing—clean a closet, bathe the dog, fold the laundry. Some people keep a list of tasks for just such an occasion, and get pleasure out of crossing something off. Simply uncluttering your personal space can be stress-relieving.

Try inspiration. Listen to soul-stirring music, take a walk on the beach and watch the sun set (or rise), visit a house of worship, pray, join a choir, listen to your favorite AA recordings, or read the *Big Book* or other recovery literature. If you can't get outside, watch some nature videos.

Try exertion. Exercise helps trigger good feelings by causing the release of endorphins, more of those "feel good" chemicals. So go for a brisk walk, a run, a bike ride, a swim. Shoot some baskets, play tennis, plant a garden, or do whatever you consider both fun and exercise. Or get your exercise along with a sense of achievement by doing physical work that needs to be done—wash windows, scrub floors, mow the lawn, wash the car.

Try meditation. A little directed thinking can do wonders.

Try relaxation. Try any activity that helps you unwind, such as yoga, sports, fishing, gardening, knitting, deep breathing, writing in your journal, hiking, golfing, birding, watching TV, reading, listening to music, hobbies, listening to recordings (AA or others), or taking a hot bath, a long drive, or a short nap.

Try supplication. Prayer, especially the Serenity Prayer, can work wonders. Try to get in touch with your Higher Power, however you interpret it. For some, anxiety and depression are related to a lack of reliance on a Higher Power; the result is that fears and expectations rule your emotions. Surrendering this emotional control can free you from feelings of anxiety and depression. Revisit your early 12-step work with your sponsor or spiritual advisor.

Try illumination. Some cases of depression, particularly in women, are related to Seasonal Affective Disorder. With winter's short days providing less light, some people get deeply depressed. Light therapy, being exposed to bright light for several hours during the day, can miraculously bring you out of the doldrums.

Try manipulation. Of your diet, that is. Sugar is sometimes at the root of depression or anxiety. Cutting it out of your diet may lift your mood.

Try more manipulation. Of your language. Ban the words "always" and "never" from your vocabulary. Turn negative thoughts into positive statements. Rather than "I can't do that," think "I can do that, if I start with this small step."

Try invention. Be creative. Build something, paint, sew, sculpt, cook, write a song, build a website, create a video of your kids or pets, start a blog. Write a poem or short story (perhaps drawing on your experiences with drugs or alcohol).

Try a little tenderness. Be kind to yourself; you deserve it. Share something special with your partner, friend, or family.

Give in. For one day, stop fighting your blues and give in to it. You'll see that the world won't fall apart if you stand on the sidelines for a day. Indulge in a little "cinematherapy." Find a tearjerker movie and cry along with the characters. Or say to yourself, "Okay, today I feel really rotten, so I'm going to go to sleep early. When I wake up tomorrow, I'm going to feel much better."

Give over. Turn whatever it is you can't handle over to your Higher Power.

But don't give up. Remember that today you may feel down, but tomorrow is a new day. These feelings have always passed before; they will this time, too.

Call for help. If you're too depressed or anxious to do any of the above, call your sponsor, an AA friend, another friend, your spouse, your doctor, or your counselor as your first line of support. (Get their numbers in your phone now—*before* you need them.) Be very clear that you are inviting them to help you, that you *want* them to help you. Sometimes, we get so emotionally disconnected that it's hard to relate to others, or tell them what we need—ironically, that's when we really need to reach out. In addition, other people may worry that they are imposing on us if they reach out to help us unsolicited. If you give people permission to help you, to get involved in your life, they often become empowered with solutions.

Call for more help. If your depression stubbornly hangs on, speak to your doctor or therapist or consult a treatment center. You may need more treatment. Also get help if your behavior or feelings indicate to you (or others) that anxiety or depression may be driving you toward a relapse.

MEDITATION, MINDFULNESS, AND OTHER PRACTICES

"Some people in my home group said they practice 'mindfulness meditation' as part of their recovery program. That sounds a bit 'out there,' and not exactly like what I've been doing in NA the last few months. But I'd like to give it a try."

Meditation and mindfulness techniques can be excellent additions to your recovery program. Many people in recovery make them a part of their daily lives and swear by their effectiveness. In fact, step 11 specifically calls for meditation.

Meditation is simply doing some directed thinking, or mind exercises, to make yourself feel better—physically, mentally, and emotionally. It's a way to tune in to yourself, or tune in to support outside yourself—to draw strength

from your Higher Power, or from God, if you are a religious person. In this hectic, always connected, multitasking world, we rarely take time to slow down and listen to our inner voices and outer support. But in recovery, it's necessary.

Mindfulness is a psychological state in which people have a particular awareness of their sensations, thoughts, and feelings, and experiences them with acceptance and without judgment. Some call it a form of "radical acceptance." In essence, you learn to pay better attention to your thoughts and feelings, dismiss distractions, and accept those thoughts without judgment. Rather than changing your thoughts, mindfulness changes your *relationship* with your thoughts. In doing so, you are able to let them go; you give them no more than a brief notice, instead of letting them grab control of your mind (and ruin your whole day). For example, some people use mindfulness to deal with cravings; with practice, when they experience cravings they are able to roll right through them without giving them undue influence or power over their lives. Others use it to reduce their susceptibility to cues and triggers, or to deal with difficult memories or self-critical thoughts.

Although people have been experiencing the benefits of meditation and mindfulness for centuries (some of these practices began as early Buddhist traditions), scientific imaging studies have now proven that they can work hand in hand with the neuroplasticity of the brain (its ability to adapt and change, which we discussed in chapter 1). With just a few weeks of practice, meditation and mindfulness can change the brain's structure and function, resulting in better focus and attention; reduced stress; increased empathy for others; better self-care, impulse control, and decision making; and growth in the areas that govern memory, learning, and emotion. There is also evidence that these practices can help with pain control, immune function, anger, depression, and anxiety—and in so doing, enhance your recovery.

You can meditate and practice mindfulness while you're sitting in your living room, lying in bed, walking on the beach, or running in the morning. As you get better at it, you'll be able to use these techniques to calm yourself in stressful situations.

There are many different approaches: relaxation meditation, contemplation meditation, life-in-order meditation, mindfulness meditation, mindfulness-based stress reduction (MBSR), and guided imagery. Some of these techniques are best mastered with the help of an expert via a recording or a class. You might even consider a weekend learning retreat with others in recovery or as part of a spiritual or recovery community.

If you're a novice, the following tips will help you get started.

- Meditation takes practice. You may not get it at first, but if you keep trying, eventually you will.

- Set aside a regular time each day for meditation. You might even integrate it into your regular personal inventory practices. Some people find the early bird catches the spirit best; they meditate in the morning, before everyone else wakes up. For others, the end of the day, when they are in bed, is most conducive to communing with themselves. Still others find that walking, running, or swimming helps them focus. It's best to choose a quiet place until you get more skilled at meditation. Experiment to find out what works for you.

- If you find it hard to tune in to yourself, tune in to someone else first by listening to AA recovery talks or by reading recovery meditation materials such as *Twenty-Four Hours a Day* or *One Day at a Time*. A soft musical background (classical, religious) or sounds-of-nature recordings help some people ease into the mood for meditation.

- Empty your mind of extraneous thoughts before beginning. There are several ways to do this. Try to breathe in and out several times, focusing on your breathing and nothing else, or close your eyes and count to one hundred.

- To set the mood, visualize a place you associate with serenity (a mountain stream, a deserted beach at sunset) or imagine yourself floating serenely on a cloud. You can focus on a painting or photo in the room or summon up a scene in your mind. Try to do more than just watch the scene from afar. Try to go there in your focused mind, then try to feel it—through sound, touch, smell, and even taste. Relax your body as well as your mind. Once your meditation is done, slowly bring your focus back to your surroundings, so your experience is truly a mini excursion to a different place.

If you meditate to music, once you have practiced it for a while, you may want to set your ring tone or text ping to a similar tone, which will remind your brain of those peaceful thoughts throughout the day. You can also record a short voice clip of your sponsor or some other inspiring person, incorporate it as part of your meditation, and then listen to it during the day for a relaxing reminder. You might also arrange to have text messages or emails with these various soothing messages sent to you automatically—either at random times of the day, or at those hours you find the hardest to get through.

A Few Meditation and Relaxation Types

There are many techniques you can use to meditate and relax. Try a few and see what works for you. Ask your friends what they like. And stretch yourself: Explore something you never thought you would do, like tai chi.

Relaxation meditation. The purpose here is to relax completely, both body and mind. You do this by emptying your mind of extraneous thoughts and focusing on breathing, on your movements if you're walking, on a peaceful scene, on a word, or on a simple, repetitive prayer or thought. For some people, yoga does the trick. For others, deep breathing or progressive muscle relaxation exercises work. For others, reading escapist literature (something that is pure fun) works.

Relaxation meditation is good for getting the kinks out on a regular basis. It's also good for reducing anxiety when you're tense. Just a minute or two of deep breathing can lower your blood pressure and reduce your stress level.

Try some simple relaxation exercises. Get into a comfortable position, close your eyes, breathe in deeply and say, "I am . . . ," then breathe out and say, ". . . relaxed." Next, say, "I am . . . calm and serene." You can stop there, or you can follow that by imagining you're breathing in and out through your feet and then, in turn, your legs, abdomen, chest, back, arms, face, and scalp—which indeed your cells are doing. Or just concentrate on tightening and then relaxing each muscle group in your body, one by one.

Contemplation meditation. In this form of meditation, you simply take some quiet time to think about the past day or days, about your failures and successes, and how you can make the next day better. If you have trouble getting started, review a recent personal inventory. You can also use contemplation meditation as a way of taking an inventory. Ask yourself, "Have I been honest in all my words and actions today? Have any of my thoughts, words, or actions benefited me (or my ego) at the expense of others?"

Life-in-order meditation. When responsibilities pile up faster than the hours in your day, it helps to take time out to reorder priorities and think about what you need to do. Have a small pad and pen handy to jot down key words during this type of meditation.

Guided imagery. With this technique, you listen to a live person or a recording that helps you focus your thoughts and direct your imagination. The speaker guides you to a relaxed state and then through a scenario, such as sitting by a lake, watching immune system cells course through your body, or seeing yourself as a healthy nonsmoker. Many guided imagery programs are tailored to people with specific conditions, such as addiction, depression, PTSD, or anxiety. Others are geared toward helping with restful sleep or simply relieving stress. Guided imagery can be an easy way to get into meditation, as you only have to sit back and listen. It is sometimes referred to as self-hypnosis.

Mindfulness-Based Stress Reduction (MBSR). This is a standardized program, typically taught as eight weekly classes. It combines mindfulness meditation techniques, yoga, and discussions.

Tai chi, yoga, or qigong. These activities all involve gentle exercise, specific movements, breathing techniques, and concentration. Some people consider them "moving meditation." Many find them very helpful for stress reduction.

For Teens and Young Adults in Recovery

I f you're a teenager or young adult with a drinking or drug problem, you might feel like you've already made such a mess of your life, it's too late to do anything about it. But that's like giving up on a book in the first few pages. You still have many chapters to go in your life story, and the quicker you change your ways, the happier and healthier—and longer—that story is likely to be.

This chapter will get you headed in the right direction. It covers many of the concerns of teens and young adults who are trying to get sober and stay that way. As you move along in recovery be sure to read other parts of this book as well. The more you know about the disease of addiction, the better your chances of beating it. With hard work, you can come out a winner.

Right now, you might think you are the only person your age with this problem. But that's far from true.

The good news is that more than half of all high school students don't drink, take drugs, or smoke. So you will be able to find plenty of sober friends—friends who want

to put their brains to work building great lives for themselves.

If you're not yet addicted— maybe you're just experimenting— there are some things we'd like you to think about. At your age, your brain is still developing, and because of that, addictive substances can alter your brain's structure and functioning much faster than if you were just a few years older. That means that right now, you are at *much* higher risk for becoming a full-blown addict or alcoholic than someone who is older. And the younger people are when they start using, the higher the risk. Addiction is much less likely when people don't start using until they are in their mid-twenties or older. In fact, most of the adults who now have a substance use disorder started when they were teenagers—and many of them have now been desperately fighting to get sober for years. Ask any one of them—that is *not* where you want to be in the future.

Are You Ready to Change? It's Time

I'M AFRAID TO GET HELP

"I know my parents are right. I've got to stop drinking and using. But I'm very nervous."

That's normal. Deciding to get help for your drinking or drug problem can be scary.

It's scary for adults, too, but as a teenager, your situation is a little different. In some ways, you have real advantages over older people.

- One advantage is that you may not be deep into denial yet. Young people are pretty good at realizing that the life they want is slipping away from them.

- Another plus is that you are still at a point in your life where learning comes easy.

- And best of all, teens who get off drugs and alcohol when they are young have a wonderful blank canvas in front of them. You have many years of life left, and the opportunity to do whatever you want with them. If you get help, every opportunity in life will still be there for you: You can get a degree, learn a trade, have a career, a family—do anything you want to do.

These things are not often true for adults who are getting sober. Many have lived an addictive life for decades, and the lies they tell themselves to keep using are deeply entrenched and hard to unlearn. They find it much harder than teens to break old habits and learn new ones. And, sadly, they often don't have the time to go back and do it all again, or fix the wreckage they've left behind.

That's not to say it will be easy for you. With fewer years behind you, you still need to develop and mature, and learn many basic living skills. Most chemically dependent teens and young adults haven't had a chance to develop a complete value system. They haven't fully learned how to organize their time, succeed in school, take care of their personal needs, and communicate skillfully and successfully with friends or family.

So in addition to working on sobriety, you will also have to take on the job of moving into adulthood.

If you continue drinking or using drugs, however, your education and career training will almost certainly be disrupted, leaving gaps in your life that may never be adequately filled. Your freedom to live your dreams will become more and more limited. Doors will start closing. Eventually, the only door left open will be the one to life as an addict—maybe an addict who is in and out of prison for the rest of his life. You really don't want that.

So get help now. The sooner, the better. You have only a short time to reap all the advantages of finding sobriety as a young person. Your life and your freedom to live it are on the line.

IT'S TOO LATE

"I'm sixteen and I've been using oxys for nearly a year. I have to stop. But a friend said that you can't get off these painkillers once you're hooked—that it's no use trying."

Doctors once thought that many drug addictions were impossible to kick, but we know now that's not true. *Millions* of people have done it. In fact, in some ways, those addicted to even the hardest drugs have an advantage over those who abuse alcohol. The effects of alcohol abuse are slower to show up, so it can take years before an alcoholic will admit there's a problem.

In contrast, many people who use drugs like cocaine, Spice, and some prescription pills know right away that they have a problem. The good news is that because a narcotics addiction comes on fast, users don't have years of a deeply entrenched addict lifestyle behind them that has to be rebuilt in recovery. So don't let anyone tell you that you can't give up these drugs. You can.

HOW TO FIND HELP

If you haven't started on the road to recovery yet, you may be feeling overwhelmed about what you should do and where you can get help. Your options for treatment will be similar to those of adults, though tailored to the special needs of young people. So start by reading chapter 1, Welcome to Recovery.

When you are ready to get started, find someone to help you.

- Talk to your parents. Be honest with them about what you've been doing and tell them you need some help. They can help you get into treatment.

- If your parents are not likely to be of much help, talk to a teacher, a school nurse or counselor, your family doctor, a coach, the parents of a friend, your therapist, an older sibling or friend, a trusted neighbor, your priest or rabbi, a grandparent, an aunt or uncle, or someone at the campus health service or a local mental health agency. Tell them you want to get sober and you need someone to help you.

- Start going to AA or NA meetings on your own (look for a group that has at least a few young people). Figure out who are the leaders in the group, the people who have a strong sobriety, and ask them for some guidance.

- Call the Substance Abuse and Mental Health Services Treatment Referral Helpline at

800-662-HELP (4357) or search online at findtreatment.samhsa .gov. You can talk to a live person who will help you find local resources.

- Also check out the resources for finding help in chapter 5.

Fitting In When You're in Recovery

YES, LIFE WILL GO ON

"I just went through a session with my parents, my dorm advisor, and our family doctor. They finally convinced me I need to stop drinking so much every weekend. But drinking to get wasted is what we do in college. I'll be the only loser who can't party."

You might think everyone else drinks or does drugs, but in fact, many people your age *don't* partake. There are many students at your school who don't rely on alcohol or drugs to have fun—kids who enjoy sports, who like to dance, listen to music, watch movies, and yes, have parties.

If you're afraid you can't be one of them, maybe it's because you've never tried. Or maybe it's because you're unsure of yourself and you're afraid to try to be one of the gang without some chemical help.

There are lots of ways you can build up your confidence:

Get involved in a recovery program. Recovery programs (for adults as well as younger people)

help build self-esteem, self-respect, and empowerment. In a recovery program, you'll be able to talk with a counselor or a doctor about those fears of not fitting in. And the longer you stay sober, the better you will feel about yourself.

Stay away from your old crowd. The kids you used to drink or do drugs with should be off-limits. This will probably be easier than you think, because once they know you are sober and plan to stay that way, they are likely to take a walk.

Clean up your online life. Like most young people, you probably live half your life online. Take some time to clean up the image you're sending out to the world. You want to attract the kind of friends who are not binge drinkers or drug users. And don't forget that someday you will be looking for a job—and most employers will check you out online. (You might think they don't look at Facebook, but they do. Not much is private these days.) Don't mess up your chances for a great career before you even get started. Unfriend all those hard-partying friends. (See more on page 233.)

Change your phone number. It will be easier to avoid the party friends if they can't call or text you. An easy way to do that is to swap your phone with your mom or dad. Trust us, Mom will find it easier than you to ignore the keg party invites. If you can't get a new phone or a new number, delete all the numbers of the people you want to avoid. Don't make it easy to fall back into your old habits.

Build a new social life around your recovery program. There are *many* other college students who've been through the same kinds of turmoil you've been through and who are now sober. You can learn a lot from them and have good times with them. They are just like the people you used to hang out with, but now none of you needs booze or drugs to have a good time. For now, just focus on building friendships with them. Your sponsor, as well as any others who help guide your recovery, should be people who are a bit older than you (young people in recovery don't usually have enough experience to be mentors). Those older folks will know how to keep your life out of the ditch.

Consider a recovery campus. If you're worried you won't be able to avoid partying at your current school, think about transfering to a school with a strong recovery program. Many schools now have them (see page 197). Some have an entire dorm set aside for those in recovery. To many kids (and adults), recovery is the hip place to be these days.

Take good care of yourself. This is something you probably weren't too good at before you got sober. Shower regularly; keep your hair clean; brush and floss your teeth. Pay attention to what you eat.

Get into fitness. Sports can make you feel better, occupy your time constructively, and start you on the road to a lifetime of fitness. Join a club or a team at your school to find others with the same interests. (See chapter 24 for more exercise tips.)

Find new role models. Look around at the kids in your school. You may be able to tell who drinks and uses drugs and who doesn't by the way they dress or wear their hair. Think about dressing like the most productive and successful kids in your school. And don't forget how many celebrities are in recovery. They are not all outspoken about it, but you can be sure that many of your favorite musicians and actors are sober.

Find some new music. You might have always listened to particular types of music when you were drinking and using drugs. Listening to those types now could be a cue that triggers a relapse (see chapter 10). If you find that escaping into a familiar beat triggers old user feelings or weakens your enthusiasm for recovery, turn it off and keep it off. If you really want to keep listening to a certain type of music, play it only occasionally, or do it in conjunction with recovery activities, such as reading recovery literature or meditating. With enough repetition and listening in a positive environment, your brain can reassociate the music with recovery.

Think about your goals in life. Who do you want to be? What do you want out of life? What do you want to contribute to society? You may not know exactly what you want, but you can start exploring. You can find some dreams to start working toward. Sober, you are more likely to be able to clarify what these goals are and then progress toward them one step at a time.

YOU *CAN* RESIST DRUGS AND ALCOHOL

"I just went back to high school after six weeks of treatment and summer vacation. What do I do when my friends ask if I want to get high?"

You are smart to think ahead. You need to make a plan to deal with this kind of situation long before it comes up, or you might have trouble refusing their offers. Peer pressure can be tough to fight, but you can resist.

All you need are the right tools. You probably got some of them in treatment, and you'll pick up others as you go to more AA or NA meetings. Talk about this issue with your counselor, your sponsor, and other kids in your school who are in recovery. Ask them exactly what they do to avoid problems. The following may also be helpful:

- Think ahead to situations you may come up against and plan exactly what you'll do in each one. Act out some scenarios with your sponsor or counselor; that will make it easier to handle them when they occur in real life. If someone approaches you, try not to look scared or nervous. Stand tall, look directly at them, and speak firmly and confidently,

leaving no doubt that you mean what you say.

- Don't get into a debate with someone who is trying to convince you to get high. Just ignore the bait; don't engage in the conversation. Change the subject or go talk with someone else.

- It takes two to make a drug deal: a seller and a buyer. Walk away and don't let that sale happen. Don't risk your recovery. Say no and leave.

- Block phone calls, texts, and emails from people you don't want to be around. Delete their contact info.

- Don't tempt yourself by looking at old party photos on Facebook. Delete them now. Untag yourself. (See more on page 233.)

- Stay away from the people and places you associate with getting high. If anyone asks, let them know you've been to treatment and are in recovery; hang out with other kids in recovery or straight kids.

- You won't be able to avoid socializing, so be sure to read the advice in chapters 10 and 11 on doing it safely and sober.

- Don't be afraid to ask for advice. If you are upset, confused, or unsure of what to do, find someone who can help you. Asking for help is a sign of strength, not weakness.

Talk with your sponsor, drug counselor, an AA friend, your guidance counselor, your clergyperson, or a teacher. If you feel comfortable doing so, speak to one or both of your parents, another relative (maybe you have one who is involved in recovery), or a sober friend's mom or dad. They were all teens once, and peer pressure was every bit as heavy then as it is now.

- Download some recovery apps for your phone. They can help you to chart your days sober, recognize your triggers, and more.

- Whenever you're tempted to get involved with drugs or alcohol again, think about the consequences. Weigh the long-term risks against the short-term benefits. Remember what life was like when you were using—a little bit of heaven, a whole lot of hell. Think about who else you'll hurt (besides yourself) if you relapse. Think about messing up your schoolwork and your future. Think about the fact that, as a young person, you are very likely to end up with a serious addiction as an adult if you continue to use now. If you think you'll need something to remind you, write up your story and tuck it away someplace safe, so you can refer to it later on. See Lest You Forget: Remembering the Bad Old Days on page 228.

- Whatever you do, don't let other kids make the decisions that can so powerfully affect your life and your health. It's your life, and you're in charge of it.

PEER PRESSURE AND BULLYING

When people talk about teens and drugs, they often refer to peer pressure. That means pressure from friends and other people your age to do something or act a certain way. You've probably seen or experienced this a lot.

Peer pressure is not always on the surface or obvious. You mention at the lunch table that you're going to study this weekend instead of going to a party, and a major eye roll from one of the supposedly cool girls clearly says to all how uncool you are. So you feel pressure to go to the party and do what you can to fit in. Or you turn down a beer at the party, and everyone laughs. Next time, you chug it, even if you didn't want it.

These days, much of the peer pressure takes place online. A teenage girl (wisely) says she's not ready for a sexual relationship, and she gets teased on Facebook or bombarded with texts about what a nerd she is. A guy says he doesn't do drugs anymore, and he gets blasted with texts about how he's just a chicken and not fun anymore. The best response is to ignore it—don't feed the trolls. Bullies want to get a rise out of you. If they don't, they'll move on. It can be really hard to not fire back, but do your best to just ignore them. Block their texts or emails. Unfriend them. Delete their messages without reading them. If they continue to bother you, print out the evidence of what they are doing and tell a trusted adult who can deal with the situation.

Some other tips for standing up to bullying:

- Stand up for others who are being bullied. Don't be a silent bystander. If someone encourages you to join in the harassment, tell them that you don't do things like that, and you wish they wouldn't either. Do what you can to break the cycle, and notify an adult about what's going on.

- Don't engage in bullying another person, even if it seems like an innocent act: You might think you are just passing around a funny video of someone, or forwarding a private text message, but that person might be feeling horribly humiliated.

- Distance yourself from the people who are doing the bullying—in person and online (see page 233 for tips on handling social media).

Think before you post. Keep your private information private. Remember that pretty much anything you post online is now out there for all the world to see, even long after you try to delete it.

You have to be a strong person to resist peer pressure to do something you know is wrong. It helps to keep in mind that, no matter what lead or leader you follow, *you* are responsible for—and will pay the price for—what you do.

START A REBELLION

Doing something because everyone else is doing it is the way of sheep, not of tough, smart people. If it's the norm to drink and use drugs in your school, start a counterrevolution. Get together with a group of friends and sign a pact, promising you won't drink, smoke, or take drugs. Get as many kids as you can to join in.

You might also get involved in local efforts to help other students avoid binge drinking (including college hazing activities that involve drinking). A number of organizations are working on these issues at schools across the country.

If you see someone who might be overdosing on drugs or alcohol, call 911—even if you are not sober yourself or if others try to discourage you from doing so. Too many young people have died because those around them were afraid to get the police involved, out of fear they would be arrested themselves for illegal drugs or underage drinking. Cold showers and hot coffee won't help. Getting medical attention will—and could—save a life. This is *not* a rare occurrence—more than 1,800 college students die of alcohol-related causes every year.

Many colleges, local communities, and states now have "medical amnesty" or Good Samaritan policies and laws that protect those who call for help. Find out what the policy is in your area, and be sure others know about it as well.

Working Things Out—at Home

"My dad's done nothing but scream since the school counselor told them I got caught with Baggies full of Oxy-Contin and Adderall. My mom just cries all the time. I'm going through treatment now, but I don't know how I can face going home."

Your parents are probably just as worried about your homecoming as you are. They're upset because they love you and are afraid of what drugs could do to you. Addiction is a fatal disease. They can't help but be painfully aware of how many kids like you are dead because of overdoses or other complications of addiction.

During treatment you'll have lots of time to think about what happened, to learn about your disease, and to evaluate yourself and your life. Your parents need to use this time to think about it, too.

You and your counselor or doctor can encourage your parents to do the following:

- Attend the family portion of your treatment program, if there is one. If not, ask if your parents can spend some time with your counselor before you go home.

- Go to Al-Anon or Nar-Anon meetings regularly. At these meetings they will find reassurance that they aren't alone. They will see that there are many of other parents in the same situation and they can all help each other.

- Read chapter 26, For Family and Friends. This chapter explains alcoholism and addiction to the family and friends of people in recovery, and has ideas for helping the whole family.

- Set up a contract for your behavior when you get back home (your counselor can help with this). The agreement needs to have pretty tight limits on spending money and credit card use (see Money Matters on page 216 for ideas on how you and your parents can put limits on your money), use of the car (if at all), curfews, and hours allowed online or on your phone.

- Your parents will be expected to give you love and the basics (food, clothing, shelter, and education), as they are legally bound to do while you are a minor, but not much more.

- You will be expected to follow the rules laid down, do your share of work around the house, do your schoolwork, and be accountable for your behavior. The more details you include in the contract, the easier it will be for everyone to keep to it.

List, for example, the specific chores you will be responsible for. This process works best when everyone gets involved, and all agree on what is expected.

For your part, you will have to be very understanding when you get home. You hurt your parents a lot. Later on, you will have to think about how you can make amends for that. Right now the best way to do that is to work hard on your recovery. You will have to understand that your parents must stop enabling you—that means they will no longer give you the kind of support that allowed you to drift into using drugs and getting away with it for so long. It may take some time for them to trust you again, and you will have to earn that trust.

Rebuilding relationships will be a very important part of your recovery. If your family has not been functioning well for a while, you could probably use some outside help with that. This is one reason why you should be in some kind of continuing care program for quite a while. When problems come up, you'll have a qualified professional to discuss them with. It may be helpful for all of the family to record some conversations at home (with everyone's approval, of course) and then listen to them with the counselor. Sometimes people don't realize that what they say can really affect other people; playing a conversation back gives them the chance to see that. You might also want to keep a journal of feelings and events to talk about with your counselor or sponsor.

Working Things Out—at School

"I'm a senior in high school, and I've been drinking since the sixth grade. My grades have been awful for years. Now that I'm sober, I want to turn things around and make my last year a good one. How can I do that and still go to AA meetings every night?"

Maybe you can't. You need to think about what your priorities are now, and what you can honestly handle. Sit down and talk about your options with your parents and your school counselor, and if possible, your drug counselor.

One option is to get a reduced class schedule for now. Or you can do some home schooling or online learning. Maybe you can graduate six months or even a year behind your class. This way you can focus on recovery without ignoring school entirely. Gradually, as your sobriety gets stronger, you'll be able to shift more of your time and energy to school.

If a part-time schedule isn't an option, you might want to ask about a six-month leave of absence. That would give you time to really concentrate on recovery. (By the way, alcoholism *is* a recognized disability, and the school system needs to accommodate your recovery.) If you do take time off, ideally you should spend several hours a day in an outpatient or continuing care program where you can build your recovery skills. You could also do some volunteer work or take on a low-stress part-time job.

The fact is that going back to school right now could be very difficult for you. Your schoolwork will surely be better than it was while you were drinking or using, but it's unlikely to be first-rate until the fog of early recovery clears. Some people find the fog hangs on as long as a year. You may also find that you have to relearn some things that you thought you knew. Things learned when you are under the influence are often lost when you get sober.

Once your recovery is more stable and you go back to school, you should be able to do well. Not only will you not be hampered by chemicals in your body, you will have learned a lot—about yourself, about dealing with other people, and about being responsible.

When you do return, it's important that a professional at your school knows about your situation and is there to help you get readjusted and deal with any problems that come up. It's best if this person is a trained alcohol and drug counselor, but it can also be a guidance counselor or school nurse.

Your first instinct might be to keep your alcoholism a secret when you go back. Not a good idea. Honesty is an important part of your recovery program, so it's best

to level with at least one person there. It would be even better for you to let everyone know. You don't have to make a major announcement, but simply mention that you are in recovery if the subject comes up. That way it will be easier for you to say no if you get invited to a party where there will be alcohol, or if someone tries to interest you in drugs in the locker room.

If the other kids know you are in recovery, you can also be a role model for those who are still drinking or using drugs, and who may want help one day.

There are probably at least a few other kids in your school who are in recovery. So there may already be an AA or NA group that meets there, at lunch or after classes. If not, you might want to start one, or start a young persons' meeting in the larger community. Talk to your school counselor about it. It would give all of you a chance to share your concerns about getting back into the swing of things at school and to support each other at this tough time. If you can't find or start a local group, be sure to check out some online options (see chapter 8).

In some schools, you may be asked to agree to a written or verbal contract that spells out what is expected of you now. It may include drug testing. If it does, think of it not as "They don't trust me!" but as a way of earning trust. The more negative drugs tests you pile up, the stronger your case for more trust and freedom.

THE
YELLOW
ZONE

Are You Ready for
the Yellow Zone?

Read these questions and discuss them with your sponsor and other advisors. In general, if you answer yes to most of the questions, you're ready to move forward.

- Do you have a stable and strong recovery well under way?

- Have you been sober and in recovery for at least eighteen months?

- Can you honestly say, "I have no desire to drink or use drugs"?

- Is the fog mostly gone?

- Have you successfully completed an initial treatment plan?

- Are you actively involved in a recovery fellowship?

- Have you honestly and completely worked through steps 1–9 (if you are involved in a 12-step fellowship)?

- Have you seen the promises of the *Big Book* come true?

- Are you ready to start working on steps 10, 11, and 12, which will help you maintain a "fit spiritual condition"?

- Do you have a relapse prevention plan in place?

- Do you have a place to live where you can continue your recovery?

- Do you believe your recovery is strong enough that you can now look at other areas (spirituality, relationships, recreational activities and socializing, education, career, finances, and physical and mental health) and start to rebuild your life?

Proceed with Caution: Build Your Life

Once you get to the Yellow Zone, your life in recovery should be feeling pretty normal and natural to you. You can ease up a bit on that intense focus on recovery that you've had for the last eighteen months or so. Of course, you can't abandon all your recovery activities (you can't *ever* do that). You may want to continue with some professional treatment. And you should definitely stay involved in your support fellowship (if you're doing a 12-step program, you still have more to do). But you can now also turn your attention to other parts of your life. The Yellow Zone is when you *proceed with caution and build (or rebuild) your life.*

Now you can put a lot of your energy into building the life you desire and making your existence more fulfilling. Now is when you can start to really work on relationships and career goals and get involved in some fun activities. It's also time to start thinking more about your physical health so you can start getting your body back into top shape.

You should be feeling much better now. Your brain is healing, and the brain fog that dogged you in early recovery has lifted, for the most part. Your cravings for alcohol or drugs are mostly gone. The depression, anger, resentment, embarrassment, and pride that were hallmarks of your early recovery have slowly melted away. The self-centered, me-first attitude that was so much a part of your addiction (and that helped you get through early recovery) has eased up.

Now you're starting to be concerned about others, about how what you say or do affects them. You've candidly evaluated your past actions toward others, your work, and other aspects of your life through a moral inventory, and have begun to look at yourself in the mirror long and honestly. You are starting to enjoy life again.

You are entering a time of growth and maturation, a time when all the richness of life (with its ups and downs), which so long eluded you, can finally be yours.

As you read about the Yellow Zone, think about what your priorities are now. What do you want to accomplish in the next few years? How do you envision your life unfolding? What do you need to get started on now? Write up a list of your personal goals in your recovery journal.

You might be anxious to leave your early sobriety behind and move on with your life. That's completely understandable. Now that you're sober, there's a great life out there, calling your name. But as always, don't rush things. It's better to take the time to build a solid recovery than to plunge headlong into trying to fix and rebuild everything in your life. There is nothing wrong with staying in the Red Zone for a while longer and continuing with a more intense focus on your recovery.

Expect to stay in the Yellow Zone until you have about four to six years of recovery.

Living Your Life, Healing Your Brain

The work you did in the Red Zone laid down a strong foundation for recovery. Keep building on that. Keep working your program.

Your brain is feeling and working much better now, but it's not completely healed yet. Now the healing will focus more on those areas that are concerned with outside-centered functions (how you interact with the world around you), rather than the self-centered functions of early recovery.

As you did in the Red Zone, keep using the power of your thoughts and actions to heal your brain and make living in recovery your normal state of mind. Remember to include your TAMERS in your daily life:

Think about recovery & Talk about recovery

Act on recovery, connect with others

Meditate & Minimize stress

Exercise & Eat well

Relax

Sleep

Following is a summary of what you need to do in the Yellow Zone.

All of these issues are addressed in the following chapters.

Recovery Treatment

If you are still in professional treatment, keep it up. But now you can shift more of the treatment focus to your relationships and other parts of your life. Any medication you use now should be only to treat illness.

Mutual-Support Fellowship and Spirituality

- Stay actively involved in AA or another fellowship; keep your mind focused on recovery and immerse yourself in a recovery-focused community.

- Meet with your sponsor regularly to talk about recovery.

- Start working on steps 10 and 11; regular inventories, prayer, and meditation all focus your mind on recovery and reinforce what you did earlier.

- Start looking for ways to help others; it's a very powerful way to keep your mind on recovery. Learn how to be a good sponsor and reach out to others (step 12).

- Maintain your spiritual practice.

Living Sober and Preventing Relapse

- Continue to surround yourself with people, places, and things that support your recovery. Live in the culture of recovery.

- Continue to be watchful of the cues and triggers that could fire up those old neural pathways of drug-seeking and cravings.

- Regularly review your plans for what you will do if you run into any of those cues and triggers, or if you have any thoughts of using.

- Do regular Recovery Zone ReChecks, to anticipate and deal with events that could disrupt your recovery before they have a chance to influence your thinking.

- You can move on to a more flexible living environment, but it should still be entirely supportive of your goals.

- Continue writing in your recovery journal. Practice gratitude every day.

Relationships, Recreation and Sober Socializing, Education, Career, and Finances

- Work at rebuilding old relationships and starting healthy new ones.

- Have some fun. Explore hobbies, sports, and other leisure activities.

- Move forward with your education or career, and start to repair finances.

- Think often about the rewards of life that you have now regained—honesty, responsibility, loving relationships, having fun sober—

THE YELLOW ZONE

as well as those areas you are still rebuilding.

- Challenge your brain with some new activities: learn to play a musical instrument, learn a new language, or plan a travel adventure.

Physical Health, Diet, Exercise, and Mental Health

- Develop a relationship with a doctor, and address any lingering health issues.

- Start learning about nutrition; nourish your body and brain so they function well.

- Explore exercise options; find something you will enjoy doing regularly.

- Set some health goals, such as losing or gaining weight and improving your cardio.

- If you have any lingering mental health issues, deal with them now.

- As always, avoid all medications that could alter moods or reality, such as sleep aids, antidepressants, and antianxiety drugs.

- Continue to use the tools you've found most helpful in avoiding or dealing with anxiety, depression, and stress.

Recovery Zone ReCheck

At least once a month, do a Recovery Zone ReCheck (see chapter 2). Assess what is going on in your life, and think about what current or upcoming events or issues could upset your recovery. Make a plan for dealing with the situation by asking yourself the ReCheck questions:

Potential effects. How might this event affect my sobriety?

Recovery Zone. Which Recovery Zone should I go back to in order to avoid a relapse, and for how long? Which recovery activities should I resume or increase in frequency?

Other actions. What else can I do to avoid a relapse?

Your Recovery Program in the Yellow Zone

n the Yellow Zone you can now ease up a bit on your recovery program. But just a *bit*. You can't ever turn your focus away from recovery altogether.

The biggest mistake people make at this point is to cut back on recovery activities. It's common to become overly confident once recovery gets more comfortable, once you've moved beyond those clenched-fist early days. It's easy to yawn at meetings and lament that the people there just "hash and rehash the same old stuff." It's tempting to forget about meetings entirely—to move on and spend more time with family and friends, just catching up and having fun. *Don't do it*. If you value your sobriety and this amazing new life you have built, don't slack off. It's okay to cut back on meetings some. But it's crucial that you stay involved in your recovery program. Keep watching for those relapse risks. Start working on the last three steps if you're in a 12-step fellowship. Reach out and sponsor others if you are ready. It will all help you to *continue* to save your life.

Keep Working Your Program

THE 12 STEPS— DON'T STOP NOW

By now, you've put in a lot of time and effort working through the first nine of the twelve steps. It might be tempting to skip over the last three, but that would be a major mistake. The last three steps are the maintenance steps—they are vitally important to your *ongoing* sobriety. While you will start to work on them now in the Yellow Zone, you should plan to make them a part of your life forever.

Below are some ideas for working steps 10 (personal inventory) and 11 (daily prayer and meditation). Step 12 involves reaching out to others in need; many people choose to do that by being a sponsor to new fellowship members. You can read more about being a sponsor in the next section.

Many people also find it's helpful to repeat the fourth step now (the moral inventory; see chapter 8). A new inventory may look very different from the one you did when your judgment was still not up to par, your psyche was focused solely on yourself, and your head was stuffed with cotton. You'll probably find that now you can remember more, evaluate better, identify behavior patterns that were invisible earlier, and see yourself and others in a very different light. Plus, the work you'll do in the Yellow Zone will mean more if it's based on an updated analysis of where you've been and where you are now. And with most of the fires in your life now extinguished, some further introspection can yield valuable insights—and big gains in your quality of life.

In fact, even once you have completed all of the steps, it's a good idea to keep them close at hand—for the rest of your life. Think of them as a prescription for living. Some of their guidance, such as meditation and helping other alcoholics, you might practice regularly. Other facets, such as doing an inventory, might be a tool that you return to as needed. Many people in recovery make a habit of reworking all of the steps every five years or so.

TAKING A PERSONAL INVENTORY (STEP 10)

Burning up your life history doesn't mean you stop looking at yourself and your life. Step 10 suggests that you continue to take a personal inventory periodically. This kind of honest tally of events and feelings allows you to analyze your actions after the emotions of an event have died down, but before they've slipped away entirely. It can also help you see when you may be ready to move forward in the Recovery Zones—and when you might soon be in danger of a relapse and need to be extra careful about your sobriety. Some people do an inventory each day; some do it once a week. It's up to you.

There are lots of ways to do a personal inventory. You can do it during a meditation session or when talking with your sponsor. You can do it with an inventory or journaling program on your computer or an app on your phone, or you can jot it down in a paper journal.

Keeping an ongoing written record of your inventory is an

especially good idea for high-risk people, those who've had a relapse, and those who have trouble being honest with themselves. It's harder to lie on paper. It's also ideal for those who want to be very thorough. A written journal can also help you review your progress over time.

If you decide on a paper journal for your inventory, buy a notebook and keep it next to your bed, near the kitchen table, or anywhere else you will be able to spend some time with it regularly. For each entry, simply record the date and then write about your activities, people you've seen, things you've accomplished, meetings you've attended, and so on. Be specific about things that may have some importance: "This morning, I got up late and was late for work." Try to record your feelings as well as activities: "I handed in my report two days early, and I was really angry at my boss for not even saying 'thank you.'" Record good feelings as well as bad ones: "I was scared to death before I gave my first talk at NA, but later I was on cloud nine."

Ask yourself the following questions as you reflect on your life:

Recovery Activities

- Did I have a plan for the day, and did I follow it?

- With whom did I spend most of my time?

- Where did I spend my time?

- Did anything threaten my sobriety recently? What?

- What specific work did I do on my recovery program (attending meetings, doing meditations, reading fellowship materials, or listening to recordings, etc.)?

- Is my attitude toward recovery constructive?

- What did I accomplish recently in regard to my recovery? Is there anything I wish I had done that I didn't do? What could I have done differently?

- What did I accomplish recently in regard to my spirituality? Is there anything I wish I had done that I didn't do? What could I have done differently?

- What do I need to add to my recovery activities in the future?

Relationships, Recreation, and Sober Socializing

- Was I honest in all my dealings?

- Have I been fair in all my interactions with others? Were there situations where I was wrong or unreasonable? Did I make amends?

- What good things happened? How did I react to them?

- Did any bad things happen? What were they? How did I react?

- What did I accomplish recently in regard to my relationships? Is there anything I wish I had done that I didn't do? What could I have done differently?

THE YELLOW ZONE

- What did I accomplish recently in regard to my recreational and social activities? Is there anything I wish I had done that I didn't do? What could I have done differently?

- What could I do in the future to improve these areas of my life?

Education, Career, and Finances

- What good things happened? How did I react to them?

- Did any bad things happen? What were they? How did I react?

- What did I accomplish recently in regard to my education, career, and finances? Is there anything I wish I had done that I didn't do? What could I have done differently?

- What could I do in the future to improve these areas of my life?

Physical and Mental Health

- What good things happened? How did I react to them?

- Did any bad things happen? What were they? How did I react?

- What did I accomplish recently in regard to my physical and mental health? What would I like to have done that I didn't do? What would I have done differently?

- What could I do in the future to improve these areas of my life?

Recovery Zones

- What Recovery Zone am I in today?

- Are there any reasons or signs I need to move back to a higher-risk Recovery Zone tomorrow or someday soon? What do I need to do to prepare for that or, if possible, avoid it?

- Are there any signs I am moving forward toward a lower-risk Recovery Zone? Is there anything more I can do now to help myself move in that direction?

- Should I move to a new Recovery Zone soon? Am I ready?

(These questions can also be found in a printer-friendly format at TheRecoveryBook.com.)

After you have taken an inventory, step away from it for some time. Later on, look over your entry and see if anything in it tells you how you are doing. Look for patterns over the previous days or weeks, and for changes from last month or the month before. Look for the character defects you listed in your inventory in step 4 and for signs that you're still in their grip. Your inventory can tell you that your recovery is going well, or that your attitudes need some work.

It may also be helpful to go over your journal periodically with another person—like your sponsor, counselor, or physician—to see if they pick up something that you've missed.

A CHECKLIST FOR PRAYER AND MEDITATION (STEP 11)

Step 11 suggests a practice of regular prayer and meditation.

Below is a checklist, adapted from the *Big Book*'s description of step 11, that can help you make this a regular part of your life.

On Waking

- Think about the twenty-four hours ahead and consider your plans for the day.

- Ask God (as you understand him) to direct your thinking.

- Ask God for inspiration.

- Relax and take it easy.

- Meditate with a prayer to be shown the next step.

- Pray to be given what is needed to take care of your problems.

- Pray for freedom from self-will, and make no requests for yourself.

Throughout the Day

- Pause when agitated or doubtful and ask God for inspiration, an intuitive thought, or a decision.

- Remind yourself that you no longer run the show.

- Humbly think, "Thy will be done."

On Retiring at Night

- Constructively review your day.

- Were you resentful, selfish, dishonest, or afraid?

- Do you owe someone an apology?

- Have you kept something to yourself that should have been discussed with someone at once?

- Were you kind and loving toward all?

- What could you have done better?

- Were you thinking of yourself most of the time or were you thinking of others?

- Ask God's forgiveness and inquire what corrective measures should be taken.

- Consider your plans for tomorrow.

- Ask God to direct your thinking.

Reach Out to Help Others Now

ARE YOU READY TO BE A SPONSOR?

"A guy I've met at a couple of NA meetings asked me to be his sponsor, but I'm not sure I'm ready."

Questioning your readiness is a good sign—you are not willing to take on this responsibility without being sure you can handle it.

For some people, it's best to wait until the Green Zone to be a sponsor. Others might be ready in the Yellow Zone—provided they have a solid, strong recovery under way

THE YELLOW ZONE

and they ease into sponsoring. The amount of time you have been sober is less important than having a program that can serve others well. Some people are ready to become sponsors at the end of a year; others aren't ready until much more time has passed.

Ask yourself these questions:

- Have you worked through at least steps 1–9? Will your own sponsor attest to that? Are you now working on steps 10, 11, and 12? (Being a sponsor is a step-12 activity.)

- Do you have a solid sobriety? Have you addressed the difficult life issues using the tools of recovery, rather than just coasting through? Is your sobriety the kind you think others could benefit from?

- Do you feel secure in your recovery? Do you and your sponsor agree that you now have a program in place that can weather upcoming storms?

- Do you have enough time to devote to being a sponsor? Will you still have enough time for restoring relationships, your career, and other aspects of your Yellow Zone work?

- Do you feel able to emotionally detach yourself from other people's problems (and maybe even start going to Al-Anon if dealing with another alcoholic/addict takes a toll on you)?

- Do you know how AA works from the perspective of an insider—someone who's participated in meetings and service work, not just observed? Have you read the *AA Service Manual*?

If you answered yes to all of these questions, then you are ready. If you didn't, give yourself and your own recovery more time. There's no rush. But whether you become a sponsor now or later, do take on that task someday. Research shows that people who sponsor others have the very best sobriety success.

///////////////////////////

"I'm a middle-aged man, and my recovery is really good. I'd like to share what I've learned by becoming a sponsor to someone else. How do I find a sponsee?"

Sometimes the sponsee (or "pigeon") finds you first—just walks up to you at a meeting and asks. Sometimes you have to take the initiative and approach a tentative newcomer. Either way, you want to be sure you have a good match. You might get your first clue to a possible sponsee from something he says at a meeting, something that you identify with and makes you think you can help him. (Also take a look at chapter 8 for a refresher on the qualities that make for a good sponsor-sponsee relationship.)

If you're asked to sponsor someone, sit down and talk with

him about his needs and how the relationship might work before deciding yes or no. If, after the discussion, you don't feel the chemistry is right, it's okay to say so. But do help the person to find the right sponsor and assure him that even if you can't be his sponsor, you can be a good friend and supporter as he gets started in recovery.

///////////////////////////

"I'm already sponsoring one woman, and another has asked me to sponsor her. How many people is it okay to sponsor?"

While you are in the Yellow Zone it's best to stick with just one sponsee. Later on, you might take on more people. But there is no simple formula for what you might be able to handle at that time. Some folks—retirees, for example, with plenty of free time and years of wisdom—manage to successfully sponsor a dozen or more, while others have their hands full with one.

How many you can take on will depend on your personality (are you overwhelmed or invigorated at having expectations and being in demand?), and on your current schedule. Whatever you do, don't increase your "case load" too quickly, and feel free to pull back at any time if you feel you are giving less than your best to all your sponsees. Your goal is to help others and yourself, not to get your name in the AA record books.

HOW TO BE A GOOD SPONSOR

"I'm not sure what to do now that I'm a sponsor. The woman I'm sponsoring has a pretty shaky recovery, and I don't want to make it worse."

Though you aren't responsible for the failure or success of those you sponsor (it's up to them), you should do the best job you can.

- Let the person you are sponsoring know that what you are doing is a critical part of your own recovery, and not taken on as a professional responsibility.

- Make yourself as available to her as you can. Arrange to meet regularly with her on a one-to-one basis. Build a personal bond with her (it will benefit you both) and suggest an agenda for keeping her recovery work constructive (step work will usually be the top priority).

- Monitor her recovery; encourage her to accomplish certain things, like working on a particular step or dealing with a barrier that is keeping her from a good recovery. Encourage her to read the *Big Book* and other materials and discuss them with others.

- Let her know about meetings, retreats, and other recovery events that may be helpful to her. Be a role model and show her how to stay actively involved in the fellowship. Encourage her to set up chairs or make coffee before a meeting, to read aloud the Serenity Prayer, the Twelve Steps, or the Twelve Traditions, and to eventually chair a meeting or give a talk. All of that will help her see that recovery is much more than just sitting in a meeting.

- Make it easier for her to get to meetings. That doesn't mean you have to drive her everywhere, but give her a lift when you can. And ask her to give you a lift from time to time.

- Introduce her to others who may be helpful to her recovery or have wrestled with problems similar to hers.

- Nudge her in the right direction, based on your own judgment of what she should be doing. But keep in mind that change is often gradual, and as long as she isn't stuck, she's okay.

- Don't play therapist. You are not a professional; it's not your job to give advice or to help the other person. Your job is to act as a nonjudgmental sounding board; to guide, not direct. For example, if your sponsee is trying to decide whether or not to end her marriage, discuss her options with her and tell her you will support her no matter what she does. Be sure to remind her that she is the one who has to live with her decision. But also remind her that you will help

her to build a recovery program that gives her the sanity to do that. (You can also help her move through the decision-making process [see chapter 18].)

- Expect that some of the issues she brings up in early recovery will be compulsive echoes of an urge to drink or use. Your attentive ear, mature behavior, and thoughtful response will help her move toward healing.

- Respect her privacy. Just as anything you hear at AA or NA is confidential, so is anything you hear from the person you are sponsoring. There are exceptions, however, when someone's safety is threatened.

- Take advantage of technology to be a better sponsor. Keep in touch by texting, email, or video chat, if that works for your sponsee. Use social media to network with others who have similar recovery interests.

- If your sponsee has insatiable needs, you don't have to be available every minute of the day and night. Sometimes a really troubled person needs two or three secondary sponsors, so when the primary sponsor isn't available others can take over. If a sponsee continues to need round-the-clock support, she probably needs professional treatment. Suggest it.

- Don't try to control. Alcoholics and addicts often try to control

YOUR RECOVERY PROGRAM 369

their world and everyone in it. Don't enable, don't hover, don't do everything for your charge, leaving her nothing to do for herself. Expect that your sponsee will take many wrong turns on her recovery journey. Guide her so she'll learn not to make the same mistake twice.

- Don't use your sponsee in the wrong way. Being a sponsor helps the sponsee, but it is mostly meant to help satisfy *your* recovery needs. You do it to maintain and strengthen your own recovery. It is a form of step-12 work or service. But if it begins to satisfy a personality need—if you use this person as a stand-in for your family, as an excuse for leaving work, as a whipping post for your own frustrations, or as a reason for not accomplishing things in your life—you are abusing your step-12 work.

- Avoid business and financial relationships with sponsees. Even lending just a few dollars here and there will taint your ability to be objective and limit your effectiveness.

Remember that sometimes it takes a fairly assertive, even aggressive, approach to get an alcoholic or addict's attention. But persistence usually pays off. Also keep in mind that you are not responsible for the sobriety of those you help. You can't take credit for their successes, and you're not responsible for their

failures, including relapses. They must be responsible for themselves.

PROTECT CONFIDENCES

Though you are not acting in a professional capacity when you sponsor an alcoholic or addict, you must remember to keep whatever you are told in this relationship strictly confidential. No doctor-patient or lawyer-client relationship is more sacred.

If a friend or family member of your sponsee asks for confidential information entrusted to you, you must say no. If, however, you feel that withholding the information would foster dishonesty or could hurt someone emotionally, encourage your sponsee to disclose it himself.

Keep in mind that being a sponsor does *not* give you any legal protection. If you see anything that seems to be ongoing criminal activity, end the relationship right away (or risk being considered an accomplice). Use your own judgment as to whether you should pass that information on to someone else.

If your sponsee divulges any information that makes you think someone is being seriously harmed, or soon will be, you might not have a legal obligation to take action (in most states sponsors are not "mandatory reporters"), but you do have a moral obligation. The need to prevent serious harm is more important than the confidentiality of your relationship. For example, do not hesitate to save a life or stop a crime (from a safe distance). If you are not ready or willing to interrupt such behavior, you may not be ready to be a sponsor.

There are a few ways you can handle such a situation:

- If the danger is not imminent, you might ask other AA members for advice. Or you might ask others in your fellowship to intervene together on this person's behavior. Another option is to talk with a physician or counselor who has experience with the issue.

- If the danger does seem imminent—for example, a spouse or child is likely to suffer physical harm—you need to act. The best option is to call the police.

- Some areas are grayer than an immediate threat: the mere suspicion of spousal or child abuse, for example. What you should do in such a situation is not always clear-cut. But if you suspect your sponsee is either an ongoing perpetrator or a victim of such acts, you should help him find a family counselor or physician to discuss the problem with. (You can also get some good advice on what to do from the experts at domestic violence and child abuse hotlines. See page 254.)

- Your sponsee needs to understand that your role is not to pass judgment, but rather to encourage him to grow, to avoid repeating past mistakes, and to recover. He needs to know that any tales he tells you about past misdeeds—that are known to have stopped with sobriety—will be held in confidence. Just as important, your sponsee needs to know you will not be a part of any dishonest or illegal activity, and that you will act on any behavior that threatens other people.

Best-case scenario: Make sure that you and your sponsee have an understanding from day one that you will protect his confidences, but not if anyone is put in danger.

HELP OTHERS IN YOUR COMMUNITY

As you move further into the Yellow Zone, you might also be interested in helping others in your community, beyond being a sponsor. That's great. Just like being a sponsor, getting involved in such activities will strengthen your own recovery. And there are many things you can do: Give talks at schools, teach drug-education classes at a women's shelter, work to get stronger alcohol- or drug-related legislation passed, and so on.

At this point, though, tiptoe into the water rather than diving in headfirst. Explore your options; look for opportunities. Try out a few different activities and see what might be a good fit for you. Try to avoid any tasks that might be stressful, tedious, or take too much time. And at first, avoid regular commitments, like teaching a class every week. You want to be wary of overextending yourself.

Later on, once you're in the Green Zone, you'll have more time and energy to help your community. You'll find lots of ideas in chapter 22.

Common Issues in the Yellow Zone

AM I CURED?

"I haven't had a drink in almost two years, and I've worked through the first nine steps with my sponsor. I can't even remember the last time I wanted a drink. Doesn't that mean I'm okay now? Can't I give up all this AA stuff—and maybe have an occasional drink at a party?"

Sorry, but no. Your reasoning *sounds* logical. You feel great; you've been sober for a fairly long time; you don't crave alcohol anymore. Therefore, you must be cured. But it could also seem logical to a person with diabetes: I haven't had a brownie in a year; my blood sugar level is just fine; I'm feeling great; I must be cured.

The logic in both cases is illusory. You feel good because you've abstained from alcohol. The person with diabetes feels good because he has controlled his diet and taken his insulin. For both of you, your diseases are controlled, but they are not yet curable.

Still, many alcoholics and addicts (and some diabetics) find it hard to accept that their disease is incurable. It's common that at this time in recovery, when things are going really well, a sense of denial rears its head once more and the person in recovery starts to think, "I never really had a problem." (There's an AA saying for this: "When health returns, the liar revives.")

You may not be able to keep your mind from speculating, but you can keep your body from acting on it. Stick to your recovery program now with even more energy than before. Review the guidelines on avoiding cravings and temptations in chapter 10, and be sure to do a Recovery Zone ReCheck with your sponsor regularly (see page 18). You may find that now, when you are feeling really great, you need even *more* support not to drink than you did a few months ago.

Bottom line, controlled drinking almost never works for alcoholics/addicts—as many who've tried it could tell you. This is as true after twenty years of sobriety as it is after one. You are *never* cured of alcoholism or addiction. Even some of the most die-hard AA old-timers have been known to slip when they got careless about working their programs—ten, twenty, even thirty years after they got into recovery. You can judge from their experiences what an "occasional drink at a party" could do to you.

FILLING IN THE BLANKS

"A lot that happened while I was drinking and using drugs is a total blank. Now that I've been sober a couple of years, my family and friends sometimes allude to things that I don't remember at all. Is it better to leave it that way?"

This is one Pandora's box worth opening. You couldn't lift the lid earlier in recovery, while you were struggling to save your life, because you weren't ready to deal with what might come swarming out. Now, however, it is okay to start looking back at what happened and at what you did—as long as you can address what comes up constructively, without reigniting fires or causing harm to others.

Explain the blanks in your memory to family and friends, and ask them to help fill those blanks in. Tell them you want to know what happened, what you did that might have hurt them, and how they felt, so you can better make amends. This will not only help you understand their feelings about the past but will also allow everyone to talk freely about it. No more walking on eggshells.

Add these incidents to your list of necessary amends, and make those amends.

CAN I CUT BACK ON MEETINGS NOW?

"I've been going to four or five meetings a week for the last year. My wife thinks it's time for me to cut back and spend more time with the family, but

I'm scared of going to fewer meetings. How many should I go to?"

That depends on your personal needs. In the Yellow Zone, as your life starts to get back on track, you'll need to find the combination of meetings and other fellowship activities that works best for you. There is no magical formula.

Many people are able to cut back on meetings once they've built a solid foundation of recovery and moved beyond the Red Zone. But most, like you, are wary. Meetings have been their lifeline for a year or more, and they wisely hesitate to let go. But they can safely loosen their grip, little by little.

Now's the time to start settling into an AA program that fits into your life, instead of fitting your life into your AA program. Your new routine might include fewer meetings, but perhaps more meditation and reading at home, a mini meeting with an AA friend over lunch each week, occasional AA retreats, talking with your sponsor often, becoming a sponsor yourself, and doing some service work. More important than going to a specific number of meetings is living the lifestyle promoted at meetings— living in the culture of recovery.

Remember, though, that cutting back to fewer meetings isn't a permanent decision. You have to be flexible; indeed, your life depends on it. You do have an illness, and if it flares up, or threatens to, you may need some extra treatment. So if you have a bad day, go to an extra meeting. If you're having problems at work, you may feel better if you go to a meeting every night for a couple of weeks. And if you or your sponsor notices that your old attitudes or behavior patterns start to reappear (if, for example, you become resentful, angry, or depressed), it will be clear that you've dipped below your "therapeutic dose" of AA. In that case, increase your meeting attendance for a while to be sure you don't slip and fall. Also be sure to do regular Recovery Zone ReChecks, so you can *anticipate* when you might need to increase your meeting attendance. And don't overlook the inspirational booster-shot value of AA conventions and retreats.

DON'T LET DOWN YOUR GUARD

"A friend in NA, who's been sober longer than I have, just had a bad slip. He's sober again, but boy, it makes me worry it will happen to me."

It can happen to anybody. There is no cure for addiction, and a fairly large percentage of those who try to get sober have one or more relapses. It's no disgrace, but it can be demoralizing. Remember, though, that it can't take away what was learned in recovery. In fact, it can teach us a great deal about how to apply that knowledge more successfully the second time around. For example, maybe the friend who slipped didn't manage to remove all temptations from his home; this time around, he's sure to be much

more careful. If you want to avoid your friend's fate, continue to work your program faithfully, go to meetings, and avoid temptations. Reread the Red Zone sections on avoiding the people and places from your time of addiction and give some more thought to what you can do to avoid a slip.

MY LIFE IS STILL NOT PERFECT

"I have been on the straight and narrow for almost two years. I'm doing everything I'm supposed to. Gone to meetings, gotten back with my wife. How come my life is still far from perfect?"

Look around you. You may see a lot of people whose lives you think are perfect, but the fact is that nobody's life is perfect. You may even think your life is still a mess. But that's okay. You can't get back everything you lost or achieve everything you dream of all at once. You are still fairly early in recovery. Remember, your goal isn't perfection, but progress—day to day, month to month, year to year. If you can look back and see progress, you're doing fine. Keep doing what you are doing.

But maybe you really don't see that you're making any progress when you compare your life now to a couple of years ago. That's not uncommon. Recovery is often a case of two steps forward, one step back. For some people, the first year or so is a case of one step forward, one step back. They finish the year

Crisis Management: Retreat to the Red Zone

You've lost your job, or you've lost your love. You're under a lot of stress, with finals coming up. You have surgery, and quite enjoy that painkiller they gave you. Whatever the situation, suddenly you feel as though you're sliding backward, and all the progress you've made in recovery is no more than a memory. Don't let those sinking feelings send you off to a relapse!

When a crisis rears up, it's time to take shelter. Head back to the safety and security of your Red Zone activities—go to more fellowship meetings, talk more with your sponsor, meditate more, read more. Do whatever it was that helped keep you sober in those early days. And don't let embarrassment, pride, or cockiness keep you from temporarily retreating. It's perfectly fine to move back there for a while. Once the crisis has passed, you can move once again into the less sheltered Yellow Zone and return to rebuilding your life.

Crises can lead to relapse, no question. The best way to deal with them, actually, is to *anticipate* them, to recognize when they are coming up in your life—long before they catch you unawares. Don't wait for a crisis to sneak up on you. Be sure to learn how to do a Recovery Zone ReCheck (chapter 2), and do it regularly.

not much advanced from day one. Sometimes this is because they were living in such a fog for so long that now they just can't handle reality and won't be able to until much more time has passed. These people often need to spend some extra time in the Red Zone to build a solid foundation for recovery. If this is your situation, don't fret. It's okay. Take the time to do the work. Don't skimp on that foundation or try to finish it in a hurry. Over the next few months you should start to see progress.

Another possibility is that you need a recovery overhaul. That may be the case if you really don't see any progress in the coming months, or if you've experienced any of the following:

- Close calls—or even a few periodic relapses

- Delayed withdrawal symptoms

- An inability to get comfortable with reality

- A lack of enthusiasm for life

- Frequent bouts of cravings, depression, anger, resentment, pride, or embarrassment

- An ongoing focus on destructive or dysfunctional self-centeredness (where your decisions seem to bring you only more misery, and you fail to show concern for others)

If you do need a recovery overhaul, it might be because you're missing one or more of the essential ingredients for a successful program. You might need some inpatient or outpatient treatment if you've never had it, or you might need to check in for a booster if you have. As strange as it may sound, inpatient treatment after a long period of sobriety can be more productive than when you are newly sober. Your brain has had some time to heal, and your decision-making skills will be sharper. You will probably also need to pay more attention to your recovery program: more meetings, more time with your sponsor, more reading, more meditation, and more basic early step work.

There's another common reason why you might be feeling stuck and "less than wonderful" right now: You might have been doing your recovery work so well and enjoying it so much that you've gotten bogged down in the comfortable and comforting Red Zone survival mode. Those blinders you put on so you could avoid outside distractions and focus on recovery can also serve to isolate you. Some people, in fact, get so involved in the security and selfishness of early sobriety that they never move past it and get into the rewards and enjoyment of life that come in the Yellow and Green Zones. So if your recovery is solid and you answered yes to most of the Are You Ready for the Yellow Zone questions on page 356, give yourself a little push into your Yellow Zone work. The rewards will be well worth the effort.

Another possibility is that you are hovering somewhere between the Red and Yellow Zones. That's normal; many people swing back and forth. One day they are stepping bravely out into the world, and the next they are back in the safe womb of early recovery. That's okay, as long as overall you're having more days in the Yellow Zone than the Red Zone, and most days you're working at moving forward, rather than curling up under the covers.

Relapse Alert

THE RISK OF RELAPSE IS ALWAYS THERE

As you progress through the zones of recovery, most of your early fears and concerns will drop away and be forgotten. One fear, however, can (and should) stay with you for the rest of your life: a healthy fear of a relapse. The risk, not surprisingly, is highest in the first few months of recovery—that time when your brain still has a lot of healing to do and your recovery skills are brand-new. The risk diminishes with time, sure, but it never goes down to zero. It never fades away completely. Many life events—good and bad—can send your risk soaring once more. Whether you left behind your drugs of choice yesterday or ten years ago, or even thirty years ago, your disease can become active again if the conditions are right. (And in fact,

THE YELLOW ZONE

the risk of relapse often rises again as someone gets into older age, due to increasing medical problems and declining mental acuity.)

A relapse is not usually a sudden occurrence, either. As you learned in chapter 10, it often starts long before you give in to your treacherous inner voice with an "Oh, what the hell! Why not?" It starts long before you pick up that drink or pill. Rather, it often starts with one of those seemingly little things that can throw off your day: feeling frustrated by a traffic jam; feeling exhausted from working too hard; feeling angry with your spouse over whose turn it is to do the dishes.

If you are familiar with the attitudes and behaviors that can lay the groundwork for a relapse, however, you can be alert to risky situations, recognize your own warning signs, and be ready to take cover and ride out the storm. Avoiding a relapse can be as simple as retreating to an earlier Recovery Zone and ramping up your program. Doing regular Recovery Zone ReChecks will also help you to anticipate problems.

In the Red Zone, you learned about some of the many cues and triggers that could lead you to relapse, such as driving past your once favorite bar, letting your emotions get the best of you, and so on. Avoiding those things should be second nature by now (but it's always good to review them regularly). Now it's time to think about some other, maybe not-so-obvious issues, as well as some new risks.

THREE SIMPLE GUIDELINES TO AVOID RELAPSE

For many people, avoiding your triggers and a subsequent relapse can be boiled down to three simple guidelines: Be honest, follow your 12-step program, and avoid all mood-altering drugs and medications. Most people who relapse have cut corners in one of those areas.

Be honest. Those with successful recoveries will testify that staying honest is a critical factor.

Dishonesty is a way of life for many active alcoholics and addicts. If it now creeps back into your life in any form, you could start falling right back down that slippery slope: denying your disease, neglecting your recovery program, rationalizing bad actions, and failing to look at yourself honestly.

How does that happen? Think about how you would feel if you cheated on your spouse or stole from your employer. Now that you are sober, you'd probably feel pretty rotten about it, or at least have some discomfort, some uneasy feelings of guilt. Those feelings are hard to live with, and the addict's tendency is to deal with them by smothering them with drugs or drowning them in gin.

Another way to be dishonest—it's less obvious, but still dishonest—is to simply avoid telling the truth. Failing to confide the truth to those trying to help you—doctors, counselors, sponsors, others in AA—can also sabotage recovery. Sometimes we lie as a way of protecting ourselves, hoping to avoid the consequences. But in the long run, the consequences of lying are always worse. We lose the respect of others. Perhaps worse, we lose self-respect.

Follow your 12-step program. By now, you are deeply involved in your fellowship. Keep it up. It will always serve you well.

Avoid all mood-altering drugs or medicines. These are probably the biggest risk to your recovery. Always, always, *always* think twice about any drugs or medications you take; in most situations, there is a safer alternative. Read more about the dangers of seemingly safe drugs on page 290, and learn about your many alternative options discussed throughout this book.

LOTS OF THINGS CAN TRIGGER A RELAPSE

What else do you need to be wary of? Here are some things to keep in mind.

HALT. If you get too Hungry, Angry, Lonely, or Tired, you may be more vulnerable to relapse.

Hungry. Eat regularly; get three nutritious meals a day, plus snacks in between to keep up your blood sugar level and ward off hunger.

Angry. Talk about your anger with supportive people and examine it honestly. Confront your anger before it has a chance to own you.

Brain studies show that anger and other emotions can act like mood-changing drugs, making people revert to more primitive survival behaviors and do things they wouldn't do otherwise.

Lonely. Stay active in a recovery community, and go to meetings often enough to keep loneliness at bay. Engage in regular social activities with recovering friends, too. When loneliness troubles you, call a sponsor or AA buddy. Don't cave in and retreat; that will only lead to more loneliness.

Tired. Avoid overdoing it at both work and play. Try not to take on more than you can handle. Exercise regularly, since moderate amounts of exercise increase energy levels. And remember, you don't have to be at the gym to get exercise. Walking up the stairs at work counts, too.

Unrequited thirst. Finding yourself thirsty with nothing to drink but a cold beer is extremely risky. So be sure that you're well supplied with frosty sodas, juice, or ice water.

Negative feelings. Resentment, ingratitude, self-pity (telling yourself you're a victim rather than someone who made poor choices related to your disease), pessimism (your glass is always half empty), impatience (you crave instant gratification—one day at a time isn't good enough), and frustration ("Why can't everything go the way I want?") are all attitudes that can undermine recovery. If you don't

THE YELLOW ZONE

acknowledge these traits and deal with them quickly and constructively (see chapter 14), they will lead you over the edge.

Unrealistic expectations. Expecting too much too soon (a trait typical of alcoholics/addicts) can lead to disappointment and resentment, which in turn can lead to the nearest bar or dealer. In early recovery to mid-recovery, it should be enough that at the end of each day you can say, "I stayed sober today." Follow the Recovery Zone System for tackling things at the right time, and see chapter 14 for dealing with expectations realistically.

Leftover issues from the Red Zone. How strong is your recovery foundation? Have you thoroughly embraced steps 1 (you admitted there was a problem and you hadn't solved it yourself), 2 (you agreed that a solution exists and that hope lies outside yourself), and 3 (you agreed it would be necessary to apply the solution to the problem in order to heal)? Did you get a sponsor and confide in him? Have you dealt with other basic issues of early recovery? If you have reservations about any of these areas, you probably have a weak foundation. That will make it tough for you to be strong when you run into difficult circumstances.

Unresolved Yellow Zone issues. If you've tried to build (or rebuild) the life you desire, but you still have unresolved problems in your relationships, your work, or other aspects of your life, those negative feelings can simmer and eventually come to a boil. If this is the case, do some more work on your Yellow Zone priorities now.

Renewing old friendships. Once recovery seems well established, it may seem silly or overly cautious to avoid the old friends you used to drink or use with. Getting together with an old friend might seem like an innocent idea, but the sneaky insanity of addiction can overcome you just when you're not looking. A good rule of thumb for situations like this is to examine your motives: Why do you really want to see her? Are you planning to do it on the sly, without your sponsor's knowledge? Have you talked about the pros and cons of such a meeting with your sponsor? Quite often you will find that unless the person you want to reconnect with is also in recovery, you're in danger of picking up where your relationship left off.

Getting back on the old merry-go-round. As your recovery progresses, you might start to feel invulnerable: "I'm doing great. Seeing some of my old playmates, visiting some of my old playgrounds, won't bother me a bit. I got through risky times when things were a lot worse than they are now." Getting that "ten feet tall and bulletproof" attitude is rather like jumping out of a plane without a parachute: People have done it and survived, but the odds are not in your favor. If you find yourself invited to a party or other event that is important to attend but you suspect could be risky, take a friend in recovery along if possible. Study the sober socializing tips in chapters 10 and 11 and use them to plan your every move ahead of time.

Remembering the old days. This is also known as "romancing the drink [or the drug]." Putting a shine on the bad old days ("Hey, remember that time when we all got loaded at that concert?") can make them suddenly seem like good old days. Don't dwell on the past. If someone else tries to romanticize your drinking or drugging days, put on the brakes with your own memories by talking it through to the results: "Yeah, and I vomited all over myself and my date." If you're the one who starts romanticizing, bring yourself up short.

Indulging in doubtful habits. Nicotine and sugar have been associated with relapse in some people. What helped to quench your cravings in early recovery could now trigger worse ones. So learn about and start to follow the life-extending, sobriety-sustaining health habits recommended in the Yellow and Green Zones. Keep an eye on any other compulsive behaviors that might crop up, such as gambling, sex, and eating. They seem to stimulate the same addiction-related chemicals and activity in the brain as drugs do, and may weaken your defenses against relapse.

Shifting the blame. If you can always find someone or something else to blame for your problems, past or present, you aren't putting the responsibility for your life where it belongs: in your own hands. By relinquishing your responsibility to deal with your life, you cave in to the irresponsible behavior of addiction. Returning to active addiction is a likely next step.

SITUATIONS THAT INVITE RELAPSE

Sometimes just plain old life itself sets you up for a relapse—certain situations will weaken your defenses. Your only protection is eternal vigilance. That means doing regular Recovery Zone ReChecks so you can see these situations coming and safely retreat to an earlier zone.

Bad times. Not surprisingly, many people relapse when something goes awry in their lives. Almost any major problem can trigger a slip, including the death of a loved one; the loss of a job; a catastrophe (a home destroyed by fire, for example); or an illness—anything from a cold to cancer. (The opposite is often true, however—many people in recovery do quite well in the bad times because they know how to move back to recovery basics.)

Good times. While you might be alert to a possible slip when things are going wrong, you're much less likely to be wary when everything's coming up daffodils—you patch up your marriage, or get a great new job. In fact, most people tend to let their guard down completely when everything is going right. They toast themselves mentally: "I'm doing great. Staying sober is easy. I don't have the problems others have. I'm in control." Or you get pulled away from recovery when you refocus on being a better parent or doing a great job at the office. Or you get a little complacent because, really, everything is just fine. Gradually, you start skipping counseling sessions and meetings and start avoiding your sponsor. Then before you know it, you've taken that mood-altering medication your doctor prescribed and you're off to the races—again.

Milestones. Being sober for thirty days, six months, one year, or five years is certainly something to celebrate. But it should also be a reminder: *Keep working your program.* A sober anniversary can be a time of confidence and elation ("Everything's going so well!"), of anxiety and depression ("Things are going too well; it can't last" or "They aren't going well enough"), or of complacency ("This sobriety is a breeze; now what?"). Unless it's also a time of caution and reflection, a recovery milestone can put recovery at risk. Many think, "Okay, I've proved I can do it. Now I can relax a little." They skip the next meeting or neglect to check in with a sponsor, and their sobriety becomes vulnerable. Many treatment programs now recognize this risk. Most programs no longer talk about graduating; instead, they celebrate a successful end of treatment with a "transition" ceremony.

The riskiest sober anniversaries, experience shows, seem to be three months, six months, and one year.

Vacations. Because vacations often take you far away from your usual support and accountability systems, they can be opportunities for a relapse. Pick your vacation destinations thoughtfully. Choose recovery-related retreats and conventions in early recovery, and later on stick to resorts and destinations that stress or support an atmosphere of sobriety. When possible, share vacations with support group friends. Stay connected with your support systems through email, texting, Skype, and other means.

Change. Starting a new relationship or breaking off an old one, switching jobs, and moving homes seem to increase the risk of relapse. They all involve ventures into the unknown, and the attendant anxiety creates an uneasy thirst. Hopefully, you were able to avoid or postpone such events while in the Red Zone. Now that you are in the Yellow Zone, you are much better equipped to deal with changes, but you need to still be alert to their potential for tripping you up.

Boredom. Once the early work of recovery is completed and most of your life is on an even keel, you may long wistfully for drama or excitement—often for the wrong kind.

Illness or physical ailments. Aches and pains—headaches, backaches, surgery, dental problems, injuries, or other physical complaints—have been linked to the start of drinking and drugging. Not surprisingly, they've been linked to relapse, too. Sometimes it's because you are feeling miserable and exhausted and your defenses are down. Sometimes it's because of the anxiety and depression an illness has triggered. All too often, however, a relapse is due to the medications your well-meaning friends or health care providers have suggested to chase the pain.

In the past, some people in recovery felt safe taking any prescribed medications; if it was prescribed by a doctor, they figured, it must be safe. This is no longer safe thinking; overdoses of prescription drugs now kill about four times as many people as overdoses of illicit drugs. Understandably, the patient dealing with a backache or other ailment wants relief. He falsely believes he can control such usage, but more often than not he finds out too late that he was wrong. The result: relapse. The fact that the drug was prescribed and used with the best of intentions, and that the relapse was accidental, doesn't help one bit. A relapse is a relapse.

So if you experience frequent headaches, intestinal disturbances, muscular spasms, or any other symptoms, be alert for signposts warning that you're speeding toward what might be called a medically prescribed relapse. If you become seriously ill and need medication for treatment or surgery, or if you're about to have a baby and think you might need pain relief in labor, be sure you and your doctor follow the guidelines discussed in chapter 24.

Unexpected exposure. You're a nurse, and you find yourself with the key to the drug cabinet. You're doing the spring cleaning, and you turn up a forgotten cache of vodka. You're visiting a friend out of town, and while brushing your teeth you stumble upon a vial of painkillers left over from his back surgery. If you don't have a workable plan for such eventualities, relapse is only a misstep away. So be sure you plan ahead and know exactly what you will do.

Triggers. Remember, they can be almost anywhere:

- Something you see: powdered sugar spilled on the table, a mug of beer on TV, a familiar-looking tattoo or body piercing

- Something you hear: music you associate with your addiction

- Something you smell: stale beer, perfume, a whiff of marijuana

- Something you taste: nonalcoholic beer, pretzels like the ones you used to eat at your favorite bar

- Something you touch: grains of sugar, a flat mirrored surface

Any of these flashback stimuli (see chapter 10 for more potential cues) could trigger a craving. Vigilance—being prepared for psychological ambushes—lessens the danger.

RELAPSE RED FLAGS

There are many behaviors that can quietly (or noisily) signal that a relapse may be imminent. If you're always on the alert for these, you'll have a better chance of heading off a slip before it happens.

Elaborate excuse-making. When you find yourself going to great lengths to rationalize or explain away your behavior—why you missed a couple of meetings, why you've been late to dinner every night for a week—you are probably tottering on the brink.

Panic. Anxiety or panic attacks, thoughts of suicide, compulsive behaviors such as gambling or promiscuous sex, and eating peculiarities are sure signs that your life is getting out of hand. They require immediate attention. If getting back to your Red Zone life-and-death priorities doesn't get you better fast, seek help from a professional.

Irresponsibility. You start avoiding your commitments, failing to do what must be done, and procrastinating through your deadlines. You do things you know are not in your own best interests, or are in the worst interests of those you care about.

Breaking the rules. The rules laid out for continuing care no longer seem to apply to you. You "forget" to engage in the recovery activities you suggest to your sponsees or new members of your group. You "stop by" your old hangouts instead of detouring around them. You find a way to justify not making amends. You stop taking inventory.

Lying low. You used to check in with your sponsor at least twice a week. Now you realize it's been more than two weeks.

Sick thinking. You start missing the action at the bar and wonder if it really was the alcohol that caused your problems. You ponder the possibility of a little "scientific experiment" in social drinking; after all, you only had a problem with cocaine, not alcohol. You feel sorry for yourself. You start to call your sponsor when temptation invades your mind—but you abruptly hang up. You act on impulse rather than with forethought.

Strapping on spare parachutes. You discover you still have your dealer's numbers on your phone, but you reason that they're important reminders of your old ways and don't delete them. You turn down a ride to a meeting with an AA friend because you know you can't stop for a drink with him "just in case" you need one. You rationalize that you need to keep those old prescription painkillers just in case you break your leg in the wilderness, yet you haven't been camping in years.

Treading water. You've hit a plateau. You follow your program faithfully, but things are not getting better. If this lack of progress continues for six months or a year, it's time to think about seeking professional help, even if you had treatment earlier. Some people are so sick initially, their ability to think so dampened by drugs, that treatment is less effective than it could have been. For them, recovery often stagnates. Once the brain is in better shape, it can absorb more than it could earlier; getting a refresher course of treatment *without waiting for a relapse* is often the way to go.

Going to hell with yourself. You find yourself forgetting to take a bath, brush your teeth, get your hair cut, wash your clothes, or see the doctor when you are ill. These kinds of behaviors often reveal a nosedive in how you feel about yourself and your recovery. The next thing you're likely to forget is your sobriety.

Switching poisons. Alcohol is your nemesis, so what could be wrong with smoking a joint or two? You're a cocaine addict who never had trouble with alcohol, so why not enjoy a glass of wine? Or prescription painkillers were your downfall, so why should a snort of coke be a problem? Sorry. It won't work.

Denial. If any of the above describes your behavior, yet you swear to anyone who will listen that you aren't at risk for relapse, you're just fooling yourself. You are very likely well on the road to a relapse.

Heading Off a Relapse

TAKE ACTION QUICKLY

What do you do if you see any of the signs that a relapse is approaching? For at least a couple of weeks, revert to an earlier Recovery Zone, as described in the Recovery Zone ReCheck plan (see chapter 2). Review the many suggestions for dealing with cravings and compulsions that you learned about in chapter 10. And try any or all of the following suggestions to avoid falling off the wagon. Remember, the compulsion to drink or use drugs will pass if you do something else.

- Call your sponsor or advisor right now. This is when all those emergency numbers in your phone come in handy. If you fail to contact the first person you call, work your way down the list until you do reach someone.

- Go to a meeting. If your usual meeting isn't on, go to one that is—across town, online, or, if necessary, in another town. Now. No excuses.

- Go to more meetings than you have been, starting now. You may have to do more than a meeting a day for a while.

- Put some space between yourself and temptation. If you're a health professional, ask a colleague to take charge of your key to the drug cabinet. Walk out of a party or other event the moment you begin to sense "that old feeling" coming on.

- Try relaxation techniques, meditation, prayer, reading (the *Big Book* or other inspirational materials), listening to talks, pick-me-ups (exercise or even some sweet snacks), or other methods of smothering a compulsion to use or drink.

- Register for an upcoming recovery weekend or retreat. Total immersion in a convivial, sharing, understanding atmosphere for forty-eight hours can be a very sobering—and fun—experience.

- Remember what pre-sobriety life was really like. Review that cache of materials you prepared in early recovery (the history, letters, photos, and videos) so you wouldn't forget all the gory details.

- Ask yourself what it is you want to get out of the drink or drug that's tempting you. Surely you can come up with a better, sober way to reach that goal.

- Close your eyes and imagine what it could be like if you use again. Pure old-fashioned fear is a very powerful force restraining people who feel a compulsion to use— fear of sliding back into hell, fear of pain and degradation, fear of dying. So whatever thoughts you are having of using, follow through in your mind to the end point—another DUI, another weekend in jail, losing your job or your relationship. Or even worse, killing an innocent child or someone's beloved pet because you drove drunk or high.

Bottom line, you need to *always* be prepared to deal with an urge to use. Have a plan in place to deal with a whole list of perilous situations: You're offered a joint by a new friend, the emergency room doc prescribes a mood-altering drug for the pain of your sprained ankle, you run into an old drinking buddy.

Know not just roughly what you would do, but precisely, including the very words you would use. Anticipate the kind of response you might get in return, and decide how you would handle it. Role-play with AA or NA friends to prepare for the real thing. Rehearsing sticky situations beforehand opens up a prepared escape route. And knowing what to expect from yourself helps you live up to those expectations.

If you feel a slip is close, consider giving yourself a "booster" at a refresher program or an in- or outpatient treatment facility. Some treatment centers do not accept sober people, and most insurance carriers will not cover treatment for someone who hasn't relapsed. But you may be able to arrange an admission for mental health reasons or for an impending relapse, and be covered that way.

If you spot a pattern of regular slips, or a cycle of periodic sobriety followed by slips, try to head them off. If, for example, you seem to relapse every six months or so, check in for a booster after four or five months. Tinkering with your body's relapse clock could block that slip.

Finally, strengthen your recovery. Thoughtfully and honestly evaluate your recovery program to find and expose the weaknesses. Then return to the Red Zone to find the best ways to overcome them. Also study chapter 5 of the *Big Book* (How It Works) and suggest discussion topics at meetings that you think will be helpful. Dropping back to square one now, before a slip, will be a lot easier, and more productive, in the long run.

IF YOU HAVE A SLIP

First of all, remember that one slip (taking that first drink or fix) does not an irreversible relapse make. A close call or an actual slip doesn't mean you're a failure; just that your program needs immediate first aid. For some people, one or more slips, or even a full-blown relapse, may become a meaningful part of their recovery process. The following steps can turn a slip into a "therapeutic slip"—a learning experience that, instead of damaging your recovery, will strengthen it.

- Recognize that you made a mistake, but that you don't have to compound it. One drink doesn't deserve another.

- Don't surrender to the "Now that I've had one, what difference will a few more make?" despair. The difference could be considerable—between being sober this time next year and being dead.

- Leave the scene, pronto. Get your sponsor or another supportive person on the phone right away, and have them talk or text with you as you make your way to safety. Get yourself to an AA meeting, your sponsor's home, the home of another AA friend, your counselor's or doctor's office, or some other safe haven. If you're at home, dump the drugs or alcohol down the toilet before you go.

- Get immediate help from whomever would be most useful in directing you back to recovery. If you haven't already reached someone, get out your phone and start calling the people on your list; keep trying until you reach someone. Don't be embarrassed to ask for help. You are not the first person to slip.

- No slip "just happens." Once the immediate crisis is over, do an inventory to try to figure out why you slipped. Look over the risky attitudes, behaviors, and situations described in the preceding pages, and see which may have been responsible for your fall. Figure out what happened so you'll know what to do in the future.

- Reinforce your recovery program as though you were starting from scratch in the Red Zone: consider some more professional treatment, go to more meetings, rework the steps, read recovery literature, do more meditations, and so on.

If You Relapse

GET HELP AS SOON AS YOU CAN

If at any time you have a full-blown return to your drinking or drug-using behavior, even only sporadically, you are in relapse. Taking action is critical to your survival.

Get short-term help. Don't think about it—just do it. As soon as you can, pull yourself together and contact your sponsor, counselor, doctor, treatment program, or another strong, reliable person. If you wait until you hit bottom again, you might not live long enough to make another stab at recovery. Really. Don't stop calling until you've reached a sympathetic and sober person who can come to you immediately. Alternatively, take a cab to an AA meeting or clubhouse.

Detox. If you had withdrawal symptoms the first time you quit, you are likely to again, even after just a short period of using alcohol or another drug. Since withdrawal symptoms are generally more severe the second (or later) time around, you may need a medical detox.

Get long-term help. If you didn't go the formal treatment route the first time around, now is a good time to try it. If you did get treatment but you lacked motivation, professional treatment can be particularly valuable now. If you really open up your mind, all the words you listened to but didn't make a part of your life then should now finally make sense.

If you have a history of periodic sobriety and relapse, getting some professional treatment now may be not only valuable but absolutely necessary for your survival. Impaired judgment from drinking could set you up for self-destructive behaviors. With the dampened inhibitions caused by alcohol and drugs, even suicide looms as a disastrous consequence. Typically, relapse and its associated mood instability is a time when many people alternately seethe with anger and wallow in self-pity.

Spotlight your shortcomings. Relapsers sometimes think they are experts on recovery and that the relapse was "just a fluke." When they're told, "What you need is ninety meetings in ninety days," their response may be, "I know what I need, and that's not it!" If that sounds like you, do your best to drop the attitude. If you want to get sober again—this time for good—the first thing you're going to have to admit is that you *don't* know everything there is to know about recovery.

So swallow your pride and start your program over from scratch; do some soul-searching to find the chinks in your recovery armor and what led to the relapse. You can go back to your old AA group, or you might want to make a fresh start at a new group, one where you aren't recognized as an old-timer. Either option is fine, as long as you find a good environment for surrender, humility, and hope; it will be the keystone to your recovery.

Refocus on recovery. For now, forget about being a sponsor or helping other people, and instead look after yourself. Even if you've been sober for years, a relapse means you have to drop everything and concentrate on the work of recovery—on Red Zone work. You'll probably complete it in less time than you did the first time around, but you'll need to take it to heart and integrate it into your life better than you did then.

Make meetings mandatory. Don't ever let going to fellowship meetings become a random activity or one of convenience; structure your life so meetings are a routine part of it. Going to the same meetings at the same time and place each day (or later on, once or twice a week) will strengthen the habit. Sticking to a routine will help you to realize when something is wrong.

Link your meeting attendance to your other daily routines. Go to a meeting on your way home from work, before you hit the gym, or en route to an evening class. That way you know where you're going in advance and don't have to make a fresh decision each time.

Unmask the villains. Take a good look at your current involvement in your fellowship. Do you regularly confer with a sponsor? Have you gotten careless about attending meetings? Do you read the *Big Book* and other literature often? Also take a good look at your life. Are your relationships healthy? Is your job on track? Do you have too much stress in your life?

Don't be embarrassed. Your friends at your fellowship know that nobody's perfect. You may feel uncomfortable having to start all over again, but mostly you will get a lot of loving support.

Think positive. Anyone can become *and stay* sober—anyone who is motivated and willing to put in the necessary hard work. This time, that anyone can be you.

TWO STRIKES— YOU'RE OUT?

The first time you get out of treatment, you're welcomed back to the world with open arms. "Hey, glad to see you got your life together! Anything I can do to help?"

Screw up later on, though, and nobody trusts you. It would be nice if everyone around you realized that relapse is not unusual with the disease of addiction and understood your slip. But that's not likely.

So instead of having others understand your situation, you are going to have to understand theirs. They trusted you to stay sober, and you didn't. Maybe not for the first time. Not surprisingly, their patience is wearing thin.

The best you can do is level with them. Tell them a relapse wasn't in your plans, but it happened. Tell them that you don't intend this to be a revolving door, that one day at a time, you're going to try with everything you can muster to stay sober again—and to regain their trust. Explain that what you've learned from your relapse will help you, but don't make any extravagant promises. (And don't say these things unless you really believe them.)

Learn, too, from the attitudes of those around you. They are telling you in the only way they know how that your relapse hurt them as well as you. Maybe their pain, coupled with your own, will help you do what is necessary to stay sober this time.

WASTED YEARS?

So you had a slip or a relapse after several years of sobriety. You may feel that you blew all that effort, that those years were a waste. They weren't. During that time your body was free from chemicals, so from the point of view of your health, they certainly weren't wasted. And from the point of view of recovery they weren't squandered, either. You learned a lot. Your drinking or drugging will never be the same, knowing what you know. It's like ending a bad marriage. If you learn from your mistakes, you can do better the next time you walk down the aisle. Learn what led up to this relapse and you'll do better next time, too.

18

Rebuilding Your Life: Relationships, Recreation, and Socializing in the Yellow Zone

///

F or a year or more now, you've been hearing: "Concentrate on your recovery, on your own needs. Healing relationships is important, but for now, just patch things up. You can fix it all later." Your family and other loved ones have heard over and over how important it is for you to focus on getting better, even if they felt left out for a while.

///

Everyone has waited—some patiently, some not so patiently—for the moment when you could switch your focus from self-healing to relationship-healing. Now, finally, it's time. (And aren't you lucky that they stood beside you for all this time? Go give them all thank-you hugs right now.)

Now is the time for you to rebuild ties with your family and friends, and to really work on those relationships—warts and all. It's also time to learn more about having some fun—sober fun, of course. If you are so inclined, you can even get out there and start dating and find a brand-new relationship.

Is It Time to Make Changes?

ARE YOU SURE YOU'RE READY?

"Following the suggestion of my sponsor, I avoided making any major decisions during my first year or so of recovery. Is now the time to start thinking about a change?"

Probably. Until now, your major goal in recovery was, wisely, to stay sober and save your life. Now it's time to put some new life in your life—and that requires making some decisions. To see if you are ready for that, take a targeted inventory.

- Has your judgment (as seen in your behavior) improved since the days when you were drinking or using? To get an accurate and fully objective assessment, you'll have to ask others—your sponsor, family members, friends, and coworkers—this question, too.

- Do you have a better idea of who you are and what your goals are? Comparing past inventories to the present will help you decide.

- Have you improved your interpersonal skills? Can you relate to others without threatening or feeling threatened?

- Are you mostly free of resentment of others?

- Do you think you'll be able to handle a decision that ends up with a bad outcome?

If you can answer yes to all these questions, then, yes, you're ripe for change and ready for decision making. In the Yellow Zone, we do suggest you rebuild your relationships, social life, career, finances, and more. But don't try to change everything all at once. Take on one issue at a time, preferably starting with a minor one (no harm done if it goes bad), and apply the following basic decision-making principles to it.

A STRATEGY FOR MAKING DECISIONS

Identify the problem or decision to be made. It could be a relatively minor decision: Should you buy a new laptop? Or it could be a major, life-altering decision: Should you move to a new town? End your marriage? Some people just let life roll over them, with no one making any decisions. Don't be one of them. This is your life to live the way you want—sober and happy. Now is the time to make that happen.

Gather data on the subject. Do some research on laptop models and prices. Look into the cost of a move and how it would affect your life, friends, family, and work. Go to a marriage counselor with your spouse to see how your marriage looks to an outsider.

Do some field research. How have other people solved similar problems? AA resources and members provide an infinite supply of case histories—through recordings and online forums, in the *Big Book*, at meetings. Whatever it is you're contemplating, you will probably find others who have been there before you. Study these case histories closely, then factor their successes or failures into your decision making—you may be able to avoid being your own lab rat.

Know your personal values and your goals. In making any decision, consider how well it plays with your values and goals. Is having a new laptop important? It might be crucial if you are exploring a new career in video production. Is saving your marriage a priority? Even if it seems irreparably broken now, a divorce with no attempt at reconciliation might be contrary to your values and the vows you made.

Knowing what you believe in and making decisions accordingly is not just a good exercise—your happiness and your life depend on it now. Honesty, safety, respect, responsibility, health, and freedom are all things you should give more than lip service to.

Look at your options. List all of the possible actions and decisions, along with the risks and the benefits of each. How will they affect you (emotionally, physically, and financially), your recovery, and other people? Will they be easily reversible, or will they be carved in stone once done?

If you buy a new laptop, it could help you explore career options, but you might not have enough money left to cover your rent. If you don't buy it, your rent will be paid but you might find it harder to start your own video company.

If you divorce, you might have a fresh new beginning, but it could mean hurting children you love or giving up a relationship that still has some meaning.

There might, of course, be a long list of risks and benefits for any one decision. Sometimes, when you look at your list you can easily see which choices are good bets (those with a long list of benefits) and which are not (those with lots of risks). Sometimes, however, the picture looks relatively balanced. Then you have to go to the next step.

Minimize risks or increase benefits, when possible. This technique can improve the odds for any decision.

For example, the financial risk of buying a new laptop could be reduced by waiting a few months for the next generation of machines to come out and then buying a discounted older model.

Carry out your decision. The best of decisions (and the worst) are meaningless unless they are implemented.

Accept responsibility for your decision. That doesn't just mean that if things go wrong, it's your fault, or that if things go well, you get a medal. Decisions are what we make them. If you decide to buy the laptop, move

THE YELLOW ZONE

to another town, or stay in that marriage, your responsibility doesn't end there. Now you have to make your decision work—for yourself and for the others involved. (Sure, it can be more comfortable to sit on the sidelines and play the victim, but remember, even the Serenity Prayer guides us to "change the things we can." And by this stage in your recovery, you should be developing some assertiveness skills.)

If you find you are making decisions without following a game plan, such as the one above, or if you recognize that a decision is rife with risks but make it anyway, you are acting compulsively—much the way you did when you drank or used drugs. This probably means there are some big holes in your recovery program, and you might need to head back to the Red Zone for a while.

Renewing Relationships

One of the main things you'll need to do as you rebuild your relationships is move beyond thinking about only yourself. That served you well in early recovery, but it's time now to focus more on the needs of others and how you can build bridges with them.

REGAINING TRUST

"You'd think that after eighteen months of sobriety I'd have won back my family's trust. But my wife and

kids still act like I'm the meth addict living on the street."

Proving that you could stay sober was just the first step in regaining the trust of those around you. It was enough in early sobriety, but it isn't enough now. Now you have to prove you're not just an addict who no longer uses but also a thoughtful, caring person.

While you were using, your behavior was certainly self-centered. It continued to be during the early—and necessarily selfish—months of recovery. Now you have to move and grow beyond your old self and start to build on top of the solid recovery foundation you've established. You need to start to show concern for others by giving yourself, your time, and your energies as gifts to those you care about.

You'll gain trust and respect most easily when you trust and respect others. You'll learn people's needs only when you start paying attention to how they feel, and to how what you do affects their feelings. Now is the time to listen, to pay more than ear service to what they say, to learn to take criticism without exploding in anger.

In the Red Zone, you built a protective wall around yourself to allow for healing. Now it's time to be more open and vulnerable, to allow for emotional growth. You may find this idea difficult, because the tendency of the addict is to be defensive, which only builds the wall higher. But by following the recommendations throughout this chapter, you *will* be able to open up communication channels. This will cause you discomfort at times, but you can handle it now. And it's the kind of pain that "hurts good"—the kind that leads to emotional gain.

DEVELOP YOUR COMMUNICATION SKILLS

Chances are, your communication skills fell to the wayside while you were in active addiction. Now is the time to brush up on how to interact with others.

Even poor communication might be better than no communication. In the first months of recovery, communication is often nonexistent, or almost so. Any communication, even if it is shaky and tentative, is a sign that a relationship is, at least, no longer completely dead.

Honesty is the best communications policy. If family members always level with each other—even when it might be painful—then they can always trust each other. That doesn't mean intentionally saying hurtful things ("You sounded like a jerk on the phone!"), but giving honest answers and opinions when asked. ("That phone call sounded annoying, but I think the person calling didn't deserve to be called names.") If you can't learn the truth from those you are close to, where else can you learn it? Another trick to foster some honest discourse: Ask for permission before you give feedback. ("Would

you like a stock phrase I use when I'm annoyed by sales calls?")

A lot is lost in translation. What you say is often not what other people hear. Likewise, what you hear is not always what other people are saying. You may have heard this before, but keep it in mind during actual conversations. "There's a great band playing downtown this week" can mean nothing more than that. But it can also mean "I'd love to see that great band." If you don't make that clear and the person you're addressing doesn't pick up on it, you may resent spending your evenings at home. Particularly when discussing serious matters, don't leave understanding to chance. Be sure you've made your point by repeating it in different ways, and then nicely ask your listener what he heard.

If you are the listener, don't try to read more—or less—into what you hear. If you have an interpretation, repeat it to the speaker to see if you have it right. If you don't, ask more questions.

Remember the saying "It's not what you say, it's how you say it." Try to always convey kindness in your voice.

Snap judgments smother discussion. If you say, "That's a stupid idea!" a few times, the person you've said it to will stop coming up with ideas, period. There will be no more communication. Say, "There you go, blowing your stack over nothing again," often enough, and the other person will begin to suppress their feelings. Instead of judging, listen to what they have to say, and accept their feelings as real and valid. Then express your own feelings or opinions. For instance: "Maybe you are right, but can I tell you what I was thinking?"

Avoid digital disasters. In a world where we are all communicating more and more via email, texting, social media, and other technological means, our intended messages often get distorted. Digital misunderstandings can quickly lead to angry arguments. In early recovery, the risk of such mishaps is particularly high: People are still relearning how to communicate, and because they have a history of poor communication, they'd often really prefer to send a quick text than talk.

If short and factual information is all you need to communicate, send a quick text. But when you need to discuss more personal or emotional subjects, try to find the time to talk in person. Or, if you really do need to communicate digitally, take the time to carefully compose your words. Then put it aside overnight and read it again in the morning. Does it still say what you intended? Will it help rebuild your relationship? Bottom line, staying in touch digitally can help restore trust and build communication skills, but never hesitate to pick up the phone or talk face-to-face about sensitive issues.

Anger breeds anger. An angry person is not a communicating person. If your partner comes home from work late and you start ranting and raving, the response will almost certainly be ranting and raving right back at you. A better option would be something like this: "I am really upset about your being late. I was afraid something had happened to you. Next time please text me so I won't worry." Rather than a rant, you're likely to get an apology. Remember—of all the feelings bottled up in families dealing with addiction, anger is the most destructive. Restoring the caring and nurturing that you lost during your active addiction can cut off the anger at its source. Plus, in the addict, anger is often just self-hate turned outward, an attempt to prevent a downslide in self-worth. As the person heals in recovery, they often find that their anger just melts away.

Knowing values is valuable. Knowing your own values and those of the person you are talking to makes communication much easier. You can measure what someone says against the values you know he holds. If, for example, you know your spouse really cares about religion, you won't assume that his glumly reported Sunday morning headache is an excuse to avoid going to church. When you sense a conflict between what the other person is saying and the values you believe he holds, raise the question and explore it. Personal values often get eroded during active addiction, so boundaries about them tend to blur. If values have been vague in your family, or they seem to have slipped in the recent past, start talking about and defining them now.

Friends—even spouses—need not agree on everything. You like burgers and she likes fish; he watches the news and you love sitcoms. They say opposites attract, and certainly some very happy marriages have been built by people with different interests and tastes. But those who succeed have something very important in common: mutual respect. Not only do they respect each other's opinions but they also listen to them without belittling.

Practice helps make perfect. Rehearse what you are going to say ahead of time. That can help make it easier to say something you might otherwise find difficult. It will also help divorce your statement from the emotions of the moment. In some cases, role-playing with a surrogate can help, too.

Rebuilding Family Ties

I DON'T KNOW WHERE TO START

"It's time for me to start pulling the family together again—meaning my husband and kids—but I don't know how or where to begin."

It all begins after you've said you're sorry. It continues with your husband and kids waking up to find

you cheerful and ready to leave for work; not hungover or still drunk from the night before.

Sobriety alone cannot reverse the damage that's been done to your family. Now that your first priority—your recovery—is well under way, you can focus on healthy communication. But you can't force-feed change down family members' throats. Improvements in family relations are most likely to occur when the whole family participates in change-making and slowly gets the feeling that things have indeed changed for the better.

Relationships must be cultivated gently and patiently. Don't expect problems that were years in the making to be resolved with a few quick hugs and kind words—no matter how sincere—just because mom's finally come home clean and sober. You may have been stoned or drunk during much of their childhood, when your children were young, immature, and very impressionable. The impact of your behavior as an addict—particularly on teenagers—may be greater than they show or you can imagine. You have your work cut out for you.

////////////////////////

"My wife and I have been separated for nearly four years. I haven't spoken to her since I got sober. Should I call just to let her know how I am?"

It's too late to rewrite history, but it may be possible to shape the future. Some relationships still have the ingredients needed for a healthy renewal in recovery. Do an inventory of the relationship before trying to reestablish communication. Was it loving, caring, and generally healthy, aside from the chemical dependence? Do unforgettable ghosts of violence, incest, or child abuse still haunt the past? Would the relationship be supportive of your newfound way of life or jeopardize it? Would harsh rejection sour your recovery at this point?

If the answers to these questions are favorable, or at least not totally negative, and you still have fond memories of your ex (and, so far as you know, she's not in a committed new relationship), it can't hurt to make contact. Usually a letter or email is least threatening; plus, it allows you to explain the reason for your contact without the phone suddenly going dead in your ear. Regrets, amends, and optimism about the future may all be part of your correspondence. But bad habits die hard, and it may be difficult to avoid manipulation, so you might want to ask your sponsor to review what you wrote before you hit Send. What happens next will depend on how your ex responds to this first peace offering. You might have the door slammed in your face. If so, at least you can go on with your life knowing you tried. Or there might be a cautious opening. In that case, take some time to explore the relationship before you decide whether or not there's a future for the two of you.

HOW A PARENT'S ADDICTION AFFECTS CHILDREN

The children of people in active addiction can experience a wide range of emotions: confusion, anger, shame, fear, guilt, anxiety, loneliness, helplessness. Some children in these households continue to do fairly well; others have a very hard time with just about everything. How and to what degree a child was affected by parental alcoholism or drug use varies, depending on many factors.

- Were both parents addicted, or just one? The emotional scarring is often more severe when it's the mother (who is often the primary caretaker) or when both parents are addicted.

- How severe were the symptoms of addiction? Generally, the more severe, the greater the impact on the child.

- Was there a strong caregiver other than the addicted parent or parents? Such a caregiver often helps to ease children's sense of hopelessness, gives, them a healthy sense of self, and improves coping skills.

- How old was the child when addiction became a problem? When did the parent get sober? The longer the parent's involvement with alcohol or drugs, and the more often they cycled through treatment attempts, the greater the child's emotional difficulties.

- What was the child's place in the family? In general, children build life skills and self-worth, and make the best of their situations, by finding roles that help them adapt. Often firstborns react differently than last-borns, and middle children differently from both.

- Was there family cohesiveness in spite of the addiction? If the family was somehow held together—usually by the nonaddicted parent or another adult in the household—problems may be less severe.

- Did the family manage to stick to its general direction and goals in spite of the addiction? The more the addiction derailed the family's goals and identity, the more difficult it is to get the children back on track.

- How did the nonaddicted parent respond to the situation? A parent who was unable to cope with not having their personal needs met can find it difficult to meet their children's needs. On the other hand, strong spouses, particularly those involved in Al-Anon, often are able to give strong support to children through their own emotional recovery, lessening the impact of the other parent's addiction.

- How much did the child understand? Was he a terrified and confused bystander who saw all and was told nothing, or was he dealt with honestly? Did he get any emotional support during the time of the addiction? This kind of support can reduce emotional scarring in children.

- Were family members allowed, even encouraged, to express feelings? In families where feelings are regularly stifled, the emotional development of children is often stunted.

- Was the child's independence fostered? Children who learn to stand on their own two feet do fairly well, even in a family suffering from chemical dependency.

- Did physical or sexual abuse compound the emotional abuse in the home? This always puts a child at higher risk for developing problems, and requires professional help. It may take some effort to uncover such abuse, since it usually occurred under intoxication; blackouts may have obliterated it from the perpetrator's memory.

- What is the educational level of the parents? Is the family financially stable? Lower education levels and lack of economic security tend to compound the negative consequences of living with a chemically dependent parent.

THE YELLOW ZONE

HELPING YOUR CHILD

While you're working on your recovery, your child will need to do some recovering, too. Don't naively assume that once you get sober, everyone in the family will feel better and all your problems related to your drinking or drug use will disappear. They won't.

If your children are old enough, don't let them indulge in such wishful thinking, either. Let them know it's going to be a long haul for everyone, but that at least now you'll all be pulling together. It will help for them to learn about alcoholism/addiction. If they are young, read to them or have them read some good children's books on the subject. If they are teenagers, they can read this book; they should also get involved in Alateen. They might also turn to some online support resources, but it's best to be very wary there. These kids are very vulnerable to manipulation, and online predators are just waiting for them. Alateen meetings—in person and online—are closely supervised by adult volunteers who have been thoroughly vetted.

What if your kids ask, "What am I supposed to tell my friends about what's been going on?" Encourage them to be honest, but say it's okay to stick to simple responses. For example, they might respond to a friend's questions with: "Thanks for asking. My mom has been sick, but she is getting treated for her illness. She's getting better." They shouldn't feel they have to hide your disease.

(Consider, too, that any young friends who are asking questions might be dealing with similar issues in their own homes and be trying to reach out for help.)

Some children will need one-on-one professional help to learn how to cope with the situation. Seek help from a counselor or therapist trained in treating children of addicted families if your children seem extremely withdrawn, are getting into trouble at school or with the police, refuse to discuss your alcoholism or addiction, or repeatedly talk about hurting themselves or wanting to die. Professional help is also an absolute necessity if they've been subjected to any sexual or physical abuse at home.

Because your children will be at high risk of marching to the same drummer you did, you should take steps to make them as drug-resistant as you can (chapter 23).

FAMILY COMMUNICATION AND DECISION MAKING

"After what seems like a lifetime of drinking and then a year of meetings every night, I came out of my fog realizing I hardly know my wife and my children. I don't even know how to talk with them."

Though you may feel a burning desire to try to fix things right now, to create one big, happy family overnight, resist it. A family in recovery is a lot like an individual in recovery. It takes a long time to heal. Relationships change and grow slowly. Suspicion and skepticism die hard. Understanding comes slowly, one day, one thoughtful loving act at a time. Since your recovery progress will influence that of your family's, they will usually be a couple of steps behind you. But there are things you can do to help nudge their recovery along:

- Be sure you have started to make amends. With your family, it will take a lot more than a simple "I'm really sorry, guys." Making "living amends" is likely to be the most meaningful. So let your actions show them how much you value them, and that you don't intend to fall into the same traps again: Treat them well every day, help out around the house, participate in family events, go to school activities, and, most of all, be there when anyone in the family needs your support.

- Be sure you have forgiven anyone in the family you harbor resentments against. If you are still angry with your wife for throwing you out when you were drunk or for spending a lot of time away from home, it's time to wipe those slates clean.

- Be sure your family understands your illness. Your explanations may fall short. Ideally, those who are old enough will have read about alcoholism and addiction here and elsewhere, spent some time with a variety of recovery recordings, and gotten involved

with Al-Anon or Alateen. If not, now is the time. A family retreat or convention with others in recovery is an ideal way for families to learn from each other in a fun, low-pressure atmosphere. Another good way is socializing with another family in the same stage of recovery, preferably one that shares interests and values similar to your own. If your family members resist learning about your illness, you might encourage them to talk with your counselor, doctor, or someone from your treatment center. Or you might try a reverse intervention (see page 402).

- Demonstrate that you've grown beyond the self-centered early stages of recovery by showing those you love that you are thinking about them. If you're forgetting birthdays and anniversaries or you fail to call home when you're delayed at work, you still have a way to go.

- Find things that you and your family members can all enjoy and plan activities around them. These should be areas where there are no obvious conflicts or threats to any of you, so the activities can be relaxing and fun for all. Relationships are most easily nurtured by building on common bonds.

- Learn to respect the individuality and autonomy of each family member. Give up your urges to

THE YELLOW ZONE

control them. This is something that addicts and their partners often have trouble with. If you can't accept the fact that your teenage children can make some decisions on their own, you may need some professional counseling. Your partner, too, may need it, if she finds it hard to stop trying to control you—as she probably tried to do for years.

- Be open to change and growth. It may not be the easiest or most comfortable thing in the world, but it is healthy and necessary. No one stays the same from year to year—at any age. Accept and applaud this in yourself as well as in your spouse and children.

- Once family communication on noncontroversial issues seems solid, you can begin to identify areas of conflict and try to work on them. But if you find that every time you try, someone (or everyone) explodes, then you should back off and not try to handle such issues on your own. Get some family counseling.

///////////////////////////

"Every time we have to make a decision in our family, there's a major blowup."

Many families in early recovery have problems communicating and making decisions. For years, there was little useful communication. Decisions were poorly thought out. The addicted person—or the

spouse or family member struggling to maintain some order—handed down decisions from above with little discussion. Or no one was in any shape to make choices, so things just happened. There may have been an ongoing struggle for control, with power, size, and lies dominating, while positive values like caring, helpfulness, and honesty were trampled underfoot.

Sobriety alone won't alter these family patterns. You'll have to work at changing them if you want everyone to see that there's a better way.

First, introduce some democracy. Suggest that you all have regular family meetings to discuss things. Call such meetings often, and include everyone in the household. Don't wait for a crisis, or even the need to decide anything. At least weekly, sit down and talk about how things are going. Review any problems or gripes that have cropped up. But also remember to hand out compliments for jobs well done and for kindness or thoughtfulness.

Set some ground rules for your meetings:

- Each speaker, no matter what age, will have their say and others will listen with respect.

- Everyone has a right to voice an opinion, but not to judge or criticize others.

- Everyone has the right to bring up items to talk about and to air problems or grievances. But personal attacks are taboo.

When you need to make a decision, follow the steps listed earlier in this chapter. Allow children, even young ones, to voice opinions and cast votes. It doesn't always have to be "one person, one vote," however. The person who is most affected by an issue should have a larger say. When making any decision, you will all need to consider health, safety, cost, family values, and the impact on recovery. Ideally, try to reach a consensus. When there is a split vote, try to resolve the issue through negotiation.

FINDING TIME FOR FAMILY FUN

"I know that I need to spend more quality time with my family. But I am so involved in NA that I don't quite know how to do this."

Your problem is shared by millions of others in 12-step programs. Here are some ideas:

- Going to meetings is still important, but you might be able to cut back a bit now, or fit your meetings into your life with a less recovery-centric focus. For example, can you go to meetings at noon or before work, rather than in the evenings, when your family would like to spend time with you? That way, you can keep up your involvement in recovery activities and expand family time, too. You should be okay as long as you are still living in a culture of recovery.

- Look at your schedule and see where you can plug in more family time. You might be able to downsize your involvement in several areas in order to free up more family time. Cut back on other outside activities (church, school, community work). Make family and recovery activities number one and two. Sometimes it will be hard to set priorities when all your options are good; that comes with the turf.

- Invite your spouse and children to some open meetings. They'll learn a lot, and it will give you more time (and empathy-building shared experiences) together.

- Invite your family to join you on weekend trips and longer vacations around recovery conferences, retreats, or other events. This, too, will add to family togetherness and will broaden their understanding of this disease.

Remember, too, that the idea of "quality time" is often misunderstood. Any time you spend with your children in a loving and caring atmosphere is quality time. You could be preparing dinner while your toddler plays a little concert with the pots and pans on the floor. Or paying bills as you answer questions from your teenager, who is deep in geometry homework. Or picking out the clothes you'll wear to work in the morning and

THE YELLOW ZONE

explaining to your ten-year-old how to coordinate colors.

There are endless ways to be part of your children's lives, even when time is limited: walking to school together, saying prayers together at bedtime, discussing the news, playing a shared video game or doing a crossword puzzle together, going to the supermarket together. It's all quality time, as long as you reach out and make contact with them. On the other hand, you could spend every minute of every day with your children and make no contact at all.

A REVERSE INTERVENTION

"My parents have been giving me a hard time ever since I started going to NA. They're embarrassed that their little girl (I'm thirty-two) says she's an alcoholic and an addict. It can't possibly be true, they say. What can I do?"

Your parents no doubt love you, but they also see you as an extension of themselves. They are having trouble dealing with the fact that this extension isn't perfect. So they prefer to deny that you have a problem. They aren't unusual. Most people in our society don't understand the disease of addiction. They see it as a moral failing, something to be ashamed of. Your parents might only start to see it in its true light if they talk to other parents going through the same thing—preferably at Al-Anon. You might try a "reverse intervention."

- Gather together a group of people, preferably the kind your parents will respect. You might include a clergyperson familiar with addiction, a doctor or counselor trained in addiction, any relatives who are supporting your recovery, and other parents who are active in Al-Anon.

- Choose a site where your parents will be comfortable. It could be their home, if you live with them, or your home. Or it could be neutral ground, such as your house of worship or family doctor's office.

- Plan out what each person will say. Ask each professional who is going to attend to be ready to talk about how alcoholism/addiction is a disease, not a moral weakness. Ask Al-Anon members to be ready to talk about how they felt when they heard about their child's problems and how they found that sharing their concerns with other parents can help.

- Write up a list of the kinds of things you were doing that convinced you that you had a problem. You don't have to include specifics if you don't want to talk about them now, but do be honest.

- Invite your parents to the location of the intervention, telling them there are some people you'd like them to meet. If they balk, you may have to spring the intervention on them as a surprise. You might invite them to your house for brunch or have your counselor suggest a meeting.

- Ask one of the professionals to guide the discussion so it won't be a direct confrontation between you and your folks.

You may succeed in getting your parents to understand your illness better and to see how Al-Anon can help them. But they may prefer to continue in their denial. If they do, you will have to steer clear of frequent contact with them; the stress could be hazardous to your recovery.

If you live with them, think about getting your own place or moving in with a friend in recovery for a while—especially if your parents refuse to get rid of any alcohol or pills around the house.

HELPING MY FAMILY GET PAST THE THINGS I DID

"While I was drinking I did some awful things to my daughter. I was arrested and went to prison for what I did—rightly so. The judge said I can now have supervised visits with her, and I'm trying to rebuild our relationship. But she won't talk to me—won't even stay in the same room with me."

You need to adjust to her feelings of fear and distrust. She doesn't trust that the abuse is over. You will have to prove it over a long period of time through your behavior toward her. This won't be easy. She is old enough to know that what you did was wrong, bad, sick. But her feelings are very confused. Certainly she hated what you did and hated you for doing it. But at some point in her life, she probably loved her father. She may be staying away from you as much because of her own mixed feelings as out of fear.

Dealing with sexual abuse is beyond the scope of groups such as AA. If both of you are not already getting therapy, it's time to look into it. You'll both need long-term professional help to deal with this situation. It can help her move past the harm that was done and develop a healthy way of looking at love, sexuality, and intimacy. It can help you understand what you did and how to prevent your behavior from recurring. You can't force her to have a relationship with you, but with therapy, you may be able to rebuild it over time.

If you don't get help, your problems could begin all over again, even if you stay sober. Or the guilt and anxiety could drive you back to drink. If your child doesn't get help, she may carry the scars of the abuse for the rest of her life. She may never be able to have a healthy relationship as an adult, may never understand what real love and intimacy are about, and may end up with someone just like dad—who drinks and abuses her. All too often, addiction triggers other self-destructive cycles, which become disasters on their own.

Your daughter, and anyone else who is dealing with this kind of a situation, can get help from the national Childhelp Child Abuse Hotline 800-4-A-CHILD (422-4453). Childhelp's website (childhelp.org) also has good resources.

Common Relationship Issues

WHAT IS NORMAL?

"I'm the alcoholic daughter of two alcoholic parents. My husband is also from an alcoholic family. We are expecting our first child and want to raise him in a healthy, well-functioning family. But we don't even know what that is."

Most alcoholics don't. And simply abstaining from alcohol and drugs doesn't mean they— or you—will automatically know what makes for a healthy and loving home. A good way to learn is to look back at your earlier life and try to figure out which parts were dysfunctional. Then go outside of your own experience to learn what constitutes a better atmosphere. Find some reputable books on family interactions and discuss them with your husband. As you build your life together, try to model your behavior on those healthier ways of relating, with regard to decision making, sharing feelings, and many other issues.

Decision making. You may have grown up in a home where family decisions were made in the heat of the battle, with the spoils of victory going to whoever shouted the loudest. Those without any power learned to meet their needs by manipulation or by going outside the family completely. These behavior patterns often persist long after the drinking or drug use stops. In a healthy and functional family, people sit down and discuss the decisions that affect everyone. Say they are trying to decide what to do on a Sunday. If there's general agreement, they go with it. If not, each member voices his or her wishes. Then they negotiate. They try to see if the decision is more important to one member of the family than to the others. The wishes of that person may get priority, or at least extra weight. They make compromises. The point is, they work out a plan where everyone's needs and desires are met somehow. Maybe not today, and maybe not completely, but eventually. No one is left out.

Control. Controlling others is another big family issue. In alcoholic/addict families, unrelenting control is usually paramount, with the addict determined to push all the buttons. Other family members are bullied into following his rules, no matter how crazy. The kids have to do their homework at a certain time, eat every string bean on the plate, play only with selected friends. The spouse has to have dinner on the table at exactly the right moment. The nonaddicted partner, while following all the rules, also tries desperately, and unsuccessfully, to control the addict. The family is in a whirlwind of chaos, and, in fact, it's the alcohol or drugs that are controlling them all.

In a healthy family, in contrast, members work well together and respect each other; they aren't heavily invested in the need to control events and one another. Both spouses have learned to let go, to give everyone the freedom to control their own lives.

Emotions. Feelings are another hot-button issue. In the addicted family, feelings are buried six feet under. What is going on (or how each family member feels about it) is rarely discussed, either within the family or with others on the outside. An artificial and transient sense of well-being is created by a conspiracy of silence. Yet each person is likely experiencing a growing sense of insecurity, inadequacy, and shame.

In healthy families, feelings are shared, expressed, and attended to as a necessary part of good family interaction. Everyone knows it is not only okay to open up and talk about what one feels inside, but it is healthy, even necessary, to do so.

Going to extremes. In the addicted family, everything is done to excess—life is lived on the edge. Healthy families do things in moderation: They get angry and have fun, spend and save, work and relax.

Family goals. Another issue you and your husband should think about: your goals for your family. All families have goals, traditions, rituals; maybe they are focused on ensuring all the kids go to college, or on religious activities, or volunteer work. In alcoholic and addict families, any goals, traditions, and rituals that were once there are usually crowded out by substance use. Children, and even parents, may become confused and uncertain as to what the family really wants and what it believes.

The healthy family has thought about and discussed what their goals are, and how they can structure their lives to meet those goals. If caring about the less fortunate is an important value, for example, they make it a family tradition to donate all their loose change in the collection plate at church each week. If education is an important value, they set aside a special time each day for family reading, studying, or learning something new.

Family resilience. All families go through good and bad times. How they deal with the down times can vary quite a bit. Illnesses, for example, tend to upset family functioning. If dad is recuperating from knee surgery, everyone has to change or add roles temporarily to compensate. Mom may have to cut down on her hours at work, and the older kids might have to take on the food shopping. This kind of temporary stress can actually strengthen a healthy family; everyone gets a charge out of pulling together, caring for each other in new ways. In the alcoholic family, however, family resilience is often minimal or nonexistent, and any upset sends the family spiraling further downward.

The best medicine for the family wounded by addiction is unconditional love, given and accepted. And time. Give yourself the time to recover from your pasts, and learn about and develop healthy ways of relating. Read everything you can about family dynamics. Also consider taking a course in parenting or functional families, or working with a therapist. The good news is you know from the start you have some learning to do—your baby will be very fortunate to grow up in such a loving and caring household, even if you don't do everything perfectly right.

///////////////////////////

"My fiancée keeps telling me that the way I relate to other people, even now that I'm sober, is very strange. She's so concerned about it that she refuses to set a wedding date."

A perceptive woman. Most alcoholics/addicts display abnormal human-relations patterns outside the family as well as within it. You go to buy a car and don't get the price you want, so you stomp out of the showroom in a fury—you think the salesman is out to get you. Or you stifle that response and feel exploited and despondent. A more normal reaction is to grant the reality that you and the dealer have different goals (you're trying to get the best deal you can and he's trying to make a living selling cars). The appropriate response would be: "Well, your price is higher than I want to pay. I'll do some more shopping around and see if I can do better."

Or your boss tells you that your most recent report isn't good enough. You react defensively, accusing others and constructing elaborate alibis for yourself. A more sensible reaction would be to rein in any anger and ask calmly, "Where did I fall short? What can I do to get my work up to speed?"

The alcoholic/addict, after years of perfecting his self-centered behavior, sometimes never manages to develop healthy negotiation skills. He tends to take criticism as a personal attack, disagreement as a personal affront, calamity as a personal assault.

By this stage of your recovery, with your brain on the mend, your judgment sounder and your ego, hopefully, stronger, it's time to start looking at such situations more rationally. If someone seems to criticize you, try to recognize that everybody gets criticized, sometimes unfairly, and to understand that it may have less to do with you than with the person dishing it out. Maybe your boss is worried about his own job. Or maybe he still drinks and resents your sobriety. Whatever the reason, your flaring up won't improve matters. Nor will it help when the criticism is justified. That's when you need to remember that nobody is always right, and that being wrong is okay. What *isn't* okay is trying to defend your position when you know you erred.

FEAR OF BECOMING VULNERABLE

"My husband claims I'm afraid to really open up to him, that I'm always afraid to try something new. Is this part of my disease?"

You don't have to be an alcoholic to be afraid to open yourself up to another person or to dread trying something new. Doing these things makes a person vulnerable, and many people fear exposing themselves to rejection or failure that way.

But you're right—you are more likely to harbor this fear if you have the disease of addiction. Alcoholics and addicts tend to be defensive, to build walls to hide the weakness of their inner resources. They fear and dam up emotions because emotions put them at risk (if you don't love, you can't lose).

The fear of being vulnerable can appear in a relationship when you hold back, reluctant to give yourself wholeheartedly and completely. Or it could show up elsewhere: a fear of meeting new people, taking a new job, going to a different AA group.

It's probably time for you to do some work on getting past your fears. Opening yourself up to emotions and new experiences, and letting yourself be vulnerable and grow emotionally, are essential to your good recovery. Allowing yourself to be vulnerable isn't easy. You will need to be at a fairly advanced and secure place in recovery. And you may have to practice quite a bit, take some baby steps, before it feels natural and nonrisky to you. ("Just for today, I'm going to completely be open and available to my husband."

If you never acknowledge your fears and accept the risks, you'll never move beyond them. You will continue to live in fear, to live a life that is about as fulfilling as watching diners through a restaurant window.

Some fears, of course, are well founded. Driving through the part of town where you used to buy drugs, or stopping off after work at a bar you frequented "just to say hi to my pals," is a risk that won't help you grow and could push you down the slippery slope to big trouble. Clearly, you need to learn to exercise good judgment in order to differentiate between a risk worth taking and one that's just plain crazy.

ACQUIRING ASSERTIVENESS

Assertiveness is not a behavior familiar to most alcoholics/addicts. Instead of being assertive, they tend to be totally passive or extremely aggressive. They often swallow their feelings and reactions until one day they explode in a ball-of-fire temper tantrum. That may not get them what they want (though it does guarantee anger and resentment from the other party), but it feels good. On the other hand, if they grit their teeth and contain their feelings, they're the ones who become angry and resentful.

Assertiveness is a way of making a point without being offensive or hurtful. How does it work? Say a husband is always late for dinner. That's been his style for years. His wife and children have always waited for him, with resentment mounting by the minute. When he finally arrives, she either rails at him, tosses his meal in his lap, or sits down to dinner simmering in silence. Then everyone is out of sorts and unhappy.

Calm assertiveness is the better way: "Honey, you were late to dinner again tonight. If you're late tomorrow, we'll have to eat without you." She is firm but not angry. The next evening, if he's late, she sits down to dinner with the kids at the agreed-upon hour. When her husband barges in with "I'm starving. Where's dinner?" her response is neither angry nor punitive, but matter-of-fact: "We've already eaten. Your dinner is in the oven." If he blows up, she leaves the room without attempting to score debating points. Using this approach, she is much more likely to get on-time family dinners than if she is aggressive or passive. But even if she doesn't, there is a lot less fighting and family turmoil, and she's no longer feeling like a bitter and resentful doormat. She's a person with some control of her life who can take pride in having changed herself.

DO A RELATIONSHIP INVENTORY

"The first year of recovery, things seemed to be going pretty smoothly with my partner. Then, bang, everything seemed to go haywire. I looked at him and said, 'Why am I living with this person?'"

Your partner is probably asking the same question. During your first year of recovery, while you just concentrated on getting better, your relationship was not your number one priority. Now, suddenly, with your sobriety solid, your neglected relationship is back on center stage, and it's getting some dismal reviews.

This is common, but it's not necessarily an ominous sign. Your relationship may seem terrible. The old relationship no longer works, and you haven't yet developed a new one. That's unsettling. The familiar status quo, bad as it was, was a known quantity. Each of you knew how to relate within it. Now you're two different people who have to get to know and learn to live with each other all over again. The first step is to honestly evaluate your relationship—to see what kinds of problems bedevil it and what can be done to remedy them.

Just as you have done a personal inventory as part of recovery work, you can do a relationship inventory. Do it as a SWOT analysis, examining the relationship's Strengths, Weaknesses, Opportunities, and Threats. Write up lists of everything you can think of in each of these areas, then stand back and look at what you have. You might see some clear solutions that will get your relationship back on track.

Consider each of these areas:

Intimacy

Sex is certainly part of intimacy, and many marriages require at least an adequate sex life to endure. But intimacy is more than that. It's being able to expose not just one's body but one's innermost being to the other person. This is tough for people who have been stuffing their feelings and lying about their thoughts for years, but it's necessary.

Expectations

Though unrealistic expectations can be a problem for anyone, they seem particularly common among addicts, possibly because they tend to be perfectionists. Inspect your expectations. Do you want too much? Do you expect your partner to be perfect? Remember that no relationship, like no life, is without its rough moments and hard times.

Psychological Baggage

Key words or phrases ("I'm thirsty," "I can't," "Don't you dare!"), key sounds (the front door slamming, a spouse crying), and key sights (a bottle of gin, a vial of pills) can all trigger memories and strong feelings from the past. Discuss with your mate the memories that each of you would be happy to forget and how you can avoid triggering them. Each of you should also learn how to deal with them if they do come up. Talking with a sponsor, friend, or therapist may help.

Physical Baggage

Debt, chronic illness, and poor occupational skills are all forms of physical baggage that can hamper a relationship. They won't go away overnight. Each must be tackled individually. Time and patience, along with problem-solving skills, will help.

A house, a child, some furnishings, a few dishes—anything that's associated with a previous relationship can lead to discord in a present one. Some of those things can be tossed out if finances permit (such as furniture or dishes), but others (such as children) obviously can't. If you remarry, a new spouse may have to learn to live in a house once shared with another, or to accept the fact that another woman's children are very important to her husband (and can grow to be important to her, too).

Air any resentments, rather than smothering them. Just saying "I hate living in her house!" or "Her paint colors drive me up the wall!" may ease the pain. Or it may lead to doing some inexpensive redecorating now and a plan for major changes later.

Fears

Everyone has them. Fears of relapse, unfaithfulness, desertion, inadequacy, crime; fear of what people are saying; fear of uncertainties about the future.

In a relationship, there are often elements that create fear about its stability. Maybe the problem is money: Your credit card debt piled up while you were using drugs, and your finances are now very shaky. So when your spouse wants to eat out, there is a fight. Or maybe she is fearful when you turn to your sponsor or an AA meeting for support rather than to her.

Sometimes just recognizing that fear exists is enough to exorcise it. More often some discussion is needed between the partners to instill comfort and reassurance so the fears can be banished forever. If your spouse knows you're worried about money and would rather not eat dinner out, she may be willing to come up with an alternative. If she admits she's jealous when you turn to your sponsor rather than to her, you can explain it's like turning to your doctor: It's part of your treatment.

Unhealthy Dependencies

If you are dependent on your partner for some secondary gain, such as prestige or lifestyle, and you feel that without that gain life would be unhappy or unrewarding, you put yourself in a weak position. It enables your partner to strap a collar around your neck, tugging at it when she wishes. If this is true in your relationship, you need to identify your area of weakness and then figure out

how to loosen the collar. If money is the matter, maybe you need to get a better job or learn how to live on less. If it's prestige—doubting yourself while basking in her reflected glory—then you have to work on developing your own sense of worth.

*Inter*dependence in a relationship is not a bad thing. In fact, it's healthy—as long as it's not heavily one-sided. Perhaps one person provides most of the financial support and the other keeps the family going emotionally and physically. This is fine—as long as each appreciates the other's contributions. If you suspect that your dependence may be out of balance, get a second opinion from your sponsor or a professional.

Support-Group Envy

At this point in the relationship, your spouse should understand the benefits you (and she, indirectly) get from your group and other recovery activities. Ideally, she should be involved in them herself, to some degree. If she knows how AA works but still feels jealous of the time you give to it, there is probably something else going on. Maybe you really aren't giving her enough time and attention; maybe you haven't conveyed your willingness to carry your fair share of family responsibilities. Or maybe she doesn't like the new you—the you who doesn't need her as much. Just as control of the chemical takes high priority in the addict's life, control of the addicted person often becomes important to the spouse. Being at least partially deprived of that role could be at the root of her feelings. In that case, get her to read chapter 26, urge her to go to Al-Anon if she hasn't already, and ask her to consider counseling.

Old Habits

Almost everyone who lives with another person finds some of that person's routines, behaviors, or habits annoying, even infuriating. The problem is worse in homes where alcohol or drugs have played a role—those behaviors are often associated with the addiction. Even long after someone has gotten into recovery, the behaviors can continue to be triggers for the reactions and defensive reflexes that were common earlier.

A vexing habit can be something as minor as leaving the cap off the toothpaste, or as emotionally major as nonchalantly coming home late or forgetting birthdays. Often the fact that the other person is upset by the behavior isn't mutually or openly acknowledged, despite the head of steam clearly building up. So the first step is to identify which behaviors irritate each of you. At an appropriate time, get it all out in the open with a constructive discussion. Then try to negotiate and work out a mutually satisfactory agreement.

It can also help to remember that wedges like these habits are really composed of two parts. One is the behavior itself, the annoying habit. The other part is the emotions, fears, and resentments that result

from dealing with the behavior. You'll need to address both parts.

Incompatible Interests

You like the symphony; he likes car races. That can spell trouble for your marriage. But it can also mean enrichment—he escorts you to the symphony, and you accompany him to the races. You'll find either that you can actually enjoy each other's interests or that an evening never seemed so long. If the latter is true, you might try exploring some new interests you can enjoy together. Occasionally you can give each other a gift of self in sharing racing or Rachmaninoff, but mostly you can each follow those interests solo—though perhaps less often than you'd like. Take it one event at a time, and you should be able to work out the differences.

Try Therapy

If after you've tried to work on these aspects of your relationship and the picture still looks bleak, seek professional help. Don't go to therapy as a last-ditch effort, but with a wholehearted commitment to try to make your partnership work. Without such a commitment, therapy is almost certain to fail. Of course, it may fail even if you give it your best shot, but at least you'll be able to look back and say you tried. And hopefully you will have learned something about yourself. Future relationships will benefit, improving the odds of your converting today's misery into tomorrow's success.

Having Fun Again

WHERE'S THE FUN?

"My first year of recovery was the toughest year of my life. But I made it through. Is it going to stay this hard? Is life ever going to be fun again?"

No and yes. No, it isn't going to always be this tough. And yes, life is going to be fun again.

In the Yellow Zone of recovery, you've reached the point where you can concentrate more on rebuilding and enjoying your life. That doesn't mean you'll wake up tomorrow to find your world is filled with puppies and sunshine. But it does mean you can start to think about more than merely surviving without drugs and alcohol. Just what direction your thoughts and actions take will depend on what sounds like fun to you. But all your fun shouldn't come from doing "fun" things. You need to learn to get more enjoyment out of life itself, to get a buzz from staying sober just as you did from drinking or using drugs. This can be tough for alcoholics/addicts, who have so long been in hot pursuit of instant pleasure, focused on cause and effect rather than process. Now it's time to focus on the joy that can come from simple, honest pleasures.

WHAT DO I DO WITH ALL THIS FREE TIME?

"I feel like I'm ready to go to fewer fellowship meetings. But I'm so used to doing that every night that I'm afraid I won't know what to do with my free time."

When you started going to meetings, you probably complained that you had no free time for anything else. Now that free time threatens, you are concerned again. That's because change, even for the better, tends to make us tense and uneasy. Moving and switching jobs, for example, both generate high stress levels. But with the right attitude, both can improve your life.

Similarly, with the right attitude, your newfound leisure time can go a long way in helping you rebuild your life. Change that transforms you as you grow in recovery is actually essential to your return to health. Welcome the challenge that more leisure time brings. Filling it fits in perfectly with two major activities of the Yellow Zone: rebuilding relationships and learning to enjoy life again.

To help rebuild your relationships, organize your free time so that you spend a lot of it with the people you are trying to bring back into your life, such as family, friends, and coworkers. Limit solitary activities, like reading or watching TV, but don't abandon them entirely if you enjoy them. If you have children, try to include them in many of the activities you choose. They have probably been the prime victims of your substance use; let them now be the beneficiaries of your recovery. But don't forget your relationship with your partner. Set aside some special time each week for the two of you alone. As you plan these outings, remember that part of your recovery now is learning how to make decisions in consultation with others. For most alcoholics/addicts, going off on one's own is an established behavior pattern. Changing that leap-before-you-talk attitude now will take a conscious effort. So when you are planning activities with family or friends, don't dictate what the activities should be. Consult the others involved, and let them take the lead often.

Some ideas for filling your time:

- Choose activities that will maintain the wall between you and dangerous playgrounds and playmates.

- Be certain your plans are within your financial means. You may still have the inclination to do things that are unrealistic. Stifle that urge to overspend.

- Avoid overprogramming. Leave some time for relaxation, some time to "do nothing." It can keep you feeling grounded and calm.

- Avoid overdoing it physically. If you've been a couch potato for a while, this is not the time to catapult yourself into strenuous physical sports and games. Those should wait for the Green Zone. Ease your way into a physically active life.

Another important aspect of your recovery is service to others. So

when you're ready for it (usually in the Green Zone), consider doing some community work.

If you're having trouble figuring out just what you want to do, try writing up an interests inventory. Think about all the things that you enjoy, or suspect you would enjoy. The possibilities now are virtually unlimited. Also factor in whether or not you have some sober friends who also might enjoy those activities. Use your inventory as a take-off point for planning activities. You may have to try out a number of possibilities before you settle on the ones you want to pursue. But even that should be fun. (However, be cautious that the old addictive you is not just looking for a way to move back in. For example, a poker game might sound like fun, but is that because you are really looking for the drinking atmosphere that often goes along with it?)

A safe way to explore new activities is to do them with a sober activity group. Ask around at your meetings to find a local group. Check out Meetup listings.

HANDLING SUCCESS

"Why is it that every time I tell my NA friends that things are going great, that I've never been so successful at sobriety, that life is great, they give me a funny look and warn me to 'Watch out'?"

Maybe they know from experience that a smooth, straight road tends to make the driver

THE YELLOW ZONE

careless, and getting careless can lead to an accident—or, in your case, a crack-up of a different sort: relapse.

That doesn't necessarily mean you're in trouble if your recovery isn't filled with bumps along the way. It just means that you can't allow yourself to be lulled into believing you are in total control and there will never be any bumps ahead. You need to stay humbled by your past and stay alert, with your eyes open every minute.

Alcoholics and addicts, so long used to bad experiences, often begin to feel uncomfortable when things go well for a while. They find themselves asking, "After everything I've done, do I really deserve this great life?" Or they start waiting for the other shoe to drop: "Things are going so well, I know it can't last." Both of these attitudes can hinder recovery.

Conversely, sometimes things go so well you start to believe that you are so smart and so unique ("terminal uniqueness," some call it) that the rules of recovery don't apply to you. You may drop values and people that were once important to you. This feeling of power, coupled with a loss of humility, can affect not just your work and your relationships, but your recovery as well. The next logical step is the dangerous thought, "Hey, I bet I could drink now without any problem!"

You don't have to fear success and happiness. You just have to learn how to handle them safely.

Remember your bad times. You may be headed in the wrong direction if you forget where you've been. Your brain is now naturally forgetting those past painful experiences and recalling them as "not so awful" after all. You need to keep those memories fresh. Remind yourself by working with others who are just getting started in recovery, by sharing your story at NA meetings and listening to the stories of others, and by looking at mementos from your past (videos, photos, pleading emails from friends, your wrecked credit report, or anything else that shows what those "good old days" were really like).

Share your wealth. Your success will mean more to your life and your recovery if you share your hard-earned wealth of experience with others. How you do that will depend on your skills, your contacts, your financial resources, and so on. Spreading the word about recovery in your community is generally best reserved for a Green Zone activity, but you can lay the groundwork now. Start exploring. See chapter 22 for some ideas.

Finding a New Relationship

ARE YOU READY FOR SOMETHING NEW?

"My longtime live-in girlfriend and I broke up when I got sober. She's still

into drugs, and I know we'll never get back together. At first I was desperate to find another woman. Now I've learned to live alone and be happy with myself. But there is still a piece missing from the vision I have for my life. I want to have a loving relationship. Is this the time? How do I do it without messing it up?"

Now that you're no longer "desperate" to find a new woman to complete your identity, you probably are ready to start looking. Like a drug, any relationship pursued compulsively to satisfy dependency needs will eventually implode. So before you build a romantic relationship, be sure you've solidly finished the work of early recovery. Don't slip into a superficial or physical relationship with the first person who comes along. Swap your old patterns of impulsivity and emotionality for depth and meaning.

To build a lasting relationship, you need the right tools. Brush up on your communication skills and think about what you're looking for in a person. To understand and remember where you're coming from, review your moral inventory. If in leafing through it you find you weren't as honest as you could have been, it's time for a rewrite. (If you missed doing one earlier, do it now—see chapter 8.) Analyze your words to see what your behavior was toward those you were attracted to, what was wrong with it, and where you can do better. Understand what you got out of relationships: which

parts were good and which bad. Think about the kind of relationship you'd like to have, the kinds of values you'd like to share, and the qualities you want to develop: perhaps the thoughtfulness of sending flowers, or of paying a compliment when you admire a new outfit, and keeping your opinion to yourself when you don't. Use this evaluation as a basis for your dating behavior now.

When you are ready to head back out there, don't start by looking for the mate of your dreams, that paragon of perfection you want to spend the rest of your life with. Try mingling in groups for a while—with couples and singles interested in a common activity. That should help you dust off your socializing skills without the pressure of one-on-one encounters. In these relatively safe group outings, take on some new challenges: Talk to people you might not usually approach and explore how their lives might enrich yours. Then, date people you like but you're not totally smitten by, giving yourself the chance to be alone with someone without stress. Should you be rejected or the evening turn out less than perfectly, the pain will be minimal. Once you've tested the dating waters casually and relearned how to relate to others, you'll be better prepared. Then you can think about going out with someone you're really interested in. Even then, don't rush the relationship. Let it develop naturally so that you're good friends before you're great lovers.

If a relationship does start to get serious, take the time to examine it objectively. Think about any potential problem areas. Friends, interests, background, religion, education, goals, and attitudes (toward money, morals, children, family, work, alcohol, and drugs) are all possible areas of disagreement. Is either of you in the relationship to fill needs that really should be met by recovery? (If you can't think of any problem areas, you aren't being honest or looking hard enough.) Map these territories, and see if you can come to an accommodation. If the relationship gets even stronger and you are considering living together or marriage, but some areas of conflict persist, get some professional counseling.

////////////////////////////

"A very nice man at my office just asked me out. I would like to date him, but what if he finds out about my history of drug use?"

He should find out about it—from you. You needn't go into great detail on a first date. Just mention that you are in recovery and you don't drink or use drugs (you surely won't be the first person he's met in recovery). Should the relationship bloom, you may want to take him to an open NA meeting, give him some reading material, and introduce him to some of your sober friends. If any of this turns him off, it's better to know it now rather than later. Whether it works out with him or not, remember that keeping your past under wraps when disclosure is appropriate can serve to make you feel ashamed and guilty. It can create doubts about the value of all the work you've done, and could jeopardize your recovery.

AN NA ROMANCE?

"I feel I'm ready for a serious relationship now. There's a young woman at my office who I'm very attracted to, but shouldn't I stick with someone who is also in NA?"

There are obvious advantages to taking up with another NA or AA member. She understands where you are coming from and where you want to go. She recognizes the importance of meetings, respects the close relationship you have with your sponsor, and appreciates the need for absolute abstention. If you both have good recoveries, you will have common values and goals, and the communication skills developed in recovery will make your lives better. You will already share a social support network that many people lack today. But there are also possible drawbacks to getting involved with someone in recovery. If either of your recoveries is shaky, if either of you has neglected portions of your program, or if either of you is en route to a slip, you could be headed for a hand-in-hand dive off the same cliff.

There are, of course, also advantages and disadvantages to seeing someone who is not affiliated with NA. She might bring some wonderful stability into your life, if she is willing to learn about chemical dependency and get involved in your recovery. On the other hand, she may not accept or understand your close ties to NA, may balk at the frequent meetings, or may be jealous of your sharing confidences with a sponsor and fellowship friends.

More important than where you meet the person you want to make a new life with is the kind of relationship you share. If it's built on a solid foundation of healthy interaction, love, common goals, and honesty, the odds of its succeeding are very good.

WARNING NOTES

What you don't know about sex can hurt you. Don't forget the following:

- Both very good and very bad sexual relationships can lead to relapse—the good sex because you associate the satisfying feelings with a drug high, the bad sex because you want to get rid of the bad feelings that follow. If you feel the urge to drink or use after sex, get in touch with your sponsor, take a cold shower, or try some of the suggestions in chapter 10.

- If you are going to have a relationship, sexual or otherwise, it should not be with someone who is using—even if you suffer from the delusion that you are the only one who can help her get sober. Really, step away from it now.

- Guilt-creating behaviors (such as cheating on a partner) can lead to relapse. Stay honest.

THE YELLOW ZONE

Rebuilding Your Life: Education, Work, and Finances in the Yellow Zone

U p to this point in your recovery, you've been repeatedly advised, "Stay put. Don't make any drastic changes in your working life." At long last that advice can be put aside. Now, if change is what you want and it makes sense, it's not only okay but it can actually be good for your recovery. It's time to decide what's next. It's time to dream about what you want to be and take steps to make it happen.

Are You Ready to Make Career Changes?

I HATE MY JOB

"I stayed with a job I really disliked during the first year of recovery because everyone said I shouldn't make any changes until I was on more solid ground. Well, I'm sober eighteen months, and I'm still unhappy at work. Can I look elsewhere now?"

H ere are some other questions to ask yourself (be sure to also get feedback from your team):

- Are your feelings about your job generating emotions, such as anger and resentment, that could jeopardize your recovery? Are these feelings related only to your job, or do you generally feel angry and resentful about other things in your life, too? If the feelings are indeed related only to your work, then switching jobs may make a lot of sense. If they aren't, changing jobs won't cure what ails you (and could make things worse). Try instead to deal with your negative emotions directly before you write that resignation letter.

- Are you expecting too much? No job is great every day. There are good and bad days in the best of jobs. In recovery, you've been trudging the road to mature living; you should now be able to take the good with the bad. Take another look at your job in the light of this basic truth.

- Is it the place where you're working that doesn't seem right, or just your own job? Would a promotion give you what you need? If you've been there a while, you probably didn't grow much in the job while you were drinking. Now that you have more than a year of responsible behavior under your belt, talk with your boss about the possibility of advancing in the company, about any education or training you might need to achieve this, and whether the company offers any help (many will pay for training). If you can't move up, what about a lateral move within the company? Sometimes just a change of duties, a change of scene, is what

you need. If not, then maybe you should move on.

- Do you have something else in mind you'd rather do? Living as a slave to alcohol or drugs almost always kills the dreams you once had. Now that you're in the Yellow Zone, it's time to start thinking about taking some chances, reaching for the stars, and getting more from your life. If you had your eyes on a particular dream job in the past, go for it now.

If you don't have something specific in mind, think about and explore some other options before burning bridges at your current job. Now that you are in a position of stable recovery and have spent some time learning about yourself, you'll have better judgment and more realistic ideas of what you might be able to do. Depending on your skills, almost any job should be open to you now.

- If you don't have the background that will allow you to walk into a new field, can you start laying the groundwork? Could you make inroads by working at an internship or networking with people in that field? Do you need retraining or more education? If so, is that an option right now? Do you have the time and the money needed? If training is needed and feasible, decide how this can best be handled, and if it can be done before you leave your present job.

- Be realistic. People with addiction often dream impossible dreams; is that what you are doing now? If you're thinking about changing fields entirely but are not sure, do some research. Talk to others who are in the field, and ask your recovery friends and your sponsor what they think about your ideas. Test the waters. Take a course or do some volunteer work in the field you're contemplating.

- Are you reading your feelings correctly? Is it really your job you hate? Or do you want to move on because you suddenly feel ready to conquer the world? Are you bored and antsy in general? If your problem isn't your job, look at other parts of your life—relationships, leisure time—and see what can be done to enhance it. If you can get everything else back on track, your job might not seem so terrible after all.

See the job hunting tips on page 422.

I LOVE MY JOB

"I just got a new job, and it's fantastic! I can't believe that it's really mine, that I'm doing just what I want after years of going nowhere."

There are two things to say to someone who has landed a great job: congratulations—and be careful. The reasons for the congratulations are obvious: You're recovering from a serious disease and now rebuilding your life. The reasons for the caution may be less obvious.

Though it's wonderful to have a job you like, it's important to keep in mind that a job can't make you happy or make your life perfect. A job is, well, a job. It shouldn't be your whole life. It's just one leg of the tripod that supports a stable, well-balanced existence. There's also the family/friends leg and the relaxation/play leg; you'll want to pay attention to all of those legs in the Yellow Zone.

And of course, they all have to rest on a strong foundation—your good recovery. Becoming too dependent on your work, leaning too hard on that leg of your tripod for your support and satisfaction, can topple you by regenerating that old familiar self-destructive trait: dependence. When we become so dependent, our self-image begins to dim: "Without this job [or spouse, or whatever], I wouldn't be a complete person." Then the fear of losing the job becomes so all-encompassing that the joy disappears and is replaced by resentment and depression. The prime source of happiness becomes a source of unhappiness.

So enjoy your job, but be sure you're getting happiness and satisfaction from other parts of your life as well: Take a course, plan a trip, take up a hobby or get involved in sports, or get active in your religious community or a volunteer organization. If you're part of a family, make time for outings with your partner or kids; if you're not, make an effort to find friends or someone special. Above all, don't neglect the recovery activities that have brought you to this point.

I'M GOING NOWHERE!

"I've been sober for nearly three years. I feel pretty good, but I still haven't gotten my act together as far as work. I keep trying different things, but I'm not finding a comfortable niche anywhere."

First of all, if you aren't sure what you want, it might help to meet with a career counselor. The perfect job may be waiting for you out there—you just need to find out what it is. A good career counselor can help you look at options. And remember, there may be more than one right solution. Alcoholics and addicts tend to think there are only right and wrong, no gray areas. With your more mature thinking now, you should be seeing that there are several career options that could work for you.

Second, it may not be the job choice that's the problem, but your own attitude. No job is always wonderful or perfect. Every job stresses us, bores us, or makes us want to punch a wall sometimes. Maybe you expect too much. Or maybe you're still nursing a lot of negativism, a quality that can sink your sobriety as well as your working life. Work harder on your recovery or, if you think it might help, see a counselor.

"I think I'm finally ready to go back to school. Are there any universities that welcome people in recovery?"

There are many, and the numbers are growing. Several schools now offer recovery campus programs; options include drug- and alcohol-free dorms, on-campus fellowship meetings, counseling, and even special recovery centers on campus. You can read more about these programs in chapter 10.

BECOMING AN ALCOHOL AND DRUG COUNSELOR

"I used to be in sales, but I never liked the work. From my experience with 12-step work, I think I would make a very good drug counselor."

Sit down with half a dozen patients in a treatment center, and five of them will tell you they want to switch careers and become substance-abuse counselors when they get out. By the time they finish treatment, only one or two still think that way. For most of those folks, the desire to help others was just a natural part of recovery. For others, their interest in counseling was a way to deny their own neediness. ("I'm not the person with the problem. These other folks are.")

If you are still interested now that you are solidly in the Yellow Zone, however, and have done a good deal of step-12 work, you can certainly consider this kind of career change. But again, you have to really examine your motives. Is it a desire to do more step-12 work? Keep in mind that that's actually selfish in nature—it's a way to secure your own recovery as much as someone else's. Trying to help others professionally before your own needs are met can do more harm than good.

Think carefully: What attracts you to this kind of work? If it's an unselfish desire to help others, that's a noble goal and one that should not be discouraged. But counselors aren't the only people who help others. Lots of jobs contribute to the good of all—police officer, teacher, waitress, social worker. Doing what you do best and doing it well is the way you can best contribute.

Another consideration: Do you really understand the nature of substance-abuse counseling? It's often a very frustrating job, because you can't "cure" your client. In a sense, your client has to cure himself. You may be able to keep this in mind when you do step-12 work and not feel responsible every time someone fails. But if you do this kind of work professionally, you're more likely to forget that, to feel guiltily responsible, or to start playing God.

There's also a high burnout rate in substance-abuse counseling, and it's especially high when the career is chosen for the wrong reasons.

If you're still convinced that the most important thing you can do with your life is help others live a life in recovery, that's certainly all to the good. But you'll need professional training. You'll need to explore your state's education and licensing requirements; they vary widely, but most states require education and experience. Some give credit for what was learned in personal recovery. You can check with the state and national associations of addiction counselors to see what is needed (see chapter 5).

If switching careers might be difficult at this point, you can satisfy your need to help others by doing volunteer work or by sponsoring several people in your fellowship.

JOB-HUNTING TIPS

Looking for a new job is always daunting. It's particularly unnerving when you are in recovery—still unsure of yourself, uneasy about how employers might view your disease. But many people in recovery land good jobs, and you can, too. In early recovery, your job served to meet your basic needs while you focused on recovery activities. Now that you are more secure in recovery, a career fills a different niche: It is part of building the life you truly desire. The following pointers should help:

Do your homework. Many alcoholics and addicts set inappropriate career goals, often because they are unable to do an accurate self-assessment. If your career goals aren't crystal clear, you may want to get some vocational counseling from someone who understands the needs of the person in recovery. You'll find programs that help people get back on their feet work-wise at treatment centers, major employers, alcohol and drug dependency advocacy agencies, and your state department of employment. The best of these programs include skills assessment, a part-time transitional work program, job-preparedness training, stress management and assertiveness training, job and job-hunting skills seminars, and placement. A nearby community college may also have some job-seeking programs.

Clean up your online reputation. These days, most employers look at the digital clues to your life: your Facebook and Twitter accounts, personal blogs, and so on. You don't have to pretend to be someone you're not, but you do want to present the best possible face to the world. See the tips on page 233 for how to clean up your online life.

Get your résumé out there. Post your résumé on as many online job boards as you can, and peruse those boards regularly for open jobs.

Network. Most jobs are not filled through advertisements. They are filled because someone knows someone. So be sure to tell everyone you know that you're looking for work. Network on Facebook with your high school and college classmates. Sign up for any private social networks of those groups. Set up a profile on LinkedIn.com and join alumni and interest groups. Join professional organizations. If you graduated from college, see if your school has programs for job-seekers; many help even those who have been out of school for many years with résumé writing, interview techniques, and more.

Network some more. If you have trouble finding an employer who doesn't freeze up at the mention of addiction, ask around at fellowship meetings for names of "recovery-friendly" employers.

Do some role-playing. Before you face any prospective employers, run through some simulated interviews with an employment counselor, your sponsor, or a friend. Be sure they hit you with some tough questions, such as "How do you explain this two-year gap in your employment history?" and "How can I be sure you are really on the mend now?"

Do it right. Neatness counts. A sloppy, skimpy résumé or poorly filled-out application will lead a prospective employer to question your ability, whether you mention your addiction problem or not.

Dress for the role. Wear to the interview whatever is appropriate for the job you are applying for.

Arrive on time. Turning up late for an interview could close down a job opportunity before you even open your mouth. In fact, be early. Better to wait than to rush in late.

Get a foot in the door. Consider volunteering, doing an internship, or getting a temp job at an organization that interests you. This will allow you to get to know people on the job, show what a skilled and conscientious worker you are, and learn more about potential jobs.

Recognize that you might not get the job. Most times there are many applicants for a single job, and all but one will be disappointed. This is not a personal judgment against those who don't succeed. Still, because rejection right now may be difficult to handle, be prepared to turn to your support network if you are turned down. Go to a meeting, call your sponsor, have lunch with a fellowship friend—and start applying for other jobs right away.

FEELING LEFT BEHIND

"All the people I went to law school with are successful attorneys now. At this point I have to start from scratch, and it doesn't make me feel too good about myself."

You have every right to feel very good about yourself. You're sober. Envying others you think are more successful is dangerous anytime, but especially in recovery. Instead, use yourself and your recent growth as a yardstick for success. Look at who you were a year or so ago, and who you are now. You have come a very long way. And you now have a great opportunity to realize your potential, more so than many people ever will. Just don't expect things to be better two weeks from Tuesday. Recovery from the gradual and complex disease of addiction is gradual and complex. Job satisfaction during that recovery can be slow to improve. For many people it still isn't there after three years of sobriety. But by six years or so, most people begin to feel more satisfaction with their jobs, as well as closer to career goals in relation to their contemporaries.

And things keep getting better from there. Right now you feel left behind; you haven't yet caught up with old friends and colleagues in material terms. But some of the assets you've built up in sobriety—self-awareness, emotional stability, improved social skills, spiritual fulfillment, an understanding of life earned the hard way, and even the ability to remain sober one day at a time—can't be bought by even the wealthiest person you know.

STARTING A BUSINESS

"My business went downhill when my drinking got really bad. I finally had to declare bankruptcy. I inherited some money, and I'd like to use it to start another business."

Answer the question of whether or not this is the right time for you to take that leap again by doing a personal/professional inventory.

- Is your recovery sound and stable? If not, the stress of starting a new business could wreck it. Talk with your sponsor and your counselor, if you have one, to get their views on whether you are ready for this kind of heavy-duty entrepreneurial effort.

- Is your health back up to speed? Do you have the energy—both emotional and physical—for this venture?

- Can your recovery tolerate the more-than-full-time demands of a business start-up? Will those demands detract from your fellowship meetings and recovery activities? Is there a way you can integrate those into your business routines?

- Can your relationships tolerate the demands of a business start-up? The Yellow Zone is when you should be setting priorities for making your life satisfying and productive. Would starting a business distract you from those important tasks?

- Do you have a sound business plan? Many communities have a small business development authority that can help with planning a new venture.

- Will the nest egg you inherited cover start-up costs and pay you an adequate salary for the next six months to a year?

- Have you carefully evaluated every aspect of your plan and gone over it with a variety of people with expertise in the field?

If the answer to any of these questions is no, then you probably should not be starting a business now. That doesn't mean you won't be ready in six months or a year. Just be sure to go slow and to evaluate every angle before taking the plunge.

If it seems sensible to go ahead, you might want to look for some help from local, state, or federal agencies, such as the Small Business Administration office in your state. Since those in recovery are covered under the Americans with Disabilities Act, you needn't worry about your history disqualifying you from getting help—as long as you remain sober. You might also want to enroll in a course about starting a business at a community college or Chamber of Commerce.

RETURNING TO HIGH-RISK WORK

"I was a pilot before I was fired for getting to the airport drunk. I've been absolutely sober for the last two years and completely out of touch with the industry. Is there any chance I can get a flying job now?"

Federal regulators have justifiably put everyone in the transportation industry under the microscope—and the breathalyzer. All people employed in this field are monitored closely for alcohol and drug problems. Luckily for you, professional pilots have some great recovery programs and organizations. Check out the HIMS program (himsprogram.com) as well as Birds of a Feather International (boaf.org), a 12-step fellowship that also welcomes other cockpit crew members.

If you adhere to a solid program of recovery, and can prove it, you

THE YELLOW ZONE

will almost certainly be able to return to flight status if you want to and are otherwise qualified. For obvious reasons, you can expect to be monitored closely and drug-tested frequently.

Fixing Finances

"I totally messed up my finances while I was drinking. In the year-plus that I've been sober, I've really tried to live within my means. I want to buy a car, but will I be able to get credit? Do I have to tell about my drinking problem?"

When you borrow money, you aren't obliged to sit in the confessional. You are, in fact, protected by law from having to divulge confidential medical information. If the question of a credit history littered with no-pays or late-pays comes up, you can say you went through a "period of illness" during which you struggled to keep up with bill payments as best you could. People (lenders) are generally more forgiving when you simply say that you had a medical problem. If the lender is still uneasy about your ability to keep to a payment schedule now, offer to take out "credit disability insurance." This policy, which adds a small fee to your payment, will make the payments for you if you are out of commission.

Applying for a loan with collateral behind it—the auto loan you're eager to get, for example—is probably ideal. In tough economic times, most car dealers are so delighted to make a sale that credit checking may be less than rigorous, and your willingness to use the dealer's in-house financing should simplify matters. Another option to rebuild your credit is to open one credit card account, make some small purchases on it, and pay it off on time every month. Once you've shown that you can make on-time payments regularly, it will be easier to get other loans. But at this point, except for necessary purchases (such as that car you need to get to work), don't overcommit yourself. This is your rebuilding time. Build up your financial status, put some money in the bank, and continue to live within your means. Once you've shown you're a solid citizen, it will be safer for you to consider getting more credit, and safer for the lender, too.

///////////////////////////

"I need to refinance my house to get my financial life in order. But I've had such terrible experiences in the past with bankers and debt collectors that I'm starting off angry—and I haven't even been turned down yet."

Before you worry about your finances, you'd better worry about your recovery. Here you are blaming bankers and debt collectors for your financial failures while you were in active addiction. Go into this with a chip on your shoulder and not only won't you get a loan but you'll build up resentments that could lead to a slip.

Think about the way you used to handle money. If you were like a lot of alcoholics/addicts, you spent your money freely (mostly on the wrong things), neglected bills and other obligations (probably including your mortgage), and ignored dunning letters and phone calls.

So before you make an appointment at the bank, clean up your attitude. Then contact the bank that holds your current mortgage and level with them. Tell them you would appreciate their advice on how you can get your financial house back in order, and ask if they would be willing to work with you. Explain that you've been ill, but you've been well now for more than a year and your disease is in remission and will stay that way as long as you continue with your program.

In most cases you will get a fair hearing. The bank, after all, is in the business of making loans. If they hold your old mortgage, they won't increase their risk very much by giving you a new one. They may want to set certain stipulations before discussing refinancing (such as a letter from your doctor, treatment program, or sponsor). Bringing such a letter with you to the meeting will help assure them of your sincerity. If you get no response from your current lender, and your credit is not completely shot, try other banks. It's best to start local, where you can meet with lenders in person.

YOUR FINANCIAL STATEMENT

To get credit you may need to present a statement showing your assets (what you own or are owed) and liabilities (what you owe). Even if you aren't trying to get credit, it's a good idea to put together such a statement to see where you stand financially.

There are several financial software programs that can assemble this information for you. For example, with Quicken software you can link to all of your financial accounts and download transactions regularly. It's then easy to get a picture of your net worth, showing all assets and liabilities. Another option is Mint.com, which is free. These programs will also help you see exactly where your money is going every month.

If you want to figure out where you stand the old-fashioned way, draw a line down the center of a sheet of paper. Label one side Assets and the other Liabilities. Under Assets, list the dollar value of savings, checking, and money market accounts; stocks and bonds; real estate; automobiles; life insurance; and any other assets you own. Under Liabilities, list your obligations: the balance on your mortgage; outstanding loans, including personal and auto loans; credit cards; alimony and child support; and anything else you owe. If your liabilities exceed your assets, you're in debt.

Then take a look at your monthly budget. Again make two columns:

Monthly Income and Monthly Expenses. Under Income, list your wages, interest, dividends, commissions, and so on. Under Expenses, list rent, mortgage and other loan payments, insurance, real estate taxes, mortgage insurance, utilities, tuition, and other regular expenses. This will give you some idea of how much money you have left each month for food, clothing, and miscellaneous expenses. If there is very little difference between income and expenses, you are overextended.

If you are living on the edge financially, take a good look at where your money is going every month, and you'll probably find some places where you can cut back. Can you cut out the cable subscription or your phone's data plan? Start cooking at home more? Get books from the library? Bring lunch to work more often?

It's a good idea to update your financial statement at least once a year, and even more often in early recovery. It might be pretty dismal at first. But as you progress in recovery and continue to repair your finances, seeing your bottom line get better and better every month will give you a nice emotional boost.

Your Health in the Yellow Zone

A s the eminent baseball philosopher and realist Yogi Berra once said, "It ain't over 'til it's over." That's true in recovery, too.

Some people find that all the symptoms that have plagued them since the day they got sober are gone by the time they reach the Yellow Zone. They feel "normal" for the first time in years.

Others are still experiencing a variety of leftover problems—occasionally physical, but often emotional or intellectual. For most, these will gradually go away over the next year, but for a few they may hang on longer.

You might be feeling pretty good right now. But as your symptoms fade, don't ignore taking care of your health. Now is the time to start taking care of your health beyond the urgent issues you addressed in the Red Zone, and to reinforce the healthy habits you've been

learning about. Find a good doctor who knows how to work with people in recovery (or at least one who is willing to learn), get a thorough checkup, and take care of any lingering health issues now.

Your Health Priorities Now

A PHYSICAL EXAM

"It's been a year since I got sober. I feel fine. Do I need to see a doctor?"

In the Yellow Zone, whether you feel fine or not, be sure to get a baseline physical exam and periodic follow-ups. Just what your exam should include, and how often you'll need to see your doctor in the future, will depend on your age, health risks, and which chemicals you used. So be sure to give your doctor an honest and complete history of your substance use. He will suggest tests and screening exams based on your age, gender, and family and personal health history. Certain illnesses are more common among those who've used alcohol or tobacco, so your checkup may also include a cardiovascular assessment, chest X-ray, careful exam of mouth and neck, liver tests (including virus testing), tests for blood in the stool, and, for women, a mammogram. The cardiovascular workup should include, at a minimum, an assessment of blood pressure and cholesterol levels. If you haven't already been tested for hepatitis C and HIV, you should do that now (see page 293).

If you experience any old or new symptoms now that are unexplained (by a virus going around, for example, or something you ate), be sure to see your doctor. They could be remnants of the damage caused by using or drinking, or they could be psychologically triggered (psychosomatic) physical ailments caused by the restructuring of your life. But they could also represent a new medical problem that needs prompt attention. Hear-no-evil denial is no stranger to people who are or have been seriously ill. It occurs with many diseases, not just addiction. Listen to the warnings your body is now able to give you.

FIND THE RIGHT DOCTOR

Not every doctor understands or wants to cope with patients who have a past troubled by alcohol- or drug-related problems. But it's critical that you find one who's willing, able, and experienced. To find some good candidates, ask for referrals from your treatment center, counselor, and friends in recovery. One option is to look for a primary care doctor who is a member of one of these organizations:

- American Board of Family Medicine (theabfm.org/diplomate/find.aspx)

- American Academy of Family Physicians (aafp.org)

- American Board of Addiction Medicine (abam.net/find-a-doctor)

- American Society of Addiction Medicine (community.asam.org/search/default.asp?m=basic)

If you can't find a primary care doctor who has experience in addiction, ask a few questions to assess a candidate's views on recovery. First, explain that you are an alcoholic or addict and that you are in recovery. Then ask:

Would you be comfortable having a sober alcoholic/addict as a patient? A negative answer should tell you to look elsewhere. Even an uneasy yes should raise doubts.

What do you see as the cause of alcoholism and addiction? The doctor who thinks it's a matter of moral weakness or lack of willpower is not for you. You want a doctor who understands that this is a chronic and primary disease, one that isn't caused by emotional or social problems (but very often *leads* to many other physical and mental issues). A doctor who doesn't understand this might prescribe drugs to cure the "emotional" problems, setting you back to where you were before you got sober. The doctor should also recognize that alcoholism/addiction is a treatable, but incurable, disease, which requires lifelong vigilance.

What is your attitude about prescribing drugs for people in recovery? A doctor who doesn't understand that *any* mood-altering drug may be risky, or who simply says, "Well, I wouldn't give him Oxycodone or Valium," is not well informed enough to protect your recovery. You want a doctor who truly understands the life-and-death risk of relapse that can result from taking any mood-altering drug, and who knows that such drugs should be used only when needed to save your life.

Have you ever been to an AA meeting? A doctor who cares enough to get familiar with 12-step fellowships will have a big advantage in treating patients in recovery.

Correct answers to these questions may not be enough; the doctor needs to follow up with correct care. A doctor who agrees that "alcoholism is a disease" and then hands you a script for tramadol (Ultram), which is an addictive narcotic, needs to be educated or dropped.

The ideal doctor will do more than provide routine care. He will:

- Be familiar with and know how to treat the residual problems of addiction (such as liver disease, neuropathy, and herpes).

- Help you deal with pain without getting hooked again—treat minor illnesses without using mood-altering drugs, and weigh the risks of using anesthesia or other drugs for serious illnesses or surgery.

- Be willing to be your advocate if you have problems at work or at home.

- Be familiar with and able to refer you to local counselors or treatment centers, if needed.

- Know enough about recovery to be able to help you over the rough spots in your program.

If you have a wonderful doctor who has no experience in treating people in recovery, see if he'll learn more about it so you can continue your relationship.

BUILD A PARTNERSHIP WITH YOUR DOCTOR

These days, good health care means building a partnership with your doctor and others.

- If your doctor doesn't already know you well, schedule a get-acquainted session so he can learn what your life was like during your active addiction, how it is now in recovery, and any major issues you want to address soon. Before your appointment, write up some notes on what you'd like to discuss and the questions you want to ask. And don't be shy about pulling out your notes during your meeting or taking notes as you two talk.

- Tell the whole truth to your doctor—about your past history, present behavior, symptoms, possible causes, and so on. If you provide only partial or incorrect information, you won't get the best possible treatment.

- Don't see any other doctors without telling your primary care doctor. Consider him the gatekeeper of all your medical care. Check any treatment, particularly if it involves medication, with your primary doctor. Any time you see another doctor or have a test done, ask that the results be sent to your primary doctor. (And keep a list of your own of all visits, tests, results, medications, and so on.)

- If your doctor suggests any medication, politely remind him that you're in recovery. Always ask if the medication is absolutely necessary and if there are any drug-free alternatives.

- Also recognize that for busy doctors, a prescription is a fast way to deal with complicated issues; one-on-one counseling is much more time-consuming. So if you decide a drug fix is not for you, let your doctor know rather than meekly accepting the prescription and then tossing it in the trash.

- Get all of your medications from one pharmacy, so the pharmacist can watch for compatibility.

- If emotional problems arise, remind your doctor that your new outlook on life allows you to see many problems as challenges that can help you grow, and you prefer to try to handle them through your recovery program or talk therapy, rather than with a drug. (Of course, serious mental illness may require medication; see chapter 13.)

- Promote your own wellness. Build a healthy lifestyle—don't smoke, eat healthily, get regular exercise, and reduce stress—and you will lower your chances of getting sick.

- Report symptoms promptly. Don't wait until bronchitis becomes pneumonia before calling the doctor.

- Follow your doctor's suggestions. Your compliance will help your doctor build trust in you. If you have reason to question his recommendations, however, or you have any concerns about the care you're getting, let your doctor know. Your relationship is a collaboration, not a one-person show.

- Offer to take your doctor to an AA or NA meeting from time to time.

- If you often find yourself disagreeing with your doctor or don't feel you're getting adequate support for your recovery, think about finding a new doctor.

Medication Concerns

CAN I TAKE PAIN MEDICATION NOW?

"I need to have some minor surgery and my doctor says it would be okay for me to take some Demerol for the pain. He said that with two years of sobriety, I shouldn't have to worry."

What you have to worry about most is your doctor's knowledge about addiction. Suggest that he read the material on pain control on page 513.

Your doctor needs to realize that right now, you are still at as much risk from mood-altering drugs as the day you got sober. And you will still be at about that much risk twenty years from now. Don't let any doctor, your friends, or that addict inside you tell you otherwise. Now is *not* the time to relax your vigilance.

If you need surgery, your best and safest bet is to follow the precautions in chapter 24.

WHY ARE YOU REALLY GOING TO THE DOCTOR?

For some people (particularly those who used prescription drugs, or got their drugs one way or another from medical sources), going to the doctor is tied in with using drugs.

If you find yourself inventing reasons to see a doctor more often than is usually necessary, ask yourself why. Could it be that the addict in you is working its way toward a relapse? There is also the risk that if a doctor gets tired of seeing you for things that don't have real medical solutions, he may prescribe something that will address your moods and open the door to relapse.

Your Primary Health Issues Now

Alcoholism and addiction leave their scars not only on your psyche but on your body. Some of their effects are long-lasting, even permanent. It's important to stay on the alert for serious medical problems that may result from past drinking or drug use. Now that you are in the Yellow Zone, you can start to address some of those less-urgent issues and rebuild your health. (If you plan to do any online health research, be sure to read the recommendations in chapter 13.)

THE YELLOW ZONE

A VARIETY OF ACHES AND PAINS

"I am still bothered by leftover symptoms from my alcohol and drug use. Is this possible?"

Considering that every one of your billions of body cells was susceptible to injury during active addiction, it isn't surprising that your body's repair crews have not yet repaired all the damage—even a year or more after you became sober. Most of the symptoms you noticed in the Red Zone will have cleared up by now. Others will go away eventually, but some of the effects of drug and alcohol use may never heal.

The symptoms most likely to have disappeared by now include abdominal soreness; acne; anemia (unless there is severe liver disease or another chronic condition); bleeding gums; breathlessness (except in smokers and those still subject to anxiety attacks); chest pain; coughing up black mucus; dry eye; dry mouth; ear inflammation; flaking of the face; fungal infections; gastritis; heartburn; increased susceptibility to infection; inflamed ears; infertility; itching; lack of coordination; leg cramps; menstrual irregularities; mouth sores; night sweats; ringing in the ears (tinnitus); shakiness; skin rashes; sore throat; tremors; and visual disturbances.

Some of the symptoms that often continue to persist well into the Yellow Zone include anxiety attacks; fatigue; flashback sensations; hemorrhoids; intellectual problems; memory problems; and sleep problems.

Other symptoms may also be hanging around now, but they are less universal, such as generalized and nonspecific aches and pains; bowel problems; bronchitis (in smokers); feminization traits (in men with severe liver damage); gout and arthritis (which usually improve but may not disappear completely); headaches; erectile dysfunction; joint and muscle problems; mild pain from old surgical scars; minor annoying sensations; muscle atrophy (but it shouldn't get progressively worse); muscle pain, weakness, and twitching (not progressive); nightmares; and nosebleeds (if drugs were snorted). A few people continue to have memory deficits at this point, but for most that will go away. Some extremely serious cases of cirrhosis may be resistant to treatment. And many people find that numbness and tingling in fingers and toes bothers them for years. It may be years, too, before anxiety attacks and other mood disturbances disappear completely and you feel your moods are well balanced. Traumatic physical injuries that occurred during addiction may be permanent.

Still, most symptoms that were noted in early recovery should be gone by now—either because they resolved, or because your body has adjusted back to a normal level of sensitivity. If they haven't, there may be another cause that's unrelated to recovery. Talk to your doctor.

LIVER DAMAGE

"I still seem to have yellowish skin and some abdominal pain. Does that mean my liver is still bad?"

Most alcoholic liver damage is reversible through sobriety. Sometimes, however, the liver will continue to deteriorate due to the progressive scarring of cirrhosis or due to viral hepatitis.

Symptoms of serious liver disease include yellowing of the skin, dark-colored urine, fatigue, enlarged visible blood vessels in the skin (particularly the nose and chest), and flushed (reddish) palms. Twitching limbs and a distinctive breath odor can also indicate liver disease.

If you have any of these symptoms, see your doctor. He can assess your liver's health by measuring the blood levels of liver enzymes (SGOT, SGPT, GGT), which are released into the blood when a liver cell dies. He can also test you for hepatitis C, which can be transmitted via contaminated needles and sexual contact, as well as other less common hepatitis viruses.

Alcoholic Liver Disease

If you were a drinker, it's likely that your problems are the result of alcohol use.

Though alcohol affects virtually every cell in the body, the liver takes the most punishment. That's because it's the liver's job to process toxic substances in the bloodstream, including alcohol and drugs, to try to render them harmless. Excesses of alcohol (as little as three drinks a day) and of some drugs taken by mouth can overtax the liver's purifying machinery, eventually causing it to malfunction.

Three kinds of liver damage commonly occur in alcoholics:

Fatty liver (steatosis). This condition is almost universal among those who drink excessively. The liver, located in the upper right abdomen, is enlarged and may be tender to pressure, but the alcoholic may notice no symptoms. The best way to treat your fatty liver is to work your recovery program. With abstinence and a healthier lifestyle, the liver almost always returns to normal. How quickly this happens depends on how much alcohol has been ingested and for how long; it can take anywhere from two weeks to many months or more. Good nutrition and moderate exercise can help speed the return of normal liver function (in particular, reducing fat in the diet may hasten the healing process). Taking too much vitamin A or B12, on the other hand, can slow down the healing or even damage the liver. Do not take anything more than a daily multivitamin unless your doctor tells you otherwise.

Alcoholic hepatitis. This condition is more severe than fatty liver. The cause isn't known for certain, but it is likely related to the immune system's response to the toxic effects of alcohol on cells. Again, there may be no symptoms, but observant friends may spot the telltale jaundice (a yellowing of the skin and the whites of the eyes), resulting from a buildup of bilirubin in the blood. Often, however, there is nausea, vomiting, and loss of appetite, as well as fatigue and malaise. There may also be pain in the upper right quarter of the abdomen, intermittent fever, and weight loss. Perhaps most dangerous and disarming is the fact that as the liver deteriorates, pain and tenderness may ease up or go away. If alcohol consumption is continued, the condition gets worse, often progressing to cirrhosis. With abstinence, about 70 percent of livers eventually return to normal, but in an unfortunate 30 percent, the condition persists.

Good nutrition can hasten healing. Treatment usually includes a low-protein, high-calorie diet, with an emphasis on thiamine and the other B vitamins, and sometimes salt restriction.

Cirrhosis. The longer an alcoholic continues to drink, the greater the chance of developing cirrhosis, the end stage of the progression that begins with a fatty liver. Women, because of their smaller size and how their bodies handle alcohol, can develop cirrhosis on less alcohol in less time. Intravenous drug use along with drinking multiplies the chances of developing cirrhosis. Hepatitis B or C infection, too, may lead to cirrhosis.

Cirrhosis kills one in ten of its victims without any warning symptoms. The other nine may have nausea, vomiting, and fatigue; abdominal pain; fever; or jaundice. A medical exam may show signs of increased blood pressure in the veins that carry blood containing the products of digestion to the liver. And because the liver plays a role in producing reproductive hormones, women may have menstrual irregularities or a complete absence of menstruation, and men may develop enlarged breasts and shrunken testicles. The most serious complication of cirrhosis is the development of liver cancer (hepatoma) down the road.

A doctor can diagnose cirrhosis based on a medical history, physical exam, blood tests, and ultrasound. A liver biopsy is needed to confirm how much damage was done.

The core of treatment is staying sober. In less severe cases, those who are completely abstinent have a 90 percent chance of survival for five years; those who are not, only a 65 percent chance. In more severe cases, the five-year survival rate is poorer: 55 percent in abstainers, 33 percent in those who continue to drink.

Treatment also includes a nutritious diet, with extra calories if needed. Depending on associated problems, treatment may also include restricted sodium or protein, medication, or other medical procedures. Cases of liver failure may respond to the use of lactulose, a nonabsorbable sugar. In a massive laxative sweep, it clears out the gastrointestinal tract, eliminating many toxic substances that the sick liver has been unable to process.

Of course, with all types of liver damage, abstinence from alcohol is essential. If you relapse, you could have irreversible liver damage. For some, a liver transplant may be an option—recovering alcoholics can be considered for transplants if they can prove six months of sobriety and have a supportive environment for recuperation—but donor organs are not always available.

Viral Hepatitis

There are five known viruses that can infect the liver: A, B, C, D, and E. All of them can cause a short-term condition: acute hepatitis. Symptoms are similar to those seen with alcoholic liver diseases and include nausea, vomiting, fever, body aches, and an inflamed liver. Many people, however, don't notice any symptoms at all. Acute hepatitis is short-lived; it goes away in a few days or weeks.

Chronic hepatitis is more worrisome. Caused by the B, C, or D viruses, it can last from several months to a lifetime and cause significant problems, including cirrhosis, liver cancer, and liver failure.

Hepatitis C is considered the most serious of these three. Because it is often passed from one person to another by sharing contaminated needles, it is a major concern for those who have used intravenous drugs. It can also be transmitted by blood transfusions and organ transplants (better screening for hepatitis C in the blood supply began in 1992). Also at high risk for the virus are people who have HIV or have gotten a tattoo or piercing with unsterile equipment. (It can also be spread by sexual contact, and by sharing toothbrushes or razors, but those cases are less common.) You cannot get it through casual contact, such as shaking hands or hugging. Today, about 3.2 million people are believed to be infected with hepatitis C, and most of them don't know it yet. Many public health experts consider this to be a major unrecognized health crisis.

Hepatitis C often causes no symptoms at all for years or even decades. When symptoms do occur it might feel like a case of the flu. Also common are fatigue, jaundice (yellowed skin and eyes), fever, achy muscles and joints, loss of appetite, nausea, and tenderness in the abdomen.

If you are at risk, ask your doctor to do a blood test. If you do test positive, you'll need to talk with your doctor about treatment options. About 15 to 25 percent of people who contract the virus will never develop the chronic infection; the virus apparently leaves the body, though researchers are not quite sure how this happens. The rest will have a chronic infection; the virus remains in the body long term. They might feel fine for years, but they are at risk for long-term health problems, including liver damage, liver failure, liver cancer, and death. In fact, hepatitis C infection is now the leading cause of liver cancer, as well as the most common reason for seeking a liver transplant.

For several years, the standard treatment for chronic hepatitis C infection has been a course of two drugs, pegylated interferon and ribavirin. They can reduce the amount of the virus in your blood (your viral load). If they work well, and your viral load is undetectable for six months after treatment, you probably will not have any serious liver problems in the future. However, these drugs do not work for everyone, and they can cause significant side effects, such as depression, fatigue, fever, nausea, and vomiting. If you have the virus but don't have any symptoms, you might want to put off treatment for now. If you do, be sure to have your doctor monitor your liver health regularly, and take care not to infect others. Use condoms, do not donate blood, and avoid sharing items like razors and toothbrushes. You should also talk with your doctor about any other medications you are taking; some, such as acetaminophen, may damage your liver. There is one possible big advantage to waiting on treatment: There are likely to be much better options available in the near future.

Hepatitis B can also be spread through contaminated needles and unprotected sex, and symptoms are similar to those of hepatitis C. It is much less common, however. Hepatitis B can also cause cirrhosis, liver failure and liver cancer. It is also treated with a long-term round of antiviral drugs. Hepatitis D is found only in those who have hepatitis B; it is treated with pegylated interferon.

Hepatitis A, which is most often spread through contaminated food or water, can also be found in those who shared needles. Hepatitis E, which is rare in the U.S., is also spread through food or water, or through sexual contact. Both hepatitis A and E usually go away on their own in a few weeks.

HEART DAMAGE

Heavy drinking and drug use can damage the heart and the blood vessels that serve it, and can raise levels of low-density lipoproteins (LDL), the "bad" cholesterol. That puts heavy drinkers at an increased risk of a heart attack. The risk will diminish as you get further into recovery. But in the meantime, be on the alert for possible signs of a heart problem: extreme shortness of breath or chest pain on exertion; swelling of the ankles, hands, or face; a racing heartbeat; a "fluttering" in the chest; and the inability to breathe comfortably when you are lying down. If you have any of these symptoms, don't panic—there may be a perfectly innocent explanation. But do check with your doctor at once.

OPTIC NEUROPATHY

The eyes do not escape the damage inflicted by alcohol. Chronic alcoholism can lead to reduced vision, blurred vision, vision distortions, spots, and diminished color vision. Smoking compounds the problem. Abstention from both alcohol and tobacco, plus a good diet, halts the progression of the condition, but sometimes residual vision loss remains.

BRITTLE BONES

"I recently fell on an icy sidewalk. It didn't seem all that bad, but I did break my arm in two places. The doctor said my bones are brittle."

Alcohol interferes with the absorption of calcium in the intestinal tract, leaving it unavailable to the bones. As a result, many drinkers—male and female, though the problem is usually worse in women—end up with brittle bones.

There are things you can do to strengthen your bones. One is to be sure you get plenty of calcium (at least 1,200 milligrams, or the equivalent of four glasses of milk, daily). You also need adequate amounts of vitamin D, which helps metabolize the calcium. If you don't get much exposure to the sun, and if you're getting your calcium from a source other than vitamin D–fortified milk, you might need to take a vitamin D supplement; ask your doctor about it.

Avoid a diet high in protein, which also seems to interfere with calcium absorption, and avoid caffeine, which does likewise. Do a lot of weight-bearing exercise—walking, biking, jogging (see chapter 24). If you're a woman near menopause, you might talk with your doctor about taking estrogen; it can enhance bone density, but it can pose other risks.

HIATAL HERNIA

A hiatal hernia occurs when a portion of the stomach pushes up through the opening in the diaphragm where the esophagus passes through. There may be no symptoms, but sometimes, particularly in alcoholics, there are symptoms of heartburn or gastric reflux. Dealing with the condition is important because the irritation of the esophagus can cause bleeding and raise the risk of esophageal cancer. You can minimize symptoms by following the tips for dealing with heartburn in chapter 24. See your doctor if they don't help.

A Healthy Lifestyle

THE CLEAN AND SOBER DIET FOR THE YELLOW ZONE

In the Red Zone you had to focus on saving your life. In the Yellow Zone, it's time to concentrate on repairing and rebuilding your life and learning to enjoy it again. It's not until the Green Zone that you will shift your focus to extending your life and making it even healthier. That is when you can put a major effort into changing your dietary ways and getting back into tip-top shape. Still, making some changes now will make that final effort easier—and help you feel better along the way.

In the Yellow Zone, continue with the basics you learned in the Clean and Sober Diet for the Red Zone: 1) plan for a safe "relapse," 2) eat three squares, 3) get plenty of fluids, 4) eat plenty of foods rich in B vitamins, 5) catch up on calcium, and 6) shun sugar.

Now add three more factors:

- Be more aware of what you eat. Once a month during the next year, keep a log or an online diary of everything that goes into your mouth for a few days. Do you seem to be eating as much, less than, or more than you thought? Do most of the items on your list look pretty nutritious? Are you eating a lot of high-fat foods or junk foods?

- Start reading labels. Learn about what's in the foods you eat—it's all there in the standard nutrition label on most foods. How much protein, carbs, and calories are in that food? What is a serving size? How much fiber is in there? This will help you build a foundation for the dietary changes you'll make later on.

- Find a good source of food. Reading labels is not going to help much if you do all of your food shopping at fast-food joints or convenience stores. It might take some effort to find good

food sources. But your body and your taste buds will thank you for the effort. Ask around to see where others in your area like to shop. If you don't have a car of your own, maybe you can line up some regular shopping outings with others from your fellowship.

EXERCISE NOW?

"My counselor said I ought to start thinking about some recreational activities. That raised a big question mark in my head. To me, recreation has always meant surfing the Internet, watching dumb videos. Besides, shouldn't I be concentrating on more serious stuff?"

Recreation—which can include music, dance, indoor games (Ping-Pong, Monopoly), outdoor games (tennis, Frisbee), hobbies (knitting, gardening), arts and crafts (photography, pottery), mild exercise (walking, bicycling), or just about anything else you enjoy—is serious stuff. It's a vital part of a healthy lifestyle—an absolutely safe relaxant and a temporary escape from problems—as well as a vital part of recovery.

But like you, most alcoholics/ addicts have trouble even contemplating recreation. The reasons are many, but each can be overcome.

Limited experience. For most alcoholics/addicts, recreation meant recreational drugs; other activities were usually limited to those that didn't take much effort, like watching TV or going to sporting events. *Solution*: Remember, there's always a first time. That goes for riding a two-wheeler, going for a hike, or doing whatever else you want to try. You've broken new ground before, and you can do it again.

Limited skills. To participate in most recreational activities, you need to have some basic skills, know the rules of the game, and be able to get along with others. Most alcoholics and addicts lack this expertise. *Solution:* They can be learned. Pick a recreational activity that sounds interesting but isn't very complicated. Learn the rules one step at a time. If you can, take lessons or get some pointers from a friend.

Limited old pals. Most of your pre-sobriety friends are probably no more adept at healthy recreation than you are. *Solution:* Share your recreational time with AA and NA friends or sober family members. Join some clubs or Meetup groups of like-minded folks (as long as they don't end their outings at a bar).

Limited time. Certified workaholics can't find time for fun—and believe they shouldn't have any. *Solution:* Remember that recreation is as important as food to your body, soul, and recovery. Make time for it.

Unlimited guilt. Most alcoholics and addicts have an I-don't-deserve-to-have-fun or a just-relaxing-like-that-must-be-bad attitude. *Solution:* Improve your self-worth (see chapter 14). Everybody deserves to have fun—you included.

Unlimited fear. If you're afraid of interacting socially without a chemical crutch, recognize that not only can you socialize without chemicals—you can socialize a whole lot better. Just look at your AA experience. And you won't have to worry the next day about what you might have done. If you're afraid of looking silly, stop worrying about how you look to others. If you goof up, poke a little fun at yourself and laugh it off. If you're afraid of having free time at all because you might fall into your old free-time ways, filling your free time with constructive activities is much safer than just letting free time happen.

Don't forget that recreation should be fun. Don't approach it with the same grim determination or compulsiveness you brought to your earlier activities. Every tennis serve doesn't have to be an ace, every swing of your golf club a hole in one. In fact, you should avoid any form of recreation or exercise that is too goal-oriented while you're in the Yellow Zone. It can turn into another addiction and can take your focus off recovery. For now, just relax and have fun.

BODY ART REMOVAL

Now that you're sober, you might be looking at those old tattoos and piercings with a twinge of regret. Most piercings will close up on their own over time if you remove the jewelry. Getting rid of tattoos is more complicated, but it can often be done with laser treatments. Ask your doctor for a referral to a dermatologist.

Mental Health

LINGERING SYMPTOMS

In the Yellow Zone you should be feeling pretty good mentally. Some people do find a few new mental health issues crop up now, such as depression and mood swings. Some ideas for coping with these are below.

////////////////////////////

"My first year or so of recovery was a breeze. Now I am suddenly feeling depressed."

In the first year of sobriety, many people are thrilled to have finally made major changes in their lives. They are high on getting sober, so to speak. At some point, however, it's time to go home and live in the real world, and that can feel like a big letdown. As a result, they may have bouts of depression or anxiety. They may feel like they have no direction in life. Now that they are finally feeling a bit stronger and are healing from addiction, they aren't sure what to do next. Others find the Yellow Zone tough because they see their new life of sobriety and moderation as "boring." Building and living in a stable life just doesn't carry with it the crisis and chaos that they have grown dependent on. They have a hard time recognizing the simple pleasures and joys of life.

Your feelings will change as your newfound recovery skills and resources kick in even more solidly. The important thing is to not let yourself stagnate in this period—that can be risky. Instead, look for some new challenges and goals—in your recovery work, your job, your relationships. If you haven't already, think about what part of your life you need to rebuild or attend to in the Yellow Zone, and make a plan for that. Add a little more fun to your routine. And remember that fulfillment in recovery is based on what you do with yourself, not on what you put into yourself.

EXAGGERATED MOOD SWINGS

"My first year of recovery went pretty well. Now, thirteen months since I quit meth, I'm crying one minute, feeling euphoric the next. I've always prided myself on my control of my emotions. It's totally gone now."

Congratulations! The fog is lifting. Your brain has probably been shrouded in the clammy mists of residual chemical damage for the past thirteen months. Prior to that, your drugs neatly anesthetized your feelings. Now the emotions you've been suppressing for years have escaped at last. Because they are unfamiliar, and you don't know yet how to deal with them, they're spilling out like jelly beans all over the floor. Not to worry—you'll learn how to handle them. It's something like the sensations when your arm "falls asleep." At first it's numb (like your emotions until now), then it tingles as circulation begins to return (that's what they're doing now), and finally it normalizes (which, soon, your emotions will do, too). If those emotions had come flying back at the start of recovery, you'd have had an even harder time dealing with them. The fog (which can last as long as a couple of years) gives you a kind of a grace period, in which nothing is felt too strongly. Problems and emotions sit quietly in the background. All you have to do is go to meetings and abstain.

Still, the "awakening" can come as a shock. Everything seems to be going so well, and suddenly reality strikes. Fortunately, you're now in a stronger position to strike back: Accept the fact that you have feelings, and that feelings are okay. Even crying is healthy—it works some chemical magic in the brain that improves your mood. Use the tips for banishing depression and anxiety and for dealing with anger in chapter 14. They will help.

LACK OF ENTHUSIASM

"My recovery is going okay. I've been sober for nearly two years. But I don't seem to have any enthusiasm for life. I'm divorced, with grown kids, and I just seem to go through the motions every day. Isn't there something more?"

Yes, life is about more than just going through the motions.

That's just what you should be finding out in the Yellow Zone. You *will* find the joy again as you continue to rebuild your life; you just need to do some exploring to find out what you want out of life and what might make it more meaningful.

Search for something that excites you and makes you want to get out of bed in the morning. It could be something you've been dreaming of for years, or something brand-new and freshly alluring. Maybe you always wanted to sing, write, or paint, but marriage and the need to earn a living stood in the way. Now you can explore those interests. If your passion is singing, join a chorus or choir—every town has one. Try your hand at writing by starting a blog. Learn to paint by taking a class. Or you can volunteer—there are thousands of different ways to help out in your community.

Or perhaps you have a newfound hankering to fly a plane or climb a mountain. Whatever your dream, you can make it come true in some way. Talk about it with your sponsor or a friend. Think about how you could prepare for and reach your goal. Try it out with small steps at first and see if it's really what you want. If it is, go for it.

But before you launch into a new venture, there are a couple of things you should know. One, getting into a really exhilarating activity (for some it's skydiving; for others it's something tamer) can trigger those old drug highs. The crash afterward can trigger cravings and relapse.

THE YELLOW ZONE

So use safeguards: Practice and share your new hobbies with others in recovery. Two, remember that while getting involved in something new can bring fun and excitement to your life, and even banish the blues, it won't bring you happiness. Happiness is something we have to find in ourselves by living our lives in a way that builds self-value. Relying on anything outside for happiness—be it a chemical, a person, a job, or a new undertaking—is risky. Your happiness lasts only until the chemical wears off, the relationship falls apart, the job becomes routine, or the new becomes old.

CHARACTERISTICS PICKED UP IN ADDICTION

Humans have a wonderful way of adjusting to their life situation in order to survive. Think about it: If you don't get enough food, your metabolism resets and burns what food you do get more slowly. In a tight situation, you get the burst of adrenaline you need to fight or flee. When you were drinking or using drugs, you probably developed some traits that guaranteed you'd get the substance you thought you needed to survive—you became self-centered, and learned to manipulate others, lie, cheat, cover up, and get by one day at a time. Most of those who survive long enough to get into treatment have really perfected those "skills."

You should be able to recognize some of those behaviors in yourself by now. And maybe you've noticed

that they became so entrenched that they haven't yet disappeared. You may even be clinging to them like old friends, possibly believing you can't live without them. But you can.

Now is the time to look at these traits and decide which ones you need to shed. You will probably notice and need to work on others, but the followong are the most common ones that people develop.

Self-centeredness. This probably was important to you not only in active addiction but in early recovery. It gave you the ability to stick to your program and to focus exclusively on getting better. It did its job. Now it's time to say good-bye to self-centeredness, to broaden your horizons some (but still focus on your recovery). Move beyond that totally self-centered mode so you can heal relationships, improve your work life, and build a better social life. If you don't, you run the risk of relapse. Start focusing on the needs of others, listening to what they have to say, and giving them help when they need it.

Deception and dishonesty. You wouldn't have survived active addiction if you had told the truth to your loved ones, your boss, your coworkers, and your dealer. But you won't survive recovery if you don't start telling the truth, the whole truth, and nothing but the truth now. Instead of covering up mistakes, try to acknowledge them and learn from them. You can't continue to manipulate others, to lie to and deceive them, and still get better. Dishonesty and recovery are strange bedfellows. One of them has to get up, get dressed, and go home.

Resentment and anger. Even these traits had a place in surviving addiction. When your life was hanging by a thread, they helped create the energy and determination to keep going just a little longer. But now that the fires are out and sanity has returned, they are not of much help. They can divert your brain from the more logical thoughts you are capable of now that you're in a safe and secure atmosphere. You'll need to move beyond those primitive, animal-like feelings. It can take a while to get there. Remembering to practice all your Yellow Zone brain-healing habits (see chapter 16) will help quite a bit here, by further restoring that "executive brain" functioning.

One-day-at-a-time lifestyle. Ironically, most alcoholics and addicts learned very well how to live one day and one fix at a time during active addiction. ("I only have enough money for today's fix." "I'm too hung over to go to work today. I'll try tomorrow.") That one-day-at-a-time philosophy is one to hang on to. It transfers easily to recovery. The difference is in the emphasis—from staying high one day at a time to staying sober one day at a time.

Changing or redirecting all of these traits may not be easy. It will take effort, thinking about each act each day. But you can do it. Look how far you've come already.

THE
―――
GREEN
―――
ZONE
―――

Are You Ready for the Green Zone?

- Do you still have a stable and strong recovery well under way?

- Have you been sober and in recovery for at least four years?

- Can you still honestly say, "I have no desire to drink or use drugs"?

- Overall, is your life full and content?

- Are you actively involved in a recovery fellowship?

- Have you honestly and completely worked through steps 1–12? Do you use their guidance in your daily life?

- Are you ready to help others experience recovery?

- Do you have a relapse prevention plan in place?

- Are you regularly doing Recovery Zone ReChecks?

- Have you rebuilt your life with regard to relationships, recreational and social activities, education, career, finances, and physical and mental health?

- Are you ready to take more action to achieve your best health, prolong your life, and live your life to the fullest?

- Are you ready to be an agent for positive change in your community?

Go: Celebrate Your Life

Once you have a few years of sobriety behind you, life will seem pretty darn good (actually, *really* good). When you've done just about everything you needed to do to rebuild your life, you'll be ready for the Green Zone. In the Green Zone, you can *go and celebrate your life* while still living in the culture of recovery.

At this point your professional treatment is probably done, though you might maintain a relationship with someone for help as needed. You're still involved in a recovery fellowship, and have worked through all the steps. Your relationships, social life, career, and finances are stable and content. You've learned how to enjoy life again. Your physical and mental health are stable as well. You have accepted yourself, unconditionally and "as is." You've become the person you really want to be.

Life is great now, but you are, of course, *always* vigilant about the risk of relapse.

In the Green Zone, you'll do what you can to further improve your health and your habits, so you can live as long as your genes, luck, and better nutrition and preventive health care will allow. It's also time to focus even more on giving back. Think now about how you can help others who are struggling to find recovery and all the good things your rich new life has given you. Everyone deserves that chance, and you can help them get there. You'll find some good options in chapter 22.

You'll probably reach the Green Zone about midway through or well into your first decade of living a sober life (maybe earlier if you've been deeply involved in a very structured and supportive recovery environment).

Living Your Life, Healing Your Brain

Your hard work in the Red and Yellow Zones helped you to build a wonderful new life. You can pull back on recovery activities somewhat now, but don't pull back so much that you are at risk of relapse. Continue to live in the culture of recovery.

Your brain should be just about back to normal once you reach the Green Zone. But it's vitally important to keep reinforcing those healing, recovery-focused pathways in your brain (otherwise they could get "pruned" away). Always remember that you are in recovery. Keep practicing those TAMERS, focusing your thoughts and actions on recovery.

Below is a summary of what you need to do in the Green Zone. These issues are explored in the following chapters.

Recovery Treatment

Maintain a relationship with a recovery professional just in case you need to turn to someone for guidance. As in the Yellow Zone, any medication you use now should be used only to treat illness.

Mutual-Support Fellowship and Spirituality

Find your own best level of participation in meetings and other recovery activities, in collaboration with your sponsor. Even if you cut back, continue to meet with your sponsor, go to meetings, and do personal inventories to keep your mind focused on recovery. Keep up with the spiritual practices that have gotten you this far. If you are getting a little bored with your fellowship meetings, you might want to take on a leadership role or other tasks to renew your interest. Think of yourself as an example of successful recovery. You now can focus even more on helping others find recovery. If possible, take on additional sponsees now. You can also make a difference in the community at large, by speaking out as a recovery activist, if you choose.

Living Sober and Preventing Relapse

As always, you need to be vigilant about anything that could trigger a relapse. You know what your triggers are, but be sure to review the earlier chapters on relapse from time to time. Also review your own plans for what you'll do if you run into any cues or triggers, or you have any thoughts of using. Be sure to do Recovery Zone ReChecks. Continue writing in your recovery journal. Practice gratitude every day.

Relationships, Recreation, Sober Socializing, Education, Career, and Finances

Your life in these areas is pretty well on track by now, so enjoy it to the fullest. Enjoy your relationships and take time to nurture them. Have fun with your recreational and social activities. Advance in your career on your own merits, and take on new challenges.

You know firsthand what addiction can do to a family, so learn all you can about how to raise substance-free children and help your loved ones avoid the troubles that nearly derailed your life.

To further foster your brain healing, think often about the many rewards of life you have regained—honesty, responsibility, loving relationships, leading a purposeful life, having fun sober, a rewarding career, better finances, renewed health. Challenge your brain with new activities.

Physical Health, Diet, Exercise, and Mental Health

Continue to work on achieving your best health. Be sure to routinely take care of preventive health care needs, such as screening exams. As always, be very careful to avoid all medications that may alter mood or reality, such as sleep aids, anti-depressants, and antianxiety drugs. Make healthy eating and regular exercise a routine part of your life. Keep working on your physical health goals, such as losing or gaining weight and improving your fitness. Let your doctor know that you are in recovery and that you will be happy to talk with other patients who would like to learn about recovery. Continue to do what's needed to maintain good mental health.

If you are still smoking, now is the time to give it up.

Recovery Zone ReCheck

Although you are in the Green Zone, you are still at risk of relapse. So continue to do Recovery Zone ReChecks regularly. Once a month or so, assess what is going on in your life, and make a plan for dealing with any potentially upsetting situations, using the ReCheck questions.

Potential effects. How might this event affect my sobriety?

Recovery Zone. Which Recovery Zone should I go back to in order to avoid a relapse, and for how long? Which recovery activities should I resume or increase in frequency?

Other actions. What else can I do to avoid a relapse?

THE GREEN ZONE

Your Recovery Program in the Green Zone

By now you've struggled through the Red Zone, literally saving your life. You made it through the Yellow Zone, repairing and rebuilding your life and learning to enjoy it in new ways. Now in the Green Zone you are ready to live a long and happy life.

You might be tempted to bow out of recovery activities altogether, but that would be a mistake.

Stay involved, even if you cut back some, because the bad days are still going to pop up, and you need to be ready to deal with them. So take some time now to think about how involved you'll be in your fellowship, and what you'll need to do to stay sober. Make a plan and stick to it.

It's also time to reach out and help others who are suffering from addiction. Maybe you'd like to take on more sponsees. Maybe start a new group, or take on an area leadership role in your fellowship. Or

maybe you'd like to get involved in your community, helping out with educational programs or raising awareness. Many communities are frantically trying to deal with the growing drug epidemic; you can use your voice and your energy to help turn the tide.

However you reach out to help others, you will also be helping your-self. As they say at AA, "You have to give it away to keep it." That's one of the key insights that led to the founding of AA. When you help other people with addiction, when you help your community under-stand the nature of addiction, you are reminded of who you are, where you came from, and what you could be again. In fact, studies show that when people help others, the givers benefit even more than the receivers. And long-term surveys have shown that one of the most important factors in recovery is sponsoring someone else.

So explore your options for giving back in this chapter, and get going.

Sticking with Recovery

CAN'T I JUST MOVE ON AND FORGET ABOUT MY OLD LIFE?

"I've got my four-year chip and feel great. I'm married to a man who didn't mind giving up an occasional beer to marry me. We're expecting a baby. I'd never want to go back to the horror that was my life before. Can't I just forget about AA and get on with my new life?"

You could, but it would be risky. It's possible that some alcoholics and addicts could survive without AA or NA. But since we don't know which ones, it's best for everyone to continue taking their "medicine"— in this case, meetings. It's like wearing a seat belt when you get into your car. You are not likely to have a car accident every time you drive, but a little preventive medicine, a bit of risk management—wearing that seat belt—could save your life just when you least expect it.

Plus, surveys have shown that giving up meetings and not helping others with addiction are the leading indicators of an imminent relapse.

It's dangerous to think that you could be one of the special ones, that you're different. It's much safer to stay involved in your fellowship, even if at a lower level of activity. If you are determined to cut back drastically, please observe the following safeguards.

- Keep to a meeting schedule, even if you go no more often than once a week. Mark your meeting on your calendar, and don't allow anything—outside of an emergency—to keep you from going.

- Go to extra meetings as soon as you start to have negative feelings that are difficult to handle, such as anger, depression, boredom, worry, or anxiety. Or—very important— when your life goes on stress overload. (That's a bonus of long-term recovery—your brain is now much better at thinking things through, so it now steers you toward good sources of help in times of stress.)

- Continue working your program: Take periodic inventories, keep a journal, meditate, and read 12-step literature. People who have incorporated 12-step practices into their daily lives typically do well, even if they cut back on meetings.

THE GREEN ZONE

- Keep a relationship going with your sponsor. Stay in close contact and meet with her periodically so she can help you spot small problems long before they grow into major problems. Give her permission to confront you if you start to stray.

- Include fellowship friends and events in your social schedule.

- Reach out and help someone occasionally, for yourself as well as the recipient.

///////////////////////////

"I've been going to NA for six years, and lately I find that I've heard it all before. I'm bored."

You could consider going to meetings in another part of town occasionally, or cutting back on meetings. But the problem may be more about your perspective at this stage of recovery, rather than the quality of the meetings. You can't change the speakers you now find boring, but you can listen differently. Next time, dissect the talk—how did the speaker find strength through their step work and other recovery practices? How could each of those elements apply to your life?

If you think meetings at your group tend to be weak, offer to serve as chair and come up with some ideas to strengthen them.

You might suggest alternative meeting formats, or some meeting topics that are relevant to things you need in your own recovery program. Maybe you can suggest that your group do more service work—taking meetings to prisons, hospitals, or other places where you are likely to find people in need. Your expertise can be harnessed now to help newcomers, who may be as disappointed with the meetings as you are—and may walk out and never come back. So instead of just thinking about it, help them (and yourself) by speaking up.

Of course, if other people are content with NA sessions that leave you feeling angry, bored, and impatient, it may be you, and not the meetings, in need of dissecting. Talk to your sponsor, do an inventory, and figure out what's behind your negative thinking. And deal with your feelings before enough resentment builds up to damage your recovery.

AM I ADDICTED TO AA?

"I know a lot of people start cutting back on AA activities after three or four years. Even after six years, I feel as though doing that would be like cutting off my arm. Could I be addicted to AA?"

Possibly, but it's sort of like being addicted to water or air. Certain things keep us alive.

Some people in recovery do substitute a dependence on AA for their dependence on chemical substances. Obviously it's a safer dependence, but it is a dependence nevertheless.

If you find that this far into your recovery, AA meetings are still more important than anything else—if AA activities interfere with your work, family life, or social development, or if all of your free-time activities involve AA—you might be using AA in an unhealthy way. In that case, you're going to meetings but probably not getting very much out of them. You're not growing as you should be, and your recovery is "stuck."

What can you do? Review the Green Zone guidelines (chapter 21). Once you have a few years in recovery, it is okay to move beyond the very restrictive practices of early sobriety you followed in the Red Zone. It's okay to open up your life. Also talk about this issue with your sponsor or with others at meetings. If you can't get unstuck, get some professional help. Of course, there are people who make AA the center of their lives, who spend most of their free time with others in the fellowship or at AA functions, and who nevertheless have a very healthy recovery. Their relationships are flourishing. Their work lives are satisfying and successful. And they find time to exercise, see a movie, enjoy a ball game, or do community service. If that's you, continue to enjoy your "addiction."

Keep Helping Others—It Helps You, Too

It's not as easy as it once was to do step-12 work—to reach out and try to help other individuals. In the old days, you could always find another drunk who was sobering up and sit with him through his home detox. Now many people go through professional detox and treatment and are not as accessible. Plus, increased security concerns mean that those who would like to volunteer at an institution such as a hospital must jump through more hoops.

But you can find opportunities. Let your home group know you are ready to help others. Offer to sit with someone going through detox at home, or to chair an AA meeting. Offer to talk one-on-one with people who are in early recovery or just thinking about getting sober. Or offer to talk with groups of people about addiction and recovery. In most cases, your offer will be snapped up quickly.

To find out where you might help, check with:

- Your family doctor.

- The local hospital—particularly if there is a busy emergency room or a detox or addiction unit.

- Detox centers.

THE GREEN ZONE

- Treatment centers, particularly those run by nonprofit groups.

- The local police precinct or legal aid group. Many police departments have trained Crisis Intervention Team (CIT) officers who respond to calls involving substance use or mental illness. They may have work you can do as a volunteer.

- Local schools that might be interested in drug and alcohol education programs.

- Your minister, rabbi, or priest. Many are interested in helping parishioners with drug and alcohol problems, but they often have little training or experience in the area.

- Prisons and jails. Most of the people in jail have addiction issues and are desperately in need of recovery. A visit from you (or a fellowship meeting you bring them) could change their lives. You can also do the same at a homeless shelter, where you are sure to find people with addiction issues.

One great way to help others is to get trained as a Peer Recovery Specialist or Recovery Coach. These programs train people who have a good recovery, teaching them exactly how they can best help others. Classes usually cover basic addiction science, ethics, communication skills, motivational techniques, and how to open doors to the places where people need help (such as doctors' offices, mental health clinics, and shelters). These kinds of training programs are becoming available in many communities.

You can also do volunteer work that is unrelated to addiction. Work at a homeless shelter or hospital, tutor adults or kids, serve on a committee at your house of worship, or deliver meals to seniors. All of these can give you a feeling of achievement, boost your self-esteem, and enrich the lives of others.

START A NEW SERVICE-ORIENTED AA GROUP

"Some friends and I have been thinking about starting a new AA group that focuses more on service. Several of us were introduced to 12-step recovery while in prison. We'd like to help others in the same situation, but sitting around waiting for them to find us is frustrating. They could really use our help, especially when they are released, but they might not even know we exist."

Starting your own 12-step group is relatively easy. It just takes two people, operating under the Twelve Traditions. And as you are thinking, it's great for the founders of a group to have a sense of common purpose.

Virtually any reason for starting a new group is a good reason, and offering fellowship to people who are in prison or were recently released certainly is one. That is, in fact, a primary purpose of AA—to "carry the message of recovery to the alcoholic who still suffers." There are many other ways to do that as well. You could set up a group that caters to beginners or professionals, men or families, gays and lesbians, the hearing-impaired, or any community. Or you could set up a group that focuses on the 12 steps or any other aspect of the program.

You can meet anywhere: in people's homes, in a hospital, in a house of worship, in the cafeteria at work, in an existing AA clubhouse. It's nice to have packets of AA materials and meeting schedules to hand out to newcomers, along with copies of the *Big Book* to sell at cost.

If you want to have meetings inside a correctional facility, it's a bit more complicated, but it's entirely possible. You will need to set it up with the agency that runs the facility and follow their rules. If you want to meet outside a facility and focus on those who were recently released, you might contact the warden or sheriff and let them know that your group exists and welcomes newcomers. They can spread the word among those who will be released soon. The Alcoholics Anonymous General Service Office (GSO) also has a lot of information on working with people in correctional facilities, as well as on starting a new group (go to aa.org and click on For Groups and Members). Later, when your group is well off the ground, you can officially register it with the GSO.

TAKE A LEADERSHIP ROLE

"I really do appreciate what others have done for me at AA. Now that I've been sober for five years, how can I show that appreciation?"

Alcoholics Anonymous is a voluntary fellowship that depends on members well into recovery to give of themselves and their time to make it work. You can show your appreciation by becoming more active in service work in AA, and by carrying AA's message to others.

AA is organized at several levels. Local groups send delegates to represent them at periodic area assemblies, and each area sends representatives to the General Service Conference, which is held in New York each year. An international convention, held every five years, attracts tens of thousands of members from around the world.

Talk with your local leaders about how you can get involved in service work; they will welcome your offer and will surely have ideas about what you can do. You can also read more about AA's structure and opportunities to get involved at aa.org. Getting involved at increasingly higher levels will be of service to others, and will also provide a valuable outlet for your growing talents and skills. Those who've taken this route usually find they get much more than they give.

THE GREEN ZONE

Be a Recovery Activist

YOU KNOW THE COST OF ADDICTION

It sounds like a typical week of daytime soaps, but it's all too real. A teacher is caught in the cross fire of two drug gangs. An elderly woman driving home from church is killed by a drunk driver. A teenager with a bright future dabbles in painkillers, graduates to heroin, and dies of an overdose just weeks before she was to leave for college. A young mother, desperate for the energy to keep up with her job and her kids, gets hooked on meth, losing everything.

The cost of alcoholism and addiction in human lives wasted, destroyed, and made miserable is enormous. Helping individuals with the disease, both by acting as a sponsor and through other means, has to be our first concern.

But this disease assaults our society in other ways, too. When an alcoholic mom shoplifts to get clothes for her kids, the store has to raise its prices. When a couple's drug use tears the family apart, their kids go into foster care and are supported by the state. A man with a crack habit goes on a burglary spree, trashing houses along the way, and everyone nearby pays more for homeowner's insurance. On any given day, scores of hospital beds are filled with people suffering from the complications of alcohol or drug abuse, increasing health costs for all. Our courts and prison systems are clogged with people who committed crimes either under the influence or to protect their drug trade.

You've heard it all before. The financial costs of alcoholism/addiction are in the hundreds of billions per year. The human costs are incalculable. Does alcoholism/addiction affect everyone in our society? You bet it does. Can each of us do something about it? You bet we can.

Once you were part of the mess. Now sober, you can be part of the cleanup. You can't do it alone—you'll need plenty of help, from government agencies, families, neighborhoods, houses of faith, law enforcement, parent groups, schools, businesses, service clubs, and health professionals. But you can do your share.

WHAT IS THE ANSWER? RECOVERY ACTIVISM

Prohibition didn't work in 1919. It just changed saloons into speakeasies and made millionaires out of mobsters. Legalizing drugs isn't the way to go, either. Alcohol, a legal drug, routinely destroys lives.

What *will* work? Changing people's attitudes. As long as drug use is acceptable to some, there will be no shortage of customers. As long as kids see alcohol as an integral part of life—in the ways we celebrate, have fun, and conduct business—they will see it as a necessity. As long as kids think of pills and other drugs as the way to deal with every bump in the road, they will turn to ever more dangerous fixes for every ache. And as long as alcoholism and addiction are seen as "someone else's problem," people will turn away from confronting the issue.

Those are the attitudes that need to change. In fact, they have already started to change. A drunken man reeling down the sidewalk is no longer seen as funny, and many people don't think nondrinkers are oddballs at all. And many others are realizing, finally, what a toll drugs are taking on everyone.

Even better, many people who are in recovery are coming out of the closet, so to speak. They have left their shame and guilt behind. They no longer feel they have to hide their disease and their struggles, and are proudly telling others about their sobriety and the miracle of recovery. Many communities are holding "recovery fairs" and "recovery celebrations." People are coming out to stand up for recovery.

Are you ready to get involved in moving things even further along this pathway? Your goal isn't to become a modern-day prohibitionist. Some people can drink lightly and safely, and they shouldn't have to suffer the evil eye if they choose to imbibe. And some of those strong narcotic painkillers *do* give blessed relief to patients with severe pain.

Instead, you can become a recovery activist. You can move us even closer to the days when being in recovery is completely respected, where not drinking is always as acceptable as drinking, and where kids know that the cool thing is to never use any drugs. You can do it by speaking out, and by proudly standing out as a person in recovery.

Exactly how you take on recovery activism will depend on you, your lifestyle, and your connections. With a problem this huge, the possibilities are endless. Do an inventory. Ask yourself, "How am I linked to society? Where can I speak out?" You might want to connect through your religious life, or work, or community service. You might choose to be a role model, a law-changer, or a public speaker. It's up to you.

Even if it's only a letter to your legislator or a local newspaper, those on the receiving end know that your emails or phone calls represent hundreds, maybe thousands of others. If each reader of this book made just one call, wrote just one message, posted to just one blog, the impact would be considerable. Just imagine if *everyone* involved in a 12-step program did the same.

WHAT ABOUT MY ANONYMITY?

If you are a member of AA, NA, Al-Anon, or a similar mutual-help group, you may be wondering if you have to adopt an alias whenever you're out crusading against the alcohol and drug plague in your community. After all, aren't you supposed to remain anonymous?

Well, "anonymous," as AA traditions define it, doesn't mean you can't get involved in community efforts under your own name. It means only that you should not talk about yourself as a member of

THE GREEN ZONE

your specific fellowship when you are speaking to the media—which includes the press, online venues, and radio or TV. You are totally free to identify yourself as a more general "person in recovery" when talking with the media.

To clarify this further, lots of public events are not media-related. So if you want to talk before a school board or at a community meeting, you can be as open as you want. (But, of course, always respect the anonymity of others.)

BE A LAW CHANGER

Legislation alone isn't going to change attitudes, but it can make a difference. Look at how common no-smoking laws are now, and how much more seriously states take drunk-driving offenses. Those changes were largely fostered by people who pushed for stronger legislation.

You can speak out in support of many different types of legislation that could help your community. For example, voice your support for:

- Rules that clarify local school policies on alcohol and drugs

- Legislation supporting better and more available effective treatment for addiction

- More low-cost sober housing for people in recovery

- Homeless shelters that include programs to help people get into recovery

- Taxes and fees that fund programs of awareness, prevention, and treatment

- Candidates who support strict drug laws as well as recovery resources

Support such efforts any way you can—for example, persuading friends in influential places, writing emails, making phone calls, joining committees, signing petitions, and sharing information on Facebook.

BE A COMMUNITY VOLUNTEER

If volunteering is a part of your life, you have many opportunities to spread the word. Whether you work with Little Leaguers or seniors or you volunteer at a school or a homeless shelter, you can use what you know about addiction to educate others. For example, you might offer to run a drug awareness day at the local high school.

One great way to help is to get involved in a local alcoholism and addiction council or recovery advocacy group. These groups help support grassroots change. They develop public policy and programs, educate communities, and provide clout for the forces trying to change attitudes.

USE THE POWER OF THE WORD

Preventing a fire makes more sense than waiting to put it out when it has grown to a four-alarmer.

As a person in recovery, you're in a position to tell your story and help others avoid the actions that put your life in harm's way. You can also use the written word to influence others—write to legislators, newspapers, and online publications.

USE THE POWER OF RELIGION

Houses of worship can do a lot in the battle against the disease of alcoholism/addiction. They can encourage support groups to meet on their premises, offer programs that increase awareness and reduce stigma about addiction, and provide nonalcoholic options for ceremonies and social functions. They can also help those in early recovery with a meal, a temporary roof over their heads, some child care, or a small job to help build a résumé.

As a person with long-term recovery, you can take a lead in making this happen.

USE THE POWER OF THE PURSE

Voting with your wallet is often as effective as entering a voting booth. How do you do that? Don't patronize the restaurant that offers deals to "buy two drinks, get a third free," lets young women drink for free, or otherwise pushes heavy drinking. Skip the grocery store that sells alcoholic "coolers" in the produce section, promoting them as something healthy. But do let the managers know why they've lost your business.

Whenever you can, spend your dollars at businesses that support the growing recovery movement, as well as those that take a responsible attitude toward alcohol and drug use. If you come across a restaurant that hosts a fund-raiser for a homeless shelter or is very vocal about checking the IDs of young people, tell the owner that you appreciate his efforts and will gladly support his business.

USE THE POWER OF THE WORKPLACE

Many of us spend at least half our waking hours at work. It is often a good place to help raise awareness of the risks of alcoholism/addiction and their effects on society. It's a particularly good place to get active if you are in a position of influence—if, for example, you are a business owner, a manager, or a union representative.

Many companies today routinely screen applicants for drugs; if yours does not, see if you can get that policy passed. You might also volunteer to help others who ask for help from the Employee Assistance Program, help to share information about addiction with coworkers, or organize fellowship meetings.

Simply letting it be known that you, a valued worker, are in recovery will send the message that those with problems should be helped to get treatment rather than being tossed out. It will send the message that hiring people in recovery is good business, and that the very qualities that keep people sober also make them excellent employees.

THE GREEN ZONE

Raising Substance-Free Kids

You might think that your own kids, having had a front-row seat to the misery brought on the family by addiction, will steer clear of alcohol and drugs. But that rarely happens. In fact, your kids are probably at higher-than-average risk of becoming dependent themselves. But just as you immunized them against childhood diseases, you can take steps to protect them from addiction.

All Kids Are at Risk for Addiction

All kids today are susceptible to the lure of mood-altering chemicals and the addiction that can follow. This is particularly true in the teenage years, because of adolescent insecurity, lack of family cohesiveness, the all-too-easy access to drugs from doctors and others, and pressure from peers and the surrounding culture.

Kids who grow up in drinking and drugging families face an even greater risk, due to both genetic and environmental factors. Genetically, if a biological parent is an addict or alcoholic, the child may have inherited that tendency. Environmentally, kids who are exposed early on to a drug-centric way of life often start using at a young age, compared to their peers. In addition, familiarity breeds comfort. These kids often are more comfortable in the familiar world of alcohol and drug use—no matter how unhappy it is—than in an unfamiliar world of abstinence. Plus, children typically are not ready to learn from the mistakes of others, particularly those of Mom or Dad.

The good news is you don't have to sit by and let your kids fall victim to the disease that ravaged your life. You can take many steps that might help them avoid wasting years in addiction.

What if you are an always-been-sober adult child of an alcoholic or addict? You still need to worry about your children. Kids often inherit traits from their grandparents. Your kids, too, should be forewarned: Abstain as you have, and they can avoid the disease.

How to Addiction-Proof Your Child

Although you can't absolutely prevent your child from falling into the same traps that you did, you can try to reduce the risk. One of the most important things you can do is be a great role model: Show them that life can be fun and exciting without drugs or alcohol. That will help instill the idea that they could miss all the fun if they do drink or use drugs.

MAKE YOUR HOME A DRUG-FREE ZONE

Making your home a drug-free zone means more than just locking the liquor cabinet. It means making it clear that drugs and alcohol have no role in your family's life. Some ideas:

- Keep your home free of alcohol and drugs. This includes prescription drugs, as much as possible. Many kids today start their drug use with prescription drugs—often pills that are found in their own homes or those of their friends. If you must keep some prescription drugs in the house, follow the security guidelines on page 210.

- Counter—by both words and actions—the common attitude that drugs can cure all ills. Many people grow up with the attitude that drugs, mood-changing or not, are always the answer, even when other options are available. They live their lives defined by chemicals. If your kids learn early that there are other solutions, they will carry that knowledge throughout their lives. Make the use of pills (even an innocent headache remedy) a last-resort treatment in your home.

- Let your children know that being drunk or high is neither funny nor acceptable, and that alcohol is not needed to celebrate or have fun. Point to some celebrities who are famously sober as examples of what cool really is.

- Don't let anyone offer a sip of beer or other alcoholic beverage to any children, no matter how adorable relatives think this is. Behaviors like that glamorize and justify chemical use. It says to kids, "Hey, this is something you can do to be more grown-up."

THE GREEN ZONE

- Strongly discourage anyone who plans to drive while using any mood-altering drug or medication, or alcohol. Also discourage anyone who plans to partake in other potentially dangerous activities while drunk, such as skiing, swimming, biking, or boating.

- Teach your children that they must never, ever get in a car with someone who has been drinking. Make it clear that it's not uncool to turn down such a ride; in fact, walking away is a very smart thing to do. Make sure they know they can always call you for a ride, even if it's the middle of the night.

- Explain to your children why your home is drug- and alcohol-free: "Our family is not like most other families. We have this illness called alcoholism (or addiction)." Explain that they are likely to have the problem, too, unless they are really careful and learn all they can about how to enjoy life without drugs and drinking. Admit to them that it won't be easy: "It's going to take all of us working and talking it out together. You'll get a lot of pressure from friends, social media, TV, wherever you go. If you see drugs at school or you're offered any, you need to let us know. We want to try to help you, to talk about how you can handle those situations."

- Stay sober and work hard at your recovery. The example you set in the past was probably pretty bad. But now you know you've got to do better, for your family as well as yourself. Keep working your program, and let your kids see how important sobriety is to you.

BE AN EFFECTIVE PARENT

We all need nurturing, love, and praise in order to thrive. If children don't get these things at home, they either become withdrawn and depressed or turn elsewhere to find them. Most often they turn to a peer group, where in order to earn their strokes they may have to do things that conflict with the values they learned at home: drink, use drugs, have sex, and so on.

So it's vitally important that you create a caring, nurturing environment for your children. In your home, children should know that whatever they do, they will always get love and moral support and that these won't be withdrawn as punishment for anything. Building a strong relationship with your children now will mean that in times of crisis your love, support, wisdom, and experience won't be shut out of your child's decision making. Here are some ideas for fostering that good relationship.

Be honest. Dishonesty is the soil in which the seeds of addiction germinate. Being honest in all your dealings with your children and others is one of the most important preventive strategies any parent can have.

Be trustworthy. Show your kids by your actions that you can be trusted to keep your word. That's the only way you can expect them to keep theirs. Parents who break their promises teach their children to do likewise. Trust your children as long as they earn that trust.

Be open about other family problems. This includes financial or job-related problems, for example. You don't have to go into great detail, or lay blame on anyone, but it's important for them to know that problems are a part of life and you don't run away from them.

Admit to making mistakes, and be willing to change course if you seem headed for disaster. Kids need to learn that everyone makes mistakes, and it's okay to admit it. Otherwise they may either try too hard to succeed or not try at all— and eventually try to cover up their normal imperfections with layers of lies or with chemicals.

Don't stifle thought and opinion in your home. Listen to your children without criticizing or discounting their views. You don't have to agree with them, but they should not feel intimidated about voicing their opinions. If you won't listen to their views, how will they possibly feel free later to stand up for themselves in front of others?

Don't stifle feelings and emotions in your home. Be sure there is plenty of hugging and laying on of hands— the warm and loving kind. Also be sure your kids know it's okay to feel and express anger, disappointment,

fear, frustration, or other negative feelings. Don't belittle, laugh at, or be angry about your child's feelings. Accept them as real and make it clear you are glad that your child feels free to express them. Mentor acceptable and constructive behavior. For example, if your child seems reluctant to express feelings or talk about a problem, try to create an opening that will make it easier: "Gee, you seem upset about something. You might feel better if you talk about it. I'm ready to listen whenever you're ready to talk."

It's also important to discuss ways to deal with feelings and to "feel better." That means figuring out why we feel the way we do and determining what actions or behaviors can alter that feeling for the better.

Make your home a place for family members to bring their concerns. If your child brings a problem home and is scolded or ridiculed, you can be sure that next time the problem simply won't come home. Your child may take it elsewhere or may not deal with it at all. If, on the other hand, you handle the small ones (about schoolwork or a friend) with sensitivity, your child is more likely to bring you the bigger problems later on.

If, during your years of substance use, your child lost faith in you as a confidant, be sure there is someone else he can talk to until you reestablish rapport. It can be someone at Alateen; a grandparent; an older sibling or other relative; a minister, priest, or rabbi; a teacher or guidance counselor; or a doctor. It needs to be someone your child likes and trusts.

Give your children your time and attention. If it seems to your kids that work, social activities, and Facebook are more important to you than the family (as drugs or alcohol once were), they may build up resentment that later shows up in rebellious behavior, including drug use. Be sure there is plenty of time for family dinners or other family events.

Attention, like love, should never be used as a bartering tool—it's a child's due. Children who get too little attention often find negative ways to get it. Flunking a course or coming home after curfew drunk tends to attract more attention from busy parents than getting straight *As* or coming home on time. Be sure to make as much fuss when you catch your kids being good as when you catch them being not so good.

Set limits and house rules. Have clear boundaries for how you expect everyone to behave. It nurtures healthy development and helps kids develop skills that will stay with them for life. Some rules can be set by adult decree; others, by family discussion. Rules should always be spelled out clearly, and everyone should be expected to follow them. The consequences when rules are broken should also be clear, specified in advance, and always carried out promptly.

Know when to say no—and mean it. If parents (perhaps wanting to be loved) never say no, then why should their children (perhaps wanting to be liked) say no when offered drugs? But pick your arenas carefully and don't say no to everything. When it's rational and safe, let the kids win a round now and then.

Set clear rules on room searches. Establish a clear family policy that says, "Because we love you and care about what happens to you, we reserve the right to search your room and your belongings if we ever think you might have a drug or alcohol problem."

Do not use any form of physical punishment, period. And be alert for signs of abuse—physical, emotional, or sexual—from others who have contact with your child. If there has been any child abuse in the past or there is any occurring now, get professional help.

PROTECT YOUR KIDS ONLINE

If your kids are tweens or teens, protecting them involves a lot more than just holding their hands while crossing the street. Parents today have to deal with a bewildering—and ever-changing—array of online programs and communities. It's up to you to set some very clear ground rules.

Rule one is to monitor your child's use of social media and other online communications. Let your kids know up front that, while you trust them to be careful online, you plan to review their accounts from time to time, including email, texting, chat, photo-sharing, and social networking sites like Facebook. Insist that they share with you the passwords to all of their online accounts as well as all devices (phones, tablets). Also let them know that if they change a password or open a new account anywhere, they need to let you know about it. Then follow through and do your reviews—on their devices or by logging into their accounts on your own computer (or, even better, both).

You don't have to scrutinize every email, text, or chat transcript, but do read enough to know what is going on in their lives. Often all may seem well on the outside, but a bit of monitoring can reveal issues or problems that you had no knowledge of. Keep an eye on who they are connecting with and what they are saying. Do the relationships seem like healthy ones? Are there any obviously inappropriate chats, such as an older teen (or even an adult) suggesting a meeting? Is there any bullying going on? Do you know personally all the people who are friends with your kids on Facebook? Are there any inappropriate pictures of your child or other people? What about any baffling messages that could be shorthand for alcohol or drug use?

Some more ideas:

- You can put limits on your child's online use by using parental controls from your phone/Internet service, an antivirus/security software, or another parental control program. For example, you can limit the hours when texting and phone calls are allowed. (A low-tech way to do this is to insist that all phones are left on the kitchen table during homework time and are charged in the kitchen overnight—not in a bedroom.)

- Use parental controls to limit the type of sites they can visit and use—even before they go exploring. Consider blocking all chat services other than Facebook, as well as all "adult" sites. You can set it up so that when they try to access a blocked site, they'll see a screen with your customized message: "This site has been blocked by Mom for your safety. If you truly need access to it, use the link below to email me about it."

- Set your control program to keep a list of all the sites your kids visit—or try to visit—and how often. That can be an eye-opener! You can even set some programs to give you a GPS reading of where your child is (or at least where his phone is).

- Some of the parental control programs will also block contact from people you have decided are inappropriate for your child. They can also send you an alert when suspicious activity occurs, such as inappropriate language.

- Be sure to explore the sites and services your kids are allowed to use and see what additional controls you might set up on them. For example, on Facebook you can set it up so all photos tagged with your child's name (posted by anyone) have to be approved before they go live. Then make sure you are the one who reviews and approves all tags. (See more on locking down accounts on page 233.)

- If you share a computer or tablet with your kids, set up password-protected accounts for everyone. That way you can limit their access while still being able to see what you want.

- Be sure to block inappropriate programs and channels on your television as well.

- Keep televisions and family computers in public areas of the house; kids are less likely to go exploring if Mom might walk into the room at any moment.

- Slowly increase your child's online access. For example, if your tween is just dying to be able to text people, start her off by allowing her to text only a few chosen people—her very cool aunt who lives far away and maybe one or two of her friends.

Just as you talk with your kids about all kinds of behavior, talk with them about what is appropriate to post online and what is not. Explain to them that pictures and videos posted online will be there *forever*, even if they think they've been deleted. Talk to them about the dangers of posting inappropriate photos, such as nude body parts, and about never making fun of anyone or bullying anyone online. Suggest they do a quick test for whatever they are thinking about posting: "Would I want Grandma to see this?" If not, chances are they shouldn't post it.

INSTILL THE TOOLS TO RESIST TEMPTATION

Many life skills and attitudes will help your children to value themselves and be able to stand up to peer pressure. You can help them develop these attributes.

Self-Worth and Self-Respect

Kids who like themselves are less likely to try to become someone else through the use of chemical substances. Those who respect themselves are less likely to allow others to push them into unwise behaviors. Here are some techniques for helping your child build a healthy sense of self-worth:

- Respect your child. If parents don't show they value a child, it will be very hard for that child to value himself.

- Be realistic about your child's abilities. Don't expect a child to behave or perform like an adult, and don't expect more than your child can give.

- Reward good behavior; applaud work well done. Catch your child being good, and reinforce this behavior with a pat on the back, a hug, a high five, or simply words of praise.

- Encourage more effort when work doesn't match ability, but never belittle. "You stupid kid—why can't you ever do anything right?" is hurtful and ineffective. Much better when the performance is mediocre is "That's not bad, but I bet you can do even better."

- Nurture innate talents (art, sports, music, writing, mechanical skills, sociability) as well as areas where your child tends to have less ability. Where there is natural ability, there should be striving for excellence; in the other areas, for competency. Becoming a proficient and successful human being builds self-worth.

- Encourage good work skills. Helping out with chores will help boost the self-esteem of children as well as make them feel more a part of the family.

Self-Reliance and Independence

You can only make your kids independent by loosening your controls. You start letting go when you first leave a baby with a sitter, when you send a preschooler off on a playdate. Then there's the first sleepover, the first after-school job. Later on, you foster self-reliance in your children when you let them make some of their own decisions and suffer the consequences of their behavior.

Self-Comforting Skills

Don't encourage the use of outside resources (such as food, drink, pacifiers, or gifts) to make an upset child feel better. Instead, offer love and support, but not to such a smothering degree that you don't allow the child a chance to work out of the misery alone. Suggest a trip to the playground; sing a song or listen to music; play catch; draw a picture; do a puzzle. Older children can go for a walk or a run, turn to music or books, or even learn to meditate. They can also learn to think through a situation and learn how to use both problem-solving and decision-making skills to deal with their feelings.

Ability to Delay Gratification

Children who are overindulged and who find their parents submissive will find it hard to delay gratification in their teen years. For instant happiness, they may turn to chemical substances. Kids need to learn that some things are worth waiting for—a hard concept to get across in this always-on world of texting, Facebook, and Twitter, but a vital one.

Impulse Control

Children who get their hearts' desires by screaming or pouting find loss of control a very useful bargaining chip. Let your children know you won't even listen to their requests until they calm down. As they get older, they also need to learn to control negative impulses.

THE GREEN ZONE

Self-control is learned best in a home that is neither overly permissive nor overly strict, and where fairness and rational behavior are the golden rule.

Mood-Maintenance Skills

A teenager doesn't need drugs to experience mood changes, but many of them turn to drugs to alter moods they are uncomfortable with. To avoid this in your family, talk about moods, mood changes, and ways of dealing with all types of emotional discomfort. Let children know it's normal to feel great some days, and not so great on other days (and that those bad days are not all bad; they can help us grow and mature). Let them know that pills are not the way to deal with those swings, no matter what they see on TV. Help your child learn about the techniques recommended in this book for avoiding and coping with extreme mood swings (good diet, exercise, meditation, good sleep habits, and antidepression activities).

Decision-Making Skills

Too many children are led into drugs because they are not used to making decisions. From earliest childhood, give your child the opportunity to make choices: "Do you want to go on the slide or the swings?" "What clothes do you want to wear today?" As your child gets older, allow more leeway in decision making (as long as health and safety are not at stake). Teenagers should be encouraged to make most basic decisions in their lives (what courses to take, which music to listen to, what apps to download). But they will need plenty of input from an understanding adult for some decisions.

Hobbies and a Healthy Social Life

Kids who are busy—with school clubs, lessons, sports, karate, youth groups, or hobbies—are less likely to turn to drugs as an escape from boredom than are kids who hang out at the mall or hole up in a room playing video games for hours on end. Encourage activities that provide healthy ways to have fun and keep busy. Also encourage those activities that include social connections and service to others, such as volunteering at an animal shelter or working at a community event.

A Set of Values

Values are taught primarily through example. But in a world where values outside the home often clash with those inside, parents also need to talk with their children about things they think are important: honesty, charity, tolerance, respect for others, concern for the environment.

A Spiritual Life

Strong religious faith of any kind can help deter drug use. If that is something you are comfortable with, pass it on to your child with love, inspiration, explanation, and information. If you are not religious, but your child wants to explore a religion, find a likeminded and trusted mentor.

Realistic Expectations

Children need to know what you've been trying to learn in recovery yourself: that nobody is perfect. Not parents. Not teachers. Not friends. And not themselves. We should all try to do our best, but shouldn't beat up on ourselves when we fall a little short. To feel good about themselves, kids need to recognize their strengths but also accept their weaknesses and mistakes. The idea that "if you're not perfect, you're nothing" is destructive to children as well as to adults.

Information

Education is one of the best weapons against drug and alcohol abuse. Ideally, education about the effects of drugs and alcohol on body and soul should begin in early childhood, but it's never too late to start.

Be sure you make it clear that beer, wine, and hard liquor all pack the same wallop—kids often don't know this and think, for example, that beer is a "safe drink." They also often think that just because a pill is prescription, it is safe; make sure they understand that this is not at all true.

Avoid scare tactics and preaching, but do talk about your own experiences. Urge your child to go to Alateen or go with you to open 12-step meetings and functions, in order to learn from others. If necessary, get your child some private tutoring from a drug counselor.

Role-Playing

Talk about situations that could arise with their friends. Ask your kids, "How do you deal with a classmate—especially one you really like—who offers you a beer at a party? Or a smoke at a football game? How do you respond when an older kid tries to bully you into taking a puff on a joint?"

Acknowledge that it is not always easy to just say no, and talk about how they can handle such situations.

Goal-Tending Skills

Goals are what keep us going and doing our best in life. We need short-term goals (getting homework done on time), medium-term goals (learning to play the piano), and long-term goals (becoming a concert pianist). Striving for unreachable goals, however, is frustrating and self-defeating (like finishing homework in the first hour after school, when pent-up energy levels are highest and the playground beckons). Goals, particularly short-term ones, should be realistic, such as finishing homework immediately after dinner, before the laptop is turned on.

WHAT DOESN'T WORK

Some parents have tried to head off problems with alcohol and drugs by telling their children, "If you want to drink or use drugs, do it at home." This almost invariably backfires, and the kids end up with serious problems. It's also a bad idea to try to give a child a "bad" experience with tobacco, alcohol, or drugs—making them use it until they feel sick. If the first use

THE GREEN ZONE

is unpleasant, a kid with an inclination toward addiction (like your own) will usually keep trying until it gets better—and it will, as tolerance develops.

Limiting drug education to "just say no" usually fails, too, because it tends to maintain the romanticism of drugs and it doesn't deal with the major drug problem in this country: alcohol. What can work is helping them develop qualities and attitudes that make drugs unnecessary in their lives.

Force and coercion are not effective measures for preventing drug or alcohol problems, either. Children who are abused may cower and submit to parental power at home. But in the long run, they are more likely to rebel and seek escape through drugs than are those who are treated with fairness and firmness.

YOU WILL SURVIVE

Being a parent is never easy. It's even tougher if you've lost some rapport with your children because of your own drug or alcohol misuse. But many of the tools you've learned in recovery can be useful in surviving as a parent. On days when you feel like locking the kids in their rooms and throwing away the key, think of some of AA's basic mottos, such as "One day at a time" and "This too shall pass." And say the Serenity Prayer. Several times.

Your Health in the Green Zone

Y ou have come so far on this journey. With a few years of sobriety behind you and most aspects of your life back on track, it's now time to do everything you can to live a long and healthy life. It's time to focus on preventive health care, clean up your diet even more and get regular exercise. It's also time to get your weight where you'd like it to be (or at least close).

And what about taking drugs? Can you now finally take a narcotic painkiller after minor surgery? Sorry, but no. Too many people relapse at this stage due to well-intentioned pain-control measures. You've got to be vigilant about your sobriety forever. That means taking those drugs only when it is absolutely necessary—we're talking life and death here. Thankfully, there are effective alternatives. Read more about recovery-safe medical and dental care, and how to handle emergencies, in Medication Concerns, page 475. And be sure to check out all the options for managing a variety of medical issues, in Nondrug Approaches to Common Medical Problems, which starts on page 494.

If you plan to do any health research online, please see Calling Dr. Google on page 286 for tips on safe searching and a list of reputable health sites.

Your Health Priorities Now

GET REGULAR CHECKUPS

O nce you're in the Green Zone, you should get into the habit of seeing your doctor periodically, even when you're feeling fine. Now that you're no longer living so close to the edge, it's time to get serious about regular screenings for serious diseases, adopting preventive health habits, and undertaking other health-promotion strategies under your doctor's guidance.

If you haven't done so already, see a doctor for at least a basic exam and to start a relationship with someone you can turn to if any health issues come up. When the doctor asks about your drug history, be sure you give a complete and honest answer. The substances you used, how you used them, and for how long will dictate what your exam should emphasize. If your drug of choice was alcohol, he will check your liver and nervous system more closely; if cocaine, your blood pressure, heart function, and nose. If you smoked your drugs, a chest X-ray or CT scan may be in order. If you injected them, you'll need tests for hepatitis B and C and HIV.

The doctor will also want to know if you've tried to get sober before, if you've been through in- or outpatient treatment for your addiction (and where), and if you are now in a continuing care program.

For ideas on how you can find a "recovery-safe" doctor, see Find the Right Doctor on page 430.

RAISE YOUR ODDS OF HAVING A LONG AND HEALTHY LIFE

Get regular exercise. Most adults should get some regular exercise. Start with the little things: Take the stairs instead of the elevator, park at the farthest corner of the parking lot when you shop, get off the bus a stop or two early and walk to your office. To further improve your cardiovascular health and reduce your risk of stroke, heart disease, and high blood pressure, set up an exercise program that includes at least two and a half hours of moderate-intensity aerobic exercise each week (or an hour and a quarter of vigorous activity). Moderate means activities such as brisk walking, ballroom dancing, and gardening. Vigorous activities include running, swimming laps, and hiking uphill. And you don't have to do it all at once; just ten minutes of activity at a time is enough to get the benefits. If you start any exercise program more strenuous than walking, be sure to get your doctor's okay first. Read more about exercise in Your Healthy Lifestyle: Exercise, on page 490.

Control your weight. Maintaining a normal body weight will reduce your risk of premature death.

Live smoke-free. Using tobacco raises your risk of dying of cancer, heart attack, and stroke. If you haven't quit smoking yet, now is the time. Read chapter 25.

Follow the Clean and Sober Diet. This diet—low in fat, salt, refined grains, and sugars, and high in fiber—isn't a panacea, but it does improve your odds of staying healthy (see page 483).

Minimize stress. Stress can have a good effect on our lives, or a deadly one. It all depends on how you handle it (see chapter 14 as well as Anxiety, page 498).

Get health screenings. When you meet with your doctor over the years, he may suggest a number of preventive health screenings, such as mammograms, oral cancer screenings, and so on.

Adopt a low-risk lifestyle. Avoid risky sex and dangerous people and places; hang out with your new sober friends and avoid those you used to drink or do drugs with.

Avoid toxins. Your brain and body will thank you if you make an effort to avoid exposure to toxins such as paint fumes, pesticides, gasoline vapors, propellants, secondhand smoke, chemicals, harsh cleaning agents, molds, unproven supplements that are not needed for medical care, and so-called "miracle" cures or treatments. You don't have to go live in the middle of the desert, but do what you can to minimize exposure. Look for greener versions, and always read labels so you know how to properly use and dispose of all cleaners, chemicals, and other items.

Medication Concerns

I n spite of the risks, it's sometimes not possible to avoid mood-altering drugs when a serious accident or illness strikes, or when surgery is necessary.

If at all possible, find out before you have a surgical procedure what kind of medication your doctors might prescribe. Read through the information below to learn about safe options. Tell the doctor handling your case (who might be a surgeon or anesthesiologist you have never met before) that you are in recovery, and you cannot use many medications. If it seems that he has little or no experience with addiction, get a second opinion from a doctor who knows what the safest medication options are for you. If you and the doctor (or dentist), after weighing risk against benefit, decide that nondrug pain relief (see Pain, page 513) won't be enough and that a prescription or other risky drug is absolutely needed, there are things you can do to avoid a relapse.

First, preparing for surgery means you are back in the Red Zone for a while. If possible, before you have surgery or start the medication, talk with your sponsor about how you will increase your recovery activities. Will you go to more meetings, talk with your sponsor daily, start working on the steps again? Draw up a formal plan for how you will handle this situation. (See Recovery Zone ReCheck, page 18.)

Second, read through the following guidelines for safe medical and dental care. There are many things you can do to help prevent a slip.

THE GREEN ZONE

SAFE MEDICAL CARE

- If you're having surgery, regional anesthesia (which numbs the area to be worked on) is preferable to general anesthesia (which puts you to sleep) when feasible.

- Ask your surgeon to request that the anesthesiologist omit the pre-op drugs (usually a sedative or narcotic) if possible. A chat with the anesthesiologist, meditation, soothing music, or saying the Serenity Prayer may do just as much for you. Also explore the possible use of hypnotism and acupuncture for drug-free or drug-reduced surgery. Guided imagery recordings that aim to relax you during surgery or medical procedures may also work wonders (start listening to them before your procedure).

- Whenever possible, have an advocate or buddy at your bedside. This can be a family member who is knowledgeable about safe medication procedures, or your sponsor or another AA or NA friend.

- When medication is necessary, if at all possible it should be in a different class from your old drug of choice. For example, if you used OxyContin, taking it or a related drug (any other narcotic), except under the most controlled conditions, could be fatal to your recovery.

- Don't accept any medication unless you're given a very convincing reason why you need it—and why your need for it overrides your risk of relapse and possibly dying from active addiction. Try to consult an American Society of Addiction Medicine physician or medical staff at a chemical dependency treatment program if you're uncertain.

- If possible, any needed medication should be administered only in a hospital, where it can be closely controlled.

- For pain relief, always ask if a non-mood-altering drug, such as ibuprofen (Motrin, Advil) or acetaminophen (Tylenol), can be used instead of a mood-altering one. Also consider nondrug treatments for pain (see Pain, page 513).

- Avoid narcotics if at all possible. You could require large doses to get any pain relief—large enough to make your doctor uncomfortable. And these large doses could be enough to trigger relapse risk, yet not enough to relieve your pain. Not a good situation, clearly. A much better option is a drug called ketorolac (Toradol). It is something of a miracle cure for pain in the addict. It is at least as effective for pain as narcotic drugs, but it is chemically similar to ibuprofen-like drugs, so it carries little, if any, relapse risk.

- If you do have to take a narcotic after surgery, a strong narcotic for a few days in the hospital will be safer than a milder one for a few weeks at home. The longer you take the drug, the greater the risk—especially if you are in charge of administering it.

- In the hospital, ask your doctor to leave standing orders that exempt you from routine sedation or sleeping pills. This kind of medicating is often more for the convenience of the staff than the benefit of patients, and it definitely is not safe for you. Have your doctor explain your situation to the nurses so you won't have medication pushed on you. Because nursing shifts change often and nurses on a new shift may not be aware of your doctor's orders, it can help to ask each nurse to read your chart before giving you any medications. The biggest risk will probably be when you're fresh out of surgery and are groggy. If an advocate is with you, he can do the talking. Another strategy that almost always works is to tape a sign on your headboard and add a note to your chart saying that you are "allergic" to sedative and narcotic drugs.

- If, in spite of your best efforts, sedative or narcotic medication is handed to you, dump it down the toilet. Don't leave the pills lying temptingly on your nightstand.

- Avoid medication "as needed by patient." Most hospitals now have patient-controlled pain med pumps. These devices allow doctors to prescribe pain medication via an intravenous pump; the patient controls the frequency of dosing, within limits. With your history, that is clearly playing with fire. If medication is needed, it's better for the nurse to deliver it, but only on a regular schedule as prescribed by your doctor. Reassess your need for pain meds every day with your doctor, and reiterate to everyone that you prefer to use nonmedical tools to control pain and you want to taper off any risky medications as quickly as possible.

- If at any point you don't understand what's happening to you, or can't get your point across to the nurses or resident, appeal to the attending doctor on call. That might not win you any popularity contests, but it won't lose you your sobriety either.

- Ideally, you should be drug-free for forty-eight hours before release from the hospital. In other words, you should be detoxed before discharge. But if your medical issue was severe or complicated and required much medication, detox alone may not be enough to prevent a relapse. Then it might help to convalesce in an addiction treatment facility for a short time. If that's not

THE GREEN ZONE

practical, make plans with your sponsor to smother you in AA friends, meetings, and materials for several weeks until the drug fog lifts completely and you leave your return trip to the Red Zone behind. In any case, the first few nights should not be spent alone, but with someone who has a solid recovery or is active in Al-Anon. Be aware that the rekindled addict in you might not be able to make the best decisions, so to protect your recovery, make plans to delegate decisions to others.

- If you have to take medication at home, don't put yourself in charge of it. Ask a nonaddicted spouse or friend familiar with the use of drugs in recovery to stay with you (or you with them). Ask them to read this section of the book. Their judgment about medications will be more objective than yours. They should dole out one dose at a time and make sure you swallow each dose on the spot. The supply of medication should not be left out in your room or bathroom, where you might be tempted to take an extra dose or two. Your friend should also keep a written record of all medications taken. Any leftovers should be disposed of safely.

- In the case of a serious mental illness, the decision to use medication (such as lithium or antidepressants) should be made with the guidance of a doctor who is well versed in addiction and who will carefully supervise its use. Do not rely on the opinions of your sponsor or others in AA or NA who may warn you to "stay away from the stuff," no matter how well-meaning. The fact is that sometimes such drugs must be used. (Of course, you must use precautions similar to those described above.) The medication and dosage should be reevaluated regularly; as soon as it ceases to be absolutely necessary, discontinue it under your doctor's care. (Read more about drugs for mental health in chapter 14, and drugs to treat addiction in chapter 5.)

SAFE DENTISTRY

The last thing most alcoholics or addicts think about when they are drinking or using is taking care of their teeth.

Then sobriety brings painful reality. Rotting teeth start to ache. Swollen, red gums feel sore. That overdue visit to the dentist becomes a necessity—and a risk.

In the Green Zone, it's time to finally get all the dental work you need done. But be sure your dentist understands what is and isn't safe for a patient in recovery. The following points are crucial if you're to keep your teeth without losing your sobriety:

- Dentists are licensed to prescribe the same medications as doctors—to sedate, tranquilize, and anesthetize—but they may be unaware of the risks of medicating a patient in recovery. If you don't forewarn your dentist, he won't know your situation. And what your dentist doesn't know can hurt you.

- Ask what type of mouthwash is used in the office. If it contains alcohol, bring your own or rinse with plain water.

- If you need repair work done, talk to your dentist ahead of time about anesthesia options. Never agree to nitrous oxide (laughing gas) or any other general anesthetic for routine dental work. A local anesthetic, such as Novocain, lidocaine, or Marcaine, which numbs the gums but not the brain, is okay. They resemble cocaine chemically but do not appear to be hazardous in recovery. If you get heart palpitations or a racing pulse with the use of lidocaine, ask if you can get it without the epinephrine component. Also safe for dental work are hypnosis and acupuncture. You can also try using guided imagery recordings focused on dental work or general relaxation.

- Do not take meperidine (Demerol), diazepam (Valium), tramadol (Ultram), acetaminophen with codeine (Tylenol 3), midazolam (Versed), or any other narcotic or tranquilizer (see Pain, page 513) either before or after a dental

procedure. Also avoid any other drug about which you have any doubts. That doesn't mean that you have to suffer. Ibuprofen (Advil, Nuprin, Motrin) is even more effective than narcotics when two or three are taken before a dental procedure and the dose is repeated six hours later. If you can't take ibuprofen, acetaminophen (Tylenol) or aspirin will relieve pain effectively enough. If these options fail to wipe out the pain completely, just remind yourself that a little pain is better than a big slip. (It's okay to take antibiotics before or after dental surgery.)

- Use nondrug treatment (such as cold therapy) when possible for pain after a dental procedure. Holding a bag of frozen peas to your jaw afterward can help quite a bit. Also try elevating your head when you sleep.

- If you need oral surgery and a local anesthetic won't suffice, check with your own doctor or one certified by ASAM to see if the planned anesthesia is appropriate, or if there might be a better way. If general anesthesia is indeed called for, it's best to perform the procedure in the hospital, following the guidelines in Safe Medical Care, above. If that's not possible, have your sponsor or another support person with you at the dental surgeon's office and plan to be surrounded by AA friends

THE GREEN ZONE

from the moment you arrive home until all aftereffects of the medication (including any cravings) have faded away. If you or your sponsor notice a return of cravings or risky thinking, implement your contingency plan—admission to a treatment center for a short stay, for example—until these effects have resolved.

SAFE HANDLING OF A MEDICAL EMERGENCY

If you twist your ankle or badly slice your finger, you'll probably head to an emergency room. But such a visit could be hazardous to your sobriety.

ER staffers are not likely to be well informed on the treatment of people in recovery. So be prepared. Carry in your wallet and your phone your sponsor's phone number and the numbers of several AA or NA friends; your doctor's number; and a copy of the Menacing Medications list on page 291. Also always carry with you a condensed version of your medical history: any medications you take, recent surgeries or diagnoses, and any other medications you need to avoid.

If possible, call your own doctor before you go to the ER. If he is available, you may be able to buy time with temporary measures—ice packs, for example—until he can come to your rescue. You may be lucky enough to have a doctor who will meet you at the ER, or at least call and tell the doctor in charge a little of your history and its risks.

If you can't reach your doctor, try to get your sponsor or another AA friend to meet you at the ER. If you are in no condition to call, ask someone else to call for you. When you get to the ER, show the staff your Menacing Medications list. If they seem to be ignoring your request to avoid those drugs, ask them to call your doctor. If the drug is for pain relief and you can grit it out, tell them you don't need it, or ask for an ibuprofen or acetaminophen instead. Ketorolac (Toradol) is also an option. It works best when the first dose is given by injection (as in the ER); later doses can be taken by mouth.

When your sponsor or another AA person gets there, he can act as your advocate. Between you, you should be able to persuade the ER staff that some drugs are very risky for you, but you may have to be very assertive. Don't worry about offending someone. This is your life at risk. Do not believe an ER doctor, no matter how wise he seems, if he says it's okay to take the drugs. It isn't. You need to always consider the risk of relapse if you take those drugs; it's usually greater than any risk you might face by doing without them.

One way to get the attention of a busy staff, wherever you are being treated, is to tell them you are "allergic" to alcohol and other drugs with a mood-altering effect (this is true—research shows that alcoholism is in part due to an allergic process in the brain). The medical and legal risks of prescribing drugs to someone who has volunteered information about an allergy will generally prevent a doctor from giving it to you, unless withholding it would be a greater threat to your life.

There may be times when a forbidden medication will have to be used—in life-and-death situations, when the pain is unbearable and nothing milder helps, or when serious mental illness is present. In any of these situations, follow the protocols discussed here as much as possible.

When the emergency is over and you're left with lingering pain, discomfort, or other symptoms, see the ideas in Nondrug Approaches to Common Medical Problems, page 494, for tips on how to cope.

Your Primary Health Issues Now

CANCER WARNING SIGNS

Alcoholics have an increased risk of certain cancers—most commonly those of the mouth, throat (pharynx), voice box (larynx), esophagus, liver, colon and rectum, breast, pancreas, and liver. Those who also smoked (tobacco, and probably marijuana) have an increased risk of cancer of the mouth and tongue, larynx, bladder, esophagus, kidneys, and lungs.

Talk with your doctor about which cancer screening tests you should have.

HAVE A SAFE AND SOBER PREGNANCY

"I've been sober for more than three years. I'm feeling fine, and would like to have a baby. Is there anything special I need to do?"

Before you start trying to conceive, do what you can to improve your health. Improve your diet. Give up smoking. Cut out or cut down on caffeine. Get into a good exercise routine. If you're over- or underweight, try to get as close to normal weight as possible. See your doctor for a preconception physical, and if you find you have any chronic conditions, such as diabetes, get them under control. You should be off all mood-altering prescription drugs by now, but if you aren't, talk with your doctor and try to get off them soon. Also, start taking a daily vitamin supplement that contains folate.

Once you start trying, avoid X-rays, unnecessary medications, cigarette smoke, and exposure to toxic chemicals.

And, of course, work hard at your recovery. A sober mom is the best gift you can give your future baby. Dad should also be sober before trying to conceive, since drugs could damage not only his fertility but the baby's future health as well.

To give your baby the best odds of being born healthy, and to be sure you come through pregnancy, labor, and delivery without hazard to your recovery, do the following:

THE GREEN ZONE

- Tell your doctor that you are in recovery; if you have an emergency later you want him to be aware of your special precautions.

- Continue to work hard on your recovery; a relapse could be disastrous for you both.

- Take childbirth classes to learn about labor and delivery, including how to deal with the pain in a natural and, if possible, drug-free way. If you don't have a spouse or partner to join you as coach, or maybe even if you do, ask your sponsor, a family member, or an AA friend to come to the classes, too. Taking a class and practicing the breathing exercises faithfully doesn't guarantee that you won't need drugs during labor and delivery, but it will improve your chances.

Talk about labor and delivery pain control options with your doctor and others before your due date.

- Line up some strategies to help you avoid using medication when you go to the hospital. Have your sponsor or another AA friend on hand, if possible. Take along some AA recordings and books. Try meditation, relaxation exercises, guided imagery, a focal point for visual concentration, counterpressure (your coach puts pressure on your back—with a rolling pin, a ball, or his hand— to counter the pressure from inside), and possibly TENS (see Pain, page 513), acupuncture, or hypnosis.

- If the pain becomes more than you feel you can bear, tell your doctor. Based on your behavior, your description of what you're feeling, and how far along you are in labor, he will decide on the wisdom of giving you medication. Your first choice should be a local anesthetic. If oral medication is needed, follow the protocols in Medication Concerns, page 475.

- A local anesthetic, such as a pudendal block (to allow for a painless episiotomy) or an epidural (which numbs your lower body but doesn't affect your mind), is safe for women in recovery. A tranquilizer or Demerol, on the other hand, should be avoided if at all possible. To avoid temptation, ask a professional familiar with your situation (such as a doctor certified by ASAM) to decide if medication is needed. The longer you've been in recovery, the higher your pain threshold will be, and the more likely you'll be able to tolerate the pain.

- If you have no other good options, let your obstetrician do whatever he thinks is needed for a safe delivery. If mood-altering drugs prove to be necessary, right after the birth you can put yourself back in the Red Zone for two to three weeks. Ramp up your recovery activities and stay there until your usual recovery thinking has returned. During that time, delegate important life decisions to your sponsor or another trusted person.

If you have a non-emergency Cesarean section, you will probably have an epidural or a spinal anesthetic. These forms of anesthesia won't significantly affect your recovery and will allow you to view the birth and feel alert after it. Don't take medication home with you for postpartum pain—it won't be good for you or, if you're nursing, for your baby.

Do remember that it's important to involve your partner in all of your preparations for childbirth, as well as in the delivery itself. If you do, you will find pregnancy a wonderful opportunity for growth in your relationship.

IF YOU ARE TERMINALLY ILL

Quality of life is paramount when there's not much of it left. For the terminal patient, there's a normal tendency to seek escape from pain through the use of narcotics.

But that's not the best place to start. Narcotics may be very effective for other patients. But for people with addiction, they often lose their effectiveness after just a few doses, especially if you had a high tolerance to them in the past. Then you're right back where you started—in pain, but now in

relapse mode, too. Sliding back into addiction will not only fail to enhance the quality of the last days of life, but it will also diminish it.

Even if you know your condition is terminal, work hard with your doctor to find relief for your symptoms without mood-altering drugs. Try the ideas in Nondrug Approaches to Common Medical Problems, on page 494, and make sure you have plenty of emotional support. And remember that pain and suffering are two different things—many of the skills and lessons you learned in your recovery program will help you to suffer much less during any illness.

Later, if narcotics become an essential last resort, at least that option has been preserved.

Your Healthy Lifestyle— the Clean and Sober Diet

EAT FOR YOUR HEALTH; EAT FOR RECOVERY

Now that you're finally in the Green Zone, it is time to really shake up your eating routine and instill some good dietary habits— habits that will serve you well for a lifetime.

When you were actively drinking or using you might have been starved for good nutrients. One reason is that alcohol's empty calories

THE GREEN ZONE

often replace the more useful elements of a normal diet.

A second reason is the damage alcohol inflicts on the body, particularly the digestive tract. It interferes with the efficient use of whatever nutrients are consumed. This results in a variety of problems: an increased risk of osteoporosis because of decreased metabolism of vitamin D; impairment of brain production of proteins; and, most commonly, deficiencies of vitamin A, folate, vitamin B6, and thiamine (B1). Deficiencies of zinc, iron, magnesium, vitamins E and K, and phosphate also are not unusual.

What food you did eat during your addiction probably bore no resemblance to a balanced diet, and poor nutrition can cause some serious damage. Too little calcium and you can develop osteoporosis (brittle bones). Too little iron: anemia. Insufficient thiamine: beriberi (with damage to the nervous system). Not enough fiber: higher risk of digestive problems and some types of cancer. Getting too much of some nutrients can also sap your health. Too many calories and you become obese and are at added risk for heart disease, stroke, diabetes, and other serious diseases. Too much fat and cholesterol, and the hazards of heart and blood vessel diseases, and some cancers, increase.

The Clean and Sober Diet is designed to overcome any malnutrition caused by your past alcohol or drug use, start you on your way to optimum health, and discourage cravings that can lead to relapse. It has the potential to improve both the quality and length of your life and enhance your recovery. Of course, no diet can guarantee a long and healthy life, or an abstinent one. But the diet that follows is designed to improve your chances of achieving both.

THE NUTRITIONAL COMMANDMENTS

In the Red and Yellow Zones, you started following some basic nutritional guidelines designed to help you curb cravings, avoid relapse, and become more aware of your diet: 1) plan for a safe "relapse," 2) eat three squares, 3) get plenty of fluids, 4) eat foods rich in B vitamins, 5) catch up on calcium, 6) shun sugar, 7) get more aware of what you eat, 8) start reading labels, and 9) find a good source of food.

Now you're ready to further expand your nutritional knowledge and change your eating behaviors. Start by absorbing and acting on these Clean and Sober nutritional commandments.

Variety Is More Than the Spice of Life

It's the key to healthy eating. No single food contains all the nutrients needed to sustain life, so eating a wide range of foods makes it much more likely you'll get those necessary nutrients over the course of a day or week.

So do what investors are supposed to do: diversify. Vary your daily intake among the Essential

Element choices (see page 486). Enjoy a wheat cereal one day, oats the next, and a seven-grainer the third. Vary dinner side dishes: brown rice, couscous, chickpeas. Do the same with all your food choices.

All Calories Are Not Created Equal

The 275 empty calories in a jelly doughnut are not equal to the 275 nutritious calories in a heaping bowl of oatmeal. Plus, the oatmeal keeps blood sugar levels stable a lot longer than the doughnut, avoiding a blood sugar dive and midmorning apathy. So choose your calories wisely. Opt for "nutrient dense" foods—the ones that are packed with vitamins, minerals, and other healthy components and have relatively few calories.

To reduce your risk of heart disease and cancer, most of your calories should come from plant sources: fruits, vegetables, whole grains, dried beans, and peas. A much smaller percentage of your calories should come from animal sources: fish, poultry, lean meats, and nonfat or low-fat dairy products. Very few of your calories should come from foods high in fat, sugar, or refined grains.

Sugar Highs Can Lead to Sugar Lows

The average American consumes 150 pounds of sugar a year, which translates to more than 750 sugar calories a day—calories that are totally lacking in nutritional value.

It's time to start changing your ways. Why?

- Sugar raises the risk of diabetes. And diabetes is a primary cause of kidney disease. You don't want to have to deal with dialysis or a kidney transplant after you've come this far.

- You could put yourself in the same nutritional boat you were in when you were using alcohol, consuming the empty calories of sugar instead of the empty calories of alcohol.

- Your body may be unable to handle sugar normally. Some researchers believe that alcoholics have either a glucose intolerance or an out-of-whack glucose metabolism. Since a steady supply of glucose in the blood is needed for good brain function, sudden dives can leave you depressed, irritable, and fatigued. That just makes you want more sugar (or alcohol). It's suspected that this seesaw effect can last for months or even years into recovery.

Others suspect there is a dysfunction in the brain that is critical to both the regulation of glucose metabolism and the production of the brain chemical serotonin (involved in mood regulation). When blood sugar drops in these people, the amount of serotonin does, too, and they can become depressed, irritable, impulsive, and even violent. This is the same area of the brain—the reward system— where alcohol and drugs exert their mood-altering effects. So you could be courting a drug or alcohol relapse by consuming even average quantities of sugar.

- You could become addicted to sugar. Some believe it's possible to become addicted to sugar just as it is to alcohol or drugs.

GET STARTED WITH BETTER FOODS

You want to improve your diet, but how do you start? Look at what you're eating now. If you're like most Americans, you may be unpleasantly surprised. If you started keeping a food diary back in the Yellow Zone, look at it now. If you didn't, keep a daily diet diary for a week. Compare what you've been eating to the Essential Elements foods below. This will give you some idea of what changes you need to make.

Next, sweep the cupboards clean. Get rid of foods with refined carbs (white flour, breads, refined cereals), sugar in any form (cookies, cakes, candy, ice cream), and hydrogenated or partially hydrogenated shortenings (those that are solid at room temperature).

Restock your shelves with whole-grain breads, cereals, and flours; peas and beans; fruit-juice-sweetened cookies and muffins; frozen fruit juice concentrates for cooking and baking; nonstick vegetable spray; and canola and olive oils. Replenish fresh fruits and vegetables regularly. Continue developing your label-reading expertise so you won't be misled by package hype.

THE ESSENTIAL ELEMENTS OF YOUR DIET

You could set up a chemistry lab in your kitchen to be sure you get all the nutrients you need every day. Or, you can just be sure to get your Essential Elements.

The portion sizes and nutritional information for the Essential Elements listed below are for fresh foods, raw or cooked, unless otherwise noted. Some foods give you double or triple credit. Broccoli, for example, qualifies as a green leafy vegetable serving, a vitamin C food serving, and a calcium serving.

Whole Grains and Legumes— 6 to 11 Servings Daily

These foods are rich in many of the nutrients that alcoholics and addicts lack, including the B vitamins and trace minerals. They are not fattening—as long as they aren't slathered with butter or drowned in rich sauces.

With occasional exceptions, all breads and cereals should be whole grain. And don't confuse these concentrated complex carbohydrates with simple carbohydrates like sugars, which should be avoided.

One complex carbohydrate serving equals: 1 slice bread; 1 small roll; or ½ bagel. Other options: 1 small pita bread; ½ cup cooked brown or wild rice, millet, kasha, unpearled barley; 1 tortilla; 2 to 6 whole wheat crackers; ½ to ⅔ cup cooked beans (kidney, lima, chickpeas, pinto) or peas (lentils, split, black-eyed); 1 ounce whole grain pasta; or 2 tablespoons wheat germ.

Calcium-Rich Foods— 2 to 5 Servings Daily

How much you need each day of calcium-rich foods depends on your age, gender, and other variables. For example, women generally require 3 servings daily, but 4 during pregnancy and 5 when nursing. Both males and females require 4 servings until they reach their mid-twenties. Anyone with a history of alcoholism probably requires more calcium rather than less, to compensate for the years their bones were deprived of the mineral by alcohol.

One calcium serving equals: 1 cup skim (nonfat) or low-fat milk or plain yogurt; ¾ cup Parmesan cheese; 1 to 1½ ounces hard cheese, such as Swiss or mozzarella; or 4 ounces canned salmon or 3 ounces canned sardines, with the bones. Other options: ¾ cup calcium-added milk or calcium-fortified orange juice; 1½ cups cooked kale, mustard, or turnip greens; 1¾ cups broccoli; 10 dried figs; or 3 cups cooked navy or pinto beans.

Vitamin C–Rich Foods— 1 to 3 Servings Daily, or More

This vitamin is important for everyone's good health. It helps normal tissues stay healthy and promotes healing of damaged tissue. It is said to be a natural mood booster, too. It's best to get your vitamin C from foods, rather than a supplement.

One vitamin C serving equals: ½ cup strawberries; 1½ cups fresh blueberries; 1½ cups most other berries; or ¼ cantaloupe. Other options: ⅛ honeydew melon; ½ grapefruit or ½ cup grapefruit juice; 1 small orange or ½ cup orange juice; 1 small kiwi; ½ large mango; ½ cup broccoli or Brussels sprouts; ⅔ cup cauliflower or kohlrabi; or 2 small tomatoes, ½ cup tomato purée, or 1 cup tomato juice.

Fruits and Vegetables— 4 to 6 Servings Daily, or More

Just like your mom always said, fruits and vegetables are packed with goodness. Eating a diet rich in fruits and veggies can lower your risk of many diseases. Eat at least 4 to 6 servings per day; some advocate 9 servings or more. Another way to measure: Try to fill half your plate with these foods. Be sure to get a lot of red, orange, and dark green vegetables. Serving sizes vary; you can eat essentially an unlimited amount of the leafy green veggies, but less of the foods that pack more calories, like avocados, or lots of carbs, like potatoes.

Protein-Rich Foods— 2 Servings Daily

This requirement is higher for pregnant women (4 full servings) and for others with special needs. It may be reduced to 1 or 1½ servings temporarily (on doctor's orders) in those with severe liver damage (vegetable protein may be tolerated better than that from animal sources). But patients with milder

THE GREEN ZONE

damage benefit from adequate protein intake, so check with your physician. Protein is particularly important in recovery because it helps keep blood sugar levels steady and repairs damaged tissue. Having some with each meal will help keep your blood sugar from dropping between meals, triggering a craving for sweets (or worse).

Iron-Rich Foods—Some Daily

Small amounts of iron are found in many of the fruits, vegetables, grains, and meats you consume every day. Eating some of the foods that are particularly rich in iron will help ensure you don't suffer from iron-deficiency anemia.

Iron-rich foods include: beef; carob flour or powder and baked goods made with them; chickpeas (garbanzo beans) and other dried peas and beans; dried fruits; Jerusalem artichokes; pumpkin seeds; sardines; soybeans, soy products (tofu, miso), and baked goods made with soy flour; and spinach.

Fat—In Limited Quantities

We used to think all fats were bad, but we now know that is not true. Too much fat in the diet is definitely bad for your health (linked to both cancer and heart disease, as well as altered blood cholesterol levels), but a diet without any fat is not good for you, either. Fats help with brain functioning and are a source of energy. They are also essential for controlling inflammation, keeping your hair and skin healthy, absorbing some vitamins, and clotting blood.

How much fat do you need? U.S. guidelines recommend the average adult consume no more than 20–35 percent of his total daily calories in the form of fat.

What kinds of fats are best? There are a few different types of fats: monounsaturated, polyunsaturated, saturated, and trans fats. To make a long story short:

- Monounsaturated and polyunsaturated fats are better for you (just remember to look for the "un" fats).

- Saturated fat intake should be minimal (no more than 10 percent of total daily calories).

- Trans fat intake should be as low as possible.

SALT

We don't need large amounts of this mineral in our diet. A lot of studies have shown that as salt intake rises, so does blood pressure. And high blood pressure puts you at risk for cardiovascular disease, kidney disease, and other ills.

The U.S. Department of Agriculture recommends no more than 2,300 milligrams (mg) of sodium a day (and less than 1,500 mg per day for people who are fifty-one and older, as well as those of any age who are African American or have high blood pressure, diabetes, or chronic kidney disease). Most of us consume about 3,400 mg per day—so it's time to cut back.

Add salt at the table rather than during cooking (most people use less this way). Use spices, herbs, lemon juice, vinegar, and other seasonings to spice up your food. Avoid salted nuts, pretzels, herring, olives, prepared salad dressings, and other highly salted foods, as well as any processed main course with more than 450 mg of sodium or side dish or dessert with more than 200 mg. Processed foods often are high in sodium and generally should be avoided.

CUT THE CAFFEINE

Caffeine (found in coffee, tea, and many soft drinks and medications) is a drug. It has some definite mood-altering effects (it peps some people up, and paradoxically calms others down), and heavy users can experience both side effects and withdrawal symptoms.

No research has linked this very common drug directly to relapse. And no research shows it is harmful in low doses. Still, there are some good reasons to eliminate caffeine from your recovery life: If you have panic attacks, agoraphobia (fear of crowded places), mood swings, or any type of anxiety disorder, they may be related to the consumption of caffeine. Since a panic attack could lead to feelings that some would treat with drugs, the caffeine could be an indirect trigger. Some people get the same kind of rush from caffeine that they get from alcohol and sugar—and the same kind of letdown later. That rush, in fact, is a very good reason to avoid those caffeine-rich energy drinks.

(Some treatment programs consider their use a relapse.)

If you are hyper, restless, or agitated, or experience sleep problems or palpitations, caffeine is the likely culprit. It may also aggravate premenstrual syndrome (PMS) or irritate a sensitive stomach (even decaf coffee may be irritating). In very large doses (more than eight cups of coffee a day), caffeine can cause a variety of serious symptoms, including restlessness, headache, disturbed sleep, heart irregularities, digestive tract irritation, diarrhea, and, in some people, delirium. That may sound like a lot of coffee, but not a few AA members drink as much at one meeting.

Cutting down on caffeine may be particularly important if you give up smoking. While you smoked, nicotine helped metabolize the caffeine more quickly. Without the nicotine, more caffeine will remain in your bloodstream longer, and you could suffer from a suddenly concentrated jolt of symptoms from the drug.

THE HERBAL TEASE

Herbal teas sound safe and natural. But herbs are drugs, and some of them have a mood-altering effect. Although many of the national brand herbal teas may be okay, avoid any that stimulate or change your mood or give your heart "skips" or palpitations. And stay away from exotic herbals, especially sassafras and comfrey, which can damage your liver—the last thing you need in recovery.

THE GREEN ZONE

Drinking green tea is safe for most people, but avoid having too much of it, as it does contain caffeine. Also avoid supplements made of green tea extract; they have been linked to liver damage.

Your Healthy Lifestyle: Exercise

Exercise can lower your weight, your blood pressure, and your cholesterol levels; reduce your risk of heart disease, diabetes, stroke, osteoporosis, and some cancers; and prolong your life. It's even been linked to a lower risk of "cognitive decline" and dementia.

Exercise can also address many of the issues you face as a person in recovery, and enhance the odds that your life will remain a long, sober one. It's the perfect replacement for the couple of drinks that helped you unwind after work. It improves self-image, chases sleep problems, enhances insulin sensitivity, and alleviates symptoms of mild to moderate depression and anxiety. It can alleviate much of the pain of mild to moderate arthritis and fibromyalgia. It helps control your weight by burning calories and speeding up metabolism, and makes stress easier to handle and reduces its effects on the body. It can preserve bone mass and reduce the risk of falling (very important for older folks). It enhances social skills and stimulates thinking.

Exercise also helps reconstruct lifestyles. A health-oriented life that builds in regular exercise usually has no room in it for the use of drugs or misuse of alcohol. Indeed, studies show improved abstinence rates for those in exercise programs compared to those who remain inactive. And it's crucial to healing your brain. Exercise improves your ability to learn and remember.

BEFORE YOU START

Before setting out on any exercise program more strenuous than walking, get your doctor's blessing. Depending on your age and condition, he may recommend you take a stress test.

PUT TOGETHER A VARIED PROGRAM

The best exercise program for you will depend on several factors—your health, your age, your personality and interests, your physical limitations or disabilities, your daily schedule, and the facilities available to you. One thing's for sure: There's a program that's right for you. The ideal program for a healthy person includes cardio, strength training, and flexibility activities. Choose activities you enjoy and can look forward to. Switch them up to avoid boredom. Take a dance class in the winter and take up running in the summer, for example. Take a kickboxing class at the gym during the week and go for a hike on the weekend. Exercise with a buddy if you enjoy company, by yourself if you're a loner. If you need structure to bolster your commitment to regular exercise, join a health club or exercise class. If you can afford it, get a personal trainer, even if it's only to help you set up a program.

Exercising with other people in recovery gives you a bonus: The time you spend exercising helps your recovery as well as your body.

Cardiovascular Exercise

Cardio workouts generally mean aerobic exercise: rhythmic, repetitive activity strenuous enough to stimulate the heart, lungs, and muscles and result in increased oxygen to the muscles. Popular aerobic exercises include walking, running, bicycling (stationary or moving), working out on an elliptical or other machine, tennis singles, cross-country skiing, rowing, jumping rope, aerobic dancing, and swimming. Most of these are also weight-bearing exercises, and will also help strengthen your bones (swimming is the exception).

Some types of aerobic exercise are safer than others. Walking and cross-country skiing, for example, are less likely to lead to injury than running. Aquatic exercise can be both aerobic and nonimpact, making it a perfect activity for people with arthritis, back pain, or other limitations.

Most adults should get at least 150 minutes of moderate-intensity cardio exercise each week, or 20 to 60 minutes of vigorous-intensity exercise. You can break it up however you want, as long as each session is at least ten minutes long. Vigorous activities include running, singles tennis, spinning, using the elliptical, and playing sports such as soccer and basketball. Moderate activities include brisk walking, mowing the grass, doubles tennis, and doing tai chi or yoga.

Resistance/Strength Training

Strength training involves working out each of the major muscle groups, usually with free weights or machines. But you don't have to be that high-tech. Results soon begin to show even with old-fashioned push-ups or chin-ups, where the weight is you, or heavy gardening, where you are shoveling and digging. Strength training is crucial: It can increase your ability to engage in an aerobic program by strengthening your muscles and endurance and reducing your risk of injury. It will also make you more fit for other tasks—such as moving furniture or carrying children. For the recovering alcoholic/addict, it's a great way to rebuild muscle mass and restore muscle tone.

Aim to train each major muscle group two or three times a week, waiting at least two days to rework each group. In other words, you can train your arms and back one day, train your legs the next day, and then return to your upper body the third day. Start with eight to twelve repetitions on each exercise, and do two to four sets of each.

Flexibility

Well-designed and properly performed stretching exercises

THE GREEN ZONE

(including yoga) enhance flexibility, maintain and extend freedom of movement, and help you dodge the stiffness that can come with age. Like strength training, flexing can improve your aerobic performance, but it's not clear that doing stretching exercises before and after your aerobic workout will prevent injury. Some studies show that done regularly, such exercise does reduce injury frequency. Aim to do some flexibility exercises at least two or three days a week.

EXERCISE SAFELY

Exercise is a lifestyle-enhancer, but like every endeavor it can involve some minor risks if you don't approach it properly. You might want to start your program working out in a class or with a personal trainer, where you will have someone guiding you and watching your technique. This is particularly useful if you are new to an activity such as weight training or yoga. You don't have to spend a lot of money on a trainer or a fancy gym membership, either. Check out city rec centers, the YMCA, and community centers, or join a running club or another outing group.

Start Slowly

If you're like a lot of alcoholics/ addicts, you tend to plunge into things headlong—new drugs, new kicks, new activities. But the physical and mood changes you're looking for with exercise will come slowly from consistent, ever-increasing efforts. If a fierce compulsion to get into shape rules your exercise plan, you're sure to do too much too soon, damage muscles and joints, and cause needless aches and pains and possibly serious side effects. Feeling discouraged could make you an early dropout—a serious side effect in itself.

So, if you've been sedentary, limit yourself to no more than five minutes of strenuous exercise the first few times out. Your body seems to be adjusting well to your chosen activity? Great. Extend that exercise period by a few minutes each day until you reach twenty to thirty minutes. If walking—a nice safe way to get started—is your exercise of choice, start with ten minutes and work up to an hour.

If you have a new pair of running shoes you're itching to use, cover half a mile by walking two blocks and then running one. In later sessions (on alternative days to avoid stress to legs and back), work up to two running and one walking, then drop the walking and, if you're having no trouble with breathlessness, keep adding blocks until you've reached your target of a couple of miles or more.

When strength training, start with the very lightest weights and work with them for several days. Increase the number of repetitions gradually over a week or more, before moving to the next size weights. When you do move up, start with just a few reps, and then work your way up again.

Start each workout slowly in order to gently stretch your muscles and start increasing your heart rate and blood flow. Walk a few blocks at a leisurely pace or pedal your stationary bike slowly. Then build up to the heart of your workout. Add five to ten minutes of lower intensity exercise at the end of your workout to cool down.

Set Realistic Goals

Alcoholics/addicts tend to think big and go to extremes: "I'm going to start running today, and by two weeks from Tuesday I'll be ready for the Ironman Triathlon." That kind of thinking will doom your program to failure and can damage the very body you are trying to get healthier. So set attainable goals and aim to meet them gradually (working with a trainer will help a lot here). Moderation should be your byword in exercise, as in everything else in your recovery. The ultimate goal is to achieve a healthy and sustainable exercise program. Don't go out to set world's records. Go out to enjoy each day's physical activity and the good feelings it brings.

Be Consistent

Exercising one week then skipping the next will avail you nothing. By the time your sedentary week is over, many of the benefits of your active one will have disappeared. Exercising like crazy for a month, then skipping two months, will do you no good physically and could increase the risk of injury. To have a beneficial effect, exercise has to be as regular as the six o'clock news, at least three times a week. Devise a plan you can follow.

Tune In to Your Body

Remember that you're not into abusing your body these days. So listen when it speaks to you through fatigue (slow down or quit for the day); pain (take the stress off the injured body part, rest up until the injury is healed, and then gradually restart exercising at a lower intensity); dizziness, light-headedness, headache, or nausea (stop, and check with the doctor if these symptoms appear again when you're working out).

If you're so winded you can't carry on a conversation while exercising, you may be overdoing it—slow down or stop. But in general, relax, enjoy, and stay loose. Don't allow a fear of injury to interfere with your concentration; because it increases muscle tension, fear will actually make you more injury-prone.

Chest pain during exertion that subsides after a few minutes of rest may be angina, a serious sign of heart disease. This pain is usually in the midline of the chest, but it can be felt in other places, such as the jaw or arm (usually the left). In this condition, fatty deposits partially block one or more arteries supplying blood to the heart. With heavy exercise, an inadequate blood flow results in pain. Many therapeutic options are available, so you should see your doctor within a day or two of experiencing angina. If the pain is severe and doesn't go away in

THE GREEN ZONE

fifteen or twenty minutes, call 911 or have someone drive you directly to the emergency room.

Adapt to Your Schedule

If you plan an exercise program that's impossible to carry out, it will be just that. So plan one that will work for you. Research shows that you can break your exercise up into small segments throughout the day with no loss of benefits. All you need is ten minutes a pop. So if you don't have time for more than a five-minute warm-up, a ten-minute run, and a quick cooldown and shower in the morning, you're fine. Just add enough segments to reach 150 minutes total per week.

If you find your exercise program is cutting into your recovery program, consider combining the two. Listen to recovery recordings while you run or walk. Watch recovery videos while on the elliptical. Get your exercise by walking, instead of driving, to fellowship meetings. Ask others in recovery to join you on a hike, and talk about your programs.

Nondrug Approaches to Common Medical Problems

FIND SOME NEW WAYS TO DEAL WITH MEDICAL ISSUES

Turn on your computer, open a magazine, or switch on the radio, and you will surely hear that there's a pill to cure whatever hurts you. It's no wonder, then, that from earliest childhood we learn to rely on the quick fix for solving our problems, rather than getting to the source of an issue and solving it. But when you're in recovery, the quick fix is no longer the best fix.

In fact, we should all see drugs and medications as a last resort in treating minor medical problems at home. Cultivating such a point of view can help everyone to avoid or leave behind the mind-set that popping a pill is the answer to virtually every problem in life. It's particularly useful in teaching children to live drug-free lives.

Just as it's important for your general health to learn to read labels in the supermarket, it's important for your recovery health to learn to read labels in the drugstore. Avoid all suspicious ingredients (including alcohol, antihistamines, codeine and other narcotics, sedatives, and stimulants) and any product that warns of drowsiness. If you are in doubt about anything, check the list of drugs that are acceptable for pilots (see Medication Concerns, page 290).

Of course, sometimes medication is necessary. So don't reject it when the benefits outweigh the risks. But think it through: Is the benefit of this drug really more important than the risk of relapse it poses? If it will save your life, it probably is. But if it's not necessary to save your life, and it has mood-altering qualities or carries any other risk of relapse, you are probably better off without it.

There are many medications that do not put recovery at risk, and which may be necessary at times. For example, antibiotics, insulin, diuretics, anticoagulants, most blood pressure medications, and heart failure medications are generally used to treat or prevent severe or potentially fatal illnesses, and are relatively safe. Alcohol-free children's medications that do not contain any other risky ingredients that alter mood or thinking, taken in doses recommended for age twelve and over, may also be okay.

Knowing what to avoid, what is safe, and what to do as a last resort to treat the most common illnesses will help safeguard your recovery. Below are lots of options for dealing with common ailments, as well as guidance on what to avoid.

Remember, you are always better off if you can eliminate the cause, rather than simply treating the symptoms.

THE BEST MEDICINE— YOUR RECOVERY PROGRAM

No matter what ails you, keeping your recovery program strong is your best medicine. More than 350 illnesses have been linked to the use of alcohol; avoiding it—one day at a time—for the rest of your life reduces your risk of all of them. Alcoholics who relapse are much more likely to die before their time

than other people. Alcoholics who stay sober eventually have a life expectancy as long as that of nonalcoholics. Experts speculate that the outlook is equally grim for those who misuse other drugs.

ALLERGIES

Treatment to avoid: Popping a pill. Particularly risky are most antihistamines, which, though they do counteract the allergic response, are mood-altering. Avoid all allergy medicines containing antihistamines, alcohol, or ephedrine or pseudoephedrine, including brompheniramine (Dimetapp), cetirizine (Zyrtec), chlorpheniramine (Chlor-Trimeton, Allerest, Contac, Coricidin, Sinutab), diphenhydramine (Benadryl, Nytol, Sominex, Tylenol PM), dimenhydrinate (Dramamine), doxylamine (Vicks NyQuil, Alka-Seltzer Plus Night), and triprolidine (Actifed). However, some allergies can cause a potentially life-threatening anaphylactic shock. This situation justifies using anything that will reverse the condition.

Treatment to substitute: First of all, before you treat, make sure you have allergies. Some symptoms of alcoholism mimic them. Alcohol can wash oils and proteins out of skin and mucous membranes, causing runny, sniffly noses, watering eyes, and peeling skin. Other drugs can cause nasal symptoms, skin rashes, and assorted allergy-like symptoms. If you are sure allergy is the problem, try a nondrug approach

THE GREEN ZONE

first. There are two ways of dealing with allergy: One is by doing
something about the allergen that
is triggering the symptoms, and the
other is by treating the person having the allergic response. It's best to
do both.

The Allergens

Try to identify what is driving your
immune system crazy. Sometimes
it's obvious (every time a cat pads
by, you sneeze). Sometimes a little
detective work is necessary. If you
think a food is causing the problem,
eliminate one or more suspects from
your diet and see if the symptoms
ease up. If they do, and they then
return when you eat the food again,
you have your culprit. If it's pollen,
note if symptoms worsen when pollen counts are high. If you always
have a reaction in one room of the
house and not others, try to figure
out what's different in that room. If
you fail to uncover the tormenting
allergen, have an allergist do skin
testing.

Once you know, or even suspect,
what the offenders are, try to eliminate them from your life. At home,
you might try to create one allergy-
free room—ideally your bedroom.
Consider the following:

- **Foods.** Avoid eating anything
  that triggers a reaction.

- **Animal dander.** Stay away from
  dogs and cats. If you have a
  pet, you may have to find a new
  home for it (unless you can be
  desensitized).

- **Indoor allergens.** Keep your
  home as dust-free as possible.
  Dust frequently with a damp
  cloth or furniture spray; vacuum
  upholstery and carpeting, damp-
  mop floors, and wash curtains
  and similar items often. Avoid
  chenille bedspreads, velour
  upholstery, and any kind of
  carpeting, draperies, and other
  items that can harbor dust,
  mites, and mold where you sleep.
  Install an air cleaner, and place
  filters over forced-air vents.
  Avoid fans (which can stir up
  allergens) and replace your air-
  conditioner filters with HEPA
  filters. If you live in a humid
  climate, use an air conditioner
  to lower the humidity in your
  home; humidity promotes the
  buildup of allergens. Rugs and
  carpets are often hideouts for
  sinister allergens. Dust, mites,
  mite and roach droppings,
  other animal debris, mold, and
  chemical residues collect in
  carpet pile and may be almost
  impossible to get out and keep
  out. Hardwood, tile, and vinyl
  flooring are good substitutes.
  If you have carpeting that can't
  be easily replaced, first try
  sprinkling borax on it. Another
  option is a sturdy plastic or
  microfiber covering on carpets;
  though less than elegant,
  it should minimize allergic
  reactions. Mites also love to live
  in your mattress and pillows.
  Plastic covers for your bedding
  may substantially improve your

allergy symptoms, if they are the culprit. Also change your linens often, and wash them in hot water—if possible, 130–140 degrees. If your fabrics can't handle hot water, put them in the freezer for forty-eight hours to kill the mites.

- **Pollen.** Allergies to pollen are very common, and usually recognizable by their seasonal appearance. Pollens from weeds, trees, and grass are the most likely to make you miserable, but there are several things you can try to keep them at bay. Watch the local pollen counts on the news or a website (try weather.com/activities/health/allergies) and do what you can to limit exposure on high pollen count days. Limit your outdoor activities to when counts are lowest—generally the afternoon or after a rainstorm. Keep your windows closed and use your air conditioner to keep indoor humidity low and to minimize circulating allergens. Shower and wash your hair at night, to avoid sleeping with the enemy. Don't hang your clothes outside to dry. When in your car, keep your windows closed and use the air conditioner. Change your car's air filter as recommended.

- **Molds.** Mold can be a problem anywhere, at any time of year, especially in damp climates. If the humidity level is too high in any part of your home, try to lower it by using a well-maintained dehumidifier, providing adequate ventilation, and making sure that steam in the kitchen, laundry, and bathrooms is vented to the outside. Use an antimold agent to carefully clean areas where molds are likely to grow (garbage cans, refrigerators, shower curtains, bathroom tiles, damp corners). Limit the number of houseplants in the rooms where you spend a lot of time, and store firewood away from the house.

  When outside, avoid damp wooded areas, particularly where fallen leaves and tree stumps have been left to decay. Be sure drainage is adequate around your house. Rake leaves frequently so they don't have time to begin to grow mold, or have someone else rake them; dispose of leaves and other garden debris promptly. Cover your child's sandbox when it rains. And allow plenty of sun to reach your property (mold thrives in the shade).

- **Bee venom.** If you've ever had a bad reaction to a bee sting, see your doctor about the possibility that you are allergic to the venom.

- **Miscellaneous allergens.** There are many other potential allergens that can be removed from your environment as necessary: wool blankets; down or feather pillows; tobacco smoke; perfumes; soaps and cosmetics.

THE GREEN ZONE

The Person

It isn't possible to eliminate all allergens from your life. Instead, you may be able to change the way you respond to them by undergoing desensitization. See your doctor about this; you'll need to be tested to have the correct allergies identified.

You can also try treating the symptoms—for example, hot showers and humidifiers for respiratory problems. Try a saline nasal spray to clear out your nose.

Last-resort treatment: If an antihistamine is required, try Claritin (loratadine) or Allegra (fexofenadine). They travel from the bloodstream into the brain only minimally and don't have as potent a mood-altering effect. Singulair (montelukast sodium) is also okay, as long as there is good monitoring. Older allergy drugs, because they typically have more severe effects on wakefulness and thinking, pose a much higher risk of relapse.

In certain cases, your doctor may suggest topical or inhaled steroids (including nasal sprays such as Flonase, Nasacort, or Rhinocort), or a short course of oral steroids. You may want to avoid nasal sprays, however, if you snorted your drugs, as using a spray could be a trigger.

ANXIETY

Treatment to avoid: Medications seem like an easy way to rid yourself of anxiety. But the easy way, as you have undoubtedly learned by now, usually isn't the best way. To protect your recovery, avoid all sedatives like benzodiazepines and other mood-altering drugs, including those containing alprazolam (Xanax), aripiprazole (Abilify), buspirne hydrochloride (BuSpar), chlordiazepoxide (Librium, Limbitrol), clorazepam (Klonopin), clorazepate (Tranxene), diazepam (Valium), flurazepam (Dalmane), halazepam (Paxipam), haloperidol (Haldol), lorazepam (Ativan), midazolam (Versed), oxazepam (Serax), prazepam (Centrax), quetiapine (Seroquel), risperidone (Risperdol), temazepam (Restoril), thioridazine (Mellaril), thiothixine (Navane), trazodone (Desyrel), triazolam (Halcion), ziprasidone (Geodon), and zolpidem (Ambien).

Treatment to substitute: Anxiety can best be eliminated by getting rid of the cause. When this isn't possible, coping with the cause and desensitizing yourself to the symptoms can lessen the anxiety. Meditation, exercise, relaxation techniques, yoga, going to a fellowship meeting, and talking to your sponsor or counselor all help. In severe cases, see a professional for more help; he may be able to help you develop some even better coping methods and avoid using drugs. For more tips, see chapter 14.

Last-resort treatment: If your anxiety is long-lasting (more than a few weeks), debilitating (interfering with your work or other parts of your life), or has you thinking self-destructive thoughts, get more help from a professional. Be sure to find someone who is experienced in working with recovering alcoholics/

addicts. Talk and behavioral therapy may be sufficient. (Do keep in mind that as your brain continues to heal, your anxiety may ease up and return to a level where it's a useful emotion.)

ARTHRITIS

Treatment to avoid: Do not use mood-altering painkillers (see Pain, page 513).

Treatment to substitute: Apply creams containing salicylates to painful joints. Heat (hot baths, whirlpools, heating pads, or an electric blanket), exercise, and weight loss (if you're overweight) may also help. There is also some evidence that a vegetarian, gluten-free diet may help reduce symptoms.

Last-resort treatment: Use aspirin, ibuprofen (Advil, Medipren, Motrin, Nuprin), or acetaminophen (Anacin III, Datril, Tylenol), as directed by your doctor. Studies show they are generally as effective as stronger drugs. When an anti-inflammatory action is needed, aspirin, ibuprofen, or other non-steroidal anti-inflammatory drugs (NSAIDs) are best.

ASTHMA

Treatment to avoid: If possible, avoid over-the-counter anti-asthma medicines. These drugs produce a stimulant side effect, usually making the user jittery.

Treatment to substitute: Preventing an asthma attack is the best way to go, since treatment always has a

risk (and because your breathing capacity may be significantly compromised by the time symptoms are very noticeable). If your attacks are caused by allergies, eliminate as many triggers as possible (see Allergies). If you have exercise-induced asthma, talk with your doctor about how you can exercise without having a flare-up. Take good care of yourself and try to avoid colds and other upper respiratory infections, as well as excessive stress, all of which can also bring on an attack.

Asthma can be a very risky illness, so rather than trying home remedies or over-the-counter treatments, work with your doctor to develop a monitoring and maintenance plan. Ask your doctor to teach you how to monitor your bronchoconstriction with a peak flow meter; it's a better way to keep an eye on things than simply watching for symptoms. You may need two different types of treatments: maintenance, which seeks to prevent symptoms, and rescue, which is used in the event of an asthma attack. For people in recovery, it's better to use ongoing maintenance therapy, rather than frequently using a rescue inhaler.

Tilade (nedocromil), an inhaled anti-inflammatory agent, is a good choice for maintenance treatment in mild cases of asthma. Another maintenance option, an inhaled steroid such as Flovent (fluticasone), Azmacort (triamcinolone), AeroBid (flunisolide), or Beclovent (beclomethasone), is more effective and

THE GREEN ZONE

relatively safe because the effect is primarily local—in the lungs. Another alternative is a medication such as Singulair (montelukast sodium).

Most rescue inhalers use albuterol, which stimulates the airway muscles to open up passages. Check the ingredients carefully, however, as some use alcohol as a propellant; avoid those. You need to keep the rescue inhaler with you at all times.

Because asthma treatment carries some risk of relapse, be sure your care is supervised by a doctor who understands this, and that you both follow the safe medication precautions in Medication Concerns, page 475.

Last-resort treatment: Other options include steroids or albuterol delivered via a nebulizer (a machine that suspends the drug in a mist that is inhaled over several minutes).

BACKACHE

Treatment to avoid: All narcotics and other risky painkillers (see Pain, page 513). Muscle relaxants are often prescribed for back pain, but they don't fix your back—they just sedate your brain. This is clearly not a good option for someone who wants to stay sober.

Treatment to substitute: Bed rest during an acute episode; slowly ramp up activities as you start to feel better. After that, focus on exercise, particularly any that aims at strengthening the abdominal muscles that support the back;

good posture (with pelvis thrust forward and spine as little curved as possible); care in bending (bend at the knees, not at the waist) and lifting (use your legs, not your back); a firm mattress (sleep with knees bent); chairs that support the spine. Many people can get relief with massage, a heating pad, hot tub soaks, or acupuncture. Also try the pain-relief tips on page 514. A physical therapist sometimes helps.

Last-resort treatment: The safer pain relievers (aspirin, acetaminophen, ibuprofen). Ibuprofen and other NSAIDs (such as naproxen) can be particularly helpful in relieving stubborn pain; they also decrease inflammation. Check with your doctor if all else fails. If you are referred to an orthopedic specialist, make sure your own physician is involved in any medication decisions. If surgery is needed, be sure to follow the safe medication recommendations on page 476. (Also, if you have a sudden backache along with fever, or with pain on urination, call your doctor. It might be a urinary tract infection.)

COLDS AND FLU

Treatment to avoid: Medications containing antihistamines (see Allergies, page 495), as well as all nasal sprays and drops or mouthwashes containing alcohol or antihistamines. Also avoid decongestants, such as phenylephrine and pseudoephedrine. And, because colds and flu are caused by viruses, skip the antibiotics.

Treatment to substitute: Adding humidity to indoor air; safe saline nose drops or sprays, such as Ayr, Ocean, and Nasal, or mix your own; menthol/eucalyptus lozenges; hot fluids (one cup per hour during the day); Vicks VapoRub; and, of course, chicken soup. Large doses of vitamin C (2,000–4,000 milligrams a day) are controversial, but some studies find this reduces symptoms. If you have a severe sore throat, see your doctor for a throat culture to make sure you don't have a strep infection.

Last-resort treatment: Decongestant nasal sprays may provide brief relief, but when their use is stopped, there is a rebound effect: Symptoms become worse than before. It may help to use such a spray two or three times to clear the sinuses and then switch over to a saline solution. For fever and aches and pains, take the safer painkillers (see Pain, page 513).

CONSTIPATION

Treatment to avoid: Chemical laxatives (such as Correctol, Ex-Lax, Feen-a-mint, Senokot) are not recommended for anyone because they can damage the bowel. They can also be habit-forming, so they are particularly unwise for people in recovery. Stool softeners such as mineral oil are also risky, because they sweep out fat-soluble vitamins (A, D, E) along with stool and, if inhaled, can damage the lungs. Old standards, such as Epsom salts and milk of magnesia, which are known as osmotic agents, are a bit

safer, but dependence on them can also develop. Least risky are bulking agents, such as bran, psyllium (Metamucil), and methyl cellulose (Citrucel), but including fiber in your diet naturally is a better alternative. If you're on a laxative, you may have to be weaned from it gradually to let your intestinal motility return to normal.

Treatment to substitute: Many people who think they are constipated really aren't. They equate infrequent bowel movements with constipation. But it's as normal to have a movement every three days as it is to have one three times a day. Only when the movement has to be forced, when there is gassiness and bloating, and when the stool itself is dry and hard is constipation present. If you're not constipated and you want to stay that way, or if you are and would rather not be, the following will all help:

- **Prompt action.** If you've got to go, go. If you don't respond to the urge to go, your body withdraws it. If you deny your body often enough the result is constipation.

- **Medication monitoring.** Something as innocent as an iron or calcium supplement or an aluminum- or calcium-based antacid can cause constipation. So can a variety of prescribed medications. If you associate constipation with a new medication, let your doctor know. Usually you can switch to a less constipating formula. (If your calcium-based antacid is the culprit, switch to one that uses magnesium.)

- **A diet high in insoluble fiber.** That means wheat bran (not oat or barley, which, though possibly helpful in reducing cholesterol, are soluble), fruits, vegetables, legumes (dried beans and peas), and whole grain cereals and breads. Particularly helpful are apples, figs, pears, prunes, prune juice, or prune juice followed by hot coffee. Any hot drink is, in fact, stimulating to the colon. Many people find that hot water with lemon juice first thing in the morning works like a charm.

- **Moderate exercise.** A good brisk walk a couple of times a day or a half-dozen sit-ups is often enough to get things moving.

- **Adequate fluid.** Well-moistened food will make its trip through your digestive tract more quickly and smoothly. Always drink at least a full cup of liquid when you have a high-fiber meal. At least six to eight glasses of water a day (we're not talking soda here) should not only help your constipation problem but keep your skin moist as well.

Last-resort treatment: If these measures fail, check with your doctor. You need a medical exam to be sure there is no underlying disorder. If the diagnosis is just garden-variety constipation, a bulking agent, stool softener, or enema may be recommended for temporary use. Lactulose is a good laxative, especially for people with liver disease. Another laxative, Miralax, can also be taken on occasion for five days.

COUGHING

Treatment to avoid: Most prescribed cough medicines are in the risky category. So are a number of over-the-counter cough preparations. Many contain alcohol, codeine, ephedrine, pseudoephedrine, hydrocodone, and/or risky antihistamines (see Allergies, page 495) or decongestants. Risky cough medications include Delsym (dextromethorphan), Dimetane-DX, Fedahist Expectorant Syrup, Robitussin, Triaminicol Multi-Symptom, Vicks Formula 44, and all multisymptom cold preparations.

Treatment to substitute: Humidification of air; bathroom steam, created by running the shower at maximum heat (but not with you in it); hot liquids (one cup per hour of chicken soup, other clear soups, tea, or fruitade made with hot water and fruit juice); Vicks VapoRub; menthol eucalyptus cough drops, hard candies, or simple throat lozenges (Cepastat, Chloraseptic); Hold cough lozenges; honey and lemon; hot shower (let water beat on your back); or an ice pack on the neck. If you have a severe cough that is not helped by these tips, use a cough medicine that has only an expectorant (guaifenesien), such as Mucinex. It will help loosen the congestion. If you're a smoker, giving up tobacco will help.

Last-resort treatment: Call the doctor if you are running a fever with the cough, if the cough is interfering with your sleep, if it persists without improvement for more than a week, or if you are coughing up sputum that is darkish yellow, greenish, blood-tinged, or has a foul odor. You may have developed a bacterial or other nonviral infection of the bronchial tubes or lungs, or another medical problem that needs attention. The right antibiotic will usually knock an infection right out and will be safe to take in recovery.

Keep in mind that a cough related to a past cocaine or marijuana habit can last weeks into recovery, and needs only symptomatic treatment.

DEPRESSION

Treatment to avoid: All stimulants, antidepressants, and other psychoactive drugs, including amitriptyline (Elavil, Endep), amphetamine and/or dextroamphetamine (Adderall, Biphetamine, Dexedrine, Obetrol), bupropion hydrochloride (Wellbutrin), citalopram (Celexa), doxepin (Sinequan), duloxetine (Cymbalta), escitalopram (Lexapro), fluoxetine hydrochloride (Prozac), imipramine (Tofranil), methamphetamine (Desoxyn), methylphenidate (Ritalin), mirtazapine (Remeron), paroxetine (Paxil), perphenazine-amitriptyline (Triavil), phenmetrazine (Preludin), sertraline (Zoloft), and trazodone.

Treatment to substitute: The first line of defense against mild depression is your recovery; research confirms that many people who stick with AA get better long-term depression improvement than people who take antidepressant medications. Also helpful are activity, people, and generally being involved in a meaningful life. So get out there and get busy. See chapter 14 for tips on banishing the blues.

Last-resort treatment: When depression becomes severe and doesn't lift, interferes with your sleeping, eating, or working, or is triggering self-destructive thoughts, get professional help. Often, talk therapy can pull you out of depression. If depression is severe and intractable, and nondrug methods are not helping, medication may be an option; see Medication Exceptions, page 292, for tips on its safe use.

DIARRHEA

Treatment to avoid: Antidiarrheals containing narcotics, phenobarbital, opium, or other risky drugs (such as Donnagel PG, Imodium A-D, Lomotil, Parepectolin).

Treatment to substitute: Bed rest and fluids (water, weak tea, Gatorade, or orange juice diluted half and half with water). Fluids are important to prevent dehydration, but avoid sugar-sweetened beverages, which can prolong diarrhea. The doctor may recommend a special oral rehydration preparation to replenish the fluids and other chemicals your body has lost (you can also make your own by dissolving ½ teaspoon

THE GREEN ZONE

of salt and 5 teaspoons of sugar in a quart of water). If you are hungry, eat plain white rice or pasta, or white toast with a fruit spread. It's not necessary to starve yourself, but avoid high-fiber foods (including fruits, vegetables other than potatoes without the skin, and whole grains), undiluted juices, and milk until bowel movements have been normal for a day or two.

Last-resort treatment: To allow nature to sweep the offending virus out of your body, do not take medication for the first six to eight hours. Then take Kaopectate or another kaolin product, or Pepto-Bismol, if needed. Call the doctor if diarrhea persists for more than two days, or if it is severe (more than two or three times an hour, or eight times a day), bloody, black, or contains worms. Also call if diarrhea is accompanied by fever over 101 degrees for more than a day, or by persistent pain in the abdomen or rectum; any of these conditions could mean you need intravenous hydration or another treatment.

EARACHES

Treatment to avoid: Risky painkillers (see Pain, page 513).

Treatment to substitute: Heat applied with heating pad set on low, a hot-water bag filled with warm water, or warm compresses, while waiting to speak to your doctor. Ear infections usually require medical attention; your doctor will probably prescribe antibiotics. If you get an earache with a head cold, try relieving middle ear pressure by holding your nose and swallowing or blowing.

Last-resort treatment: The safer pain medications (acetaminophen, ibuprofen).

HEADACHES

Treatment to avoid: All risky painkillers (see Pain, page 513).

Treatment to substitute: "Take two aspirin" is the classic prescription for headache, but that shouldn't be your first choice. Initially, try prevention. To minimize the likelihood of headache, try to figure out what triggers your headache and what you can avoid in the future. Often a heightened sensitivity to life situations will trigger a "stress" headache. Also, "vascular" headaches, similar to migraines, are not uncommon while your body adjusts to living without drugs. Headaches generally ease up over time as your conscious or subconscious drug-seeking thoughts change to the healthier thoughts and attitudes of recovery. In the meantime, try the following:

- **Eat regularly.** Many headaches are hunger-related.

- **Exercise regularly.** This may reduce tension and, with it, headaches related to stress.

- **Relax regularly.** Several powerful muscles connect to the sides and base of the skull. If you have difficulty relaxing, these muscles tense up and pull constantly. The result: a headache. Learning and practicing relaxation techniques (see chapter 14) will help not just with headaches, but with many other aspects of your recovery as well. Using your leisure time for pleasurable activities will also help you relax and reduce the chances of tension-caused headaches. Pursue active hobbies that allow you to interact with others in a healthy fashion (hiking, volunteer work) or produce results (fresh-caught fish, a bevy of beautiful photos, homemade bread); they are better in the long run than passively watching videos or sports. But it's certainly okay to collapse in front of the tube or hang out on Facebook once in a while after a tough day.

- **Get adequate rest and sleep.** Lack of sleep and insufficient rest can make your head pound.

- **Attend fellowship meetings regularly.** Headaches are less likely to be a problem if you unload the feelings that may be causing them.

- **Cope with problems promptly.** The stress of accumulated worries can lead to headaches. Sometimes you just have to accept your problems; your recovery program will help you do that.

- **Avoid noisy stores and loud music.**

- **Avoid stuffy quarters.** Working, sleeping, or living in a warm, smoky, poorly ventilated space can lead to headaches. Keep windows open and the air circulating at home and at work. If you can't open the windows at work, try to take a walk during your lunch break.

- **Avoid allergens.** If you have a history of allergies, you may get sinus headaches from exposure to a variety of substances, including tobacco smoke, dust, dust mites, dog dander, perfume, and incense. See Allergies, page 495.

- **Avoid entirely, or at least reduce, caffeine intake and cigarette or cigar smoking.** Both caffeine and nicotine can cause rebound headaches.

- **Avoid refined sugar.** In some people, sugar can lead to lightheadedness or headache, possibly caused by a seesaw effect: a rapid rise in blood sugar levels shortly after ingestion of the substance, followed by a sudden drop a while later.

If you do get a headache, try the following:

- Lie down in a quiet, dark room with your eyes closed.

- Meditate or do relaxation exercises; listen to guided imagery.

- Eat if you think you have a hunger headache. But don't overeat.

- If you suspect anxiety or tension is the culprit, deal with the problem that's plaguing you.

THE GREEN ZONE

- If stuffy indoor air is making your head spin, open the windows or go outside.

- If your sinuses are pounding, try a heating pad, hot compresses, or alternating thirty-second hot and cold compresses to the affected area for ten minutes, four times a day.

- Try cold: Apply an ice pack or "ice-pillow" to the nape of your neck or your forehead. Or apply heat (see Pain, page 513) and then get your partner, a friend, or a masseuse to follow with a good rubdown.

- Try acupressure: Squeeze the web of skin between your thumb and index finger.

Last-resort treatment: If nothing else helps, you can now take two ibuprofen or acetaminophen. If your headaches are severe enough to warrant a trip to the doctor, ask about migraine medications in the triptan class (Imitrex, Relpax, Zomig). Some headaches in recovery are not true migraines, but if they have a vascular component they may respond to these treatments. If you suffer from persistent headaches, or headaches accompanied by nausea and/or vomiting, disturbed vision (double vision, for example), or poor coordination (unrelated to your addiction), see your doctor immediately.

HEARTBURN
See Indigestion.

HEMORRHOIDS
Treatment to avoid: Any painkillers listed as dangerous on page 513.

Treatment to substitute: To avoid hemorrhoids or minimize symptomsr, try the following:

- Avoid the straining that comes with constipation by keeping regular.

- Eat a diet rich in vitamin C (which keeps blood vessels healthy).

- Avoid any food that seems to make your hemorrhoids worse (sometimes tomato sauce or other acidic foods do).

- Keep the rectal area clean (use moistened, unscented white toilet tissue, or a bidet).

- Avoid long periods of standing or sitting; break them up by walking around. Rest or sleep on your side, rather than your back, and sit on a doughnut-shaped rubber cushion, if necessary, to keep pressure off rectal veins.

- Apply heat or cold, whichever is more comfortable (an ice pack, a warm sitz bath), or alternating heat and cold, when hemorrhoids flare.

- For relief, use Tucks (individual cleansing pads), or medicated suppositories or topical anesthetics if recommended by your physician. If your hemorrhoids protrude, swallow your embarrassment and ask your doctor to show you how to tuck them back in.

Last-resort treatment: Most of the time, hemorrhoids cause discomfort, itching and some bleeding. They are a nuisance, but not usually an urgent medical crisis. However, they do need medical intervention in two situations. The first is when blood in a hemorrhoid vein clots. The inflammation can be very painful; if the condition is not manageable with safe pain medication, the "thrombosed hemorrhoid" needs to be evacuated surgically. (The doctor may suggest narcotics or other pain relievers for this pain; that is not a good option for you, clearly. Ask if he can prescribe Toradol instead. It's a safe alternative.) The second situation is when severe bleeding poses a risk in itself. Unfortunately, hemorrhoids and their complications are more common in alcoholics and addicts, because the liver damage they often have puts excess pressure on the anal veins, expanding them and contributing to the condition. If you spot any rectal bleeding, consult your doctor.

INDIGESTION, HEARTBURN, AND GAS

Treatment to avoid: Risky pain medication (see Pain, page 513); any drug used to treat irritable bowel syndrome and similar conditions containing belladonna, ergotamine, or phenobarbital; other gastrointestinal medications containing risky ingredients (Phazyme PB). Also avoid aspirin and ibuprofen and other NSAIDs, which could upset your stomach even further.

Treatment to substitute: For occasional indigestion or heartburn: Exercise patience or try a safe antacid. You could also try a banana, which can often relieve simple GI discomfort. Or a diet 7UP or Sprite, which some people find work as well as Alka-Seltzer and are certainly tastier.

For frequent indigestion or heartburn: Avoid any food or beverage that you've noticed causes discomfort. Possible offenders include alcohol, of course; hot, spicy, highly seasoned, fried, or fatty foods (including nuts); processed meats, such as hot dogs, bologna, sausage, and bacon; chocolate, coffee, and carbonated beverages; citrus fruits and juices; and spearmint and peppermint (even in gum). Also avoid smoking, which encourages the production of stomach acids; pressure on the stomach, from tight belts and garments or from bending at the waist (bend at the knees instead); and stress, particularly at mealtimes. Eat several smaller meals rather than three big ones (but be careful not to eat more total food). Relax, if possible, for half an hour after each meal, and lose weight if you need to. Sleep with your head elevated four to six inches (use a large pillow or wedge or books under your mattress).

THE GREEN ZONE

Last-resort treatment: Try an antacid, such as Maalox, Mylanta, Gaviscon, or Phazyme (but not Phazyme PB). Best are those that are low in sodium. Magnesium or aluminum-based antacids are more effective than calcium antacids, which cause a rebound in stomach acidity. Over-the-counter medicines such as ranitidine (Zantac), famotidine (Pepcid), lansoprazole (Prevacid), and omeprazole (Prilosec) work in a couple of different ways, but all are effective and relatively safe for those in recovery, if you need medication. Your body will build resistance to each of them, so limit your use to short periods or rotate them every couple of weeks. If these measures don't help, or you find you need to use these medications for more than several months, see your doctor. Persistent indigestion, vomiting, or a change in your bowel habits requires medical evaluation.

INJURY, MINOR

Treatment to avoid: All risky pain relievers (see Pain, page 513). Theoretically, some first-aid creams and sprays containing alcohol could be a problem. Practically (unless you're spraying your throat), they are probably okay. But when in doubt, do without. For example, to clean a minor wound when the skin is broken, use an iodine-based product like povidone-iodine 10 percent (Betadine) for disinfecting rather than alcohol-based witch hazel.

Treatment to substitute: For minor traumatic injuries, try RICE (rest, ice, compression, and elevation). Compression is a good first-aid technique. It will stop bleeding (apply pressure directly to the wound) as well as reduce the swelling of a sprained ankle or injury (use an elastic bandage or tie a towel around the affected body part). Elevating the area will also diminish pain and swelling. Also see nondrug methods of pain relief on page 514.

Last-resort treatment: The safer pain relievers (see Pain, page 513). Check with the doctor if symptoms don't improve or they get worse in the hours after injury. If a sprain still hurts after three or four days or you are having significant functional impairment, get it checked out. It could be a fracture.

IRRITABLE BOWEL SYNDROME

Treatment to avoid: Most drugs used to treat irritable bowel syndrome and similar conditions (Lomotil, other medicines with an opiate base, any sedatives, Donnatal).

Treatment to substitute: Try stress reduction, relaxation, a diet high in insoluble fiber, and eliminating tobacco, caffeine, and other stimulants, and possibly sorbitol. Some people also get relief by eliminating milk products, using only those with added lactase (the enzyme that helps digest milk sugar), or taking lactase tablets (Lactaid) before consuming dairy products.

Last-resort treatment: For severe pain, acetaminophen (Tylenol) will help. Nonsteroidal anti-inflammatory drugs (NSAIDs) such as ibuprofen may also give some pain relief, but they can also irritate your stomach and make it hurt even worse. Probiotics, bacteria that supplement the bacteria that should be thriving in your GI tract, often reduce symptoms significantly and can be used safely in recovery. If the symptoms don't go away, a full GI checkup by your physician may be necessary.

KIDNEY STONES

The pain of kidney (renal) stones usually begins in the back, just below the ribs on one side or the other. As the stone moves from the kidney to the bladder, down the ureter, the pain (a stabbing type that tends to come in waves) travels with it around to the groin and down one side of the abdomen. It's reputed to be the most excruciating pain that humans experience, except for childbirth. The pain may continue over a period of hours or days, which is why it presents a special problem for the person in recovery. Strong pain relief is usually indicated. Fortunately, Toradol, a prescription NSAID, usually works as well as morphine for acute pain. If your doctor suggests a narcotic or another drug on our risky list, stand your ground and ask for Toradol.

Sometimes, nothing but a narcotic will help, however. If that is the case, no matter how long you have been sober, you should consider yourself back in the Red Zone (see chapter 2 on doing Recovery Zone ReChecks). You have to assume that the judgment necessary for maintaining your sobriety will be lost. To reduce the risk that your sobriety will be lost with it, increase your program activities. Stay in close contact with your sponsor, your addiction physician or counselor, and your fellowship group (maybe go to a meeting every day). Read up on the Red Zone guidelines and take all of the precautions suggested for those who are brand-new to recovery.

If you have an episode of kidney stones, drink a lot of water (at least eight to ten glasses a day) and call a urologist for expert help. The stones usually pass by themselves. If not, you will need help getting rid of them. The longer you are in pain, the more likely you will need heavy-duty pain relief. In some cases, a technique known as ultrasonic lithotripsy, which pulverizes the stones into small particles that pass in the urine, can eliminate the need for surgery and lessen the amount of drugs needed. Sometimes, however, there's no choice but to surgically remove a stone.

Each recurrence puts your recovery in jeopardy. So it's important to find a urologist who will work with you to fully resolve this issue, and to prevent it in the future. It's also important to find out what type of stone it was, as that may point to how you can prevent the problem in the future. To capture a stone,

THE GREEN ZONE

urinate through a fine strainer until after the stone is passed. Any solid material in the urine will end up in the strainer. Carefully put the stone or stones in a container and bring it to your doctor. The type of stone will dictate how you can avoid a recurrence. For example, if it is primarily calcium, you may have to cut down on your intake of this mineral. Drinking plenty of fluids, especially in hot weather, may also help reduce the chance of more kidney stones developing.

MENOPAUSE

Treatment to avoid: Menopause can cause a number of bothersome symptoms, such as hot flashes, mood swings, sleep disturbances, and night sweats. The symptoms themselves present no real medical concerns (they are a normal part of aging), but the discomfort and annoyance they bring has the potential to work against a good recovery program. They could chip away at a positive recovery attitude, and could also prompt a doctor unfamiliar with recovery to prescribe medications that increase relapse risk (such as antidepressants or antianxiety medications). If you see a doctor about menopausal symptoms, be sure he knows you are in recovery and you do not want any of those medications.

Treatment to substitute: The symptoms will eventually go away, though it might take several months or even years. That is little comfort when you are sweating through the sheets night after night. Some recovery-safe remedies:

- **Night sweats.** Wear light wicking clothing at bedtime and try running a fan to cool yourself off. Wicking materials draw sweat away from the body, leaving you cooler and drier. If you don't find any wicking pajamas, lots of clothes made for outdoor activities and working out are designed to do this as well. Also try wicking sheets.

- **Sleeping problems.** See Sleep sections on pages 519 and 521.

- **Mood problems.** The same techniques that help your mood issues in recovery can help here. Check out the ideas for easing anxiety, fatigue, irritability, and depression throughout this book. More exercise and eating a healthy diet may also help.

- **Sexual changes.** If dryness is a problem, try a lubricant during sex as well as a vaginal moisturizer for other times, such as Replens or K-Y Long-lasting Vaginal Moisturizer. Also ask your doctor about a low-dose vaginal estrogen cream; it is limited to a local effect, so does not pose the same risks as oral estrogen therapy.

- **Urinary incontinence.** Some women have minor incontinence at menopause. Wear a mini-pad to avoid accidents. Do Kegel exercises to tone up those pelvic floor muscles. (Find your relevant muscles by stopping the flow of urine. Then when you are not urinating, practice contracting and releasing those same muscles. Hold the contractions for 2 to 3 seconds and release. Do 10 repetitions at a time, several times a day.) Avoid food and drinks that have a high acid content, such as tomatoes, oranges, and grapefruit, as they can irritate the bladder. Also cut back on caffeine; it can be an irritant. If the incontinence is severe and disabling (you are afraid to leave the house because you might have an accident), talk with your doctor about it. There are some very effective medical treatments available.

- **Bone density.** Alcoholism and menopause both increase the risk of osteoporosis (a disease in which your bones become weak and are at higher risk of fracture). Sobriety and regular exercise can help improve your bone health and lower this risk, but your risk may never go back to where it would have been without drinking. Get a bone density exam (a simple X-ray) early in menopause as a baseline measurement, and ask your doctor if you need prescription medication to prevent bone loss.

- **General remedies.** Try adding natural estrogen (phytoestrogen) to your diet. Soy milk, soy nuts, miso, tempeh, and tofu all contain soy, and pose no risk to recovery. (Note, however, that the safety and effectiveness of soy supplementation has not been scientifically established.) Be wary of using any herbal remedies for symptom relief, as some have been linked to liver problems. Most women who are in menopause or are post-menopausal should take 1,200 mg of calcium and 600 units of vitamin D daily.

Last-resort treatment: Hormone replacement therapy (HRT) is not routinely recommended because it increases the risks of blood clots, heart disease, heart attack, stroke, some forms of cancer, and other serious conditions. But if your menopausal symptoms are severe, they could be a risk to a quality recovery, so a short-term course of HRT may be advisable, particularly in early recovery. (Be sure to talk with your doctor about any other risk factors you have before starting HRT. Let him know that you are in recovery; alcoholism increases the risk of cardiovascular disease and several cancers, which could be raised even further by adding HRT.)

If you do take any type of HRT, start with the lowest dose possible.

MENSTRUAL/ PREMENSTRUAL DISCOMFORT

Treatment to avoid: Medications containing pyrilamine maleate (Midol, Premsyn PMS, Pamprin), anti-depressants, and benzodiazepines.

THE GREEN ZONE

Treatment to substitute: Reduce or eliminate sugar, caffeine, and chocolate (it contains theobromine, a caffeine-related compound, which can act as a stimulant). Increase your calcium intake; drink plenty of fluids; work some exercise into your daily schedule. Some women find that vitamin E supplements (200 to 400 I.U. daily) or raspberry leaf tea help, too (but don't drink the tea if you might be pregnant). When tension strikes, try meditation and other anti-anxiety weapons. Reduce your schedule when you expect symptoms to be most debilitating. For pain, try a hot-water bottle across your abdomen or other appropriate pain-relief techniques (see Pain).

Last-resort treatment: If pain and cramping are interfering with your life, take Motrin or another ibuprofen-only preparation (Advil, Nuprin). If the symptoms are predictable and severe, a preemptive strike with one of these might help.

MOTION SICKNESS

Treatment to avoid: Most motion-sickness preparations, including those containing cyclizine lactate (Marezine), dimenhydrinate (Dramamine), meclizine hydrochloride (Bonine), ondansetron (Zofran), or promethazine (Phenergan). Also avoid patches that contain drugs such as scopolamine; these drugs are absorbed through the skin into the bloodstream.

Treatment to substitute: To reduce the risk of motion sickness, don't read or do close work while in motion; in a car, do the driving yourself, or sit in the middle front seat; don't ride on a full stomach; keep your eyes on the horizon; nap for most of the trip, when possible. Also try two capsules of ginger as a preventive measure. If you are aboard ship, stay on deck in the fresh air and nibble on dry crackers to suppress nausea. Long popular with sailors, elastic bands (Sea-Bands) worn on the wrists apply a kind of acupressure and often help prevent motion sickness. They are available in drugstores. You can also try pressing two fingers on the inside of your wrist; like the Sea-Bands, this applies acupressure.

Last-resort treatment: If nausea and vomiting when traveling are a serious problem, you can use Emetrol liquid, which acts locally and works well for many people. Check with your physician if nothing else banishes queasiness.

NAUSEA AND VOMITING

Treatment to avoid: Most anti-nausea drugs, including Atarax, Benadryl, Compazine, Dramamine, Marezine, Phenergan, Thorazine, Vistaril, and Zofran.

Treatment to substitute: Sea-Bands (see Motion Sickness) reduce or eliminate nausea in many people. Modify your diet: To keep body fluid levels normal, drink water if it stays down (small sips every fifteen minutes may work better than large gulps); otherwise, suck on ice chips (fluid is important to prevent dehydration). Consider using a rehydrating solution, such as Gatorade or a home-made solution (see Diarrhea, page 503). Gradually add light, nonfatty foods (such as plain gelatin dessert, clear soup, toast, or fruit) as vomiting ceases. Also try cold foods like Popsicles; they are less upsetting than others. Stay as inactive as possible until symptoms improve; rest in bed if you can.

Last-resort treatment: If vomiting continues for more than twenty-four hours, is bloody, has a foul odor, or is accompanied by severe pain, call the doctor. You may need intravenous hydration or surgical intervention.

ORAL HYGIENE

Treatment to avoid: Stay away from products containing alcohol; most popular brands of mouthwash and a few toothpastes do (including Aim, Pepsodent, and Close-Up). Even if you don't swallow the product, it will still get into your bloodstream through membranes in your mouth and throat. Read labels.

Treatment to substitute: Rinse your mouth regularly with a solution of salt water or baking soda and water (½ teaspoon salt or baking soda to 1 cup water) or use Oxyfresh, Tom's of Maine mouthwash, or another alcohol-free brand of mouthwash. However, getting in the mouthwash habit can be a slippery slope, because many of them do contain alcohol. You can keep your mouth fresh, and your gums and teeth healthy—and never need mouthwash—if you eat a nutritious, low-sugar diet, floss

regularly, and brush twice a day (both your teeth and your tongue).

Last-resort treatment: See your doctor if you can't rid yourself of mouth odor. Intractable odor probably does not originate in the mouth, but elsewhere in the digestive tract.

PAIN

Treatment to avoid: Even inno-cent-sounding pain relievers such as ibuprofen and Tylenol can pose some risk in recovery, particularly when they are laced with other ingredients, such as codeine, antihistamines, sedatives, or caffeine. Avoid any form of aspirin or acetaminophen or any other pain medication that has added caffeine (such as Excedrin); prescription analgesics containing codeine (such as Empirin with codeine, Fiorinal with codeine, Phenaphen, Robitussin A-C, and Tylenol 3); diprenorphine hydrochloride; hydrocodone; meperidine hydrochloride; methadone hydrochloride; morphine or hydromorphone; oxycodone; tramadol (Ultram); and pentazocine (Talwin).

Also avoid all narcotics, including the natural ones: opium (Donnagel, Dover's Powder, Paregoric, Parepectolin) and opium derivatives, such as codeine, OxyContin, morphine (MS-Contin, Roxanol, Roxanol-SR), and hydromorphone (Dilaudid). Also avoid synthetics: butorphanol (Stadol); fentanyl and methadone (Dolophine, Methadose); hydrocodone and phenyltoloxamine

(Tussionex); meperidine (Demerol, Mepergan); oxycodone or oxycodone hydrochloride (Percodan, Percocet, Tylox); oxymorphone hydrochloride (Numorphan); pentazocine/naloxone (Talwin). (New pain meds are likely to be invented in the future, of course. Your safest bet is to avoid them, too.)

Treatment to substitute: Pain experts are starting to realize that narcotic drugs, though sometimes useful in the short run, are not the best way to deal with pain, especially chronic pain that is not caused by cancer. Narcotics, for example, don't zap the sources of pain—they just eliminate your perception of it. But because they make you less aware of the pain, your body is fooled into cutting down on the natural painkillers it produces. As a result, when you stop taking the narcotics, the pain is more severe because your body isn't turning out enough of its own chemicals to relieve it. So you take more narcotics, and a dangerous cycle of even more suffering begins.

This cycle tends to occur with any kind of medication used to treat chronic pain. At first it helps; then gradually, as emotional and physical resistance develops, more and more medication is needed to get relief. This increasing reliance on drugs when better options exist is equivalent to relapse for someone in recovery, and it can bring other addictive behavior on its coattails. So if your pain is going to stay with you, learn to handle it with a better option than

medication. Mild pain won't kill you, but a relapse very well might. (See also specific recommendations for short-term severe pain conditions such as kidney stones [page 509], terminal illness [page 483], childbirth [page 481], surgery [page 476], dental care [page 478], and medical emergencies [page 480].)

There are a great many drug-free ways to deal with pain, some simple, others rather complicated, all worth trying before resorting to medication.

- **Acupuncture and acupressure.** Some kinds of pain, especially those in which there is a localized area of tenderness within the region of a muscle spasm, respond dramatically to these ancient Chinese arts. While acupuncture is done with needles and requires an expert, acupressure can sometimes be performed by kneading or massaging the pressure points—which anyone taught to locate them can do.

- **Aloe vera.** For the pain of simple burns (and to speed healing), applying the juice from a broken leaf of the aloe plant seems to be very effective. Keep a plant handy or purchase a first-aid cream or spray containing aloe.

- **Biofeedback.** This technique seems to work especially well for pain related to tension. Through a system of sensors attached to the skin and a device that registers body response, you can learn to control certain involuntary functions and ward off certain types of headache.

- **Chiropractic manipulation.** Chiropractors can often help with back and musculoskeletal-related pain. But be sure you have an accurate diagnosis of your problem before accepting chiropractic treatment, and ideally, ask your doctor for a referral so that you can feel confident about the chiropractor you see.

- **Cold therapy.** Cold therapy not only dulls the pain of an injury but it can also, by reducing blood flow, decrease swelling and bruising. It's most effective during the first thirty-six to forty-eight hours after an injury, or until swelling subsides. Treat bruised areas promptly with a cold pack. A bag of frozen peas wrapped in a towel will mold nicely to the shape of the area being treated. Or use ice cubes in a sealable plastic bag, or a reusable ice pack. Apply the cold pack for ten to twenty minutes every hour or two while you're awake, until the pain and swelling are gone. Alternatively, an injured foot or hand can be soaked in ice water for up to fifteen minutes at a time. Repeat every hour or two.

  Minor burns can also be treated with cold therapy. Soak immediately in icy water or apply cool compresses until the pain

diminishes (usually about half an hour, though sometimes pain can persist for hours).

  Do not apply cold therapy if you are hypersensitive to cold or have poor circulation (if you have Raynaud's disease, for example), or if the wound is open or already blistered.

- **Elevation.** In infection, surgery, or trauma, swelling of the affected area often stretches the pain receptors, which transmit messages of dismay to the brain that are interpreted as pain. Elevating the injured part of the body above the level of your heart allows the circulatory system to absorb more tissue fluid and reduce the swelling, lessening the nerve stimulation. This means less pain for you.

- **Elimination.** Try to eliminate the cause of the pain. If it's a hunger headache, eat. If it's back trouble, get a new mattress, a better office chair, or more comfortable walking shoes, and improve your posture and your abdominal muscle strength (by doing safe sit-ups with your knees drawn up, for example). If it's tension-triggered pain—in your neck, for example—do relaxation exercises.

- **Exercise.** Keeping your body in good shape with exercise can help prevent painful injury. It can also reduce the likelihood of pain (such as backache) that comes from poor muscle tone. Exercise is often a very

THE GREEN ZONE

Beware of an Overdose

Aspirin, ibuprofen, and acetaminophen are "safer" painkillers. But that doesn't mean you can pop them like candy. All can have serious side effects when taken in large quantities, especially on an empty stomach. Aspirin and ibuprofen can irritate the digestive tract and cause internal bleeding. Those in the NSAID category (such as ibuprofen) can cause kidney damage and increased blood pressure. Acetaminophen can cause liver damage, which is particularly risky in alcoholics and addicts, as they often have compromised liver function. In more sensitive people, even normal doses of acetaminophen can be hazardous, so it should be used only with careful attention to the dosage; never take it in larger-than-recommended doses.

relax tense muscles, and reduce stiffness, as well as help reduce pain. Heat is best for treating back or muscle pain, inflammatory-related problems such as arthritis, and injuries once the swelling has subsided (usually after 36 to 48 hours). Moist heat (from a warm compress, moist heating pad, shower, or bath) often works better than dry. Check with your doctor to learn which form of heat (or cold) works best in which situations.

Always wrap heating pads and hot water bottles in a towel to prevent burns, and limit applications to 20 to 30 minutes. Avoid heat therapy if you have a fever, internal or external bleeding, or an infection. If you have a heart condition, check with your doctor before using a hot tub or whirlpool. If you are pregnant, avoid heat therapy to your torso.

- **Hydrotherapy.** Whirlpool baths are best, but any hot bath can help relieve muscle pain, as well as tension and insomnia. A heating pad applied after the bath provides additional comfort.

- **Hypnosis and guided imagery.** If chronic pain is the problem, hypnotism can sometimes make it bearable. See a doctor familiar with hypnosis, or a reputable hypnotist your doctor recommends. Also check out guided imagery recordings that address pain. (See chapter 14.)

successful treatment for muscle pain. Low-impact exercise, such as swimming, may help arthritis pain. Even simple stretches and range of motion exercises can yield results.

- **Heat therapy.** Heat—in the form of a heating pad, hot water bottle, warm compress, or hot bath, or a combination of these—can speed healing,

- **Ice.** See Cold therapy.

- **Immobilization.** Keeping an injured arm, ankle, finger, or leg immobilized will often reduce the pain and encourage initial healing.

- **Massage.** A good massage can often reduce tension and pain. If you can't afford a professional, ask your partner or a friend to learn the tricks of the trade.

- **Meditation.** Meditation isn't a cure-all, but it can help in a battle against pain (see chapter 14).

- **Physical therapy.** A licensed physical therapist can often help reduce pain.

- **Placebo.** Anything that you are truly convinced will relieve your pain will likely work. Once you have a good recovery under way, your brain gets back to producing its own pain-relieving chemicals, such as endorphins. Then you can use the power of your own thoughts to "pump in" those drugs. Think positive, pain-free thoughts, and your brain follows along with the drugs. Go back to negative thoughts, however, and your brain will drag you back down again. Your powerful brain can generally give you at least half as much benefit as any drug treatment.

- **Relaxation.** Relaxation comes in many packages—a movie, a concert, a good book, a leisurely walk, playing catch with the kids. Learn what it is that truly relaxes

you, and try it even before pain begins to nag.

- **Rest.** While not a panacea, rest seems to be good for most things that ail us, pain included. Whether you're dealing with a running injury or a headache, time out for rest usually helps reduce the discomfort. Going forward with exercise or other activities in spite of the pain may seem gutsy, but it's usually a bad move.

- **TENS (transcutaneous electric nerve stimulation).** This method of pain relief relies on low-level electrical stimulation delivered to the skin by a special device. It's believed that this stimulation either blocks the transfer of pain impulses (because the nerves can carry only one message at a time) or promotes the release of pain-relieving endorphins. It has been used with varying degrees of success for various kinds of chronic pain, as well as for dental work, childbirth, and back pain.

- **Ultrasound.** Deep, penetrating sound waves can often unknot muscle spasms and relieve the pain that accompanies them. This, of course, must be done by a professional. Ask your physician or physical therapist for a recommendation.

- **Venting.** If the pain is caused by fear or worry (a tension headache, neck pain, or upset stomach, for example), talking about the problem often helps. In such cases the pain is only the symptom; your body is saying, "Hey, something is wrong!" and it's the underlying cause that needs treating.

Last-resort treatment: If you do decide you need medication for acute or short-term pain, you may be pleasantly surprised at how effective several of the over-the-counter medications can be. While you were drinking or using, you probably found little relief from them, because alcohol or other drugs were interfering with the brain mechanisms that deal with pain (as well as those that deal with anxiety and depression). Now that you're in recovery, aspirin, ibuprofen, naproxen, and even acetaminophen can bring dramatic relief. Take (as directed) aspirin (Bayer, Bufferin, Ascriptin, Ecotrin, Empirin, and generics); acetaminophen (Tylenol, Panadol, Tylophen, Datril, and generics); ibuprofen (Advil, Nuprin, Motrin, Genpril, Medipren, and generics); or magnesium salicylate (MST, Nuprin Backache Caplet). Take these medications after eating, not on an empty stomach, and follow with a full glass of water.

Though these drugs are not normally addictive, remember that the illness of addiction is in the person, not the drug. So take them *only* when absolutely necessary. Use the nondrug therapies as your first lines of defense, and reserve the medications for times when nothing else will work. Do not take these painkillers in anticipation of pain that might never occur. Such self-medicating can spur a return to addictive behaviors—you would be using drugs to solve problems that might not even exist. (However, it's probably okay to take them before an in-office surgical procedure, if a doctor or dentist suggests it.)

Even extremely severe pain can now be treated without a narcotic. Toradol, an oral or injectable non-steroidal anti-inflammatory drug (much like ibuprofen), is highly effective in treating pain and doesn't carry any greater risk of relapse than other NSAIDs. It can cause bleeding and kidney damage, however, so it must be used only when really necessary and for no more than five days. Most severe pain should be improved by then.

Any other pain medication should only be taken as described in Medication Concerns, page 475.

SKIN PROBLEMS

Treatment to avoid: If you are taking Antabuse to help you not drink, avoid all creams, lotions, ointments, and sunscreens that contain alcohol. It can be absorbed through the skin, so applying these could make you sick. They are probably not a problem for others.

Treatment to substitute: Moisturize dry skin daily, avoid very hot showers or baths, use a mild soap or cleanser only as needed, and try to reduce indoor dryness in the winter.

To minimize acne, keep skin clean with a mild cleanser or soap (such as Dove). Don't pick at or squeeze pimples. Treat breakouts with over-the-counter benzoyl peroxide preparations. Start with a low-concentration (2.5 percent) gel or wash; work up to a higher concentration as needed (maximum 10 percent) but back down if skin gets very irritated. If that doesn't seem effective, your doctor may prescribe a topical antibiotic, such as erythromycin or clindamycin, to spread on affected areas. Dietary changes aren't necessary unless you note a link between a particular food and an eruption.

You can speed the departure of skin rashes by using very mild hypoallergenic soap, such as Basic or Neutrogena, and using it only where your body is really dirty or smelly. Baking soda or Aveeno (colloidal oatmeal) in your bath water may also help. If the rash is allergic in nature, an over-the-counter cortisone cream may alleviate it. If it is caused by a fungus (as are athlete's foot and jock itch), an over-the-counter antifungal preparation, such as Tinactin, Micatin, or Lamisil may help. Don't stop applying such a medication as soon as the rash is gone; continue it for an extra week or two to lower the risk of a recurrence. Sometimes a minor rash can become infected with the bacteria normally in residence on skin. In many cases, warm compresses or soaks can nip such an infection early; you can also try a topical antiseptic such as povidone-iodine (Betadine) solution. Intense redness, pain, or pus, however, usually indicates problems that need medical attention.

The development of cold sores or fever blisters caused by herpes simplex virus 1 can sometimes be blocked by taking lactobacillus tablets or capsules at the first twinge. Over-the-counter ointments may also help. They can also be treated with Zovirax or another antiviral medication.

Last-resort treatment: When all else fails in eliminating acne, a fungal infection, or recurrent herpes outbreaks, an antibiotic, antifungal, steroid, or antiviral medication taken by mouth may be prescribed.

SLEEP PROBLEMS: TOO LITTLE

Treatment to avoid: All sedatives and sleeping pill medications, including chloral hydrate (Noctec), eszopiclone (Lunesta), ramelteon (Rozerem), zaleplo (Sonata), zolpidem (Ambien), and flurazepam (Dalmane); any medication in the barbiturate category, including pentobarbital (Nembutal), phenobarbital, and secobarbital/amobarbital; temazepam (Restoril); trazodone (Desyrel), and triazolam (Halcion). All nonprescription sleeping preparations, including those containing diphenhydramine (Benadryl, Nervine, Nytol, Sominex 2) and doxylamine succinate (Unisom). And please note: The use of sleeping pills has been associated with a dramatic increase in death rates, even in people who are not addicts. They should be considered very

THE GREEN ZONE

dangerous for those in recovery, especially since safer and effective alternatives are available.

Treatment to substitute: The most effective ways to improve sleep in the long run, you may be surprised to learn, do not come in a bottle. Keep in mind that worrying about not sleeping tends to compound the problem. Lying in bed and thinking "I won't be able to fall asleep" often converts anxiety into reality. The following sleep hygiene tips should help:

■ Have a regular going-to-bed routine. Go to bed at the same time each night—at least as often as you can. Use standard sleep-inducing tricks at bedtime: a warm bath or leisurely shower, reading, soothing music, a back rub, cuddling with someone you love, making love, meditation and relaxation techniques (see chapter 14), prayer, warm milk, or counting backward from one hundred.

■ If sleeplessness has become a habit, you might try to break the habit by changing your going-to-bed routine as much as possible; even consider changing the location of your bed.

■ Have an active day. Get up at the same time every morning (even if you tossed and turned all night); make a point of getting out and spending time with friends or family (isolation may contribute to sleeplessness). Get in some moderate exercise daily; it will make it easier to sleep at night. But don't nap during the day or exercise just before bedtime.

■ Try to eliminate the stress and anxiety that may be keeping you awake (see the tips for dealing with stress in chapter 14). Get rid of underlying problems when you can. And if you can't, make a monumental effort not to take them to bed with you. Distract your mind with an engrossing TV show or book, with meditation, or with recovery recordings.

■ Be sure your sleeping quarters are conducive to sleep. That means the room should be dark, neither too hot nor too cold, and quiet (though not necessarily silent; white noise from a fan or a phone app, for example, may help you sleep). If light streaming through a window is interfering with your sleep, try heavier window coverings (look for curtains designed to block the light) or wear an eye mask. If noise from outside is the culprit, block it out with ear plugs or white noise. Shut down your phone completely so the texting pings and the glowing light don't wake you up. If you use your phone to run a white noise app, shut down the text and email pings and turn down the brightness.

■ The mattress should be comfortable and not lumpy, the linens neat and smooth. But don't cover your head with the blankets, since this can reduce oxygen and increase carbon dioxide intake, leading to headache and sometimes abnormal heartbeat, both of which can keep you awake.

- Find your natural sleep rhythm. You'll sleep best when your temperature drops; take it hourly for a few days to determine when this happens during the day. Try to time your bedtime accordingly. If your internal clock is set inconveniently—for sleep from 2 a.m. to 10 a.m., for example— you might try to reprogram it via chronotherapy, a method that attempts to manipulate your internal clock. (But remember that what is considered normal varies widely. For some, an afternoon nap combined with nighttime sleep works perfectly.)

- Try a different bed. Restless twist-and-turn sleep can be created by pressure points on a mattress. If you suspect this is the source of your problem, turn the mattress over or add a sculptured foam pad called an "egg-crate mattress"; or buy a new mattress or switch to a waterbed or a large air mattress.

- Late in the day, avoid foods that tend to give you indigestion or reflux (which can interfere with sleep). Also avoid a heavy meal just before you turn in. And of course keep away from caffeine, at least from early afternoon on; its effects may not strike

until eight hours or more after it enters your system.

- Before bedtime, avoid things that tend to stimulate: loud music or entertainment, scary or thriller shows, animated or angry discussions, and strenuous physical exercise. If you've been to an exciting movie, meeting, or sports event, take some time to unwind (with a bath, book, music, or yoga) before bed.

- Comfort yourself with the thought that if you're in bed with your eyes closed, even if you're awake, you're getting rest.

- Don't just lie there. If you are very restless and sleep doesn't come in 15 to 30 minutes, get up and do something. Watch TV, read some AA literature or a relaxing novel, do last night's dishes, or sort the laundry.

Last-resort treatment: If these suggestions don't alleviate your sleeping problem, a medical workup is probably in order. If your symptoms are not directly traceable to withdrawal, you might need to do a sleep study to rule out sleep apnea (the only medically risky cause of insomnia).

SLEEP PROBLEMS: TOO MUCH

Treatment to avoid: All stimulants and antidepressants, including caffeine. If you're gulping coffee or energy drinks to stay awake, you're using them as a drug. Beware. The relapse train may have already left the station.

THE GREEN ZONE

Treatment to substitute: Maintaining a healthy schedule and sleep pattern demands a certain amount of self-discipline—something few active alcoholics/addicts have ever developed. But it's never too late to begin. Start keeping track of your daily schedule with a calendar. Schedule early-morning activities (such as fishing, shopping, hiking, or fellowship meetings) that will lure you out of bed. Get an alarm clock or app that has a snooze alarm (which will wake you a second time if you don't get up at the first signal). If you usually just shut off the alarm clock and turn over, have a friend or neighbor call or stop by to be sure you get up and get dressed. If you aren't working, fill your days with meaningful pursuits: meetings, visiting friends, classes, good works. Try exercising early in the morning. Also try to avoid heavy meals, which can make you drowsy. Try to keep your activities consecutive, so you won't be tempted to go home and crash between them. For example, plan to meet a couple of friends after work for dinner and then go right to a meeting, followed by a snack with your sponsor.

Last-resort treatment: If these suggestions don't help, see your doctor.

SORE THROAT

Treatment to avoid: Gargles or mouthwashes containing alcohol; risky pain relievers (see Pain, page 513).

Treatment to substitute: Gargling with warm salt water (1 teaspoon salt to 1 glass water) or diluted hydrogen peroxide (use a 3 percent solution diluted with an equal amount of water, or dilute according to instructions); sucking on lozenges, such as Chloraseptic, Cepastat, or Sucrets; or an ice pack to the neck.

Last-resort treatment: Most sore throats are caused by viruses and require no drug treatment; but if your doctor diagnoses a strep throat, antibiotics are recommended. Report to your doctor any sore throat that is accompanied by a fever or swollen glands, or that interferes with swallowing.

VAGINAL INFECTION

Treatment to avoid: All risky painkillers (see Pain, page 513), sedatives, and anti-anxiety drugs. If you have pain along with vaginal symptoms, see a doctor; it could be a serious condition that needs immediate evaluation.

Treatment to substitute: The best treatment for vaginal infections is prevention. To avoid this problem, or hasten its departure:

- Keep the vaginal area clean and dry. Always wipe from front to back after using the toilet, to avoid spreading germs. Rinse thoroughly after showering or bathing, and avoid deodorant soaps, bubble baths, perfumes, or other potential irritants.

- Wear breathable underwear.

- Avoid tight clothing.

- Follow the Clean and Sober Diet. Be particularly sure to keep your sugar intake low—sugar may provide a breeding ground for yeast (candida) infections. Eating a daily cup of yogurt with live cultures may also help.

- Consider over-the-counter treatments; some work very well. The first time you have symptoms that could indicate a vaginal infection, see your doctor to be sure of what it is. If it recurs, you may be able to treat it yourself with an over-the-counter product. Preparations called imidazoles are very effective: Tioconazole 6.5% 1 day; Vagistat-1, Monistat-1, Monistat-3, Monistat-3 suppositories, Clotrimazole 2% 3 days; Monistat-7, Clotrimazole 1% 7 days.

Last-resort treatment: See your doctor if symptoms reappear or don't resolve with an over-the-counter product. Failure to fully treat some types of vaginal infection can increase your risk of HIV infection and other STDs.

WEIGHT CONTROL

Treatment to avoid: Many prescription appetite suppressants, including amphetamines, dextro-amphetamines, methamphetamine, or other stimulant derivatives. Also stay away from over-the-counter or "natural" weight-loss medications of any kind. The ingredients in these are often unpredictable, and they may contain prohibited or addictive substances. Avoid fasting and liquid diet plans. Fasting could lead to drug craving, and the quick-fix weight loss is usually gained back just as quickly.

Treatment to substitute: Reducing caloric intake (by reducing food intake) and upping caloric outgo (through increasing exercise). For many people, Weight Watchers and Overeaters Anonymous are very helpful.

Last-resort treatment: If you are extremely obese or are having a difficult time taking weight off, your weight-loss program should be supervised by a physician who specializes in the treatment of obesity without drugs. In the most extreme cases (when the obesity could be more dangerous than the potentially fatal risk of relapse), bariatric surgery may be an option. However, researchers have found that such surgery can turbocharge latent addictive tendencies—many who have had the procedure fall back into active alcoholism.

THE GREEN ZONE

Time to Quit Smoking

You've already given up at least one old friend—alcohol or another addictive substance. Why should you have to give up this last dependency, one you may be clinging to for dear life? For just that reason: dear life. In the U.S., tobacco use is the major cause of people dying before their time. Now that you have a strong, well-established sobriety under way, it's time to do everything you can to live a long and happy life. That includes giving up smoking. We've organized this chapter along the lines of the familiar trio of phrases that precedes a race. In this case, it's the race for your life.

- On Your Mark: Why do you want to quit? What is your motivation?

- Get Set: Figure out your personal quit plan. Get your tools lined up and ready to go.

- Go: Quit day. Take off, and don't look back. Run for your health.

You succeeded in giving up drugs or alcohol. You can do this, too. And if you tried to quit in the past and were unsuccessful, don't despair. It often takes a few tries. It's all part of the process of becoming a nonsmoker.

On Your Mark: Deciding to Quit

SMOKING AND YOUR RECOVERY

As you've probably noticed, a lot of people in recovery smoke. For some, it serves as a new crutch, something to lean on when drugs and alcohol are off-limits. For others, it's a nice bonding tool— lighting up with other fellowship members after meetings is a way to get to know people and form relationships.

Now that your recovery is stable, however, this final addiction is probably starting to feel like an anchor around your neck. You are likely sick and tired of trying to find places where you can smoke, are tired of the mess and the smell, and are thinking—at least a tiny bit—about what you might be doing to your health.

For people in recovery, giving up smoking may be both harder and easier than it is for others. Harder because it has become a substitute for other substances (and nicotine *is* an addictive drug; research shows it may be just as addictive as alcohol, cocaine, and heroin). But easier because the very same principles you used to break other addictions can now be applied to smoking. In a way, by learning about and embracing the principles of recovery, you've already done some of the hard work of quitting.

So as you start to think about quitting smoking, know that you already have an edge:

- You know it won't be enough just to stop smoking; you will have to reorganize your life to be tobacco-free—again changing those people and places who tempt you and maybe even your daily schedule.

- You know you won't be able to have a smoke now and then because, just like the idea of having one drink, that could reignite your addiction.

- You know you can successfully change your life and your

identity. You did it once when you became a sober person. Now you can do it again to become a nonsmoker.

- And, maybe best of all, you've already developed a whole suite of coping skills to use when those cravings arise or you feel tense.

WHY QUIT? THE GOOD NEWS

You know smoking is bad for your health. You don't need us to lecture you on that. So let's start with the good news—all of the positive things that can happen when you quit. First of all, you won't be exposing your body to more than 7,000 chemicals with every puff (hundreds of them are toxic, and 70 of them can cause cancer).

Once you quit—no matter how long you've been smoking or how old you are—you reduce your risk of many health problems and increase your potential life span.

- Within a few minutes, your heart rate slows to more normal levels.

- Within a day, the level of carbon monoxide in your blood drops to normal.

- After three months, your circulation and lung function improve.

- After nine months, you'll be breathing easier and coughing less.

- After a year, your risk of coronary heart disease is cut in half.

THE GREEN ZONE

- After five years, your risk of some cancers (mouth, throat, esophagus, and bladder) is cut in half, and your risk of cervical cancer is back to normal.

- After five years, your risk of stroke is back to normal.

- After ten years, your risk of dying of lung cancer is cut in half.

- After fifteen years, your risk of coronary heart disease is back to normal.

Of course, there are also many benefits not related to health.

- You won't have to always be searching for a place where you can smoke.

- Your teeth will look better.

- Food will taste better.

- People won't roll their eyes at you every time you sneak a smoke.

- You'll be free of those jittery urges to smoke.

- Everything about you will smell better (hair, clothes, breath, car, home, etc.).

- You'll be more attractive and kissing will be more fun.

Plus, you will save a ton of money. A pack of smokes typically costs $7 or $8 now. If you smoke an $8 pack each day, you're spending $2,920 on cigarettes each year.

Another huge benefit is that quitting now can act like a booster shot for sobriety. Some people,

once they've been sober a while, get a little complacent. They go to fewer meetings, maybe take sobriety for granted. Taking on a campaign to quit smoking, using the tools you have learned in recovery, can help reengage your mind in your sobriety, reinforcing that new wiring you laid down in the past few years. And that's a very good thing.

Best of all, you will be able to proudly call yourself a nonsmoker. Remember how great you felt when you finally got into recovery? Like you were on top of the world? You can feel that way again.

THE HEALTH RISKS

Yes, you know smoking is bad for you. Let's do a quick review of the health risks anyway.

Smokers die, on average, ten years earlier than nonsmokers. In the U.S., tobacco is linked directly or indirectly to more than 440,000 deaths each year. That's one out of every five deaths—more than due to HIV, the use of alcohol or illegal drugs, suicides, murders, and car crashes combined. And for every person who dies due to smoking, twenty others are dealing with a serious illness because of it.

You know that smoking can cause lung cancer. In fact, it is responsible for 80 to 90 percent of all cases of lung cancer. It has also been linked to cancers of the esophagus, mouth, pancreas, kidney, bladder, cervix, voice box, stomach, and throat, as well as acute myeloid leukemia, a blood cancer.

Smoking also causes other serious and disabling lung diseases, such as emphysema and chronic bronchitis, as well as heart disease, stroke, aortic aneurysm, and osteoporosis—all potential killers.

Then there are the nonfatal effects: wrinkled skin, yellow teeth and fingers, tobacco breath and stale-smelling clothing, and deadened taste buds and sense of smell. In teens, it can also stunt the growth of your brain, raise your blood pressure, and raise your risk of blood clots (a particular worry if you are using a hormone-based birth control, such as the pill).

Cigarette smoke seems to interfere with the way the body deals with certain nutrients (vitamin C, for example), drugs (caffeine, for one), and some medications. The painkilling effect of analgesics, for example, is weaker in smokers, so they need larger dosages. If you smoke and have to take medication for surgery or some other reason, you might need higher than normal doses, which could wreck your successful recovery.

STILL NOT READY?

If you've read this far, but you're still not sure you're ready to quit, dig a little deeper. Look at those who have managed to give up smoking. Imagine your world without tobacco. Think about how sweet life would be as a nonsmoker. Pray for the desire to stop, meditate on it, and keep an eye out for a sign that it's time to stop.

Get Set: Preparing to Kick the Habit

WHAT IS YOUR QUIT PLAN?

Once you've decided to quit, you'll need a plan of action. In other words, you don't have to quit cold turkey this instant. It's better to prepare yourself for a quit date and work up to it. Here are some basic steps to follow:

1. Analyze your smoking habits.

2. Start changing your thinking.

3. Choose your tools.

4. Start changing your habits.

5. Set a quit date.

6. Quit.

Within this basic plan there are many tools that might help you quit; what works for you may not work for others. Some people find that looking at pictures of diseased lungs helps, while others would rather focus on the positive aspects of quitting, on becoming a nonsmoker. Some people find it helps to focus on being around for a far-off event, such as a grandchild's high school graduation, while others like to focus on a physical goal, such as how much better they'll feel when they go backpacking next summer.

Read through the next sections and think about what might work for you. Then write up your own plan of action for those six steps.

THE GREEN ZONE

ANALYZE YOUR HABIT

Many smokers don't even think about when or why they smoke. It's just automatic. But recognizing those habits will help you break them. So start paying attention to your smoking.

- Track your habit for a week or more. Write down each cigarette you smoke and when, where, with whom, and why you smoked it. Get to know your routines around smoking, your preferences. Also note how badly you needed each cigarette, on a scale of 1 to 3 (with 3 indicating the greatest need). Keeping a diary will help you see how much you are smoking, which smokes will be easier to give up, and which routines you'll need to change.

- In your diary, try to note what motivates you each time you light up: Is it nicotine cravings, oral gratification, to keep your hands busy, to steady your nerves, to ease anxiety, or simply for pleasure? Or is it just a habit at certain times?

- Are you truly addicted to tobacco? Do you smoke every day? Do you have to have a cigarette when you get up in the morning? Do you find yourself lighting up almost every hour or two during the day? If not, you may not be physically addicted, and chances are good that you can give it up more easily than

you thought. Of course, this isn't likely if you've been smoking for a long time. Most people in recovery are every bit as addicted to tobacco as they were to their other drugs of choice.

START CHANGING YOUR THINKING

Just as you successfully changed from an active alcoholic or addict into a sober person, you can change from a smoker to a nonsmoker.

- Start thinking of yourself as a nonsmoker. Repeat ten or more times every morning, evening, and right before you fall asleep, "I am a nonsmoker," or "I don't smoke." Just as with addiction recovery, your thoughts can change your brain. Focus your TAMERS practice on your smoking habit for now.

- Use positive reinforcement to enhance your image of yourself as a nonsmoker. Imagine yourself enjoying not smoking, breathing clean, fresh air, enjoying food more, and feeling new bursts of energy.

- Reject tobacco as your "friend." Many smokers have an emotional attachment to their cigarettes that is akin to a friendship—or almost a love affair. They think of tobacco as loyal in difficult times, available for support when times are bad, and nonjudgmental when other friends are gone. A big step toward giving up tobacco is changing your relationship with it. See it as your enemy, your worst nightmare.

- Think about why you want to quit. Do you want your kids or partner to be proud of you? Are you getting ready for a special event? Do you want to feel more in control of your life? Do you just want to get rid of this last nagging addiction? Do you want to save money for a new car or a down payment on a home? Do you want to improve your health?

- Write down your reasons for quitting on a card and carry it with you. Attach the card to your cigarette pack with a rubber band. Whenever you reach for a cigarette, read the card. Also post it on your bathroom mirror, in your car, on the refrigerator, next to your computer, or wherever you will see it regularly. (You can also record videos of your reasons for quitting. See the apps in Choose Your Tools, page 530.)

- Shift your addiction frame of reference. Think of nicotine as your drug of choice, of smoking as your active addiction, and of yourself as an addict with a desire to stop smoking.

- Start going to more 12-step meetings to refresh your recovery program and tools. You may find it hard to talk about your nicotine addiction in AA meetings (unless you can relate it to your alcoholism, others may consider it off topic). Another option is to start going to Nicotine Anonymous meetings.

- Make use of the tools that can help change your thinking, such as counseling, group therapy, meditation, and hypnosis. You might also find support in the aftercare or continuing care meetings of your treatment center.

- Remind yourself regularly about all the health risks of smoking and the benefits of quitting. Read everything you can find about the hazards of smoking.

- Reinforce the notion that smoking is a dirty habit by not emptying your ashtrays (in your car, at home) and keeping windows closed.

- Remind yourself how awful smoking is by taking a day to overdo it: Smoke at least double your usual quota of cigarettes, smoke until your eyes and throat are irritated, until the very thought of another cigarette alarms you. (If the feeling stays with you the next day, try to go cold turkey.)

- Set up a Google alert that searches for "dangers of smoking" or something similar. Your email inbox will be filled with news about the dangers—day after day.

THE GREEN ZONE

CHOOSE YOUR TOOLS: PATCHES, GUM, APPS

There are many tools that can help you quit, such as nicotine replacement therapy (patches, gum), phone apps, counseling, and more. Medication taken orally is also an option. A note of caution, however: For people in recovery, medication should be a last resort. If you need something other than abstinence, try nicotine replacement therapy before trying medication.

Consider some of the options below—long before your quit date. If you find something you think will work for you, add it to your written quit plan, and get things ready before your quit date arrives. For example, you might need to lay in a supply of patches, sign up for text messages, schedule an appointment with your therapist or doctor, or decide on a mutual quit date with a buddy. Don't leave your planning to the last minute and then use that as an excuse to not quit. Be ready.

Nicotine Replacement Therapy

Nicotine is a drug, and you are probably addicted to it. Nicotine replacement products, such as patches, give you a small dose of nicotine, easing the symptoms of withdrawal. They allow the smoker to give up the most dangerous part of the habit (the smoke-filled lungs), and also break the behavioral habits, while temporarily continuing to get a fix.

Over-the-counter (nonprescription) options include the skin patch, gum, and lozenges. With a prescription, you can also get an inhaler or nasal spray system. Many people use a combination, such as patch each day, plus gum or a spray when they have a strong "breakthrough" craving.

Nicotine patches are applied to the skin. They typically come in three steps, or strengths: 21 mg, 14 mg, and 7 mg. You start with the strongest version, then taper down to the weakest over a few weeks or months. Eventually, they are eliminated entirely. The patch has a fairly high success rate, and some people find them easier to use than the gum.

If you use the gum, you have to follow directions carefully (it's not like chewing Chiclets) or you could end up with side effects, such as nausea. Chew it slowly and intermittently (off and on) and tuck it in your cheek between chews. Wait at least 15 minutes after you eat or drink.

Most people find that starting with twelve pieces a day (each chewed when you crave a smoke) works to replace the nicotine they've been getting from tobacco. The frequency is gradually whittled down to zero. As use is tapered off, you may need to cut the gum into smaller pieces. Gum should not be used for more than six months.

All of these substitution methods are more effective when tied to a formal smoking-cessation program, such as counseling.

However, this route isn't for everybody. Those who have certain heart conditions and pregnant women and nursing mothers should not use nicotine replacement products. It may also be risky to smoke while wearing the patch.

While these medications are available without a prescription, it's always best to talk with your doctor before you start using them. And be aware that if you snorted your former drugs of choice, using a nasal spray could be a trigger for you.

Some people are now using electronic cigarettes to continue to get a dose of nicotine. These devices, usually battery operated, turn the nicotine into a vapor that is inhaled. The U.S. Food and Drug Administration says these products have not been studied, and it's not known if they are safe. They are banned in some areas. For a person in recovery who smoked their drugs, they also pose the risk of triggering addictive behavior. Some people do find them to be a helpful tool for quitting, however, sometimes as an alternative to the patch.

Prescription Medications

Two medications often used to help people quit are bupropion SR (Zyban) and varenicline tartrate (Chantix). They can ease the withdrawal symptoms and urges to smoke. Bupropion can be used along with nicotine replacement products. Varenicline can also block the effects of nicotine if you start smoking again.

Think twice before you take prescription drugs for your smoking habit, however. In fact, consider them a last resort. They can trigger a relapse. These medications should be used only if no other method has worked for you, and only if continuing to smoke is a bigger immediate risk to your health than a relapse would be. Be especially wary if your old drugs of choice were pills; taking any pills now could act as a trigger. Plus, as a person in recovery, you don't want to come this far only to revive the idea that outside drugs (or alcohol) are the answer to every ache.

These drugs do have some side effects, and should be used only with your doctor's guidance. Also be sure to read Medication Concerns on page 290 precautions on taking any drugs.

Organizations and Apps

Many organizations have materials to help you quit.

- Smokefree.gov is sponsored by the National Cancer Institute (part of the U.S. National Institutes of Health) and other organizations. It has a wealth of free materials, including guides to quitting, quizzes, journals, and help via instant messaging. It also offers free phone apps that will help you monitor your progress, track your cravings, and calculate your savings; some apps also give you tips for dealing with cravings, and even post your progress to your social media accounts. One app also allows you to record video messages to serve as reminders of why you want to quit. This site also has a texting service that will send regular messages of encouragement to your mobile device (text QUIT to IQUIT [47848], or sign up at smokefree .gov/smokefreetxt).

- Two other NIH sites have materials tailored for women (women.smokefree.gov) and teens (teen.smokefree.gov).

- If you're in the military, check out Quit Tobacco, Make Everyone Proud (ucanquit2.org) from the U.S. Department of Defense. It offers information on quitting, group coaching, personalized training materials, and more. If you are enrolled in Tricare, you have access to live online chat help as well as phone support 24 hours a day (North Region: 866-459-8766; South Region: 877-414-9949; West Region: 888-713-4597). If you're a veteran enrolled in the VA Health Care System, you can call 877-222-8387 for help.

- The National Cancer Institute has phone and online counselors (English and Spanish) who can help you find information and explore options for quitting. Call 877-44U-QUIT (877-448-7848) or go to cancer.gov/cancertopics/ tobacco/smoking (click on LiveHelp Online Chat).

- Contact your free state quitline at 800-QUIT-NOW (800-784-8669). Trained "quit counselors" can help you explore your motivations to quit and your triggers, devise a personalized quit plan, and give you support and encouragement. In most cases you'll be connected to a program in your own state.

- The American Cancer Society has a Guide to Quitting Smoking at cancer.org/healthy/stayawayfrom tobacco/guidetoquittingsmoking /index, or by calling 800-ACS-2345 or your local ACS affiliate.

- Want to hear how other people managed to quit? The U.S. Centers for Disease Control has posted videos of real quitters at Tips From Former Smokers (cdc .gov/tobacco/campaign/tips).

Group Therapy and Support Programs

Success rates are much higher when a smoker attends a clinic or group program.

- The American Lung Association offers a Freedom From Smoking program. Call the Lung HelpLine at 800-LUNG-USA (800-586-4872) or go to lung.org/stop-smoking/how-to-quit/freedom-from-smoking.

- The American Cancer Society offers Fresh Start support groups at workplaces. See Workplace Solutions at acsworkplacesolutions.com/

freshstart.asp or call 800-ACS-2345 (800-227-2345).

- Nicotine Anonymous uses a 12-step approach to quitting smoking. Go to nicotine-anonymous.org.

- Many local medical centers also offer smoking cessation programs. Call your local hospital or county health department to see what is available.

Individual Therapy

A wide range of psychotherapeutic and behavior modification approaches are available, with varying success. Therapy is most successful when the client is motivated and the therapist is experienced. Hypnosis works for some people, but it should be administered only by a licensed physician or therapist. Acupuncture also works for some people. (To find practitioners in these areas, ask around at your fellowship meetings, and also see the listings in chapter 5.)

Guided visualization also helps some people. Check out the options at healthjourneys.com.

Buddy Up

You can improve your chances of quitting if you find others willing to quit with you. Set a joint quit date, talk to each other several times a week, get together for lunch regularly, and send encouraging text messages.

You can also get online support from others who are trying to quit, such as in the American Lung Association's Freedom From Smoking program (facing page), or on quitnet.com.

Another option is to find a sponsor who will focus on your habit—someone who's successfully quit and is willing to talk you through your own journey.

Inpatient Treatment

When all else fails, inpatient treatment may work. Provided at some treatment centers, it is modeled on drug and alcohol treatment but usually lasts no more than a week. Aftercare at Nicotine Anonymous or another group program is usually recommended.

START CHANGING YOUR HABITS

Start shaking up your smoking routines, before your quit date.

Go back to your smoking diary and look at the situations that trigger your desire to smoke. Start changing those habits now. Do you always have a cigarette with your morning coffee? Switch to tea. Do you always have a cigarette when you talk on the phone? Try to make your calls from a smoke-free zone. Is your lunch break always a time to light up at work? Take a walk instead. Is the end of a meal the signal to pull out a pack? Get up from the table as soon as you've had your last bite.

Another way to change those ingrained habits is to make smoking a chore. Put your cigarettes in an inconvenient place; keep matches and cigarettes in different rooms;

THE GREEN ZONE

if you're right-handed, smoke with your left hand. Smoke only standing up, or only in a place you dislike, such as the garage.

By now you are probably getting at least somewhat sick of your relationship with nicotine. You might not see those smokes as so much of a friend anymore, so keep cutting down how much you smoke:

- Before you light up, read your reasons for quitting card.

- Try to wait ten minutes before lighting up. After a few days, extend that to fifteen minutes, then half an hour, and so on.

- Have your first cigarette of the day later and later in the morning.

- Looking at your diary again, figure out which cigarettes you are least dependent on. Try eliminating them now by first asking yourself, "Do I really need this cigarette?"

- When you do light up, smoke only half of the cigarette.

Postponing lighting up may allow the craving to pass without your yielding to it. This will also help you reduce the number of cigarettes you smoke, and thus taper your intake of nicotine, before you quit.

Get rid of all your smoking paraphernalia now, too: lighters, matches, ashtrays, and so on. Some other actions you can start now:

- Find some things you can substitute for cigarettes (gum, raw vegetables) and start using them occasionally.

- Switch to low-tar cigarettes, preferably a brand you don't like, as you get closer to your quit date.

- Think about taking up yoga, reviving your meditation practice, or doing whatever else helps you relax.

- Spend more time at places where smoking is prohibited, and avoid locales you associate with smoking.

- If the AA meeting you usually go to is not nonsmoking, find one that is.

- If you must be somewhere where smoking is permitted, stick with the nonsmokers.

- If smoking is permitted where you work, set your own limits and make your own rules—decide, for example, that you will smoke only on breaks.

- Ask friends not to smoke around you, and stay away from friends who can't oblige.

- If you have more than two cups of coffee a day or the equivalent in other caffeinated beverages (sodas, teas, and so on), start to cut back on your caffeine intake over a period of several weeks to prevent caffeine rebound as your nicotine intake drops.

SET A QUIT DATE

Once you have done all of your preparation, it's time to choose a quit date.

You can pick a particular date in advance: a family birthday, a holiday, the first day of the next month, or the next Great American Smokeout in November. If you think it might help, plan to quit while you're on vacation. A totally different environment, a place where you've never smoked and where your daily routine is completely different, may make quitting easier. (Or on a day when you feel awful, you can just say to yourself, "Today I feel lousy. Smoking is the main reason, and I'm not going to smoke anymore.")

Announce your quit date publicly. Tell friends, family, and coworkers you are planning to quit and when. If you are participating in an online forum for quitters, announce it there. Announce it on Facebook, on other social media sites, and any other way you can think of.

As your quit day approaches, get your teeth cleaned and whitened at the dentist's office and resolve to keep them that way. (Brushing after each meal will also reinforce the idea of keeping your mouth fresh, and you'll be less likely to want to foul it with tobacco.) Air out your car, your home, and your clothing.

GO: Quit Day

ON THE BIG DAY AND SOON AFTER

You are now a nonsmoker. Relish your new identity. Change your self-image, as well as the image others have of you, to nonsmoker. When the subject comes up, instead of saying "I'm trying to quit," say assertively, "I don't smoke."

You are likely to have some cravings, and you may also feel out of sorts without a cigarette in your hand. So continue the preparatory behaviors on the facing page (change people and places you associate with smoking; make smoking difficult; think of the rewards of not smoking; substitute other forms of gratification; and so on).

Also, stay busy, especially in the first few days. Exercise, even if it's only a walk around the block. Drink lots of water; it helps to flush nicotine out of your system. A tall, cold drink of water may even banish a craving for a cigarette. Check in with your quit buddy or sponsor regularly. Spend as much time as you can with friends who don't smoke. Listen to meditation or visualization recordings. Go to a movie or take a class at the gym.

Apply what you learned during your drug or alcohol recovery to giving up tobacco. This is just another addiction and should be treated as such. But keep in mind that though you may be able to take your other addictions one day at a time, you may have to stay away from cigarettes just minutes at a time.

If you have a craving, tell yourself you can wait for that smoke. Do something else instead. The craving will pass whether you smoke or not. Select the substitute activity that

THE GREEN ZONE

most fulfills the need you think you smoked for.

Substitutes include:

- **Relaxers.** If you smoked to calm your nerves, try relaxation exercises and other routes to calm (see chapter 14). When a craving strikes, sit down and relax your body. Slowly inhale deeply, then exhale. Repeat until the urge fades.

- **Mouth fillers.** Try raw veggies, chewing gum or mints, or a plastic straw.

- **Hand busiers.** Keep your hands occupied with knitting, needlework, or drawing. Do a jigsaw puzzle; play solitaire or video games; take up a musical instrument; try simple carpentry; finger worry beads or a rosary; roll a couple of marbles or modeling clay around in your hand; or make paper airplanes.

- **Mind occupiers.** Read, learn some new software, edit your digital photos, study a foreign language, do volunteer work, take a course—anything that will require you to concentrate and keep your mind focused.

- **Short-term distractors.** When a craving stirs, get up and go for a walk; dance; turn down the lights and make love; take a leisurely bath; go for a bus ride or go anywhere else that smoking is prohibited; do some research for the vacation you're going to take with the money

you save; or catch up with friends on Facebook.

Reward yourself for your abstention. This will also improve the odds of success. Spend some of your new-found savings on tangible rewards, such as a movie, new clothes, or a ball game. Or give yourself a psychic reward: Tell yourself how proud you are of yourself and how proud others are of you, or how you and your home smell and look better. When eating, notice how good food tastes and smells. Every day, remind yourself how much money you're saving. Put what you would have spent on tobacco in a piggy bank, and use the savings for something special.

Be persistent. If at first you don't succeed, try again. And again. You can do it—millions of people have. And don't despair if you do slip and have a cigarette; just remember that you don't have to have two. Call your sponsor, your quit buddy, or your state's quitline (see page 532) to talk about it. Learn from your slip.

DEALING WITH NICOTINE WITHDRAWAL

As with any addiction, giving up nicotine invites a bombardment of withdrawal symptoms. Not everyone experiences every symptom. Some lucky people breeze through withdrawal feeling nothing but regret at losing a friend they've relied on, while others have a tougher time.

Nicotine is a psychoactive substance that works at specific sites in the brain as a relaxant, while paradoxically acting elsewhere in the body as a stimulant—accelerating heartbeat, elevating blood pressure, and giving a generalized lift. The body responds to the withdrawal of the drug in many ways; some of them are uncomfortable but none are life-threatening. The most common:

- A decrease in heart rate and blood pressure

- Tingling or numbness in the extremities as circulation improves

- Difficulty sleeping; vivid smoking dreams

- Restlessness

- Increased coughing

- Dry mouth

- Slight sore throat, and possibly sore gums and tongue

- Fluid retention

- Psychological distress, including intense cravings, nervousness and tension, depression (possibly with bouts of crying), fatigue, irritability, light-headedness, and aggressiveness

- Impairment of both physical and mental performance, with a lack of concentration

Less common symptoms include headaches, muscle aches, and constipation and other intestinal ills.

You may have all or only a few of these unsettling phenomena. As with any withdrawal symptoms, there are ways to minimize the discomfort. To reduce nervousness (by slowing the release of stored nicotine into your bloodstream), increase your intake of fruit, fruit juice, milk, and mixed greens, and cut back on meat, poultry, fish, and cheese. Avoid caffeine, which can add to the jitters. Get plenty of rest (to counter fatigue) and exercise (to replace the kick you used to get from nicotine). Let your mind go fallow for a few days, if necessary, doing mindless tasks or wandering around a shopping mall or some other place where smoking is prohibited.

The worst of withdrawal lasts only a few days to a few weeks.

THE GREEN ZONE

CHAPTER

For Family and Friends

I f you live with or care deeply about someone who is an addict or alcoholic, you know how this disease can turn everything upside down. You may have been dealing with the fallout for years—binges of drinking or drug use, lost jobs, damaged relationships, wrecked cars, ruined finances. And lying. So much lying. Your loved one may have turned into someone you hardly recognize.

You know that addiction has greatly altered your loved one's behavior. What you may not realize is that it has also had a big impact on your own outlook on life and behavior. Your loved one's addiction is a disease, and any time a serious illness strikes, whether it's cancer, Alzheimer's, or something else, everyone close to the patient is affected. The same is true when the illness is chemical dependency. Everyone in your family, as well as other people in your lives, has been affected by addiction in some way. Now you all need to work on getting your lives back to some kind of normal. With recovery, you'll all have a chance to rebuild and reinvigo-rate your relationships, but this will work only if everyone works hard at overcoming the insidious effects of this disease.

So where do you start? We suggest you first learn about addiction and understand that it really is a disease and how it has affected your loved one. Read chapter 1, Welcome to Recovery. Then read chapter 2, Your Recovery Plan, to get an overview of what it means to get into a life in recovery (it's much more than just getting sober). Chapter 2 will also introduce you to the Recovery Zone System, which provides a blueprint for tackling the issues of recovery one by one without getting overwhelmed. Then come back to this chapter, to better understand your role in everything—and how you can and cannot help your loved one.

All the other chapters, while aimed at the person in recovery, will also help you. They'll give you a better understanding of what the alcoholic/addict is going through, and also teach you about the many options for treatment, how AA and other fellowships work, and much more.

A quick warning here—we hope that your loved one will eventually be putting a lot of time and effort into his recovery. So much time and effort that you might again feel left out, just when you thought you'd all turned a corner. Understanding how recovery works should make things easier on you and help you to be patient with the process. Remember, your loved one has a brain disease. You can hate the disease while still loving the person.

How Addiction and Alcoholism Affect Relationships

FAMILY DYNAMICS

Sometimes we don't realize how much our actions can affect those we are close to.

Think of your family as a many-armed, multilayered mobile, like one that hangs over a baby's crib. Balancing at the end of each arm is a fam-

ily member, living his or her own life. Every move, every action by one person sends his own arm into motion. But that exerts a force on all the other arms—and family members—forcing everyone to react.

Say that, for months or years, everyone has been humming along fine, handling their jobs, relationships, health, and other parts of their lives without any major upheavals. The family mobile is balanced, with each arm making only minor swings up and down.

Then one member of the family is diagnosed with a serious illness and their spot on the mobile starts to swing wildly. That greatly upsets the balance of everyone else connected to them, leading to a wide range of reactions. Some family members do all they can to help the patient. Others retreat in confusion and distress. Some experience feelings of denial, anger, anxiety, or depression. It will be a long time before things settle down and everyone's life is back in balance.

It's the same when the disease is addiction. One person in motion affects all the others.

In this case, however, the impacts are often felt long before a diagnosis is made. While the disease is developing and the forces are still small, family dynamics and relationships start to shift—long before anyone realizes there is a serious problem. Gradually, the family begins to change as the drinking or drug use takes over. Family members have all kinds of reactions to what is going on, including super responsibility and powerlessness; self-blame or blaming the alcoholic; anger and forgiveness; hurt and fear. They try to manipulate, reason with, beg, or browbeat the addict into cleaning up his or her act, almost always unsuccessfully.

As the disease progresses, the family starts to look like a mobile in a wind storm. The arms are flailing about wildly, and nothing is working as it should. The addict loses more and more control over his own life while, ironically, often taking control of the tangled and distorted lives of everyone else. Everyone is living a life filled with trauma and destruction—which can cause long-lasting psychological damage.

The family is likely to remain wildly out of balance for quite a long time, until the addict is diagnosed and enters into treatment and recovery.

CODEPENDENCY

Other people on the mobile, those whose lives are swinging wildly out of control due to their relationships with the addict/alcoholic, are often called codependent. That's because, just like the addict, they too have a dependency—not on a substance, but on the addict himself. Their lives end up revolving around that of the addict, and they change their own behavior to try to cope with the stress and unpredictability of life with a chemically dependent person.

This can take many forms:

Covering up. The addict makes liars of us all. When a substance abuse problem occurs, family members usually step in to try to fix it. They do this as much to cover their own embarrassment, guilt, and shame as to cover up for the addict.

If the sick family member is too hung over to go to work, the partner delivers an excuse to the boss. If dad forgets Little League practice, his son tells the coach he's out of town. If money is spent wildly, cuts are made elsewhere.

The addiction and its damaging consequences are covered up. Painful feelings are suppressed. Trauma and distress intensify, but it's all kept under wraps.

In effect, well-meaning family members and others help the addict/alcoholic to sail merrily along, even while his disease is getting much worse. And this unwitting conspiracy to cover up the embarrassing damage makes it difficult for anyone, particularly the foggy-thinking alcoholic, to realize he has a really big problem.

Rationalizing. Rather than acknowledge the addict's increasing disability as the disease runs wildly out of control, family members try to explain it away: "He's under a lot of pressure right now." "It's those awful friends she hangs out with."

Withdrawing. If a man fears his partner will have two cocktails too many and make a scene when they go out with friends, they stop going out. If a young girl can't be sure her dad won't be stoned when she gets home from school, she never invites her friends over.

Blaming. Family members search their own psyches for an explanation. They blame themselves for the catastrophe that has overtaken their home: "Maybe I haven't been helpful enough [or loving enough, or trusting enough, or made enough money]." Some come to think there's nothing wrong with the person who is misusing substances. Instead, as their own behavior becomes so distorted and the addict's rationalizing so convincing, they start to think *they* are the problem. Of course, at the same time they might also blame the addict: "You ruined our lives. You messed up our kids." Others try to place the blame on other friends or family members, or on society.

Haranguing and controlling. As it becomes more obvious that something is really wrong, there is a lot of shouting and begging. Everyone accuses the others of crimes. One or more family members may try to control the erratic alcoholic— sometimes to the point of obsession. They are always unsuccessful in the long run. But there may be enough seeming victories that the manipulation goes on.

Checking out. When they fail to help their sick loved ones with kindness or to change them with sound and fury, some family members simply give up. They check out, either physically by staying away from home a lot or moving out, or emotionally by withdrawing into themselves. They go on with their own lives as best they can.

All of these approaches, unfortunately, are doomed to failure. Rather than helping, they allow the addict/alcoholic to continue toward his inevitable fall. Over time, any friction that might have led to positive changes has faded away. The addict is left with no responsibilities or expectations, and no accountability for his actions. The destructive spiral of drinking and drugging accelerates.

At the same time, the effects on everyone else have worsened, too. Others in the family keep scrambling, trying to take up the slack. Stress and responsibility are shifted away from the sick member to others. The family gets even further out of balance.

Even once the addict/alcoholic gets sober, these imbalances in family dynamics don't go away overnight. Extensive therapy may be needed to help the family regain its balance, and that takes time and effort. In effect, the entire family needs to enter into recovery.

ENABLING

Closely related to codependency is the concept of enabling. Those who live or work with addicted people tend to adapt in such a way that they make it easier for the addict— they enable them—to continue their self-destructive spiral. Spouses take over the responsibilities of the sick partner, forgive unforgivable behavior, live under crazy conditions, and keep trying to be loving and caring in the face of abuse. Parents close their eyes to odd behavior, hand out big allowances, and write absence notes for questionable illnesses. They are all enslaved to the disease of addiction, failing to hold the addict accountable for his actions and fooling themselves into thinking they are saving the person they love.

KIDS ARE AFFECTED, TOO

Whether they withdraw or act out, most children in families with addiction suffer from severe embarrassment and shame because of their parent's behavior. They see the knowing looks and hear the whispered comments. And they cringe. Even the silence of kind friends who try to look the other way can be painful.

To compound their misery, these kids usually feel guilty about being ashamed. They feel they are betraying the family when they fail to defend Mom or Dad to friends or strangers. Once they are old enough, they often take sides, cutting themselves off from either their friends or their family.

But these kids might be most upset and confused by the uncertainties and inconsistencies of their seesaw lives. They are confused by role reversals, such as when the non-addicted parent has to jump in and take over the tasks of the addicted one.

Then there are the dramatic mood swings: Mommy is loving when sober, withdrawn when drunk. Daddy is friendly when off drugs, violent when he "needs them." There are dramatic swings in atmospheric pressure: The home is sometimes morosely silent and at other times an angry and tumultuous parental battlefield. Sometimes the parents turn the kids into pawns: Drunk dad treats them to ice cream and toys, eroding mom's efforts to instill discipline and structure.

Perhaps most damaging of all, there are the swings from bright hope (when a parent promises to stay sober) to darkest despair (when the promise is broken). This behavior damages the child's self-image ("If Mommy really loved me, or if I were really good, she would stop drinking"), and builds a basic distrust (which unless reversed can color all future relationships). It also increases guilt and confusion; the child hates and fears the father when he's drunk, but loves the very same person when he's sober.

Because their emotional resources can't fix their problems, children in these families may also experience physical symptoms related to the dysfunction—sleeplessness, night terrors, unexplained aches and pains, upset stomachs, and so on.

DENIAL

Even in the midst of all this turmoil, addicts, and often other family members, will swear up and down that there is no problem. This group insanity often develops into what's called a "merry-go-round of denial."

"I've been going to AA for six months. I know I'm an alcoholic. But my wife still drinks herself sick every night, and takes pills, too. Why can't she see what's happening?"

Your wife isn't ready to admit that she's sick. Her denial of her condition is a very common symptom of the disease of addiction. While it might seem that she is just being stubborn, that's not the case. More likely, her inability to see what is happening is due to the effects of alcohol and drugs on her brain. The "higher thinking" part of her brain may realize she has a problem, but another part, the one associated with primitive survival needs, has an irresistible need for alcohol and drugs. The brain can't hold on to these two contradictory beliefs for very long, and the survival brain usually wins out. The fleeting thought that she might have a problem is gone in a flash.

Getting Help for Your Loved One

IF THEY REALIZE THEY NEED HELP

In the best of circumstances, your loved one will finally see for himself that it's time to do something about his drinking or drug use. To get there, he'll need to take three important steps. You can play a supporting role in each step, but you can't control the situation.

1. Recognition. First of all, he has to recognize there is a problem, that his drinking or drug use has gotten out of control. The light may dawn when a boss orders him to shape up or ship out. Or when a close friend takes him aside and urges him to seek help. Or maybe when you finally take on that thankless task yourself. However it happens, your addicted family member may be the last to know there's a problem—or at least the last to admit it.

2. Acceptance. Next, the addict must be willing to accept the diagnosis of alcoholic or addict. Many people simply reach the point where, on their own, they're ready to throw in the towel and declare, "I am an alcoholic." Others are more tentative and will say only, "If you think I am an addict, then I will stop using drugs." This is still a form of denial, but it opens the door a tiny bit.

3. A decision to get help. It's not enough for the addict to say, "Okay, I'll stop." That's only the very first step; the most basic foundation of a new life. Now he must formulate a plan for getting help, for building a life that no longer needs alcohol or drugs. It all starts with detox and the initial professional treatment, if any (the Red Zone chapters outline many options). It most likely also includes getting involved in a recovery fellowship.

You may be a key person in helping decide which recovery options make the most sense, given your knowledge of the addicted person and the severity of his or her problem, as well as your knowledge of finances, insurance, and so on. Ideally, these decisions will be made with the help of a trained professional (doctor, psychologist, cleric, or counselor), other family members, and of course the addict himself.

If your loved one sees this search as building a "therapeutic alliance" with people he trusts, he is more likely to embrace the process.

WHEN THEY DON'T AGREE THEY NEED HELP: INCHING TOWARD RECOVERY

Of course, many alcoholics and addicts will not readily accept that they have a problem. And as you surely know by now, you can't force someone to face up to his problem and embrace recovery. You've done all the crying and shouting already, and it didn't help.

So what can you do to help nudge someone in the right direction—and maintain your own sanity at the same time?

Calmly discuss your feelings. Drinking and drug use usually put feelings on the back burner. If you're being hurt by someone's addiction, talk about it calmly and rationally, avoiding anger, accusations, ultimatums, and nagging. Let him know the pain you feel because of your love for him; it may make it easier for him to address the problem. (See tips on how to have a motivational rather than confrontational conversation on page 105.)

For some people, it's easier to accept the idea that they are "at risk" of chemical dependency. Admitting that you are an alcoholic or addict can be very hard; the diagnosis often carries shame and guilt. If you instead gently raise the issue, saying, "Honey, I'm afraid you may be at risk of developing a problem," he may be more open to taking a closer look at his behavior.

Give him a copy of this book. If he learns about addiction, and sees that it really is a disease, he may start to recognize that he does have a problem. If he refuses to accept the book, leave it out where he can read it when he thinks no one is looking.

Be ready to respond to silent cries for help. The husband who's using meth "accidentally" leaves some in the family car. The young man who's drinking too much keeps complaining to his girlfriend about vague symptoms. They're trying to call attention to their misery in the only way they know how. Your loved one may do the same one day. Be on the lookout for these cries for help, and be ready to respond with some constructive options.

- Suggest the two of you have a heart-to-heart talk about what's going on, and look at options for recovery.

- Suggest you both go to an open AA or NA meeting, just to see what it's like.

- Urge him to talk with his doctor, minister, therapist, or a counselor.

- Ask a friend who is in recovery to talk with him.

Do an intervention. If he continues to deny that anything is wrong, consider an intervention. First let him know you are looking into your options for doing one. Assure him it is because you love him and care about the relationship. Give him some time to see that you really are serious about taking this step. If he continues to resist getting help, plan the intervention and carry it out. Even if it doesn't work right away, you've planted a seed for future salvation and will know that you've done everything you could.

Go to Al-Anon or another family-support group. You aren't responsible for your loved one's recovery, but you are responsible for your own. At Al-Anon and in other groups you will meet others who are facing the same problems you are struggling with. Their love and support will guide and strengthen you, whether your partner gives up drinking or not and whether you leave him or not.

Involuntary treatment. In many states, an addict or alcoholic can be involuntarily committed to treatment. If you think you might need to pursue this option at some point, be sure to first get involved in your own support fellowship; that way you will have the knowledge and skills that will enable you to seriously commit to that action and be prepared for the consequences. Not surprisingly, someone who is not ready to seek treatment on their own might not be too happy to be forced into it. They may even react violently when they are released. So be sure you want to go through with it before you take action. (The decision will probably be easier if you truly fear they will die soon without treatment.) The legal procedures vary quite a bit from state to state, and can be rather complicated. For guidance on what is required in your area, start by calling your local police department or mental health clinic.

SHOULD WE DO AN INTERVENTION?

If someone you love has a drug or alcohol problem and continues to deny it, or they have a relapse and refuse to admit it, an intervention might be your best option.

What Is an Intervention?

An intervention is a process in which people try to help an alcoholic or addict realize he has a problem and persuade him to get treatment. Family members, close friends, and sometimes a professional facilitator meet one or more times to talk about the issues. The process then concludes with a meeting with the alcoholic/addict and a plea to get help.

An intervention should stress the importance of the family's pain and needs. Family members are allowed to spell out their feelings and frustrations with a supportive group present to help them make their case. But it is not the time to beat up on the person, to punish or get even. The purpose of an intervention is to help, out of love and concern.

About nine out of ten interventions succeed in getting an addict into treatment. But even those that don't succeed can be therapeutic. They give family members the feeling that, no matter what happens, at least they tried. They have expressed their love and concern for their loved one, and did all they could to help him.

A really successful intervention helps not only the alcoholic, but those around him. It stresses the importance of their needs and persuades them that, whether or not their loved one agrees to treatment, they need to change their own lives. It can be liberating, since it provides a forum where they can finally tell the alcoholic how they've suffered. During the intervention process, family and friends can also take a stand to start healing themselves, or at least to withdraw from being part of the problem through their silence or enabling.

When Is an Intervention a Good Idea?

It can help when an addict has rejected other unmistakable attempts or suggestions to get treatment, is practicing denial and self-deception, and there are no other strong factors (such as job, medical, or legal problems) to motivate him to seek treatment.

When Is an Intervention Not a Good Idea?

It might not work when there is little ammunition with which to approach the person in trouble. An intervention usually takes place after personal and direct attempts to confront your loved one have been attempted and failed, and when you have many examples of addictive and harmful behavior.

Do We Need Professional Help?

If your family relationships are fairly strong and the person you are trying to reach does not have a history of mental problems, violence, or self-destructive behavior, family and friends may be able to handle the intervention alone, perhaps with coaching from a professional. It's usually better and more effective, however, to hire a professional to set up the intervention and take part in it. This is especially true if you suspect that the addict might blow up or otherwise react badly.

Who Should Participate?

Pick people who are closest to the addict and the most influential. These could be family members, close friends, a clergyperson, a doctor, business associates, and others. Bringing in people from outside the family helps by making it clear it's not just family members who know about the problem and are concerned. The group should be large enough to have an impact and to show there is some interest and power behind the effort. But it should be small enough to still be personal and manageable and not overwhelm your target (usually no more than eight).

Don't invite anyone who might have a drinking or drug problem of his own. Also exclude those who always trigger anger in the alcoholic/addict. Young children should not attend. Older children and teens, however, can be very effective.

Does the Intervention Need to Be a Surprise?

Not always. Strategies for running interventions have improved greatly over the years, and a new "invitational" type of intervention has proven very successful. In this approach, the addict or alcoholic is told up front that the people who care about him are planning an intervention. He is invited to take part in the whole process, which might include several meetings.

HOW TO STAGE AN INTERVENTION

There are typically nine steps to an intervention.

1. Decide if an intervention is appropriate. If you believe a child, partner, family member, or close friend is in need of help and he refuses to seek it voluntarily, or if a person in recovery has a relapse and is not seeking help, discuss the situation with one or two other key players. If you agree that an intervention is needed, continue with the next step.

2. Make a list of all potential participants.

3. Contact a professional who is experienced in running interventions. To find one, ask for referrals from friends who are involved in AA, NA, or Al-Anon, an addiction specialist, or a local treatment program (but not one you intend to use, as that could create a conflict of interest). You can also contact the American Society of Addiction Medicine (ASAM), or a local alcohol awareness council. See chapter 5 for the types of health care professionals who work in addiction.

Before you hire someone, ask about costs and manner of payment, and learn about his credentials and methods. Talk to him in person and see if he comes across in a loving, compassionate way and will be able to direct family energy constructively.

The fee for an intervention, which usually covers two or three planning sessions and arranging some logistics, can range from $750 to more than $4,000. Some community groups offer this service for less or even at no cost. People who are in recovery may also help run informal interventions as part of their step-12 work.

4. Arrange a preliminary planning and education meeting. Have the professional there to explain how the intervention will work and to provide some alcohol and drug education. He can also explain the workings of treatment, AA, and Al-Anon.

Have everyone who will be at the intervention write up some past events when they were hurt by the addict's alcohol- or drug-related behavior. Each incident should be a firsthand experience and include:

- When and where it took place

- What the behavior was

- How it related to alcohol or drug use

- How it affected them (for example, embarrassing, dangerous, or financially damaging)

- How it made the person recounting the story feel

When possible, be specific about how much alcohol or cocaine or pills were consumed. Use recent incidents rather than those that can be dismissed as ancient history.

Warn all participants to avoid bringing up issues (such as an affair) that are not common knowledge and could stun the subject or other participants.

5. Get the facts on treatment. You can't just surround the drinker or drug user and say, "You've got to get treatment." Someone who has been blind to the need for treatment is in no condition to research the options. Deciding to get sober will be hard enough. So before you confront them, line up some treatment options.

Read the earlier chapters on treatment and explore your options, including inpatient treatment, outpatient treatment, and individual therapy, as well as AA, NA, or other mutual support programs.

Talk with people at various treatment options. Speak directly to potential therapists as well as staff at treatment centers. For some questions to ask, see chapter 5 on how to assess treatment facilities and options. Don't sign up with the first treatment center or therapist you interview. By the time you've talked with several people and inspected three or four facilities, you will have spotted strengths and flaws you wouldn't have noticed earlier, and you'll be almost an expert.

Also find out how the treatment can be paid for. Citing the cost of treatment is a popular way to squirm out of getting help. (See Paying for Treatment, page 93.)

Consider the logistics. The addict is also likely to come up with a long list of reasons why he can't go to treatment, so be sure to block all those potential escape routes. Find out if he can get time off from work (as discreetly as you can), and whether there is a bed available at an inpatient center, if that's the choice. Look at both business and family responsibilities and see how they can all be met or put off while the patient is getting sober.

6. Hold a rehearsal. A rehearsal will lower the stress at the actual intervention, helping everyone feel calmer, better prepared, and more confident. It also allows the family to confront in advance the emotions stirred up by the process. If these were to surface at the actual intervention, the whole process could be endangered. Everyone who is going to be at the actual intervention should be at the rehearsal. Someone who is not familiar with the process could wreck it.

Have one of the participants play the role of the addict. Bring out every piece of information you might bring up at the intervention. In turn, each person should:

- Present the items on their lists of past events, calmly and in a nonjudgmental way, just as they would present information suggesting that a family member has another disease.

- Talk about how the drinking or drug use has affected them personally, how they have been hurt, upset, angered, embarrassed, or frightened by it, and how it is running or ruining their lives.

- State what the consequences will be if the subject refuses to stop drinking or using drugs. These should not be a cluster of idle threats, but specific actions each of you is willing to take. Depending on the situation, they might include separation, divorce, loss of custody or access to children, loss of employment, loss of financial support, eviction from the home, and so on.

- Close with a plea for the alcoholic/addict to get help.

If during the rehearsal some people seem unsure about the process, are afraid of angering or alienating the alcoholic, or unexpectedly play defender, ask them not to attend the real thing. By general agreement, edit out weak or unconvincing episodes of drug use and drinking. If information comes up that could be very upsetting to the addict, don't use it too early in the intervention. It may be more effective later—especially if he is reluctant to get help. If facts upsetting to those at the rehearsal come up, they will need to be dealt with, too—by the professional present or by another counselor.

7. Make final preparations. Before the intervention, as needed, reserve space for your loved one at a treatment center (if inpatient treatment is the chosen option), make an appointment for him with a therapist or at an outpatient clinic, and pack his bags. Arrange details such as transportation, pet care, childcare, or time off work. Do whatever is necessary to make it easy to get the person into treatment right away if the intervention is successful.

8. Set up the intervention. Choose a spot the subject can get to easily. Ideally, it should be neutral territory—a doctor's office, a church meeting room. If you think it will be impossible to get him there, you can do it at home as a last resort.

The room should be chosen and arranged so there is no easy escape. If violence is likely, make sure there are no weapons nearby.

Pick a time when all essential players can be present. Getting the star there, of course, will be a challenge, if he doesn't know what is going on. One approach is to say that you've been seeing a counselor (the intervention counselor) as a family "to deal with the problems you've created in our lives," and that you would like him to join you for a one-time-only meeting. Then, with the time and place set, extend the invitation to that meeting. Try to be up front, but do whatever is necessary to get him to the intervention.

If you have no luck in getting him to come to a meeting, you may have to approach him on his own turf. Pick a time when you're sure he will be at home and is likely to be most lucid. Then have all the participants converge on the house together. If your subject retreats to the bedroom, follow. If he tries to escape through the front door, block it if you can, but if there is any threat of violence, or you fear the situation could lead to violence, let him leave.

9. Do your lifesaving work. Calmly have each participant talk about past events and potential consequences, as rehearsed earlier. Each person should end with a plea to get help. Reading from prepared notes will reduce anxiety and make certain that nothing important is left out. Be sure to constantly emphasize the love and concern of everyone.

When everyone is finished, the intervention professional or whoever is running the meeting should ask, "Is this how you want to live your life?" and urge the subject to "please get help." He should also clearly again spell out the consequences if help isn't sought—but only if everyone is really ready to follow through on them.

POSSIBLE INTERVENTION OUTCOMES

In the majority of cases, when an intervention is carefully planned and well executed, the alcoholic or addict agrees to go into treatment. A well-orchestrated intervention leaves little room for failure.

Sometimes, however, the response is, "I promise, I'll stop drinking—but on my own." How do you respond then? You can remind him about the number of times he's made—and broken—that promise. If his answer is still an adamant "No, I'm not going to treatment," you may be forced to say, "Okay, one more try." But try to get him to promise that if there is any further drinking or drug use, he will then get treatment. You can suggest that in the meantime, going to AA or NA meetings will help him.

What if your loved one bolts out the door, flatly refuses to make any changes in his life, or refuses to acknowledge that there is a problem? Even then, the intervention has not been a complete failure.

First, you've planted some important seeds, and possibly helped the addict to move closer to the day when he will be ready to seek help. Second, you've done your very best to help, so you don't have to feel responsible if your family member continues his self-destructive behavior. Third, you have all finally recognized the problem for what it is, and brought it out into the open, and now you all can—and should—take steps to help yourselves.

You will, however, have to follow through on your decided-upon consequences. That might be very hard for some people to carry though, but it must be done.

PROTECT YOUR FINANCES

If you are financially tied to an addict or alcoholic who is still using, you should do what you can to separate your finances from his. Set up your own checking account and start depositing your paycheck or other income there. Set up your own savings account and credit cards. Secure every account you can think of that he might have had access to, including little-used IRAs and savings accounts. Change your passwords, move the accounts, hide your checkbook. If you shop online and have your credit card numbers stored online at various sites, take them off the sites, and also change your passwords. Set up a separate user account on your computer, protect it with a password, and be sure you always sign out when you leave the computer. Also hide (or keep very close track of) any valuables that could easily be removed from the house and sold or pawned for cash. If you have joint accounts, you may be able to move all of the funds into a different account without his permission (state laws vary). Ask for some advice on this at your bank, or talk with a lawyer.

As your last step, cut off his access to any of your accounts he had permission to use, and take back any credit cards, debit cards, ATM cards, or checks he had in his possession. If he has just the credit card account numbers, you'll need to change those to prevent online purchases. You want to do as much as you can to secure your money before he realizes what you are doing.

Also see page 216 for ideas on how you can limit and monitor his spending if you have any joint accounts (for example, you can get text alerts whenever he uses a credit card).

PREVENT AN OVERDOSE DEATH

Thousands of people die of opioid/narcotic overdoses every year. Take too much of these all-too-available drugs, and breathing and the heart can slow down or stop altogether. In many cases, however, this can be reversed—and a death averted—with an injection or nasal squirt of a prescription drug called naloxone (Narcan). Many emergency staffs (first responders, paramedics) have been trained to treat overdoses, and they carry naloxone in their drug kits.

If someone has overdosed on drugs or alcohol, call 911. You may be able to save their life. If you are also high, call 911 anyway. In many states, you are protected from prosecution if you've been using illegal drugs or drinking underage.

If someone you know is continuing to use opioids and is at risk of overdose, you may want to get an overdose reversal kit. Also call your local first responders and make sure they have the drug on hand and have been trained to use it.

Find out more at SAMHSA Opioid Overdose Toolkit (store .samhsa.gov/product/Opioid -Overdose-Prevention-Toolkit/ SMA13-4742), or at Project Lazarus (projectlazarus.org).

If They Won't Stop

SHE WON'T ADMIT THERE IS A PROBLEM

"My mother and I keep arguing about the martini she has every night before dinner. I've measured the gin in it, and it's more like a triple martini. As soon as she drinks it, her memory goes completely, and it seems her memory in general is worse. How can I get her to stop drinking?"

Tell your mother that alcohol causes premature aging of the brain, and that it is very likely the cause of her memory problems. Even small amounts of alcohol can masquerade as senile dementia. If concern about memory loss isn't enough to scare her into sobriety, then she has an alcohol problem.

Talk to her doctor if you can. (Due to medical privacy laws, he may not be able to share details of your mother's medical history with you, but you can tell him about your concerns.) He may be able to prescribe sobriety for health reasons.

If that doesn't work, try to persuade your mother to try going sober for just a couple of months. During that time, keep track of her memory lapses. Have things improved? If so, you should be able to persuade her to continue abstaining in order to keep her brain as healthy as possible.

CONTINUED DRINKING

"My wife has gone to AA a few times to please me, but she hasn't stopped drinking. Her drinking doesn't seem to bother her, but it's driving me crazy."

Be grateful for the AA meetings your spouse did attend. Once an alcoholic goes to AA or to treatment, even under duress, they are never the same. The AA or NA experience may not have kept your wife sober this time, but it can sure ruin her future drinking. That's because some of the foundation for substance abuse has been undermined permanently—she now knows that help is available. Going to AA or treatment and just looking around at all those people in recovery grinning and hugging tells her that when she's ready for it, there is a way out, that addiction is not the only way to live. No matter how bad things get for her, she will know that where there is life, there is hope.

CAPTURE THE MOMENT

If a family member or close friend is not yet sober, record their actions. Get a photo or video of them looking their worst: coming in from an all-night drunk, standing next to a smashed-up car, or just looking dazed and out of it. These records will be valuable tools to use later, when a craving threatens to sabotage recovery.

When Your Child Is in Trouble

DO YOU SUSPECT YOUR CHILD IS DRINKING OR USING DRUGS?

Parents who spend a lot of time listening to and talking with their kids are more likely to be tuned in to what's normal behavior and what's not. Still, even actively involved parents may miss—or subconsciously deny—the earliest signs of substance use.

Some of the clues kids exhibit when using drugs or alcohol are fairly obvious:

- Many hours spent alone, especially in their room; ongoing isolation from the rest of the family. This is particularly suspicious in a child who hasn't been a loner up until now.

- Resistance to talking with or confiding in parents; secretiveness, especially in a child who had previously been open.

- A change for the worse in performance and attendance at school or a job or other responsibilities, or in dress, hygiene, or grooming.

- Frequent memory lapses, lack of concentration, or unusual sleepiness.

- A change to friends you find unacceptable.

- Pronounced mood swings with more irritability, hostile outbursts, and rebelliousness.

- Lying, usually in order to cover up drinking or drug use, as well as the source of money or new possessions. Stealing, shoplifting, or run-ins with the police. Cash, prescription drugs, liquor, or valuables may vanish.

- Extreme or obsessive guarding of personal space and possessions. Teens will often hide alcohol, drugs, and drug paraphernalia in their rooms or backpacks.

- Giving up healthy activities, such as sports, school clubs, religious activities, or hobbies.

- Physical symptoms, such as dilated or pinpoint pupils, bloodshot eyes, nosebleeds, appetite changes, digestive problems, excessive yawning, or the shakes.

- Breaking curfew.

- Extreme tattoos or body piercings.

However, you shouldn't jump to the conclusion that your child is using if you see such behavior. These signs can also be due to illness or a family disruption such as divorce.

Some behaviors leave little room for doubt.

- Alcohol on the breath.

- Obvious hangovers, blackouts, drunken or high behavior, slurred speech, poor coordination, or frequent vomiting.

- Drugs and paraphernalia stashed in pockets, drawers, backpacks, or other hideaways: seeds or leaves, rolling papers, a roach clip (small metal holder for marijuana), hand-rolled cigarettes, empty cans bent in the middle and covered with soot and pinholes (a homemade crack pipe), small plastic bags of white powder, glass pipes or tubes (for snorting or smoking drugs), plumbing fixture joints (for cooking up vapor to inhale), empty glassine capsules, steel wool pads (to hold a drug in place in a pipe), glass tubes (used as pipes), or even whip cream chargers for huffing.

Should you search your child's room, backpack, car, or phone? Some parents will say, "I couldn't breach my son's trust by searching his room." You are the adult and you are responsible for what your children do—including their possession of an illegal substance. Drug laws are more punitive than ever before, and often the judicial discretion allowed in the past, which sometimes got both parents and kids off the hook, is no more. If your child has cocaine or hash hidden in a dresser drawer, you could be held responsible. Ideally, you let them know long ago that they were to share all of their social media account passwords with you. Use them now to see what is going on. If they changed the passwords, insist they give you the new ones, and if they refuse, remove the devices.

THE STAGES OF TEEN DRUG USE

Experimenting. There is strong peer pressure to dabble recreationally in drugs. It is usually limited to weekends, and in most cases, there is no lasting change in behavior.

Actively seeking drugs. The child moves toward dependence when drugs are used to produce good feelings, to enhance athletic or academic performance, or to relieve stress. Use usually spreads to midweek, and there may be marked changes in behavior and school performance. (At this point, you need to get them some help immediately.)

Desperately seeking drugs. Now there is a complete loss of control over drug use. Attempts to limit use can cause withdrawal symptoms, including depression, moodiness, and irritability. Other signs of drug use may be noticed, including the sudden disappearance of money or household goods to pay for drugs.

YOU NEED TO TAKE ACTION

If you do suspect your son or daughter is using drugs or alcohol, don't hesitate to bring up the subject. Addiction lives in secrets. The sooner the problem is brought out into the light of day, the better the chances that your child will live to have a healthy future. Raising the subject will be easier if you already have good communication in the family. It will also be easier if you raise the issue at a time when no one is in a hurry to go somewhere else. Avoid doing it when everybody is tired or out of sorts.

Sit down with your child and raise the issue calmly. Don't do it when he seems to be drunk or high, or when you are angry. Lay out your observations and concerns, and give him plenty of opportunity to respond to you. Listen. And listen some more. Pay attention to his body language, his facial expressions, and what he is not saying.

If He Wants to Talk

It's possible he will be grateful that you want to help. He may feel out of control and appreciate your offer of support. If so, talk about how you can seek help together.

If your child has only been experimenting with alcohol or drugs, it might be just a phase. Older teens and young adults do go through a developmental period known as "emerging adulthood," where they separate themselves from their parents and earlier relationships. This can come out as rebellion, misbehavior, anger, and experimentation. Many kids will make it through this phase safely into adulthood, older and wiser and without the disease of addiction. If you think this might be the case, taking your child to an open AA or other 12-step fellowship meeting may be a way for him to learn more about what can happen if his use continues unabated.

But getting an evaluation by a professional is also important. You and your child might both be only too happy to pass things off as "just a phase," so don't rely on your own judgment here. Get help from an expert. This can be done by your doctor, a school drug counselor, a therapist or addiction counselor, or perhaps a clergyperson. Teen drug counseling is best provided by someone trained in both child/adolescent therapy and drug rehabilitation.

Of course, if you know or strongly suspect your child has gone beyond experimenting, you must move quickly to get help from a professional and decide on the best course of treatment.

How do you find a professional who can help steer your family through this? Again, start with your family doctor; if he is not knowledgeable about addiction, ask for some referrals. You can also contact a nearby rehab facility, a local mental health agency, a private therapist, or a specialized addiction therapist. Get involved in a family-support group and ask the people you meet there for ideas. If you are in recovery yourself, you might ask for advice from your own counselor, teenagers you know from your own mutual-support network, or their parents. Ask for referrals from friends, relatives, and coworkers who you know have had similar issues in their families. Call your insurance company for referrals to local facilities and experts. Also see chapter 5 for other types of professionals you might contact for help, and how you can find them. If an intervention seems in order, see Getting Help for Your Loved One (page 543) for how to arrange one.

Professional treatment options for teens are similar to those for adults, but with some important caveats. You can read more about treatment options and how to find a good program in chapter 5, and the special issues that arise when placing teens in treatment.

Also be sure to read about the unique issues that face teenagers in recovery, in chapter 15. It will help you understand more about how this all looks from his perspective.

If Your Child Refuses to Talk

Of course, when you sit down to talk, your child may not only be ungrateful—he may be furious with you. If you're in recovery yourself, he may turn it back on you: "Look who's lecturing!" You may get an outright denial that doesn't ring true or an admission-but-no-problem defense, in which case you're at a standoff.

If this is the case, don't drop the issue, and don't start a shouting match. Instead, make plans to call in an objective professional to referee. Explain to your child, "I don't think you're a bad person. But I do think you're a person who needs help. I know you think there's no problem now, and maybe there isn't. But let's get an impartial opinion."

Make it clear that you're going to see a counselor not because you're sure your child has a drug problem, but because you aren't able to agree on the subject. This gets rid of your adversarial roles and allows you to slip into a supportive role. If your child still refuses to own up to the behavior and your suspicions are shared by the counselor, you can implement a drug-screening plan to settle the matter (such as random home screening at your request; see Home Drug Testing, page 253). If your child refuses, you can assume a drug test would be positive. If he balks at seeing a counselor, you can also assume a problem exists.

As the parent, you then must take steps to see that your child is treated—ideally at an inpatient setting, away from the distractions that have already helped lead him astray. An outpatient setting (where your child lives at home) is not likely to help if he has not yet agreed that there is a problem or that he needs help. Waiting for him to "hit bottom" or respond to outpatient behavioral therapy could be very dangerous, or even fatal. Far too many teens die of overdoses of alcohol or drugs, or in other situations (such as car accidents) that are related to substance use. Bottom line, a very assertive approach to the problem is the only safe approach.

TREATMENT FOR TEENS

The quality of the treatment program you choose for your teenager can make the difference between success and failure. The program should do more than get kids off alcohol and drugs. It should teach them about the risks of untreated addiction and the rewards of abstinent recovery. It also needs to help them learn all about mutual-support fellowships and professional resources, and instill the skills they need to live a drug-free life.

All of the standards for judging a treatment program in chapter 5 also apply to choosing one for your teenager. But there are some additional issues that might need to be addressed.

First, because your child is a teenager, there are different issues he and you might be concerned about: peer pressure, continuing his education, fitting in with the family, separating himself from the family as he gets older, behavioral issues such as acting out, and so on. A program that is experienced in working with teens will know how to address these.

Second, the attitude toward teenage alcoholics/addicts is often much more punitive than toward chemically dependent adults. Frustrated parents, teachers, counselors, and law enforcement staff just want to send them away to be "fixed." So these kids often wind up at boot camp programs that are rigid and harsh, where punishment is the prime teaching tool and children are deprived of their rights. Studies have shown, however, that these programs do not work, and they can make a child's problems even worse.

What kids do need is a secure and trustworthy environment where they can feel safe about exposing their vulnerabilities. For most, a better choice is a more relaxed program that allows them some responsibilities and demands accountability. In most cases, a mixed-age patient population is most beneficial, but there are also some fine programs designed especially for teens. Take a close look at any program before you send your child there. Discuss the options with your doctor or the therapist who is advising you. Also talk to former patients and their parents; that will often give you a better view of the program than speaking only to staff.

If your child is in trouble with the law, see if there is a juvenile drug court available in your area. Getting involved in such a program may provide your child with treatment, social services, and other help. Read more about drug courts on page 280.

You might also come across some wilderness-based programs, which challenge kids to survive under tough conditions. Although these may have appeal in certain cases, they don't offer a realistic transition to living in recovery in the real world. They are better saved for later on, if your teen wants an outdoor challenge once his recovery is well under way. Of course, beware any that have a punitive, boot camp–like atmosphere.

CAN YOU AFFORD TREATMENT?

The cost of treatment for substance misuse can seem astronomical to the average family. But the cost of not getting treatment can be a child's life.

Even in the short term, there can be enormous costs if you choose to "wait until things get worse." You could spend thousands in lawyer's fees, auto repair, insurance premiums, tuition spent in vain, and money and goods stolen from the family. There are nonfinancial risks, too: kids hurting themselves or others, flunking out of school, losing a chance to get into a good college, getting pregnant or getting someone else pregnant, or becoming infected with HIV or hepatitis C. Can you afford to get treatment for your teenager? The question should really be: Can you afford not to get treatment?

If your health insurance doesn't cover treatment and you don't have the financial resources to pay for it yourself, there are other options. Get advice from:

- Your local department of youth services

- The counselor at your child's school

- An employee assistance program at work

- Your doctor, clergyperson, or therapist

- Friends or family members who have gone through similar issues

- One or more local drug programs or hotlines

- Local treatment programs (some have scholarships)

- The SAMHSA Treatment Referral Helpline: 800-662-HELP (4357) or 800-487-4889 (TDD), findtreatment.samhsa.gov

- Your state substance abuse agency: findtreatment.samhsa .gov/locator/stateagencies

- The National Council on Alcoholism and Drug Dependence: ncadd.org, 800-NCA-CALL (622-3255)

SET GROUND RULES FOR YOUR HOME

Whether or not your child goes to treatment, if you strongly suspect or know he has a problem, you should start adopting some ground rules for your home right now.

There should be a strict rule of no alcohol or drugs in the house for anyone, including parents, even if they are not addicts or alcoholics.

In addition:

- Dispose of or lock up all prescription drugs.

- Get rid of all guns and other obvious weapons.

- To prevent thefts of items that might be sold for money, lock up valuables outside the home. Keep a close eye on all credit cards and checks, as well as small electronics such as tablets and laptops. You might lock everything in a cabinet and check things out to family members as needed.

- Change your online passwords to protect bank accounts as well as any sites where you have shopped online and your credit card information might be stored. Always be sure you log out of any online shopping and financial sites before you leave the computer.

- Get a copy of your credit report to see if any new accounts have been opened in your name without your approval.

You should also set up specific ground rules governing behavior—in effect, a contract between you and your child. This is probably best done with the guidance of your child's therapist or drug counselor. This contract should specify the responsibilities of all parties, in writing, with every detail spelled out. For example, the parents may agree to continue to provide food, clothing, shelter, education, and medical care. The child's half of the bargain will be abstaining from alcohol and drugs and following all house rules. He may be required to participate in recovery activities and follow specific rules for socializing, schoolwork, an outside job, curfew hours, household responsibilities, and car-use privileges (these probably shouldn't be reinstated without a lengthy period of sobriety and good behavior). Insist that he share all passwords to all online accounts (social media, photo sharing, email, texting, and so on), and let him know you will monitor his online activities at random.

The contract should also include guidelines for monitoring and accountability: Will there be random drug testing? How will you know if he went to his NA meeting?

You'll also need to list specific consequences if your child does not live up to the contract. These can range from loss of privileges for getting home late to commitment for treatment to—harsh as it may sound—being turned over to the police for using prohibited substances. This should only be a last resort, since this kind of situation puts troubled kids together with other troubled kids—and often results in only more trouble.

The contract should specify the ways in which the child's good behavior—staying sober, regular school attendance and improved grades, having negative drug screens, attending AA meetings—can gradually earn him additional privileges.

If there are infractions, respond quickly. Children don't benefit when their parents let them get away with breaking their word. The teenager has to learn that in the end, no one can pull him out of addiction but himself.

Grown children who live at home, or who return home in trouble, should also be required to agree to a contract that includes abstinence. And they should be evicted if they fail to live up to their part of the bargain. Continue to be available for constructive help when needed (like driving your child to a treatment center), but don't let yourself or your financial resources be used to enable drinking or drug use. If you cover any expenses, make the payments directly; never hand cash or credit cards over to a person who is using.

Parents who turn to eviction as a last resort may feel both a sense of relief and a sense of guilt. It's okay to feel relief—you've gone through a terrible time. Having this child out of your life for the time being will remove an immediate burden, from your shoulders if not your heart. But while relief is warranted, guilt is not. You did the best you could; no one can do more than that.

You will need to explain what is happening to other children in the family. They should be invited to attend Alateen, Al-Anon, or open AA or NA meetings, and be given counseling as needed. Also expect them to meet the same standards set for the sick child: no alcohol, no drugs, clear-cut hours, and so on.

If you are in recovery yourself, you'll have to continue to work hard on your own program throughout all of this. Nothing will be more beneficial to your child in the long run. If the stress of your child's substance use seems to be threatening your sobriety, go to more AA or NA meetings, start going to Al-Anon or Nar-Anon meetings, or seek additional counseling. Or do all three.

Understanding the Zones of Recovery—and Your Role in Each

Recovery from alcoholism and addiction is a lifetime process—it never ends. Your loved one will always be in recovery. But he won't always be in the early stages of recovery, when things can be quite difficult and relapse seems just around the corner.

The Recovery Zone System, which Dr. Al developed after many years of working with alcoholics and addicts, divides recovery into three distinct zones, and offers guidance on what issues to tackle when. Understanding this system will help you know what to expect in these early days, as well as years down the road. (See also chapter 2, which has more details on the system, as well as chapters 3, 16, and 21, the guides to each zone.)

THE RED ZONE

The Red Zone is the first stage of recovery, the lifesaving zone. It includes several important facets of recovery: making a commitment to sobriety, detox and withdrawal, initial professional treatment (if any), getting involved in a mutual-support fellowship such as AA, and learning how to live as a person in recovery (and stay there). It usually lasts for eighteen months or so.

- Detox is the initial period when your loved one stops taking drugs or drinking and waits for what is still in the body to exit. Some people have an extremely difficult time with detox, suffering through major withdrawal symptoms; others have a much easier time. Before your loved one goes through detox, read up on what it's like (see chapter 6).

- The initial professional treatment, if any, may take a few weeks to a few months or longer, depending on the options chosen. Read more in chapters 5 and 7.

- Getting involved in a mutual-support fellowship program will take up quite a bit of your loved one's time and energy now. (Read more about AA and other fellowships in chapters 8 and 9.)

- Your loved one will also be learning how to live in the culture of recovery—identifying the triggers that can lead to a relapse, and learning how to deal with them; relearning how to deal with emotions, as well as family, friends, and coworkers; getting back into a work routine; and maybe taking small steps toward sober socializing. Making major changes or repairs to his life—such as new relationships, going back to school, or a career shift—will have to wait, for the most part. It's easy to feel resentful about all of this, but it really is necessary. (Chapters 10 through 15 cover those issues, and more.)

In the Red Zone, the person in recovery is making life-and-death choices. It really is that important. He needs to focus entirely on getting well, on laying down a solid foundation upon which he can build a meaningful life. If he fails to stay sober, his addiction might well kill him.

So it's important for everyone who cares about him to respect his need to pursue sobriety as faithfully and as single-mindedly as he once pursued his drugs of choice, even though it will mean many hours spent at fellowship meetings.

Your Loved One in the Red Zone

You will probably find that sober, your partner, parent, sibling, or child is a "new" person. Not necessarily better, at least at first, but certainly different. You knew what to expect when drugs or alcohol were in control, and you learned to adapt (as best you could). Now you have to start learning what to expect from this new sober person.

For a while it may be like living with a stranger. That won't be easy. This stranger may seem unstable at times, even act drunk or high. In early recovery, the body is in a recuperating mode (sleeping a lot is common), the mind is cloudy, and behavior is unpredictable. Emotions can be explosive. For a long time, he used chemicals to smother or deal with his feelings. Now those feelings are suddenly reappearing, and he doesn't know what to do with them. Don't be thrown by the fact that your partner is chipper and smiling one day and depressed the next. Try not to worry when your teenager comes home from school day after day and crashes on the couch instead of hanging out with friends. For most people it takes a good year, sometimes much longer, for the mind to clear and emotions to level off. We used to think that the brain was pretty much set in stone once fully grown. We now know that it can change throughout a lifetime. In recovery, the brain is being rewired for sobriety, and this takes time. (Read more about the brain in recovery in chapter 1.)

It may look to you like he is floundering or has no direction in life—at work, at school, in his social life. But that's normal behavior in early recovery. At this point he is focusing on getting better. Everything else has to wait. The self-centeredness you probably came to hate is still there, but now it's directed toward renewal instead of destruction. This attitude is likely to continue throughout the Red Zone.

Family and Friends' Response in the Red Zone

Family members and friends may all react differently to recovery. Many will be genuinely pleased. Spouses whose marriages were clearly doomed by substance use are often cheered by the possibility of recovery. Parents who felt embarrassed, guilty, and disappointed when their child was drinking or using drugs often feel cautiously optimistic. They think maybe those hopes they abandoned long ago may yet be fulfilled. Friends may figure they finally have their long-lost buddy back.

But though everyone claims to be pleased about sobriety, many really aren't. Some of those close to the patient may harbor subconscious resentments. This is particularly true when the patient's active addiction satisfied a personal need.

For example, a husband took over the family finances while his wife was drinking, and found he liked it. Now he is annoyed by the idea of handing financial control back to her. A mother felt needed again when her broke, drug-using daughter moved back home. Now she fears loneliness when the girl sobers up, finds a job, and wants to move in with a friend.

Sometimes recovery is subconsciously resented and resisted by a family member whose life revolved around Al-Anon. "If he gets sober, what will I have to do? Everything I worked so hard to adjust to will change, and I'll have to start all over again."

Other times, family members resist one's recovery because it threatens their own untreated addictions.

If it seems that anyone in the family is consciously or subconsciously fighting recovery, get some counseling. That kind of attitude can sabotage a fragile recovery.

Your Relationship in the Red Zone

In this early stage, when recovery is just getting a foothold, your expectations may be on a collision course with reality. You might expect that with sobriety comes a perfect relationship, a perfect home life at last. But in reality, of course, there is no such thing.

Sometimes there is a brief honeymoon, with everyone on their best behavior to avoid triggering a slip. Everything seems perfect. But it isn't real, and it rarely lasts.

There are too many unresolved issues that still need to be addressed: resentment, guilt, anger, or money or job troubles. You may want you and your loved one to start working on those things right now. You may want to fix everything that went wrong right now. You may want your best friend to go on that long-postponed ski vacation now. But if it's at all possible, wait. Wait until your loved one gets into the next stage of recovery, the Yellow Zone, when his focus will be on rebuilding

his life. He will be much more ready and able to tackle all of those things then.

You will also need time for your own healing. Most people who stick with someone—whether it's a partner, child, sibling, parent, or friend—as they get into recovery have to go through their own healing process and make their own adjustments to a new life. Getting involved in Al-Anon, Nar-Anon, or another support fellowship will help you do that.

Finding that sobriety doesn't mean a suddenly perfect relationship often comes as both a surprise and a disappointment. Even more surprising, it might seem to you like your relationship is getting worse rather than better. But if you find your loved one distant at first, don't be alarmed. Those in early recovery have to put their best efforts into staying sober, into literally staying alive. That means that when you want to talk or go out to dinner or have friends over for an evening, he may not have the time or the physical or psychic energy to participate. His life is focused on the activities and behaviors of sobriety.

That doesn't mean there will be no time at all for your relationship. It's a good idea to plan to spend some together regularly—listening to music, going on family outings, or whatever you enjoy doing jointly. Take every opportunity to go to meetings together, get together with friends from AA or Al-Anon, watch AA videos, or read meditations.

Your goal now is to find some common areas of life that you can enjoy together, to gently start rebuilding your relationship. Leave the thorny issues alone for now—you can address them later on, once you have all learned some advanced recovery skills.

In a sense, you need to get to know one another again. Without the alcohol or drugs in your lives, you are truly different people. You are now tied together with different strings. If it's your mate who's recovering, it's like the early stages of courting, where you go slowly and try to learn what you can about the other person. If it's a child or parent, it's as though you're starting fresh with a new family and have to get acquainted. If it's a friend, you'll also be starting from scratch. It's hard, but starting from neutral territory has some real benefits. You can toss away old feelings and animosities and try to be the person you always wanted to be, but couldn't quite manage to be. Work toward real communication, but understand that you probably won't get there until sometime after the first sober year.

Your Role in the Red Zone

Read all the chapters on the Red Zone (chapters 3–15) so you know what goes on in early recovery and what you can expect. If honesty fell victim to addiction (as it usually does), start resurrecting it, not just with your loved one in recovery but with everyone else in your lives.

Cooperate in making the house an alcohol- and drug-free zone. And if you do the cooking, be sure you know about the relapse traps in some foods (chapter 10). You can also help strengthen recovery by introducing the Clean and Sober Diet. Help your loved one anticipate and avoid other situations where he might be tempted to relapse.

Don't try to choreograph his recovery—you can't control his every move. Taking on the tasks of recovery is his job, even if you are the parent. It's not your job to get him to meetings or to counseling sessions (unless a nondriver asks for a ride). Nor are you expected to check for alcohol on the breath or run a home drug test every night—though in some cases this may be part of a parent-child or spouse-spouse agreement when trust has not yet returned. Instead, work on improving yourself through your own 12-step program.

THE YELLOW ZONE

The next phase, the Yellow Zone, is all about rebuilding the life that was derailed.

The person in recovery now takes steps to make his life everything he wants it to be. He is still involved in his recovery fellowship, and perhaps is sponsoring others. He is restoring and rebuilding relationships, reevaluating career goals and making moves in that arena, and getting back into enjoying life through relaxation and recreational activities. He is also doing what's needed to further restore his physical and mental health. And he is restoring his spiritual life. Think of the Yellow Zone as a construction zone.

To learn about the kinds of problems and feelings that crop up for many people in this stage, read chapters 16 through 20.

Your Role in the Yellow Zone

The Yellow Zone is also a very important time for you and your relationship with the chemical-dependent person in your life. Now it's time to start the real work of rebuilding your life together. You'll both have to be open, sharing, caring, thoughtful, forgiving, and, most of all, not controlling. You will have to learn how to communicate again (chapter 18) and how to express your feelings without anger. You'll have to learn how to have fun together again, and how to run a household together again.

If your loved one seems to still be struggling with issues that could threaten his sobriety, talk to him about maybe refocusing or renewing the work he did in the Red Zone. He might need to further strengthen his foundation before he can rebuild a relationship with you.

Take a look at the Are You Ready questions for the Yellow Zone (chapter 16). They help people determine if they are ready for the Yellow Zone. You can't know what exactly is in your loved one's head and heart, so you can't answer the questions for him, but you might be able to help him assess where he is now, to see if

he really is ready to move forward. Go through the questions together, talk about them, or suggest that he talk about them with his sponsor or counselor.

You should also learn about the Recovery Zone ReCheck process and how that works (chapter 2). It's a simple system that helps people in recovery to anticipate—and avoid—situations that could lead to a relapse. As someone who is intimately involved in this person's life, you can help with that process.

THE GREEN ZONE

The Green Zone is all about extending and enjoying the life that was saved in the Red Zone and rebuilt and revitalized in the Yellow Zone. It is the equivalent of a normal life, but with an ongoing recognition of recovery issues and a clear sense of purpose.

Now is the time for the person in recovery to truly enjoy his life: to participate fully in relationships, recreational activities, and his career. It's also time for him to do even more to live as long as he can: Follow the Clean and Sober Diet, quit smoking, start exercising, get rid of (or finish gaining) those last nagging pounds, and take care of preventive health maintenance.

The Green Zone is also the time when he can focus even more on sharing the gift of recovery, both by sponsoring people and by fostering changes in the community.

The Green Zone will continue for the rest of his life. To

learn more, read chapters 21 through 25.

Your Role in the Green Zone

Now is the time for you to also reap the rewards of your earlier hard work. It's time to live your life to the fullest, and be the healthiest and happiest you can be.

You are every bit as important to the success of the person in recovery now as you were earlier. Maybe even more so. Talk about what each of you would like to do to make your lives better, and how you will make those changes. Find ways to work toward your goals together.

For example, it's nearly impossible for one person in a home to change his eating habits if no one else goes along with it. So if you live with the person in recovery, adopt the Clean and Sober Diet and encourage everyone in the household to give it a try. It's also difficult to stop smoking if those near you are still puffing away. So again, make it a project for the whole family, or the whole gang of friends or coworkers.

Your continued support of his fellowship activities is also important now. Most people maintain their sobriety better when they don't detach themselves completely from AA or NA. If he hears complaints about his fellowship taking up too much of his time, he could drop out. In the long run, that could be bad for everyone. He will also now be spending time trying to help others find recovery, and trying to make a difference in the world. Why not join him?

Your Concerns, Actions, and Emotions

HELPING YOUR PARTNER IN TREATMENT

"My wife is about to enter a residential treatment program. I want to know what I can do to help her. She's fighting an addiction to painkillers— the drugs she was prescribed after surgery a few years ago."

Though she will have to fight her own battle, there are several things you can do to support her.

Stand behind her. When she goes to treatment, she needs to feel that you fully support her struggles to engage in recovery. Don't belittle her or try to shame her.

Keep the home fires blazing. Your wife will have enough to deal with without worrying that things could fall apart while she's away. So assure her that everything on the home front will be fine. If you have kids or pets, make plans for their care so she won't have any concerns about them. If you need to take time off from work, you might be able to make use of the Family and Medical Leave Act. This law is designed to help families who are dealing with tough situations, such as those brought on by medical problems. It allows you to take unpaid, but job-protected, time off. Your family doctor or a doctor at the treatment center can verify that there is a family illness that needs your attention. You do not have to tell your employer the nature of the illness. (See Treatment Confidentiality, page 92.)

Clear out all drugs. Carefully search your home for alcohol, pills, other drugs, and drug paraphernalia. It might be stashed in odd places, so search everywhere and get rid of everything you find.

Keep in touch. Writing to your wife, rather than phoning her or having a video chat, is probably the best way to keep in touch for now. There are several reasons for this.

In early recovery, memories are short, and feelings are volatile. Things may be said on the phone in anger or in haste—things that neither of you would put in writing. In addition, phone calls can be distracting to someone in treatment, and a phone conversation can be played back mentally and distorted by the participants. A letter or card is much harder to misinterpret. It remains exactly as it was written, and a counselor or friend can help interpret it if there is any doubt. In addition, a letter will not distract from her other treatment activities, and can even be reviewed by the staff or other patients as part of therapy. Many treatment programs recognize this, and limit or prohibit phone calls and encourage letters.

Write letters that are honest and newsy. Express your feelings and concerns, but before you raise issues that could be distracting or embit-

tering, check with your spouse's counselor. The counselor (who in a way will be counseling both of you) will let you know just how much you should be involved in treatment.

The counselor or nursing staff may be able to let you know how your wife is doing, but privacy laws might prohibit them from giving you updates. In most cases, staff can share information only if a patient has agreed to it. In turn, you can provide insights that may be helpful to those treating her. If at any time during treatment you discover something about her substance use or behavior that you think could be useful in her care, get in touch with the counselor and fill her in. And get in touch right away if you see any signs that she's just going through the motions of complying with the program, rather than taking it to heart. If her letters are filled with resentment and anger toward you, or seem designed to make you feel guilty, take a step back. Recognize that they are coming from someone who is going through a very tough time, and who is searching for meaning during what are probably the most difficult days of her life. Speak to her counselor about them.

But keep away. Many treatment centers do not permit any visiting until the family session at the end of treatment. Even if the facility your wife is in allows it, you should consider staying away—especially early in treatment, when visits tend to trigger addictive behavior and arguments. You'll both be doing some changing in this period; you'll appreciate the differences more fully if you don't see each other for a while. Plus, some of the really bad feelings of the past may fade away while you're apart. Also, if you haven't seen each other for a few weeks, the reunion may even rekindle some of those loving feelings that were lost in the storm of addiction.

Help yourself. You're likely to feel left out at this time. Until now you've been heavily involved in trying to help your spouse one way or another. Now someone else has taken over. You may actually find yourself feeling jealous of her counselors and thinking that someone else might succeed where you failed. But getting your spouse well wasn't your responsibility. It isn't even the responsibility of the counselor, who will only be guiding her (and who has had a lot of professional training). The addicted person herself needs to do the work that leads to healing.

You may feel a whole host of other emotions—anxiety, denial, anger, guilt, resentment, fear. Though these emotions are par for the course, they won't make you too pleasant to come home to, and learning to deal with them will help you both recover. Now is an ideal time to do this, and there's no better place to begin than at Al-Anon. If after several Al-Anon meetings you are still anxious, or if you're

feeling as if all the worries are on your shoulders while your spouse is being catered to in a fantasyland treatment center, look into some therapy for yourself. Al-Anon friends are likely to have some good recommendations of therapists with experience in this area.

Help others. You may not be the only one suffering the effects of your spouse's alcoholism. If there are children, young or adult, they're certainly not unscathed. The same may be true of your wife's parents, siblings, and close friends. You can help them by guiding everyone toward appropriate resources: Nar-Anon or Al-Anon for adults, Narateen or Alateen for teenagers (or other family-support groups), and therapy for those who need extra help.

Participate in the family program. You may be nervous about taking part in the family segment of the treatment program. But chances are you will quickly settle into the routine and appreciate the experience. Along with the relatives and friends of other patients, you'll discuss and learn a lot about your own needs, those of the patient, and those of other family members. You'll also learn a lot about your own substance use, and whether it is a problem.

Before you and the patient zero in on the flaws in your relationship, you will both be encouraged to grow separately. You may explore issues through counseling, group discussions, classes, and support from staff, other family members, and other patients. Now's the time to ask about the things you might unwittingly do to sabotage recovery, and how you can avoid being an enabler. Talk to staff people who are members of Al-Anon, and if there are Al-Anon meetings nearby or at the center, go to some.

Even the best of family sessions won't solve all your problems. A lot of unfinished business will remain that you'll both need to work on later. A weak family program—and there are some—may leave you feeling frustrated, uneasy, guilty, and unsure how to proceed when you leave. If you feel your concerns were not addressed well during family treatment, get some more help.

SHOULD YOU KEEP ALCOHOL OR DRUGS AT HOME?

"My husband is now gung ho for sobriety, and he wants me to get rid of all the liquor in the house. I don't see why our friends or I can't enjoy a drink in our home."

This question is addressed in chapter 10, but it bears repeating: The best show of support you can give a family member who has a drug or alcohol problem is to remove all mood-altering drugs and alcohol from the home. Period. If you're unwilling to clear out the liquor, you should think about why you feel that way. Some possibilities are below.

A conscious or subconscious wish to sabotage your spouse's recovery. This is not out of malice but out of fear. Fear that if your spouse gets sober, your life will change.

It's a realistic concern. But if you both work at it, the change should be for the better.

An inability to give up or change your role in the relationship. Over the years, you managed to develop your own identity as his problems continued to alienate you in the relationship. But standing your ground now will only create rigidity and distrust between you. As his recovery progresses, the behaviors that worked for you in the past will need to be reexamined. You'll both need to open up in order to rebuild your relationship.

A desire to make your spouse suffer as you've suffered. Fired by normal resentments, you ask, "Why should I make it easy for him by making our home an alcohol-free zone?" The answer is obvious. If he fails in his attempt to stay sober, you will suffer, too.

An inability to face giving up liquor yourself. If you feel you can't live in an alcohol-free house, you may have an alcohol problem, too. A person who is truly a social drinker can take booze or leave it. If you can't leave it, or have trouble leaving it, think about going to some AA meetings. It's not unusual to see several family members all getting into recovery together.

Get rid of the drugs, too. Those painkillers left over from your back surgery—the pills you forgot about long ago—could be the trigger to a relapse (or the first step in a young visitor's addiction). So go through your closets and medicine cabinets and get rid of whatever you can.

Al-Anon and Other Support Fellowships

AL-ANON, NAR-ANON, AND OTHER MUTUAL-SUPPORT FAMILY FELLOWSHIPS

Al-Anon, Nar-Anon, and other family-support groups are to you what AA or NA is to the alcoholic/addict in your life: a mutual-support fellowship. These resources remind you that you're not alone and offer structured advice from those who have been through it before you. They help you learn that, when it comes to your loved one's addiction, "I didn't cause it, I can't control it, and I can't cure it."

Al-Anon and Nar-Anon are 12-step programs run entirely by the members. You'll get the most out of them if you go to meetings regularly, find a sponsor, and work the steps. Other groups don't use the 12 steps, but they can also be quite helpful.

To find an Al-Anon meeting, go to al-anonfamilygroups.org/how-to-find-a-meeting, or call 888-4AL-ANON (425-2666). Al-Anon also has many online, email, and phone meetings, all in several languages.

Nar-Anon information can be found at nar-anon.org. You can also call them at 800-477-6291.

If your loved one also has a mental illness, you may find the National Alliance on Mental Illness (NAMI) helpful. Contact them at nami.org or at 800-950-NAMI (6264).

As with AA groups, Al-Anon and Nar-Anon groups are diverse and take on many different personalities. You may need to try out a few different groups to find one that fits you well. If you find these programs are just too painful right now, go to some open AA or NA meetings. They can be a good introduction to recovery, while keeping you out of the hot seat for now.

AL-ANON'S TWELVE STEPS

Al-Anon's Twelve Steps are virtually identical to those of AA:

1. We admitted we were powerless over alcohol—that our lives had become unmanageable.

2. Came to believe that a Power greater than ourselves could restore us to sanity.

3. Made a decision to turn our will and our lives over to the care of God *as we understood Him.*

4. Made a searching and fearless moral inventory of ourselves.

5. Admitted to God, to ourselves, and to another human being the exact nature of our wrongs.

6. Were entirely ready to have God remove all these defects of character.

7. Humbly asked Him to remove our shortcomings.

8. Made a list of all persons we had harmed, and became willing to make amends to them all.

9. Made direct amends to such people wherever possible, except when to do so would injure them or others.

10. Continued to take personal inventory and when we were wrong promptly admitted it.

11. Sought through prayer and meditation to improve our conscious contact with God *as we understood Him*, praying only for knowledge of His will for us and the power to carry that out.

12. Having had a spiritual awakening as the result of these steps, we tried to carry this message to others, and to practice these principles in all our affairs.

ALATEEN AND NARATEEN

Alateen is a division of Al-Anon for teenagers who are affected by someone else's drinking (such as a parent, stepparent, grandparent, aunt, uncle, sibling, or close friend). Each group is sponsored by an active adult member of Al-Anon. The sponsor is present at all meetings but does not run them. Narateen is the Nar-Anon division for teenagers; its meetings are also supervised by adults.

The purpose of these meetings is to give kids the chance to discuss their experiences; to help each other understand the disease of addiction and the phases of recovery; and to share effective ways of coping with their problems in substance-using families. Like Al-Anon and Nar-Anon, Alateen and Narateen are based on the 12 steps. Ideally, regular attendance at meetings helps young people to put their loved one's condition in perspective and achieve some order in their own chaotic lives.

Alateen and Narateen are important forums for kids, giving them a chance to voice their thoughts in a safe, nonjudgmental atmosphere, often for the first time in their lives. These kids have often not been able to express their feelings at home and have avoided discussing their problems with friends at school. At meetings they find kids just like themselves, with the same feelings and fears. The mutual support found can lessen the loneliness they feel. It can also increase their feelings of self-worth by helping them understand that they aren't responsible for how others act, that other people have had the same experiences, and that they aren't stupid or worthless.

Bringing high-risk teens together doesn't automatically provide a magic cure, however. A poorly supervised group can, in fact, act as an enabler to support teen drinking or drug use, instead of helping the kids deal with their problems.

So try to pick a well-chaperoned group that discourages such thinking (talk with the chaperone to find out more about the meeting). Discussions should focus on the experience of living in a family with alcoholism or addiction and on looking at the damage that's been done. Groups where the discussion centers on chemical thrill-seeking, or where drinking and drug use are romanticized, could seduce a child who hasn't yet dabbled in alcohol or drugs.

If your teenagers balk at going to Alateen or Narateen, you might let them do a test run at a weekend recovery retreat in a fun location. Or take them along to an AA/Al-Anon or NA/Nar-Anon convention; they often include meetings and talks for young people. These events give teens a chance to meet others in a similar situation in neutral territory, which they might find less intimidating or embarrassing than going to a group near home. They might then go home ready to try a group in the neighborhood. Attending open or family AA or NA meetings with you can also be helpful as a learning experience.

If your child is a tween or younger, there aren't a lot of readily available 12-step resources. Some communities have informal groups. Most often these are little more than babysitting services. But even getting kids involved in simple adult-led activities such as talking about, or drawing pictures about, their experiences in an alcoholic home can be enlightening for others in the family and therapeutic for the child. Some treatment centers, such as the Betty Ford Center, do have excellent programs for young children. Ask about such programs when you are looking at treatment options.

Children who have significant emotional problems or have been subject to any kind of abuse, no matter their age, need more than Alateen or Narateen. They should see a therapist who is experienced in dealing with children from families with alcohol or drug problems.

IS AL-ANON RIGHT FOR ME?

"My daughter's drug counselor said I should go to Al-Anon. Isn't that group for family members of alcoholics, not drug addicts?"

The largest single segment in Al-Anon is family members and friends of alcoholics, but these days about a third of all members are there because of someone's drug use. (Besides, most drug users also have an alcohol problem.)

You'll find strong support from other Al-Anon members. They are there to get help for themselves and to help others, and many have had experiences like yours. You may fear that even though Al-Anon worked for them, it won't work for you, that if you change yourself or the way things are done in your family, everything will fall apart. Talk to those members about your fears. They probably felt the same way when they first put a tentative foot inside the door of a meeting, or sat in the back row hoping no one would recognize them. But they found out that the program could work for them—and it can work for you.

Of course, you can also try Nar-Anon meetings, if there are any in your area.

////////////////////////////////

"Isn't Nar-Anon mostly for spouses? Will it help me as a parent?"

It will help. But you might also look for a Nar-Anon group that is made up mostly of parents and focuses on their special interests and concerns. Many parents have found that these kinds of groups are very helpful. If there are several Nar-Anon groups in your community, try a few different meetings and see if you can find such a group.

If you can't find one, you can always suggest parenting issues as a topic for a meeting. You might also look for other parent members and set up a regular parents-in-Nar-Anon meeting. Through discussions of the members' experiences, you can look at issues such as balancing detachment and control with a teenager; dealing with addicted teens in school; how members have used guidance from teachers and school counselors; situations that had impacts on other children in the family; and emotions stirred up by undesirable friends. Rather than replacing regular Nar-Anon meetings, these meetings should supplement them.

Even if you don't seem to be getting help from Nar-Anon at first, keep going. One day the light may suddenly switch on and you will find the help you need. If not, consider professional therapy.

TAKE CARE OF YOURSELF

"My husband hasn't had a drink or taken any pills in three months. This is his longest period of sobriety in fifteen years, and the kids and I thought our lives would finally be good again. But things seem just as bad as before—maybe even worse. I'm so tired of this."

Giving up alcohol and drugs is only the first step on the long road of recovery. Your husband, and your family, won't be healed overnight. In fact, things might get worse before they get better. He will have to put in the time and effort to build a solid recovery.

What you can do is take care of yourself and your children during this difficult time. Start going to Al-Anon or Nar-Anon meetings. There you'll learn how you can make it through from others who have had the same struggles.

Below are some basic principles that can also help. Absorb them; think about them; make them part of your life.

Each of us is responsible for our own behavior. You were not responsible for your spouse's drinking or drug use (or that of anyone else in your family), and you aren't responsible for his sobriety now. He's the one who swallowed the pills and lifted the glass to his lips. He's the one who has to develop the recovery skills to make sure it never happens again. You are responsible only for what you do.

Your behavior is the only yardstick by which you should judge yourself. If your partner (or your child or your parent) behaves badly, you may feel sad about it. But since it isn't your responsibility, you shouldn't feel guilty. Just keep tabs on yourself. If you are doing what you should be doing, you're doing all that can be expected.

We can't control or change others. It always seems so easy when we're young and still believe in fairy tales. We fall in love with the guy who drinks too much or the girl who got hooked on meth and we're sure that, with our love, we can change them. Of course, we can't. But we keep trying, and usually make things worse. In recovery you have to accept that if your spouse is to stay sober, he will have to do it on his own. You can't be responsible.

We shouldn't rely on others for our happiness. Until now you probably let your moods be dictated by his behavior. You were miserable when your husband was drinking and happy when he was sober. From now on, try to get your happiness from what you do. Remember, the alcoholic/addict in your family didn't get sick to make you miserable and he isn't trying to get well to make

you happy (or shouldn't be). He should be doing it for himself. And you should also do what you must to make your life better.

If he doesn't show up in time for a party or event, go yourself. If you enjoy music and he doesn't, it's okay to go to a concert on your own or with friends. Be as nice to yourself as you've been to other people—even spoil yourself occasionally. You deserve it, and it will help build your own sense of self-worth. Without feeling good about yourself, you won't be able to feel truly good about anyone else. It will also make "detachment with love" possible.

You have to separate the disease from the person. If a family member has Alzheimer's, you hate the disease but you don't stop loving the person. It's the same when the disease is addiction.

Recovery is a slow process. Just as if he'd been through major surgery, it will take time for your partner to heal. So try to be patient.

DISCOMFORT WITH AL-ANON

"I'm very uneasy about going to Al-Anon or Nar-Anon. From what I've heard, it sounds like a lot of simplistic and mindless spiritual hocus-pocus."

Rely on the evidence of your own ears and eyes. Yes, you may be uncomfortable at the first few meetings. That's natural. But eventually, what you'll find there is peace of mind and down-to-earth practicality—not mindlessness. You will hear stories just like your own, from people who have felt the same pain you have, the same frustrations. You'll discover that the only difference between you and those who are regulars at these meetings is that they've learned how to deal with the problems of chemical dependency in their families in a healthy way. And you can do that as well.

So don't allow your wariness of spirituality deprive you of the benefits of Al-Anon or Nar-Anon. If the first group you go to seems too focused on the spiritual for your liking, try another. If that's not an option, just work on ignoring those aspects of the meetings. Reading the material on spirituality for the alcoholic/addict in this book may also help (chapters 8 and 9). You'll see that the subject can be interpreted in many ways, and that even those who consider themselves non-spiritual can be very successful in AA, NA, Al-Anon, and Nar-Anon if they try. If there are other family-support groups in your area, give them a try, too.

Look upon your fellowship meetings as sanity-saving medicine. There, you will find a big dose of good humor, common sense, and open-arms friendship.

NAR-ANON RESENTMENT

"I resent being told I should go to Nar-Anon. My husband is the sick one."

Your feeling is a natural one and is not uncommon. But the more that is known about the disease of addiction, the more it's seen to affect everyone in the family. Including you.

You've probably heard of the term *codependency*. What happens is people develop their own emotional symptoms as a result of their association with an alcoholic or addict. They get thrown into the role of saving and protecting that person. They get emotionally entwined with him and his actions, as a result of their feelings of love, care, and commitment. Their own identity comes to depend on the behavior of the alcoholic/addict— they are codependent. As time goes by, love, expectations, guilt, shame, and embarrassment all grow. They become barriers to facing the problem and finding solutions.

This scenario may be what you and your family are experiencing. Nar-Anon can help you deal with all of that and have a happier, more sane life, whether or not your husband gets any help himself. At least give it a try.

Plus, your seeking help can help him. At Nar-Anon, family members learn to stop enabling. They learn to put a stop to the destructive interactions like those you may be living with, and they turn their own lives around. The addict then often finds himself without the supports that have kept the roof from caving in on him. And then he has a choice: Clean up the wreckage of his life or, eventually, die pinned beneath it. Indeed, when family members get help, the odds rise that the addict will also look for help.

Also, if he gets involved in recovery and in NA and you don't go to Nar-Anon, he'll grow and mature and you'll stay just where you are, left behind. That isn't good for a relationship. Many have floundered because one partner refused to work at getting better.

Rebuilding Your Family—or Not

HOW CAN I TRUST AGAIN?

"My husband lied so much in the past that I don't trust him to tell me the truth. He hasn't had a drink in weeks. But every time I see him go down the street in the direction of the liquor store I panic, even though that's the only way he can get anywhere from our house."

After years of watching what your husband does, you've become conditioned to expect the worst when he walks out the door. It will take a lot of time and loving attention for you to become "reconditioned," to change your gut reactions to your husband's behavior. You will have to see for yourself that—time after time—his old behaviors, the ones you fear, don't occur.

The first step to breaking this pattern is to talk about your feelings at a support fellowship, such as Al-Anon. You'll find that a lack of trust is common. It takes a long time to regain that trust, but one day you realize that you're not automatically breaking into a sweat when your spouse heads in a dangerous direction, or comes home late, or forgets an appointment.

NOW HE'S ADDICTED TO NA

"Now that my husband is finally off drugs, I think he has a new addiction: Narcotics Anonymous. It doesn't matter what else is going on in our lives, he's got to go to NA. NA is obviously more important than me or our children—and I've become resentful."

You probably wouldn't be resentful if your husband had a stroke and needed to go to physical therapy every day. Your husband has a potentially fatal disease, and NA is a vital part of his treatment. It's lifesaving therapy for him, and right now it has to take priority over anything that is not absolutely necessary to keep him alive. This is particularly true when he's in early recovery.

There are ways to make this time easier on everyone in the family.

- Go to an NA meeting with him.

- Take your kids along as well, if they are old enough to sit quietly and understand some of what is going on—usually about age seven and older.

- Go to Nar-Anon or Al-Anon meetings yourself to unload

some of that resentment and to get the support you need to keep recovery a primary focus for you.

- Build some time into your schedule for the two of you to spend alone talking over the events of the day, discussing your reactions to and feelings about them, and maybe reading some meditations or prayers together. Whatever you choose to do, turn off the TV and your phones. Focus on each other.

- Set up a special family outing at least once a week. Choose something you can all enjoy.

Also, evaluate your feelings honestly. Could you be resentful because his support meetings and the people there have done for your husband what you couldn't do? Many spouses and family members feel that way about treatment, meetings, sponsors, and counselors. It's understandable, but it's not productive. Because of your close relationship to him, you can't possibly do what an objective professional or a fellow NA or AA member can do. Accepting that fact will help you feel better about your spouse's NA experience, as well as about yourself.

SOBRIETY AND SEX

"Since my partner stopped drinking, she hasn't had any interest in sex."

Don't take it personally. Very few people in early recovery are interested in making love. There are many reasons, some related to hormonal changes, some to psychological and emotional unreadiness, and some to relationship factors. You can speed your partner's return to a healthy sex life in several ways:

- Read chapter 11 so you understand completely what is going on—for her and for you.

- Rekindle romance by reminding her how it was when you first met—without pressure.

- If you think she may be worried about having contracted a sexually transmitted disease (or if you are worried that she may have), ask her to talk with her doctor about testing.

- Give it time. Like everything else in recovery, rebuilding your sex life is a slow and steady process that takes patience.

- Work on the relationship. Work on communication, trust, and enjoying each other in other ways.

- If the lack of a sex life is interfering with your relationship or with recovery, or if it persists into the second half of the year, get professional help.

HOW MUCH SHOULD WE HELP OUR CHILD?

"Our son is in an outpatient drug treatment program and is doing well. He's found a job, but he needs a car to get there. Of course he doesn't have a penny, and his credit is shot. We can afford to buy him a used car— but should we?"

Parents with kids in recovery have to walk a very narrow line between helping and enabling. Sure, your child may need help, especially if his life has been a mess for a couple of years or more. But you've got to avoid giving the kind of help that will enable him to go back to using drugs.

First of all, offer only no-frills assistance. Limit it to the necessities: food, basic clothing, shelter, transportation, maybe a prepaid cell phone with minimal minutes. Second, if he's living at home, have him contribute to his room and board. Also expect him to be a participating family member, helping with the shopping, cooking, dishes, yard work, or wherever else his help is needed.

Finally, make your help contingent on his sticking to his treatment plan. If he stops going to counseling sessions or meetings, or starts seeing old using friends, cut off your help immediately. If you want, you can also tell him he will need to agree to random drug tests (see Home Drug Testing, page 253), and any test failures will also mean an end to your help.

If you do buy him a car, keep it in your name and register him as one of the drivers. Build in a goal for him to strive for. Let him know that at a certain point in his recovery, perhaps after two years of sobriety, you will consider signing the car over to him.

///////////////////////////

"Our nineteen-year-old daughter is in an outpatient treatment program and living at home. I tried to sit down with her and make a schedule to be sure she gets to meetings and therapy. My husband says to let her handle it herself."

Your husband is right. Your daughter has to get herself to meetings—it's not your job. In fact, the less involved you are in managing her recovery program, the better. You can provide food, shelter, medical care, and schooling, if that's the deal, but otherwise it's time to let go.

There is an exception to this "hands-off" rule: When an alcoholic/addict is suffering from organic brain damage and memory is poor, it's okay to remind him about a meeting or to call his sponsor when it seems necessary.

HE'S HAVING SELF-DESTRUCTIVE THOUGHTS

"My boyfriend has been sober for six months, but he still seems depressed a lot of the time. Several times he's hinted about feelings of not wanting to live. How seriously should I take such comments?"

Very seriously. Many people who talk about suicide do attempt it, and suicide is especially common among alcoholics and addicts, even those in recovery. So try to get some professional help for your boyfriend right away. Call the National Suicide Prevention Lifeline (800-273-8255) and ask them for advice (also see Suicide Prevention and Crisis Intervention Lifelines, page 119). Find out what you can about local mental health resources (see chapter

5) and urge your boyfriend to seek help. If he threatens to do anything, call 911 immediately or take him to a hospital emergency room or mental health crisis center. Don't delay. (Find out now where the closest facilities are.)

WHAT ABOUT A RECONCILIATION?

"My husband has been an alcoholic for years. I finally threw him out of the house more than a year ago, and I thought, 'Good riddance.' Now he calls and says he's been in treatment for alcoholism and he's sober and wants to see me and the children. I still say, 'Good riddance.'"

Who can blame you? This man was destroying your family and you're not willing to risk his coming back and doing even more damage.

On the other hand, he may no longer be the same person you've known in recent years. Treatment often changes people completely, not only bringing them back to their pre-drinking selves, but also making them better human beings than they ever were before.

Still, if you don't want to see your husband, no one can force you. Of course, the courts may force you to allow him to see his children. But do you want it to come to that? Do you want this kind of contention between you? A better course may be to agree to a meeting with him, perhaps in the presence of a counselor or therapist. Talk about the issues between you, the problems you see as insurmountable. If the first meeting goes well, maybe you'll agree to further counseling. Keeping an open mind could eventually lead to opening your heart. If it doesn't, it could at least lead to a more amicable separation.

SORRY, BUT I'VE HAD ENOUGH

"My father has been a drug addict for as long as I can remember. Now he's finally gone to treatment and says he's doing well, but Mom and I feel that we've had enough and we don't want him back in the house."

Think about what you're saying. For years while this guy was doing drugs, you let him live with you. Now that he's hoping to turn his life around and behave himself, you want him out. Does that make sense?

We do understand where you are coming from. Your feelings are echoed angrily in thousands of other homes every day, probably for several reasons:

- Fear—is he really going to go straight?

- Resentment and anger— rejection is a way to get even.

- Role changes—now that he's promising to behave, the delicate balance of relationships in the family is likely to change.

- Change, even if there's a chance it might be for the better, is always unsettling.

But your father has a disease. Now, when he's trying to do something about it, is not the time to bar the door against his return. Now is the time to give him your support. Try to stick together as a family or, at the very least, keep your options open until you've given his sobriety a chance and can better judge whether or not all the hurts can be mended. If you really don't want him to live in your home when he leaves treatment, urge him to find a sober-living residence where he can stay for a few months.

In the meantime, learn all you can about his disease. Go to Nar-Anon or Al-Anon. If you need it, get professional help. But don't throw in the towel until you've all had a chance to clean up your lives. Good stuff could be underneath.

Relapse

IF THERE IS A SLIP

Many alcoholics and addicts have a small slip or a full relapse at some point, most often early in recovery. Family and friends need to be alert for the most obvious warning signs: The person in recovery starts feeling sorry for himself, muses about missing the action at the bar, talks about the good times. He starts wondering, "Am I really an alcoholic?" "Did I really need to give up drugs?"

Read chapter 10 to learn more about what can trigger a relapse, what the warning signs of trouble are, how to head off a relapse, and what the person in recovery needs to do if one occurs.

Also read about how the Recovery Zone System (chapter 2) can help your loved one to avoid a slip by doing regular Recovery Zone ReChecks to anticipate any events that could trip him up.

One of the most important things you can do—whether there is a slip or not—is to continue to take care of yourself and your healing, and to continue to go to Al-Anon or Nar-Anon meetings. This will help reinforce the positive recovery environment. In fact, keeping your focus on recovery may help your partner avoid a relapse once his newfound focus on it wanes.

///////////////////////////

"My father was doing really well once he started to go to AA, but then he went to an office Christmas party and came home smashed. My mom and I are crushed and don't know what to do. Should we have stopped him from going to the party?"

Your distress is understandable but not constructive. If you've been going to Al-Anon or Alateen, you know that you can't control an alcoholic and you're not responsible for his actions.

Your attitude, however, will make a difference. Don't cry, argue with him, or threaten him over this slip, or allow it to break your heart or spirit. A slip or two along the road to sobriety is not unusual. (In fact, it's best to have a contingency plan ready for such occasions. If you don't have one yet, set one up soon; see A Contingency Plan for Slips, page 582, for some ideas.)

For now, let your father know that you aren't shocked or disappointed (though you may indeed be very upset), and that you're still there to support his recovery. You could also explain that you're nervous when he doesn't go to meetings, distressed when he drinks, and worried about the impact of his behavior on the family. Make it clear that whatever his reason or excuse for drinking, it's not good enough.

Let's hope that this was just a momentary slip and your father will get right back on the wagon. But if he heads for the corner bar tomorrow, bite your tongue, even though you will really want to say something to him. Don't tell him to call his sponsor or to go to a meeting. That's his responsibility. And it could backfire—he might go out to drink to spite you.

It's tough, but you and your mother need to detach yourselves from this situation, to look at it from the point of view of innocent bystanders. That's healthier for you than taking your father's drinking as somehow your responsibility. If you had tried to stop him from going to the party, that wouldn't have worked. You can't put him in mothballs.

This situation isn't easy for you. But if we want the dignity to live our own lives as we see fit, we have to give the same opportunity to those we love.

IF THERE IS A RELAPSE

"My boyfriend just relapsed for the second time—just when things were going well. I'm so angry I could scream!"

Go to a fellowship meeting, or sound off in an online forum instead. Post something on your blog. Go for a run around the block or try some meditation. If you absolutely have to scream, lock yourself in the bathroom to do it.

Fight the urge to scream at your boyfriend. It might give you a momentary sense of satisfaction, but in the long run, it won't help either of you. Anger and screaming beget anger and screaming. Certainly you should express your feelings, but calm down and think before you speak or act. An alcoholic/addict is much more likely to criticize himself if others don't beat up on him first.

But remember, if he wants to kill himself with chemicals, you can't stop him. If he hasn't been in treatment, you might try an intervention aimed at getting him into an inpatient program (see Getting Help for Your Loved One, page 543).

///////////////////////////

"The guy I live with went through a treatment program because his employer insisted. Now he's drinking and using drugs again, as if he didn't learn anything."

It's doubtful that he didn't learn anything, no matter how scornful he may be of the experience. There's one thing that treatment is guaranteed to do: destroy one's innocence about alcoholism or drug addiction.

Your friend can never again drink or use as casually and obliviously as he did before. He's been told what he's doing to himself and the nature of his disease. Best of all, a door will have opened. He will know where to turn for help when he's ready. That doesn't guarantee he will seek help at some point, but it improves the odds.

A CONTINGENCY PLAN FOR SLIPS

The best way to deal with a slip is to prevent it (see chapter 10). The next best way is to agree up front what will happen if a slip does occur—to form a contingency plan.

At some point early in your loved one's recovery, everyone closely involved should sit down and discuss what will happen if there's a slip. You can even write up a formal plan, called an "advance directive" or a "recovery action plan." If possible, also get some input from an addiction professional. You might want to have it drawn up by a lawyer, to have even more power in case a relapse gets really ugly.

Your plan needs to be tailored to the individual and the situation. For example, you could let your husband know that if he starts using again, you will call his boss and say, "Joe is operating heavy machinery under the influence again." Or your

girlfriend could agree that if she has a slip, she will go to the inpatient treatment program she's been trying to avoid by going to NA. Or you could make it clear to an adult child who's just gone through treatment that if he slips, he's out of the house, with no phone, car, or credit cards. Whatever the plan, it should be put into effect right away if a relapse occurs. If you did an intervention, you might include the specific contingencies you agreed upon at that time.

MATTERS OF LIFE AND DEATH

Does it ever make sense to step in to prevent your loved one from self-destructing? Sometimes. If your partner, parent, child, sibling, or friend is high on drugs or alcohol and about to drive a car, taking away the keys could save a life—or several lives. Likewise, if he intends to work at any safety-sensitive job while under the influence, you can prevent a catastrophe by notifying a supervisor. If suicide or violence is threatened, call the police.

Ideally, it's best to discuss these types of situations when your loved one is in a moment of relative sobriety, but even if you haven't, you have a moral responsibility to take action. Taking action when necessary will help to put a stop to the games an alcoholic/addict tries to play with your emotions. Plus, if something bad does happen, you will know you did what you could to avoid it, and you didn't cover it up. You will be able to live guilt-free.

Afterword

They say in the rooms of 12-step fellowships that "sobriety isn't everything, it's the only thing." And to be sure you don't lose it, they remind you of a pivotal meditation: "God [or my Higher Power], I appreciate your giving me the ability to laugh. But don't ever let me forget when I cried."

Your future looks bright now, and understandably, the bad old days of drinking and drugging are something you'd just as soon forget. But remembering those days, remembering the moment that made you realize you'd had enough or that sent you shakily off to your first meeting, can strengthen your recovery and help keep you sober.

Something else worth remembering is a comment heard over and over at the annual gatherings of Willingway alumni:

"When I first came here ten [or twenty or thirty] years ago, I was full of self-pity. I felt like I was a victim with nothing to look forward to but pain and misery. I learned so much in recovery—how to deal with problems instead of drowning them, why I spent so much time lying and drinking and using—that now I can honestly say I'm glad alcoholism and drugs messed up my life. It made the rest of my life so much better. It gave me an incredible gift that I could pass on to the next generation. Even with all the pain and misery, I wouldn't change a thing."

The hard work of recovery turns negatives into positives and pain into gain. We hope that whatever you've learned will always be a part of your life. And that you, too, will pass it on to others.

Here's a quick summary of what will help you continue to meet the challenges ahead. One day at a time, you need to:

- Stay sober. (Without sobriety, nothing else will have any value.)

- Retain your honesty. (It will never lead you astray.)

- Continue to learn and grow. (That's what keeps us young and alive as long as we live.)

- Care for yourself, body and soul. (No one can do this as well as you can.)

- Nurture your relationships—they'll enrich your life. (But no relationship is perfect all the time; they all need care and effort to flourish.)

- Hang on to your fellowship group ties—both to keep your own recovery healthy and to return the favor to others who are new to recovery.

- Continue to work your recovery program as you have refined it in the Green Zone, and do regular Recovery Zone ReChecks to ward off relapses.

- Keep your brain focused on recovery by practicing your TAMERS every day.

- Work toward making your life and those of others better. But always remember: It's progress, not perfection.

You'll know it's all working for you when you can sum it up the way Dr. John Mooney (our all-time favorite optimist) often did:

"Recovery means being able to look back at the end of any day of your life— good, bad, even terrible—and say of it, 'How about that? Another sober day. Ain't life great?'"

Acknowledgments

As anyone who has ever tried to kick an addiction knows, recovery is a lot easier when you have a good support group. When writing a book on recovery, you need a good support group, too. We had the best—for both editions of *The Recovery Book*.

Our heartfelt thanks go to the many people in the recovery community who so generously shared their stories and knowledge: the entire Willingway family of staff, patients, alumni, and friends; the Willingway Foundation Board; the residents and staff of Lee Street Recovery Residence, Louie's House, and the Healing Place of Wake County; Judge Robbie Turner and the staff of the Effingham County Drug Court; Dan and Agnes O'Laughlin and supporters of Recovery Africa; the National Health Service staff in County Durham, UK; the addiction medicine physicians of Like Minded Docs; the Raleigh Continuing Care group of Willingway; Dana Archibald; Fred Barber; Cindy Bernhardt; Ken Blackman; Bill Borchert; Gene Botwright; Heath Browning; Chris Budnick; Susan Burton; Jenn Buzzi; Greg Caudill; Fulton Crews; Carole Delongchamps; Emily Eisenhart; John Elford; Greg Evans; Andy Finley; Brett F.; Bob Gwyther; Ruby Hamilton; Paula K.; Doug Jackson; Judith Landau; Robert Malik; Tennie McCarty; Jerry Moe; Jamie Norton; Robert Piubeni; Terry Rustin; Janet Salvio-Littlejohn; Raymond Scott; Kurt Shafer; Alana Smith; Tom Smith; Tracie Smith; Joe Sweeney; Jim Tracy; Charlie Wagner; Shawn Williams; John Williamson; and many others who met with us in focus groups and elsewhere.

We would also like to thank Harry Haroutunian, M.D., of the Betty Ford Center, for writing such a heartfelt foreword; our agent, Arnold Goodman; and everyone at Workman Publishing.

We are also indebted to our personal support networks, who saw us through many long days, late nights, and missed vacations:

Al J. Mooney, M.D.: My very tolerant and supportive wife, Jane, and our children John and Rachel and their families, who all permitted me to steal precious moments from grandkids to complete this project. Also, my parents, Dr. John and Dot Mooney, for instilling in me a passion for helping any alcoholic who still suffers.

Catherine Dold: My family: Mom, Dad, Bruce, Lisa, Eileen, Bob, Megan, Kristen, Katherine, and Susan, as well as the amazing women of Boulder Media Women.

Howard Eisenberg: My late wife, Arlene Eisenberg, who was the coauthor of the first edition. Her classic *What to Expect* series gave Dr. Al the idea of writing a book that would tell people what to expect on the bumpy road to recovery, and her uncommon sense and organizational skills launched that first edition.

AL J. MOONEY, M.D.
CATHERINE DOLD
HOWARD EISENBERG

Recovery Resources

For more resources, please see TheRecoveryBook.com/Resources.

General Addiction and Recovery Resources

ABOUT ADDICTION AND RECOVERY

Commonly Abused Drugs: drugabuse.gov/drugs-abuse/commonly-abused-drugs

Drug Facts: drugabuse.gov/publications/term/160/DrugFacts

Drug Guide: drugfree.org/drug-guide

National Council on Alcoholism and Drug Dependence: ncadd.org

National Institute on Alcohol Abuse and Alcoholism: niaaa.nih.gov

National Institute on Drug Abuse: drugabuse.gov

Substance Abuse and Mental Health Services Administration: samhsa.gov

What Is Addiction? casacolumbia.org/addiction

HEALTH EFFECTS

Alcohol and Health: niaaa.nih.gov/alcohol-health

Drugs, Brains, and Behavior: The Science of Addiction: drugabuse.gov/publications/science-addiction

Medical Consequences of Drug Abuse: drugabuse.gov/related-topics/medical-consequences-drug-abuse

Addiction Treatment

ABOUT TREATMENT

How to Find Quality Addiction Treatment: casacolumbia.org/addiction-treatment/patient-guide

National Drug Abuse Treatment Clinical Trials Network:
drugabuse.gov/about-nida/organization/cctn/ctn

Principles of Adolescent Substance Use Disorder Treatment: A Research-Based Guide:
drugabuse.gov/publications/principles-adolescent-substance-use-disorder-treatment
-research-based-guide

Principles of Drug Addiction Treatment: A Research-Based Guide:
drugabuse.gov/publications/principles-drug-addiction-treatment

Seeking Drug Abuse Treatment: Know What to Ask:
drugabuse.gov/publications/seeking-drug-abuse-treatment

FIND ADDICTION PROFESSIONALS (see chapter 5)

FIND TREATMENT PROGRAMS (see chapter 5)

PAYING FOR TREATMENT

Disabled American Veterans: dav.org

Family and Medical Leave Act: dol.gov/whd/fmla

Medicaid: medicaid.gov

Medicare Rights Center: medicarerights.org

Veterans Benefits: va.gov/healthbenefits

TREATMENT CONFIDENTIALITY

Health Information Privacy:
hhs.gov/ocr/privacy/hipaa/understanding/consumers/index.html

Mutual Help Groups

12-STEP FELLOWSHIPS

AA Grapevine: aagrapevine.org

Alcoholics Anonymous: aa.org, aa-intergroup.org

Cocaine Anonymous: ca.org

Crystal Meth Anonymous: crystalmeth.org

Dual Recovery Anonymous: draonline.org

Marijuana Anonymous: marijuana-anonymous.org

Narcotics Anonymous: na.org

OTHER MUTUAL HELP GROUPS

LifeRing: lifering.org

Rational Recovery: rational.org

Secular Organizations for Sobriety: cfiwest.org/sos

Smart Recovery: smartrecovery.org

Women for Sobriety: womenforsobriety.org

Living in Sobriety

DRUG TESTING

Drugs of Abuse Home Use Test:
fda.gov/MedicalDevices/ProductsandMedicalProcedures/InVitroDiagnostics/
HomeUseTests/ucm125722.htm

Drugs of Abuse Testing:
labtestsonline.org/understanding/analytes/drug-abuse/tab/test

Drug Testing: workplace.samhsa.gov/Dtesting.html

Frequently Asked Questions About Drug Testing in Schools:
drugabuse.gov/related-topics/drug-testing/faq-drug-testing-in-schools

LEGAL ISSUES

Are You in Recovery From Alcohol or Drug Problems? Know Your Rights:
store.samhsa.gov/product/Are-You-in-Recovery-from-Alcohol-or-Drug-Problems-Know-Your
-Rights/PHD1091

**Are You in Recovery From Alcohol or Drug Problems? Know Your Rights—Rights for
Individuals on Medication-Assisted Treatment:**
store.samhsa.gov/product/Rights-for-Individuals-on-Medication-Assisted-Treatment/
SMA09-4449

Justice for Vets: justiceforvets.org

Legal Action Center: lac.org

Low-cost Legal Services: LawHelp.org

National Association of Drug Court Professionals: nadcp.org/nadcp-home

National Drug Court Institute: ndci.org

National Drug Court Resource Center: ndcrc.org

Tribal Healing to Wellness Courts: wellnesscourts.org

NETWORKS, NEWS, AND TOOLS

After Party Chat: afterpartychat.com

Association of Recovery Community Organizations:
facesandvoicesofrecovery.org/who/arco

Betty Ford Center Chat: bettyfordcenteralumni.org/chat

Faces and Voices of Recovery: facesandvoicesofrecovery.org

Get Into Recovery: getintorecovery.com

Global Recovery Initiative: globalrecoveryinitiative.org

Hazelden Social Community: hazeldensocial.org/community/community-home

In The Rooms: intherooms.com

MADD: madd.org

Many Faces 1 Voice: manyfaces1voice.org

Medical Amnesty Initiative: medicalamnesty.org

National Recovery Month: recoverymonth.gov

Phoenix Multisport: phoenixmultisport.org

Physicians for Responsible Opioid Prescribing: supportprop.org

Shatterproof: shatterproof.org

Sober Nation: sobernation.com

Sober Recovery: soberrecovery.com/forums

Sobriety Calculator: aagrapevine.org/sobriety-calculator

The Fix: thefix.com

Transforming Youth Recovery: transformingyouthrecovery.org

Young People in Recovery: youngpeopleinrecovery.org

MEDICATION SAFETY

DailyMed: dailymed.nlm.nih.gov/dailymed/about.cfm

DEA National Prescription Drug Take-Back Day:
deadiversion.usdoj.gov/drug_disposal/takeback

The Medicine Abuse Project: medicineabuseproject.org

OTHER 12-STEP FELLOWSHIPS

Chronic Pain Anonymous: chronicpainanonymous.org

Debtors Anonymous: debtorsanonymous.org

Emotions Anonymous: emotionsanonymous.org

Gamblers Anonymous: gamblersanonymous.org

Overeaters Anonymous: oa.org

Sex Addicts Anonymous: saa-recovery.org

Sex and Love Addicts Anonymous: slaafws.org

Workaholics Anonymous: workaholics-anonymous.org

RECOVERY SCHOOLS

Association of Recovery in Higher Education: collegiaterecovery.org/programs

Association of Recovery Schools: recoveryschools.org

Transforming Youth Recovery: transformingyouthrecovery.org

SOBER LIVING

California Sober Living Environments: caarr.org/sober-living/sles.html

Find Sober Living: findsoberliving.com

Homelessness Resource Center: homeless.samhsa.gov

National Alliance for Recovery Residences: narronline.org

Oxford House: oxfordhouse.org

SPECIALIZED COMMUNITIES

12 Steps for Christians: 12stepsforchristians.com

AA Agnostica: aaagnostica.org

Anesthetists in Recovery: aana.com/resources2/peer-assistance/Pages/default.aspx

Association of Recovering Motorcyclists: arm-intl.com

Birds of a Feather International (pilots): boaf.org

Buddhist Recovery Network: buddhistrecovery.org

Celebrate Recovery (Christian): celebraterecovery.com

Chabad (Jewish): chabad.org/library/article_cdo/aid/714274/jewish/Jewish-Recovery.htm

Christian Recovery International: christianrecovery.com

Clergy Recovery Network: clergyrecovery.com

Federation of State Physician Health Programs: fsphp.org

Fellowship of Recovering Lutheran Clergy: frlc.org

Five-O at the BigHouse (law): five-oatthebighouse.com

International Doctors in AA: idaa.org

International Lawyers in Alcoholics Anonymous: ilaa.org/home

JACS (Jewish): jbfcs.org//JACS

Millati Islami World Services: millatiislami.org

National Asian Pacific American Families Against Substance Abuse: napafasa.org

National Association for Christian Recovery: nacr.org

National Association of Lesbian, Gay, Bisexual, Transgender Addiction Professionals and Their Allies: nalgap.org

Pharmacists Recovery Network: usaprn.org

Pride Institute (LGBT): pride-institute.com

Recovering Women Riders: rwr.arm-intl.com

Seniors in Sobriety: seniorsinsobriety.org

Sober Bikers United: soberbikersunited.org

Substance and Alcohol Intervention Services for the Deaf: rit.edu/ntid/saisd/home

The Calix Society (Catholics): calixsociety.org

Wellbriety (Native American): wellbriety.com

White Bison (Native American): whitebison.org/index.php

Women's Recovery: womensrecovery.org

Young People in Recovery: youngpeopleinrecovery.org

For Family and Friends

MUTUAL-HELP GROUPS

Adult Children of Alcoholics: adultchildren.org

Al-Anon Family Groups: al-anon.alateen.org

Codependents Anonymous World Fellowship: coda.org

Families Anonymous: familiesanonymous.org

NACoA Just 4 Kids: nacoa.org/kidspage.html

Nar-Anon, Narateen: nar-anon.org/naranon

National Association for Children of Alcoholics: nacoa.org

FAMILY RELATIONSHIPS

Dignity USA (LGBTQ Catholic): dignityusa.org

Family & Relationships: apa.org/helpcenter/family

More Light Presbyterian: mlp.org

National Association for Children of Alcoholics: nacoa.org

Parents, Families and Friends of Lesbians and Gays: pflag.org

DRUG PREVENTION

Brain Power: drugabuse.gov/brain-power

Drugs: Shatter the Myths: drugabuse.gov/publications/drugs-shatter-myths

Family Checkup: Positive Parenting Prevents Drug Abuse:
drugabuse.gov/family-checkup

National Substance Abuse Prevention Month:
samhsa.gov/prevention/nationalpreventionmonth

Parenting to Prevent Childhood Alcohol Abuse:
pubs.niaaa.nih.gov/publications/adolescentflyer/adolflyer.htm

Partnership for Drug-Free Kids: drugfree.org

Stop Underage Drinking: stopalcoholabuse.gov/default.aspx

The Cool Spot: thecoolspot.gov/index.asp

The Medicine Abuse Project: medicineabuseproject.org

PEER PRESSURE AND ONLINE SAFETY

Cyberbullying Toolkit: commonsensemedia.org/educators/cyberbullying-toolkit

Digital Citizenship: Resource Roundup:
edutopia.org/cyberbullying-internet-digital-citizenship-resources

Family Online Safety Institute: fosi.org

It Gets Better Project: itgetsbetter.org

Kind Campaign: kindcampaign.com/about

Resources to Fight Bullying and Harassment at School:
edutopia.org/bullying-resources

StopBullying.gov: stopbullying.gov

For Teens and Young Adults

TEENS AND YOUNG ADULTS

Above the Influence: abovetheinfluence.com

College Drinking: collegedrinkingprevention.gov

Half of Us: halfofus.com

National Institute on Drug Abuse for Teens: teens.drugabuse.gov

Students Against Destructive Decisions: sadd.org

The Jed Foundation: jedfoundation.org

The Meth Project: methproject.org

Health Resources

HEALTH INFORMATION (see chapter 13)

QUITTING SMOKING (see chapter 25)

MENTAL HEALTH INFORMATION

American Psychiatric Association: psychiatry.org/mental-health/key-topics/finding-help

American Psychological Association: apa.org/helpcenter/index.aspx

Depression: nlm.nih.gov/medlineplus/depression.html

Mental Health: nlm.nih.gov/medlineplus/mentalhealth.html

Mental Health America: mentalhealthamerica.net

Mental Health Treatment Facility Locator:
findtreatment.samhsa.gov/MHTreatmentLocator/faces/quickSearch.jspx

National Alliance on Mental Illness: nami.org

National Institute of Mental Health: nimh.nih.gov/health/index.shtml

NONDRUG REMEDIES

Complementary and Alternative Medicine:
nlm.nih.gov/medlineplus/complementaryandalternativemedicine.html

Health Journeys: healthjourneys.com

Herbs and Supplements: nlm.nih.gov/medlineplus/druginfo/herb_All.html

Meditation: An Introduction: nccam.nih.gov/health/meditation/overview.htm

BODY ART REMOVAL

Piercing and Tattoos: nlm.nih.gov/medlineplus/piercingandtattoos.html

Unwanted Tattoos: asds.net/TattooRemovalInformation.aspx

Crisis Resources

SUICIDE PREVENTION AND CRISIS INTERVENTION LIFELINES (see chapter 6, page 119)

If anyone is in immediate crisis, call 911.

CHILD ABUSE, DOMESTIC VIOLENCE, RUNAWAYS

Childhelp Child Abuse Hotline: 800-4-A-CHILD (800-422-4453)
childhelp.org

Love Is Respect: loveisrespect.org
866-331-9474; text "loveis" to 22522
loveisrespect.org/get-help/contact-us/chat-with-us

National Dating Abuse Helpline: ndah.org

National Domestic Violence Hotline: 800-799-SAFE (800-799-7233)
thehotline.org/help/resources
contact@thehotline.org

National Runaway Safeline: 800-786-2929
1800runaway.org

National Safe Place: TXT 4 HELP Teenagers: If you need help, text "safe" and your current location (address/city/state) to 69866.
nationalsafeplace.org

National Sexual Assault Hotline: 800-656-HOPE (800-656-4673)

Rape, Abuse and Incest National Network (RAINN): rainn.org

Safe Helpline (for military): safehelpline.org
877-995-5247
Instant messaging: safehelpline.org
Safe Helpline app: create a personalized self-care plan
Text your zip code to 55-247 (inside U.S.) or 202-470-5546 (outside U.S.)

Womenshealth.gov: State Resources Regarding Violence Against Women:
womenshealth.gov/violence-against-women/get-help-for-violence/resources-by-state
-violence-against-women.cfm

Index

D

About the Authors

AL J. MOONEY, M.D., is an internationally recognized expert in the field of addiction and recovery. He has been involved in this field since he was a teenager, when his parents founded an addiction treatment center, Willingway Hospital. Dr. Mooney was CEO of the hospital for many years, and is currently the Director of Addiction Medicine and Recovery at Willingway. He has been instrumental in establishing recovery programs and awareness in Egypt, Bosnia, and Ghana, and worked with Georgia Southern University to establish one of the first recovery campuses. He currently serves as medical director for The Healing Place of Wake County (NC), a homeless shelter that features a peer-driven residential recovery program.

Dr. Mooney is an Inaugural Diplomat in the American Board of Addiction Medicine, and helped establish the certification standards for the specialty. He was one of the first U.S. physicians certified in Addiction Medicine, and has served as a board member for the American Society of Addiction Medicine. His medical career has included service at state and private hospitals, community organizations, mental health agencies, volunteer associations, and homeless shelters. He lives in Cary, North Carolina.

CATHERINE DOLD, a freelance writer, has covered health and environmental issues for *The New York Times*, *Smithsonian*, *Discover*, *Audubon*, *Cosmopolitan*, and many other publications, as well as for several major medical organizations. She is a graduate of New York University's Science, Health and Environmental Reporting Program. Ms. Dold lives in Boulder, Colorado.

HOWARD EISENBERG has written hundreds of magazine articles, written for TV and radio, and authored six books, including the bestselling *How to Be Your Own Doctor (Sometimes)*. Mr. Eisenberg lives in New York City.

Dr. Al Mooney is available for select speaking engagements. Please contact speakersbureau@workman.com.

βτ
9/14

362.2927 Mooney, Al J.
M   The recovery book.

DATE			

BAKER & TAYLOR